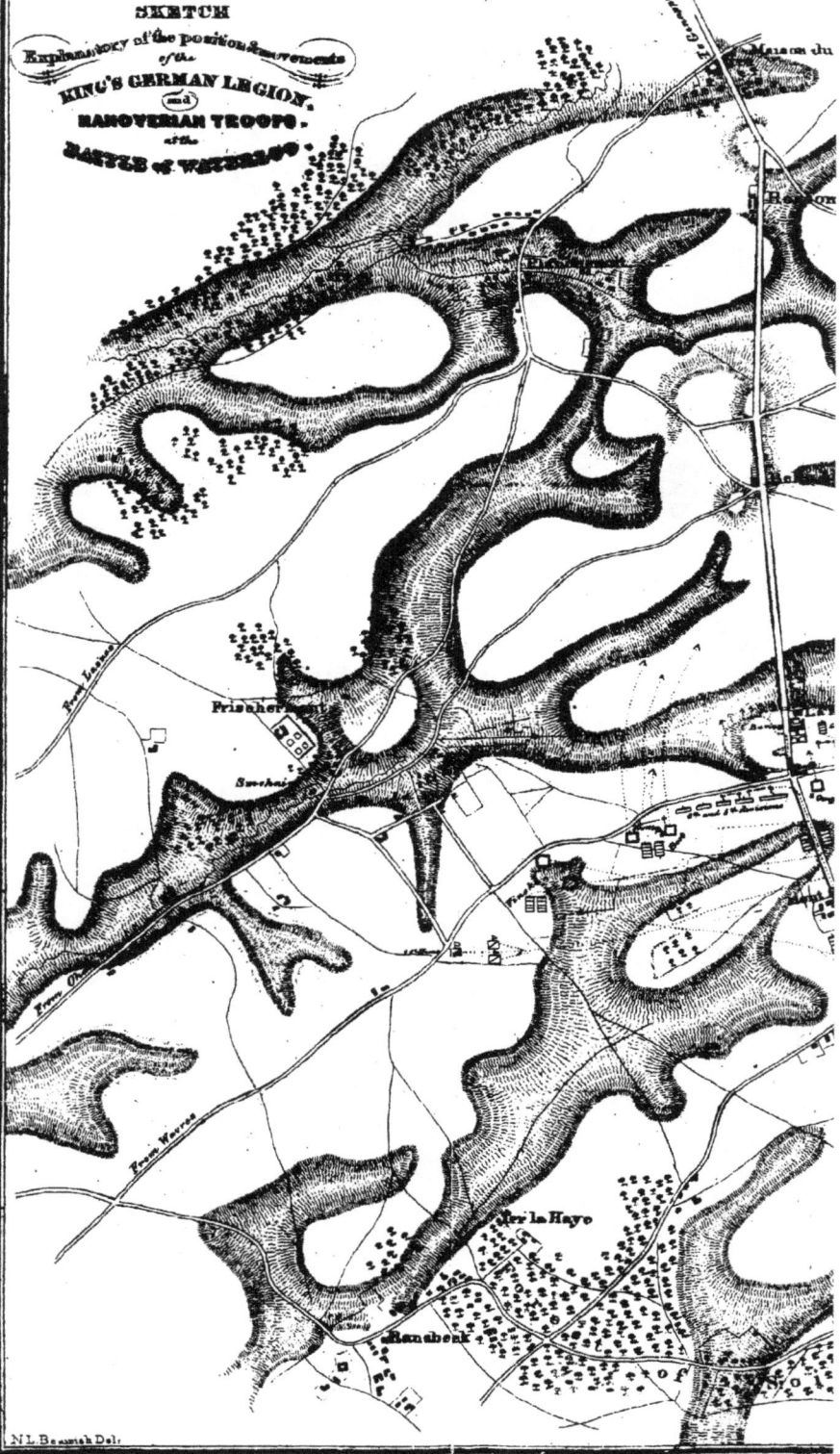

Plate IV to face the Title

SKETCH
Explanatory of the position & movements
of the
KING'S GERMAN LEGION,
and
HANOVERIAN TROOPS,
at the
BATTLE of WATERLOO

Maison du

H...on

Prisher...

Smohni

From Louva...

From O...

From Wavre

La Haye

Smohn

N. L. Beamish Del.

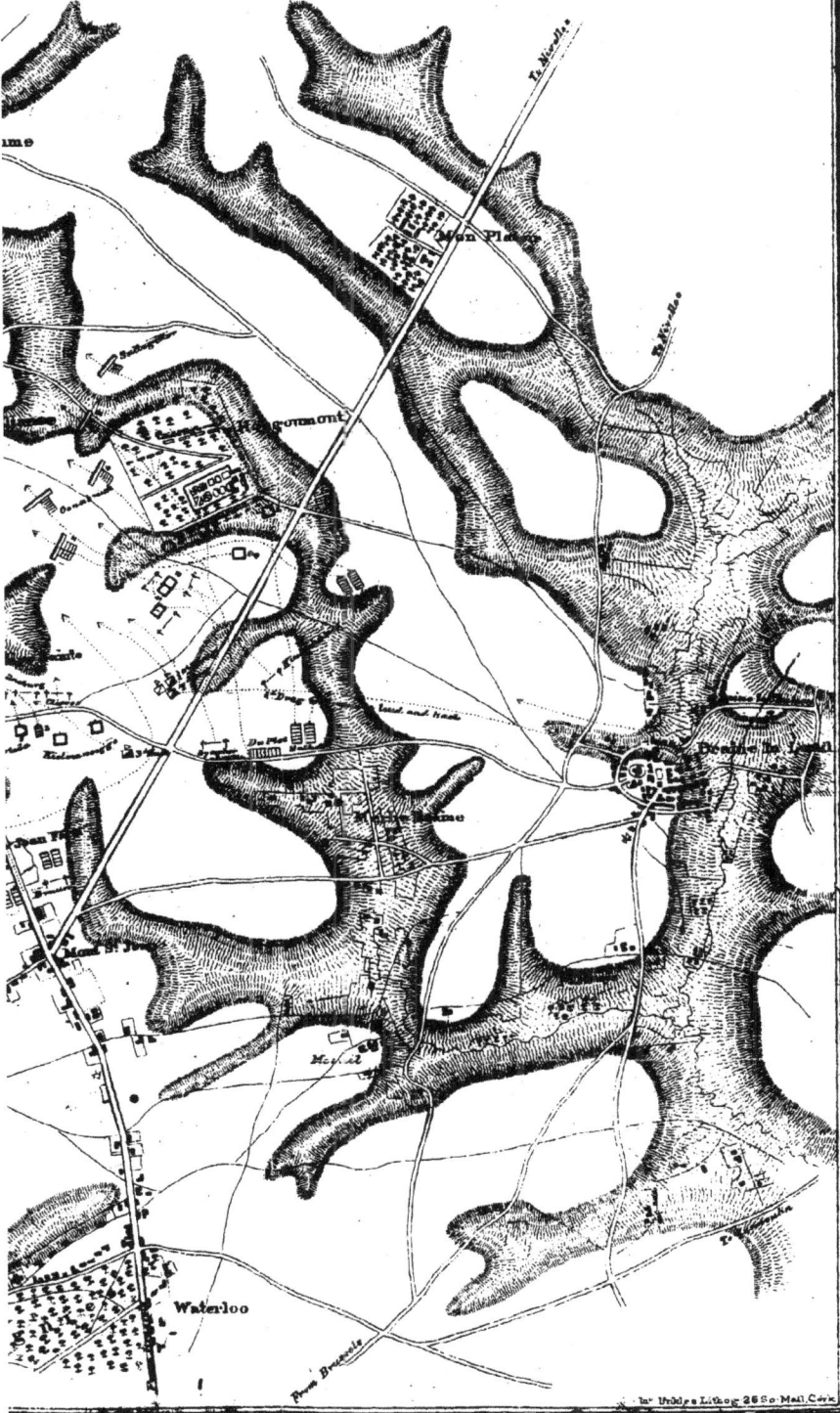

HISTORY

OF THE

KING'S GERMAN LEGION,

BY

N. LUDLOW BEAMISH, F.R.S.

LATE MAJOR UNATTACHED.

"Wir, wir haben seinem Glanz und Schimmer
Nichts, als die Müh' und als die Schmerzen,
Und wofür wir uns halten in unserm Herzen."—SCHILLER

VOL. II.

The Naval & Military Press Ltd

Published by

The Naval & Military Press Ltd
Unit 5 Riverside
Bellbrook Industrial Estate
Uckfield, East Sussex
TN22 1QQ England

Tel: +44 (0) 1825 749494
www.naval–military-press.com

Cover image: The storming of La Haye Sainte by Richard Knötel, German artist and pioneer of the study of military uniform. La Haye Sainte was the crucial position at the centre of Wellington's position at the Battle of Waterloo.

NOTICE.

Various circumstances over which the author had no control, have delayed until the present period the publication of this volume. Amongst others the length of time occupied in the collection and investigation of documents and details. This laborious task has been principally carried on by captain CHRISTOPH HEISE, of the Hanoverian rifle guards, who also has prepared the elaborate lists, containing summaries of the services and casualties of the corps, which will be found in the appendix. It would be an unpardonable omission on the part of the author, did he not further add, that to this able, patriotic, and indefatigable officer, the King's German Legion are mainly indebted for the completion of this history.

Cork, Sept. 1837.

TABLE OF CONTENTS.

CHAPTER III.

CHAPTER IV.

CHAPTER V.

CHAPTER VI.

CHAPTER VII.

CHAPTER VIII.

CHAPTER IX.

CHAPTER X.

CHAPTER XI.

CHAPTER XII.

CHAPTER XIII.

CHAPTER XIV.

CHAPTER XV.

CHAPTER XVI.

CHAPTER XVII.

APPENDIX.

RETURNS.

List of additional printed works, and Manuscripts to which reference is made in this volume.

PRINTED WORKS.

No. 1.   Journals of sieges carried on by the army under the duke of Wellington in Spain, between the years 1811 and 1814, with notes, by colonel John T. Jones, corps of royal engineers, aide de camp to the King. second edition, 2 vols. London, 1827.

2.   History of the war in the Peninsula and in the south of France, from the year 1807 to the year 1814, by W. F. P. Napier, C. B. colonel h. p. forty-third regiment, member of the royal Swedish academy of military sciences. Vols. IV. and V. London 1834 and 1836.

3.   Bulletins of the campaigns of the British troops from 1811 to 1815, compiled from the London Gazettes.

4.   Reminiscences of a Subaltern [United Service Journal 1831, Part III.]

5.   Abriss der Operationen der englisch-portugiesischen armee, unter dem unmittelbaren commando lord Wellington's, vom 1st Juni 1812. vom general major Hartmann des Königl. hannov. Artillerie. (Hannoversches militairisches Journal 1834.)

6.   Beiträge zur Geschichte des Krieges auf der pyrenäischen Halbinsel, in den Jahren 1809 bis 1813. ibid.

7.   Der Feldzug in Mecklenburg und Holstein im Jahr 1813, 1 Heft, Berlin, 1817.

8.   Geschichte des Armee-Korps unter den Befehlen des General-lieutenants Grafen von Wallmoden-Gimborn, an der Nieder-Elbe und in den Niederlanden vom April 1813 bis zum Mai 1814. (Oestreichische militairische Zeitschrift, Wien, 1827.)

MANUSCRIPTS.

PLATES AND PLANS.

ERRATA.

Page 9, line 21, *for* "Badajos" *read* "Rodrigo."
— 45, — 28, *for* "13th" *read* "30th."
— 105, — 8, *for* "second" *read* "first."
— 201, — 27, *for* "battalions" *read* "batteries."
— 223, — 7, *after* "lieutenant" *insert* " Wolrabe and Wahrendorf,"
        and *for* "fourteen men were wounded," *read* "forty-
        four non-commissioned officers and men were wounded,
        besides seven men killed."
— 228, — 9, *dele* "Wolrabe and Wahrendorf."
— 231, — 9, *for* "out of," *read* "into."
— 251, — 19, *after* "the" *insert* "skirmishers of."
— ibid — 20, *for* "colonel du Plat" *read* "captain Bacmeister."
— 265, — 14, *before* "a Portuguese regiment" *insert* "detachment of,"
        and add "Note: captain Decken was present as a spec-
        tator, and, having had his horse killed, led the attack
        on foot."
— 272, margin, *for* " 1813" *read* " 1814."
— 279, line 4, *for* "two hundred and seventy-nine *read* "thirteen hundred"
— 283, margin, *for* "1813," *read* "1814."
— 307, line 6, *for* "von Hohnstedt" *read* "von Hohnhorst."
— 309, margin, *for* " March" *read* " April."
— 330, line 12, by a communication received from major von Heimburg,
        since the text was printed, it appears that the statement
        made here relative to the battalions, Lüneburg and
        Osterode is incorrect, and that it was a battalion of the
        5th division, formed in square, which poured such an
        effective fire upon the French cavalry, at this period of
        the day.
— 356, line 2, *dele* " captain Sander."
— 371, 18 & 19, *dele* "von Bothmer, von Witte, Meyer, Winekler."
— 387, — 5, *for* " Elba" *read* " St. Helena."

APPENDIX.

— 418, — 2, *for* "2d line" *read* " 2d light," and add to " officers
        wounded": " lieut. Mielmann, artillery, slightly."
— ibid, 1st drag. *for* " 24 rank and file, and 23 horses wounded," *read* " 34
        rank and file, and 43 horses wounded."
— ibid, 2d drag. *for* " 19 rank and file killed," *read* " 20 rank and file
        killed," and *for* " 27 horses killed," 23 wounded,"
        read " 28 killed, and 29 wounded," and alter total
        accordingly.

ERRATA.

Page 437, end of page, *for* " W. Maling," *read* " T. Maling."
— 438, line 12, *for* " expenditure," *read* " expedition."
— 442, 2 & 3, *dele* " captain F. Wyncken, and lieut. Holtzermann,"
— ibid, ... 6, *for* " Marwedel," *read* " Mervede."
— ibid, ...20, *for* " Scharnhorst," *read* " Schauroth."
— 514, ...17, *for* " St. Sebastian," *read* " St. Etienne."
— 16, ...21, *for* " Marwedel," *read* " Mervede."
Return XX, *for* " George Klingsöhr," *read* " Charles Helmrich."

COMPLETE LIST, &c.

No. 1, place * *after* " R. St. A. O."
— 32, ditto, *before* " No."
— 33, ditto,
— 38, ditto,
—260, ditto,
—272, *for* " Hons." *read* " Hans."

DIRECTIONS FOR THE BINDER.

CORRESPONDENCE RELATIVE TO THE BATTLE OF TALAVERA.

Letter from Major-General von Berger to the Author.

TRANSLATION.

SIR,

The officers of the King's German Legion must acknowledge with the most lively thanks, and some degree of shame, that you, a stranger, have undertaken to write the history of their corps, and thereby to erect a lasting testimonial of its services.

From the 1st volume of the work, which appeared about two years since, it is evident with what difficulties you have had to contend in the execution of it, and it is, indeed, a matter of astonishment that you have succeeded in so great a measure, in extracting the truth and forming a connected whole from the various—perhaps often contradictory accounts, journals and notes of which your materials were composed. It could not, however, but arise that, in the description of individual occurrences, these fragments should have led you into errors which, had you been able to avail yourself of better sources of information, would, doubtless, have been avoided.

With reluctance have I decided upon addressing you respecting one of these statements, because it partly concerns myself personally, and in the refutation of it, I must come forward, in some degree, as my own panegyrist, which, during my service of nearly fifty-five years, I have never allowed myself to do. But called upon by many of the officers of the 7th line battalion of the Legion, which corps I had long the honor to command, I am induced to take this step, and I venture to hope that it will prove as unobjectionable to yourself, as incapable of being misunderstood.

In describing the battle of Talavera you have stated, on the authority of lieutenant (afterwards captain) Stutzer, that the 7th line battalion of the Legion, which, with part of the 5th battalion, were thrown into disorder by an unexpected attack of the enemy, fired upon the skirmishers of the 1st line battalion, commanded by lieutenant von Holle. This is entirely without foundation; for I had strictly forbidden the men to fire, having learned that some of our troops had been sent to fall upon the enemy's flank.

The disorder, also, into which the 7th battalion fell, was not so great as your description would imply. The greater part of the battalion remained in the position which had been assigned to it, and defended itself in so determined a manner that the men were at close quarters *(Handgemein)* with the enemy, and, having no room to fire, were obliged to use the butt-ends of their musquets. In proof of this I have only to add, that two or three french officers were stripped of the decoration of the legion of honour by some of my men, and two of the enemy, who had remained behind in the 7th battalion, were made prisoners. The singular incident also occurred to myself, that my horse, which had been hit by a ball, sprung forward and carried me into the midst of an enemy's battalion; I however, succeeded in turning him round, and came back to the 7th battalion, when he fell dead under me.

This attack was not altogether unexpected by me; for, some time before, I observed, although it was almost dark, an enemy's column move against our left wing. I pointed this out to the brigadier and requested that he would provide me with support, but he would not be convinced of what I had stated, nor would he even allow the battalion to stand up and meet the charge of the enemy, because general Sherbrooke, who commanded the division, had ordered the troops to lie down. If, under these circumstances, the battalion should have entirely given way, no reproach could, therefore, be attached to it; for, left to itself, it could not possibly long withstand the main column of general Lapisse, which consisted of at least, 2000 men.

We lost on this occasion from 30 to 40 men in killed and wounded. After general Hill had repulsed the enemy, I received orders to throw back the battalion some hundred paces and align it with the 5th battalion.

The description is further incorrect in stating that the 5th line battalion formed the left wing of the German brigades. The 7th battalion stood on the flank, the battalions being placed in the order of their numbers. This can, if necessary, be corroborated by general Donkin, who was by me a short time before the enemy's attack, and talked with me about the precarious *(misslich)* situation in which I was placed with my battalion.

Whether, as the history further states, captain Langrehr, on the renewal of the action, the morning of the 28th July, rushed forward against the enemy at the head of the 5th battalion, with the colour in his hand, I can neither assert nor deny ; but that I seized the colour of the 7th battalion, in order to raise the courage of the men, which I believed to have sunk from the occurrence of the preceding evening, the officers of the battalion yet living cannot deny : several written certificates of this fact have been already forwarded to captain Heise. To my no small satisfaction the whole battalion marched gallantly forward, and we succeeded in driving back the enemy, who suffered considerable loss. I should never have mentioned this last circumstance, the relation of which would probably have brought upon me the reproach of vain-glory, had not, in the description of this battle, the 7th battalion been represented in so little favourable a light. This alone has led me to state every thing that could tend to the honor of this truly brave battalion. For the same reason I will also add that general Sherbrooke, under whose orders both brigades of the Legion stood, came to me after the attack, and said, " your battalion this morning gloriously revenged the check which it undeservedly suffered the evening before."

You will, Sir, no doubt, excuse my having gone so much at length into this matter. As officer commanding the late 7th line battalion of the Legion I felt it was my duty to do so, and I venture to hope that in the 2d volume of your work, you will either insert this letter, or, in some other manner, correct the erroneous statements respecting this battalion.

I have the honor to be,
With the greatest respect,
Sir,
Your most obedient servant,
A von Berger,
Major-General.

Nienburg, Dec. 3, 1834.

3

Hanover, Dec. 7th 1834.

SIR,

I have the honor to acknowledge the receipt of your letter of the 3d inst., and beg to thank you for the favorable terms in which you have been good enough to notice the 1st volume of my History of the King's German Legion. The difficulties with which I had to contend in the compilation of the work, you duly appreciate, and you do me no more than justice in believing, that had more copious details of the achievements of the corps been placed at my disposal, some errors and omissions which, I regret to learn, appear in the text, would have been avoided.

I shall not fail to append your description of the part taken by the 7th line battalion of the Legion at the battle of Talavera to the forthcoming volume of the work, and I trust that this document, in conjunction with a statement from major von Holle on the same subject, will be found fully to redeem the errors, to which you have, with so much courtesy, called my attention.

I have the honor to be,
        Sir,
    Your most obedient servant,
            N. LUDLOW BEAMISH.

To Major-General von Berger.
&c.   &c.   &c.

Statement of major von Holle.

TRANSLATION.

The surprise of the night of the 29th July was related to me in the manner I have stated, by my late brother, lieutenant Charles von Holle, who was then wounded; namely :—

He was sent down the hill with his few skirmishers to plant outposts, and came upon the enemy's column of apparently nine battalions, which, charging up the hill with a tremendous fire of musquetry, drove his detachment before them, exactly upon the 7th battalion of the Legion.

The 7th battalion, half asleep upon the ground, suddenly received a shower of balls, which it immediately returned, without being aware that the skirmishers were still in its front. From this fire of the battalion, my brother received a ball through his cap.

Such accidents are unavoidable in night attacks, and many of the most distinguished English regiments committed the same mistake on this night.

My brother stated explicitly, that he observed major von Berger and lieutenant Delius, several times endeavouring to lead forward the 7th battalion, without being able to distinguish any other officers in the night.

On the morning of the 28th, when the attack on the enemy's column was made, the 5th battalion stood in the centre, and the 7th battalion on the left, the skirmishers on the right wing of the line.

That captain Langrehr seized the colours of the 5th battalion and thus led it into the midst of the enemy's column ;—that the corps of skirmishers under major von Wurmb fell upon the same in the left flank, and that both corps made frightful havoc among the enemy's ranks with the bayonet and butt-end of the musquet—are facts which can be corroborated by every officer present of both corps now living.

That major von Berger in like manner led the 7th battalion against the left flank of the enemy's column is by no means at variance with this statement.

The fact of captain Langrehr having led the 5th battalion as above mentioned, being, until now, unknown to the officers of the 7th battalion, furnishes the best excuse for my being, until now, ignorant of the fact related with regard to the 7th battalion ; more particularly as the officers of the 7th battalion had a better opportunity of observing the 5th, than I had of observing the 7th, being more to the right of the line.

An officer who was present in this battle declared to me, in reply to my enquiry, that he knew of the 7th battalion having fallen upon the enemy's column in the same manner as the 5th, which circumstance I have therefore much pleasure in adding to this statement.

FERDINAND VON HOLLE,

Major, R.L.

Hanover, Dec. 23d 1834.

HISTORY

KING'S GERMAN LEGION.

CHAPTER I.

THE possession of Badajos being now of the greatest importance to the further operations of the allied army, Lord Wellington determined upon at once proceeding with the siege. Want of time and means precluded the possibility of a regular attack being made against the body of the place, and it was, therefore, decided that simultaneous attacks should be directed against fort Christoval and the Castle.

A battering train was accordingly prepared; the artillery and engineer force was increased, and on the 25th of May the seventh division under general Houston invested fort Christoval. The batteries on both sides were completed on the night of the 2d of June; and a breach in the fort having been considered practicable on the 6th, an assault was ordered to be made that night.

1811.

May.

Jones's
Journals
of Sieges
in Spain.

But between dark and the period which had been fixed for the attack, the garrison had cleared away the rubbish from the foot of the breach, and when the advance arrived, they found it impracticable. An attempt was then made to enter by escalade, but the ladders with which the troops were provided, having been only intended to aid in mounting the breach, proved too short, and the garrison, overwhelming the assailants with various missiles, obliged them finally to retire with the loss of twelve killed and ninety wounded. A second attempt was made on the night of the 9th, when four hundred men marched to the assault, but the garrison of the fort had been considerably augmented, and they received the assailants with such resistance, aided by a mass of shells and combustibles, that after braving destruction until forty were killed, and one hundred wounded, the remainder were ordered to retire.

Lord Wellington now seeing the impossibility of obtaining possession of fort Christoval without advancing to the crest of the glacis, and having received intimation of the approach of the enemy in force, determined upon turning the siege into a blockade.

The northern branch of the allied army under general Spenser, now retired before the enemy into the Alemtejo, and Marmont was enabled to open his communications with Soult.

The officers of the King's German Legion employed

upon these operations against Badajos were; of the engineers, captains Meinecke and Wedekind, and of the artillery, captain Cleves. The successful manner in which the latter officer conducted the operations which were committed to him on the right bank of the Guadiana, met with the particular notice of the commander in chief.*

It is here necessary to detail some changes which, about this time, took place among those regiments and brigades of the legion which were employed in the Peninsula.

The first hussars, which, since the battle of Fuentes Onoro, had been occupied with the outpost duty in front of Ciudad Rodrigo, broke up from their cantonments there on the 31st of May, and, accompanying the march of general Spenser's army, came into quarters at Portalegre on the 23d of June. Three troops of the second hussars, which had been brought from the depôt of that regiment in England, also joined the army of the Alemtejo. They were formed into two weak squadrons under captain Wiering, and with the thirteenth English light dragoons, made out a light cavalry brigade, which was commanded by major-general Long. Major von dem Bussche was afterwards removed from Cadiz to take the command of these squadrons.

The eleventh light dragoons took the place of the

Journal of 1st Hussars MSS.

Journal of 2d Hussars MSS.

---

* Captain Cleves of the Hanoverian artillery, conducted that department on the right of the Guadiana with great success."—*Lord Wellington's Despatch.*

sixteenth in the brigade of general Anson, who also was relieved in his command by major-general Victor von Alten.

The detachments of the light infantry brigade of the legion, which, it is to be remembered, had been attached to the northern army, as an independent corps of skirmishers under major von Wurmb, were also transferred to the Alemtejo, and, after an absence of more than two years from their brigade, joined it at Campo Major on the 21st. These battalions were, soon after, brigaded with a battalion of Brunswick light infantry, and together with one English and one Portuguese brigade, placed in the seventh division under the command of major-general Sontag.* The seventh line battalion of the legion was broken up to supply the deficiencies in the three other line battalions, which were then serving in the Peninsula; and the officers, non-commissioned officers and staff, were sent to England to form a new regiment.

Journal of
2d Hussars
MSS.

The services of the second hussars were soon called into action; for the French were busy with the relief of Badajos, and kept a strong force of cavalry in motion in its vicinity. On the 13th the enemy were fallen in with by a patrole of this regiment under lieutenant Meister, who put the French

---

* English Brigade—51st, 68th, and Chasseurs Britanniques.—3 battalions.
German do. 1st & 2d light batt. K. G. L. & Brunswickers 3 do.
Portuguese do. 4th Caçadores, 7th and 8th Regiments, 3 do.

9 battalions

dragoons to flight, and brought in six men and ten
horses prisoners: the lieutenant and four horses
were wounded.

On the following day the enemy appeared with so
strong a force of cavalry and horse-artillery that
general Long deemed it advisable to retire across
the Guadiana, and the brigade bivouacked near
Elvas, where it was joined by the eleventh English
dragoons.

Lord Wellington had been attentively watching
the movements of the French army, and when Soult's
advanced guard had reached los Santos, leaving the
third and seventh divisions to maintain the blockade
of Badajos, he concentrated the covering army at
Albuera, which position, expecting a battle, he had
entrenched. The English commander hoped to engage Soult separately, but the cautious manner in
which the French marshal moved, prevented his
object from being accomplished, and on the 17th
the allies passed the Guadiana, raising the blockade
on the previous day.

The united French armies entered Badajos on the
19th, at a moment when the governor, despairing
of success, was preparing means of escape. Lord
Wellington now placed his troops on both sides of
the Caya, with cavalry posts towards its mouth, and
on the Guadiana, in front of Elvas. The French,
driving these outposts before them, pushed their
cavalry across the Guadiana on the 21st, when part
of general Long's brigade was brought into an affair
of more than ordinary importance.

1811.

June.

Journal of
2d Hussars
MSS.

On this day the second hussars of the legion held the outposts at Quinta de Gremezia, between Elvas and Badajos; their outlying picquet, under lieutenant von Issendorf, was advanced towards the Guadiana, and their left flank was protected by a squadron of the eleventh dragoons, posted towards Badajos.

Early on the morning of the 22d, soon after Issendorf's picquet had been relieved by a picquet of the same regiment under lieutenant von Stoltzenberg, and was already in march to the rear, the relief was attacked by a superior force of French cavalry and driven back. Issendorf, on being informed of the circumstance, instantly wheeled his men about, and hurried to the assistance of his comrade, and the two picquets then uniting, succeeded in keeping the enemy in check until captain Schulze with about half of the hussar detachment, was able to come up. To these lieutenant Crawford of the eleventh, who was also on his return from duty, voluntarily added his picquet, and, thus reinforced, Schulze charged two squadrons of Polish lancers, which formed the enemy's advance, put them to flight, and took three officers, and several men and horses prisoners.

Unfortunately, however, the victors were imprudent enough to follow up the pursuit; for several fresh columns of the enemy soon appeared advancing to the support of the lancers; and although captain Wiering brought up the rest of the hussars from Quinta de Gremezia, the whole were obliged to

retreat, and in the passing of a ravine, they suffered
considerably. However on reaching the village they
again made front, and the enemy halted; and soon
afterwards, the eleventh appearing on the Elvas
road, the French withdrew altogether. In this affair,
captain Wiering, lieutenants Borchers and von
Gruben of the hussars were wounded, two men were
killed, and about twenty were wounded and taken.

On their way back the enemy fell in with the Notes of
squadron of the eleventh, which, as has been stated, lieut.-col.
von Issen-
was posted on the left of the German picquet, and dorf.
MSS.
whose commander, probably expecting that general
Long would advance with the whole brigade, had
retained his position. On seeing the French, he
mistook them for Spanish cavalry, but soon discovering his error, gallantly charged the enemy's
column, and broke through two squadrons. Here,
however, his brave fellows became surrounded, and
the whole squadron, consisting of about seventy men
and horses, were obliged to surrender.

The French troops were now quartered along the
Napier.
Guadiana, above and below Badajos, and Lord Wellington's situation became critical. The enemy were
before him, with a far superior force, particularly in
cavalry; the Portuguese government had utterly
neglected their fortresses, and almost starved their
troops; many of the British lay sick and wounded,
and the military chest was empty. But the firmness
of the British commander was not shaken, and notwithstanding all the complicated difficulties of his

situation, he was ready to accept battle on the banks of the Caya. Soult, however, declined the risque; the defeats of Busaco, Sabugal, Fuentes and Albuera had not yet been forgotten by his troops, and although superior in physical superiority, the moral force of his army was not such as to warrant him in venturing on a pitched battle.

Lord Wellington now sought to divert the attention of the enemy from his front, by concerting with the Spanish general Blake, an irruption into Seville, with a view to the dispersion of the French army before Cadiz, and in pursuance of this plan, Blake crossed the Guadiana on the 22d. Soult hearing of his march, moved with the left of his army and some cavalry upon Seville; Marmont, also, prepared to retire; and thus, although Blake's injudicious proceedings prevented the main object of the operation from being accomplished, Lord Wellington's plan was so far successful as to break up the great army in his front.

Soult routed the Spaniards at Baza on the 9th of August, and soon after, cleared the whole eastern frontier of Andalusia; meantime Marmont retired gradually from Badajos and quartered the greater part of his troops in the valley of the Tagus. The allied army was thus relieved of the presence of the French, and having been also reinforced by detachments from England, Lord Wellington resolved to adopt a new system of operations.

Leaving general Hill with ten thousand infantry,

a division of cavalry, and four batteries of artillery in the neighbourhood of Portalegre and Estremoz, he determined upon placing the rest of the army in quarters at Castello da Vide, Marvao, and other places near the Tagus. He hoped to find an opportunity of taking Ciudad Rodrigo before Marmont could come to its assistance, and for this purpose, caused a battering train to be secretly brought to Lamego, and necessary stores for a siege to be transported from thence to Villa Ponto near Celerico.

The allies broke up from the Caya on the 21st of July, and in the beginning of August, when Lord Wellington had reason to believe that Ciudad Rodrigo was in want of provisions, he suddenly crossed the Tagus and marched towards that fortress. This march had the double object of saving Galicia by menacing the rear of an army under Dorsenne, which was then invading it, and of relieving Murcia from the operations of Soult, by drawing away part of the supporting army to the protection of Badajos.

Wellington arrived upon the Coa about the 8th of August, but found that the French had provisioned the fortress for two months, a few days before his arrival; he therefore quartered the troops near the sources of the Coa and Agueda, close to the line of communication between Marmont and Dorsenne.

The preparations for the siege went on briskly until the British commander learned that the disposable force of the enemy was too great to admit of his attacking the place, and he, therefore, resolved upon substituting a blockade.

The allied cavalry at the outposts were now kept on the alert. A picquet of twenty men, composed of equal numbers of the first hussars and eleventh dragoons, under the command of an officer of the eleventh, was surprized at St. Martin de Trebejo on the 15th, and nearly half of the party made prisoners.

On this occasion a hussar named Nebel, displayed a degree of gallantry and presence of mind that deserves notice. The officer in command of the picquet had been led by the reports of his patroles to believe that the enemy were not within six leagues of the village, and therefore allowed his men to draw their rations; but no sooner were they thus engaged when an outcry was heard signifying that the French were in the place. The men instantly hurried to their horses. The hussars, heedless of a sharp fire of musquetry which followed them into the stable, and continued to fall upon them there, bridled their horses, mounted, and rode boldly out. Their serjeant had been hit in the bridle arm, and their corporal, together with nearly the whole of the eleventh, had been taken prisoners, when Nebel, seizing the bridle of the wounded serjeant's horse, led him forward exclaiming "the first hussars don't surrender," and forcing his way through the musquetry fire, which had already wounded five of his comrades, brought off the rest of the hussars in safety!

Although Marmont had established his communication with Dorsenne, the blockade of Rodrigo was
accomplished by the allies. Head quarters were
fixed at Fuente Guinaldo; the fifth division was
placed at Perales; the first, now under general Graham, occupied Pennemacor; a battery of artillery
was withdrawn from general Hill's corps, as well as
three brigades which with a Portuguese regiment,
were placed in advance of Castello Branco to protect
magazines; while, at the same time, every necessary
arrangement for carrying on the siege was in progress.

After the blockade had continued for six weeks,
the garrison were in want of provisions, and
Marmont, who had now fifty thousand men in
the valley of the Tagus, concerted an operation
for their succour. Large convoys were collected
at Bejar and Salamanca, and on the 21st September
fifty-four thousand infantry, six thousand cavalry,
and one hundred pieces of artillery were collected
to cover their introduction to the fortress.

The British commander immediately collected his
scattered troops, and placed them in the following
order:—

The third division, reinforced by three squadrons
of the first hussars, and two squadrons of the
eleventh dragoons under major-general Victor von
Alten, formed the centre upon the heights of El-Bodon
and Pastores, which commanded a view of the whole
plain round the fortress. The light division with
some cavalry and guns, formed the right wing, and

Margin notes:
1811.

August.

Napier.

September

Journal of Victor Alten's brigade MSS.

Napier.

was posted beyond the Agueda, in such a position as to be able to observe an enemy coming from the eastern passes of the mountains. The sixth division and general Anson's brigade of cavalry composed the left wing, which, under the orders of general Graham, was stationed at Espeja, with advanced posts at Carpio and Marialva; the Partida of Julian Sanchez was on the left of these, spread, in observation, along the lower Agueda; the seventh division was at Alamedillo; the first division at Nave d' Aver; the fifth at San Payo, and general Hill approached nearer to the Tagus in readiness to give further aid.

Fuente Guinaldo being the pivot of Lord Wellington's operations, he had constructed there three field redoubts, with a view to impose upon the enemy, and so gain time to assemble his troops, preparatory to further dispositions.

The French having communicated with the garrison, and examined the position of the light division, crossed the hill with six thousand cavalry and four divisions of infantry on the 24th and introduced a convoy into the fortress. They placed some troops in observation at the Vadilla ford, and, it was expected, would not advance further; however, soon after daybreak on the 25th, the outposts of the left wing were driven from Carpio across the Azava, and pursued by the French lancers until two squadrons of English dragoons, aided by the flanking fire of some infantry in a wood, beat back the enemy, and reoccupied the post.

While this skirmish was taking place on the left, 1811. fourteen battalions of infantry, thirty squadrons of September cavalry, and twelve guns passed the Agueda under Montbrun and marched for Guinaldo, taking the road which led direct over the heights of

EL BODON.

The position of El Bodon was at this moment held Journal of lieut.-col. Ernest Poten, MSS. by five weak squadrons of Victor Alten's brigade, numbering about three hundred and forty horses; one battalion of the fifth regiment under major Ridge, and two batteries of Portuguese artillery under major Victor von Arentschild.

The ground is a rocky ridge, intersected by stony defiles, and on the right of this chain, where the crest of a gentle declivity offered a favourable position, Arentschild's guns were placed, supported by the fifth regiment,; two squadrons of the hussars under captains Poten and Bergmann occupied the high road in the centre; in rear of these stood two squadrons of the eleventh, and the remaining squadron of hussars under captain von Gruben, lay in a small hollow of the ground upon the left.

This small body of troops was supported in the rear by the twenty-first Portuguese, the seventy-seventh British, and the remainder of the third division, but the greater part of the regiments and brigades were at too great a distance to admit of their

affording any immediate assistance to the troops in
advance.

Upwards of two thousand French cavalry led by
Montbrun in person, and followed by infantry and
artillery, moved rapidly in three columns upon the
allied position. The centre horsemen, taking the
high road, came on with all the confidence which
their numerical superiority inspired, direct against
the advanced squadron of hussars commanded by
Ernest Poten. To have awaited their charge would
have been destruction to the German squadron, and
Poten, with that firmness and intrepidity which is so
often found an overmatch for physical force, allowing
the enemy to come within fifty paces of his front,
dashed suddenly against the head of the column,
and drove it upon the rear. Bergmann immediately
brought forward his squadron to follow up the
attack, and both uniting in vigorous charges against
the dense mass, forced down the enemy to a considerable distance, crowding the French horsemen
upon each other, and rolling up the whole in the
greatest confusion.

While the hussars were thus engaged with the
enemy's centre, the left column had attacked the
Portuguese batteries, and the right column the
squadron of captain von Gruben. Arentschild met the
assailants with showers of grape, and his artillery
men stoutly maintained their fire; but Montbrun's
horsemen, forcing onward, cut down one-half of these
brave fellows at their guns, and two pieces fell into

possession of the enemy. Their triumph was, however, short, for the fifth regiment, led on by the intrepid major Ridge, advanced in line and attacked the cavalry! Pouring a murderous fire upon the French squadrons, they then charged them with the bayonet, and forcing the astonished horsemen down the hill, retook the guns, and now joined by the seventy-seventh regiment, led them to the rear in safety.

1811.

September

Reminiscences of a Subaltern.

Gruben's squadron repelled the attack of the enemy's right column, and the British dragoons nobly supported their German comrades in the centre, but fresh masses of Montbrun's horsemen, with many a chivalrous officer in front, continued to issue from the broken columns, and to demand new exertions from the allied squadrons. The combat now became general throughout the whole line. Quickly rallying after each charge, Alten's little force dashed again and again upon the opposing columns, and men and horses fell thick upon the heights.* Thus the action continued for several hours. Poten had lost his right arm; Bergmann had received a mortal wound; forty-four non-commissioned officers and soldiers, and fifty-two horses of the German squadrons alone lay stretched upon the field, and the British dragoons had suffered in equal proportion; but still, rallying behind the infantry squares,

Poten's Journal. MSS.

---

* The late Sir Frederick Arentschild, who commanded the hussars, and was not given to exaggerate, declared immediately after the combat, that the allied squadrons made not less than *forty* charges on this day.

Appendix
No. I.

the undaunted horsemen maintained a bold front, and notwithstanding the immense superiority of the enemy, would have held their ground, had not Lord Wellington, seeing that the combat would become still more unequal by the arrival of the enemy's infantry before the British reinforcements could come up, ordered the troops to withdraw.

It was three o'clock before the retrograde movement was commenced, and it proceeded in the greatest possible order, the infantry marching in square, supported by Alten's squadrons and Arentschild's artillery. The French cavalry rode fiercely towards the British square which formed the rear guard; but this composed of the two weak battalions of the fifth and seventy-seventh regiments met the threatened onset with firmness. The French horsemen charged with furious valour, riding up boldly to the bayonets, and menacing, at the same time, three faces of the square, but the intrepid battalions received them with all the confidence of British infantry, and pouring a well-directed fire among the venturous troopers, as they approached, the horsemen turned and the battalions remained unbroken.

The remaining brigades of the division at length came up, and the whole retreated across the plain. The French cavalry followed, swarming around the columns in retreat, and a quick fire from their artillery swept the British ranks, but undismayed, the steady soldiers retained their invincible formation,

and thus traversing an open country of nearly six 1811.
miles in extent, while their dead and wounded September
comrades fell fast before the cannon fire, they
reached, about four o'clock, the intrenched position
of Guinaldo.

The French are supposed to have lost nearly one Correspon-
thousand men in this combat, and fifteen or twenty dence of
colonel von
officers of cavalry, who had been gallanty conspicuous Linsingen.
MSS.
in leading their squadrons to the charge, are stated
to have fallen before the allied troops.

In a general order issued by Lord Wellington, Appendix
No. 1.
on the 2d October, the attention of the whole army
was directed to the conduct of the troops which had
been engaged at El Bodon, as affording "a memorable example of what can be effected by steadiness,
discipline and confidence." "It is impossible," says
the British commander, "that any troops, can at any
time, be exposed to the attack of numbers relatively
greater than those which attacked the troops under
major-general Colville, and major-general Alten on
the 25th of September, and the Commander of the
forces recommends the conduct of these troops to the
particular attention of the officers and soldiers of the
army, as an example to be followed in all such
circumstances."

CHAPTER II.

1811.
—————
September
Napier.
The position of Guinaldo was held by not more
than fourteen thousand men, and no part of the rest
of the army was nearer than ten miles. On the 26th,
the day following the combat of El Bodon, Marmont
brought sixty thousand men together in front of
Guinaldo, and Lord Wellington's situation became
critical. In the evening however, he was joined by
the light division; but Marmont's ignorance of the
true situation of the allies alone saved their little
army from molestation.

During the night of the 26th, the British commander skilfully united his whole force twelve miles
behind Guinaldo. Marmont little aware of this
favorable moment for embarrassing the allied troops,
also retired, and continued his retrogade movement
until, to his surprise, he learned that the British
army, with their divisions widely separated, were in
full retreat. He then resumed his former front; but
Wellington had already taken up a strong position
behind the Villa-maior.

The French followed on the morning of the 27th,
and, about ten o'clock, part of the fourth division
became engaged in a sharp affair at Aldea da Ponte.

This village was twice alternately taken and retaken by the contending troops, and the fight was continued with obstinacy until evening, when the allies retired; and the morning of the 28th the whole army occupied a new position in front of the Coa.

1811.

September

The British are stated to have lost two hundred men, and the French nearly double that number in this combat. Captain Sympher's battery of artillery was the only part of the German troops engaged, and with the exception of a nine-pounder being disabled by the blowing up of the vent, sustained no loss. Marmont also retired on the 28th, and, on the following day, the allied army withdrew into cantonments on the Coa, with head quarters at Frenada. The blockade of Ciudad Rodrigo was, however, resumed; Victor Alten's brigade of cavalry, which, owing to the severe illness of its chief, had been placed under the temporary command of colonel Cumming of the eleventh dragoons—took charge of the advanced line of posts, and was spread along the country from Gallegos to Guinaldo. This brigade, suffering from the general sickness which pervaded the army, as well as from its late losses at El Bodon, was now reduced to six squadrons, and the duty became consequently severe, On the 22d of October it was at length relieved by the heavy cavalry brigade of major-general Slade, and towards the end of the following month, Alten's squadrons marched into their long promised cantonments in the valley of the Zezere.

Correspondence of captain Sympher. MSS.

Journal of colonel von Linsingen. MSS.

October.

While the northern army was thus observing the fortress of Ciudad Rodrigo, and endeavouring to recruit its strength for further active operations, the Alemtejo corps under general Hill, was employed in a brilliant enterprise in the south, where some of the German troops had also the good fortune to be engaged.

It should be premised that major Hartmann was attached to this part of the army as commandant of artillery, with lieutenant Mielmann as his adjutant; and lieutenant-colonel Offeney of the Legion staff, acted as deputy-quarter-master-general. The detachment of the second hussars was now under the command of major von dem Bussche, who joined the corps at Villa Viçosa on the 22d August, and these squadrons had been so reduced by service and sickness, that they did not muster more than one hundred and sixty horses.

Correspondence of col. Offeney MSS. A French army-corps under Girard had been ordered to levy contributions on the inhabitants of Caceres, at which place was stationed the main body of the army of Castanos under the count de Penne Villemur; and Girard, crossing the Guadiana, about the middle of October, drove the count to Aliseda, and afterwards to the Casa de Cantillana. Thus situated, Castanos applied for support to general Hill, who, having obtained Lord Wellington's sanction to drive back Girard, if he could do so without risk, made immediate arrangements for attacking the intruders.

On the 22d of October therefore, the cavalry

brigade of major-general Long, the infantry brigades 1811.
of generals Howard and Campbell, colonels Wilson, October.
Byng and Ashworth, with two batteries of artillery Offeney's
under major Hartmann, set out from Portalegre, and correspon-
the same day reached Codicera. On the 23d they MSS.
were at Albuquerque, and on the following day at
Aliseda, and the Casa de Cantillana. The enemy's
advance was at Aroya de Puerco, from whence, on the
25th, they retreated to Caceres, leaving an advanced
guard of three hundred cavalry and a few infantry at
Malpartida.

In the evening of the 25th the British right column
from Aliseda crossed the Salor river, and halted
within a league of that place, while the left column
advanced to Aroya de Puerco. At two o'Clock on
the following morning both columns marched for
Malpartida, out of which about day-break, the German
hussars drove the enemy's cavalry, and the French
retreated towards Montanches. On the 27th general
Hill moved upon Aldea da Cano, with the intention
of cutting off the enemy's retreat, but on arriving here
he learned that they had left Montanches late on the
previous day. He therefore, marched on to the Casa
de don Antonio, where, the information having been
confirmed, he decided upon pushing on the same night
to Alcuescar. Here Bussche arrived with the hussars
in the afternoon, and discovered that the French were
at Aroya Molinos, a short league distant, and general
Hill therefore, determined upon halting at Alcuescar
for the night.

1811.

October.

Offeney's
correspon-
dence.
MSS.

The weather was dark and tempestuous, but no
fires were allowed in the camp, and the troops were
placed carefully out of the enemy's view. At two
o'clock in the morning the whole moved forward in
one column for Aroya, within a mile of which, two
columns of infantry and one of cavalry were formed;
the right wing was then directed to turn the village,
the left wing to attack it in front, and the cavalry to
advance along the plain in the centre.

During these arrangements, a heavy storm of rain
set in, which so completely concealed the movements
of the troops, that they entered the village without
their approach having been observed by the enemy.
Part of the French corps had already marched out,
but about two thousand five hundred infantry, and
four hundred cavalry were still left, and these were in
the act of filing out of the place on the road to Merida,
as the British appeared.

Narrative
of general
von dem
Bussche.
MSS.

The surprise was complete—the enemy hurried
away in all directions. Bussche's hussars, having a
squadron of the ninth dragoons under captain Gore in
reserve, came up with their cavalry, and captain
Schultze, forward in the pursuit, gallantly led his
squadron over a flooded ravine, and charged the
French rear-guard; while Issendorf passing with a
detachment lower down threatened their flank. A
wild flight ensued: the hussars followed, and closing
upon the 20th and 26th French dragoons, fell heavily
upon their disordered ranks. The chace thus continued for nearly two miles, when some fresh squadrons

appeared in support of the fugitives, and they attempted to re-form. Bussche now drew aside the German squadron, and gave that of the ninth an opportunity to charge. The French received the attack with a pistol fire, but soon gave way to the British squadron, and seeing their flank threatened by the detachment under Issendorf, while the main body of the hussars had again formed in front, they hurried off to Merida.

1811.

October.

Bussche's Narrative. MSS.

Bussche's squadrons being now fatigued, he could only send forward a small detachment of the hussars to follow up the pursuit; but these, under lieutenant Borchers, brought in several prisoners, horses, and a quantity of baggage.

While the allied cavalry were thus engaged, the remainder of the troops were in close pursuit of the enemy's infantry, who endeavoured to make their escape over the neighbouring mountains; but the British battalions followed too close at their heels to admit of this attempt being successful, and nearly the whole were captured. The commanding general Girard was wounded, and among the officers taken were colonel the Prince d' Aremberg, commanding the 27th chasseurs; colonel Hutry the chief of the staff, and colonel Vechet commanding the 34th infantry of the line. The cavalry had also to boast of the capture of the general of brigade Brun, who was ridden over by the hussars, and picked up by the ninth. Upwards of two hundred prisoners, among whom were ten officers, were taken by Bussche's

1811.
_____
October.
squadrons; and the thirteenth English dragoons bore off two guns and a howitzer, being the whole of the enemy's artillery,

Bussche's
Narrative.
MSS.
The loss of the British did not exceed seventy;[*] of the legion, major von dem Bussche, captain Schulze, and thirteen hussars were wounded, four horses were killed, seven wounded, and four taken.

In the course of the following month the detachment of the second hussars was re-inforced, and became two squadrons of two hundred and twenty effective horses.

Napier.
The surprise at Aroya had the effect of putting all the French troops in motion, and a powerful attack seemed to be intended upon general Hill; at the same time Soult directed his operations against Ballasteros, and the fortress of Tarifa; and part of Marmont's army marched to the aid of Suchet in Valentia.

General Hill's corps was therefore put in movement to make a diversion, and entered Estremadura by Albuquerque on the 27th of December. Having heard that notwithstanding their late disaster, the enemy were not vigilant, Hill hoped, by forced marches, to effect another surprise, and pushing on by Villar del Rey and San Vicente, his advanced
Bussche's
Narrative.
MSS.
guard, consisting of a detachment of the hussars under lieutenant von Stoltzenberg, came upon the French vedettes at La Nava on the morning of the 29th. But the alarm was soon given, and a battalion

[*] Napier

of the enemy's infantry, which had bivouacked in the place, was enabled to turn out and form square, before the rest of general Long's brigade could come up.

1811.

December.

Bussche's
Narrative.
MSS.

The enemy's square took post in a cork wood, where the obstruction of shrubs and hollows presented considerable difficulties to the approach of cavalry; however two squadrons of the thirteenth dragoons and one squadron of the german hussars were ordered to attack the square.

Captain Cleve commanded the german squadron, and led it boldly forward in open column of divisions against one angle of the square; but the lower branches of the cork trees impeded his course, and the loose files of the adjoining squadron created disorder on his flank, and a compact formation could not be maintained. However he pushed gallantly on, received the first fire of the square without much loss, and half of his first division came within a few yards of the enemy. Here, impeded by the difficulties of the ground, they received the second fire of the square and lieutenant von Estorff, and several men were wounded; the horses of captain Cleve, lieutenants von Stoltzenberg, Estorff, and Tümmel were also hit; some of the men now flew off to the flank, and the few brave fellows who were enabled to reach the bayonets of the enemy, not being sufficient to make any impression upon the square, were nearly all struck down.

The charge of the thirteenth was alike unsuccessful,

1812.

January

Bussche's
Narrative.
MSS.

and attended with considerable loss, and the French battalion eventually effected its retreat to Merida, having sustained little injury.

The hussars lost several horses in this ill-judged attack; three men were killed, and one officer, seventeen men, and twenty-eight horses were wounded: many of the men severely.

General Hill's corps reached Merida on the following day, but the place had already been abandoned by the enemy. On the 1st of January the advanced guard of hussars drove in the French picquet at Torre Mexia, and pursued it to Almandralejo, where the enemy, having a strong force of cavalry and infantry, the hussars were obliged to await the arrival of support. But the main body of the corps, being impeded by deep roads, was yet two leagues distant, and the hussars under captains Cleve and Bussche had to sustain a continued skirmish of nearly six hours, opposed to more than double their number of the enemy's cavalry, before any reinforcement reached them. They, however, maintained a bold front, and manfully held their ground until the arrival of the supports, when the French withdrew to Zafra.

The horse of lieutenant von Gruben was killed under him, and that of captain von dem Bussche was wounded on this occasion; but the entire loss of the hussar squadrons, did not exceed four horses killed, and six men and five horses wounded.

The continued bad condition of the roads and state of the weather now caused general Hill to halt, and

1812.

January

Bussche's
Narrative.
MSS.

he sent forward a small body of troops under colonel Abercrombie to follow the enemy's rear guard. These, consisting of the two german squadrons, the fourth regiment of Portuguese cavalry, the twenty-eight English infantry and three guns, reached Fuente del Maestre on the evening of the 3d, and the advanced guard of hussars soon fell in with the twenty-seventh French dragoons, who had pushed forward a strong squadron to meet their advance, keeping a reserve in ambuscade. Major Bussche quickly passed the whole of the hussars to the front, and directing captain Cleve to charge the French squadron, held the other in reserve. Cleve was in the act of forming up his squadron for the attack, when the French, availing themselves of the favourable opportunity, threatened to charge the Germans in flank, but this intelligent officer expertly wheeling his squadron round, anticipated the enemy's charge, and fell upon them. The French awaited the attack, and standing firm, the contest was doubtful, when a movement of the reserve squadron under captain Werner Bussche, added to the appearance of some Portuguese cavalry in support, put the enemy to flight; and they hurried off to Los Santos, leaving two officers, thirty-five men, and eighteen horses in the hands of the hussars, whose loss did not exceed one man and four horses killed, and fourteen men and four horses wounded.

During this affair a soldier of the second hussars named Olvermann, exhibited a fine trait of gallantry and devotion to his officer: captain Cleve, being

1812.

January.

Bussche's
Narrative.
MSS.

prominent in the charge, became surrounded by French horsemen, and was in great personal danger, when Olvermann, forcing his way to the spot, cut from their horses two French dragoons, by whom Cleve was immediately threatened, and brought his captain off in safety! The hussar's gallantry was properly rewarded by immediate promotion.

The French were now in full retreat for Monasterio, and the object for which general Hill's corps had been moved up from Portalegre having been thus accomplished, it returned to its former cantonments: meantime an important conquest had been achieved by the main army.

CHAPTER III.

During the latter winter months Lord Wellington had skilfully managed to secure the dilapidated fortress of Almeida from sudden attacks, and to collect there a battering train and stores preparatory to his intended siege of Ciudad Rodrigo.

1812.

January

It was decided that the attack upon this fortress should be made against the north front, where two hills called the upper and lower Teson commanded the place. On the highest of these hills the French had erected a small redoubt, and this was supported by two guns and a howizer in battery, on the roof of the fortified convent of St. Francisco, which, together with two other fortified convents, called Santa Cruz and St. Domingo, formed the principal security of the suburbs.

Jones's Sieges.

The weather being excessively cold, and no cover of any sort for the troops being at hand, it was regulated that they should remain cantoned in the nearest villages, and that the duties of the siege should be taken by the light, first, third, and fourth divisions alternately every twenty-four hours.

In conformity with this plan the divisions in rear began to close up on the fifth of January, and at

noon on the eighth, the light division commenced
the investment.

Journals of
Line Bat-
talions.
Correspon-
dence of
captain
Sympher.
MSS.
The German troops employed in the siege were the
first, second, and fifth line battalions, and captain
Sympher's battery of artillery of the legion. The
former were cantoned at Alameda, about three leagues
from the fortress; the latter acted in conjunction with
the British artillery against the defences of the place,
and the light battalions were engaged in observing
the banks of the Agueda.

The first object of the besiegers was to obtain
possession of the redoubt on the upper Teson, and
this was ordered to be stormed on the evening of the
eighth. The operation was entrusted to four companies of the light division under lieutenant-colonel
Colborn of the 52d, who entered by escalade soon
after eight o'clock in the evening, and after a short
resistance and little loss, succeeded in attaining possession of the redoubt. A lodgment was immediately
formed on its right, and a communication opened
with the rear.

On the following day the work was deepened, and
the direction of the first parallel, as well as the positions for the batteries were marked out, without
much injury having been sustained by the enemy's
fire; and the operations went rapidly forward.

On the thirteenth Lord Wellington received information which led him to believe that Marmont would
advance to the relief of the place before the approaches
could be regularly formed, and having ascertained

that it was practicable to form a breach from the first parallel, he decided upon immediately opening from thence on the body of the place.

1812.
January.
Jones's
Sieges.

The fortified convent of Santa Cruz, in which the garrison maintained a strong guard, commanded the spot to which it was proposed to bring the right of the second parallel, and the possession of it became, therefore, indispensable to further proceedings. The post was ordered to be stormed; and for this purpose, three hundred men, composed of the corps of skirmishers and detachments of the line battalions of the legion, with one company of the sixtieth; the whole under the command of captain la Roche de Stackenfels of the first line battalion of the legion, were ordered to make the assault, on the evening of the thirteenth. Under a heavy fire from the fortress, the advance, consisting of the skirmishers of the first line battalion under lieutenant Charles von Holle, forced the palisades by which the convent was surrounded, and, appearing unexpectedly in the place, surprised the defenders, who fled, leaving behind their arms, baggage and accoutrements.

Notes of
major von
Holle.
MSS.

On this occasion, three men were killed, and lieutenant Lewis von Witte and thirty-four men of the legion were wounded; and on the following day lieutenant Hüneeken, a fine young officer of the first line battalion, had the misfortune, when employed in the trenches, to lose both legs by a shell, and was further obliged to suffer amputation.

Journals of
Line Bat-
talions.
MSS.

The approaches to the second parallel were now

1812.
January.
carried forward by the flying sap, and in the course of the night a lodgment was made in the convent.

Jones's
Sieges.
A bad custom had prevailed of the division on duty being withdrawn from the trenches as soon as the relieving division was seen to approach, and the enemy taking advantage of this favorable moment on the morning of the 14th, made a sortie between ten and eleven o'clock, with about five hundred men. They succeeded in upsetting most of the gabions that had been placed during the preceding night in advance of the first parallel, and some of the assailants even penetrated into the parallel itself; a few of the workmen however, spiritedly collected together by an officer of engineers, manned the parapets and kept up a Journals of
Line Bat-
talions.
MSS. steady fire, and, the detachments under captain la Roche quickly coming to their aid, the intruders were driven back.

This evening the convent of St. Francisco was escaladed by a party of the fortieth regiment, which immediately established itself in the suburbs.

Jones's
Sieges.
On the fifteenth, twenty-three twenty-four pounders and two eighteen pounders were in battery; they continued to fire throughout the day, and the main scarp was soon expected to fall. An additional battery for seven twenty-four pounders was now marked out, with the intention of forming a second breach to aid the operations against any retrenchments which might be made in rear of the principal point of attack.

On the seventeenth the second parallel was pushed

forward to its full extent on the top of the lower 1812.
Teson, within one hundred and eighty yards of the January.
body of the place, and the second breach was effected
opposite the Francisco convent. Upon this one nine Sympher's Correspondence. MSS.
pounder and one howitzer of captain Sympher's battery,
under lieutenant Schultzer, were employed to fire,
while the remainder of the officers and men of the
battery, were sent to aid the service of the guns in
the first parallel.

On the 19th, both breaches were pronounced Jones's Sieges.
practicable, and Lord Wellington ordered the attack
to be made at seven o'clock in the evening.

The operation was entrusted to the third and light
divisions under generals Craufurd and M'Kinnon,
and the Portuguese brigade of general Pack ; the two
former were to storm the breaches ; the Portuguese
brigade to escalade by the gate of St. Jago. The
assault was completely successful. In vain the enemy
took shelter behind deep retrenchments, with which
they had fortified the great breach, and desperately
opposed the furious onset of the third division ; in Napier.
vain was the smaller breach blocked up, and the
intrepid leader of the light division stormers, struck
down among his gallant men:—the right flank of the
retrenchment was gained, and the defenders, abandoning their works, fled before the British bayonets
into the town. Meantime Pack's Portuguese were
also within the walls, and before night Ciudad
Rodrigo was in full possession of the allies.

The brave commanders of the light and third

1812.

January. divisions fell in this assault, and the whole loss of the allies was estimated at ninety officers, and twelve hundred men.

The loss of that part of the German legion that was engaged in the siege, amounted to thirteen men killed, and two officers and seventy-five men wounded.

Fifteen hundred of the enemy were made prisoners; three hundred were killed and wounded, and above one hundred and fifty pieces of artillery were captured.

The siege of Ciudad Rodrigo having been thus brought to a successful close, Lord Wellington's attention was now directed towards Badajos.

Jones's Sieges. Preliminary measures for the renewal of this siege were already in progress. Stores and tools had been brought up from Lisbon to Setuval, and from thence February. to Alcacer do Sal during the month of February, and, by the eighth of March, fifty-two pieces of ordnance were collected at Elvas.

These preparations were carried on under the direction of lieutenant-colonel Dickson, who, in addition to the officers of the English and Portuguese artillery, Narrative of general Hartmann. MSS. was assisted by captain von Rettberg and lieutenants Lüchow and Thiele of the German artillery, together with the second company of that corps.

Major Hartmann received the command of the artillery of the third, fourth, and fifth divisions, of the army, but continued to accompany the fourth division.

On the 5th of March, Lord Wellington, having been relieved from the embarrassment of Marmont's troops, which were spread out in order to obtain

provisions, gave up Ciudad Rodrigo to Castanos, and 1812.
leaving the first German hussars under Victor Alten March.
in front of the fortress, put the rest of the army in
march for the Alemtejo.

The British commander arrived at Elvas on the Jones's Sieges.
11th of March, and, on the 16th, Badajos was invested
by the third, fourth, and light divisions, and one
squadron of Portuguese cavalry. General Graham,
who had relieved sir Brent Spencer, and become
second in command of the army, moved upon Llerena with the first, sixth, and seventh divisions, and
two brigades of cavalry, and the corps of sir Rowland
Hill was directed upon Almendralejo.

The first and second dragoons of the legion had, Appendix. No. II.
in compliance with their earnest request to be employed on active service, been at length removed
from Ireland, and joined the army at Estremoz, on
the 23d, under the command of major-general
von Bock. Including this brigade, the cavalry of
the covering corps amounted to five thousand horses, Napier.
and the whole allied army numbered about fifty-one
thousand sabres and bayonets.

The following officers of the German artillery and Hart-mann's Narrative. MSS.
engineers were attached to the besieging force :—

King's German Artillery.
Captain von Rettberg,
———— Daniel,
Lieutenant Lüchow,
————— Thiele,
————— von Goeben,
Engineers—Captain Wedekind

The French had strengthened Badajos considerably since the sieges of last year, and the only practicable points of attack seemed to be the south-east front, where an unfinished counterguard and ravelin permitted the main scarp of the bastion of la Trinidad to be seen from the hill on which fort Picurina is situated. Upon this hill, therefore, it was decided that the first parallel should be formed, embracing the fort, which was to be carried by assault; after which, the right face of the bastion la Trinidad, the opposite flank of the bastion Santa Maria, and the curtain between these, were to be breached from the Picurina hill.

Ground was broken in front of fort Picurina on the night of the 17th, and the work of the trenches proceeded successfully until the night of the 19th, when the garrison making a sortie with fifteen hundred infantry and forty cavalry, surprised the guard and working party, and drove them out of the parallel in great disorder. The men were, however, soon rallied by their officers, and the asailants were driven back, but not without the loss of one hundred and fifty in killed and wounded on the side of the besiegers: the commanding engineer, lieutenant-colonel Fletcher was severely wounded on this occasion.

The operations were now impeded by heavy rains, which, filling the trenches with water, caused considerable delay. On the 22d, a further interruption was experienced from the destructive fire of three field pieces, which the enemy had brought to bear upon the parallel from the right bank of the Guadiana, and the fifth division was, therefore, or- dered up from Campo Mayor to invest the place on that side of the river,

The trenches were this day again filled with water; the pontoon bridge across the Guadiana was carried away by the floods; several of the pontoons were sunk, and serious apprehensions were entertained of the besiegers being obliged to withdraw. On the 23d, however, the weather cleared, and the batteries were expected to open on the following day; but again the rains impeded the work, and it was eleven o'clock on the 25th, before the firing commenced.

Fort Picurina was assaulted and carried by storm the same evening after an obstinate resistance, which cost the besiegers nineteen officers and three hundred men in killed and wounded.

A lodgment was immediately formed in the fort; a connexion made between it and the first parallel, and, during the night, three new batteries of the second parallel were traced out.

The garrison now for the first time perceiving the real points of attack, began to repair those parts of the defences against which it was directed, and worked hard to raise the unfinished ravelin and counterguard in front of the bastion of la Trinidad. They made great progress in this effort during the night of the 31st, in consequence of the besiegers' enfilading batteries not having been sufficiently active; and this brought forth the animadversion of the commanding officer in an order issued on the first of April, in which, however, an honorable exeception was made to the battery commanded by lieutenant von Goeben.

On the night of the 2d of April, a bold attempt was made by the besiegers to draw off an inundation which had been formed in front of the place by blowing up the dam that retained the water in the ditch of the lunette St Roque; but the powder could not be placed in the proper position, and the attempt failed.

Marshal Soult now advanced to Llerena with an army to raise the siege, and the covering corps under Sir Rowland Hill, therefore, fell back on Talavera, while the fifth division under General Leith came to the support of the besiegers.

By the evening of the 5th, practicable breaches had been made in the bastions of Santa Maria and la Trinidad; but Lord Wellington, having observed that formidable preparations for their defence, had been made by the enemy, determined to delay the attack until a third breach, according to the original plan, should have been formed in the curtain. This was accomplished by the evening of the 6th, and the assault was ordered to be made that night.

The plan of attack was that the castle on the east, and the bastion of San Vicente on the west side of the fortress should be entered by escalade, while

the three breaches at the south-east angle were
to be stormed; the lunette of San Roque was
also to be carried by assault, and false attacks
were directed to be made on the Pardaleras outwork, and the bridge-head on the right bank of the
Guadiana.

All were ready at the appointed hour:—the lunette
was quickly carried by the guards of the trenches,
and the third division, marching to the escalade of the
castle, attempted to place their ladders against its
wall. The defenders armed with various destructive
missiles, long resisted these attempts, but at length,
the personal exertions of a few intrepid officers of the
division, overcame every obstacle, and the troops
established themselves in the work. In this attack
lieutenant von Goeben of the German artillery was
wounded.

The light and fourth divisions, to whom the
storming of the breaches had been committed, met
with obstacles not to be overcome, and after the most
devoted gallantry; tremendous loss, and exhibitions
of individual heroism which has never been surpassed,
they were withdrawn, at midnight, from the murderous gulph, with orders to form before day-break for a
fresh effort.

But, meantime, the bastion of San Vincente had
been entered by the fifth division, and the besiegers
being now in possession of both flanks of the fortress,
the enemy abandoned the defenses in confusion; the
light and fourth divisions rushed in at the breaches,

1812.

March.

Jones's
Sieges.

and the governor, retiring to fort Christoval, surrendered to the British chief, on the following day.

The total loss of the allies in this sanguinary siege, amounted to seventy-two officers, and nine hundred and sixty-three men killed; three hundred and six officers, and three thousand four hundred and eighty-three men wounded, and about one hundred missing.

While that part of the army to which the siege of Badajos had been entrusted, was employed in the arduous duties which have just been detailed, the light battalions of the legion were, in conjunction with other regiments, engaged in some unsuccessful attempts to surprise the French at Llerena, and that neighbourhood.

Journal of
major Rautenberg;
Narrative
of colonel
C. Wyneckon;
Notes of
captain C.
Heise.
MSS.

The first of these expeditions was made under lieut.-colonel Mitchell of the fifty-first, who, with the weak battalion of that regiment, numbering about two hundred men, and a detachment, of one hundred and seventy of the legion, under captain Cropp, set out from Puebla de Sancho Perez on the 20th of March, for the purpose of surprising a French detachment, which was supposed to be in Llerena. At one o'clock on the following morning, the troops reached Villa Garcia, where they were to be joined by a squadron of cavalry, but these not arriving after a considerable delay, colonel Mitchell pushed on with the infantry alone. It was daylight before they reached Llerena, and here the cavalry coming up, the whole immediately entered the place. But lo! only four Frenchmen were to be found, and these,

probably to avoid being taken, gave themselves up 1812.
as deserters.   March.

The governor of the place, imagining that he saw Rauten-
berg's
Journal,
&c. &c.
MSS. in colonel Mitchell's detachment, the advance guard of the British army, came forth in full costume to welcome the troops, who met with the most hospitable treatment from the inhabitants. Luckily, about eight o'clock, colonel Mitchell received information which prevented his corps from being surprised in the midst of their festivities; for it appeared that the enemy who had only retired a few leagues from the place, had been considerably reinforced, and projected returning the compliment, which the British intended for them, on the following morning. No time was lost, therefore, in assembling the troops, and they made good their retreat to Usagre, three leagues distant, without molestation. The Spanish commandant, hurrying after them, stated that Drouet had entered the place with two thousand men, half an hour after their departure.

An attempt was now made by colonel Mitchell to surprise another detachment of the enemy in the village of Hortachos, but here also the design was anticipated, and the French marched out some hours before the arrival of the allies. The troops therefore returned to Villa France on the 24th.

After these failures an expedition on a more extended scale was planned by sir Thomas Graham. This consisted of the sixth and seventh divisions of the army, with a brigade of cavalry, and two batteries of

1812.

March.

Rauten-
berg's
Journal,
&c. &c.
MSS.

horse artillery, the whole of which, having been assembled at Usagre in the afternoon of the 25th March, moved from thence at ten o'clock, for Villa Garcia, where they arrived at one on the following morning. Here general Graham made his dispositions for the intended surprise, and, about two o'clock, the corps set out for Llerena, distant about four English miles.

The main body of the infantry marched in one column on the high road; the cavalry were on the left, together with the first light battalion of the legion, with orders to enter the town from the Andalusian side; while the second light battalion, which it was intended should enter the town on the opposite side, marched on the right. In front of the main column was an advanced guard of twenty-five men of the first light battalion of the legion, with a few English dragoons; and some distance in rear of this detachment, rode Sir Thomas Graham, Sir Stapleton Cotton, general Bernewitz of the Brunswick corps, and several officers of the staff.

The night which, at starting, was illumined by a fine moon, soon became obscure, and before the troops had marched more than a mile, they were completely in the dark.

Just at this moment, a patrole of the enemy's cavalry, which had been lying in ambush near the line of march, availing themselves of the darkness, rushed suddenly upon the advanced guard, and drove them, together with the staff, in full speed back upon the

column, upsetting Sir Stapleton Cotton, general
Bernewitz, and other officers of the suite. *

Owing to the darkness of the night, the cause of
this sudden retreat and overthrow of the staff, was
not discernible to the troops in rear, but lieutenant
Rantenberg, who commanded the leading section of
the first light battalion of the legion, seeing drawn
swords, horse-hair plumes, and long tailed horses
approaching him at a rapid rate, did not hesitate to
draw up his men, and order them to fire. The French
horsemen immediately wheeled off towards the fifty-
first regiment, which was marching at the head of
the column, and they also fired. Upon this, the
regiments in rear, concluding that the divisions had
been attacked, commenced defending themselves in
various ways, according to their notions of the nature of the assault, Some sent forth a desultory fire
in the direction of their front, many of the shot from
which, falling among the flanking battalions and
squadrons, brought down several men, and caused the
horses to break their ranks; others formed square
and prepared to receive cavalry, while a crowd of
starved dogs, which had been wandering about the
road in search of their masters, setting up a loud
yell, added to the confusion. Nor was this otherwise ludicrous affair unattended with loss; for the

---

* General Bernewitz, on rising from the dust, was not a little alarmed at
seeing, as he imagined, his great coat pierced in many places by musquet balls;
however, on examination, the injury proved to have been committed by *horse
shoes!*

1812.

March.

Rauten-
berg's
Journal,
&c. &c.
MSS.

assistant-surgeon and two soldiers of the fifty-first regiment were killed; a serjeant of the first light battalion of the legion was shot through the chest, and others were wounded.

Order being restored, the march was resumed, and the troops arrived before Llerena without further molestation. It was now daybreak, and the main column halting before the place, the artillery opened a fire upon what appeared to be a strong line of infantry; but the obscurity of the morning had caused an ocular delusion, for after a few shots, this formidable opponent proved to be a stone wall! Meantime the cavalry had ascertained that the enemy were in full march for Azugal, on the other side of the town. The troops were now too fatigued to attempt a pursuit, and although two companies from the first division, which had also arrived in the place, were sent after the fugitives, they returned without success.

Narrative
of colonel
von Linsin-
gen.
MSS.

It has been stated that the first hussars of the legion under Victor Alten, were left in front of Ciudad Rodrigo, on the departure of the main army for the siege of Badajos.

The first hussars were, at this period, reduced to three squadrons, and did not number more than three hundred horses.* General Alten's instructions were

---

* Not " six hundred" as stated by Colonel Napier (History of the War in the Peninsula, Vol. 4. p. 441.) ; nor can the historian be justified in saying that, on Marmont coming close to Ciudad Rodrigo, " Victor Alten immediately crossed the Agueda, and retreated at once to Castello Branco." It will be seen that general Alten crossed the Agueda when his retreat upon Castello Branco was threatened to be cut off, and that instead of retiring *at once* to that place, he withdrew leisurely, making short marches, and stopping one entire day in the neighbourhood of Sabugal.

to remain in close observation of the enemy; to transmit to the British head quarters every possible information that he could obtain respecting their
movements or intentions, and to endeavour to make
Marmont believe that a strong British force remained
still in his neighbourhood; should the main body
of the French corps then in the province of Salamanca, either advance into Portugal, or march in
any other direction towards Estremadura, he was
to follow the allied army by Castello Branco.

1812.

March.

Narrative.
of colonel
von Lin-
singen.
MSS.

To forward these intentions general Alten sent a
party of hussars under lieutenant von Wisch into
the Serra de Francia, and another party towards
Tamames. Wisch remained in the neighbourhood
of Bejar and the Puerta de Bagnos until the
end of the month, and sent in every information
that could be required respecting the enemy's movements.

On the 27th of March, the French troops at Bejar,
reinforced by two regiments, advanced to Miranda
del Castenar, and a brigade of cavalry with guns
passed the Tormes.

On the 29th, the enemy pushed on to the Yeltes
river, and Alten withdrew the hussars to Pedro
de Toro.

The French were reported to have nine thousand
infantry and nine hundred cavalry in advance of the
Tormes; and on the 13th one column, marching
by Zamarra, moved towards the fords of the Agueda
at Pastores. Alten seeing that this movement of

1812.

April.

Linsin-
gen's nar-
rative.
MSS.

the enemy would, if he remained in front of Ciudad Rodrigo, endanger his retreat upon Castello Branco, withdrew the main body of the hussars to El Bodon, and Espeja, leaving a captain and fifty horses in the suburbs of Rodrigo, with advanced posts on the road to Tenebron and St. Espirito, while another detachment was sent to observe the fords of Pastores, and Caridad.

On the following day the hussar picquets in front of Rodrigo were attacked, and after some skirmishing, driven in by a superior force of the enemy's cavalry, while, at the same time, both French infantry and cavalry were seen moving towards the ford of Pastores. Alten, therefore, called in the captains picquet from Rodrigo, and, the parties which had been in observation in the enemy's rear having now also joined him, the three squadrons were concentrated in the neighbourhood of El Bodon. On the 1st of April his head quarters were removed to Alfayates; the following day to Sabugal; and on the 3d to Beinguerenza, where the regiment halted the whole of the following day. During these marches parties of observation had been always left a considerable distance in the rear, to watch the enemy's movements; and on the 5th, when general Alten's head quarters were transferred to Pedragoa, it was reported to him that a body of French infantry and cavalry had advanced to Sabugal, but afterwards returned towards Guinaldo. This led to various conjectures as to the enemy's intentions, and Alten, thinking it probable that the French might come upon his flank by Fundao and Alpedrinho, decided upon marching the following day to Castello Branco. Here he halted during the 7th; and, considering that the duty, which had been entrusted to him, was now fulfilled, he passed the Tagus at Villa Velha on the 8th, and the next day marched to Niza. Here, he received a communication from general le Cor, who commanded a brigade of Portuguese militia in Castello Branco, confirming his supposition as to the movements of the enemy, who, it appeared, had arrived at Fundao in considerable force. An officer's party of hussars was immediately sent back to general le Cor, to meet the enemy's advanced guard; and early on the 11th, Alten, having received Lord Wellington's orders to return to Castello Branco, re-crossed the Tagus, and arrived in time to cover the retreat of the militia upon Sarnades, to which place both the Portuguese and hussars now retired. It appeared that the French, having driven in the hussar detachment, which met their advance on the Alpedrinho road the preceding day, had entered Castello Branco the same evening, and occupied the place in considerable force. On the 12th, general Alten advanced from Sarnades, and found several squadrons of cavalry and a battalion of infantry drawn out before Castello Branco. A slight skirmish took place, in which the leading hussars under cornet Blumenhagen, driving the enemy's advanced guard upon the main body, made one prisoner; but the French maintained their

1812.

April.

Linsingen's narrative, MSS.

1812. position, and the hussars leaving picquets in front of
April. the enemy's advance, returned to Sarnades.   On the
13th, however, the fall of Badajos having become
Linsingens
Narrative.
MSS. known, the French evacuated Castello Branco
altogether; the hussars entered it the same day at
nine o'clock, and the enemy retiring to Pedragoa,
remained there until the advance of the allied army
came up on the 16th.

Soult, who had collected his army at Villafranca
on the 8th of April, finding that Badajos had
fallen, retired before daylight on the following day
Sir S. Cot-
ton's Des-
patch. towards the frontiers of Andalusia.   The British
cavalry followed under Sir Stapleton Cotton, and
coming up with the cavalry of Drouet's corps between
Usagre and Llerena, on the 11th, pursued them to
the latter place, and captured more than a hundred
men and horses, including four officers.   On this
occasion the intelligence and activity of captain
George von der Decken of the first hussars, who had
been appointed aide-de-camp to Sir Stapleton Cotton
in the preceding August, gave much aid to an effective movement which was made upon the enemy's
flank, by part of the brigade of general le Marchant.

Welling-
ton's
Despatch. The British army continued their march, the
French retiring before them, and head quarters
reached Alfayates on the 24th.

The troops now requiring rest after their severe
winter campaign, were put into cantonments on the
Douro, Mondego, and Tagus, with outposts on the
Agueda.   Every exertion was made to refit them for

active movements, and Lord Wellington prepared his plans for a more extended scale of operations than he had been hitherto enabled to undertake.

1812.

April.

About this period major-general Charles von Alten received the highly flattering appointment of the command of the distinguished light division, which had been deprived of its able chief in the storming of Ciudad Rodrigo. On the 6th of May the major-general took leave of the light brigade of the legion, and on the 8th, accompanied by his aide-de-camp captain Baring, proceeded for his new command. The departure of general Alten was a source of regret to the whole of the seventh division, and much as his old corps must have participated in the honor which this selection of their chief conferred upon the King's German Legion, they could not but deplore the loss of a commanding officer, who, while he strictly maintained the discipline, knew also how to secure the affection of his soldiers.

Rauten-
berg's
Journal.
MSS.

On the breaking up of the army from the Guadiana, major Hartmann received orders to repair to the head-quarters of the fifth division, for the purpose of endeavouring to put into good order the battery of artillery which was attached to it. He took charge of the battery at Momenta de Beira on the 3d of May, and remained there until the end of the month, when, being relieved by captain Lawson, he returned to the fourth division.

Narrative
of general
Hartmann.
MSS.

Lord Wellington decided upon manœuvering against that part of the enemy's force which was on the right bank of the Tagus, and in order to prevent

the ready communication of this army with that on

the south side of the river, he directed general Hill to march with part of his corps from Almendralejo, and destroy the enemy's posts and bridge of communication over the Tagus at Almaraz.

These works consisted of two forts called Napoleon and Ragusa, and a bridge head. Fort Napoleon, situated on the south side of the river, was an irregular work, having a retrenchment and palisaded ditch across its rear, and, in the interior, a loop-holed tower secured by a draw-bridge; the scarp of the exterior work, however, was weakened by a wide berm which divided it into two steps.

Fort Ragusa, on the north bank, was a redoubt of respectable profile, having also a loop-holed tower in the interior, but being situated too far from the river to protect the bridge, a flêche had been constructed on the bank which also served to flank the fort.

The road which led to these posts from the south, passed over an extensive range of mountains crowned by the old tower of Miravete, at the distance of four or five miles from the bridge, and this road offered the only practicable pass for artillery or wheel carriages; but the tower was surrounded by a wall and rampart twelve feet high, upon which were mounted seven or eight pieces of ordnance. A large house standing on the road had also been fortified; and two small works between the house and the tower, completed a strong line of defence across the pass.

Another approach to the bridge was afforded by a way over the Puerto de Cueva, three or four miles to the eastward of Miravete; but this was totally impracticable for artillery, and the descent towards Almaraz was little better than a goat's path.

The nature of the defences of Miravete, and the works at Almaraz were imperfectly known to Sir Rowland Hill, but having heard of the pass over the Puerto Cueva, he determined upon taking general Howard's brigade by this road to attack the bridge, while colonel Wilson's should attack the castle, and the Portuguese advance by the high road.

Conformable to this arrangement, the troops marched at seven o'clock on the evening of the 16th, carrying with them ladders, crow-bars, felling-axes, and every thing necessary for the destruction of the works. Two detachments of artillery accompanied each brigade under the respective commands of lieutenant Love of the English, and lieutenant Thiele of the German artillery.

The column which marched by the pass of Cueva was misled by the guide, and the descent was steep, rocky, and intricate. This occasioned such delay in the movements of the troops, that it was broad daylight before they had arrived within five miles of the bridge. Hill, therefore, seeing no hope of effecting a surprise, drew back the column behind the heights, where they bivouacked out of sight of the enemy.

The troops intended for the attack of the castle, delayed by the weight of the ladders and the length

1812.

May.

Jones's
Sieges.

Colonel
Dickson's
Report.
MSS.

of the road, were also unable to reach their destina-

tion before daylight, and the defences were then found so strong; the approach so difficult; and the enemy so well prepared to resist the attack, that general Chowne who commanded the column, did not consider it prudent to proceed without further instructions.

Jones's
Sieges.

The pass of Miravete was also deemed impracticable by the centre column; and now a careful examination of the heights was made, with a view to discover a passage for the artillery into the valley of Almaraz, and to ascertain the possibility of forcing the principal pass.

The result was so unsatisfactory, that the undertaking must have been altogether abandoned, had not general Hill, with great enterprise, decided upon the bold step of attempting to carry the works by escalade, and he immediately made arrangements for assaulting fort Napoleon and the bridge-head.

Colonel
Dickson's
Report.
MSS.

It was proposed that the troops should descend the mountain in the night, and come suddenly upon the forts at daylight, while the bridge and its defences were also to be assailed, and a false attack made upon the castle of Miravete.

Jones's
Sieges.

The assaulting column under general Howard, reinforced by the sixth Portuguese, a company of the sixtieth riflemen, and Thiele's detachment of artillery, began to descend the mountain at nine o'clock in the evening of the 18th, and the advance arrived near fort Napoleon at day-break; but owing to the difficulties of the roads, the rear of

the column could not close up before eight o'clock, 1812.
and by this time the garrison were put on the alert May.
by the false attack on Miravete, which, as had been Jones's
concerted, commenced soon after day-break. Sieges.

Regardless, however, of the enemy's fire, which opened upon them as soon as they were discovered, the assailants deliberately descended the ditch, and placing their ladders against the scarp, got footing on the berm. From thence, pulling the ladders up after them, they mounted to the parapet, and driving back the defenders, followed close after them into the retrenchment. Here a sharp contest took place, in which the French commandant was wounded and made prisoner; and overpowering numbers of the assailants entering the fort, the garrison without availing themselves of the security of the tower, abandoned the work altogether, and took refuge in the bridge-head. The assailants forced in here with the fugitives, who now crowded on the bridge and sought to escape across the river; but the foremost cut away some of the boats, and several men and officers were drowned; then the remainder, about two hundred and fifty in number, fell into the hands of the victors.

Meantime, the garrison of fort Ragusa had kept Colonel Dickson's Report. MSS.
up a brisk fire upon the advancing troops, and they now opened upon fort Napoleon; but lieutenants Thiele and Love, with wonderful rapidity, turned the guns of Napoleon against Ragusa, and sent forth such an active and well directed fire, that in conjunction with the approach of the infantry to the

bridge, it forced the garrison from the fort, and the
whole fled towards Naval Moral.

The destruction of the enemy's works was now
commenced, and lieutenant Thiele was charged with
that of the tower, magazines and ordnance, in fort
Ragusa.

He soon effectually disabled the guns, and proceeded to blow up the tower and magazines, in the
former of which was lodged from eight to ten hundred weight of powder. The best dispositions had
been made by him for this purpose, but over anxious
for the success of the operation, and impatient
at the slow progress of the port-fire, which he had
laid to the train, he was imprudent enough to enter
the tower with a lighted match. This, it is supposed,
communicated instantly with some loose powder at
the entrance; for scarce had he set foot upon the
threshold, when the whole building flew into the
air. The destruction of the tower was complete, but
the devoted soldier was blown to atoms!

Few individuals have been more deservedly re-
gretted than this young officer. Ever zealous and
intelligent, he had secured the esteem, and received
the marked aknowledgments of the superior officers
under whom he had served, and gave promise of
becoming distinguished in a profession, to the duties
of which his energies were entirely directed.

The tower of fort Ragusa being levelled to the
ground, the bridge as well as all the adjacent buildings and magazines were blown up, and early on the

following morning, the works of fort Napoleon shared the same fate.   On the 20th, the troops repassed the mountains, and the following day returned to Truxillo.

The total loss of the allies in this expedition was two officers and thirty-one men killed, and thirteen officers and a hundred and thirty-one men wounded.

1812.

May.

Jones's Sieges.

CHAPTER IV.

1812.

June.

Jones's
Sieges.

The ready communication of the French armies on the north and south of the Tagus having been prevented by the destruction of the works at Almaraz, Lord Wellington proceeded to dislodge the enemy from the town of Salamanca.

Considerable depôts had been collected at this place; and for their protection, as well as to command the passage of the Tormes, the French had constructed formidable works.

These consisted of a fort on the north-west of the town formed out of the convent of San Vicente, and two redoubts on the south side, formed also from convents, and called St. Cajetano, and la Merced.

The army crossed the Agueda on the 13th of June, and on the 16th reached the Valmusa river, about six miles from Salamanca.

Journal of
colonel von
Linsingen.
MSS.

Victor Alten's brigade of cavalry, which formed the advanced guard, drove the French horsemen before them on the 16th up to the forts, and made a few prisoners, but not without the loss of some horses killed; and cornets Leonhardt, Holtzermann, and Behrens, together with several men, were wounded.

The enemy evacuated Salamanca the same night, leaving a garrison of eight hundred men in the forts. These were immediately invested by the sixth division under general Clinton, and the rest of the army were placed in position on the heights of San Christoval, to cover the attack.

Deficiency of means prevented the possibility of any extended plan of attack being carried into operation against the works, and it was therefore proposed merely to breach the main wall of San Vicente, and, as soon as possible, to give the assault.

Accordingly, on the night of the 17th, the construction of a battery was commenced in a favorable position two hundred and fifty yards from the wall; but the fire of musquetry which fell upon it from the fort; the shortness of the night, and the inexperience of the workmen, prevented much progress from being made, and it was attempted to blow in the counterscarp. This also proved unsuccessful; at length, on the morning of the 18th, the light brigade of the legion, having been ordered at the particular request of general Clinton, to take the duties of the picquets and firing parties, three hundred men, under the command of captains Rautenberg and Holtzermann, were posted among the ruins, and these by a continued and well-directed fire, kept up throughout the night, nearly silenced the defenders by the following morning. The effective service rendered on this occasion by the German troops obtained for them the personal thanks of brigadier-general Bowes, who commanded in the trenches.

1812.

June.

Jones's
Sieges.

Journal of
major Rau-
tenberg
MSS.

1812.

June.

On the morning of the 19th, the detachment was relieved by an equal body of troops from the same brigade, and the battery being finished, opened upon the wall of the convent with seven pieces of ordnance.

Linsingens
Journal.
MSS.

Marmont now moved up his army to the support of the forts, and in the afternoon of the 20th, sent a strong body of cavalry, supported by infantry, and artillery, to Morisco and Castellanos, two villages immediately in front of the allied position. Victor Alten's brigade, which had been posted here, was immediately attacked, and, being overmatched in numbers, retired towards the hills beyond Morisco. Here the British artillery checked the enemy's advance, and they bivouacked for the night behind the villages. In this retrograde movement Alten's brigade was exposed to a heavy cannon fire, and suffered some loss.

On the 21st, Marmont made a reconnoisance of the British right wing from the heights leading to Aldea Lingua and the river Tormes, and established an infantry post upon a hill in front of Morisco, which commanded the right of the allied position. A squadron of the first hussars, which was sent in this direction, became engaged in a sharp skirmish, and had six men and thirteen horses wounded; and Lord Wellington, seeing that the post was likely to give serious annoyance to the allies, placed a detachment of cavalry and infantry under Victor Alten, for the purpose of dislodging the enemy on the following day.

This detachment consisted of two companies of the 1812. legion light brigade, under captains Frederick and June. Christian Wynecken; one troop of the eleventh dragoons, and another of the first hussars; and about Narrative. of col. C. Wynecken MSS. half-past eight o'clock on the morning of the 22d, the hill was attacked by the two companies in front and flank, and brilliantly carried in full view of both armies; the enemy retiring to Morisco.

But Marmont, had, on this day, been considerably reinforced, and soon a fresh battalion came forth from the village, supported by a troop of cavalry, and sought to regain the post. The eleventh quickly disposed of the enemy's horsemen, who, in their hurry to avoid the British charge, actually cleared a ditch; but their infantry too far out-numbered the legion detachment to admit of a successful resistance, and Alten directed them to withdraw. In this movement they experienced some loss; the troop of hussars now charged the French battalion in flank, but was unable to prevent it from occupying the hill.

It was already ten o'clock, and Wellington, who had been a witness of what had occurred, immediately ordered up the whole of the seventh division. These marching straight upon the hill, with the legion and Brunswick light infantry on their flank, soon caused the intruders to retire to the village. Here, however, a skirmishing fire was kept up for some time by the enemy's riflemen, and captain von Reiche, of the Brunswickers, who commanded the

1812.

June.

German skirmishers, was mortally wounded. The entire casualties of the legion in the affair, were three men killed, captain Frederick Wynecken, lieutenants Lemmers and M'Glashen, and seventeen men wounded, the officers severely; and several men and horses of the hussars wounded.

Wellington's Despatch.

The enemy retired during the night, and on the following evening took post with their right on the heights near Cabeza Villosa, and their left at Huerta on the Tormes, intending to communicate with the garrison in the forts. Lord Wellington, therefore, changed his front, placing the right of the army at Santa Marta, with advanced posts at Aldea Lingua, and he sent Bock's brigade of German cavalry across the Tormes, to observe the passages of that river.

About two o'clock on the morning of the 24th, the enemy crossed the Tormes at Huerta, with a strong force of cavalry, infantry, and artillery, and gave every demonstration of intending a general movement. Bock's dragoons, which consisted of only six squadrons, necessarily commenced their retreat, and this movement was executed in a manner which called forth the marked approbation of Lord Wellington. Two

Journals of 1st and 2d. Dragoons. MSS.

divisions of infantry and a brigade of cavalry had been sent across the river at Santa Marta, to the support of the German horsemen, but more than half a mile of ground was to be crossed before they could reach these troops, and the enemy pressed on with an overpowering force of all arms, supported by a heavy

cannonade. The steadiness of the German brigade 1812.
however, aided by the judicious disposition of the June.
squadrons, made by colonel de Jonquiéres of the Journal of
second regiment, enabled Bock to keep this formi- Brigade; Notes of
dable force in check, until reinforcements arrived to Baron Marschalk.
his assistance. Then the enemy ceased to advance, MSS.
and, observing the dispositions which Wellington
had made for their reception, they returned in the
evening to Huerta, and recrossed the river. The
Germans had three men and seven horses killed, two
men and four horses wounded, and five men were taken.

From want of the means of attack, the operations Jones's Sieges.
against the forts had made but slow progress. An
attempt to carry the Cajetano by storm on the 23d,
proved unsuccessful, and the besiegers had suffered
considerable loss; at length, on the 27th, a breach
in this work became practicable, and the same day a
tremendous fire broke out in the convent of San
Vicente, which the garrison found impossible to
subdue.

Flags of truce were now sent out from both the
forts, and an attempt was made to treat for their surrender; but, the governor having refused the terms
offered by Lord Wellington, Cajetano was immediately carried by assault, and the whole fell into
possession of the besiegers.

Besides seven hundred prisoners, thirty guns, and Napier.
a quantity of stores, a free passage across the Tormes
was secured to the allied army by this capture; the
besiegers, however, lost upwards of three hundred

1812.

June.

men; and, since the passage of the Tormes, nearly five hundred had fallen: among the officers wounded during the siege, was lieutenant Scharnhorst of the

Journal of
artillery.
MSS.

German artillery, who was unfortunately deprived of the use of an eye.

Linsingens
Journal.
MSS.

The French army retired during the night of the 27th in the direction of Toro and Tordesillas, and were followed by Victor Alten's cavalry through Huerta, Babila-fuente, Villeria and Cantalpinas. Thirty-three prisoners were captured by the advance of the brigade, which halted for the night at San Morales and Aldea Rubia.

On the 29th the allied army was put in motion in three columns, taking the several roads of Toro, Valladolid and Medina del Campo. Victor Alten's cavalry, supported by the light division and a battery of artillery, formed the advance of the centre column, which was directed upon Valladolid, and came up with the enemy's rear guard, consisting of seven or eight squadrons, and a strong column of infantry,

July.

before Rueda on the 2d of July. The French drew up before the place and seemed inclined to make a stand, but the English battery having been brought to the front, a short experience of its well directed fire, caused their retreat to be resumed. Alten's brigade followed, led by the hussars, who, attacking the retiring squadrons in detached bodies, killed and wounded more than fifty men, and took two serjeants and ten men prisoners, with the trifling loss of one man wounded and five horses killed.

The other columns of the army being too far apart to admit of an immediate junction being made, Lord Wellington was not enabled to bring up a sufficient body of troops in time to molest the enemy in their passage of the Duero; and crossing that river, they took up a position with their right opposite Pollos, the centre at Tordesillas, and the left at Simancas on the Pisuerga.

1812.

July.

Welling-on's Des-pa'ch.

The enemy being now in a position which commanded the passage of the Duero, the British commander did not think it advisable with his present means, to push the allied troops further, and head quarters were established at Rueda. Little change took place in the relative positions of the contending armies till the middle of the month, when Marmont, having been reinforced by a strong body of cavalry and the division of general Bonnet, again commenced manœuvering.

During this interval an alteration was made in the brigading of the British cavalry which transferred the eleventh dragoons to general Anson's brigade, the fourteenth taking its place in the brigade of Victor Alten.

By the 16th Marmont had concentrated his army between Toro and San Roman, and the same evening sent a considerable body across the Duero at Toro. Wellington therefore, moved the allied troops to the left, with the intention of assembling them on the Guarena; but, on the following day, Marmont, by a forced march, crossed the river, and collected the whole of his army at Nava del Rey, thus opening his communication with Madrid, from which he expected to be joined by the army of the centre.

Despatch.   Lord Wellington now took measures to provide for his retreat and the junction of his divisions, moving the fifth division to Tordesillas de la Orden, and general le Marchant's, Victor Alten's, and Bock's brigades of cavalry to Alaejos.

But the fourth and light divisions, and Anson's cavalry, which, in conformity with the plan to concentrate on the Guarena, had marched to Castrejon on the night of the 16th, were attacked at day-break on the morning of the 18th, and the left of the allied position was turned. The enemy's whole army now forced on in overpowering numbers, and the British divisions became critically circumstanced; however, although pressed in flank and rear, they retired in admirable order to Tordesillas, and from thence, having been reinforced by the rest of the cavalry, to the left bank of the Guarena, where the whole army was united.

Wellington now placed the fifth, fourth, and light divisions upon the heights of Canizal, with Victor Alten's cavalry, supported by the third dragoons, in front of their left flank, in the valley. The enemy formed on the opposite bank, and seeking to turn the allied left, sent forward the cavalry division of Boyer, supported by a battalion of infantry and three guns, to pass the river by the ford in front. Arrived on the left bank, the French

Journal of major Cordemann. MSS.

general hastily formed his division in a crowded
column, close upon the right of the infantry battalion,
intending to deploy his horsemen to that flank. Alten
perceiving that his opponent had thus limited himself
to one flank for deployment, and that his column was
much crowded, determined to frustrate his intentions,
and wheeling the allied squadrons to the left, he
set off at a gallop; formed line in front of the French
column; advanced in echelon to the charge, and falling furiously upon the head and flank of the French
crowded mass, rendered every effort of their general
to extricate his cavalry perfectly fruitless.

Now ensued a fierce contest, hand to hand, among
the rival horsemen, and many officers and men fell
on both sides. Ninety-four prisoners were brought
in by the allied cavalry, among whom was the enemy's general of brigade, Carrier, who, gallantly
defending himself in the thickest of the fight, was
disarmed by a hussar named Becker, and brought
off a captive.

But the French infantry closed up to support
their cavalry, and Alten drew back his horsemen
before the advancing mass. Arrived on the brow of
the hill, he had the satisfaction to see the third dragoons trotting along the valley. The French also
got a view of the scarlet uniforms, and pulled up.
Alten instantly formed his brigade in front and on
the flanks of the third dragoons, and the whole moving forward to renew the fight, the French horsemen
took refuge behind their infantry.

1812.

July.

Corde-
mann's
Journal.
MSS.

Guelphic
Archives.
MSS.

Journal of
colonel von
Linsingen.
MSS.

E

1812.

July.

Welling-
ton's
Despatch.

Linsingens
Journal.
MSS.

Against these, part of the fourth division had been sent, and the enemy being attacked with the bayonet, were completely routed. A squadron of the hussars followed up the fugitives, and returned with two hundred and forty prisoners.

The French cavalry officers admitted that this combat cost them three hundred men ; but the loss of the allies in the whole operations of the day was estimated at more than five hundred. Of Victor Alten's brigade eighteen men were killed and seventy wounded, besides captain Brotherton of the fourteenth, major Krauchenberg, captains Aly, and Müller and lieutenant von der Wisch of the hussars, all wounded.

During the remainder of this day, as well as the morning of the 19th, little change took place in the relative positions of the contending armies ; but in the afternoon, Marmont, having made a movement for the apparent purpose of turning the British right wing, Wellington crossed the upper Guarena at Vallesa and El Olmo, with the whole of the allied army, and made every preparation for the general action in which he expected to be engaged in the plain of Vallesa, on the following morning. Soon after day-break, however, Marmont again changed his dispositions, moving to his left along the heights of Guarena, and eventually he crossed that river below Canta la Piedra, and encamped at Babila-fuente and Villa-ruela.

The British commander, therefore, made a corresponding movement to his right by Cantalpinos, and encamped at Cabeza Villosa, sending the sixth division and Alten's cavalry to Aldea Lingua, with one squadron of the fourteenth and one of the hussars under major von Gruben pushed across the Tormes to Calvarasso de abaxo.

These movements of the contending armies furnished an interesting spectacle. Separated only by gentle elevations of ground which stretched towards the Tormes, they marched in parallel columns with all the order of a parade movement, but ready at any moment to wheel up and change the bloodless scene into a fierce fight. Marmont's object was to outflank the British, and cut off their communication with Salamanca and Rodrigo, and pressing on with this intent he continued to extend his left flank, while Wellington at once penetrating his adversary's views, maintained a corresponding movement with the allied right.

With the exception of one division, the French force crossed the Tormes in the afternoon of the 21st between Alba de Tormes and Huerta, and encamped at the edge of a forest, which extends from the river to Calvarasso de ariba. The main body of the allied army also crossed the same evening, in the neighbourhood of the town ; the third division and D'Urban's cavalry remaining on the right bank. Napier.

Marmont extended his left along the edge of the forest, menacing the allied line of communication with Rodrigo. In the night, information was received that nearly two thousand cavalry and twenty

1812.   guns would join the French on the 22d or 23d, and

July.   Lord Wellington, therefore, determined, unless he

Napier.   was attacked, or that Marmont committed some
glaring error, to retire before the expected reinforcements could arrive.

The position taken up by the allied army was
marked on the right by one of two small hills called
the Arapiles, and on the left by the ford of Santa

Linsin-   Martha; the villages of Calvarasso de abaxo and
gen's Jour-
nal. MSS. Pelabravo, in front of this line were occupied by
the German hussars and the fourteenth dragoons,
and the outposts stood close to those of the French
along the roads leading to Alba and Huerta.

Abriss der   The ground contained within the angle formed by
Operation-
en der en.   the Tormes, between Alba de Tormes and Salamanca
glisch-por-
tugiesisch- is of a peculiar character. At, and in the neigh-
en Armee*   bourhood of Alba, steep isolated hillocks interspersed
with rugged water courses, mark the surface of the
country, while down the river north-east ward towards
Calvarasso de abaxo, it descends into a level plain.
The ground again rises towards Calvarasso de ariba,
and on the higher features of the ridge, which approach the Tormes, it is covered with thick wood.
Through this runs the high road from Alba de
Tormes to Salamanca, reaching the open country
about a mile from Calvarasso de ariba, where also the
road from Huerta to Mozarbes crosses the great road.
Between Calvarasso de ariba and the river Zurguen,

* By major-general Sir Julius Hartmann, K. C. B.—See Hannoversches
militairisches Journal, 1831.

whose deep channel winds round in a circuit of four
leagues from Mozarbes to Salamanca, a high table
land rises, which, although broken on its south-
eastern and south-western boundaries, by various
irregular elevations and deep water-courses, presents
in the summer season, no serious impediment to the
movement of troops. On that side of the plateau
immediately over Calvarasso de ariba, and about
half a league from thence in the direction of Mozarbes,
stand the two Arapiles, which, as has been stated,
marked the British right. These hills are of a circular form, steep and rugged in ascent, and on the
summit, of very limited circuit. They are about six
hundred paces distant from each other, being divided
by a stony ravine through which runs a narrow
road. The hill which lay nearest to the British
right, has a slight command over the other, which,
however, has the advantage of being flatter and more
roomy. Below these hills, and situated on the bed of
a stream which crosses the plateau in a diagonal
course, lies the little village of Arapiles, and the
narrow road which has already been described, crossing the rivulet by a bridge, runs through the village.

The Arapiles formed, therefore, the key of Lord
Wellington's position.

After a violent storm of rain, accompanied by extraordinary coruscations in the air, which, frightening
the horses and oxen, caused some destruction and
much confusion in both armies, the morning of the
22d of July opened clear and bright upon the assem-

bled hosts which were about to be engaged in the

battle of

SALAMANCA.

Linsingens
Journal.
MSS.

The French troops in front of the allied left wing were in motion at day-break to their left. The hussars followed their movements from Calvarasso de abaxo by Pelabravo towards Calvarasso de ariba, maintaïng a continued skirmish with their flanking parties. In the wood near the latter place, the skirmish became hot, and the German riflemen of the seventh division were sent to support the hussars. Victor Alten, being desirous to ascertain the nature of the movements of the French columns, which were covered by skirmishers, and obscured by the wood, went forward to the front of the line, in order to obtain a clear view; and there, about eight o'clock, received a wound, which obliged him immediately to leave the field.* The command of his brigade, there-

* General Alten's wound was caused by a carbine ball, which penetrating the thigh, grazed the bone, and the effusion of blood was, with difficulty, so far stopped as to allow of his being taken on horse-back to Salamanca, where, about ten o'clock, the wound was dressed. Before leaving the field, the general directed his aide-de-camp captain Linsingen, whom he left with colonel Arentschild, to inform him immediately if any doubt should be entertained of the result of the action, as he would, on no account, fall into the hands of the French. About three o'clock Linsingen sent word that the event was doubtful. Alten instantly rose, and although told by the surgeon that by displacing the bandage, his life would be endangered, he insisted upon being dressed and placed upon his horse; and the general had actually ridden a mile out of the town on the Rodrigo road, when another messenger reached him, saying that the order to attack had been given, and no doubt was entertained of the result being favorable to the allies. Unwilling, however, to return without more accurate information, he remained for some time on the spot; until judging by the sound of the firing in the attack of the third division, that the enemy were in retreat, he quietly returned to his quarters, having been on horse-back nearly two hours. Fortunately no bad consequences resulted from the zealous imprudence of the gallant general.

fore, devolved upon lieutenant colonel von Arentschild, and that of the first hussars upon major von Gruben. The enemy soon brought up infantry and artillery to this point, and Arentschild's brigade withdrew, leaving the skirmish to be maintained by the fourth caçadores and the light troops of the seventh division. Shortly after, the cavalry brigade, with the exception of two squadrons of the fourteenth,* was removed to the extreme right of the line.

The Arapiles were still unoccupied: but soon a swarm of French riflemen, which had been concealed in a hollow of the ground near Calvarasso de ariba, rushed forward to secure one of these important heights. Captain Sympher's battery of the fourth division was immediately hurried off to defeat the enemy's object, but the French being nearer to the hill, gained its summit before he could offer any resistance. Sympher, however, made an excellent disposition of his guns, placing them above the village of Arapiles, in such positions as to command the passage between the heights and part of the approach to that which had just been seized by the enemy. Meantime the smaller hill was secured by a battery of horse-artillery, and soon a cannonade opened from these neighbouring points.

Abriss der
Operation-
en, &c.

The French being now in possession of one of the Arapiles, it would have been difficult for the allies to retreat during daylight; for Marmont, by extending

Napier.

* These two squadrons rejoined the brigade in the afternoon.

1812.
July.
Abriss der Operationen. &c.

his left, and collecting a force behind the hill which he had secured, could make a dangerous rush upon them during the movement. Wellington, therefore, threw back his right flank to the heights behind the village of Arapiles, placing the fourth division on the edge of the plain above the place, and the light cavalry brigade under Arentschild in observation on its right. As the enemy's meditated attack became more developed, the remaining divisions of the army were collected in this direction ; the third division also, with D'Urban's cavalry were brought across the river and posted in a wood near Aldea Tejada, and Bock's heavy brigade of German cavalry was stationed in observation on the left.

Napier.

Thus the new position of the allies had its left on the nearer Arapiles, and its right on Aldea Tejada.

Journal of captain count Wallmoden. MSS.

During the execution of these changes the skirmishing continued without intermission in front, and a squadron of the German hussars, which was employed to cover the station of the British commander, becoming engaged in an unequal contest with the enemy's light troops, suffered some loss. Lieutenant Bobers of the regiment, however, made a gallant reprisal, attacking a superior number of the enemy with twenty hussars ; rescuing a wounded man from the middle of the enemy's ranks, and bringing off several prisoners.

Napier.

From the nature of the ground occupied by the allied army, the greater part of the troops were concealed from the view of the enemy; and those which ap-

peared, seemed to be directed in retreat towards the 1812.
Rodrigo road. About twelve o'clock Marmont brought July.
up two additional divisions to the French Arapiles, Napier.
thinking that Wellington would attempt to seize it
in order to protect his retreat; however no attack
was made by the allies, and the French general,
fearing they would retreat before his own dispositions
were completed, directed Thomieres division of infantry, with fifty guns and the light cavalry to threaten
the Rodrigo road; intending when Wellington should
move against this force, to fall upon his flank from
the Arapiles.

About three o'clock the French left was seen in
motion towards the Rodrigo road. This caused a
considerable extension of their line, and a large interval
was observed by Wellington between the French left
and centre. The British commander eagerly seized
the favorable occasion which was thus presented to
him for becoming the aggressor, and made immediate
dispositions for attack.

The fifth division was placed behind the village Abriss der
of Arapiles, on the right of the fourth, with the sixth Operation-
en, &c.
and seventh divisions, Bradford's Portuguese, and
the Spaniards of Don Carlos d'Espana in second line;
these were intended to attack the enemy's centre.
The third division, flanked on the right by D'Urban's
and Arentschild's cavalry, supported by Anson's brigade, were to turn the left; the heavy dragoons under
Le Marchant were to charge on the left of the third
division; Pack's Portuguese brigade, supported by

1812.

July.

the first division, were to storm the French Arapiles; and the light division, as well as the German heavy cavalry, were to remain in reserve upon the left.

Napier.

It was four o'clock before these dispositions were completed, and Marmont with his army separated into three parts, now saw, to his dismay, the allies advancing against his detached troops. He instantly sent out officers to hasten up his centre from the forest and stop the progress of his left; but it was too late: the third division was already closing upon Thomieres, and Marmont, hurrying to the spot, was struck down by a shell and dangerously wounded.

Linsingens
Journal.
MSS.

The march of the third division with D'Urban's and Arentschild's horsemen was covered by the deep ravine of the Zurguen—along the left bank of which marched the cavalry—until they reached the heights occupied by the enemy's advanced left flank. Here the French infantry made a determined resistance to the skirmishers and leading regiments of the third division, and their cavalry, consisting of six squadrons stood boldly behind a ravine, or dry bed of a rivulet, prepared to oppose the progress of Arentschild's brigade. The ravine was deep; its opposite bank rose extremely high, and the difficulty of passing a body of cavalry across it, in front of an enemy was manifest. Arentschild, however, did not hesitate to make his dispositions for the charge, and directing Gruben to file the hussars across from the centre of squadrons, he followed with two squadrons of the fourteenth as reserve. The hussars were quickly

formed on the other side, and charging, completely 1812.
broke the enemy's line, but lo! a second line ap- July.
peared advancing to the support of the first, and the Linsin-
gen's Jour-
hussars were, in their turn, obliged to give way. nal. MSS.
Their situation became now critical; for the deep
ravine was in their front, and a superior force of the
enemy close at their heels, with every prospect of
precipitating them into the hollow. The intelligence
and presence of mind of the officers, however, saved
the regiment. Gallopping forward at full speed
before their retreating troops, to the edge of the
ravine, they there faced about and sought to reform
the scattered squadrons. The dispersed horsemen
instantly obeyed the rallying call of the bugle;—a
connected body was soon brought together; and the
brigade dashing forward with a united impulse, drove
back their astonished opponents.*

Meantime the third division had completely succeeded, and having easily repulsed a feeble attack of
some cavalry squadrons, rolled up the extended left
wing of the enemy's infantry. Le Marchant's heavy
horsemen now charged the mass, and finished their discomfiture; and many seeking to escape through the
vale of the Zurguen, fell into the hands of D'Urban's

* By a strange error, or omission in the reports made to Lord Wellington,
the "two squadrons of the fourteenth dragoons" are represented in his lordship's
despatch as "successfully defeating every attempt of the enemy on the flank of
the third division," and no mention whatever is made of the German hussars,
who were the principal opponents of the French cavalry on this point, the
fourteenth being held in reserve after the first charge.—See colonel
Arentschild's Despatch, Appendix V.

1812.

July.

Appendix
No. V.

and Arentschild's victorious horsemen. Another attempt was now made by the French cavalry in an open space in the wood, where several squadrons of their third regiment of hussars formed up, and having made some impression upon the Portuguese cavalry, threatened the scattered hussars and fourteenth. The officers of Arentschild's brigade immediately rallied a body of the allied horsemen, strong enough to meet the attack, and anticipating the enemy's charge, put them to flight. This was the last attempt of the French cavalry on this part of the field, from which they entirely disappeared; and the allied squadrons now followed the infantry.

Napier.

After the first shock of the third division, the fourth and fifth, passed the village of Arapiles under a tremendous cannonade, and drove back the French troops step by step to the southern and eastern heights. Pack's Portuguese assailed the French Arapiles; but the defenders fought bravely, and Clausel, who had become the chief after Marmont's fall, made great exertions to restore the battle, and had already rallied the broken troops.

Abriss der
Operation-
en, &c.

Pack's attack on the Arapiles failed, and the fourth division severely pressed was obliged to give way; but fortunately, a judicious disposition of the left brigade of the fifth division, made by Marshal Beresford, checked the enemy's progress, and Wellington ordering up the sixth division to this point, the allies regained the advantage.

The skirmishers of the first, second, and fifth line battalions of the legion under captain la Roche, were opposed to a swarm of the enemy's tirailleurs on this occasion, and contributed much to the success which attended the attack made by the brigade of the fifth division.

The enemy's right wing being still uninjured, Clausel formed a new position upon the flank, drawing up his troops in front of the wood, upon the high ridge looking down upon the allied line. To turn the right of this formation the first and light divisions, together with two brigades and Sympher's battery of the fourth division, were brought up, while the sixth division, supported by the third and fifth, were ordered to attack it in front. This movement was completely successful, and the enemy now giving way on all sides, fled through the wood towards the fords of the Tormes, followed by the allied troops.

Here again the line battalions of the legion, which formed the advance of the column, were much distinguished. Out of a hundred and twenty men the skirmishers lost thirty-three in killed and wounded; captain Scharnhorst, and lieutenants von Brandis, and Ripke were also wounded on this occasion, the latter mortally; and the legion had farther to deplore the loss of the gallant captain Langrehr of the fifth battalion.

Concluding that the Spaniards still held possession of the castle of Alba de Tormes, Lord Wellington believed that the passages of the river below this

1812.

July.

Notes of major von Holle. MSS.

Despatch. Abriss der Operationen, &c.

Notes of major von Holle. MSS.

1812.

July.

Abriss der
Operation-
en, &c.

point were alone open to the enemy; he therefore directed the first and light divisions, a brigade with Sympher's battery of the fourth division, and some squadrons of cavalry, to follow in pursuit on the road to Huerta; but the castle of Alba had been abandoned by the Spaniards, and the enemy taking that road, and being favored by the darkness of the night, escaped with less loss of prisoners than might have been expected.

Linsingens
Journal.
MSS.

During these movements Arentschild's brigade continued to operate on the right of the advancing infantry, and, following up the pursuit, captured two guns which had been abandoned by the enemy. About ten o'clock the French were distinctly heard crossing the bridge at Alba, and the hussars returned to the scene of their late exertions in the wood near the Zurguen. At day-break on the following morning it was ascertained that the routed army had taken the road to Peneranda.*

---

* During the advance of the line battalions of the legion at the close of the day, serjeant Scheidemann, with twenty skirmishers of the second battalion, became separated from the rest of his company by the difficulties of the ground, and followed independently in pursuit. He drove before him a superior number of the enemy's infantry, and, falling in with a squadron of English dragoons, mainly contributed to the dispersion of another body, which had formed square in a wood. The serjeant now sought to rejoin his battalion, and coming up with an officer's detachment of the legion, also on its return, undertook to lead the way, marching with six men about a hundred paces in front. It was dark; the road led through a wood ; after some time he found that his party was again isolated; and to increase his difficulties, eleven French infantry soldiers appeared in his front !—however, Scheidemann encouraging his men, attacked the enemy, and brought the whole in prisoners.—Guelphic Archives, MSS.

The loss of the allies in this battle exceeded five thousand men. The casualties of the legion were ten men and three officers killed, one major-general, and twelve other officers, seven serjeants and ninety-eight rank and file wounded, besides sixteen horses killed and twenty wounded.

The total loss of the enemy was not ascertained. It has been rated so high as nineteen thousand men, among whom were three general officers killed, and four wounded. Seven thousand prisoners fell into the hands of the allies, besides twenty guns, two eagles, and eleven standards.

1812.

July.

Appendix,
No. VI.

CHAPTER V.

1812.

July.

Journals of
1st and 2d
dragoons.
MSS.

Before day-break on the morning of the 23d of July, the first and second dragoons of the legion, forming the brigade of major-general von Bock, which, as has been stated, was held in reserve upon the left of the allied army during the battle of Salamanca, received orders to break up from their bivouack at Pelabravo, and follow in pursuit of the enemy.

Arrived on the Tormes they were joined by the light cavalry brigade of major-general Anson, as well as by the first and light divisions. The two brigades passed in review before Lord Wellington, and little doubt was entertained of an attack upon the enemy's rear-guard being meditated by the British chief.

Awaiting the passage of the infantry caused some delay at the ford near Babila-fuente, and it was eight o'clock before they reached the right bank of the Tormes.

The wreck of the beaten French army under Clausel, had taken the road to Peneranda by the village of Garcia Hernandez. The approach from the Tormes in this direction was through a narrow marshy valley, along which ran a small rivulet bounded by steep banks. The road was rough and stony, and so confined as to cause a great extension and consequent delay of the cavalry in their march, and nearly an hour elapsed before the head of the column had cleared the defile and reached the stony plain beyond it.

The German dragoons under Bock formed the rear of the cavalry column, having Anson's light brigade in front, and soon the whole were in full trot towards the village of

GARCIA HERNANDEZ.

After proceeding about a league in this direction, the leading brigade came in sight of the enemy, who were found advantageously posted with some squadrons of cavalry in line on the plain in front, several battalions of infantry in square on the heights in advance and to the right of these, and some guns in the intervals.

Narratives of lieut. col Frederick von Uslar Gleichen; major Bendix von der Decken and major von Witzendorf. MSS.

The French infantry and artillery being, at first, concealed by the inequalities of the ground, the brigades were ordered by Lord Wellington to attack the cavalry, and their pace was accordingly increased to a gallop. The German regiments, confined by the narrowness of the valley, had been unable during their progress through it, to move upon a larger front than sections of threes, and now, being in echelon of squadrons, they attempted to form line upon the first squadron without halting. Hurried forward, however, by the excitement of the moment, the leading

1812.

July.

Narratives of lieut.-col von Uslar-- Gleichen, &c. MSS.

squadron of the first regiment under captain von Hattorf—having also in front, general Bock; the field officers of the regiment, and lieutenant-colonel May, of the English artillery, who brought the order from Lord Wellington*—dashed on without waiting for the remaing squadrons, and made straight for the enemy's cavalry.

The left wing of the French horsemen retired from the charge of Anson's brigade, and those in front went about on the approach of Hattorf's squadron; but in the pursuit the flank of the squadron became exposed to the fire of the infantry on the heights, by which colonel May and several men and horses were wounded, and the pursuit was discontinued.

Captain Gustavus von der Decken, who commanded the third or left squadron of the regiment, seeing that if he advanced according to the order given, his flank would be exposed to the fire of a dense infantry square, formed the daring resolution of attacking it with his single squadron.

This square stood on the lower slope of the heights, and obedient to the signal of their chief, the German troopers advanced against it with order and determination, while a deafening peal of musquetry from the

* Bock was near-sighted, and not being aware of the proximity of the enemy, when colonel May brought him the order to charge, added, after expressing his readiness to comply;—"but you will be good enough to shew us the enemy" To this request colonel May readily assented, and gallantly accompanied the first squadron in the charge, where he was severely wounded. When afterwards relating the circumstance, the gallant colonel was wont jestingly to add :—"That was what I got by playing the dragoon, and leading the Germans."

enemy greeted their approach. Arrived within a
hundred yards of the point of attack, the gallant squadron officer, struck by a ball in the knee, fell mortally
wounded, and lieutenant von Voss, with several
men and horses, were killed; but instantly, captain
von Uslar Gleichen, who commanded the left troop,
dashing forward, placed himself at the head of the
squadron, and re-animating his followers by words
and example, while another shower of bullets carried
destruction among their ranks, the intrepid soldiers
forced onward, and bringing up their right flank,
appeared before the enemy's bayonets on two sides
of the square.

The two front ranks, kneeling, presented a double
row of deadly steel, while in rear of these, the steady
musquets of four standing ranks were levelled at the
devoted horsemen. At this critical moment, when
the sword was about to be matched against the fire-
lock, and the chivalrous horseman against the firm
foot soldier—when victory hung yet in equal scales—
an accidental shot from the kneeling ranks, which
killing a horse, caused it and the rider to fall upon
the bayonets—gave the triumph to the dragoons!

For a path was now opened, and the impatient
troopers rushing in amid the blazing fire, while
men and horses fell fast before the musquets of the
French infantry, their firm formation was destroyed,
and the whole battalion were either cut down or
taken prisoners.

Captain von Reitzenstein, who commanded the

1812.

July.

Narratives
of lieut.-col
von Uslar--
Gleichen,
&c. MSS.

1812.

July.

Narratives
of lieut.-col
von Uslar--
Gleichen,
&c. MSS.
second squadron, seeing the success which had attended the daring onset of his comrades on the left,
and being also impeded in his forward movement by
the difficulties of the ground, decided upon following
up the discomfiture of the infantry, and attempting
the second square, which stood on the edge of the
heights.   He was received with a steady and destructive fire, by which lieutenant Heugel was killed,
and lieutenant Tappe severely wounded; but the moral
force of the French infantry had been shaken by the
fearful overthrow which they had just witnessed, and
some timid individuals leaving their ranks, Reitzenstein rushed in with his ready followers; the square
broke, and the greater part of the battalion was cut
down or captured.

Journal of
2d Dra-
goons. No.
2. MSS.
A third square was instantly formed by those few
who had escaped from destruction, and some cavalry
came to their support.   Against these captain Baron
Marschalck led the third squadron of the second
regiment, and, being joined by the left troop of the
second squadron under lieutenant Fumetty, charged
and dispersed the enemy's cavalry; then riding boldly
at the infantry, broke and completely overthrew
them.

The wreck of the routed battalions now rallied and
attempted to make a stand on a rising ground near
the high road to Peneranda, where they again formed
a connected body.   Marschalck and Fumetty led their
troopers a second time to the charge, but their little
force had become too much reduced, and the horses

were too fatigued to admit of any impression being made upon the enemy. The French received the attack as well with a heavy fire as with a shower of stones, to which they now had recource; captain von Uslar was killed, lieutenant Fumetty was wounded, and several men and horses were struck down. No farther attempt was made by the dragoons, and the enemy resumed their retreat.

The loss of the German brigade in this brilliant combat, was four officers, forty-eight non-commissioned officers and soldiers, and sixty-seven horses killed; two officers, fifty-six non-commissioned officers and soldiers, and forty-six horses wounded, and six men and four horses taken.

The French had few killed in proportion to their numbers; but many of the prisoners, the whole of whom amounted to nearly fourteen hundred, were wounded: among the captives was the chevalier Mollard, who commanded the brigade.

The conduct of the heavy dragoons of the legion in the combat of Garcia Hernandez has been the theme of general admiration; even a French historian has eulogised their gallantry.* Lord Wellington signified his satisfaction by appointing a guard of

1812.

July.

Journal of 2d dragoons, No. 2. MSS.

Appendix. No. VII.

* "L' Angleterre entretenait aussi deux regimens de dragons et trois de hussards, appartenant au corps étranger, dit King's German Legion. Ils ont surpassé la cavallerie nationale pour le service des avant gardes et pour la bataille. La charge la plus audacieuse de la guerre d' Espagne a été fournie, ainsi que nous le verrons en son lieu, le lendemain de la bataille des Arapiles, par l' Hanovrien Bock, à la tête de la brigade pesante de la legion Allemande." Histoire de la guerre de la Peninsule sous Napoleon &c. &c. par le general Foy, Tome 1, p. 290—1.

honour from the brigade to attend his person; he
also granted them two days rest on the field of battle,
and in his official account of the combat, thus alluded
to the achievement of the German dragoons :—

"I have never witnessed a more gallant charge
than was made upon the enemy's infantry by the
heavy brigade of the King's German Legion under
major-general von Bock, which was completely successful, and the whole body of infantry, consisting of
three battalions of the enemy's first division, were
made prisoners."

Soon after this memorable combat, the officers of
the legion were granted permanent rank in the British army; which distinction was communicated to
the corps in the following notification from the War-
Office :—

War-Office, 10th August, 1812.

"In consideration of the King's German Legion
having so frequently distinguished themselves against
the enemy, and particularly upon the occasion of the
late victory obtained near Salamanca, His Royal
Highness the Prince Regent is pleased, in the name
and on the behalf of his Majesty, to command that the
officers who are now serving with temporary rank in
the several regiments of that corps, shall have permanent rank in the British army from the date of their
respective commissions."

The British army continued its march in pursuit
of the enemy towards the Duero, Victor Alten's
brigade of cavalry under Arentschild, forming the

advanced guard. On the 25th the brigade entered 1812.
Arevalo, and here it was reported that King Joseph, July.
with about ten thousand men, had been at Blasco Linsingens
Sancho, three leagues distant on the Avila road, the Journal. MSS.
preceding night. As this village lay in rear of his
line of march, Arentschild halted the brigade and
sent out a patrole in that direction, as well as parties
of observation on the Segovia and Olmedo roads.

The rear-guard of the beaten army took advantage
of the respite thus afforded them, and halted about
four miles distant on the road to Olmedo; but the
hussars were not idle, and cornet Blumenhagen, who
had the command of the party sent in this direction,
brought in thirty prisoners. In the evening this list Guelphic archives.
was increased to nearly sixty; for, to the astonish- MSS.
ment of all the brigade, the patrole which had been
sent to Blasco Sancho, consisting of only a corporal
and five men, returned bringing two officers and
twenty-three well mounted troopers! These belonged
to a corps of Spanish chasseurs, which had been
lately equipped for the service of King Joseph, and
were under the command of French officers at
Blasco-Sancho, where they were surprised by the
patrole. In this enterprise a private of the German
hussars named Kastorff was the principal actor.
After capturing four chasseurs who were posted as
vedettes outside the village, he proceeded to a house
in which the rest of the detachment were stationed,
and directing two of his comrades to fire through
the windows, entered the house alone, and single

handed drove two officers, five non-commissioned officers and eighteen chasseurs, from one room to another, until at length, completely intimidated, they surrendered! Twenty-nine horses were found in the stables, and the whole were safely delivered at the head-quarters of the brigade. This exploit was considered worthy of notice in Lord Wellington's official despatch, and by the special order of the commander-in-chief, the gallant hussar was promoted to the rank of corporal.

On the 27th, part of the French army crossed the Duero, and the following day Lord Wellington's head-quarters were at Olmedo. King Joseph, with the army of the centre was at Segovia the same night, with the apparent intention of diverting the allied troops from the pursuit of the beaten army; but in this he did not succeed, and the British advanced divisions having crossed the Eresma and Ceja rivers on the 29th, the enemy's rear-guard retired across the Duero, and following the main body towards Villa Vanez, abandoned Valladolid, and left seventeen pieces of cannon, numerous stores, and eight hundred sick and wounded in the hands of the allies. Three hundred prisoners were also taken on the following day, and the British entering Valladolid, were enthusiastically received by the inhabitants.

The army of Marmont having been thus driven from the Duero, Lord Wellington directed his attention to that of King Joseph, and leaving his advanced guard and left wing to continue the pursuit

towards Burgos, he moved the right wing to Cuellar, 1812.
where head-quarters were fixed on the 1st of August. August.
The same day Joseph Bonaparte retired from Segovia
and crossed the Guadarama mountains. Welling- Despatch.
ton now seeing that little was to be feared from
Marmont's army, determined upon either bringing the
king to a general action, or forcing him to quit Madrid; so leaving Cuellar on the 6th, he marched to
Segovia, and halted at St. Ildefonso on the 8th, to
allow time for the rest of the army to come up.

General D'Urban's brigade, (consisting of three
regiments of Portuguese cavalry); the first light battalion of the German legion, and captain M'Donald's
battery of horse artillery, passed the Guadarama, Narratives of lieut. col Frederick von Uslar Gleichen; lieut.-col. Christian Wynecken major von Witzen-orf, and captain Kuhls, MSS.
without opposition, by the 9th, and the following day
bivouacked at the Puente de Ratamar. On the 11th
they were joined by the heavy cavalry brigade of the
legion under colonel de Jonquiéres,* and the whole
advanced on the road to Madrid. The cavalry soon
fell in with the enemy's rear-guard, and a distant
skirmish was kept up to the village of Las Rosas,
from whence the enemy retired through Majalahonda Journals of 1st and 2d Dragoons. MSS.
towards Naval Carnero, on the right of the road to
Madrid.

They were followed by the allied cavalry and artillery to Majalahonda, a village about two miles from

---

* In consequence of Sir Stapleton Cotton having been disabled by a wound
the temporary command of the allied cavalry devolved upon major-general
von Bock, who was succeeded in command of the German heavy cavalry brigade by colonel de Jonquiéres.

1812.

August.

Narratives
of lieut.-col
von Uslar--
Gleichen,
&c. MSS.

Las Rosas. Here the Portuguese brigade and four of the guns were halted, while the German dragoons were ordered back to Las Rosas, where also the light battalion had been halted.

Bock's brigade had not been unsaddled for several days, and were much in need of rest. General D'Urban, therefore, directed that they should take the present opportunity of obtaining some relief. The strong brigade of Portuguese cavalry, and the British guns in front formed an out-post fully sufficient to secure them against any sudden attack, and to provide still further against a surprise, colonel de Jonquiéres obtained permission to place a picquet of forty dragoons under lieutenant Kuhls in front of the Portuguese : the remaining two guns were posted on the road to Madrid.

Kuhls tracked the enemy for four miles on the road to Toledo, and charging boldly in front of a defile, killed and wounded several of the rear guard ; but about three o'clock in the afternoon, the French horsemen returned, reinforced by a battalion of infantry and some guns, and the Germans fell back upon a Portuguese picquet in front of

MAJALAHONDA.

The enemy's leading squadrons came confidently forward, leaving the main body at a considerable distance, and D'Urban seeing the favorable opportunity which this disposition offered for an attack,

directed the Portuguese to charge. Led on boldly
by their officers they advanced in good order, and
with every demonstration of making a resolute assault,
but just at the moment when contact was to be
expected, and before they had actually reached the
enemy's squadrons, they suddenly wheeled about,
and abandoning their gallant officers, and leaving the
British guns to their fate,* they fled in disorder
through Majalahonda, and continuing their disgrace-
ful flight, gallopped back the whole way to Las Rosas.

Kuhls vainly endeavoured to stop the French
horsemen, and was thrice wounded in his efforts to
check the pursuit; but the numbers were too unequal,
and after the most resolute conduct on the part of his
men, aided by the gallant bearing of cornet Dröge,
who commanded the support, he made for Las Rosas,
cutting his way through the enemy's scattered troopers

Meantime the rest of the German brigade, little
anticipating any demand upon their services, while
three regiments of cavalry and four guns were posted
two miles in their front, were quietly occupied with
their stable duties in various parts of the village, many
of the men in their shirts and trousers. Kuhls had
sent in several reports of the enemy's movements, but
colonel de Jonquiéres, relying upon D'Urban's cavalry, and the orders which he had received, made

1812.

August.

Narratives
of lient.-col
von Uslar--
Gleichen,
&c. MSS.

---

* By the exertions of captain M'Donald and his officers and men, the guns
were moved off, but owing to the inequalies of the ground, the carriage of one
was broken, and two others were overturned. These fell into the hands of the
enemy, and were found the next day in Majalahonda with the carriages
burnt.—Despatch.

1812.

August.

Narratives
of lieut.-col
von Uslar--
Gleichen,
&c. MSS.

no preparations to meet an attack, and the brigade was completely surprised. The alarm was sounded;—two companies of the light battalion which were stationed in the lower part of the village, soon stood to their arms;—the dragoons hastened to saddle, and every exertion was made on the part of the officers to receive the threatened onset.

But the German troopers were too dispersed to admit of any effective number being soon assembled, and although captains von Reitzenstein and Marschalck with wonderful activity and presence of mind, brought together a few men of their squadrons, and bravely meeting the French horsemen, attempted to check their progress at the entrance of the village, they were overpowered by numbers, and the elated enemy, following up their successes at a rapid rate, crowded into the place, and appeared suddenly in an open space which divided the upper from the lower part of the village. Here the main body of the first light battalion, together with the baggage of the whole was stationed, and the French riding wildly about, caused great confusion, took some prisoners,* and wounded seven men of the battalion; but the companies quickly formed in the open space and drove back the horsemen. By this time the dragoons were

---

* Among others the black big drummer of the battalion, who, together with the donkey on which the drum was carried was taken prisoner. On the following morning, however, as the battalion was entering Madrid, the regimental march was heard distinctly accompanied on the drum, and soon, to their mutual joy, appeared the black, urging his donkey to the utmost with one hand, and beating time with the other.

all mounted, and quickly assembling in bodies of tens and twenties, as their scattered position alone admitted, they rode boldly against the intruders and drove them out. The brigade was then formed, and soon the two regiments appeared in their full strength of four squadrons* on the road in front of Las Rosas.

1812.

August.

Narratives of lieut.-col von Uslar-- Gleichen, &c. MSS.

The Portuguese cavalry now took courage and came up on the left of the Germans, forming with them an oblique line, having the left thrown forward. Scarce was this effected, when the enemy advanced on a front of two squadrons, at a slow pace, bringing forward their right against the Portuguese and opening a fire from the captured guns. The allies rode out bravely to meet the threatened attack, but just when the pace had been increased to the charge, and the Portuguese brigade had arrived within twenty or thirty paces of the enemy, they again deserted their officers, wheeled about, and fled back to the village!

The left flank of the German brigade was now completely exposed to the enemy, by whom they were nearly surrounded, and no alternative remained for them but a rapid retreat, which was immediately commenced in column of squadrons.

The French pressed on, and falling upon their rear took some prisoners, among whom was colonel de Jonquiéres commanding the brigade. Near the village the Germans made front, and the leading squadron of the second regiment under captain

* Since the combat of Garcia Hernandez the brigade had been reduced from six to four squadrons.

1812.

August.

Narratives
of lieut.-col
von Uslar--
Gleichen,
&c. MSS.

Friesland,* joined by the picquet under Kuhls, charging with impetuosity, killed and wounded several of the enemy. The second squadron under captain von Lenthe, together with the picquet, now advanced to the charge; the opposing squadron-officer rode forward and confidently called upon Lenthe to surrender; but Wolbers, a bold soldier, springing from the ranks, cut the haughty captain from his horse, and the French squadron gave way.† Thus the pursuit was checked, and the heavy cavalry brigade of general Ponsonby appearing at the same time in sight, behind Las Rosas, the French withdrew to Majalahonda.

In this unfortunate combat the German dragoons had several casualties. Cornet Kohlstedt and twelve men were killed, captain von Uslar-Gleichen, captain von Hattorf, lieutenants von Witzendorf, Poten, Kuhls, five serjeants and thirty dragoons were wounded, the greater number of the officers severely; ten horses were killed, twelve wounded, and six men and twelve horses were taken.

Lord Wellington expressed his high satisfaction at the gallant conduct of the German brigade under such trying circumstances, and directed that they

* Captain Friesland, who had been long suffering from fever, fell in the charge and was replaced on his horse by a brave dragoon named Schlütter.

† Sergeant Feldmann of the first dragoons, as well as sergeant Erdfelder and private Becker of the second regiment, were conspicuous for their gallantry in this combat; the first rescued part of the regimental baggage; Erdfelder cut a flank officer from his horse; and Becker, rushing into the midst of the enemy's horsemen, laid about him until, covered with wounds, he was obliged to be carried from the field.—Guelphic Archives. MSS.

should form the advanced guard of the army, on its 1812.
entrance into Madrid the following day. August.

The British troops entered Madrid on the 12th of Welling-ton's des-patch.
August, and were welcomed with every possible
demonstration of joy by the inhabitants. Joseph
Bonaparte had retired on the preceding night with
the main body of his army upon Aranjuez, leaving
in the fortified enclosure of the Retiro, a garrison
of two thousand men. On the 14th, the interior
wall having been forced, and arrangements made for
storming the place, the garrison surrendered, and a
hundred and eighty-nine pieces of brass ordnance, nine
hundred barrels of powder, twenty thousand stand of
arms, and a quantity of various stores came into
possession of the allies.

Soon after this event the enemy abandoned Toledo;
and the garrison of Guadalaxara, consisting of seven
hundred men surrendered to the Empecinado by
capitulation. The accounts from the south were
also satisfactory; the enemy abandoned their works
before Cadiz on the 24th; blew up the castle of
Niebla; and the city of Seville, defended by eight Colonel Skerrett's despatch.
French battalions and two regiments of dragoons,
was carried by assault on the 27th, by the small
corps of colonel Skerrett, who made nearly two hundred prisoners, without experiencing any material
loss. The gallant conduct of a detachment of the
second hussars of the legion under cornet Wieboldt,
on this occasion, was specially noticed in colonel
Skerrett's despatch.

1812.
September
Welling-
ton's
despatch.
Joseph Bonaparte continued his march towards Valentia, and on the 19th, his rear guard was reported to be at La Roda. Meantime the enemy's troops at Valladolid advanced, and drove in Anson's picquet at Tudela, while another body under general Foy carried off the garrison of Toro. This general now marched to La Baneza with the intention of relieving the garrison of Astorga, but these, to the number of one thousand two hundred men, surrendered to the Spaniards on the 19th, and when the French arrived on the 21st, they found the place abandoned. Foy then returned to the Esla, and carrying off the garrison of Zamora on the 29th, marched for Tordesillas.

Napier.
Lord Wellington quitted Madrid on the 1st of September to direct the movements of the troops, which he had ordered to be collected at Arevalo. This force, amounting to only twenty-one thousand men, moved from thence on the 4th, and on the 6th passed the Duero. The French retreated slowly through the valleys of Pisuerga and Arlanzan, where the natural impediments of the ground enabled Clausel to baffle the efforts of his adversary. By protracted flank marches alone could the enemy be dislodged; the French general many times offered battle; and it was not until Wellington was reinforced on the 16th by eleven thousand Spanish infantry, three hundred cavalry, and eight guns, that Clausel gave up all offensive demonstration, and retreated through Burgos to Breviesca.

'Two divisions had been left in Madrid under Charles Alten; sir Rowland Hill was directed to cover the capital on the south, by taking post on the river Jarama; and the Spanish general Ballasteros was requested to co-operate with Hill in case of Madrid being menaced by Soult.

1812.

September

Welling-
ton's des-
patch.

It was on the night of the 17th that the French retired to Breviesca, and they were reported to have left a garrison of two thousand five hundred men in the castle of Burgos. The allies crossed the Arlanzon on the 19th, and immediately invested the fortress.

The troops employed in the duties of the siege were the first and sixth divisions of infantry under generals Campbell and Clinton, and the Portuguese brigades of generals Pack and Bradford, composing a force of twelve thousand men: the remainder of the army was advanced in front of Monasterio to cover the attack.

Jones's
Sieges.

Three advanced flêches on the heights of St. Michael, were immediately taken possession of by the investing corps, and after a good deal of skirmishing, the advanced posts and sentries were fixed on various points of the heights.

SIEGE OF THE CASTLE OF BURGOS.

The castle of Burgos is situated upon an oblong conical hill which is divided on the south by a deep ravine from the neighbouring heights of St. Michael. The defences were found to form three different lines;

the first was an old escarp wall, improved by shot proof parapets and palisaded at the salient and re-entering angles; the second was a palisaded re-trenchment; and the third was a similar line of defence, having on its highest point an interior retrenchment formed out of the old keep, and called battery Napoleon.

Except on the side of the hill of St. Michael this fortified post had a complete command; the summit of St. Michael, however, which was less than three hundred yards distant, was nearly on a level with the upper works of the castle, and this hill was occupied by a hornwork of large dimensions and difficult of access in front, but the branches were imperfect, and the rear had been only temporarily closed by a strong palisading.

The project of attack was to assault and make a lodgement in the horn-work of St. Michael the first night, and, on the following night, to commence a battery which should see under the south end of the church of La Blanca; where the smallness of the front, the steep fall of the hill, and the faulty nature of the lines presented the most favorable point of attack. A communication was then to be made from the suburbs of St. Pedro, and a parallel established connected with the upper works. From this parallel the work was to be approached by sap, and from thence galleries run under the escarp, where breaches by mines were to be made, and a lodgement being formed on the first line of defence, the second and third were to be from thence successively battered and assaulted.

The horn-work of St. Michael was attacked on the evening of the 19th by three different storming parties, directed against the two demi-bastions and the gorge. The two front attacks were unsuccessful and the assailants suffered considerable loss, but the third party, led by the gallant major Cocks of the 79th, entered at the gorge, and putting the garrison to flight, carried the work.

Seven field pieces were here captured, and the enemy admitted having sustained a loss of six officers and one hundred and thirty-seven men killed and wounded, but that of the allies was considerably greater, being six officers and sixty-five men killed, and fifteen officers and three hundred and thirty-four men wounded.

A lodgement was immediately formed, and a battery was commenced on the night of the 20th. This was armed with five guns on the night of the 22d, and another battery, intended to bring down the keep, was commenced at the gorge of the horn-work.

The artillery of the besiegers consisted of only three eighteen-pounder guns, and five twenty-four-pounder howitzers. These limited means would, it was evident, lead to a protracted siege, were the operations to be conducted systematically, and Lord Wellington, therefore, in order to abridge the proceedings, and save the troops from unnecessary fatigue, determined upon making an effort to carry the exterior line of defence by escalade.

1812.

September

Jones's
sieges.

Journals of
line batta-
lions.MSS.

Jones's
Sieges.

For this purpose a body of four hundred men,
composed of about equal numbers of the guards,
Scotch brigade, and King's German Legion, the latter
under captain von Scharnhorst, were provided with ladders, and directed to march at midnight on the 23d,
into a hollow road which ran from the suburb of St.
Pedro parallel to, and within about sixty yards of the
foot of the wall to be scaled. Half the party were
to arrange themselves in line so as to fire over a bank
against the work, while the rest, divided into sections
were to advance under cover of the bank, and rearing
their ladders against the wall, mount to the assault.
The firing party was afterwards to become a working
party, and form a ramp, and to aid these a larger
working party was held in reserve. A Portuguese
battalion was, at the same time, ordered to favour
the escalade by assaulting the same line on its left
flank, where the defences were weak.

The Portuguese were checked by the fire from a
guard-house on the line, and never entered the ditch.
The escalading party under major Laurie of the 79th
reached the wall, and reared their ladders almost
without opposition, but the main body, advancing
on a front of four men, had lengthened out so considerably before they reached the spot, that, on the
garrison opening a fire, much confusion arose in their
endeavours to close up; and the firing party, never
taking post on the bank, pushed with the rest into
the ditch. Several gallant attempts were now made
to ascend the ladders, and some individuals gained

a momentary footing, but the garrison, mounting on
the top of the parapet, bayonetted the foremost down,
and then pouring a fire of musquetry, as well as a
number of shells and combustibles among the assailants, killed the commanding officer, and caused great
destruction.

Hesitation ensued ; for it could not be immediately
ascertained who was the next senior officer, and for
more than a quarter of an hour the troops had to
await the determination of this point, exposed to the
destructive efforts of the garrison. At length the
question was decided, and the necessity for retiring
appearing evident to all the officers, the detachment
withdrew, leaving nearly half its numbers killed or
wounded before the wall.

Captain von Scharnhorst and lieutenant Hansing
of the second line battalion of the legion fell in this
unfortunate attempt, and the loss of the detachment in
non-commissioned officers and men was considerable.

The attempt at escalade having thus proved unsuccessful, the original plan of forming breaches by
mines was adopted.

On the morning of the 25th, the sap had been
advanced to within sixty feet of the exterior wall of
the place, and a gallery was therefore commenced
from its head towards the wall; and on the following
night with a view to form a gallery for a second
mine, a trench was made on the right of the first
parallel.

In consequence of the workmen being unaccus-

1812.

September

Jones's
Sieges.

Journals of
line batta-
lions. MSS

tomed to military mining, and being badly provided with tools, these operations proceeded slowly; however the enemy appeared to anticipate the loss of their outer line, and now directed all their exertions to the defence of the second.

About noon on the 29th, the miners at the first gallery had reached the foundation of the escarp wall of the castle; a chamber was, therefore, made and charged, and at midnight, a storming party of three hundred men having paraded in the trenches with a working party in their rear prepared to form a lodgement, the mine was sprung. The explosion brought down the wall and formed a practicable breach, and the assault was ordered to be made. The advance of five men mounted the breach without opposition, but the supporting body, taking a wrong direction, reached the wall where it was uninjured, and the officer who commanded it reported that the mine had taken no effect : the storming party were, therefore, ordered to retire.

These protracted and unsuccessful operations had begun to discourage the troops. They had been exposed for twelve days to a close and well-directed fire from the castle, and the discharge of musquetry from behind a stockade on the outer line was so accurate, that every man was struck down who offered the least object to the marksmen. To overcome this fire, the guns of the first battery were opened upon the stockade, and after three hours firing, it was completely demolished.

Every exertion was now made to forward the con- 1812.
struction of the second mine, and lest it should fail, September
a third battery was commenced immediately under Jones's
Sieges.
the outer defences of the castle. This was rapidly
executed; but just as it was about to open on the
morning of the 1st of October, the enemy brought so
hot a fire to bear upon it from the place, that Lord
Wellington ordered the battery to be evacuated.
The parapet was soon after nearly demolished by
the enemy's fire, and most of the guns were disabled.

A fourth battery was, therefore, commenced on the
left; but scarce had sufficient cover for the men been
thrown up, and the guns removed, when the enemy
concentrated such a mass of fire upon the spot, that
it became evident the guns could never be served.
The idea of employing ordnance on this point was
now abandoned altogether.

Meantime the second mine was proceeded with,
and having been completed by the 4th, a fire was
opened upon the first breach, the ascent to which had
been rendered difficult by the garrison, and it was
arranged that the second mine should be sprung, and
both breaches stormed at five o'clock in the afternoon.

These operations were entrusted to the twenty- Journals of
line batta-
fourth regiment; supported by a reserve in the trenches lions MSS.
which included two officers and sixty men of the
German line brigade. The mine was sprung at the
appointed time and formed an excellent breach,

1812.

October.

Jones's
Sieges.
The troops instantly rushed to the assault, and overcoming every obstacle, established themselves on both points of the enemy's exterior defences with little loss.

The working parties were immediately ordered to form lodgements on both breaches, but having been employed in support of the storming parties, some confusion and delay arose in separating them, and they were imprudent enough to leave their arms at Journals of line batta-lions. MSS the foot of the breach. About midnight the enemy made a sortie on the workmen at the left breach, who now ran to fetch their arms. Lieutenant Boyd of the first line battalion of the legion, hurried with a covering party to the spot, and, uniting with the workmen, succeeded in driving back the assailants. These impediments, however, and the continued fire from the place, much impeded the work, and but a small front of entrenchment was obtained before morning.

Lieutenant Meyer of the first line battalion of the legion was mortally wounded in this assault, six men of the brigade were killed, and lieutenant Schauroth of the fifth line battalion and eleven men were wounded.

Jones's
Sieges.
Arrangements were now made for the attack of the enemy's second line of defence. Batteries were prepared to breach the re-entering angle formed by the junction of the first and second lines, and it was intended to try and burn the church of La Blanca with hot shot. Meantime working parties were employed in improving the lodgements on the breaches,

and turning the parapet of the exterior line into a
parallel against the place.

1812.

October.

Correspon-
dence of
general
Löw MSS.

But in the afternoon of the 5th the garrison made
a sortie with three hundred men against both breaches
and gaining possession of the first, overthrew the
gabions, ruined the lodgement, and carried off the
tools. They failed, however, in their attempt upon the
other breach, for major von Robertson of the second
line battalion of the legion, who commanded in the
trenches, aided by the exertions of the other officers,
was enabled to rally the broken detachments, and
drive back the intruders from this point. The loss
of the allies, however, exceeded one hundred and
fifty men, among whom were captains Langrehr of
the second, and lieutenant von Goeben of the fifth
line battalion, both severely wounded, besides twenty
serjeants and soldiers of the German brigade.

Batteries were opened against the second line of
defence on the 6th; and on the following day considerable impression had been made upon that part of
the wall intended to be breached. The approaches by
sap were also carried to within thirty yards of the
covered way.

At two o'clock on the morning of the 8th, the
garrison made another sortie with four hundred men,
which, aided by the darkness, and a heavy fall of rain,
overthrew the advanced covering parties, and drove the
guard and workmen from the summit of the outer line.
Lieutenant-colonel Cocks, who commanded in the
trenches, and had been promoted for his distinguished

Jones's
Sieges.

Löw's correspondence MSS.

conduct on the 19th of September, was killed in the onset, and many men, with nearly the whole of the officers were struck down; then lieutenant Beuermann of the second line battalion of the legion spiritedly rallied the rest, and a brave serjeant of the same battalion * animating them by his example, the assailants were attacked with the bayonet, and driven off. But they had already levelled the work ; the tools were carried away, and more than two hundred of the besiegers had fallen.

Jones's Sieges.

Löw's correspondence MSS.

The loss of the legion was considerable :—Captain von Saffe, of the first line battalion was killed; lieutenant Wynckler of the fifth line battalion was taken prisoner; captain Lodders and lieutenant Wynecken were severely wounded; forty-six non-commissioned officers and soldiers of the German detachment alone, were killed, and sixty-three were wounded.

Jones's Sieges.

After the severe loss sustained by the besiegers on this occasion, no further attempts were made to push the works beyond the outer line.

In the evening the new breach was pronounced practicable, and during the night a communication was made for the purpose of bringing a fire of musquetry to bear upon it; but the expenditure of small arm ammunition had been so great, that this could not be prudently continued, and it was found necessary to send to the rear for a fresh supply.

---

* Ludwig Floerke, who, for his gallant conduct on this day, received the thanks of his commanding officer in the regimental orders, and was appointed colour sergeant of the battalion.—Guelphic Archives, MSS.

Meantime the besieged were preparing for an
obstinate defence. They contrived to clear away
about eight feet of the top of the new breach, and to
form a small trench at the back of the rubbish,
which enabled them to work under cover.

On the 15th a fire was opened from four guns upon
the wall of the keep, but such a return was made
that the guns were soon silenced, and they were now
directed against the breach. The efforts of the
artillery to burn the church of La Blanca were also
unsuccessful.

A gallery had been commenced on the 9th, from
the nearest houses of the town towards the church of
St. Roman, which the garrison held as a post, and
by the 16th, a mine was formed and loaded under
the church. On the following day the batteries fired
with great effect upon the new breach and second
line, and Lord Wellington, having examined the
injuries done to the defences, determined upon a
general attack, which he directed to be made at half
past four o'clock in the afternoon of the 18th.

It was arranged that, at this hour, the mine under
the church of St. Roman should be sprung, and the
breach stormed which should be thereby caused;
and after the explosion, the second line was to be
entered both by escalade and at the breach.

The troops selected to storm the breach in the
second line were three hundred of the German brigade under major von Wurmb; while at the same
time two hundred of the guards were to enter by

1812.

October.

Narrative
of captain
Hesse.
MSS.

escalade on their right. The Germans were divided into two principal bodies, consisting of two hundred men, under the immediate command of major Wurmb, and the reserve of one hundred men under captain Breymann. The reserve was placed in a trench, on the high ground in front of the breach, with directions to support the assault by firing over the heads of the stormers; and these were to advance in three separate detachments, which, after gaining the breach, were to turn to their left, and force a stockade, which the enemy had erected across the ditch, between the second and third line.

Notes of
major von
Rettberg
and major
Wichmann
MSS.

Lieutenant Hesse of the second line battalion commanded the forlorn hope of the German stormers, and, the mine having been sprung at the appointed hour, this intrepid officer led his detachment up the breach in the most gallant style, gained the summit with little loss, and pushed on for the stock-

ade. Here a strong body of the enemy was posted, and a destructive fire falling upon the Germans, some gave way and joined the guards, who had succeeded on the right; however, the rear detachments coming up, the enemy were driven from the stockade, and the Germans endeavoured to tear down the barrier. This was found impracticable; and now the enemy assembling in great force behind the third line, sent a mass of shells and combustibles among the assailants, and caused great destruction. But Wurmb's bold soldiers were not to be deterred, and attacking the third line with desperate valour, three officers and

several men actually gained the summit! Their
triumph was however, short; for the guards, after October.
the most gallant and successful attack, being unsup- Hesse's
ported, had been obliged to give way, and an over- MSS.
powering mass of the enemy now rushed down upon
the Germans. These, left also without support,
were unable to maintain the unequal contest, and,
after all their officers had been either killed or wounded, they were forced back through the breach; and
although the explosion of the mine had enabled the
assailants to make a lodgement in the ruins, it was
found necessary to abandon the attack.

The gallant Wurmb, a distinguished officer, fell Journals of
line batta-
in this assault; lieutenant Bothmer was killed; cap- lions MSS.
tain Bacmeister was mortally, and captain La
Roche dangerously wounded; lieutenants Hesse,
Quade, and Schlaeger were all wounded, the two
former severely, and seventy-five non-commissioned
officers and soldiers were killed and wounded.*

The conduct of the guards and German legion in
this last attempt upon the castle of Burgos, drew
forth the following emphatic expressions of approval
from Lord Wellington.

"It is impossible to represent in adequate terms Despatch.
my sense of the conduct of the guards and German
legion upon this occasion, and I am quite satisfied
that if it had been possible to maintain the posts

---

* The distinguished gallantry of lieutenant Hesse in leading the German
attack, obtained for him the tardy, but well merited acknowledgement, of
promotion in the Hanoverian army at the end of the war.

which they had gained with so much gallantry, these troops would have maintained them."

The French now advanced in considerable force to the relief of the place, and reports from sir Rowland Hill stated the enemy's intentions of moving towards the Tagus. Lord Wellington, therefore, fearing that Hill might be obliged to retire, and the besieging army thus become insulated, determined upon raising the siege; and the troops, breaking up on the night of the 20th, marched back towards the Duero.

Thus ended the unfortunate operations against Burgos, which failed principally in consequence of the deficiency of the siege establishment. The sappers and miners were but half instructed; they were ill provided with tools, and great delay was the consequence. The artillery force was also inadequate; and thus a beseiging army which, provided with sufficient means of attack, could have carried the fortress in ten days, was, after the labour of a month, and the loss of two thousand men, obliged eventually to abandon the attempt.

During the whole of the siege, the weather was most severe. In many places the ground was literally knee-deep, and the troops were unprovided with tents or shelter of any kind: many of the Germans dug holes in elevated places, to protect themselves from the continued rain.

The entire loss of the three weak battalions of the German legion which were employed before Burgos, amounted to five officers, seven sergeants and one hundred and nine men killed; and fourteen officers, eight sergeants and two hundred and twenty-five men wounded and taken; making an aggregate of nineteen officers and three hundred and forty-nine non-commissioned officers and soldiers.

1812.

October.

Appendix.
No. VIII.

The British troops were so judiciously withdrawn on the night of the 20th, that the French did not become acquainted with the movement until the 22d, when they followed, and on that day encamped with ten thousand men on the other side of the town.

The allied army gained Cellada del Camino and Hornillos the same evening, and on the following day resumed their retreat. The light cavalry brigade under general Anson, and light infantry brigade of the legion under colonel Halkett together with some horse artillery formed the rear-guard; a body of guerilla cavalry marched on their left, on the other side of the Arlanzon; and Bock's brigade was halted as support, at the

Journal of
major Rau-
tenberg;
Narrative
of captain
C. Heise;
Journals of
1st and 2d
dragoons :
MSS.

VENTA DEL POZO.

Lord Wellington was desirous that his principal force should be able to make good way to the rear, and gain the village of Torquemada, about seven leagues distant, without molestation. He, therefore, ordered the brigades of Anson and Halkett to remain in front of Cellada until the enemy should advance.

1812.

October.

Journal of
major Rau-
tenberg,
&c. MSS.

Halkett placed the light infantry brigade of the legion behind a brook, on the banks of which, hid by bushes that screened its sides, the second light battalion was concealed. In front of this brook, and on ground favorable to their movement, stood Anson's cavalry. Were they attacked, a flanking fire could be poured upon the assailants from the concealed infantry, or if a retrograde movement was found necessary, their retreat could be covered by the same means. The first light battalion occupied the village of Cellada as a reserve.

Contrary to general expectation, at about nine o'clock in the morning, Anson's outposts were driven in, and the cavalry on both sides became engaged. The unexpected fire from the German battalion in ambuscade, favoured the British attack, and the enemy's cavalry obliged to give way, contented themselves with observing their opponents at a short distance.

But, having been re-inforced, they again advanced and seemed to threaten surrounding the British position ; seeing which, sir Stapleton Cotton, who commanded the rear-guard, ordered it to retire, and the troops drew back to about half a league behind Cellada. Here the light battalions occupied a height on the left of the high road, while the cavalry halted on their right and front in the plain.

The French, having now a clear field, moved rapidly forward, and driving before them the guerilla cavalry, appeared in considerable force, although at

some distance on the left of the rear-guard. The 1812.
light battalions were, therefore, ordered to form October.
square, and lord Wellington, after reconnoitering Journal of major Rautenberg &c. MSS.
the enemy from the height on which the German
infantry were posted, gave instant orders that they
should retreat, and endeavour to secure the march
of the cavalry by occupying a pass near the village
of Villadrigo, about four miles distant.

Anson's light cavalry now advanced on the left, and
by frequently charging the French squadrons, which
continued to press forward in superior force, enabled
the German battalions to preserve a well ordered
retreat; and they had already arrived within a quarter
of an hour's march of the pass, when they had the
satisfaction to find themselves still farther supported
by their countrymen of the heavy cavalry brigade,
which, formed and halted in line, awaited their
approach.

Bock's brigade was well placed for checking the
farther advance of the enemy, having on its right
the river Arlanzon, and about five or six hundred
paces in front, a canal, over which a small bridge
united the high road from Cellada to Villadrigo.

Unfortunately the German squadrons did not receive orders to attack until Anson's brigade, pressed
on all sides, had fallen back upon them, and the
French cavalry, having crossed the bridge, had
formed *en muraille* on the opposite side of the canal.

Then it was that Bock was ordered to charge,
and although the enemy's first line was broken,

1812.

October.

Journal of
major Rau-
tenberg &c.
MSS.
and a considerable impression made upon their second line by his gallant troopers, who cut down many officers and men and suffered a severe loss, superior numbers obliged them to retire.

Meantime the light battalions had continued their retreat, marching in columns at quarter distance, and prepared at the shortest notice to form square. The second was about two hundred yards in rear of the first battalion when the heavy brigade was forced to give way, and, passing the latter battalion in double-quick time, it endeavoured to reach some ruins situated about five hundred yards in front.

The French, following the allied cavalry, now came upon the first battalion, which immediately halted,—formed square, and firmly sustained the first charge of the enemy's horsemen.

The second light battalion was unable to reach the ruins before the approach of the French, and having arrived at about a hundred and fifty yards from the village, also halted and formed square,

Both battalions then retired through Villadrigo, retaining their formation, and the first battalion had just emerged from the village, when the French cavalry again advancing to the charge, both squares drew up, and prepared to receive them.

The first battalion square received the enemy's charge upon its right and rear faces, which sustained the attack with their previous firmness, and the French troopers unable to make any impression, after a considerable loss, transferred their attack to the second battalion. Here also they completely failed; a murderous fire poured steadily upon the horsemen, forbid any nearer approach, and the discountenanced squadrons retired, fallen men and horses marking their discomfiture.

1812.

October.

Journal of major Rautenberg &c. MSS.

A renewal of the attack being expected, both squares remained stationary, and the enemy forming in masses upon their rear and right, appeared to contemplate another charge.

But a volley from the rear ranks of both squares soon sent the assailants off at a trot to a respectful distance, and the allied cavalry having been, by this time, restored to order, the French were kept effectually in check during the remainder of the day, and the rear-guard resumed its march without further molestation.

The retreat was continued without intermission for more than two hours, at the expiration of which time a halt was made in order to refresh the troops. Colonel Halkett now communicated to the German battalions lord Wellington's thanks for the gallant manner in which they had covered the retreat of the cavalry; a double allowance of spirits was ordered to be issued to the men, after their arrival at Torquemada, which they reached at two o'clock on the following morning, and the fatigues of the combat were soon forgotten.

The cavalry were the principal sufferers of the legion at the Venta del Poço, the light battalions having only had a few men wounded. The heavy brigade, however, lost major Fischer of the first, and lieutenant Droege of the second dragoons; major von Meydell, captain von Lenthe, lieutenants von der Decken, Phibbs, Schaeffer, von Hugo, and cornet Massow were all wounded, captain von Lenthe and lieutenant Schaeffer being also taken prisoners; eleven men and twenty horses were killed; thirty-six men and thirty-three horses wounded, and thirty-nine men were taken.

Some fine traits of gallantry were exhibited during this combat: sir Stapleton Cotton being involved in the mêlée after the failure of the allied attack, would have been struck down by a French dragoon, had not his orderly, a gallant soldier of the first hussars named Schutte, interposed, and cut the assailant from his horse; captain von der Decken, the general's aide-de-camp, was rescued from the enemy's hands by an intrepid officer of the twelfth English dragoons; and captain von Reitzenstein owed his safety to corporal Hofmeister, and another brave man of his regiment.

The loss of the French was considerable: in one regiment alone nearly all the officers were wounded; and although Bock's troopers were overpowered, the nature of the wounds which their opponents received, shewed how fiercely they had fought.*

* "Votre Excellence jugera de l' acharnement avec lequel on s'est battu, lorsqu'elle apprendra que le brave colonel Beteille et six officiers de la legion de Gens d'armerie ont été blessés; que dans le 15r. Regt. de Chasseurs, le colonel et tous les officiers, excepté deux, ont reçu des coups de sabre ou des contusions, et que les lanciers de Berg ont eu dans leur Escadrons plusieurs officiers blessés."—General Caffarelli's despatch.

The troops continued their march on the 24th, and on the following day were placed in position on the Carrion, the right being at Duenas, and the left at Villa-muriel. Here they were joined by a bri- gade of guards which had been disembarked at Corunna, and lord Dalhousie, under whose orders it had marched, was appointed to the command of the seventh division, which general Hope's state of health had obliged him to leave in the preceding month. After an unsuccessful attack upon the left of the allied army, which was gallantly repulsed by the fifth division, the enemy passed the Carrion at Palentia. The left of the allies was now thrown back, and the bridge of Villa-muriel was destroyed; but the enemy discovering a ford, passed over a strong body of infantry and cavalry. These were attacked by the allies and driven across the river with considerable loss, but the fire upon the British left had been very severe throughout the day, and their loss was proportionably great.

Lord Wellington broke up from the Carrion on the 26th, and marched to Cabeçon del Campo, crossing the Pisuerga river. The enemy placed themselves opposite on the following day, shewing a considerable force, particularly in cavalry, which could not be estimated at less than five thousand horses. They now commenced a sharp cannonade on various parts of the allied line, which caused some loss, and colonel Robe commanding the artillery, was severely wounded

Previous to the departure of lord Wellington from

Madrid, he had left directions for destroying the arsenal and fortified post of the Retiro should it be found necessary.

These works formed a triple line of defence. The exterior was made up of the palace of the Retiro, the museum, and the park wall; the second was a field profile of nine fronts, having on one front a ravelin and advanced lunette, and the interior defence was an octagonal star-fort, almost the whole interior of which was occupied by a large square building, originally a porcelain manufactory and called the

CASA DE LA CHINA.

This was the principal enclosure, and contained within it, barracks, hospitals, armories, public offices, and extensive military magazines. The museum contained the forges and wheel makers shops; the palace had been used as a barrack for both cavalry and infantry, and the adjoining sheds and coach-houses were filled with caissons and other military carriages, together with a vast quantity of timber applicable to the construction of ordnance.

The execution of this responsible duty was entrusted to lieutenant-colonel Hartmann* of the German artillery, who was directed to make such arrangements of the ordnance and stores as would provide either for their preservation, or for the facility of destroying the whole at a short notice.

* Major Hartmann had the honor to be included in the brevet which came out soon after the battle of Salamanca.

Special modes of operation were also laid down 1812.
for his guidance, among which, it was directed that October.
the guns should be placed upon the ground in such
relative positions as that the fire of one should des- Appendix No. IX.
troy the other; and that, in the explosion of the
powder, all risk of injuring the town should be
carefully avoided.

To aid colonel Hartmann in the execution of Beiträge zur Ges-
these operations, captain Cleeves, lieutenant von chichte des Krieges.
Scharnhorst, two non-commissioned officers and four
gunners of the German artillery, together with Mr.
Sparkes an assistant commissary, and messrs. Atkinson
and Causton, clerks of stores, were placed under his
orders, and he lost no time in making all suitable
arrangements.

The powder, small arms, gun ammunition, and all
combustibles were placed in the interior court of the
Casa de la China; the ordnance in the court between
the interior house and the great building; the gun
carriages, ammunition waggons, carts, and timber
between this building and the parapet of the interior
fort; and the building itself was mined under the four
angles and one pier of the archway.

With the exception of one Portuguese regiment,
the troops under Charles Alten left Madrid on the
23d, to join the corps of general Hill. The mines
under la China were then loaded, the trains prepared,
and the various stores arranged for ignition.

At ten o'clock on the morning of the 29th, colonel
Hartmann received orders to begin the destruction

1812.

October.

Beiträge
zur Ge-
chichte des
Krieges.

of the stores. To ensure the safety of the town as well as that of the people at work, he proceeded with the various objects in regular succession, destroying first the combustibles, musquet barrels and locks, and then loading the ordnance. These labours continued until evening, when the nature of the work obliged him to postpone further operations until daylight.

A heavy fall of rain during the night rendered the proceedings difficult on the following morning, as the train became wet before the port-fire could be applied, and great delay was the consequence. It was now attempted to explode the guns according to the proscribed instruction, but the numerous splinters of shot, and the quantities of bricks, stones, and timber which were brought down from every part of the building, rendered this operation so extremely dangerous, while, at the same time, it did not produce the desired effect, that colonel Hartmann decided upon giving up the attempt, and directed the guns to be fired singly. This arrangement was necessarily the cause of still farther delay, and prevented the possibility of the work being concluded before night, as had been contemplated.

Meantime the buildings within the exterior line, and the palisades were ignited, and by five o'clock in the afternoon, above one hundred pieces of ordnance had been completely destroyed.

Colonel Hartmann having now learned that no British troops were between the ford of the Arganda

and the town, the possibility of the French entering
Madrid before the whole of his instructions had been
complied with, became evident to him; he, therefore, Beiträge
justly considering the destruction of the buildings and zur Geschichte des
gun carriages of more importance than that of the Krieges.
guns, which by spiking could at least be made
temporarily unserviceable,—directed the firing to
cease, and the mines to be prepared for explosion.
This operation was directed by captain Cleeves, and,
with the exception of the mine under the right front
angle of the building,—the train of which was broken
by the adjoining mine exploding too soon,—it was
completely successful. The remaining guns, about
fifty in number, were spiked or hidden in the shores;
the carriages and carts were then fired, and the
whole was kept in a continued blaze during the whole
of the night.

These various and hazardous operations had all
been effected without any serious accident, but in the
explosion of the last house the loss of two valuable
lives was unfortunately sustained. This house was
a slight arched building situated in front of the entrance gate of la China, and had been used as a
depôt for the different combustibles employed in the
destruction of the works; which being completed, it
was directed to be fired by igniting some fascines
and other timber, that were placed in a corner of
the building. Mr. Atkinson was charged with the
superintendence of this explosion, and both he and
Mr. Causton were so imprudent as to enter the house

1812.

October.

Beiträge
zur Ges-
chichte des
Krieges.
with lighted port-fires, without the precaution of
having had the floor previously cleared of the loose
powder.   An immediate explosion was the consequence, and the two unfortunate youg men were
crushed to death under the ruins.

The remainder of the troops received orders to
leave Madrid at five o'clock in the afternoon of the
31st, accompanied by colonel Hartmann and his
assistants.   Finding that the rear-guard was halted
at a short distance from the town, Hartmann applied for general Hill's permission to attempt the
explosion of the mine which had failed.   This was
the more important as a quantity of musquets and
small arms had been placed near it for the purpose of
being destroyed at the same time.   General Hill
having assented, the operation was entrusted to captain Cleeves, who, accompanied by four mounted men,
and protected by the cavalry picquets, returned to the
arsenal, and quickly renewing the train, effected the
explosion.   Unfortunately, owing to the too rapid
ignition of the port-fire, the gallant officer was severely burned in the hands and face, and suffered
serious injuries in the head.

On the evening of this day Hill's corps was drawn
towards the Guadarama pass, and the French resumed their occupation of the capital on the following
morning.

Napier.   It has been stated that the allies crossed the Pisuerga on the 26th of October.   On the following
day the whole French army appeared in front of

Cabezon, and their numbers shewed lord Wellington that he could not permanently maintain either the Pisuerga or the Duero. Wishing, however, to gain time, he held his position, and when the French extended their right, with a view to dislodge the allies, he directed the bridges of Valladolid and Simancas to be destroyed.

The latter operation was entrusted to colonel Halkett, who, with the two light battalions of the German legion, a battalion of Brunswickers, and two guns, proceeded down the right bank of the river on the 27th, and took post near Simancas. On the following morning, the French, availing themselves of a thick fog, pushed forward a strong reconnoitering party towards the German outposts, and taking prisoners a corporal and three men of the advanced patrole, nearly captured the outlying picquet. Towards noon, some of the enemy's staff officers appeared upon the heights, which commanded the bridge of Simancas, and a corps of at least six thousand men were seen, formed in column of attack.

Rauten-
berg's,
Journal.
MSS.

Halkett immediately took the two light battalions of the legion across the river, leaving the Brunswickers on the right bank. The enemy's guns now opened, while their skirmishers, debouching from a defile, crowded towards the bridge. The Brunswickers were then also withdrawn. Halkett had made all the necessary arrangements for destroying the bridge, and wisely concluding that, on its explosion, the enemy would try that of Tordesillas, he

Wyneck-
en's narra-
tive. MSS.

1812.

October.

Wynec-
ken's nar-
rative.
MSS.

directed colonel von Hertzberg to take on the Brunswick battalion to that point.   This being done, the
train was lighted, but some delay occurring in the
explosion, the French tirailleurs were enabled to fire
from the centre of the bridge before the mine sprung,
and bringing also two guns to bear upon the legion
battalions, some men were wounded.   The bridge,
however, at length, blew up, and the enemy, quickly
retiring, proceeded down the river towards Tordesillas. Two companies of the legion brigade were now
placed on picquet, while the remainder retired to a
pine wood about a mile in the rear, and bivouacked
for the night.   On the morning of the 29th the guns
and picquet united in firing upon the enemy's rear-
guard and baggage as they passed, and the brigade
marching in the evening to Villa Nueva, arrived in
front of Tordesillas on the morning of the 30th.

The bridge here had been destroyed in the preceding June; but the French contrived to render it passable to foot passengers, by laying boards
across the broken arches, and a strong picquet was
stationed there for its defence.   The Brunswickers
had been directed to take post in the ruins and
prevent the enemy from repairing the bridge; but a

Napier.

daring exploit of sixty French officers and non-
commissioned officers, who, swimming the river,
surprised their post, obliged them to retire.

Narrative
of captain
Walther.
MSS.

When Halkett arrived, he sent out fifty men from
each battalion of the legion under captain Cropp,
who placing them across a deep road way, which

led to the bridge, sent patroles in front and flank to 1812.
ascertain the enemy's movements. October.

The most advanced of these patroles soon sent in
word that a strong detachment of the enemy had Walther's narrative MSS.
crossed the bridge, and was moving, apparently with
the intention of surrounding the German picquet by
its left flank. This was considered a false alarm,
caused by a picquet of Portuguese caçadores, which
was expected on the left, and, unfortunately, it remained unnoticed; for just as Cropp's detachment
was leaving the road, and about to take post in an
adjoining wood, the French appeared in the rear,
and fell upon the Germans so suddenly, and with so
much violence, that the picquet was broken and
dispersed, and nearly sixty men made prisoners.

Lord Wellington had destroyed the bridges at Val- Napier.
ladolid and Cabezon, and crossed the Duero on the 29th;
and now hearing of the French exploit at Tordesillas,
he marched by his left to the heights between that
place and Rueda, and presenting a bold front to the
enemy checked their farther progress. The bridges
of Toro and Zamora were now also destroyed, and
the communications insured with general Hill.

CHAPTER VI.

In order to bring up the movements of the second
hussars of the legion to the present period, it will be
necessary to go back to the operations of general
Hill's corps during the month of March.

To this corps, it will be remembered, were attached two squadrons of the second hussars under major von dem Bussche. On the 16th of
March a movement having been made towards
Merida, the advanced guard of hussars under cornet
von Thümmel discovered a strong French post consisting of cavalry and infantry, about three leagues
from the place.   A single vedette stood carelessly by
his horse upon a height near the road to La Nava.
The hussars immediately gave chace to the vedette,
and gallopping with him into the town, took prisoners three officers, and several troopers.   The
rest managed to turn out and form squadron on
the bridge, where Thümmel charged them twice
with success, and following up his advantage, although wounded, drove the whole to the other side
of the Guadiana.   Here the French had a strong
corps of infantry, and five hundred cavalry, and the
infantry advanced to cross the river, but the rest of

general Long's brigade appearing in sight, they fell
back, and marched to Almandralejo.

On the 26th, information having been received
that a strong body of the enemy's cavalry was stationed
at Don-Benito, the hussars were directed to march
to that place, and a detachment of infantry to follow
by the way of Mongabril.

An open country exposed the march of the Germans
whose approach was immediately notified to the
enemy by their vedettes, and they retired behind the
place. The hussars bivouaced in front on the Merida
road. Towards evening the infantry came up and
also prepared to bivouac, sending some riflemen
into Don-Benito, where they took post behind a
wall.

The approach of night had concealed the arrival of
the English infantry from the enemy, who being now
reinforced, advanced from the place with the intention of surprising the hussars. To their astonishment, however, they were saluted on the way by a
sharp fire from the riflemen, which so disconcerted
them, that they hurried off to La Nava and Campa-
nario, leaving several killed and prisoners in the
hands of the allies.

In the course of the following month the enemy's
cavalry returned to Don-Benito, and an expedition
consisting of the German hussars, the ninth dragoons
and a battery of artillery, was sent under sir William
Erskine, to reconnoitre their movements; but again
they withdrew to La Nava, and a skirmish only took

1812.

Bussche's
Narrative
MSS.

place, in which a few of the hussars were wounded.

On the 1st of July the enemy's cavalry, with artillery advanced to Corte de Pelleas, and drove back a regiment of Portuguese horse, which was stationed there; but the English and German squadrons hurrying to their aid, the French marched to Santa Martha. Here some Spanish squadrons were stationed, which giving way, were driven by the enemy up to the British bivouac near Albuera, where they captured an infantry picquet. The hussars had at this moment just reached the bivouac on their return from Corte de Pelleas, but instantly remounting, they sallied forth, to re-take the picquet. Serjeant-major Klare, who marched in command of the leading sections, rode boldly forward, charged the enemy's advanced guard, and cut down several of them, and the rest of the brigade, then coming up, drove back the assailants, who were thus prevented from surprising the English cavalry, then bivouaced in an adjacent wood. The Spanish squadrons suffered considerably on this occasion; the hussars had only two men wounded and one horse killed.

On the 3d of July, the French and allied cavalry had some sharp skirmishing at Villa-Alba, where the hussars had two men and one horse killed, and two men and three horses wounded. A few days afterwards near Usagre, they lost four horses. The enemy's cavalry now moved to Llera and Valentia, followed by general Long's brigade, which, on the 12th, reached Berlanga.

On the morning of the 24th, two regiments of French dragoons, and one regiment of chasseurs under general Lallemand, drove in the Portuguese picquet from Hinojosa to Ribera, where four squadrons of Portuguese cavalry were stationed under colonel Campbell. His force being so inferior to that of the enemy, he retired upon Villafranca, from whence general Long's brigade advanced, accompanied by a battery of artillery. The enemy withdrew beyond the defile of Ribera, through which Long advanced, and pushing his squadrons round the town, attacked the enemy with spirit, while the artillery fired with effect from some high ground on the Villafranca side of the defile. The French gave way and retired rapidly on Hinojosa. A squadron of the hussars under major von Wissel dashing forward in pursuit, became exposed to the attacks of a strong column of the enemy's cavalry, which they bravely repulsed, and driving the French horsemen into the defile, pursued them on the road to Llera and Valentia de Torres. The French had thirty men and a number of horses killed, and eleven men and thirty horses were taken. The loss of the allied brigade was inconsiderable; of the hussars three men and five horses were wounded. The enemy now retired to Llera, and the allied cavalry again occupied Villafranca de los Barros.*

1812

Sir Wm. Erskine's despatch.

Bussche's Narrative MSS.

Narrative of general von Wissel MSS.

* The following incident was as creditable to the French general as complimentary to the German hussars :—

Two hussars had been sent from Ribera with despatches, and on their return, were quietly watering their horses at a brook outside the town, be-

1

1812.

Bussche's
narrative.
MSS.

On the 1st of August, immediately after the ninth dragoons had been relieved on the out posts by the hussars, the enemy advanced from Hornachos towards Ribera with one thousand infantry, six hundred cavalry and two guns, for the purpose of foraging. The main body of general Hill's corps being at a considerable distance it was important that the French should be kept in check, until re-inforcements could arrive. This was a duty of no little difficulty; for the hussars weakened by sickness, and having three picquets detached, could not, at this moment, oppose more than a hundred horses to the enemy. They were, however, joined by a picquet of the ninth dragoons that had just been relieved, and the officer commanding which, spiritedly brought his party to their support.

In order to conceal the weakness of his squadrons from the enemy, Bussche kept them on the heights of Ribera, scattering the men about in various directions; causing signals to be sounded, and all the appearance of a considerable cavalry force to be assumed by moving the files from one side of the hill to the other.

lieving that the place was still occupied by the allies, when suddenly they were surprised by the French; disarmed, and dismounted, and brought prisoners to general Lallemand. The general interrogated them, and having ascertained to what regiment they belonged, directed that their arms and horses should be immediately restored; and giving them permission to depart, desired that they should tell their commanding officer, "that it gave him pleasure to shew his respect for the German hussars, by thus allowing them to return to their regiment."—Bussche's Narrative. MSS.

The skirmishers had to sustain a severe and unequal contest, and many times it was found necessary
to form up and charge the advancing horsemen, Bussche's
which was always done with success. Lieutenant narrative. MSS.
Charles von Gruben directed these operations, and
with such a degree of judgment and gallantry, that
the enemy failed in every attempt to drive back the
hussars. This fatiguing contest had continued for
several hours, and the skirmishers were relieved,
but their zealous officer, disdaining repose, insisted
on continuing his exertions: an additional officer
was, however, sent forward to his aid. Gruben now
redoubled his labours; made the men take steady
aim at their opponents, and being himself a good
marksman, exemplified his instructions by a few
well-directed shots at the opposing line. This drew
upon him the attention of the enemy; his horse was
soon hit, and shortly after, a fatal bullet struck the
gallant youth to the earth!

The hussars had now maintained the post for
nearly five hours, when sir William Erskine arriving,
ordered them to retire, and, abandoning the heights,
they formed upon the reserve squadrons behind a
brook, which was approached by a defile. The
enemy now for the first time got a full view of the
little force with which they had been vainly contending, and dashed down the hill with rage and
mortification upon the rear-guard, which quickly
retired through the defile. The French followed in
mass, and crowding forward towards the reserve,

obliged the whole to retire at a rapid pace, and with some loss; an effort was made to check the pursuit, but the numbers were too disproportionate, and the hussars continued to retreat. An officer's picquet was now placed in a wood, but in view of the enemy, who again intimidated by appearances ceased to press on, and the rest of the brigade soon coming up, they eventually returned to Hornachos, leaving two officers and several men killed and wounded.

The loss of the hussars in this skirmish was one officer, one man and four horses killed, and ten men and eight horses wounded. The officer, lieutenant von Gruben was a most promising young man, of great natural ability, and who, on this day, had particularly distinguished himself. The esteem in which he was held was fully testified by the attendance of nearly all the officers of general Hill's corps at his interment on the following day.

Towards the latter end of the month, Hill's force was united at Usagre and Villagarcia, for the purpose of co-operating with the main army. About this period major Bussche was reluctantly obliged to give up his command of the hussars, in consequence of ill health, and major von Wissel became commanding officer of the detachment.

On the 20th of October, the two squadrons received orders to join the brigade of Victor Alten, and having been reinforced by the third squadron

from Cadiz,* they arrived at Villaverde near Ma- 1812.
drid, by the end of the month.

October.

Sir Rowland Hill continued his march from Ma- Welling-
drid towards Arevalo, slowly followed by the enemy. despatch.
He had intended destroying the Puente larga, but
the mine failed, and the enemy having collected
large bodies of troops between the bridge and Aranjuez they attacked the British post on the bridge,
but were repulsed with considerable loss. The ca- Linsingens
valry brigade of Victor Alten formed the rear-guard MSS.
of general Hill's corps, which passed the Guadarama
on the 3d of November, and reached Villacastrin
without molestation. On the 4th the rear squadron

* The third squadron under captain Friederichs had, since the battle of
Barossa, been actively employed in operations carried on by colonel Skerrett
against Tarifa, Niebla and Seville. During the investment of Tarifa by the
French (Nov. 1811.) Lieutenant Koch having been sent with a detachment
of sixty hussars to reconnoitre towards Frasinas, fell in with an enemy's patrole of a hundred dragoons and as many infantry, the former being posted
on an open height, with the infantry in rear flanked by a wood. The hussars
were debouching from a defile when the enemy were thus discovered, and
Koch instantly led them forward at speed against the French cavalry, which
gave way, and were driven back upon their infantry by the hussars. The
whole of the French detachment then retired, and the hussars returned to
Tarifa, surprising on the march a small French picquet, who throwing down
their arms, fled to the mountains.

On the 20th December, (1811) when the French advancing, drove in the
Spanish picquets, the officer commanding, deserted by his men, would have
been taken prisoner, had not sergeant Storch and four hussars, hurrying to
his assistance, driven back the enemy, who lost five men. By a well-timed
charge of a detachment of twenty hussars under cornet Wiebold during the
taking of Seville, in the following August (1812), in which a sergeant and
two hussars were killed, the French were prevented from blowing up the
bridge of that town.

This squadron was so reduced in horses by the various and severe duties in
which it had been engaged, that it was found necessary to supply it with a
remount of thirty-six Spanish horses.—Journal of 2d Hussars, MSS.

of hussars under lieutenant Baring, being pressed by the enemy's advance, made front at a bridge near Villacastrin, charged the French horsemen and drove them back with loss. The following day a squadron of the second hussars under lieutenant Koch brought up the rear, and became engaged in a sharp skirmish, during which the lieutenant cut a French officer from his horse. This was between Villacastrin and Villanueva. In the evening a picquet of twenty-two of the same squadron under lieutenant Grahn checked the enemy's progress in a very remarkable manner. This picquet took up a position in the hollow of a deep road-way, or defile, flanked by thickly wooded heights, and leading from a ford of the Adaja river. The French, having reconnoitered the position of the picquet, formed in a dense column on the opposite bank to the number of from twelve to fifteen squadrons; Grahn, seeing the unequal contest with which he was threatened, directed his men to put a second ball into their carbines, and, extending his little force in such a manner as to give it the protection of the wood, he sent a report of his situation to the brigade, then at Villanueva, about a league distant, and firmly awaited the enemy's advance. A French squadron soon appeared in motion, and crossing the ford, pressed into the defile. The hussars now opened their carbine fire, which, wounding several men and horses, caused such a panic among the assailants that nearly the half of them immedi-

Narrative of captain Grahn. MSS.

ately recrossed the river; the rest sought out for other approaches to the position of the picquet, but without success, and the enemy seeing that the Germans were neither to be forced in front or flank, quietly dismounted and did not seem disposed to renew the assault. Nearly an hour had thus passed, when Grahn, having received orders to join the brigade, left four men as rear-guard in the defile, and set off to the rear at a trot. The French were no sooner aware of this movement than they hurried after him, and the little rear-guard were on the point of being made prisoners, when Grahn, facing his detachment about, rode boldly against the enemy's advance, drove them back, and brought off his men in safety. The French now retired, and the picquet rejoined the brigade without further molestation.

Lord Wellington finding that the bridge of Toro Napier. had been repaired on the 4th, and that the enemy might, therefore, fall upon his rear, while Soult, moving by Fontiveros, could reach the Tormes, directed general Hill to march direct upon Alba; and breaking up from his own position in front of Tordesillas, on the 6th, he put the army in march for Despatch the heights of San Christoval. Here they arrived on the 8th, and the same day Hill's corps passed the Tormes, the cavalry brigade of general Long remaining on the right bank. On the morning of the 10th, Long's cavalry were obliged to retire through Alba, and in the course of that day, the enemy's whole army approached the British position. Twenty

1812.
November.
Napier.

pieces of cannon were opened upon the troops at Alba, and more than a hundred men fell on the side of the allies; but they defended the post with such vigour that the enemy did not venture on an assault, and the next morning they withdrew.

On the 14th, the French crossed the Tormes about seven miles above Alba, and took up a position at Mozarbes. Wellington was therefore obliged to withdraw his troops, and by the following morning he united the allied army in the position of the Arapiles, hoping that the enemy would give battle there. But Soult commenced fortifying Mozarbes, and, extending his left, threatened the allied line of retreat; wherefore the British commander, feeling himself too weak to attack, threw his army into column, and boldly passing the enemy's left flank, gained the Valmusa river, the same night.

Linsingens
Journal.
MSS.

The march was continued towards Rodrigo on the following day, Victor Alten's cavalry forming the rear-guard. This brigade consisted only of six squadrons; one having been left at Morisco, and another at Aldea Lingua. About noon it reached Matilla, in front of which Alten posted one squadron, with a line of out-posts in advance. About three o'clock the French came on with fourteen squadrons, drove in the out-posts, and advanced rapidly on the brigade, which lay in a wood in rear of the town. Alten instantly met the attack with his left wing, composed of two squadrons of the fourteenth and one squadron of the second hussars, seeing which the

Polish lancers that were opposed to him went about. 1812.
The allied horsemen followed, dealing out sabre blows November.
with considerable effect; but a strong reserve appear- Linsingens
ing in support of the enemy, they were recalled. Journal.
MSS.
The French now again made front, and followed
closely on the heels of the allied squadrons, until
checked by the fire of an infantry picquet from the
wood. Alten now ordered forward his right wing
consisting of the first hussars, who attacked a body
of chasseurs in their front, and drove them back in
confusion; but the general, concluding that the enemy
had guns with their reserve, here checked the
pursuit, and halted his brigade. The French
cavalry had several men and horses wounded in
this day's skirmish, besides some loss in prisoners.
The loss of the hussars was eight or ten wounded,
and the fourteenth had two men killed and two
wounded.*

---

* Colonel Waters of the British staff, was left sick in a village through
which the rear squadron of hussars under captain Aly marched on the 15th,
and Aly, knowing the loss which the army would sustain, if the gallant officer
fell into the enemy's hands, directed a bold and intelligent hussar of the
squadron, named Christian Ellicrott to try and bring him off. The squadron
passed on, while the hussar repairing to colonel Waters's quarters, dressed
him; got his horse ready, and, conducting him out of the village, sought to
join the squadron; but the French had already intercepted their march, and no
means of escape offered but by taking a circuitous course towards the army.
The state of colonel Waters's health did not admit of his riding fast, and by
the time they had reached a village, where the invalid halted for refreshment,
while the hussar went to look out for a ford in a river that was to be crossed,
the enemy had also arrived in the place. No ford could be found, and both
were obliged to swim their horses across the stream. The French now nearly
surrounded them, and colonel Waters being much exhausted from the over
exertion which he had undergone, found himself unable to proceed, and lay
concealed for an entire day, guarded by his faithful attendant. The journey
was then resumed, and after several days march, during which they had to cross
other rivers, and were in constant danger of falling into the enemy's hands,
the trusty hussar brought his charge safe back to the allied army.—Guelphic
Archives, MSS.

The retreat was continued through a wooded country,

the right of the allied army being covered by the

light division, and the left by the cavalry. The centre column was commanded by sir Edward Paget, who, in riding to the rear to ascertain the cause of an interval which appeared between his divisions, had the misfortune to fall into the enemy's hands, and was made prisoner.

The stragglers on this day were numerous, and great irregularity prevailed among the allied troops; many left their ranks in pursuit of swine which abounded in the neighbouring forest, and two thousand are stated to have been captured by the enemy,

besides a quantity of baggage. On reaching the high table land above the Huebra, the French took advantage of the ground to cannonade the light division; but Alten led his gallant followers down to the stream amid the unceasing cannon fire, with a degree of coolness and order worthy of the highest praise, and they gained the opposite bank with little

loss. Now, however, the enemy made an attempt to force the fords, and keeping up a plunging fire upon the light and seventh divisions, nearly three hundred men were killed and wounded.

On the 18th, the wearied soldiers had to traverse marshy plains, which exhausted their strength, and the number of stragglers increased to a considerable extent; many also, tempted as on the preceding day, by large herds of swine, broke away from the ranks to satisfy their hunger, and serious consequences might have resulted if the point of retreat had been much farther distant. However, the French halted on the Huebra, and, on the 19th, the allied troops reached Ciudad Rodrigo ; the whole army then passed the Agueda ; and on the 20th, the several divisions marched into their respective winter quarters in Portugal.

1812.

November.

Wellington's despatch.

CHAPTER VII.

OPERATIONS IN THE NORTH OF GERMANY.

The disasters of the French army in 1812 formed the elements of a result little apprehended by its ambitious leader.   The devoted sacrifice of Moskow, and the premature rigour of a northern winter, had driven back, and finally caused the flight and ruin of the invading forces ; the victors followed, and, completing their successes on the banks of the Beresina, pressed after the fugitives to those of the Saale.   Here the extraordinary efforts of Napoleon had collected fresh troops, and a new army under Murat was brought into the field.   Other reinforcements under his personal command, advanced from the Rhine, and it was evident, that, although the usurper had been driven from the greater part of his German conquests, he was fully determined on making a desperate effort to regain them.

But, in the beginning of the succeeding year a spirit arose in the north of Germany which sealed Napoleon's downfall.   The king of Prussia, weary of the thraldom under which he had been so long forced to bend, and seeing the favorable opportunity which presented itself for liberating his exhausted domi-

nions from the invader's yoke, summoned his subjects
to take up arms in defence of their king and country,
and on the 22d of February, 1813, concluded a
treaty of alliance with the emperor of Russia. The
Hanseatic states now rose; Sweden also joined the
allies ;—Hanover, Mecklenburg, Dessau, Cöthen,
proclaimed their independence; and soon the wild
plains and dark recesses of northern Germany re-
sounded with the cry of "Freedom" and "Fatherland."

For the purpose of forwarding this popular demonstration in the north, the allies came to the determination of placing a separate corps upon the lower
Elbe, which, in conjunction with the Swedes, was to
act under the chief command of the Prince Royal of
Sweden, the immediate direction of the corps being
entrusted to lieutenant-general count Wallmoden
Gimborn.*

The basis of this corps was composed of the Russian detachment of generals Dörnberg, Tettenborn,
and Czernicheff, which consisted principally of Cossack Pulks. To these were added, towards the end
of April, the new formed Hanseatic legion, consisting

---

* General Wallmoden was the the eldest son of the Field Marshal who
commanded the Hanoverian army in 1803. He had been for some years in
the Austrian service, which he left for the Russian service about the commencement of Napoleon's invasion of that country. He then came over to
England, and having been selected by the British Government as eminently qualified to direct the proposed operations in the north of Germany,
received the local rank of lieutenant-general in the British service, (his
commission bearing date, January 21st 1812,) and at the decease of major-
general von Bock, he was appointed, (March, 1814,) colonel commandant of
the 1st dragoons King's German Legion. In June 1815, general Wallmoden retired from the British service and returned to the Austrian.

1813. of three battalions of infantry, and eight hundred

April. cavalry; five battalions of Hanoverian infantry, two
hundred hussars, and a few riflemen; three battalions
Der Feld-
zug in Mec-
klenburg,
&c. of Mecklenburghers; a Prussian and a Dessau battalion, and one battalion of Russian riflemen. The greater part of these were new levies, having been raised
within a few weeks, and the whole amounted to about
five thousand six hundred infantry, and six thousand
cavalry.

An agreement had also been entered into between
England and Russia for the formation of a corps of
ten thousand men, to be raised from among the
Russian prisoners of war, and to be called the
Russian German Legion.

Marquess
of London-
derry's
narrative of
the War in
Germany
and France Military stores and equipments of all sorts were
promptly and abundantly furnished to these troops
by the British government, which also agreed to
give two millions sterling for their maintenance;
two millions more were allotted to Russia and
Prussia, besides five hundred thousand pounds for the
support of the Russian fleet. In return Russia was
to employ two hundred thousand men, and Prussia
one hundred thousand in active operations against
the enemy.

Der Feld-
zug in
Mecklen-
burg, &c. The desultory nature of the intended operations in
the north of Germany caused the troops which were
employed there to be much dispersed, and consequently reduced those which remained under the
immediate command of general Wallmoden to a very
inconsiderable and ineffective body. With these, how-

ever, he was required to support Hamburg, and 1813.
secure the Elbe, as well as to cover the rear of April.
Bulow's Russian corps, then operating near Berlin.

To aid the organization of the new levies, a Narrative of captain
detachment of the King's German Legion was ordered Dehnel. MSS.
to embark for the north of Germany. The troops
were selected from the two light battalions, and the
first, second and fifth line battalions, making together
about four hundred men, which were placed under
the command of lieutenant-colonel Martin; a detachment of the first hussars under lieutenant Krauchenberg, were added, as also six guns and fifty artillery-
men under captain Wiering. The whole embarked
at Sheerness, under the command of general Lyon,
on the 6th of April, and reached Hamburg on the
29th.

A separation of the corps now took place, the
infantry having been previously formed into two
light and two line companies. The line companies,
under major Müller, joined the line battalion of
Lauenburg, which was then being organized under
major von Berger at Bergedorf; the first light
battalion company under captain Holtzermann, was
attached to the Lauenburg light battalion, and the
second light battalion company under captain
Schaumann, to the light battalion of Bremen and
Verden, both then stationed on the Wilhelmsburg
island, for the defence of Hamburg, which city was
occupied by the Russian corps of general Tettenborn.

The movements of the French towards the Elbe,

made it necessary for the detachments and new levies that were dispersed through the Electorate of Hanover, to cross that river, which they did at Boitzenburg, Artlenburg and Harburg without loss.

Der Feld-
zug in
Mecklen-
burg &c.
Napoleon had, by this time, brought up his reinforcements to Erfurth, and Davoust, who commanded the French troops in the north of Germany, held possession of Lüneburg, Harburg, Stade, and Cuxhaven. He was busily endeavouring to collect boats, of which the precautionary measures of Tettenborn had stripped the left bank of the river, and reinforcements daily arriving to the French, Hamburg became in a perilous position.

On the night of the 8th of May an attempt was made by the enemy's troops at Harburg under Vandamme, upon the islands of Wilhelmsburg and Ochsenwerder, and the allies were driven back to Vödel, a small village situated on that extremity of the Wilhelmsburg immediately opposite Hamburg. Great consternation now arose in the town, and many of the citizens fled, with their most valuable effects, to Altona. Towards noon, however, the allies were re-inforced, and a detachment from Ochsenwerder, attacking the enemy in the rear and right flank, rendered valuable aid to count Kielmansegges' riflemen, who were much pressed. The enemy were finally driven back to Harburg, and the island, although, in the short time, thoroughly plundered by the French, fell again into possession of the allies.

This affair cost the allies eighty men in killed and wounded, but the French are supposed to have lost a hundred.

Major von Berger, on being informed of the attack, marched up from Bergedorf with the troops under his orders, and falling upon the enemy's post at Fünf-hausen, drove them back, but with the loss of from twenty to thirty men in killed and wounded.

A few days afterwards, the allies having been obliged to evacuate the Hope entrenchment, opposite to Zollenspieker, major von Berger learned from an interrupted despatch addressed to general Vandamme from marshal Davoust, that the former had been directed to attempt the passage of the Elbe at Zollenspieker; he therefore sent forward the troops under his command, with all possible secrecy, and placed them behind the Elbe dyke.

Before day-break the enemy were heard embarking, and they landed from two to three hundred men upon a small island near Zollenspieker. Their boats had gone back to bring over additional troops, when Berger, seizing the favorable moment, sent over captain Lucadon with a few hundred men, while, to prevent the arrival of the enemy's reinforcements, a fire was opened upon the river from a twenty-four pounder battery at Zollenspieker.

The French, seeing the difficulty of their position, defended themselves to the utmost, and Berger found it necessary to reinforce Lucadon with some more companies of the Lauenburg battalion. After

K

an obstinate contest, stoutly maintained on both sides, the allies charged with the bayonet and the French gave way. Several attempted to escape by swimming, but were drowned, and the rest, laying down their arms, surrendered as prisoners of war.

The loss of the legion light company and Lauenburg battalion on this occasion, was from eighteen to twenty in killed and wounded, among whom were lieutenant Bachelle of the seventh line battalion, and lieutenant von Issendorf of the Lauenburg regiment, both severely wounded. The French lost about seventy in killed and wounded; and five officers, twelve non-commissioned officers, and one hundred and eighty men were brought off prisoners by the Germans.

In other parts of the river the allies were not so fortunate. Count Kielmansegge had been obliged, in consequence of the state of his health, to give up the command of the troops on the Wilhelmsburg island on the evening of the 10th, and a field officer of the Hanseatic corps became director of the allied movements. Another plan of operations was immediately adopted; the small islands of Neuhof, Altenwerder and Finckenwerder, which had been occupied by the Mecklenburghers, were evacuated; the troops were fatigued with useless marching, and counter-marching, and finally, a council of war was called together to determine on the best course of proceeding. This served but to increase the confusion; no measures were taken to oppose the

expected attack of the enemy, and a general mistrust
and want of confidence pervaded the troops. At
length, towards midnight on the 10th, they were
ordered to fall back upon Vödel, thus as it were
inviting the enemy to advance and take possession of
the most important island in the Elbe!

The French were not slow in availing themselves
of the invitation, and, before the morning of the 12th
they occupied the whole island, with the exception
of the small spot at Vödel to which the allies had
retired. Here some miserable entrenchments were
hurriedly thrown up.

In the afternoon of the following day the troops
received orders to advance and drive back the enemy.
The attack was injudiciously conducted; close formed
masses of men being marched along the dyke against
a strong line of French skirmishers, whose certain
aim threw the columns into disorder before they
were brought into action. Fresh troops were sent
forward to repair the evil, but these being also
paraded along the dyke, became involved in the same
confusion. To complete the failure, the Hanseatic
commandant went over to the enemy;* and now the
allies pressed by numbers, and in danger of being
surrounded, retired with precipitation upon Vödel,
and endeavoured to embark for the Hamburg shore.
The confusion increased, the French crowding after

1813.

May
Bieder-
mann's
Journal.

Narrative
of lieut.
Müller.
MSS.

---

* Journal of lieutenant Biedermann, who adds that "another scoundrel
who was about to follow the example of his chief, was shot by the allied
riflemen.—Vol. 1, page 154.

the fugitives; and it was mainly owing to the exertions of captain Schaumann, lieutenant Biedermann, and the company of the second light battalion of the legion under their command, that the greater part of the allied troops were, eventually, enabled to embark. It often happened in the course of the retreat, that one side of a house served as a protection to the allies, and the other to the enemy. Lieutenant Müller, with a few of the Bremen and Verden battalion, and others who rallied round him, joined the legion detachment, and assisted to cover the retreat; the wretched entrenchment at Vödel afforded but a short protection, and now all hurried to the boats. Many, unable to obtain room, attempted to swim across, and were either drowned or shot by the enemy's tirailleurs. Biedermann, after the most indefatigable exertions in rallying and encouraging his men attempted to reach one of the boats by swimming, but the weight of his clothes kept him down, and he was with difficulty brought to the French side by his comrades. This gallant officer, with several others who had been left behind, were ultimately obliged to wade up to their necks in the river in order to reach a boat, and secure their conveyance to the Hamburg side.

This unfortunate affair cost the allies many men; the Hamburg Burgher-guard alone are supposed to have lost two hundred.

The allies were now deprived unexpectedly of a considerable part of their force on the islands; for the Danes, who had been latterly acting with them, were suddenly removed on the 19th. This was supposed to have been caused by the failure of the negociation which was then pending in London, for the cession of Norway to Sweden. A body of Swedes came to replace the Danes; but these also were removed on the 25th, and Hamburg was thus left to the ineffective force of Tettenborn and the new levies.

The allies now took post on Ochsenwerder, Billwerder and the adjacent islands.

Two companies of the Lauenburg battalion formed the out posts on the outer dam of the Ochsenwerder island, immediately opposite to Wilhelmsburg. In support of these stood the legion line detachment, being about one hundred and thirty men under lieutenant Dehnel, stationed in a church-yard; and the main body of the Lauenburg battalion lay in Eichbaum, on the right bank of the river, under major Müller; a few Cossacks were stationed on the flanks of the out posts.

Late in the evening of the 28th Müller was informed of the enemy's intention to attack Ochsenwerder, to which island he therefore, immediately sent the remainder of his force, and repaired himself to the out posts.

About four in the morning they were suddenly called into action by the hot fire of some howitzers which were directed upon the village; and it soon appeared that the enemy, favored by a fog, had crossed over, to the number of about two hundred men, and

1813.

May.

Dehnel's
narrative
MSS.

landed, without having been observed by the Lauen
burghers on the dam.

Müller instantly formed up his troops to oppose
their progress, but the young Lauenburghers, never
having been before exposed to cannon fire, were
thrown into confusion, and a second detachment of
the enemy having landed, the out posts gave way,
carrying with them a company which was placed
behind the dam, and the whole fell back in disorder
upon the reserve.

Müller immediately formed a line of skirmishers
of about forty men under ensign Shultze, and was
about to support them with the main body of the legion
detachment and a few Lauenburg companies, when
some shells falling among the close ranks of the latter
caused such confusion, that a forward movement
was impracticable. The Lauenburg officers' made
every effort to rally their men, but the young soldiers
having been only four weeks bearing arms, and now
for the first time exposed to cannon fire, while they
were unprovided with artillery, did not recover the
alarm until a retrograde movement to Eichbaum was
effected; and having crossed the river here, order
was restored.

The defence of the island was therefore, now
left almost entirely to the detachment of the legion,
who boldly advanced to the attack; but the French
had, by this time, brought over nearly two thousand
men, and no impression could be made by the detachment against such a superior force. They

therefore, fell back to where the ground offered some protection, and awaited reinforcements, for which major Müller had applied to general Tettenborn.

1813.

May.

A hot fire was now opened on the legion by the French masses, but every effort of the enemy to drive them from their ground was fruitless. Their numbers were, however, fast diminishing, and no reinforcements had arrived. Dehnel was now obliged to take off part of the detachment, in order to meet the enemy's attempt to turn their right wing, and Müller drew back the rest by the high road, upon the village, hoping to maintain the entrance until a support should arrive.

Notes of colonel Müller. MSS.

The contest was renewed at the village with the same fury; Dehnel was still engaged with a superior force of the enemy on the flank, which nothing but the greatest efforts could have so long kept back; however, the French at length became so strong in front, that Müller decided upon retreating to the ferry.

The retreat was conducted with perfect order; the irregularities of the ground offering many points of protection, every yard was disputed, and it became even necessary to resume the offensive, for when arrived at the ferry the boats were awaiting the reinforcements at the other side.

A desperate effort was therefore now required to maintain the ground, and Dehnel, with distinguished gallantry, led forward a small body of men, which falling upon the assailants on their right flank, checked the pursuit. The effort was, however,

1813.

May.

Colonel
Müller's
notes.
MSS.

but temporary, for the enemy, crowding on with a far superior force, pressed the legion troops on all sides, and they were eventually obliged to hurry to the boats. Another difficulty here, presented itself, for the boats were found insufficient to accommodate the whole of the men, and several were left behind. These endeavoured to shelter themselves in the thick underwood with which the bank was covered, but they would have all fallen into the enemy's hands, had not Dehnel, at the greatest personal risk, taken back a boat to their assistance, and covered by the fire of some Russian guns from Eichbaum, succeeded in getting them embarked. The French now mounted the dam, and poured a merciless fire upon the boats, by which many casualties were occasioned. A hot tirailleur fire from both sides of the river terminated this unfortunate combat, in which the legion detachment lost nearly half its numbers in killed, wounded, and prisoners.

The troops under major Müller were now relieved by a Prussian battalion, and returned to their former quarters at Bergedorf.

General Wallmoden had in vain endeavoured to obtain assistance for Hamburg from the Swedes. The Crown Prince tenaciously holding by a treaty according to which one hundred thousand men were to be placed under his command, refused to act until its conditions had been fulfilled, and even went so far as to deprive the Swedish general Döbeln of his command, for having, at the earnest solicitation of generals Wallmoden and Tettenborn, sent, previous to the arrival of the Crown Prince, some Swedish battalions to the assistance of Hamburg.

Tettenborn was thus left with a garrison of not more than three thousand five hundred men to defend that city, and, seeing himself threatened on one side by the Danes and on the other side by the French,—a united attack from whom he was now hourly to expect, and which he would have been quite unable to sustain,—he determined upon evacuating the place, and on the night of the 29th, withdrew to Lauenburg. The enemy's advanced guard followed the next morning, and coming up with the battalion of Bork at the Nettelburg sluice, pressed after the Russian skirmishers; but the battalion quickly faced about, attacked the French with the bayonet, and caused them a loss of two hundred men. Wallmoden brought together the troops of Tettenborn and Dörnberg at Lauenburg on the night of the 31st, and placed his out posts at Bergedorf; on this day the Danes entered Hamburg, and the same evening Davoust made his triumphal entry into the place, at the head of thirty battalions.

Geschichte des Armee-korps unter den Befeh-len des General, lieutenants Grafen von Wallmo-den Gim-born.

Napoleon, having sent proposals to the Emperor Alexander for an armistice, preparatory to a congress for a general peace, a cessation of hostilities now took place, and the armistice was ratified on the 4th of June. The lines of demarcation on each side proceeded from the frontiers of Bohemia to the Oder, and from thence down the Elbe to its mouth, leaving a neutral territory between, comprising Breslau; and the whole of the allied army were to withdraw to the right bank of the Elbe. The termination of the armistice was fixed for the 20th July, and six days' notice of the recommencement of hostilities was to be given.

CHAPTER VIII.

PENINSULAR CAMPAIGN OF 1813.

During the sojourn of the allied troops in winter
quarters after the retreat from Burgos, active exertions
were made by the marquis of Wellington for opening
the next campaign with an increased force and on
an improved system. Reinforcements of cavalry,
infantry, and artillery were sent from England; a
pontoon train was prepared; the heavy camp kettles
were replaced by small portable ones, and tents,—
a valuable addition to the equipments—were issued
to the troops. The great-coats were discontinued,
blankets being furnished in their room, and the
latter were so arranged that, in case of the mules not
being able to come up with the tents, they might be
substituted in place of them.

The winter quarters were not without their
enjoyments; dinners, balls, and even theatrical representations enlivened the long evenings. The proximity of their quarters led to much friendly intercourse
between the first hussars of the legion, and the
English light division; the commandant of Almeida

1813.

Journal of
major Rau-
tenberg.
MSS.

Journal of
captain
count
Wallmo-
den. MSS.

also aided in upholding the social circle, and, altogether, the short days and long nights passed over with a degree of gaiety, that could scarcely, under the circumstances, have been expected.

Previous to the opening of the campaign of 1813, the following changes were made in the regiments and brigades of the King's German Legion:—

In consequence of the second hussars being much reduced by the severe service in which they had been engaged during the preceding campaign, the horses of the regiment were transferred to the other cavalry regiments of the army, and the officers and men sent to England to be remounted. Painful as it was for the officers to see their gallant corps thus broken up, it was satisfactory to them to receive the high testimonials of the regiment which were published to the army both by the commander in chief, and the general commanding the cavalry on this occasion.

The light brigade of the legion was added to the line brigade in the first division, which thus contained five battalions of German infantry; major-general Löw, having been obliged to return to England, in consequence of ill health, the command of these battalions devolved on major-general von Hinüber, until whose return from Sicily, they were placed under the orders of lieutenant-colonel Halkett.

The artillery of the army had been considerably increased, and a strong reserve of this force organized. The reserve was placed under the direction of lieute-nant-colonel Hartmann, and consisted of three nine pounder batteries, and one eighteen pounder siege battery; numerous waggons for the conveyance of arms and ammunition were attached to the reserve, each division under the charge of an officer's detachment of artillery, and to this service the officers and men of the two companies of German artillery, which had been previously stationed in and about Lisbon, were appointed.

A veteran battalion was directed to be formed from the worn-out men of the different regiments of the legion. This establishment was first fixed at four hundred and fifty, but was ultimately augmented to ten companies of one hundred rank and file each; a depôt company and an independent garrison company, which had been for some years in existence, were incorporated with this battalion, and the command of the whole was given to lieutenant-colonel de Belleville.

Appendix No. XII.

Large draughts for the army in Germany had reduced the French effective force in Spain to one hundred and ninety-seven thousand men, and, of these sixty-eight thousand were in Aragon, Catalonia, and Valentia; so that not more than one hundred and twenty-nine thousand could be brought into operation against Wellington. But the allied force had been considerably augmented; nearly two hundred thousand troops were ready to take the field; the Anglo-Portuguese alone numbered seventy thousand; on each flank there was a British fleet, and Wellington could now look forward with confidence to a decisive and glorious campaign.

Napier.

1813.

Febrnary.

Journal of
captain
Busmann.
MSS.

March

In the beginning of this year part of the third battery of German artillery, which continued to serve in Sicily under the command of captain Busmann, was engaged in an expedition against the small island of Ponza, which was taken on the 27th of February by the allied troops, and four hundred prisoners, several pieces of cannon, besides arms and ammunition were captured. Captain Busmann was afterwards appointed to the command of the artillery in the citadel of Messina. *

No hostile movement of any importance occurred in the Spanish peninsula until the month of March, when part of the Anglo-Sicilian corps, which had been sent to the eastern coast of Spain in the preceding August, became engaged, together with the Spanish army of general Elio, in some active operations against the French force under Suchet in Valentia.

The fourth and sixth line battalions of the legion; the skirmishers of the third and eighth line battalions, and some artillery men of the third battery of German artillery formed part of the Anglo-Sicilian corps, which was commanded by lieutenant-general sir John Murray. The whole allied force, including the Spaniards under Elio, amounted to thirty thou-

---

* Serjeant Bösenberg of captain Busmann's battery, held, for three years, the responsible situation of instructor and superintendent to a company of Marine artillery, which was destined to man the flotilla and rocket battery. He commanded part of the latter in an affair at Pietro Negro in Calabria on the 15th of February, where he was wounded, and in acknowledgement of his services was presented with the medal of St. Ferdinand by the King of the Sicilies.

1813.

April,

Napier.

sand men; that of the French did not exceed eighteen thousand, but the allied troops were a mixture of various nations, very ineffective in cavalry, and dissention, ignorance and treachery were among them. Suchet had formed an entrenched camp in the neighbourhood of the Xucar river, and occupied Alcoy, Biar, Castalla, and other places in its front. On the 6th of March the allies advanced and drove the French from Alcoy, and, on the 15th, they occupied villages beyond that place. The English general now hesitated as to his further movements; but at length he concentrated the army at Castalla on the 10th of April.

The walled town of Villena in front of this place, was garrisoned by a fine Spanish regiment one thousand strong, and three or four thousand of Elio's troops were pushed forward to Yecla on the left. The latter were surprised by the French division of Harispe on the night of the 11th, and Suchet, assembling a strong force at Fuente de la Higuera, marched straight upon Caudete, and drew up two divisions and his heavy cavalry in order of battle there.

Murray brought up the allied horse, and a brigade of infantry to support the troops at Villena; but towards evening Suchet advanced, and the English general retired with the cavalry through the pass of Biar, leaving the infantry under colonel Adam in front of the pass.

Narrative
of captain
Wm. Appuhn.
MSS.

Colonel Adam's force consisted of the second battalion of the 27th regiment, the skirmishers of the

1813.

April.

Appuhn's
narrative.
MSS.
third and eighth line battalions of the legion, under captains Lueder and Brauns; the Calabrian free corps; the first Italian regiment; a troop of foreign hussars, and four mountain guns. Adam was directed to fall back upon Castalla if attacked, disputing the ground with the enemy, and a space was reserved for his troops in the line of battle which Murray had drawn out about three miles from the pass of Biar.

Napier.
Elio refused to allow the British general to draw off the garrison of Villena, and this fine regiment was consequently, obliged to surrender; and, about noon on the 12th, Suchet came down upon Adam with

Appuhn's
narrative.
MSS.
a force of from five to six thousand men. The allied brigade retired gradually to a range of heights between Biar and Castalla, and about two o'clock a fierce skirmish commenced with the enemy's advance. The two German companies, the light company of the twenty-seventh, and the flankers of the Italian regiment were principally engaged in this contest, which was maintained for five hours, with the greatest gallantry, and colonel Adam retired in good order to the ground which had been allotted to him in the

Journal of
6th line
battalion.
MSS.
position of the main army. This was attacked by Suchet on the following day, when the Germans were again hotly engaged, and detachments of the line brigade under captain Heise of the fourth, and Brandis of the sixth battalion were much distinguished.

Napier.
The enemy were repulsed at every point; a brilliant charge of the twenty-seventh regiment carried

destruction into their ranks, and Suchet in vain en- 1813.
deavoured to restore the battle. A general attack of April.
the allies would now have driven the French upon Napier.
Biar in confusion, and completed the victory, but
the favorable moment was neglected, and they
retired in order towards the pass. The quartermaster general Donkin took upon himself to send
forward three battalions and eight guns in pursuit,
and these were beginning to press heavily upon
the retreating troops, when they were ordered
to be withdrawn, and Suchet, taking up a position
across the defile, retired in the night to Fuente
de la Higuera.

Sir John Murray estimated the loss of the French
in this action at three thousand men, but Suchet rated
it at only eight hundred.

The allies lost more than six hundred; of the Appuhn's narrative.
legion, lieutenant Haslebach and eleven men were
killed, and lieutenants von Freytag, William Appuhn,
three sergeants and thirty-four men were wounded.

Lieutenant Appuhn besides being severely wounded,
had the misfortune to fall into the hands of the enemy,
but owing to the care of a faithful soldier of his company named Kölle, who remained by him when he
was left behind by the French as irrecoverable at
Villena, he was brought back to his corps on the
14th.

During the action of the 13th, twelve skirmishers Guelphic archives. MSS.
of the fourth battalion of the legion, who had been
detached to the left, not being able to extricate them-

selves from the rough ground, took shelter in a large wine press, where they were surrounded by the enemy. Encouraged by one of the party, named Schneider, they maintained themselves in this position for a considerable time, refusing all offers of capitulation, until they were eventually relieved by the twenty-seventh regiment which came to their assistance.

The campaign of the main army was opened by the marquis of Wellington about the end of April.

Napier.

His plan was to pass the Duero within the Portuguese frontier, with a part of his army; to ascend the right bank of the river towards Zamora, and then crossing the Esla, to unite with the Galician forces, while the remainder of the troops, advancing from the Agueda, should force the passage of the Tormes. By these movements he hoped to surprise King Joseph, turn the Duero and Pisuerga, and drive the French in confusion over the Carion; thence marching onward, he calculated upon turning the enemy's right flank, and gaining additional help from the Spanish irregulars; while the neighbouring ports on the coast would furnish him with supplies.

Rautenberg's Journal. MSS.

In conformity with this plan Bock's heavy cavalry brigade of the legion, the English hussars, Anson's cavalry, and five divisions of infantry, including the German battalions, were sent across the Duero under sir Thomas Graham, their march being directed through the Tras os Montes upon the Esla river.

The cavalry brigade of Victor Alten, the household cavalry, the second, third, and light divisions, and a corps of Spaniards, marched, under the immediate command of the marquis Wellington, upon Salamanca, to which point also the corps of Sir Rowland Hill was directed; and these two corps, forming the centre, and right of the allied army, were united at Salamanca on the 26th of May.

The French evacuated this town on the approach of the allies, but, lingering upon the high ground in the neighbourhood during the night, gave generals Fane and Victor Alten an opportunity of charging them with the cavalry, and taking two hundred prisoners. Seven tumbrils of ammunition, some baggage, provisions and other stores were also taken, and the enemy retired by the road of Babila fuente.

Welling-
ton's
despatch.

Napoleon had recommended King Joseph to concentrate his forces towards the Tormes, but this advice had been neglected; the troops were scattered; no definite plan of operations had been decided on; and the King and his generals were completely in the dark, both as to the movements of the allied army, and the designs of its chief.

Napier.

The right wing under Wellington was now halted to admit of Graham's corps gaining the enemys flank by Miranda de Douro and Carvajales.

This was an undertaking of no ordinary difficulty; for the Tras os montes had been hitherto considered a region nearly impracticable even for small bodies of troops, and now forty thousand men of all arms, with a cumbrous train of pontoons were to be carried through it. However the various difficulties of the

1813.

May.

Rauten-
berg's
Journal.
MSS.

Journals of
1st and 2d
dragoons.
MSS.

Welling-
ton's des-
patch.

June.

Corde-
mann's
Journal.
MSS.

march were surmounted in an admirable manner by the allied troops, and on the 30th, they reached the Esla. Here the flooded state of the stream presented new obstacles; the fords were deep and dangerous, and several men and horses were carried down by the violence of the current, and dashed against the rocks; among others four men and five horses of the German dragoons were thus lost; however by the 31st, the greater part of the corps passed the river, and they immediately advanced upon Zamora.

This place, as well as Toro was now abandoned by the enemy, and destroying the bridges there they retired upon Morales. Here their rear-guard was attacked by the English hussar brigade under colonel Grant; several of the enemy were killed, and nearly two hundred were made prisoners.

Lord Wellington halted on the 3d of June at Toro, in order to bring up the light division, and the troops under general Hill, but moved forward on the 4th. On the 7th a patrole of the first hussars was attacked by a superior force of the enemy on the Burgos road, but a squadron of the regiment under lieutenant Cordemann advancing to its relief, the French troopers were overthrown, and their leader was cut from his horse by lieutenant Blumenhagen.

By the 10th the left wing of the army had passed the Pisuerga, and on the 12th the light division under Charles Alten, the cavalry brigade of Victor Alten, those of Fane, Ponsonby and Grant,

the second British, Morillo's Spanish, and the
Conde d' Amarantes Portuguese divisions, the whole
under sir Rowland Hill,—advanced towards Burgos.

Victor Alten came up with the enemy's rear-guard,
which he attacked, and captured one officer and ten
men, together with a gun; the loss of the brigade
was not considerable.

The enemy were found posted in force on the
heights of Hormaza, their right being at that village,
and their left in front of Estepar. The English
hussars, Ponsonby's cavalry, and the light division
under Charles Alten turned their right, while Victor
Alten's cavalry, and a brigade of the second division
moved up the heights from Hormaza, and the
remainder of the troops under Hill threatened
the heights of Estepar. These movements immediately dislodged the enemy from their position,
and, pressed by the allied cavalry of the left and
centre, they retreated across the Arlanzon, on the
high road to Burgos.

In the course of the night the whole French army
retired through Burgos, destroying the castle, and
abandoning all the works which they had constructed
there with so much labour, and at so much expense.

Their retreat was continued towards the Ebro by
the high road to Breviesca and Miranda; Wellington
now moved the allied army to the left, and crossing
the country by a route not less difficult than that
taken by the troops in their march to the Esla,
succeeded in passing the Ebro by the 15th.

On the following day the enemy assembled in considerable force at Espejo, and posted a division with some cavalry at Frias. These troops marched on the 18th, the first upon Osma, and the other upon St. Millan. The Espejo corps was met by the troops under Sir Thomas Graham, which entered Osma nearly at the same time with the French, and were immediately attacked; but the enemy were obliged to give way and being followed by the allies, they retired with the loss of a hundred men through the hills to Subijana on the Bayas.

The French troops that marched to St. Millan were attacked by Charles Alten, who drove them from the place, and afterwards cut off the rear brigade of the French division, killing and wounding many, and taking three hundred prisoners.

On the 19th the allies advanced to the river Bayas, on the left of which they found the enemy's rear-guard strongly posted, its right being covered by Subijana, and its left by the heights in front of Pobes.

The light division under Charles Alten turned the enemy's left, while the fourth under general Cole attacked them in front, and they were driven back upon the main body of the army, which was then in march from Pancorbo to Vittoria.

This night King Joseph concentrated all his forces at Vittoria, and placed them in order of battle, and Wellington, closing up his rear on the following day, proceeded to reconnoitre the enemy's position.

He found the French occupying a line of nearly

eight miles in extent, in front of Vittoria, their left
rested upon the heights of La Puebla de Arlanzon,
extending from thence across the valley of the Zadorra,
to the village of Arunes; their right was stationed
near Vittoria; the right of the centre occupied a
height which commanded the valley of the Zadorra,
and the reserve was stationed at the village of
Gamarrah, in rear of the left.

The allied army exceeded eighty thousand men
with ninety guns; the French force scarcely amounted to sixty thousand, but in the number and size of
their guns they had the advantage.

The French position was attacked by the allied
army on the 21st. The operations commenced by
sir Rowland Hill obtaining possession of the heights
of San Puebla, which he effected after an obstinate
contest and severe loss. Under cover of these heights
he passed the Zadorra at LaPuebla, and the defile
formed by the heights and the river; then attacking
the post at Subijana de Alava, in front of the enemy's
line, he got possession of that village. The fourth
and light divisions now passed the river at Nanclares,
and Tres Puentes, and almost at the same time, the
third and seventh divisions crossed higher up. These
four divisions formed the centre of the army, and
were destined to attack the heights on which stood
the right of the enemy's centre, while general Hill
should attack the left. The enemy, however, did
not await the threatened onset; their line had been
much weakened by detaching troops to the posts

1813

June.

Welling-
ton's
despatch.

Napier.

Despatch.

1813.

June.

Welling-
ton's
despatch.

taken by sir Rowland Hill, and they commenced their retreat for Vittoria,—but in good order. The allies followed, marching in echelon over the hilly ground. Meantime sir Thomas Graham, who commanded the left of the allied army, moved upon Vittoria by the Bilboa road. Here the enemy had a division of infantry and some cavalry strongly posted upon heights covering the village of Gamarrah Mayor, both which village and Abechuco were strongly occupied as tetes de pont to the bridges which crossed the Zadorra there.

The heights were gallantly stormed by the Portuguese and Spanish troops under major-general Oswald, after which the village of Gamarrah Mayor was carried by general Robinson's brigade of the fifth division: sir Thomas Graham then proceeded to attack Abechuco with the first division.

Journal of
major Rau-
tenberg.

Protected by the fire of two batteries of artillery, the light brigade of the legion under colonel Halkett, advanced against this village; captain Christian Wynecken's company of the first light battalion first crossed the river, and coming suddenly upon the place, the French took fright, and left four guns and a howitzer in the hands of the battalion.

Despatch

These movements intercepted the enemy's line of retreat by the high road to France, and they were obliged to turn off towards Pampluna. Two divisions of their infantry were still in reserve, but as soon as their centre and left had been driven through Vittoria by the troops which marched against them, the remaining divisions under Sir Thomas Graham, immediately crossed the river, and the whole then co-operated in the pursuit, which was continued until dark.

The retreat of the French was so rapid that they were unable to bring away their artillery or baggage; and one hundred and fifty-one pieces of brass ordnance, four hundred caissons; a quantity of ammunition and baggage, as well as treasure to a considerable amount, fell into the hands of the victors: among other spoils was the baton of marshal Jourdan, King Joseph's lieutenant.

Despatch.

The loss of the allies in this battle, did not exceed five thousand in killed and wounded, and that of the enemy by no means corresponded with their defeat, being only six thousand, exclusive of prisoners. The German troops were but partially engaged and had few casualties, the principal loss falling upon the light brigade; among the wounded was lieutenant Hedemann of the first light battalion.

Gazette.

Napier.

An extraordinary performance of one of the first hussars during the fight, deserves to be recorded: This man, named Blanke, had volunteered to accompany an English staff officer, who, having become separated from his brigade, was endeavouring to find it; their road lay through a wood, in which four French chasseurs suddenly advanced from a by-way, and came upon the hussar, who rode a short distance in front. Blanke immediately shouted to the officer to make his escape, and dashing against the chasseurs,

Guelphic archives.

MSS.

kept them in check until he was out of sight. During this time the gallant hussar had wounded two of his opponents, but received a cut on the left shoulder, and now seeing the officer safe, he suddenly turned his horse, which was fortunately an animal of great speed, and urging him to his utmost, effected his escape!*

The full tide of victory had now turned in favor of Wellington; King Joseph at the head of a hundred and twenty thousand veteran troops, had, in the short space of six weeks, been driven from the Esla to the Ebro, through a country favorable for defence; and in the battle of Vittoria, had sustained one of the most complete defeats which marked the successes of the British arms in Spain.

* Serjeants Schrader and Kohlenberg, corporal Briethaupt, and hussars Heuer, Bliedong, Grane and Göhrder of the first hussars were all, about this period, distinguished by daring exploits on the outposts. The particulars of these, as well as other achievements of the non-commissioned officers and men of the legion, not mentioned in the text, will be found in the Appendix.

CHAPTER IX.

OPERATIONS UNDER GENERAL WALLMODEN.

1813.

A second detachment of the legion was sent to the north of Germany about the middle of May. This consisted of fourteen officers, ten non-commissioned officers and sixty men under the command of lieutenant-colonel Hugh Halkett, together with a party of the second dragoons under lieutenant Küster; and sailing from England on the 15th of May, they arrived, after having been long delayed by contrary winds, at Wismar in Mecklenburg on the 20th of June.

Colonel Halkett was immediately appointed to the command of a Hanoverian brigade, and several of the non-commissioned officers and men were distributed among the new levies. The rest were united with that part of the first detachment of the legion, which had not been broken up, forming together a body of about four hundred men, which, divided into two light and two line companies, were placed under the command of captain Philip Holtzermann.

These companies were principally kept at head-

May.
Narrative
of captain
Langwerth
MSS.

quarters, where they formed a sort of body-guard to the commander-in-chief, and took part in the various engagements that afterwards took place.

Notes of
captain
Dehnel.
MSS.

Some of the officers, however, were transferred to the Hanoverian levies: lieutenants von Windheim and Bachelle of the seventh line battalion, were appointed captains in the Lauenburg battalion; lieutenant Dehnel of the third line, was attached to a six pounder battery of artillery, which, manned partly by legion artillery-men, was placed under the command of captain Wiering; lieutenant Poten of the seventh line, was attached to the English rocket battery; and captains Schaumann and von Saffe of the second light and first line battalions were appointed aide-de-camps to colonels Halkett and Martin.

Lord Londonderry's
narrative

The armistice was prolonged to the 10th of August. This interval gave the officers in command of the new levies, an opportunity of forwarding their organization, which was not neglected. General von Arentschild, a Hanoverian in the Russian service, who had been appointed to the command of the Russian German legion, arrived and took the direction of that corps. The Hanseatic legion was placed under the orders of major-general von Dörnberg; the Hanoverian levies under major-general Lyon; all these corps were taken into British pay, and they advanced rapidly in discipline. The Russian German legion in particular was brought forward with a degree of rapidity highly creditable to the distinguished officer at its head; and altogether there was every

1883.

July.

reason to suppose, that the effective force in the pay of England would soon amount to twenty thousand men.

The Swedes under the Prince Royal, amounted to Lord London- derry's narrative about four thousand five hundred cavalry, and twenty-eight thousand infantry; but the conduct and language of their prince was calculated to create doubts as to the line of proceeding which he intended to pursue. His Royal Highness talked eloquently and scientifically on the subject of the proposed movements, but he did not appear anxious to procure his Swedes a very prominent position in the combinations.

Another reinforcement, consisting of the third hussars of the King's German legion under lieutenant-colonel Töbing, two batteries of German artillery under major Brückmann; the seventy-third English regiment, and half a battery of Rockets under lieutenant Strangways, landed at Wismar on the 8th of August, and joined the corps under general Wallmoden.

After having been left in a state of complete uncertainty as to the part which it was intended should be taken by the northern army, Wallmoden was suddenly directed on the 5th of August to repair to Stralsund, and receive directions from the Crown Prince of Sweden as to his operations. Here he was informed that his corps, augmented by the Swedish division of general Vegesack to twenty or twenty-four thousand men, was to cover the right wing of the northern army, which was then being assembled

Geschichte des Armee-korps unter den Befeh-len des General-lieutenants Grafen von Wallmo-den Gim-born.

1813.

August.

Geschichte
des Armee-
korps &c.

near Berlin and Brandenburg. At the commencement of hostilities he was to attack the enemy between the Elbe and Trave, and either put them to the route, or force them to take shelter in the fortresses of Hamburg, Lubeck, Glückstadt and Rendsburg. In case of being attacked by a superior force, he was to retire, sending general Vegesack with eight thousand infantry and two thousand cavalry behind the Stecknitz in order to cover Swedish Pomerania. If the enemy pressed on, Vegesack was to retire under the cannon of Stralsund and the bridge-head of Danholm, where the Swedish flotilla and a corps of four thousand English and Swedes would, it was presumed, be sufficient to route an army of forty thousand men; should Wallmoden not find himself in a position to relieve Pomerania, he was to retire upon the northern army and join the Crown Prince, and were the operations of this army successful, he was to cross the Elbe, and operate on the enemy's lines of communication, leaving, however, the division of Vegesack upon the Stecknitz, in order to keep in check the garrisons of Hamburg and Lübeck.

In accordance with this arrangement, Vegesack was directed to occupy the camp between Wismar and the village of Mecklenburg, with the Swedish and Mecklenburg troops, pushing small detachments to the lake of Schwerin, and the road from Gadebusch. Wallmoden was to place his troops on the left of the Swedes at Wittenburg,

Boitzenburg, or behind the lake of Schaal, so that he might threaten the passage of the Stecknitz at Boitzenburg, Mölln and Ratzeburg. Wallmoden therefore, placed his line of out-posts along the Stecknitz, and appointed the neighbourhood of Wittenburg and Hagenow as the points of assembly for his corps, and Grevismühlen for that of the Swedes: the line of retreat for the former was Neustadt, Wittslock and Oranienburg; and for the Swedes Wismar, Rostock and Stralsund.

The army-corps of Wallmoden amounted at this period, to about eighteen thousand infantry, six thousand four hundred cavalry, and sixty guns; of the latter, however, not more than forty were effective, and the new raised Hanseatic and Hanoverian cavalry were principally armed with pikes. Lützow's corps,—an enthusiastic band of youthful volunteers,*—was

---

* The corps of Lützow, called also the "Black chasseurs" and "Lützow's wild chace" (*Wilde Jagd*) was one of those volunteer corps which the patriotic spirit of the youths of Germany called into existence, when Napoleon's retreat from Moscow awakened within them the hope of freeing their country from his usurpation. It was raised in Silesia by the distinguished officer whose name it bore, under the authority of the King of Prussia, and young men of the most respectable families in the land flocked eagerly to Lützow's standard. The corps consisted of a division of riflemen, one fourth of whom were mounted; four squadrons of cavalry, three battalions of infantry, and a few guns, and it was particularly destined to act as a partisan force in rear of the French army.

In the mounted riflemen of Lützow's corps, served THEODORE KÖRNER, one of the most interesting characters which the "war of freedom" produced. Körner was a native of Dresden, where his father, known as the friend of Goethe and Schiller,—also a political writer of some celebrity,—held an official situation. After a careful private education under the most eminent professors of the academy of Dresden, the young Körner entered, at the age of seventeen, the university of Leipsic. His father intended him for a scientific profession, for which he evinced considerable capacity; but a strong poetical in not much better condition; train carriages were altogether wanting, as well as Hospitals, and the whole establishment of a general staff and commissariat.

With these mixed and imperfect materials Wallmoden was called upon to oppose an army nearly double

temperament, which had shewn itself in his earliest years, and every day became more developed, presented an insurmountable obstacle to the pursuit of studies so little suited to his genius; and after a short residence at the universities of Leipsic, Freiberg, and Berlin, he repaired in 1811 to Vienna, and gave himself up altogether to poetry, and the drama:

His first dramatic pieces were most favorably received; others soon followed, and the facility with which he composed was so great, that in the short space of four years he is stated to have sent forth no less than sixteen dramatic works, besides three novels, and various fugitive pieces. Music was also with him a favorite resource, and he composed several vocal pieces for the guitar, which he was wont to sing with much effect in the domestic circles of his friends.

A deep feeling of enthusiastic patriotism pervaded the poetical compositions of Theodore Körner, shewing also a mind filled with the noblest sentiments, strong religious impressions, and an ardent love of liberty. But Körner's patriotism was not of *words*:—The year 1813 brought with it the cry of "Freedom" into his fatherland; the standard of liberty had been raised among the youths of Silesia, and the enthusiastic poet, taking his sword and lyre, joined the brave band of Lützow, then engaged in operating upon the rear of the French army. He became Lützow's aide-de-camp, and entered into the daring movements of a partisan soldier, with all the energy of his nature. In the combat of Kitzen he was severely wounded, and narrowly escaped falling into the enemy's hands. After the armistice, Lützow's corps joined the army of Wallmoden, in Mecklenburg;—Körner despising danger, was ever foremost in the fight, and on the 26th of August, 1813, in a skirmish between Gadebusch and Schwerin, the devoted youth was struck down by a musquet ball, and almost instantly expired.

Full of youth and promise,—the noblest feelings,—the purest patriotism, Körner has left a name identified with the cause of freedom and the emancipation of his country. He fought with a degree of reckless valour, bordering on desperation. Entertaining a deep rooted hatred of the French, he gave the whole force of his physical and mental powers to free his country from their dominion. His vivid imagination, fed by the clash of arms, and the thunder of actual warfare, burst forth in glowing verses which, like those of Tyrtæus, animating his comrades to martial enterprise, in number; for Davoust's disposable force, including the Danes, was not less than thirty-six thousand infantry, three thousand three hundred and fifty cavalry, and one hundred and eight pieces of cannon; and added to these were forty gun boats on the Elbe. The French troops were, no doubt, also new levies,

diffused amongst them the spirit of his own enthusiasm. His most celebrated Lyric the "Sword Song," was written and read to his companions only an hour before his death. Covered with oak leaves and attended by all the officers of Lützow's corps, his body was carried to the village of Wöbbelin, where under an old oak,—the German emblem of liberty,—it was interred with military honors. The reigning duke of Mecklenburg after proposing to Körner's father that the body of his son should be placed in the royal vault, presented him with a piece of ground surrounding the grave, in the middle of which, a monument of cast iron has been erected to his memory. Theodore's sister, the only remaining child of his afflicted parents, followed him to the same grave in March 1815; and in May 1830, the worthy father, one of the most estimable and enlightened men in Germany, was also laid by the side of his patriot son.

Körner's most popular poems are those published at Berlin under the title of *Leier und Schwert*, and which in 1834, had passed through seven editions; two volumes of his posthumous poems have also been published, besides the dramatic pieces already mentioned.

M. Saint-Marc Girardin has thus eloquently drawn the character of Körner :—

It was his patriotism and enthusiasm that formed the genius of Körner. He was not a Tyrtæus of the closet, who composed warlike songs by his fireside ; he was a soldier—a volunteer of the *Black Chasseurs*; the sword by his side, the rifle at his back, he enrolled himself to save his country—to punish her tyrants. Poet and soldier, his genius and his courage warmed with the fire of war; for all was poetry to him: the flash of the musquet was the spark of liberty; the blood which reddened the plains was the purple of Aurora—the Aurora of freedom !"—[Friedlaender's L' Allemagne. Real. Encyclopædie, art. Körner. Notes of captain Dehnel. MSS.]

But our distinguished country-woman Felicia Hemans has cast one of the sweetest flowers on the grave of THEODORE KÖRNER :—

A song for the death day of the brave,
A song of pride!
For him that went to a hero's grave
With the sword—his bride !

M

but they were fully equipped; provided with all necessary stores and equipages, and commanded by such men as Loison, Thiebaut, Pecheux, L'allemand: the Danes were under Prince Charles of Hessia.

He went, with his noble heart unworn,
  And pure and high;
An eagle stooping from clouds of morn,
  Only to die !

He went, with the lyre whose lofty tone,
  Beneath his hand,
Had thrill'd to the name of his God alone,
  And his Fatherland.

And with all his glorious feelings yet
  In their day-springs glow,
Like a southern stream that no frost hath met
  To chain its flow!

A song for the death day of the brave.
  A song of pride !
For him that went to a hero's grave
  With the sword—his bride.

He hath left a voice in his trumpet lays,
  To turn the flight,
And a spirit to shine thro' the after days,
  As a watch-fire's light:

And a grief in his father's soul to rest
  Midst all high thought,
And a memory unto his mother's breast
  With healing fraught.

And a name and fame above the blight
  Of earthly breath
Beautiful—beautiful and bright
  In life and death!

A song for the death-day of the brave,
  A song of pride!
For him that went to a hero's grave
  With the sword—his bride!

FOR THE DEATH-DAY OF THEODORE KÖRNER.

Under these unequal circumstances of the contend- 1813. ing forces, it was to be presumed that the French August. would act on the offensive, and Wallmoden looked, Geschichte therefore, to the river Stecknitz as the line of defence des Armee-korps &c. upon which he could place the most dependence.

This river running into the Elbe at Lauenburg, forms a good line of defence between that place and Lübeck, while on the east, and nearly parallel with the river, a second line is formed by the rivers Schaal and Wakenitz. Lauenburg being the most important point and well suited to the construction of a bridge-head, works were thrown up there for the support of the out posts, the command of which was given to general Tettenborn, and the place itself was held by the corps of Lützow and Reiche* with five guns; Mölln was occupied with a small force, and the Cossack cavalry were collected behind Büchen, where the bridge was destroyed. The Swedish out-posts stretched towards the Baltic by Ratzeburg, Schönberg, and Dassow, the main body of that army being at Grevismühlen; the Russian German legion were stationed between Schwerin and Witten-burg; the Hanoverian and Hanseatic troops at Grabow; the cavalry under general von Dörnberg, stood in the plain between Zarrentin and Büchen, ready to aid the troops of Tettenborn; Ratzeburg was occupied by two companies; about five hundred Hanoverian and Hanseatic riflemen under count

* The corps of Reiche was a volunteer corps formed under similar circum-stances to that of Lützow

Kielmansegge, lay between Boitzenburg and Dömitz,
to keep up a communication with the troops which
stood towards Magdeburg; and the head-quarters of
the army were fixed at Hagenow.

Davoust drew together his principal force at
Bergedorf, Schwartzenbeck, and Lübeck; Hamburg
was garrisoned by regimental depôts, dismounted
cavalry and others, to the amount of ten or twelve
thousand men; the place itself was, by great labour,
transformed into a fortress, and furnished with three
hundred pieces of cannon; and a series of bridge
heads and block houses united it with the castle of
Harburg, which had been rendered an important
work. The fort of Travemunde, and the fortresses
of Rendsburg and Glückstadt were also available to
the marshal, whose movements, thus secured, were
to be expected either towards Stralsund, the principal
depôt of the Swedes, and the point of junction with
England, or direct upon Berlin, threatening the rear
of the northern army.

Wallmoden broke up from his cantonments on
the 6th of September, and encamped his troops in
the places which had been appointed for them:
meantime the northern army had prepared for the
commencement of hostilities.

It soon became evident, that the principal force
under Davoust was directed against the left wing of
Wallmoden's army, and it was to be presumed that a
movement upon Berlin was the object of the French
marshal. He proceeded, however, with extreme

caution, marching scarcely one German mile in the
day, and seemed to be awaiting either instructions
from his emperor, or the result of the operations of
the grand army.

Wallmoden, therefore, decided upon assuming the offensive, and by availing himself of a position between Vellahn and Kammin, opposing the enemy's progress in the direction of Wettenburg and Hagenow.

A range of hills which runs from Goldenbow towards Vellahn, formed the centre of his position, in which he placed the main body of the Russian German legion, the corps of Lützow and Reiche, and the cavalry of Dörnberg and Tettenborn; Kammin was held by another battalion of the Russian legion; and in the plain which stretches from this place towards the lake of Schaal, which flanked the right, some light cavalry were posted. The left of the position was protected by woods and marshes, which extended from Vellahn towards the Elbe, and the whole force in position numbered about six thousand infantry, three thousand cavalry and twelve guns.

In the afternoon of the 21st, the enemy passed the Schaal at Schildstedt, one column advancing by the road from Kammin to Wittenburg, while two others moved on the cross roads towards Vellahn and Goldenbow. Upon the latter place, which was held by the second hussar regiment of the Russian German legion, they opened a heavy cannon fire; but the

troops steadily maintained their ground, and Dorn-
berg bringing up the third hussars of the King's
German legion, two squadrons of Hanoverian cavalry, and four guns, the contest was continued with
great violence. The infantry now advanced on both
sides and the action became general. Tettenborn,
by a rapid movement, brought three of his Cossack
regiments upon the enemy's right flank, which produced considerable alarm, and towards evening, the
troops at this point retired into the wood on the
Schaal.

But meantime four of the enemy's battalions had
attacked Kammin, and the battalion stationed there
was, after a long resistance, obliged to yield to superior numbers.

The same night, however, a squadron of the allied
cavalry entered the place, and spread such alarm
among the French, that they abandoned the village,
and their whole line partaking of the effect, retired a
considerable distance.

Wallmoden had thus succeeded in checking the
progress of the enemy, and establishing the character
of his army; but the French had brought up not less
than twenty-thousand men on this occasion, and
although the bravery of his troops had enabled the
allied general to keep this large force in check with a
corps scarce one-third of its strength, he could not
expect to be able to maintain his ground against
such superior numbers, and he retired on the 22d
to Hagenow, placing the out posts at Toddin.

This action cost the French four hundred men in killed and wounded, while the loss of the allies did not exceed two hundred men and seventy horses.*

1813.

August.

Geschichte des Armee-korps, &c.

Wallmoden now collected his infantry at Lüb-below, and placed his cavalry on the plains of Kraak, resolved not to retire further unless pressed by a superior force. The French marshal, however, moved but a small part of his army in that direction, and directed the main body of his troops upon Schwerin. Wallmoden, therefore, moved his cavalry towards Ranskow, and sent orders to general Vege-sack to press forward and intercept Davoust, should his march be continued from Schwerin upon Rostock and Güstrow.

On the 24th the marshal had his head-quarters in Schwerin, and the troops were encamped between the lakes, the French at Neumühlen, and the Danes at Wittenforden. He still held Boitzenburg, keeping up his communication by Ratzeburg and Gadebusch.

The allied corps remained in position at Lübelow, and a chain of light troops surrounded the enemy's lines; the cavalry kept up continued skirmishing

---

* The result of this affair ill accorded with the calculations of Napoleon, who seems to have considered the army of Wallmoden entitled to little respect. In an intercepted letter which was sent from the Emperor to Davoust on the 17th from Bautzen, we find the following character given of Wallmoden's corps. "Je suppose qu' aujourd'hui ou demain vous aurez attaqué ce qui est devant vous ; si l' ennemi vous est inferieur en force, ne vous laisser pas mas-quer par un petit nombre, et par un canaille telle que les Anseates, la legion, et le trouppes de Wallmoden. Il n' y a de bonnes trouppes contre vous que les Suedes, et a peu pres le quart de ce qu' a Bulow, qui est trouppe de ligne.

and false attacks, and even went so far as to establish themselves in a wood close to the enemy's posts.

Meantime, the army of the north had been engaged with marshal Oudinot, and a decisive victory was obtained by the allies at Gross Beeren on the 23d. On the 27th the division of Gerard was surprised by general Hirschfeldt, and driven back with considerable loss, and the enemy having collected into an intrenched camp at Thiesen and Eupern, a second battle was to be expected in that quarter.

During these events the Crown Prince of Sweden had been informed of the operations on the Stecknitz, and he directed colonel Marvitz, who had been sent with four battalions and four squadrons of the Prussian corps of Puttlitz to Havelberg, to proceed to the aid of general Wallmoden in case of necessity, intending, should Davoust commence serious operations, that the whole corps should be placed under the orders of the allied general.

But it was now reported that Davoust intended to abandon the right bank of the Elbe, and send a considerable force towards Magdeburg; Wallmoden was, therefore, directed to unite with Marvitz at Havelberg, and, leaving six or seven thousand men under Vegesack for the defence of Pomerania and Mecklenburg, to attack the enemy when in march from Magdeburg to Brandenburg.

This report of Davoust's movements however, proved false, and the order was countermanded. Far from such intentions it appeared that he had col-

lected all his forces on the right bank of the Elbe, 1813.
and was in motion with the greater part against August.
Wallmoden. Hearing this, the Crown Prince promised Geschichte des Armee-korps, &c.
to send a corps of from twenty-four to twenty-five
thousand men to his aid, provided that the allied
corps united with the Mecklenburg *levee en masse*
was unable to check the progress of the enemy:
colonel Marwitz was, at the same time, moved to
Lenzen in order to be nearer at hand.

But the last movement of Davoust to Schwerin
rendered these arrangements void, and Wallmoden
took up a position between Wöbbelin and Lübbelow,
resting his right on the Lowitz marsh. In this
position he first received the Crown Prince's orders
to unite with Marwitz, and move on Brandenburg.
He accordingly broke up on the 26th, and was about
to continue his march to Lenzen on the 28th, when
he received the countermand, which luckily arrived
in time to admit of his returning to his position at
Wöbbelin before the enemy had been made aware of
his march. The allied troops now occupied Wittenburg, and disturbed the enemy's posts towards
Gadebusch and Ratzeburg; couriers and convoys
were daily captured; a French post at Hohen Vicheln
was surprised by the Hanseatic cavalry; many
prisoners were made, and the enemy harrassed in all
directions.

Davoust now sent the division of Loison to Wismar,
which so alarmed general Vegesack, that he retired
to Rostock, and the division of L' Allemand followed

him to Kröpelin; but now better informed of the real strength of the enemy, the Swedish general faced about, attacked the French brigade at Kröpelin, and New-Bukow, and driving them back, followed them to Wismar. Loison now sent up reinforcements, and the Swedes were again obliged to evacuate the place on the 31st.

While these movements were in progress on the right bank of the Elbe, an operation of some importance was effected by the allied troops on the opposite bank of the river. Davoust kept up his communications with Magdeburg by means of a chain of posts which ran from opposite Boitzenburg by Bleckede to below Dömitz, and these were defended by intrenchments. Count Kielmansegge, who was in observation at Dömitz with about five hundred men, secretly prepared to pass the river, and on the 25th of August, two hundred of the Hanoverian riflemen and Russian legion crossed the Elbe, surprised the enemy's post at Gastow, and drove them to Dannenberg, and here, to the number of two or three hundred men, they placed themselves in a fortified tower. The Hanoverian riflemen supported by the Russian legion, stormed this place, killed forty-four of the garrison, and captured three officers and one hundred and forty-four men, with the loss of only two officers and twenty-five men to the victors. The French now evacuated all their posts as far as Bleckede, and thus gave up the communication with Magdeburg. Leaving one hundred men in Dannenberg, Kielmansegge now pushed forward his patroles to Celle, and the enemy's line of communication with Bremen; and Davoust evacuating Boitzenburg, drew the post which had been stationed there behind the Stecknitz.

1813.

August.

Geschichte des Armee-korps, &c.

The French marshal was now placed in an awkward predicament; for his lines of communication with Magdeburg having been cut off, he was deprived of all means of obtaining intelligence from the upper Elbe, and he became inactive, doubtful, and apprehensive of venturing on any operation against his opponent.

Wallmoden was, therefore, encouraged to resume the offensive, and he resolved, by a rapid flank march, to unite his troops with the Swedish division, at Warin, and, in a combine movement, to attack Loison at Wismar. To conceal his design he directed that the advanced guard of Tettenborn should make a false attack on the enemy's camp on the night of the 1st of September; great alarm was thus caused at this point, and the general breaking up from Wöbbelin on the following day, marched his infantry by the Löwitz marsh to Friederichsruhe, and the cavalry to Wessen; and on the 3d he reached Warin. Here, however, he learned that, on the preceding night, Schwerin had been evacuated by the enemy, who had retired upon Gadebusch and Rhena. Wallmoden immediately changed the direction of his march and hurried to Schwerin, where the Cossacks had already arrived, while the remaining part of the advanced guard followed the enemy.

Davoust's proceedings now became quite inexplicable: after a long state of inactivity, he calls in
Loison's division from Wismar without any apparent
cause, retires himself from Schwerin, and, sending
the Danes to Schönberg, marches the French
towards Mölln and Ratzeburg. This retrogade movement led Wallmoden to believe that it had been
caused by the operations of the grand army, and that
Davoust was about to send part of his force towards
the scene of operations. He therefore, resolved upon
attempting to intercept his march, and leaving the
Swedes and the division of Tettenborn to observe the
enemy, he marched with the rest of his corps to
Ludwigslust, and on the following day to Dömitz.

Meantime the troops of Tettenborn and Vegesack
followed close on the heels of the enemy. The Cossacks and Lützow's corps attacked the rear-guard of
the column which marched upon Mölln with repeated
success, killing and wounding more than one thousand men, and making five hundred prisoners. The
Hanseatic cavalry under major Arnim, followed the
Danes, who retired upon Lübeck, with equal vigour,
but their gallant leader was struck down by a cannon
shot close to the gates of that town.

Davoust now placed his troops in position behind
the Stecknitz, having his head-quarters at Ratzeburg
and occupying Lübeck and Travemunde with strong
garrisons. The Danes encamped at Oldeslohe;
both positions were covered by marshes and lakes,
rendering them quite unassailable, and the allied

advance therefore, took up their former posts at
Boitzenburg and Grevismühlen.

1813.

September

Geschichte des Armee-korps, &c.

Wallmoden now made every preparation for passing his army over the Elbe at Dömitz, where he proceeded to construct a bridge of boats, and bridge-head. Count Kielmansegge remained at Dannenberg with one battalion and one squadron, and after repeated applications to the Crown Prince for reinforcements, Wallmoden was at length strengthened on the 6th by two battalions and two squadrons of Prussian Landwehr, with two guns.*

Meantime the intelligence from the grand northern army had been most cheering. The Silesian corps under Blucher had gained an important victory over Macdonald on the Katzbach on the 26th; twelve thousand men under Vandamme surrendered to the allies at Kulm on the 30th, and the battle of Dennewitz on the 6th of September, where Ney was defeated by the Crown Prince and Bülow with the loss of fifteen thousand men and eighty pieces of cannon, amply compensated for the ill fortune of the allies before Dresden in the preceding month.

Davoust remaining still inactive, Wallmoden returned on the 10th to Hagenow, and on the following day made a reconnoisance of the enemy's position on the Stecknitz, while Vegesack advanced to Schönberg and Rhena.

The ground on which the enemy stood was so situated as not to admit of any good general view of

* Der Feldzug in Mecklenburg &c.

their position, but it was evident that from their strong intrenchments and the natural defences in their front, no attack could be made upon them with any prospect of success; but the separation of part of the French corps soon gave Wallmoden the opportunity which he sought.

By an intercepted letter found on the person of a French artillery officer, who was taken prisoner near Mölln on the 12th, it appeared that Davoust was about to detach part of the division of general Pecheux across the Elbe. No time was, therefore, to be lost, and Wallmoden made the whole of the troops under his orders break up from Hagenow and Wittenburg the same night, and march for Dömitz, where the bridge of boats was already prepared.

The reference in the intercepted letter was confirmed by a notification which, it was ascertained, had been received by the authorities on the left bank of the river, directing preparations to be made for the reception of a corps of ten thousand men, and it further appeared that the object of this movement was to clear the neighbourhood of Magdeburg of the allied troops. A tempting opportunity was thus offered to Wallmoden to strike a blow; but it was not unattended with considerable risk; for the greater part of his troops would be thus removed from their line of defence,—brought across a great river, and placed several marches from the point of passing, as well as from the rest of the corps, which meantime, would have to observe an enemy far superior in force.

These were serious considerations, and such as, under other circumstances would, perhaps, have been sufficient to deter the general from risking the expedition; but encouraged by the timid and irresolute conduct of his opponent during the preceding operations, he felt that he was justified in making the attempt.

Leaving, therefore, the Swedish division, and about six thousand of the new levies, with a regiment of Cossacks and two guns to observe the enemy's line on the Stecknitz, he assembled at Dömitz the following force :—

CAVALRY.

Three regiments of Cossacks ....general Tettenborn.

3d hussars, King's German Legion........major Küper.*

1st hussars, Russian German Legion.

Hussars of Estorf.†

INFANTRY.

HANOVERIANS....MAJOR-GENERAL LYON.

1st brigade, three battalions........lieut.-colonel Halkett.

2d brigade, three battalions........lieut.-colonel Martin.

Six battalions Russian German Legion..general von Arentschild.

The 73d English regiment......lieut.-colonel Harris.

Lützow's volunteers, one battalion.

Reiche's volunteers, one battalion

---

* Colonel von Töbing was taken ill at Wismar soon after the arrival of the regiment, and soon after died.

† The hussars of Estorf were new raised regular cavalry, which afterwards became the 4th Hanoverian hussars, and now form with the 3d hussars of the late King's German Legion, the third Hanoverian light dragoons.

September

ARTILLERY.

KING'S GERMAN ARTILLERY..MAJOR BRUCKMANN.

    Six six-pounders........captain Augustus Sympher.

    Six six-pounders........captain Kuhlmann.

    One battery Hanoverian artillery....captain Wiering.

There were twelve other guns, and half a battery of English rockets, making altogether about five thousand infantry, two thousand eight hundred cavalry and twenty-eight guns. With this force Wallmoden passed the Elbe by the bridge of boats at Dömitz on the night of the 14th and encamped the following day near Dannenberg. The advanced-guard under Tettenborn was pushed on to the Göhrde forest, beyond which, at Dahlenburg, one hundred Cossacks were posted.

The enemy's troops amounting to seven or eight thousand men, and eight guns under Pecheux, had crossed the Elbe at Zollenspieker on the day previous, and advancing to Dahlenburg they drove in the Cossacks, and occupied the Göhrde with their advance. The main body encamped behind the forest and near the village of Oldendorf, where a piece of table land, separated from the forest by deep ravines and similarly secured on the flanks, offered an excellent position.

Calculating that the enemy would continue in march on the 16th, Wallmoden closed up the main body of his corps to the vanguard at about five miles from the Göhrde and so placed it that, covered by the inequalities of the ground, he could attack the enemy in march before they were aware of his presence. The advance of Cossacks remained in front to mask this manœuvre; and to cover the retreat two battalions and three squadrons were left in Dannenberg.

The Cossacks were driven into Metzingen, half-way towards the position of the main body, on the morning of the 16th, but noon had arrived without any further movement on the part of the enemy. This led Wallmoden to fear that the French general was either about to retreat, or contemplated involving the allied troops in protracted manœuvres on the left bank of the Elbe; he, therefore, took the opinion of his general officers upon the most advisable course to pursue, and, it being decided that the allies should fall upon the enemy without delay,*—immediately made the following dispositions for the attack:—

Six battalions and one regiment of cavalry of the Russian German Legion, together with captain Kuhlmann's battery of horse artillery of the King's German Legion were to march under general von Arentschildt through the left side of the forest, taking the roads by Rieberau and Röthen, and moving upon the enemy's left flank and rear, which they were to attack at the same moment that the centre column, consisting of Tettenborn's Cossacks, the main part of the artillery, and the Hanoverian infantry under general Lyon,—advancing by the high

1813.

September

Geschichte des Armee-korps, &c.

General Wallmo-den's des-patch.
Journals of 3d hussars and Horse artillery MSS.

* Narrative of Forester Schickendanz.

Lüneburg road, were to fall upon his front. The
remainder of the cavalry under general Dörnberg,
with captain Sympher's battery of artillery and
the English rockets, were to flank the attack
on the right, and thus a simultaneous assault
upon the enemy's flanks, rear and centre, was to
be effected.

BATTLE OF THE GOHRDE.

The troops under Arentschildt having a great
detour to make before they could arrive at the point
of attack, were put in march at twelve o'clock, and
one hour afterwards, the columns of Dörnberg and
Lyon advanced on the right and centre.

Geschichte   Just at the moment when the advance-guard of
des Armee-
korps, &c. the centre column had commenced skirmishing with
the enemy's light troops in the forest, the sound of
cannon fire was heard to come from the other side of
the Elbe, in the neighbourhood of Boitzenburg,
plainly denoting an attack of the enemy in that
quarter.   Wallmoden, however, did not allow himself to be embarrassed by the difficulties to which this
movement might naturally have been expected to
give rise, but directed the light troops of Lützow and
Reiche to press forward into the forest, while Tettenborn's Cossacks advanced on their flank. The enemy
retired, skirmishing, and covered by their cavalry,
upon the main body, the strong position of which
become now fully visible to the allied commander.

In front was a deep marsh, which stretching towards the Elbe and Bleckede, was lost in a hollow intersected with clefts and trees. The village of Lüben was before their left, and that of Oldendorf in front of their right wing; the troops were drawn out in line upon the table land behind these villages, having their artillery in front, and no sooner did the advance of the allies appear than a heavy fire was opened upon them.

Tettenborn replied from four guns, with which captain Wiering's battery, sent forward by general Lyon, soon united its fire, and in about half an hour Arentschildt, leading his columns from the forest, brought his artillery also into action.

The French surprised at seeing a large body of Wallmo-den's despatch. infantry where they only expected light troops, began to make immediate dispositions for retreat; the absence of their general, however, who was in front with his advanced posts, delayed these movements, and he had scarce arrived, when the allies commenced the attack.

Arentschildt's infantry charging with the bayonet Narrative of general von Arents-child. MSS on the left, gained possession of the villages of Oldendorf and Eichdorf, while the cavalry of Dörnberg on the right assailed the opposite flank. Arentschildt's battalions met with a fierce resistance, and nearly one hundred of his brave followers were killed and wounded; but the enemy's column had been shaken by the charge, and bringing up his regiment of hussars, they, in a most gallant assault, completed the defeat of the opposing mass.

1813.
September Dreading now the onset of Dörnberg's cavalry on the left, the French formed their columns into squares, and commenced a well ordered retreat, pouring a murderous fire from each square, as it successively fell back.

Journals of major Heise, and 3d hussars MSS. The fire of the horse artillery and rockets was brought to bear upon the enemy, but it had produced little effect, when the third hussars of the King's German Legion were ordered to charge. Led on by major Küper, the hussars rode boldly forward against the square which was in advance; but a hollow way not visible at a distance, appeared, on a nearer approach, to run in front of the square, and the squadrons, being unable to pass it, failed in the intended attack, while captain von Beila and several men and horses were wounded by the enemy's fire.

Moving, however, round the left flank of the enemy, three squadrons of the hussars formed in front of one of the rear squares, which they charged with distinguished gallantry and complete success, but experienced the loss of captain von Hugo, and cornet Bremer killed, and captains von Both and Heise wounded, besides many men and horses. The re-
Guelphic archives. MSS. maining squadrons now broke a third square, and a bold soldier of the fifth squadron, named Heymann, seizing the enemy's general Milozinsky, dragged him, with the aid of sergeant Wedemeyer from the midst of the disordered troops.*

* Corporals Duntemann and Schaper, as well as hussars Stenzig and Schwan were also conspicuous for their gallantry in the attack on the enemy's squares.—Guelphic Archives MSS.

Meantime the square against which the first at-tack of the hussars had failed, was charged by the infantry brigade of lieutenant-colonel Hugh Halkett, consisting of the battalions of Lauenburg, Langrehr, and Benningsen, which falling fiercely upon the enemy with the bayonet, forced them to give way, and the hussars pressed after the fugitives.

1813.

September

Narrative of captain Brandis. MSS.

Wallmo-den's des-patch.

The French continued to form again in the rear, and they maintained an obstinate resistance in retreat, until the repeated charges of the allies, and the destructive fire of their artillery and rockets, spread such terror through the retiring ranks, that order could no longer be preserved, and breaking, they fled in all directions.

This general disorder soon communicated itself to the troops which had been placed to cover their retreat, and the pursuit having been pushed on to Nahrendorf, the enemy found themselves cut off from the road to Dahlenburg, and obliged to retire by Bleckede,—their general, stripped of his horses and baggage, saving himself on foot. About half-past seven in the evening, Wallmoden committed the pursuit to the Cossacks and drew back the remainder of the troops to the Göhrde castle, where they encamped.

The French crossed the Elbe at Zollenspieker on the following morning, and Tettenborn advancing to Harburg, cut off all their communications with the left bank of that river.

The loss of the enemy in this engagement amounted

to nearly two thousand men in killed and wounded,

besides fifteen hundred prisoners; among the latter

were the general Milozinsky, colonel Fitzjames aide-de-camp to general Pecheux, colonel Bourdon, and several other officers. Eight pieces of cannon and twelve ammunition waggons were also captured by the allies.

The loss of the allied corps amounted to fifty officers, five hundred men, and two hundred horses; of the King's German Legion, the third hussars were the principal sufferers; captain von Hugo, cornet Bremer, eleven rank and file, and forty-seven horses were killed, and captains von Beila, von Both, Heise, adjutant von Bruggemann, lieutenant von Humboldt, cornet Oelkers, sixty-four rank and file, and seventy-six horses were wounded.

From want of waggons, many of the wounded were obliged to be left on the field during the night, when the rain fell in torrents, and in the course of the following week, captains Beila, von Both, and nine hussars of the third died of their wounds.

CHAPTER X.

On the morning following the battle of the Göhrde Wallmoden received information which removed all alarm as to the operations of the enemy on the right bank of the river, during the action of the 16th. It appeared that, on that day, a body of the French consisting of two battalions, a few cavalry and two guns, had advanced from Lauenburg, and attacked the detachment of Lützow's corps, which was stationed in Boitzenburg; but a reinforcement having been rapidly sent to their aid, the French retired without further delay.

On the 18th, the enemy advanced from Mölln and Ratzeburg, and moving upon Zarrentin, attacked with superior numbers, the troops of Lützow's corps which were stationed there under major von Petersdorf, and drove them back to Wittenburg. General Dörnberg was, therefore, directed to break up with his cavalry, horse artillery, and a few light battalions, and march upon Vellahn and Kammin to the assistance of Petersdorf; but Davoust remained inactive at Zarrentin, and finally withdrew on the 21st behind the Stecknitz, without having attempted any renewal of the attack.

1813.

September

Geschichte des Armeekorps &c.

Wallmoden now placed his troops in cantonments
between Dömitz and Boitzenburg, the hussars of the
Russian legion took the out posts at Kammin
and Boitzenburg ; Tettenborn remained in Lüneburg, and count Kielmansegge in Dannenberg, while
the out posts of the latter were pushed on to Uelzen
and Celle and his patroles went as far as Hanover
and the Weser.

Towards the end of September the Crown Prince
signified to general Wallmoden his wish that Davoust
or at least the Danes, should be attacked by the allied
corps.   In reply, Wallmoden represented the strong
position of the French marshal, and his superiority
in infantry and artillery ; and as to the Danes, that
their junction with the French, prevented the possibility of attacking them singly.   The Crown Prince,
however, with inexplicable pertinacity, maintained
his notion that the enemy ought to be attacked, and
notwithstanding the remonstrances of Wallmoden,
in which he clearly shewed as well the little chance
of success in an attack upon their strong position, as
the profitless result to the allies of even a fortunate
encounter,—His Royal Highness would still have a
battle, and preparations were accordingly made to
comply with his expressed desire.

For this purpose nearly the whole of Wallmoden's
troops were concentrated on the right bank of the
Elbe, and put in motion towards the Stecknitz.   For
the protection of the left bank, there only remained
the detachment of count Kielmansegge at Dannen-

berg; a few Cossacks, and a battalion of the Russian legion, which was stationed at the bridge-head of Dömitz.

As a support to the proposed operations, the Crown Prince promised, first the division of Puttlitz, and afterwards the brigade of Marwitz, but neither appear to have received any orders on the subject, and the brigade of Marwitz was three marches distant. Wallmoden's reserve was, therefore, limited to the Mecklenburg *levee en masse,* a nominal force armed with pikes and which had in a great measure, been already broken up.

The general, therefore, found himself in the disagreeable position of having to execute an undertaking which he considered impracticable; fortunately, however, on the night of the 4th of October, he received a despatch from the Crown Prince, which, while it urged him to the proposed attempt, left him free to act according to circumstances.

In order, as far as possible, to comply with the wishes of the Swedish chief, Wallmoden directed a simultaneous attack to be made on the enemy's posts at Büchen, and Ziethen on the night of the 5th; the former under general Dörnberg, and the other under Vegesack. Both proved, as was to be expected, completely fruitless. Dörnberg advanced with six battalions, two squadrons and two battalions of artillery upon Büchen, and attempted to pass the river; but the approach to it was along a narrow dam, defended by two strong redoubts, and no efforts of

Geschichte des Armee-korps, &c.

his batteries or riflemen could silence the enemy's guns; he therefore, retired, after losing three officers and forty men. Vegesack was still more unfortunate, losing seven officers and one hundred and fifty men; another unsuccessful attempt was made by general Dörnberg on the 7th, and now Wallmoden, considering that he had made sufficient sacrifices to the wishes of the Crown Prince, placed his troops in cantonments behind the Boitze, the head-quarters being at Kammin; and Vegesack concentrated his Swedes at Gadebusch and Rhena.

Feldzug in Mecklenburg &c.
Davoust still remained on the defensive; the absence of all the allied troops for some days from the left bank of the Elbe, had not given him courage to attempt the re-establishment of his posts there; and Wallmoden, tempted by this apathy of his opponent, decided upon making an effort to get possession of Bremen, and destroy the French communications with the Weser.

The command of this expedition was given to Tettenborn, who, taking with him nine hundred Cossacks, three hundred regular cavalry, six hundred infantry, and four guns, cut off the enemy's lines of communication for a distance of twenty miles; masked the fort of Rottenburg; drove the French into Bremen, and finally, bombarding that place on the 15th, forced a garrison nearly double the number of his troops, to terms of capitulation.

Wallmoden had now to maintain the whole line from Bremen to Lübeck against the superior force of the enemy; but Davoust's listlessness favored the allied troops, and they continued to hold their position undisturbed.

The victory of Leipsic on the 18th and 19th of October, when Napoleon was defeated by the allied sovereigns with immense loss, gave a new character to the general operations, and the conquering armies advanced towards the Rhine.* Wallmoden now took possession of Hanover; strengthened the garrison of Lüneburg, and alarmed the fortresses of Hopt and Harburg, while Tettenborn extending his troops to the Weser, took Minden, and drove the French out of all that neighbourhood.

Der Feldzug in Mecklenburg &c.

Notwithstanding these vigorous and effective operations on the part of the allied corps, the French marshal remained unmoved in his strong holds; nor did he shew any symptom of activity until the approach of the army under the Crown Prince on the 12th of November, when, breaking up from his camp at Ratzeburg, he retired entirely behind the Stecknitz. This led to a reconnoisance on the part of the allies; and, on the 14th, a sharp skirmish took place near Mölln, when the Hanseatic infantry experienced a loss of seven officers and one hundred men in killed and wounded.

---

* Lieutenant Charles Poten of the seventh line battalion, served with an English rocket battery at the battle of Leipsic, being the only officer of the legion present in that action. He had accompanied lieutenant-colonel Hugh Halkett to Mecklenburg in April, and was appointed in September to conduct the rocket battery to the grand army in Saxony.

1813.

October.

Journal of
3d hussars.
MSS.
The first squadron of the third hussars formed part of a body of cavalry, under count Nostitz, which in the beginning of this month, attacked the enemy's horse at Winsen on the Luhe; and a superior force of the French cavalry was charged with great success by the hussar squadron.

Der Feld-
zug in
Mecklen-
burg &c.
Towards the end of the month the Swedish, and some Russian troops passed the Elbe at Boitzenburg, while others blockaded Hopt and Harburg; upon this Davoust seemed suddenly roused, and taking with him the French troops only, he broke up from the Stecknitz and threw himself into Hamburg. Here he was blockaded by the corps of Woronzow amounting to six or seven thousand men, to which was added the force of Lützow; and these so completely kept him in check, that his operations were limited to the defence of the place.

The Danes thus deserted by the French, retired into Holstein under the command of Prince Frederick of Hessia. Wallmoden now concentrated his army on the lakes of Ratzeburg and Schaal, and on the 4th of December passed the Stecknitz, as the left wing, or advance of the army of the Crown Prince, who had brought up his whole force before Lübeck.

The manner in which count Wallmoden had conducted this campaign in Mecklenburg, was highly creditable to his military reputation. Opposed to a force superior both in number and organization to his own, it could not have been considered unwarrantable if he had found himself compelled to yield to that superiority; Davoust could then have marched unhindered upon Berlin or Magdeburg,—checked the Prussian troops, and the northern army in their advance, and perhaps, have given a different turn to the battle of Leipsic; but instead of this we find the French marshal shut up behind his entrenchments; his communications cut off,—his detached corps beaten;—the entire country from the Elbe to the Weser cleared of his troops, and finally a separation of his army effected which rendered both wings an easy conquest for the allied arms.

The corps of Woronzow was relieved by that of general Benningsen in its observation of Hamburg, towards the end of December, and the former joined the left wing of the army of the Crown Prince.

On the 2d of December, the Swedish army was concentrated about Mölln and Boitzenburg; that of Wallmoden around Ratzeburg.

The latter corps consisted of:—

Squadrons.	Battalions.	Guns.		
8	7	16	Russian German Legion.	Geschichte des Armee-korps, &c.
6	7	6	New raised Hanoverians.	
6	2	18	Hanseatics.	
6	1	12	King's German Legion.	

making together ten thousand four hundred infantry, two thousand four hundred cavalry, and fifty-two guns: the Swedish division of Vegesack stood towards Lübeck.

On the 3d the Crown Prince arrived, and arranged
with general Wallmoden the plan of the intended
movements. These, he proposed should be carried
into Holstein and directed against the Danish corps,
which being defeated, he presumed that Denmark
would come to terms of peace.

In furtherance of this plan, Wallmoden was to
advance rapidly across the Stecknitz to Oldeslohe,
and turn the enemy's left, while the Swedes attacked
them at Lübeck;   and thus the Danish communications with the fortress of Rendsburg would be cut off.
Wallmoden, having the most difficult part of the
operations entrusted to him, while he was provided
with the smallest force, applied to the Crown Prince
for the assistance of the corps of Vegesack.   His
Royal Highness assented, and further promised him
the aid of an additional brigade, or division if required: The Crown Prince also engaged, should
Lübeck not capitulate, to take the place by storm,
and for this purpose he brought up before it the
whole Swedish army, amounting to twenty thousand men.

The Danes about twelve thousand men under
Prince Frederick of Hessia had retired behind the
Trave, their left resting on the strong fortress of
Lübeck, and their right on Oldeslohe, where their
head-quarters were stationed.

The vanguard of Wallmoden's corps under Dörnberg, had crossed the Stecknitz on the 3d, and taken
post at Klinktrade on the road to Oldeslohe; the

main body was between that river and Ratzeburg, head-quarters being at Culpin, and the following day they were to cross and concentrate at Sieben-bäumen, while the advanced-guard moved on to Oldeslohe. Dörnberg, proceeding on his march for the latter place, came upon the enemy about noon in the neighbourhood of Siebenbäumen and Steinhorst, to which position a body of about three thousand men had been sent forward.

1813.

December.

Der Feld-
zug in
Mecklen-
burg &c.

A thick fog prevented him from learning the enemy's strength, and he, therefore, limited himself to maintaining the village of Deutch-Booden. He was weak in infantry, and the fog, broken ground, and deep roads, rendered his cavalry and artillery of little service.

The enemy advanced in force, and an obstinate contest took place in the village, where the allies lost some officers, and upwards of fifty men in killed and wounded. In consequence of the state of the roads, Wallmoden was unable to reach Siebenbäu-men until late in the evening, when he immediately reinforced Dörnberg with a few battalions, and only awaited some intelligence of the approach of Vege-sack's division, to continue his march.

The addition of this force he considered indispen-sable to his operations; for Tettenborn's troops, three battalions of Lützow's, and one of Reiche's corps being now attached to the troops of Woronzow, his infantry was reduced to sixteen weak battalions, numbering not more than six thousand men, and

the ground was not suited to the operations of
cavalry.

He waited until the morning of the 6th for the
promised reinforcement of Vegesack's division, but
without effect; the Crown Prince kept them all before Lübeck, and the consequence was, that the
Danes thus gaining time, retired in the night of the
5th from Oldeslohe, and the Trave, and moved upon
Segeberg.

The garrison of Lübeck capitulated on the 6th,
but were allowed to march out with a condition
that they were not to be followed for twenty-four
hours! Thus the whole Danish force was enabled
to gain a march upon the allies.

Wallmoden now gave up all hope of seeing the
division of Vegesack, which, in consequence of having been delayed before Lübeck, was nearly two
marches in the rear, and resuming his route on the
6th, he proceeded with the advanced-guard to Oldeslohe, the main body following.

Oldeslohe was found deserted by the enemy;
Dörnberg was, therefore, sent forward in pursuit
with four battalions and eight squadrons towards
Segeberg, while the main body took the direction of
Nehrs. On the 7th Dörnberg found that the enemy
instead of taking the direction of Neumünster from
Segeberg, as he expected, turned towards Kiel; he,
therefore left the further pursuit to the Swedes, whose
advanced-guard approached Segeberg in the forenoon
of that day, and moved upon Neumünster, where,

on the same evening, the corps of Wallmoden was
concentrated.

1813.

December.

On the 8th it advanced in the direction of
Rendsburg and the Eyder. Meantime the enemy had
arrived in Kiel; the Swedish advanced-guard followed slowly, and the main body still slower, the
Crown Prince not reaching Neumünster with the
head-quarters before the 10th.

The Swedish cavalry had, however, an opportunity of attacking the enemy's rear-guard on the 7th
at Bornhöot, when they attempted to prevent their
passage of the Brambeck. The Danes brought up
three battalions, two regiments of cavalry and six
guns, and after a contest, which cost them the loss of
their artillery and three hundred prisoners, and the
Swedes three officers and over two hundred men,
they retired upon Ploen.

Geschichte
des Armee-
korps, &c.

Although the Crown Prince had been the cause of
general Wallmoden's delay at Siebenbäumen, by
withholding the division of Vegesack, he continued
to urge the general to a rapid movement upon Rendsburg, and thus on the 6th and 7th, wrote from his
head-quarters at Lübeck:—

"The Danes have received no reinforcements.
Rendsburg is without guns, provisions, or garrison; Glückstadt is also without troops and must
fall. Nothing is to be apprehended from Hamburg,
as Davoust will be sufficiently kept in check by
Woronzow. The Danish army, with the garrison of
Lübeck does not amount to more than twelve thou-

sand men and is completely dispirited, Tettenborn's Cossacks out-flank them on one side, and Skiölde-brands cavalry on the other. The corps of Wallmoden united with these two divisions, is fully equal to cope with the enemy."

Der Feld-zug, in Mecklen-burg &c. Having arrived at the Eyder on the 8th, Wallmoden judged it advisable to send only an advanced-guard across the river, in order to observe the movements of the enemy; and accordingly, on the following day general Dörnberg was sent towards the bridge of Cluvensik. A strong detachment was placed at Aechtenwerder towards Kiel, and another towards Rendsburg in observation of that fortress. All the howitzers of the corps were sent with this detach-ment in order that a cannonade might be opened upon the place; the remainder of the troops followed the advance. The bridge of Cluvensik was found occupied by riflemen and two guns, which were sur-prised, and about one hundred prisoners, together with the guns, were captured. Arrived on the other side of the river, the detachment was met by a body of troops which had been sent to the relief of the post at Cluvensik. These the allied ad-vance also dispersed, and took from them seven pieces of artillery.

General Dörnberg now thinking it probable that the enemy would retire from Kiel upon Sleswig, sent his patroles on that road in the direction of Eckernförde, taking post with the remainder of his troops, more to the left, with the intention of pre-

venting the enemy's retreat upon Rendsburg, should
they seek to gain that place from Eckernförde.

The patroles fell in with the enemy's baggage near
Eckernförde and, as it afterwards appeared, occupied
themselves more with plunder, than in gaining information of the Danish movements;—which neglect
proved fatal to the allied corps.

Wallmoden concentrated the rest of his troops at
Cluvensik, in readiness either to follow Dörnberg, or
support the detachment at Aechtenwerder, as might
be required. On the evening of the 9th he learned
from intercepted letters, that the enemy had left Kiel
that morning, crossed the Eyder, and broken the
bridge, but in what direction they had marched remained unknown. Neither Dörnberg nor the Swedes
sent in any information on this point, and it was
only conjectured that they had retired by Eckernförde.

Wallmoden, therefore, decided upon marching
towards the latter place and sent an intimation to
general Skiöldebrand, who commanded the Swedish
advanced guard, to that effect.

Having called in all his detachments to Cluvensik, he set forward on the morning of the 10th, with
the advanced guard, leaving directions that the whole
should follow on the arrival of the detachments. He
was proceeding by Sehestedt, and had already passed
that place about a mile, when suddenly, the advanced
guard of the Danes appeared in sight. These troops
had left Kiel on the 9th, taking the road to Rendsburg,

and owing to the neglect of Dörnberg's patroles, had arrived thus far without any intimation of their approach having been given to the allies.

Wallmoden was accompanied by an aide-de-camp only, when he thus came upon the enemy's advance, and he had scarcely time to despatch an officer with intelligence to general Dörnberg, and make some hasty dispositions for meeting the threatened attack, when the Danes advanced in force upon the village.

He succeeded, however, in placing a few squadrons and one battalion in Sehestedt before the enemy reached it; and for the moment, their progress was checked.

It was to be presumed that Dörnberg's patroles would have given him intimation of this unexpected movement of the enemy, and Wallmoden held the village in the full expectation that some steps would be speedily taken by that general to restore the communication and enable him to oppose a more effective force to the assailants. He supported the troops in the village with as many as could be spared from the rear, without depriving himself of a reserve; but the battalion from Rendsburg arrived so late at Cluvensik, that only five battalions could be pushed forward, and the enemy gradually bringing up their whole force, the allied battalions were quite insufficient to oppose any effective resistance; and about ten o'clock, Sehestedt was carried by the Danes. In consequence of the unsuitable nature of the ground Wallmoden had withdrawn his cavalry, and the

enemy, availing themselves of the circumstance,
pressed after the allied battalions with impetuosity,
captured two guns and obliged them to retire upon
their reserve at Osterode near the bridge of Cluvensik.
Here the contest was renewed. Detachments of the
Russian hussars and afterwards, of the Mecklenburg
mounted riflemen, which Vegesack had sent forward
from Nortop, rushed upon the Danish infantry and
forced their way nearly to the village. The detachment of the King's German Legion under captain Narrative
of captain
Holtzermann, also advanced, and, supported by the Langwerth
MSS.
battalion of Lauenburg, moved forward in skirmishing
order, and drove back a column of infantry which
was advancing along the high road ; but in retiring
before the Danish horsemen across an open space,
the rear fell into disorder, and captain Holtzermann
had the misfortune to fall into the enemy's hands.
A charge of a squadron of Mecklenburg mounted
riflemen, however, enabled the legion again to
assume the offensive, and the contest was continued
with various fortune for some time longer. But the
enemy had lined the hedges and ditches on the sides Der Feldzug in
of the road with infantry, who poured a destructive Mecklenburg &c.
fire upon the allied troops ; these being so far
inferior, in number to their opponents, were eventually obliged to give way ; and the Danes succeeded
in resuming their march on Rendsburg.

The loss in this combat was considerable on both
sides, but from the contradictory statements which
have been put forward, it is difficult to offer an accu-

1813.

December.

Der Feld-
zug in
Mecklen-
burg &c.
rate estimate of it. A Danish account of the action exaggerates the loss of the allies to three thousand five hundred men, while it reduces that of the Danes to five hundred and forty-eight!* It seems probable that the loss on each side was about one thousand. The allies lost also two guns, which fell into the enemy's hands on the charge of their cavalry, and the same number was captured from the Danes; but one of these was afterwards retaken. Among the prisoners made by the enemy was prince Gustavus of Mecklenburg who commanded the mounted riflemen. Of the legion detachment, lieutenant Macdonald and several other officers were wounded, and captain Holtzermann and nine men were made prisoners.

Towards evening Sehestedt was completely evacuated by the enemy, and Wallmoden's communication was open with Dörnberg; however, nothing was to be heard or seen of this general, nor were his patroles to be met with up to a late hour that night.

The officer who had been sent by Wallmoden to general Skiöldebrand commanding the Swedish advanced guard, returned in the night with a reply, saying that he had received no orders to pass the Eyder! and that, the enemy had broken down the bridge.

This passive conduct of the Swedes was the more unexpected by general Wallmoden, as his orders had

* Bericht von dem Treffen bei Sehestedt von C. F. von Höegh, capitain im Königlich: danischen Infanterie Regimente Oldenburg. Ritter.

always pointed to the passage of the Eyder, and the
carrying on of rapid offensive operations. He had
engaged in the affair of Sehestedt with the well
grounded supposition that the enemy's columns would
at the same time, have been pressed by the Swedish
advanced corps of cavalry; but instead of this, he
finds himself not only deprived of the assistance of
Vegesack, but separated from one wing of his own
corps,—completely deserted by the Swedes, and left,
finally, to oppose the whole Danish force with eight
battalions. The consequence was that a considerable
number of men had been sacrificed to no purpose; for
the Danes effected their object of throwing themselves
into Rendsburg, and the garrison there being thus
augmented, no prospect of succeeding against the
place could be entertained by the allied commander.

The first intelligence from general Dörnberg came
in on the 11th, when it appeared that, in consequence
of the neglect of his patroles, he had remained unin-
formed of the enemy's movements, and, according to
the previous understanding had directed his main
attention to Eckernförde, following on that route with
the rest of his corps. Even the firing which he heard
in the direction of Sehestedt on the 10th, did not
divert him; for he considered it to be a demonstration made by the enemy for the purpose of drawing
off the attention of the allies from their real object of
attack. At length, however, he discovered his mistake, and countermarched upon Schestedt; but it
was too late, for the enemy's rear-guard had already

1813.

December.

Der Feld-
zug in
Mecklen-
burg &c,

marched out.   Considering that his communications
with Wallmoden were destroyed, he now moved
his troops on the road leading from Rendsburg to
Sleswig; but here again the enemy had taken post,
and he was obliged to dislodge them from Cropp
during the night.   At length, orders reached him
directing his return to Cluvensick, where he arrived
on the evening of the 11th : Vegesack's corps came
up in the afternoon of the same day.

The addition to the garrison of Rendsburg of a
corps of ten thousand men prevented Wallmoden
from doing more than observing the place, and he
took up an extended position at Cluvensik, Emken-
torf, and Nortorf.   A strong detachment was placed
on the other side of the Eyder to prevent any communication between the fortress and Sleswig, and head
quarters were established at Shirensee.   Meantime
the Swedish army continued to move forward slowly
towards Kiel, and the advance first passed the Eyder
on the 11th.

On the 12th, negociations for peace were commenced with the Danish government, and on the
15th, an armistice of fourteen days was agreed upon,
according to which Rendsburg was to remain in a state
of blockade, and part of the duchy of Sleswig to be
occupied : Frederickstadt and Glückstadt had previously capitulated to the Swedes.

The corps of Wallmoden had experienced the most
unmerited ill fortune in the late movements.   If the
Crown Prince had allowed Vegesack to unite his

troops with those of Wallmoden at the proper time;
if general Dörnberg had obtained timely intelligence
of the Danish movements, and placed himself in close
communication with Wallmoden,—the whole corps
would have been able, early on the 10th, to take up
a strong position between the Witten lake and the
old Eyder, about half a mile on the other side of
Sehestedt, and then could have opposed an effective
barrier to the enemy's march upon Rendsburg. Had
the Danes attempted to retreat, this could not have
been accomplished before the numerous cavalry and
light artillery of the allies without great loss; more
particularly, if the Swedish advanced cavalry under
Skiöldebrand, as might have been expected, had passed
the Eyder at Kiel early on the 10th, and moved upon
the enemy's rear. In that case the retreat of the Danes
would have been entirely cut off, and a capitulation
would most probably, have been concluded on the field.

The armistice terminated on the 5th of January
without the negociations for peace having been
brought to a successful close, and the troops were,
therefore, concentrated for further operations. On
the 9th, however, negociations were again opened; a
second suspension of arms took place, and this terminated with a treaty of peace, which was concluded at
Kiel on the 16th.

Wallmoden's corps remained in the neighbourhood
of Neumünster until the 17th, and on the following
day, marched for Buxtehude. On the 21st, one part
crossed the Elbe over the ice at Blankenese and ano-

ther at Zollenspieker, and both were united at Winsen
and Buxtehude where they were placed in cantonments.

The third hussars, and the horse artillery of the
King's German Legion were now separated from the
allied corps, and directed to join the army then
operating in Holland under the command of general
Graham.

CHAPTER XI.

OPERATIONS IN THE PENINSULA.

1813.

June.

We left the allied troops in the peninsula at the close of their brilliant achievement at Vittoria, on the 21st of June, when the French after one of the most complete discomfitures which they had yet sustained, fled in disorder to the fortress of Pampluna. On the 23d, a corps under sir Thomas Graham was detached to intercept a French force which, under general Foy, was retreating by Tolosa; the fifth division was left at Salvatierra; and Wellington followed King Joseph with the rest of the army. Journal of major Cordemann. MSS.

The first hussars of the legion under Victor Alten led the advance, and coming up with the enemy's rear-guard on the 23d, overthrew them, and made many prisoners.* On the following day the hussars

* An hussar officer was, on this occasion, witness to a scene which shewed in strong colours, the hatred and revengeful feeling which the barbarities of the French had excited in the minds of the Spanish people :—The house of a miller had been burned by the enemy during the night, and, on the following morning, the miller was seen dragging a French soldier, whom he had, with the assistance of some peasants, secured by a rope, towards the mill-dam, into which they straightway threw the prisoner. The mill-wheel went round; but the Frenchman could swim, and was making the best of his way to the bank, when the peasants assailed him with stones, and continued to shower them upon the unfortunate man until he was quite dead.—Journal of major Cordemann.

1813.

June.

Corde-
mann's
Journal,
MSS.

and light division formed the allied advance, the first squadron under lieutenant Schaumann, and one battalion of the ninety-fifth being in front. About ten in the morning about five thousand of the enemy's infantry, and a few squadrons of cavalry were found in position across the high road leading to Pampluna; and here, one gun and a howitzer, all that they had saved from the wreck of Vittoria, were placed.

The light division under Charles Alten, in their usual gallant style, soon dislodged the enemy, and the hussars and horse artillery dashing after them with rapidity, deprived the beaten army of their last gun. The loss of the French was considerable. According to their general custom of placing the German troops in the most exposed situations, the contingent of Nassau formed their rear-guard, and followed the main body in a dense column on the Pampluna road. The British horse artillery, closing up, poured a terrific fire into the ranks of these unfortunate men; scarce a shot missed its aim; one single ball was seen at once to deprive five infantry soldiers of both legs, taking the first under the hip, and the fifth under the chin! So great in deed was the torture experienced by these poor creatures, that, as the hussars rode by, they implored them as countrymen, to put an end to their torments by at once depriving them of life. This could not, of course, be complied with, and the whole road presented a frightful spectacle of mutilated human beings in the most excruciating endurance.

Clausel approached Vittoria the day after the
battle, with part of the army of the north, and one
division of the army of Portugal; but on learning Welling-
the result of the action of the 21st, he countermarched ton's des-patch.
upon Logrono. The main body of the French army
continued its retreat into France by the road of
Roncesvalles; and Pampluna was invested by the
allies on the 26th.

Sir Thomas Graham's corps included the light and General Graham's
line brigades of the German legion under colonel despatch. Narrative
Halkett. It was directed to march by the Puerta St. of colonel Wyneckeu
Adrian on Villafranca, but the weather and roads Notes of capt.Chris-
were so extremely unfavorable that the legion light toph Heise. MSS.
brigade alone, which formed the advanced guard, was
enabled to pass the mountain on that day, and it was
not until late on the 24th, that the general could
bring up on the road from Seguna to Villafranca, a
brigade of British light dragoons, and two Portuguese
brigades of infantry.

The rear of the enemy's column was at this time
passing on the great road which leads from Villareal
to Villafranca, and occupied in considerable force,
some very strong ground on the right of the great road
and of the river Oria, in front of the village of
Olaverria and about two miles from Villafranca.

General Bradford's brigade marched by Olaverria,
and was employed to dislodge the enemy on the right,
while the remainder of the troops advanced by the
high road. This was defended by tirailleurs from
the heights, and a strong body of troops posted at the

1813.

June.

Graham's
despatch,
&c.
village of Veasayn; and these the enemy continued to reinforce. Graham, therefore, determined to push forward with all expedition, by the high road, and directed colonel Halkett to advance with his light brigade on this service.

The legion battalions were flanked by some companies of Pack's Portuguese brigade, and they had not proceeded far when the advanced guard found the enemy in possession of a bridge on the high road. The French advance was immediately attacked, and driven in by the first light battalion and the Portuguese, while the second light battalion was detached to the right to seek another passage. The French about five thousand strong, had taken post behind a wall near the bridge, with their left flank on the river and their right on the road; a strong body of skirmishers was thrown out in front and on the hills to their right, and the town of Villafranca was immediately in their rear.

Wyneck-
en's
narrative,
MSS.
The German light battalions instantly commenced the attack. The first and second companies of the first battalion, which, in conjunction with the Portuguese, had taken the bridge, pursued the enemy's tirailleurs to the plain between the road and the river; the third and eighth companies held the road; the fifth and sixth moved upon the hill; and the fourth and seventh, after having passed the bridge, were sent down the stream to facilitate the passage of the second battalion.

This battalion, after passing the river, also operated

on the enemy's left, while the Portuguese caçadores moved upon the opposite flank. But the French would not commit themselves in a combat, and retired through Villafranca covered by skirmishers. The Prince of Reuss, who held the rank of major in the second light battalion of the legion, as well as lieutenant Frederick Kessler, and fourteen men, were wounded on this occasion.

1813.

June.

Wyneck-en's narrative, MSS.

Supported by some cavalry, the enemy held a turnpike house for a short time, but finally withdrew, uttering loud shouts of exultation; on the Germans entering the house, they found an unfortunate Spaniard (probably the owner) hanging by his sash from the ceiling the body was still warm. The French now retired rapidly, throwing away their havresacks, clothes, and even their knapsacks, and hurrying through Villafranca, where the pursuit ended. The Spanish corps of Longa, as well as the head of Giron's corps joined general Graham in the course of the evening.

On the following morning the enemy evacuated Celequia, and took up a very strong position between that place and Tolosa, crossing the Pampluna road. Longa's corps was therefore, marched towards Lizarga, to turn the enemy's left, while Mendizabel was directed to send some battalions from Aspeytea, to turn their right, which rested on a high mountain, with an inaccessible ravine in front.

Graham's despatch.

The French were driven from an important hill, lying between the Pampluna and Vittoria roads, by

1813, some companies of the guards and caçadores, and
June. the hill was immediately occupied by general Brad-
Graham's despatch, ford's brigade, supported by the line battalions of the
legion. A general attack commenced about half-past
six o'clock in the evening, when four guns of the
British horse-artillery, supported by an escort of the
sixteenth dragoons, and the legion light brigade, were
brought rapidly forward on the high road; these were
followed by the brigade of guards, and the division
of Giron, while two Spanish battalions and one Portuguese advanced on the left, and the line brigade
of the legion under colonel Halkett on the right.

It had been arranged that the Spanish battalions
were to attack as they arrived, and thus give the
signal for a general attack; and when within six
hundred yards of

TOLOSA

Wyneck-en's narrative, &c. MSS. the advance of the legion under colonel Ompteda was
halted, where a bend in the road concealed them from
the place, in order to give the Spaniards time to
comply with their instructions.

These did not, however, proceed with that prompt-
ness which general Graham considered necessary,
for the advance of the legion had not halted a quarter
of an hour when, addressing colonel Ompteda, who
commanded the first light battalion, he said, " you see
the Spaniards do not go on as they ought, therefore
your battalion must take the place.—Go on."

In compliance with these orders colonel Ompteda 1813.
directed two companies to move forward under captain June.
Christian Wynecken, but they had not advanced far, Wyneck-
when they became exposed to the fire of the town, and en's
narrative,
it was ascertained that the gate was barricaded. The MSS.
place also was found to be much more capable of
defence than was at first expected, for besides being
barricaded, both the Vittoria and Pampluna gates
were flanked by convents and other large buildings
occupied by the enemy, and the town was no where
open.

To avoid the fire from the gate, Wynecken's
leading company jumped over a low wall to the left,
and crept along under its protection ; but after they
had reached within a short distance of the town, an
insurmountable obstacle presented itself, being the
high wall of a convent, and the men were obliged to
return to the road : an operation attended with considerable difficulty, in consequence of the road being
much higher than the ground upon which they
stood.

Immediately on gaining the road the gallant riflemen dashed forward boldly against the Vittoria gate;
but the strong defences there rendered their success
impossible, and they quickly took shelter in the
court yard of a convent which stood on the left.
Into this place the supporting company followed,
and the rest of the battalion sought the same protection.

The convent was about twenty-five paces distant

P

1813,

June.

See Plan.

from the gate, having a narrow passage leading from its court towards the town; but the principal entrance to the building was from the road, and the whole enclosure, including a vineyard, was surrounded by a high wall.

Wyneck-
en's
narrative,
MSS.

The Vittoria gate was defended by strong palisades, and behind these stout planks were placed for the protection of the defenders; upon the wall above the gate stood a large battering cannon; on each angle of the front was a strong block house furnished with loop-holes; on the left of the town ran a deep and dirty canal, which emptied itself into a river on the French side, and near the junction of these, a small draw-bridge which also was defended by a block house, led by another gate into the place.

Heise's
Notes.
MSS.

No infantry alone could be fairly expected to force such defences; however, Ompteda, a fine soldier, who never shrunk from danger or difficulties, assembled his battalion in the convent yard, and led forward three companies against the place with signal bravery and resolution. No sooner had the devoted soldiers shewn themselves on the road, when a fire went forth from the gate and block houses which swept their ranks;—many men fell;—the rest dispersed; some sought shelter in the canal, and others in a house which lay farther on upon the left; among those who took shelter in the canal were lieutenants Fincke, and Christoph Heise, with about eighteen men of the battalion, and their situation became critical; for one block house took them in front, and another in rear, while the fire from the houses of the town came upon their right, and that of the Spaniards, who mistook them for French, upon their left! The consequence was, that nearly every individual of the party was either killed or wounded.

Meantime the skirmishers of the line battalions driving in the enemy from the Pampluna road, and neighbouring heights, pressed after them towards the entrance on that side of the town. They made some stand at a bridge, where captain Claus von der Decken, who commanded the leading company, was wounded,—but soon gave way to the skirmishers of the brigade under captain Charles Langrehr, supported by two companies of the fifth line battalion under captain Bacmeister, and hurrying into the place, opened a destructive fire upon the Germans from a convent which commanded the gate. Several officers and men were struck down, and no means being at hand to force the entrance, the assailants took shelter behind some houses in front. By this time a nine pounder had been brought up, under the support of the second light battalion, to the Vittoria gate, which was at length burst open, and the enemy's fire now slackening at the Pampluna entrance, the pioneers of the line battalions effected an opening there also.

The French immediately hurried out of the town; but it was now late; the darkness rendered it impossible to distinguish the troops of the different nations, and the enemy were, therefore, enabled to

Notes of major von Holle, and capt. Hesse MSS.

effect their escape with much less loss than they
would otherwise have sustained.

The casualties of the legion in this assault, and
more particularly of the first light battalion, were
considerable:—Out of fifty men of the eighth company
which formed Wynecken's advance at the Vittoria
gate, twenty-one were killed and wounded; captains
Cropp and Wynecken, lieutenants Heise, Heugel,
Fincke, Wolrabe, Wahrendorf, with fifty-eight non-
commissioned officers and men of this battalion
alone, were wounded, three of the officers severely ;
captain Cropp afterwards died of his wounds, and
lieutenant Heugel, who was shot in the arm, was
obliged to undergoe amputation.

In the line battalions captains Langrehr, Beuermann
and Bacmeister, and lieutenant Ferdinand von Holle
were all severely wounded; lieutenant Boyd was also
wounded, and this brigade lost in the whole nine
non-commissioned officers and men killed, and fifty-
six wounded.

Altogether in the operation against Tolosa, the five
weak battalions of the legion had nineteen non-commissioned officers and men killed, fourteen officers
and one hundred and fourteen men wounded, a loss,
which, it may be presumed, would have been in a
great measure, avoided, had a more matured plan of
operation been adopted against the place.

Sir Thomas Graham continued to pursue the enemy
by the high road to France, and dislodge them from
all the positions which they took up. On the 2d of

July they were attacked by a Spanish brigade under
Castanos, who drove them across the Bidassoa by the
bridge of Irun; Castro and the town and fort of
Guetaria were also evacuated, the garrisons escaping
by sea to Santoria and St. Sebastian; the castle of
Pancorbo, in which the French had left a body of
seven hundred men when they retired across the
Ebro, was carried by the Conde d'Abisbal on the
28th; and, on the3 0th, Longa obtained possession of
Passages, the harbour of which became of great value
to the allies during their succeeding operations.

Clausel having remained until late on the 25th of
June at Logrono, Lord Wellington conceived the project of intercepting his retreat, and therefore moved
the light, third, fourth, and seventh divisions, with the
household and general D'Urban's cavalry towards
that place; the French general however, made some
extraordinary forced marches, and arrived at Tudela
on the evening of the 27th, followed by Mina and
the cavalry of Don Julian Sanchez. He then crossed
the Ebro, but hearing of the proximity of the British,
retraced his steps, and marched to Zaragossa. Mina
followed, and succeeded in taking three hundred
prisoners, besides two guns, and some stores which he
found in Tudela; general Clinton also took five guns
in Logrono: meantime the troops under sir Rowland
Hill kept up the blockade of Pampluna, and moved
to the head of the Bidassoa.

While a series of successes were thus attending
the operations of the allied troops in the north of

Spain, an expedition directed by sir John Murray on the eastern coast, met with the most unlooked for and unfortunate result.

In pursuance of lord Wellington's orders sir John Murray had, on the 3d of June, landed on the coast of Catalonia, with the mixed force under his command, and invested Taragona; a detachment which he sent forward to fort St. Felippe on the Col de Balaquer, succeeded in capturing that post; by the 8th, fort Royal, an outwork of the fortress, was practicably breached, and, on the 11th, two heavy batteries were opened against the body of the place. But meantime reports reached the English general that Suchet and Maurice Mathieu were hastening from Valentia and Barcelona, with an overpowering force, to the relief of the fortress. Murray's disposable field army

amounted to sixteen thousand men, but of these only three thousand, including the fourth and sixth line battalions of the German legion under colonel von Hohnstedt—were troops upon whom he could depend, and the French were reported to be advancing with upwards of twenty thousand; wherefore, becoming alarmed, he raised the siege, embarked his troops, and, in his extreme haste, left nineteen pieces of

artillery in the trenches. Sir John Murray's conduct became afterwards the subject of investigation before a court martial, which did not censure him for raising the siege, or embarking his troops; but he was found guilty of abandoning artillery and stores which he might have carried away in safety.

Lord William Bentinck arrived from Sicily on the 17th, and taking the command of the allied troops at Alicant, proceeded to carry lord Wellington's instructions into execution; but the result of the battle of Vittoria soon changed the face of affairs in this part of Spain, and on the 5th of July, Suchet evacuated Valentia altogether.

The right and left of the main French army had been withdrawn quite out of France, but the centre still held possession of the rich valley of Bastan, whose fertility and strong positions the enemy did not seem inclined to forego. However sir Rowland Hill, having been relieved from the blockade of Pampluna by the Spanish army of reserve under the Conde d' Abisbal, dislodged them successively from all their possessions, and on the 7th of July, the advance of the allied army stood triumphant on the frontiers of France.

Mina, having been joined by Duran in the neighbourhood of Zaragossa, attacked the French division of general Paris on the 8th, and obliged him to retire, leaving a garrison in a redoubt. Duran was left to reduce this work, while Mina, with his cavalry, and that of Julian Sanchez followed Paris, and took from him many prisoners and a quantity of baggage, besides intercepting a convoy; Paris arrived at Jaca on the 14th, bringing with him the garrisons of Ayerba, Huesca and others, and continued his retreat into France.

Lord Wellington now prepared for commencing

operations against St. Sebastian, into which fortress
the enemy had thrown a garrison of three thousand
five hundred men, on their retreat after the battle of
Vittoria. The place was closely invested on the land
side by sir Thomas Graham with the left wing of the
allied army, and on the sea side it was blockaded
by a British squadron under sir George Collyer.

CHAPTER XII.

SIEGE OF SAINT SEBASTIAN.

The town and citadel of St. Sebastian are situated on a peninsula projecting to the northward; on this and the western side it is washed by the sea, and on the eastern side by the river Urumea.

The works on the southern or land front consisted of a single line of defence exceeding three hundred and fifty yards in length, with a flat bastion in the centre covered by a hornwork; but those on the western and eastern sides were simple rampart walls, indifferently flanked, without any obstacle in front, and on the eastern side the wall was seen to its base from a range of sand-hills on the opposite side of the river, called the Chofre sand-hills.

The citadel, called fort la Mota, is a small work situated on a rocky height at the northern extremity of the peninsula, and the whole of this eminence is cut off from the town by a defensive line covered with batteries which plunge into the lower defences of the place.

The plan of attack determined on by Lord Wellington was to form two breaches in the town wall

1813.

July.

Jones's
Sieges.

from batteries on the Chofre sand-hills, and to storm
them as soon as practicable by an advance along the
left bank of the Urumea, which was passable at low
water.   It was also determined to construct batteries
on the heights of St. Bartolomeo, where a post had
been formed by a convent and a small redoubt about
seven hundred yards in advance of the town: there
was also a temporary circular work, formed of casks,
from which it would be necessary to dislodge the
enemy.

Lieutenant-colonel Hartmann of the German artillery was appointed to the command of the artillery
of the left wing, and lieutenants Mielmann and von
Goeben of the same corps were also employed in this
part of the attack.

The investing corps was composed of the fifth
division under major-general Oswald, and the Portuguese brigades of generals Bradford and Wilson,
forming a force of about nine thousand men, which
was placed under the chief command of sir Thomas
Graham.

On the night of the 11th of July two batteries
were commenced against the convent of St. Bartolomeo, which were completed by the 13th, and on the
same day four batteries were marked out on the
Chofre sand hills, directed against the eastern wall.

The batteries against the convent were opened at
day-light on the 14th; by the 16th a large portion
of the front of the building was practicably breached,
and at ten o'clock on the following day, both the

convent and redoubt were carried by assault with little opposition; the assailants, however, in pushing forward to meet a body of the garrison which was advancing from the town to the support of the convent, became exposed to a severe fire from the place, and being also attacked by the enemy, they were driven back with some loss.

1813.

July.

Jones's
Sieges.

The attack on the redoubt was most effectively supported by the fire of two heavy six-pounders from the right under the direction of lieutenant Mielmann of the German artillery, who was severely wounded on this occasion.

The light and line brigades of the legion had been employed with the rest of the first division, in covering the great road leading from Irun to Oyarzun, but this day, (the 17th) they were moved in to the neighbourhood of the fortress for the purpose of assisting in the trenches, and they continued to supply detachments for this service during the rest of the siege.

Journals of
brigades
MSS.

The heights of St Bartolomeo having been gained, two batteries were immediately commenced there to enfilade and take in reverse the defences of the place. A lodgement was also made in the suburb of St. Martin, and the batteries on the Chofre sand-hills were completed.

Jones's
Sieges

Those on the isthmus were armed on the 19th, and the charge given to lieutenant-colonel Hartmann.

At eight on the morning of the 20th, the besiegers' batteries opened against the place, and a considerable impression was made upon the wall and parapet; the fire of the garrison, however, disabled and injured several of the guns, and the nature of the ground rendered it impracticable to employ the low ship guns which had been brought up from the fleet for that purpose.

The circular redoubt was abandoned by the garrison this evening, and at ten o'clock on the following day, the place was summoned; but the governor refused to receive the letter, and the besiegers' fire was resumed. A drain having been discovered leading from the town, it was determined to form a mine at its extremity in the counterscarp, where its explosion might throw up sufficient rubbish to form a road over the ditch.

Early on the morning of the 23d, a breach between two towers on the east front was considered practicable, and the fire of the batteries was turned to make a second breach on the same front, where the wall was weaker. This was effected the same evening, and a fire having been opened against the defences, arrangements were made for assaulting the breaches on the following morning.

But the houses in the neighbourhood of the principal breach had caught fire in the afternoon of the 23d, and the flames spreading rapidly, appeared to form an obstacle to the advance of the assailants. The assault was, therefore, postponed until the morning of the 25th, on which day at day-break, it was calculated that the tide would admit of the

troops passing along the strand to the foot of the
eastern wall.

The fifth division was entrusted with the assault,
and were to file out of the right of the parallel on the
isthmus, on the explosion of the mine which had
been formed at the counterscarp of the horn work.

The column assembled in the trenches at five
o'clock in the morning. The mine was sprung, and
blowing down a considerable portion of the counterscarp and glacis of the hornwork, created so much
astonishment among the garrison, that they abandoned the eastern parapet for a moment, and the
right wing of the leading battalions reached the foot
of the principal breach, before any very heavy fire
could be brought upon them.

The advance immediately scrambled down the
ruins into the houses, but the burning materials and
the thick smoke which here presented itself, caused
the men to hesitate, and they commenced firing from
the crest of the breach. Major Fraser who commanded the advance was killed;—disorder then spread
amongst his followers;—the exertions of the besiegers
were resumed, and soon the assailants, falling
into utter confusion, sought shelter in the trenches.
A few, yet undismayed, remained with lieutenant
Jones of the engineers on the breach, awaiting the
arrival of the support, but before these reached the
spot, the gallant men were nearly all wounded, and
the besiegers, descending the breach, carried many
of them away prisoners.

The left wing of the storming party, as well as a battalion, which was destined for the assault of the lesser breach, seeing the fate of the first, also returned to the trenches, and now forty-four officers and three hundred and eighty men having been killed, wounded and taken, all further attempts upon St. Sebastian were, for the present, abandoned.

Lord Wellington, on learning the result of this assault, and examining into his means, decided that no attack should be again made until the arrival of the additional ordnance and ammunition, which was expected from England; finding also that the troops had been much discouraged by what had occurred, and not being altogether satisfied with the assault, he directed that a body of volunteers should be obtained from the army generally, to form the assailants for the next attack: meantime the place was strictly blockaded.

When Napoleon learned the mortifying defeat which his troops had sustained at Vittoria, he despatched marshal Soult from Saxony to take the command in the Peninsula, and endeavour to regain his lost conquests. Soult arrived on the 13th of July; every exertion was immediately made for the equipment of the several corps of the French army; supplies were speedily collected at St. Jean Pied de Port, and the marshal, now designated by the title of "lieutenant of the Emperor," projected the relief of Pampluna, and the re-establishment of his army on the line of the Ebro.

1813.

July.

At this time the allied troops were posted in the different passes of the Pyrenees, with mutual communications between each part ; the right wing covered the direct approaches to Pampluna, while the left wing guarded the line of the Bidassoa, and carried on the operations against St. Sebastian.

To effect his first object of relieving Pampluna, Soult placed his reserve under Villatte in the camp of Urogne upon the right flank, to guard the line of the Bidassoa. and withdrew his right wing to the neighbourhood of St. Jean Pied de Port. Here uniting it with his left, and part of the centre, he led the whole forward in person on the 25th of July, to attack the right wing of the allies in the pass of Roncesvalles, while count d'Erlon, with two divisions, was, at the same time, to make an attack on the troops under sir Rowland Hill in the passes of Maya.

Batty's western Pyrenees.

The enemy came upon the detached brigades which guarded the passes, in overpowering numbers, and forced the right wing to retire ; Hill, however, was enabled to check count d'Erlon, but the retreat of the right wing obliged him to make a corresponding movement, and he withdrew to a strong position at Irueta, resting his left upon the Bidassoa. The allied right wing continued to retreat on the two following days and the French had approached to within a few miles of Pampluna on the 28th, when Soult directed an attack to made from the right of his position in the valley of Lanz. Fortunately on that morning,

the sixth division under general Pack arriving at the
scene of action, quickly formed across the valley,
and by its vigorous resistance, aided by the fourth
division under general Cole on the right, completely
defeated the enemy's intentions. Soult next attacked
the allied centre, but here the fourth division repulsed all his efforts, and the arrival of the seventh
division at Marcalain, giving unity of action to the
allies, the enemy's further progress was effectually
prevented.

Lord Wellington now determined upon assuming
the offensive, and attacking the troops in his immediate front, although the position which they occupied
seemed almost impregnable. With this view he
directed the third division under sir Thomas Picton
to move, on the 30th, upon the French left, whilst
Lord Dalhousie, by turning their right in the valley
of Lantz, should threaten their centre. These dispositions had the desired effect: the allies, becoming
the assailants, dislodged the enemy from every
position where they attempted to make a stand, and
pressing close on the retiring columns as they hurried through the valley of Bastan on the 31st, made
many prisoners, and eventually established themselves in nearly the same positions which they held
before the attack of the 25th.

The fourth foot battery of German artillery under
the command of major Sympher, took an active and
efficient part in these several attacks: this battery
was attached to the fourth division, whose brilliant

charges on the 28th mainly contributed to the success
of the allies on that day. On this occasion the legion
lost an officer of considerable merit in captain Avemann of the first line battalion, who was acting as
brigade-major to major-general Anson.

Captain Augustus Heise of the second light battalion of the legion, served as deputy-assistant-adjutant
general to the second division during these operations,
and was mentioned in terms of high commendation
by major-general Pringle, on whom the command of
that division devolved in the attack of the 31st.

The present operations being carried on in a mountainous country, no opportunity offered for the application
of cavalry, and the movements of the hussars and heavy
cavalry brigade of the legion at this period present
little of interest or importance; lieutenant Cordemann
was honored by being selected to attend sir Rowland
Hill with a detachment of hussars during the action
of the 30th, and was the channel of communication
between that general and the commander-in-chief;
an incident also occurred at the hussar out-posts, in
which this officer was engaged, and which may serve
to illustrate the degree of vigilance and intelligence
required for such duties :—

On the night of the 28th lieutenant Cordemann
was placed with a squadron of the first hussars on
the outlying picquet, which was stationed on the road
from Lizasso to Erasum; the surrounding country
was mountainous and woody; towards evening
the enemy's infantry encamped in the wood, on both

(marginal notes) 1813. July. General Hill's despatch. Journal of major Cordemann. MSS.

Q

sides of the road, and sent out a strong picquet to meet that of the hussars,

About eleven o'clock a loud shouting was heard to proceed from the wood in rear of the enemy's flank, accompanied by signals on the bugle. Unable to imagine what was thereby denoted, but conceiving it possible that the enemy might contemplate a night attack, Cordemann directed his squadron to mount, and proceeded to reconnoitre the enemy's camp. There all was quiet, yet the noise and bugle sounds continued and, strange to hear, the latter appeared to be similar to those used in the English service. Determined to investigate this unusual occurrence, Cordemann took with him eight of his boldest and most expert men, and, directing the rest to give him notice by firing if they were attacked, he penetrated into the wood, and proceeded to patrole in the direction from whence the sounds came. In about half an hour infantry were discovered, but in what force, or whether friend or foe was not perceptible. Cordemann now halted his men, and riding forward alone, challenged the unknown parties in English; no answer was returned; he then tried Portuguese, and to his great satisfaction, was answered by the commandant of the second Portuguese caçadores. This battalion had, it appeared, been detached on the 28th, and owing to the rapid advance of the enemy was cut off from the rest of the allied army, which it now sought to find by making the English bugle sounds. Cordemann immediately conducted

the battalion to his squadron, and from thence sent 1813.
a hussar to guide it to Lizasso, which place he July.
requested the Portuguese colonel would maintain Corde-mann's Journal.
until the hussars, who, it was to be expected would
be attacked on the following morning, should have
reached it.

According to expectation the picquet was attacked
in great force by the French infantry at day-break;
one column advanced by the road, while two others
moved in parallel directions through the wood. No
resistance could be effectively offered by the hussar
squadron to such a force, and they retired upon Lizasso, having had several horses wounded by the
enemy's skirmishers; the French, favored by the
ground, followed rapidly, but to their great surprise,
were received in front of Lizasso by the caçadores.
These, arriving on the previous night, had barricaded
the place, and loop-holed many of the houses, and
now poured such a hot fire upon the enemy that they
halted, and allowed the allied troops to retire without
further interruption : the caçadores had about twenty
killed and wounded, but the loss of the enemy was
considerably greater.

During these operations in the Pyrenees, strong
reinforcements of guns, ammunition and besieging
means had arrived at St. Sebastian, and on the 24th
of August the siege was vigorously re-commenced.

In addition to the officers of the German artillery Narrative of general Hartmann. MSS.
which have been already mentioned as employed
before the fortress, major Sympher, captain Daniel

and lieutenants Blumenbach and Hartmann of the fourth battery were added; the batteries on the isthmus were placed under the special charge of colonel Hartmann; and major Sympher took the direction of the batteries on the right alternately with major Buckner of the English artillery.

On the 26th of August fifty-seven pieces of ordnance opened against the place; the fire from the right was most effective, but that from the other flank was at too great a distance to do much injury, and another battery was therefore constructed within three hundred yards of the fortress.

On this night the rocky island of Santa Clara at the entrance of the harbour, where the garrison maintained a post, was surprised and taken by a detachment of the British naval and military force; and as this island enfiladed and saw in reverse the defences of the castle, it was decided to construct a battery there.

In order to induce the garrison to blow up their mines, and shew the nature and degree of the fire which they would be able to bring on an assaulting column, a false attack was made at ten o'clock on the night of the 29th, but although considerable alarm was produced in the place, the defenders were too cautious to expose their powers. On the 30th the breaches appeared practicable, and Lord Wellington, having inspected them, decided that the assault should be given at eleven o'clock in the forenoon of the following day, when the state of the tide

would admit of the troops passing under the left
branch of the hornwork to the breaches. In order
to make debouches for the troops, it was necessary
to break through the sea-wall between the left salient
angles of the hornwork and the trenches; and for
this purpose three mines were constructed in the advanced sap; these were sprung at two o'clock in the
morning of the 31st; the sea-wall was thereby thrown
completely down, and by ten o'clock a good passage
was formed for the troops.

1813.

July.

Jones's
Sieges.

FINAL ASSAULT OF SAINT SEBASTIAN.

The column of attack was formed of the second
brigade of the fifth division, which was immediately
supported by seven hundred and fifty volunteers,
composed of one hundred and fifty men of the light
division, two hundred of the guards, and the same
number of the German legion and fourth division;
the remainder of the fifth division was in reserve, as
well as a battalion of Portuguese caçadores, and the
whole were placed under the direction of lieutenant-
general sir James Leith.

The German detachment consisted of equal numbers of the light and line brigades of the legion, and
included the following officers:—

Journals of
battalions
MSS.

Major Gerber,............ 5th line battalion, commanding.
Captain Christian Wynecken, 1st light battalion.
Captain Heine, ... 1st line battalion.
Lieutenant Elderhost,...... 1st light battalion.
Lieutenant von Rossing,. .. 1st line battalion.

1813.

August.

Notes of
colonel C.
Wynecken
MSS.

The detachment of the light battalions was attached to that of the light division, which was directed to cover the left flank of the column during its advance, and particularly to fire upon the defenders of the hornwork, the left angle of which took the assailants in flank; and the detachment of the line battalions, as well as that of the guards, and fourth division, were placed in support of the fifth division.

Jones's
Sieges.

Precisely at eleven o'clock the columns of assault filed out of the trenches. The tide having ebbed for some time, they were enabled to proceed along the strand between the river and the wall; but immediately on the advance of the column, the garrison exploded two mines under the left demi-bastion of the hornwork, which blew down the wall, and killed or buried twenty or thirty of the assailants. Notwithstanding this explosion, and a general fire which immediately followed, the advance reached the breach between the towers in the best order, and gallantly mounted to the summit; but here they were met by such destructive discharges of musquetry from a parallel retrenchment that the foremost ranks were nearly annihilated.

Both officers and men, however, boldly attempted to close with their opponents, but it was soon discovered that the rampart along the interior of the breach, was retained by a wall from fifteen to twenty five feet high, at the bottom of which every kind of obstacle was placed, and that all communication with

1813.

August.

Jones's
Sieges.

the town by the flanks of the breach was cut off.
The only possibility which appeared of descending
into the town was by means of the ruined buildings
which, in some places, united with the high wall at
the back of the breach; but this descent, as well as
the summit of the breach, and almost every point from
whence the approaches could be seen, was strongly
manned with infantry, who poured a murderous fire
on the assailants, while the batteries in the castle
kept up an incessant discharge of grape and shells.

The gallant soldiers who headed the assault continued their desperate efforts and fresh troops filed
out of the trenches to replace the casualties; the Wyneck-
en's notes,
MSS.
volunteers now also joined in the close conflict on the
breach, and the German detachments sought bravely
to gain a footing; but in vain!—destruction spread
amongst the crowded ranks of the assailants as they
became exposed to the insurmountable obstacles
which met their progress;—no man outlived the at- General
Graham's
despatch.
Jones's
Sieges.
tempt to gain the ridge, and the devoted soldiers were
seen vainly struggling at the summit of the breach,
or lying dead or wounded at the bottom.

Nearly two hours of the most sanguinary conflict
had thus passed, and there was every reason to fear
that the contest would be prolonged until the rising
tide would oblige the assailants to retire, when a
detachment of Portuguese under major Snodgrass
forded the river in beautiful order, and attacked the
right breach, and a second column followed to the
support of the main assault; but these efforts did no

more than feed the attack ; the garrison retained
their posts, and continued their fire, and the fortress
was yet to be won.

Sir Thomas Graham seeing now the desperate
state of the beseigers, conceived the venturous experi-
ment of employing the breaching batteries in aid of
the assailants, and having consulted with colonel
Dickson, who commanded the artillery, upon the
practicability of doing so with safety to the allied
troops, he directed that the whole force of the batteries on the Chofre sand-hills, should be brought to
bear on the defences above the breach in the south-
east angle of the work.

In a few moments forty-seven pieces of artillery
opened against the traverse in rear of the breach.
This was a critical operation, for the shot passed
immediately over the heads of the troops who were
engaged in the attack, and the slightest deviation
would have been fatal to them; however, the prac-
tice of five days continued firing had given the
artillery officers so precise a knowledge of the range,
that no casualties occurred among the assailants, and
the fire was directed with such effect, that the garrison were obliged to retire behind more distant cover
and slacken their musquetry fire. The right battery
on the isthmus also joined in this operation with
great effect, its guns being directed against the south-
east angle, and the interior of one of the eastern
breaches : the riflemen in the advanced trench also
picked off many of the defenders.

A tremendous explosion along the ramparts soon 1813
shewed the result of the well-directed fire of the allied August.
artillery. The whole of the combustible materials, Jones's
Sieges.
which the enemy had accumulated there for the de-
fence of the traverses and interior works, ignited, and
exploding along the entire extent of the high curtain,
killed and wounded many of the defenders, and threw
the rest into the greatest confusion. The assailants,
taking immediate advantage of the effect, renewed
their efforts, and impetuously rushing forward, obtained possession of the first traverse. Here a fierce
conflict ensued; but the defenders were driven back,
and abandoning the ravelin and hornwork, they withdrew also from the retrenchment of the eastern breach.
The troops instantly lowered themselves down by
the ruins, and forced in by the other breaches in
rapid succession;—then vigorously following up their
success, at length obliged the garrison to take refuge
in the castle, and convent of St. Teresa, leaving seven
hundred prisoners in the hands of the allies.

Batteries were now erected by the besiegers on the
works of the town, and a powerful bombardment
was commenced against the castle. This was continued for eight days, forming a concentrated fire,
which proved irresistible, and on the 9th of September the garrison, consisting of eighty officers and
one thousand seven hundred and fifty-six men, laid
down their arms to the allied troops.

The casualties of the assailants in this protracted
siege amounted to two hundred and ten officers, and

1813.

September

Jones's
Sieges.

Guelphic
Archives,
MSS.

Journals of
battalions,
MSS.

three thousand five hundred and seventy men ; the assault on the 31st of August alone cost the besiegers more than five hundred killed, and fifteen hundred wounded; and had not a mine been accidentally discovered, which the garrison had formed under the breach, the whole body of the assailants must inevitably have perished upon that occasion. Sir James Leith while conducting the attack with great judgment and gallantry, fell severely wounded, and was indebted to his orderly, Henry Voigt, of the first hussars, for a safe conveyance through the enemy's fire. The legion lost captain Heine of the first line battalion, who was mortally wounded in the breach on the 31st of August ; lieutenant von Rossing of the same battalion was also wounded, and inclusive of these officers, the German detachments had nineteen men killed and forty-eight wounded.

CHAPTER XIII.

We must again revert to the allied army on the Catalonian coast, which under lord William Bentinck became engaged with the French under marshal Suchet, after the departure of sir John Murray.

In the beginning of August lord William had prepared for besieging Tarragona, but Suchet advanced to its relief with an army of twenty thousand men, and the British general, not considering his mixed corps equal to contend with so strong and well organized a force, withdrew to Cambrills. Suchet immediately destroyed the works of Tarragona, took away the garrison and threw up redoubts which covered Barcelona; the allied troops then returned to Tarragona, the harbour of which was a valuable rendezvous for the British fleet, and in the beginning of September lord William Bentinck moved forward to Villafranca and pushed on an advanced corps to Ordal. This corps consisted of the second battalion of the twenty-seventh regiment, the fourth line battalion of the legion under colonel du Plat; the Calabrian free corps, and three Spanish battalions. About midnight on the 12th of September these troops were attacked by the enemy in great

1813.

September

Captain
Müller's
despatch.

force, and the advance became involved in a serious contest. An old redoubt which commanded the main road from Barcelona to Villafranca was occupied by two companies of the twenty-seventh, the skirmishers of the fourth battalion of the legion under lieutenant Bacmeister, and those of de Rolls corps under captain Müller, who commanded the whole. This small force, numbering about eleven hundred men, resisted for a considerable time, the repeated attacks of the enemy, but being at length overpowered by numbers and reduced by various casualties, they were obliged to abandon the work and retire. Captain Müller, however, rallied his men behind some old ruins, and having been joined by the Spanish battalions on his left, the whole charged and regained a part of the position. Again they were driven from this post, and a second time also did they recover it ; but meantime, the French had swept round by the right and turned their flank, which obliged the gallant detachment to retire with precipitation. Their opponents now came on in such force, that the allied troops found it necessary to disperse among the mountains in order to secure their safety, and four guns fell into the hands of the enemy.

Lord Bentinck immediately put the whole army in motion for the coast; Suchet's cavalry pressed closely after, but the Brunswick hussars charging with distinguished gallantry, kept them in check ; many times did these brave men stop the threatened onset of the French troopers by anticipating their attack ; even the formidable cuirassiers were forced to give way, and towards midnight Suchet, giving up the pursuit, allowed the allies to proceed unmolested to Siljas, from whence they embarked on the night of the 13th.

Twenty-five men of the fourth line battalion were killed, and eleven wounded in this affair; lieutenants Graaffe and Bacmeister of the same battalion were severely wounded, and the injury sustained by the former was so severe that he soon after died.

The fall of St. Sebastian opened a passage to the Batty's western Pyrenees. left wing of the allied army, and the marquis of Wellington prepared to cross the frontier. Until the surrender of Pampluna, however, no extended plan of operations could with safety be commenced, and he therefore, only proposed, as a preparatory step, to cross the Bidassoa with the left wing of the army, and occupy a range of heights extending from the great mountain of La Rhune to the sea. The 7th of October was fixed for this operation, when it was directed that the British and Portuguese under sir Thomas Graham should cross by fords at the lower part of the river opposite Andaye, while the Spaniards under Don Manuel Frere, crossed higher up in front of Buriston; the light division under Charles Alten were at the same time to attack the enemy's posts in the mountains of Commissari, and pass of Bera, while the Spaniards under Giron on the extreme right, assailed the position of La Rhune.

Fording the Bidassoa in the presence of an enemy

1813.

October.

Batty's
Western
Pyrenees
is an operation of no ordinary difficulty for a large army, and requires the greatest unity of action and precision of arrangement; for the tide rises sixteen feet, and the least accident or delay, might not only defeat the object, but cause serious consequences.

On this occasion the well concerted movements of the different columns were attended with complete success. Soon after seven o'clock on the appointed day, it being then low water, a rocket was fired off as a signal, and the several columns, preceded by their light troops, crossed the sands and entered the

Journal of
major Rau-
tenberg.
MSS.
river. The first division, led by the light battalions of the German legion formed the two centre columns; these had to wade up to their middle in water, and several of the men were wounded, and fell into the

Batty's
Western
Pyrenees.
stream; so great, however, had been the caution observed in the preparatory steps, that the heads of the columns were nearly half over, before the enemy noticed their approach, and commenced firing; but the light troops soon gained the opposite side, and attacking the French picquets with rapidity, drove them from the various natural defences behind which they had been posted, and the main columns following steadily, took up their formation for attack. A pontoon bridge, was now laid down for the passage of the artillery, and cannon from the heights of St. Marzial covered these movements.

The operations succeeded at every point. The fifth division dislodged the enemy from each successive position which they took up, and the light division

was equally fortunate, on the mountain of Commissari. The French at this part were strongly en- October.
trenched, and their hut camps, situated on a rocky Batty's
steep, were fortified and defended by works at every Pyrenees.
eminence; the attack of these was, consequently
attended with great hazard, and the bold and determined conduct of the allied troops, who charged
repeatedly with the bayonet, could alone have overcome the obstacles with which they were opposed.

Nothing could exceed the gallantry of the light
division both at this point and the pass of Bera, and
Lord Wellington expressed his sense of the able
manner in which their movements were conducted
by major-general von Alten.*

The Spaniards in attempting to gain possession of
La Rhune were not at first so successful as the troops
on the left; a post on the summit of the mountain
made a short resistance, and it was not until the
following morning,—having bravely continued their
attacks throughout the night,—that they eventually
gained possession of the post.

The whole loss of the allies in this operation did
not exceed one thousand five hundred and sixty, including officers, of which number the legion formed Rautenberg's
one hundred and twenty-three, the casualties falling Journal.
MSS.
principally in the first light battalion; lieutenant
von Klencke of this battalion was killed, captain
Rautenberg was severely wounded, and captain

* "I am particularly indebted to major-general Alten for the manner in
which he executed this service." Marquis of Wellington's Despatch.

Hulsemann, lieutenants Wahrendorf, and Gibson, and sixty-three non-commissioned officers and men were also wounded; lieutenants Lemmers, Atkins, and Marwedel, with thirty-six non-commissioned officers and men of the second light battalion were wounded, as also lieutenant Hesse of the second line battalion.

The French now retreated to a position in front of St. Jean de Luz, and formed upon a strong range of heights covering that town, the whole front of which was entrenched and defended by a series of redoubts. The allies encamped upon the ground which they had gained, and here Lord Wellington decided upon remaining until after the fall of Pampluna.

Towards the close of October the French were observed making great exertions to complete their defensive works. Soult had failed in every attempt to relieve Pampluna, and at length on the 31st, after a blockade of four months, the garrison, having exhausted all their provisions, surrendered to Don Carlos d'Espana. The covering army under sir Rowland Hill was thus liberated, and preparations were immediately made by the British chief for renewing hostilities.

The intrenchments in front of the enemy's right wing were considered by Lord Wellington too strong to admit of an attack in front, and he therefore decided upon assaulting the centre and left; but here also the French position was guarded by a strong line of redoubts and intrenchments.

The assault of the enemy's line was fixed for the

morning of the 10th of November, when, soon after three o'clock, the troops began to descend from the heights. They silently advanced to the verge of the line of out-picquets, each brigade arriving at its appointed station an hour before dawn, when all were ordered to lie on the ground with the utmost silence until the signal should be given for the attack.

The right wing under sir Rowland Hill was concentrated in the valley of Bastan; the right centre under marshal Beresford in the valleys between the mountain of La Rhune and the pass of Echelar; the light division under Charles Alten formed the left centre, supported by the Spanish corps of general Longa, and was assembled in front of the pass of Bera; the space between the right and left centre was occupied by the Spanish army of reserve under Don Pedro Giron, and that between the left centre and left wing of the army by the Spaniards under Don Manuel Freyre.

The left wing under sir John Hope,* consisting of the first division under major-general Howard (including the infantry of the King's German Legion under major-general Hinüber), and the fifth division under major-general Hay, together with lord Aylmer's brigade, occupied the whole space from thence to the sea,

* Sir Thomas Graham had left the seat of war after the passage of the Bidassoa, to take the command of an expedition intended for the liberation of Holland, and sir John Hope succeeded to the command of the left wing of the allied army.

R

Sir Stapleton Cotton supported the centre with Victor Alten's brigade of light cavalry. General Vandeleur's brigade supported the right of the first division, and part of the heavy cavalry brigade of the legion was on the left.

The French had constructed a redoubt round the ruins of a small chapel, upon a ridge of hills in advance of their right, which was supported by a force of four hundred men stationed close in the rear. A battery was thrown up by the allies within a short distance of the redoubt, and from this point the attack on the enemy's out-posts was commenced.

A little before sunrise some British guns opened upon the redoubt, and the whole line was soon called into action. A warm cannonade ensued, but after some time, the British artillery had nearly silenced that of the enemy in the redoubt, and now the light brigade of the German legion under colonel Halkett, moving round the hill, menaced the rear of the French, while the picquets made a sharp attack upon their front.

Exposed to a hot fire of musquetry from the intrenchments, the troops rushed forward, and soon gaining possession of the advanced post, drove the French down the hill, to the verge of the fortified position.

The light troops of the brigades on the left also drove in the picquets in their front; the village of Urogne was carried, and the fifth division pushed forward to the inundations which covered the intrenchment in front of Ciboure, and the heights in advance of fort Socoa.

While these successful advances were going on upon the left, the first brigade of guards under colonel Maitland, and the three line battalions of the German legion under general Hinüber marched against the formidable intrenchments which covered the heights immediately behind Urogne, and extended along the hills towards Ascain. The legion battalions were on the left, the guards on the right; and upon the right of these was the Portuguese brigade of general Wilson. Opposite to the point from whence they advanced the French had constructed a remarkably strong redoubt to cover the approach to their position by the Bera road; this was opposed by a battery of British artillery from the opposite hill, and a hot cannonade ensued; but although suffering much from the British guns, and the fire of the skirmishers of the guards and legion, the enemy tenaciously defended this post.

Meantime, the principal movements of the day had been carried on with complete success upon the right and centre. Sir Rowland Hill attacked the enemy's intrenchments on the left bank of the Nivelle, while the Spaniards under Morillo moved against the village of Ainhouë; the centre under marshal Beresford attacked the French centre in the camp of Sarré, and the light division under Charles Alten assaulted and carried the intrenchments upon la Petite la Rhune; and then, supported by Longa's Spaniards, attacked the redoubt opposite the same mountain.

On all points these movements were attended with

success. By a tenacious defence of a redoubt in the centre, the enemy gave time for the troops under Beresford to get so far into their rear that retreat became impracticable, and a whole battalion, nearly six hundred strong, was captured.

Soult did not appear to have discovered the object of his antagonist's movements until one o'clock in the day, when he detached a division from his right wing to support the centre; but it came too late, and the allies, pursuing their successes, crossed the Nivelle, and separated the French centre from their left.

The second and sixth divisions under generals Stewart and Clinton, and the Portuguese division under general Hamilton, now attacked the enemy's left wing in the strong fortified position behind Ainhoüe and successively dislodged them from three redoubts contiguous to the Nivelle.* Sir Rowland Hill then directed a part of these troops to push forward in the direction of Souraide and Espelette, and thus compelled the extreme left of the enemy to take refuge in the mountains towards St. Jean Pied de Port.

The centre of the allied army crossed the Nivelle opposite St. Pé, and thus a considerable part was

---

* Corporal Rangenier of the first hussars was orderly to general Clinton, and distinguished himself by capturing a gun at the head of a detachment of the seventy-second regiment. Guelphic archives. ·MSS.

established in rear of the French right wing; night
now put an end to the pursuit and the allies bivouacked on the ground which they had so bravely won.

The total loss of the British and Portuguese in this
action did not exceed two thousand six hundred officers
and soldiers.   Lieutenant Boyd of the first line bat- Appendix No. XIII.
talion, and twenty-eight men of the German battalions
were killed, and five officers and one hundred and
twenty-five men were wounded; the chief casualties
occurred in the second light battalion; among the
officers were three severely wounded, and captain
von Heimbruch of the first light battalion lost his
left arm.*

The French right wing retreated during the night
from its position in front of St. Jean de Luz and the
lower Nivelle, leaving about fifty pieces of cannon in
the works, but they injured the bridges to such an
extent that sir John Hope was unable to press upon
the retiring columns.

It was noon on the 11th before a flying bridge
could be constructed for the passage of the artillery;
the greater part of the troops forded the river, and
as the ford was broad enough to admit of their crossing by platoons, the passage was effected in the
greatest order; torrents of rain fell, but the soldiers
buoyant under their late successes, moved on in the

* A company of the second light battalion of the legion under lieutenant
Behne, having been driven back during the action of the 10th, and its commander severely wounded, and about to fall into the hands of the enemy;
corporal Hofmeister gallantly rallied a few of the men, and rescued his officer.
Guelphic archives MSS.

highest spirits. The left wing bivouacked for the night on a ridge of hills extending from Guethary towards Espelette. The weather became now so severe, breaking up the roads and swelling the rivulets, that Lord Wellington did not deem it expedient to attempt any further advance for the present, and on the 18th of November, the army was placed in cantonments, head-quarters being established at St. Jean de Luz.

The French now withdrew the greater part of their troops into an intrenched camp in front of Bayonne, guarding, however, the right bank of the Nive, and communicating by patroles with a division at St. Jean Pied de Port. The allies formed a line of out-posts for the protection of their cantonments, and thus things remained until a favourable change of weather in the beginning of December enabled the troops to resume their march. Lord Wellington's object was to endeavour to establish the right wing of his army on the opposite bank of the Nive in such a manner as would interrupt the direct communication between Bayonne and St. Jean Pied de Port; on the 9th of December, accordingly, the left wing, under sir John Hope moved forward by the great road leading from St. Jean de Luz towards Bayonne, while Charles Alten with the light division, advanced from Bassusarry along the road leading from St. Pé. These movements were made for the purpose of menacing the enemy's intrenched camp, and withdrawing their immediate attention

from that part of their army which occupied the
right bank of the Nive, and against which the principal attack under marshal Beresford and sir Rowland
Hill was directed.

About three o'clock in the morning the troops of
the left wing commenced their march on the road to
Bayonne. The rain fell heavily, tearing up the road
and rendering their progress difficult and fatiguing;
at dawn, however, it ceased, and the whole of the
first and fifth divisions having assembled, they moved
forward in columns of battalions, headed by the light
brigade of the German legion, the skirmishers of
the legion line battalions, and the light companies of
the fifth division,—the whole forming a chain of
skirmishers in front of the column.

Soon after eight o'clock the allied line of light
troops commenced a spirited fire on those of the
enemy; but these tenaciously held their ground,
contesting every point that afforded shelter, and from
whence they could take deliberate aim. Aided
by the British artillery, however, the allied skirmishers advanced, and, the columns following, the
enemy retreated before them to Anglet. About one
o'clock the first division gained the heights on the
right of the Bayonne road opposite Anglet, the light
infantry driving the enemy down the slopes to the
intrenched camp, and the fifth division made equal
progress on the left.

While the left wing of the army under sir John
Hope was thus engaged, the light division under

general Alten, making a corresponding advance, gallantly drove the enemy from behind a deep morass which covered their advanced posts in front of Bassussary, and compelled them to retreat to the intrenched camp near the chateau de Marac.

Meantime Beresford had crossed the Nive at Ustaritz, while Hill attacked the troops stationed behind that river, opposite Cambo ; these operations were attended with complete success, and the enemy became enclosed in a sort of crescent before Bayonne.

Major Augustus Heise of the second light battalion of the legion, who served as assistant adjutant-general to the second division and had distinguished himself throughout the whole of these operations, was severely wounded in this attack.

It had been previously arranged that the left wing should retire to its old position as soon as the right wing had accomplished its object, and at six o'clock in the evening they commenced their march towards the cantonments ; it was quite dark, the rain fell in torrents, and the road had been so broken up by artillery, and the passage of troops, as to be nearly impassable. Many men fell down completely exhausted by the road side, and the fatigued state in which the whole arrived at St. Jean de Luz, after having been on foot for nearly twenty-four hours, may well be imagined.

At dawn on the 10th, the enemy moved out of Bayonne and attacked the allied left wing. They advanced in two strong columns, the first by the great road from Bayonne against the outposts of the fifth division, the second by the plateau of Bassussary against the light division, which lay intrenched in the village of Arcangues : they also shewed an intention of penetrating towards Arbonne in rear of the two divisions. 1813.

December.
Batty's western Pyrenees.

The attack on the fifth division was severe, the brunt of the action falling on the first Portuguese brigade, and that of general Robinson which moved up to its support, and the exposed situation of these troops caused them a considerable loss. But the allies made a gallant reprisal : the enemy were advancing through an orchard and thick coppice wood against Barouillet, when a Portuguese regiment from the left flank, led forward by captain George Decken,*—who, with great gallantry and intelligence volunteered his services at the critical moment— wheeled round upon their rear, and the ninth regiment in like manner, attacked them from the right. The French, in order to avoid being cut off, faced about, and meeting with the furious attack of the two regiments, suffered considerable loss : the gallant captain Decken was severely wounded. Wellington's despatch.
Batty.
Notes of captain Christoph Heise, MSS.
Rigel's sieben jährigen Kampf.

About mid-day the allies were reinforced at this point by the guards, and the enemy were obliged to give up the contest, with the loss of nearly five hundred prisoners. Batty.
Despatch.

Meantime sir Rowland Hill, finding that the main

---

* Of the first German hussars, aide-de-camp to sir Stapleton Cotton.

part of the French troops had been withdrawn from
the heights of Monguerre, advanced to that position,
and established his right upon the left bank of the
Adour, his centre upon the heights in front of Vieux
Monguerre, and his left upon the Nive, opposite
Villefranque, where a pontoon bridge kept up a
communication with the rest of the army.   Thus the
allies became posted upon the circumference of a
circle, of which Bayonne formed the centre; but their
communications were divided by the Nive, and they
had the worst possible roads to march in case of
support being required on either flank: great facilities
were therefore afforded to the enemy for making
separate atttacks on the allied army.

At the close of the contest of this day, and about
an hour before dusk, the regiments of Frankfort and
Nassau-Usingen under the command of colonel
Kruse, instead of returning to Bayonne with the rest
of the French troops came over to the allies, and
joined the liberators of their country.

The first division occupied Bidart during the night
of the 10th, to be in readiness to support the fifth in
case of a renewal of the attack on the following
morning; but the French withdrew at night, and in
the morning, the light troops of the fifth division
drove in their picquets.   All was quiet until two
o'clock on the 11th, when the enemy commenced a
furious attack along the Bayonne road, driving in the
picquets on their supports.   Although this was
unexpected, and the men had actually gone out to

cut wood for cooking, in a few moments the whole
line was in perfect order, and ready to receive their
opponents. The Portuguese and fifth division again
sustained the enemy's onset with firmness, and after
a severe contest, continued until night, both armies
remained in the position which they had before
occupied.

A hot skirmish was kept up during a great part of
the 12th; some brave officers were killed and many
wounded, but no serious attack was made by the
enemy, and the left wing maintained its position.
Conceiving now that the attention of the British
commander was chiefly occupied in securing the
defence of his left, Soult withdrew the great body of
his army within the intrenched camp at Bayonne,
leaving merely a chain of out posts in front of sir
John Hope's corps; but Wellington penetrated his
adversary's design, and made immediate preparations
to support the troops under Hill, which he concluded
would be now attacked.

These anticipations were quickly verified. Soon
after eight o'clock on the 13th, the out-posts on the
great road leading from St. Jean Pied de Port through
St Pierre to Bayonne were sharply attacked by
overwhelming numbers of French tirailleurs, who
followed by their columns, crowded up the long slopes
in front of the centre position of the allies, while a
large body at the same time advanced against the
left centre. A most destructive fire was opened from
the British and Portuguese batteries upon the French

columns, causing great havoc in their ranks; the light companies of general Barnes's brigade were driven back by the masses of the enemy, who succeeded in establishing themselves upon a height close to the position, and here a long and obstinate contest was kept up. At length a gallant charge of the ninety-second Highlanders, supported by the Portuguese, drove the enemy from the position.

The attack upon the left centre was equally formidable, and the troops in the other parts of the line were also sharply engaged; but on all points the enemy were defeated, suffering immense loss in each attack, and notwithstanding his great superiority in numbers, Soult completely failed in his design.

Hill now resolved to dislodge the French from the ground in front of their intrenched camp, where they still remained in force, and general Byng was directed to lead the attack with his brigade. The gallant general executed this task in the most heroic manner, carrying in his own hands the colours of the sixty-sixth regiment, and planting them on the hill which formed the enemy's position. The French were now driven down within the suburb of St. Pierre; all their attempts to recover this point were repulsed, and Soult became at length convinced of the utter hopelessness of any further effort to regain his lost ground.

The French marshal therefore withdrew his troops in the night within their intrenched camp, and Hill established his advanced posts opposite to the valley of St. Pierre.

1813.

December.

Batty's
western
Pyrenees.

Thus brilliantly terminated the harrassing contest in which the army had been engaged for the last five days; but these important results were attended with serious losses.

One hundred and sixty-nine officers and two thousand five hundred and sixteen non-commissioned officers and soldiers were killed, wounded and taken of the British alone, and the total casualties of the allied troops amounted to the enormous total of, three hundred and two officers, and four thousand seven hundred and twenty-seven non-commissioned officers and soldiers.

But the loss of the enemy was still greater: in the battle of the 13th, the ground was covered with their slain, and their whole loss in the five days contest is supposed to have amounted to six thousand men.

The casualties of the German legion were principally confined to the light brigade. Captain Frederick Wynecken, lieutenants Elderhorst, M'Bean and Meyer were wounded, the latter severely, five men were killed and sixty-one serjeants and soldiers were wounded.

The first division now marched back to its old cantonments, and head quarters were re-established at St. Jean de Luz. To guard against surprise, telegraphic signal stations were formed at the churches of Guethary, Arcangues, and Vieux Monguerre which communicated with another at St. Jean de Luz. By these means notice could be immediately given at head-quarters of any movement which the enemy might undertake, and thus time afforded to the British chief to meet his opponent's designs.

It is necessary here to state some changes and casualties which, towards the close of this year, occurred in the German legion.

A want of efficient light cavalry existing in the allied army, the first and second dragoons, which since their formation had been equipped and employed as heavy cavalry, were, by an order of the 25th of December, directed to be henceforth called the first and second light dragoons of the King's German legion, and equipped accordingly.

Major-general von Bock, who commanded this brigade, obtained leave of absence to visit Germany after the cessation of hostilities in December, and embarked at Passages together with captain Hodenberg of the first dragoons his brigade-major, and captain Bock of the second dragoons his aide-de-camp; but these officers were destined never to rejoin their corps; for the vessel was overtaken by a storm in the bay of Biscay, where she foundered, and every soul perished.

The gallant colonel von Arentschildt of the first hussars after conducting his distinguished regiment throughout the whole of the Peninsular campaign in a manner which repeatedly drew forth the marked approbation of the commander in chief, was obliged to yield to the broken state of his health, and, giving up the command of the regiment to major von

Gruben, he sought to re-establish his strength at
Lecumberris in the rear; the command of Bock's
brigade devolved upon lieutenant-colonel von Bulow;
general Victor Alten obtained leave of absence to
visit England, and the command of his brigade, now
consisting of the first hussars of the legion, and the
eighteenth English hussars, was entrusted to colonel
Vivian.

CHAPTER XIV.

The cessation of hostilities was employed by the British chief in giving a more complete and effective organization to the allied army. Several reinforcements had arrived at Passages, and the numerical strength of the British being considerably increased, a new arrangement of corps became necessary. The whole allied force was divided into three columns, the first or right wing under sir Rowland Hill, the second or centre under sir William Beresford, and the third or left wing under sir John Hope; the reserve was formed of the Spaniards and one division of Portuguese.

The infantry of the legion was formed into two brigades under major-general Hinüber and lieutenant colonel Louis von dem Bussche, the former commanding the line, and the latter the light battalions, and both remained in the first division now commanded by sir John Hope. The artillery, consisting of major Sympher's battery, remained attached to the fourth division, and the cavalry consisting of general Bock's brigade under lieutenant-colonel von Bülow, and the first hussars under major von Gruben formed part of the great cavalry division commanded by sir Stapleton Cotton.

The artillery of the left wing was placed under the command of colonel Hartmann of the German artillery, who also was subsequently entrusted with all the artillery arrangements connected with the intended siege of Bayonne.

A great difficulty was at this period found in providing forage for the cavalry horses. Corn or hay was not to be procured, and it was found necessary to have recourse to turnips and furze in order to support the horses. The extraordinary good condition of the German cavalry under these difficult circumstances, was a theme of general admiration, and drew forth expressions of surprise from the general commanding the cavalry. But the fact was that the German dragoons with that consideration for the horse which characterizes their nation, had sacrificed their own wants to produce this effect, giving their rations of bread to the horses, and preferring rather to live in a state of comparative starvation, than to see their faithful beasts become emaciated, and unequal to the service which they might be called upon to perform.

The new year opened with most active operations. General Buchan's brigade had been stationed at la Bastide, on the right bank of the Joyeuse river, and on the 3d of January it was attacked by the troops under Clausel, who succeeded in establishing themselves upon the heights of la Costa on its left bank. The alarm was immediately given at St. Jean de Luz; the centre and right were concentrated, and on the following day the guards and German infantry took up the alignement of the left wing, relieving the fifth division.

Lord Wellington intended to have attacked the enemy on the 5th, but the state of the weather obliged him to defer it until the following day, when the third and fourth divisions, supported by general Buchan's Portuguese and the heavy cavalry brigade of general Fane, drove back the French from the ground to which they had advanced, and the allied troops resumed their former position without loss.

The outposts of the left wing were now employed in the construction of a large redoubt on the table land behind Barouillet, as well as in the formation of a strong line of intrenchments along the whole front of the left wing, with batteries for artillery. This work was continued until the 21st, when the enemy withdrew nearly all their outposts in front of the intrenched camp.

The inclemency of the weather now checked the further operations of the allies, and it was not until the 15th of February that the troops were again put in motion.   On this day the guards and line brigades of the legion took up a position on the table land in the neighbourhood of Biaritz, their left extending to the sea, and their right communicating with the fifth division, which occupied a line along the plateau of Bassussarry to the Nive: the light brigade of the legion with the light companies of the guards held the outposts in front of the first division.

The heights of Monguerre were occupied by the
fourth division, communicating on the Nive with the
fifth, and resting its right on the Adour; thus three
divisions of the army effectually observed Bayonne,
and Wellington was enabled to employ the rest of
his troops against Soult, who, leaving the defence of
Bayonne to a garrison of ten thousand men under
general Thouvenot, assembled the remainder of his
army behind the Gave de Pau, Gave d' Oleron, and
the Bidouze.

Sir Rowland Hill had driven in the French
outposts on the Joyeuse on the 14th, and a movement
having been then made upon the enemy's left at
Hellete, Harispe was obliged to retreat towards St.
Palais, and Mina's Spaniards, who had been driven
by him into the passes of the Pyrenees in the
preceding month, were now enabled to descend from
the mountains and blockade St. Jean Pied de
Port. General Hill pursued the enemy to Garris on
the 15th, and the following day he crossed the
Bidouze.

The French now retired behind the Gave de
Mouleon, and nearly at the same moment the British
crossed at Arriverette. Here the enemy made some
resistance, but eventually retired behind the Gave d'
Oleron, and took up a position at Sauveterre covering
the road leading to Orthes.

The right of the allied centre was now moved up
to support sir Rowland Hill, and on the 21st, the
light division under Charles Alten, and the sixth

division under general Clinton, were united to the right wing, Orders were also given for the left wing to pass the Adour, and the division of Spaniards under Freyre, which had returned within the Spanish frontier, crossed the Bidassoa, and again encamped on the French territory.

At midnight on the 22d, the first division of the allied army filed into the great road leading to Bayonne. Owing to the extreme darkness of the night, some difficulty and delay was experienced by the troops, but before day-break the whole reached the sand hills which bound the coast from the vicinity of Biaritz to the mouth of the Adour: from these hills to the enemy's intrenched camp, stretches a large pine wood called the Bois de Bayonne.

The enemy's picquets were dislodged on the morning of the 23d by the light brigade of the legion under colonel Bussche; and the line brigade under general Hinüber, together with the second brigade of guards under general Stopford moved towards the mouth of the Adour, accompanied by a train of pontoons and a battery of horse artillery. The first brigade of guards marched at the same time through the Bois de Bayonne, taking with them the eighteen pounders, and the whole debouched from the wood nearly opposite to Boucaut. The heavy guns were then brought to the bank of the Adour, and placed in battery on the extreme left, fronting the right of the intrenched camp, and a brigade of guards was placed behind some sand hills close to the marsh which

protected the enemy's front. Meantime the Spanish
corps advanced to the heights above Anglet, while
lord Aylmer's brigade and the Portuguese completed
the line to the Nive; the fifth division drove in the
picquets between the Nive and the Adour on the
other side, and thus Bayonne became closely invested
by the allied left wing.

1814.

February.

Batty's
western
Pyrenees.

Previous to these movements preparations had been
made for the formation of a bridge across the Adour,
which it was proposed to construct of Spanish
chasse marcè, being decked vessels of from thirty to
fifty tons burthen; these were to have come round
to the mouth of the Adour on the 23d, under the
protection of the British squadron, but contrary winds
delayed their arrival until the 25th.

In order to secure a footing on the right bank prior
to the arrival of the bridge vessels, it was determined
to attempt conveying over a detachment of troops.
The river was about three hundred yards wide at
this point, and the current ran at the rate of seven
miles an hour at ebb tide. The only means for
crossing at the disposal of the allies were five pontoons
and four small boats which the men had carried on
their shoulders across the sand hills, and with these
they proceeded to attempt the passage. Fortunately
the attention of the garrison was completely occupied
by the demonstration upon their camp, and the
movement of the right wing under sir Rowland Hill;
the width and depth of the river, and its rapid current,
were also obstacles which naturally prevented them

from directing their observation to the movements of
sir John Hope's corps, and its position was completely
concealed from the view of Bayonne by a bend in the
river, and the large wood on the right.

A brisk fire was kept up by the batteries of the
left wing upon the enemy's intrenched camp during
the whole morning of the 23d, and some rockets
discharged amongst the gun-boats produced great
consternation.* While their attention was thus
occupied, every effort was made to ferry over
the troops at the mouth of the river, and before
evening six companies of guards, and two companies
of the sixtieth, together with a few rockets, amounting

* The flag-staff at the stern of a French corvette was carried away by an
eighteen pound shot, and the ensign which it bore, fell into the water; seeing
which a private of the first light battalion of the legion, named Lehmann,
throwing off his accoutrements, jumped into the river and made for the flag.
A heavy fire of musquetry was immediately poured upon him from the deck of
the corvette, but being an expert swimmer, he evaded the shot, and brought
away the flag in triumph. This exploit was rewarded by a liberal subscription
from the officers who witnessed it, and Lehmann, a social spirit, employed the
donation in treating the men of his company to a bottle of Lafitte each. This
brave fellow was also a singular character: Previous to entering the legion,
he had served in the West Indies, and there acquired a taste for strong liquors,
but he never suffered this propensity to interfere with his duty, and, after
receiving the balance of his pay, used regularly to apply for leave of absence
from evening roll call, and quietly spend his money in one sitting. Wishing
to re-visit his home and friends in Hanover, after the cessation of hostilities
in 1814, he took his discharge from the legion, and was considered to have left
the service altogether; but on the 17th of June 1815, just after the first light
battalion had arrived in the position of Waterloo, Lehmann made his appearance, and offered his services as a volunteer in the company to which he
formerly belonged! They were accepted; but the gallant soldier shared the
fate of many a brave man in the fierce contest of the following day, and fell,—
although a simple Hanoverian rifleman,—worthy of a place among the best
and bravest of his distinguished comrades.—Notes of captain Christoph
Heise. MSS.

altogether to about five hundred men, were conveyed to the right bank. The French now discovered their neglect, and sent down two battalions amounting to upwards of one hundred and thirty men, to oppose the British.

General Stopford, who commanded the detachment, made the most judicious dispositions of his little force, and two batteries of artillery were so placed on the left bank as to flank the assailants. These, however had little effect, but the rocket men placed themselves between the enemy and the detachment, and when the French, advancing in full confidence, had arrived within three or four hundred yards of the British line, a few rockets thrown into the midst of the dense columns, spread such consternation amongst their ranks, that facing about, they retreated in the greatest disorder. The rocket men followed, and now the extraordinary scene presented itself, of a strong body of infantry flying before some dozen assailants. But the new and formidable weapon with which these were furnished, had struck terror into the enemy, and they did not stop until they reached the citadel, while twenty-five of their body, the greater part badly wounded, fell into the hands of the detachment.*

Correspondence of general Hinüber. Narrative of general Hartmann. Notes of captain Christoph Heise. MSS.

The following day the remainder of the first division was ferried across, and the same afternoon the flotilla appeared in the offing. A bar of sand

---

* The French say that they would certainly have beaten the British detachment on this occasion, had it not been for these *diables de fusées*; one rocket alone is stated to have killed nine men.—Hartmann's Narrative,—Heise's Notes. MSS.

which extends from the right bank of the river
nearly across its mouth renders the entrance to the
Adour extremely dangerous, and a tremendous surf,
accompanied by a heavy gale of wind, now rolled
over the bar, presenting fearful difficulties to the
vessels. Several boats were swamped in the surf,
or upset and their crews drowned, but the intrepidity
and perseverance of the English naval officers was not
to be deterred, and the weather moderating towards
evening, a long line of chasse marée's passed safely
across the bar, and sailed up the river.

On the 25th, the first division advanced towards
the citadel, pivoting its right flank on the Adour, and
the left extending to the great road leading from
Bayonne to Bourdeaux ; it closed into the verge of a
deep marshy ravine, which separates the high ground
about the citadel from the surrounding country, and
thus intercepted the enemy's communications with
the open country to the north of the Adour, and
completed the investment of the camp and fortress.

During these movements a feint attack was kept
up against the intrenched camp from the opposite
side of the river, and the construction of the bridge
was carried on with rapidity. This was completed
by the afternoon of the 26th, when a firm passage,
equal to support the weight of artillery, was fully
established.

The successful advance of the right and centre had
separated the main body of the allies from the left
wing, which now became an independent corps

unconnected with the other operations. Soult 1814.
continued to give way before the British chief, and February.
his left having been turned by the passage of the Batty's
Gave d' Oleron by sir Rowland Hill on the 24th, he western
Pyrenees
retreated in the night to Orthes, and took up a strong
position behind the Gave de Pau.   This was attacked
by the allies on the 27th, when, after an obstinate
contest, the French were defeated, and Soult was
obliged to fall back upon St. Sever.

In this action, major Sympher's battery of German Narrative
of major
Daniel.
MSS.
artillery, which was attached to the fourth division,
bore a distinguished part.   Placed in a narrow
ravine on the left, where it was exposed to the
crossing fire of the enemy's guns, it had many
difficulties to contend with, and suffered considerable
loss, but the gallantry and persevering activity of the
officers and men, brought the guns to bear with
effect, and it continued throughout the day to pour a
destructive fire into the enemy's ranks.   These honors
were, however, clouded by the loss of the brave
major Sympher.   While at the head of the battery,
and in the act of ordering up one of the guns from
the rear, he was struck by a cannon shot in the chest,
and instantly deprived of life.

Soult's retreat was at first conducted with good
order, his troops manfully contesting the ground, but
Hill threatened his rear by a parallel line of march,
and the French then sought safety in flight, hastening to reach Sault de Navailles before the allies.
The cavalry under sir Stapleton Cotton, pressed close

on their rear, but they succeeded in passing the little
river in front of Sault, before Hill could come up.
Six pieces of cannon and many prisoners were taken
from the enemy; the allies had about one hundred
and eighty killed and one thousand two hundred
wounded. Among the officers severely wounded was
captain George von der Decken, aide-de-camp to sir
Stapleton Cotton.

On this day, the troops of the left were also put in
motion. The object of sir John Hope was to make
a closer investment of the citadel of Bayonne and
gain possession of the intrenched heights of St.
Étienne which are situated close to the place, and in
some measure, command it.

Correspon-
dence of
general
Hinüber.
Notes of
lieutenant-
colonels
Wynecken
and von
Rettberg.
MSS,
It was arranged that the centre of the enemy's
position at St. Étienne should be attacked by the line
brigade of the King's German Legion, under major-
general Hinüber; the right, by the light brigade
under colonel Bussche, and the left by the guards;
it so happened, however, that the movement against
the centre was commenced before that against the
flanks, and the brunt of the action fell upon the line
battalions of the legion.

No sooner did the enemy discover the advance of
the German troops than they opened a hot fire upon
them, their picquets disputing the ground from behind
the garden walls of the numerous villas on the heights,
while a heavy fire was poured down from the village
and fortified church of St. Etienne, as well as from
the line of intrenchments on the Bourdeaux road.

General Hinüber immediately decided upon 1813.
storming the village which was the key to the enemy's February.
position, and lieutenant-colonel Bodecker of the first
line battalion was directed to conduct the attack. Hinüber's correspon- dence, &c.
This officer accordingly advanced with six companies MSS.
of his battalion, supported by the fifth line battalion,
while the light battalions under Bussche pressed
forward on his left, and pushing vigorously up the
heights, he carried the place in the most gallant
manner. At the same time the skirmishers of the
first and fifth battalions, under captain von Rettberg
and lieutenants von Brandis and Wilding, supported
by the companies of captains von Borstel and
Hodenberg, and the second line battalion under
lieutenant-colonel von Beck attacked the intrenchments on the Bourdeaux road. These intrenchments
were extremely strong, all the contiguous houses
being loop-holed, but the brave assailants stormed
them with the bayonet, captured a gun, and made
prisoners of two officers and about forty men. This
assault brought the troops within two hundred yards
of the advanced works of the citadel, from whence a
galling fire was poured upon them, and, for the
moment, they were unable to bring away the gun.

About five o'clock in the afternoon, a strong
column of the enemy was seen again advancing from
the citadel to retake the position. These were
immediately met by the skirmishers of the first and
second line battalions, part of those of the fifth under
colonel Ompteda, and the companies of captains

1814.

February.

Hinüber's
correspon-
dence, &c.
MSS.
Purgold and Wenkstern of the second line battalion. A general charge was made by these troops against the enemy with the bayonet, which drove them back, but unwilling to relinquish so important a position, they rallied in the course of half an hour, and renewed the attempt. The same troops again charged and put them to flight, rushing on with a degree of impetuosity that was not to be withstood, and on this occasion they brought away the gun,

The brigades now maintained the post with the same determined spirit which they had shewn in the attack, and no farther effort to regain it was this day made by the enemy.

The loss of the legion on the 27th, was extremely severe. The officers, setting a noble example to their men, exposed themselves with a degree of intrepidity which nothing could exceed, and justly entitled them to a high place in the official account of the engage-

Appendix
No. XIV.
ment. Lieutenant Charles Meyer of the second line battalion was killed, and lieutenants Heimbruch of the first, and Witzendorf of the second light battalion were mortally wounded ; major Chuden, captains Rautenberg, Frederick Wynecken, Petersdorff, Borstel, Rettberg, William Rautenberg, Linsingen ; lieutenants Wolrabe, Fahle, Tobin, Holtzermann, Atkins, Witzendorf, Marwedel, Rossing, Wilding, Drysdale, Wichmann, Decken, Augustus Meyer, Rothard, Schauroth, Korsham, and Klinsöhr were all wounded, the greater number severely ; general Hinüber received a contusion, and altogether the killed, wounded

and prisoners in the five battalions, amounted to not
less than three hundred and twenty-eight officers
and soldiers.*

On the morning of the 28th, the enemy made a partial sortie, falling upon the picquets under captain Christian Wynecken, of the first light battalion; the attack was bravely repulsed, but not without some loss to the Germans in killed and wounded: among the former was lieutenant Elderhorst.

A new line was now taken up by the allied pic- quets, which confined the enemy still closer within the place. The right, formed of the guards, rested on the Verrerie de St. Bernard close to the Adour; from thence the line ran in a curve to St. Etieune, which was held by the infantry of the German legion, and the Portuguese formed the termination on the left, which also rested on the Adour, about a mile above the suburb of St. Esprit.

Preparations were now made for commencing the siege. Lieutenant-colonel Hartmann of the German artillery was entrusted with the chief direction of the artillery and engineer departments, and under the vigilant superintendence of this able officer, the necessary operations went rapidly forward.

The duty of the troops became extremely harassing; the weather was most inclement, and the work of the trenches could only be done with safety during

---

* The total absence of any mention of the German legion in the official despatch which reported these operations to the British government, gave rise to a correspondence between general Hinüber, his Royal Highness the Duke of Cambridge, and the adjutant-general of the allied troops, which will be found in the appendix.—See No. XIV. B.

the night : added to this was the danger of surprise, and the possibility of the enemy attempting to destroy the bridge of vessels and thus cut off the principal line of communication for the allied troops. So many were the casualties to which this part of the army were exposed, and so urgent the necessity for constant vigilance, that during the whole period of the investment, the men were never permitted to take off their clothes.

The accuracy of the French artillery-men in pointing their guns was conspicuous. It frequently happened that men were shot while stepping from behind the walls and hedges which had concealed them ; a remarkable instance of this occurred in the case of a soldier of the German legion, who had been posted at the angle of a large house with directions to look round the corner from time to time, but on no account to remain exposed. Unfortunately he placed one leg beyond the angle of the building, and in a moment it was carried off by a cannon shot. Lieu-

tenant Charles Hedemann, a promising young officer of the first light battalion, lost his leg by a twenty-four pound shot on the 30th, and died in consequence. Similar instances occurred in other regiments; in short no man could venture to shew himself for a moment, and it was found necessary in order to obtain a knowledge of the enemy's movements, and to gain timely information of any attempt against the bridge, to establish a code of signals between the besiegers and the gun boats that were stationed in the river.

Great scarcity of provisions was at this time experienced in the army, and the prices of all articles became exorbitant; but by degrees the peasantry brought in their produce to the village of Boucaut, and a tolerable market was established there; the prices, however, continued enormous, the most trifling article invariably costing three times its real value.

While the left wing of the army was thus engaged in the investment of Bayonne, the marquess of Wellington was successfully following up the victory which he had recently gained at Orthes. Sir Rowland Hill overtook that part of Soult's force which retreated by Aire, and after a sharp contest drove it from its position. Bock's cavalry brigade of the legion under lieutenant-colonel von Bülow is mentioned by Lord Wellington as having made a "most handsome movement" on the 19th March upon the enemy's rear guard, driving them through the vineyards and town of Vic Bigorre, where they had taken up a strong position. The German dragoons had seven men and twelve horses killed, twenty-two men and fifteen horses wounded, and captain Seyer was taken prisoner.*

The main body of the enemy marched upon St. Sever, and then turning suddenly round, remounted

1814.

February.

Batty's western Pyrenees.

Journal. of brigade. MSS.

* Corporal Hofmeister of the first dragoons led the advanced guard of captain Fisscher's squadron, and dashing forward with three men against the enemy's advance, in the most intrepid manner, he forced a defile, cut a French officer from his horse, and opened a path for the squadron, which charging, overthrew a superior number of the enemy's chasseurs.—Guelphic Archives. MSS.

the course of the Adour towards Tarbes. This move-

ment laid open to the allies the direct road to Bour-

deaux and Lord Wellington immediately detached marshal Beresford with a part of the troops to that city which he entered on the 12th of March. The British squadron under admiral Penrose entered the river on the 27th, and soon after, the Gironde was open from its mouth to Bourdeaux.

The Duke of Angouleme and a small suite had arrived at St. Jean de Luz from England in the beginning of January, and the news of his presence spreading over the country, the people in many places publicly expressed their sentiments in favour of the royal family. Numerous desertions now thinned the ranks of the French army, and every where the inhabitants welcomed the advance of the allies. Part of Suchet's army from Catalonia had joined Soult, but but this was not sufficient to check the victorious career of Wellington. Backed by his gallant army, and encouraged by the almost universal sentiments of the French nation, he carried on his successful progress in the south of France, harassing the French marshal at every step, and every day becoming more effective in the numbers and condition of his troops.

At this time the allied sovereigns leading great masses of men, were rapidly advancing upon the French capital. All attempts to bring Napoleon to such terms as were consistent with the security and interests of Europe, had been unavailing, and they marched on in the full confidence of being able to dictate a peace at Paris. On the morning of the 31st of March they entered that capital; a capitulation was signed;—a provisional government formed; and by a decree of the conservative senate of the 2d of April, Napoleon was declared to be dispossessed of the throne of France, and all hereditary rights were pronounced to be abolished in his family. The fallen Emperor made strong efforts to renounce the crown in favour of his son, but eventually submitted to the stipulation, that the island of Elba should be his sole territory and residence for the remainder of his life,—a suitable allowance being made him, as well as the Ex-empress, who was further to receive the duchies of Parma and Placentia.

The intelligence of these events had not, however, yet reached the south, and the operations of Wellington's army were carried on with undiminished vigour. Every preparation for the siege of Bayonne was made by the corps under sir John Hope, while the main army continued to press rapidly after Soult. This general had taken up a position at Tarbes, on the right bank of the Adour, which was to have been attacked by the allies on the 20th of March, but the marshal seeing the danger with which he was threatened, withdrew in the night and commenced a retrograde movement upon Thoulouse, which he reached on the 24th. The allies followed, but owing to the bad state of the roads, did not arrive before the town until the 27th, when they

Wellington's despatch.

T

found the enemy busied in fortifying every approach to the position which they had taken up in front of that place.

CHAPTER XV.

1814.
April.
Welling-
ton's des-
patch.
Memoirs of
Welling-
ton.

'The town of Thoulouse is surrounded on three sides by the canal of Languedoc and the Garonne, on the left bank of which river the fortified suburb of St. Cyprien formed a good bridge-head.　Each bridge of the canal was also fortified, and defended by the guns of the town.　Between the canal and the river Ers on the eastward runs a range of heights over which pass all the roads to the town from this direction, and these the enemy had fortified with five redoubts connected by lines of intrenchment.

As the roads from Ariege to Thoulouse were impracticable for cavalry and artillery, and nearly so for infantry, lord Wellington had no alternative but to attack Soult in this formidable position.　After some unsuccessful attempts to establish a bridge, and find a practicable approach to Thoulouse from the right bank of the Garonne, a pontoon bridge was laid down on the 4th of April across the river below the town, and here the troops under marshal Beresford commenced crossing the same day.　The third and sixth divisions, with some light cavalry filed over in safety, but as soon as the artillery of

1814.
April.
Narrative
of major
Daniel.
MSS.

these divisions was brought upon the bridge, it gave way, and it was found necessary to have the horses and limbers removed and the guns taken over by the men. The fourth division now passed, leaving captain Daniel's battery on the left bank. At this moment the stream began to rise, and it was at great risk that Daniel was enabled to bring over four of his guns, leaving the other two under lieutenant Hartmann, on the left bank. The river now rose to such a height that it became necessary to remove part of the bridge, and the light division as well as the Spaniards were prevented from crossing; so that only about fifteen thousand men, thirty guns and a few light cavalry were on the right bank, exposed to the risk of being attacked by a superior force of the enemy.

Luckily the French were too much occupied in completing their intrenchments to direct attention to Beresford's troops, who took up their quarters without molestation, in a small town about two miles on the road to Montauban, while the Spaniards and light division resumed their communication with general Hill, who stood in front of St. Cyprien.

By the 8th the river had fallen sufficiently to admit of the pontoons being replaced, and lieutenant Hartmann was enabled to join the battery; the Spaniards under Freyre and the Portuguese artillery under Victor Arentschild also crossed to the right bank.

These troops immediately moved forward to the neighbourhood of the town, and the eighteenth hussars under colonel Vivian, with captain Poten's squadron of the first German hussars, boldly charging a superior body of the enemy's horse, drove them from the village of Croix d' Orade, made several prisoners and gained possession of an important bridge over the Ers, which led to the enemy's position. The allied squadrons lost a few men and horses, and colonel Vivian was severely wounded.* The pontoon bridge was now removed and laid down higher up the river near Ausonne, where the light and third divisions crossed on the 10th, and the whole corps was united for the intended attack.

The plan of operations was that marshal Beresford should cross the Ers with the fourth and sixth divisions at the bridge of Croix d' Orade, gain the heights of Mont-blanc, and marching, up the river, turn the enemy's right, while the Spanish corps, supported by the British cavalry should attack the front. Sir Stapleton Cotton was to follow the movements of Beresford, with a cavalry brigade, and the first hussars of the legion with the eighteenth hussars were, under the command of major von

* A picquet of eight men of the first hussars under sergeant Westermann gave considerable effect to the charge of the eighteenth, by crossing a wide and deep ditch which covered the enemy's flank, and threatening an attack. Westermann's brave and skilful conduct drew forth the approbation of colonel Vivian, who made a public acknowledgment of the services of the gallant sergeant after the affair.—Guelphic Archives. MSS.

Gruben,* to observe the movements of the enemy's cavalry on both banks of the Ers, and beyond the allied left wing.

The third and light divisions under generals Picton, and Charles Alten, and the brigade of German dragoons under lieutenant-colonel von Bülow were to observe the enemy on the lower part of the canal, and threaten the bridge-head, while general Hill menaced the suburb on the left bank of the Garonne.

These arrangements were forthwith carried into effect. Beresford crossed the Ers, and his columns, led by the fourth division, carried the heights of Mont-blanc with great spirit. He then moved up the river, crossing a most difficult country, while the Spaniards and Portuguese artillery prepared to attack the front. The fourth and sixth divisions carried the heights on the enemy's right, as well as the redoubt which covered and protected that flank, but the right of general Freyre's division was repulsed, and, with the exception of one regiment, the whole corps was driven back upon the Ers with heavy loss. The Spanish staff officers made the most gallant exertions to restore order, and the Portuguese artillery under Arentschild firmly maintained their ground, but the French forcing on with impetuosity,

* Colonel Arentschild had been removed to the command of the German heavy brigade on the 10th of March; but after colonel Vivian had been wounded, on the 8th, was appointed to the command of his brigade. He was called upon however, to remain in personal attendance on lord Wellington during the battle of Thoulouse, and consequently the command of the hussar brigade devolved upon major von Gruben, and that of the first hussars on captain Ernest Poten.

received no check from these efforts, and the two English divisions might have been cut off from the Ers bridge, had not the light division under Charles Alten aided by the continued support of the Portuguese artillery under Victor Arentschild, boldly advancing, checked the pursuit; and the French were driven back into their position.

The fourth and sixth divisions under Beresford ascended the steep heights on the right, with the greatest gallantry, and established themselves on the enemy's line, where they awaited the arrival of the guns. These had hitherto been directed against the redoubts from the deep ground below, and the German battery under captain Daniel was distinguished for the skill and gallantry which its officers displayed in maintaining a most effective fire from so unfavourable a position. The delay occasioned by the removal of the guns, caused a momentary suspension of the attack, and Soult employed the interval in strengthening his reserves in rear of the heights: meantime general Picton had suffered a severe check at the canal bridge near the Garonne.

Captain Daniel's battery; that of the sixth division and a six pounder battery of horse artillery were soon in motion for the heights, but the approach was extremely difficult; the German battery being in advance, was stopped by a deep ditch, in order to cross which, it was necessary to unyoke the horses, and carry over the guns by hand; the English horse battery in attempting to dash across, broke

Daniel's
narrative.
MSS.

1814.

April.

Memoirs of
Welling-
ton.

some shafts, and the horses of the other were so exhausted, that the assistance of captain Daniel's team was required in order to get the guns over.

Supported by their artillery, the two divisions now advanced in line against the redoubts, while the Spaniards being re-formed, moved against the enemy's front, supported by Arentschild's guns. The French anticipating the attack, rushed forward and assailed the sixth division in front and flank, and a furious struggle ensued, but the British bayonets prevailed; the enemy were driven back in confusion, and the two principal redoubts, as well as the fortified houses in the centre of their position, were carried by general Pack's brigade. Soult was still unwilling to relinquish his strong works, and forming a new line, made desperate efforts to regain the redoubts, but without effect; the sixth division, following up its successes, continued to press along the ridge of heights from the left, while the Spaniards and Portuguese artillery steadily assailed the front, and case shot and Shrapnel shells from the English and German batteries swept the enemy's ranks or

Daniel's
narrative.
MSS.

damaged their guns. It was about this time that the battery of the sixth division was ordered to the support of general Pack's brigade, but the horses were so unequal to the work that it fell upon the German battery of the fourth division. Two guns were accordingly ordered forward under lieutenant Blumenbach, and this brave and talented young officer was receiving instructions from captain Daniel

as to the position which he was to take up, when a
cannon shot felled him to the earth.

This was one of the last shots fired by the French,
who seeing the preparations which the allied troops
were making for carrrying the rest of their position,
abandoned the remaining redoubts, and rapidly
passing the canal, took shelter in the city.

Although this action did not give much scope for
the operations of cavalry, a squadron of the first
hussars of the legion, under captain Schaumann was
much distinguished: the hussar brigade under major
von Gruben, it will be remembered, was directed to
observe the movements of the enemy's cavalry on the
allied left; and in the course of these operations it
had occasion to file over a small wooden bridge in a
valley. Captain Schaumann's squadron formed the
advanced guard, and, having passed the bridge, it
advanced by divisions towards some heights which
were occupied by the enemy's skirmishers. These
fell back as the squadron approached, and discovered
an entire French hussar regiment, formed in close
column upon a broad deep road, bounded by hedges,
and having one squadron pushed forward in front:
this regiment covered the road from St. Martin. In
order to reach the enemy it was necessary for
Schaumann to break his squadron into sections of
threes, which dangerous evolution before an enemy
he accomplished without interruption, and was
enabled to form line about one hundred and fifty
paces from the French squadron. His force

did not exceed twenty-eight file, while that of the enemy's advance was far superior in number and also outflanked him ; however, Schaumann boldly led his squadron forward at full speed against his opponents. The French awaited the charge, pouring in a heavy carbine fire among the German hussars as they approached; but undismayed, these bold horsemen pressed on, and came upon the French squadron with such effect, that it was thrown back upon the column in its rear, and the whole fell into confusion. The column being unable to deploy, horses and men were crushed together in frightful disorder ; many sprung from their saddles and ran away, leaving the rest to the mercy of the hussars, and finally the scattered troopers reached an open plain, where they managed to reform, but the hussars continuing to advance, the French soon gave up this position, and retreated towards Thoulouse, blowing up a bridge, and thus securing themselves from further molestation.

Nearly fifty of the enemy were taken prisoners on this occasion, and several men were killed and wounded ; others lost their horses, glad to escape on foot; altogether the entire loss of the French squadrons is supposed to have been not less than a hundred men, while that of the Germans did not exceed five or six men killed, and a few horses wounded: lieutenant Conrad Poten was also wounded.

Schaumann's squadron was now moved to the left, towards the bridge of Montaudran, over which a

broad road led to Thoulouse; and here it was
reinforced by the remainder of the regiment under
captain Poten. This bridge was strongly barricaded
with casks filled with earth, and was defended by
the twenty-second regiment of French chasseurs; but
a few spirited fellows of Schaumann's squadron
volunteered to remove the casks, and jumping from
their horses, although exposed to a sharp carbine fire,
they succeeded in throwing some of them into the
river, and thus opened a passage for the rest of the
troops.* Poten now led the hussars forward,—
charged boldly the opposing squadrons, and driving
them rapidly across the plain, caused the whole to
take shelter under their guns : at this moment the
fourth division carried the first redoubt, and the
action became general.†

On the morning of the 11th, a troop of the hussars
was sent to Longa, from whence a detachment under
lieutenant Blumenhagen, advancing to the village of
Caramin, surprised a picquet of thirty *gens d'armes*,
and made the whole prisoners : colonel Arentschild
this day resumed the command of the brigade.

---

* Hussars Gothard and Mertens are mentioned as having been prominent
on this occasion. Guelphic Archives. MSS.

† The distinguished gallantry of captains Schaumann and Poten and the
first hussars of the legion on this day, was published in terms of high
approbation by sir Stapleton Cotton, in the cavalry orders of the 11th of
April ; this was followed on the 14th, by a farewell letter of acknowledgment
of the general services of the regiment during the war, addressed to colonel
Arentschild : a testimonial of military merit which can hardly be exceeded.—
See Appendix XV. and XVI.

1814.

April.

Poten's
Journal.
MSS.

At four o'clock on the morning of the 12th, the French blew up the bridge over the canal, and they were soon seen in full retreat on the road to Villefranche. The broken bridge was made passable with all expedition, and captain Poten received orders to follow the enemy with his squadron of hussars. On arriving at Bassiege sir Stapleton Cotton directed one troop to be detached to some heights on the left, where the general himself repaired for the purpose of reconnoitering, while Poten pressing forward on the high road with the rest, came up with the enemy's rearguard of cavalry, about half a mile beyond the place. The French were marching in column of divisions, and Poten, having first ascertained that he had only cavalry to deal with, ventured to charge the column with his single half squadron. The two leading divisions were overthrown, and crowding back upon the rear in confusion, the whole hurried on in retreat; Poten followed to the village of Ville Nouvelle, about two miles distant, where some infantry appearing in support of the enemy, he withdrew; but twenty-seven captured men and twenty-five horses, bore testimony to his daring attack.

Sherer.

The victory of Thoulouse cost the allies more than six thousand five hundred men, in killed wounded and missing; among these were several superior

Batty.

officers, and it was a cause for deep regret to learn by the arrival of two accredited officers from Paris, on the evening of the 12th,—bringing intelligence of

the termination of the war,—that a timely intimation 1811.
of the proceedings there, would have prevented this April.
fierce and sanguinary battle.

The same officers, colonel Cooke, and the French Batty.
colonel St. Simon, sent forward a communication to
sir John Hope, as they passed through Bourdeaux ;
but it was not official, and that general did not feel
himself authorized in doing more than directing the
officers at his out-posts to communicate the intelligence to the French officers on the advanced picquets.
The enemy however, paid no attention to the notice,
but seemed, on the contrary, determined to take
advantage of the absence of any official intelligence,
by commencing more active hostilities.

At one o'clock in the morning of the 14th, a Narratives
of majors
von Einem
and Heim-
burg MSS.
Batty's
western
Pyrenees.
Correspon-
dence of
general von
Hinüber.
MSS.
Notes of
colonel
William
von der
Decken.
MSS.
deserter from the garrison of Bayonne presented himself at the British outposts. He was immediately taken
to general Hay, who commanded the picquets, to
whom he related "that the garrison intended to make
a sally,—that they were already drawn out in the
market place for that purpose,—that an extra
allowance of spirits had been issued to the men, and
that the attack would be first made upon the Spanish
posts, on the other side of the Adour." General Hay
having but an imperfect knowledge of the French
language, was not able thoroughly to understand this
communication, and sent the man to general Hinüber,
who interrogated him, and immediately sent his
brigade-major, captain von Drechsel, with the
particulars to general Hay.

However, notwithstanding this warning, and whatever measures may have been taken to meet the threatened attack, the British picquets, composed of the first brigade of the fifth division, were surprised.

The French, commencing about three o'clock with a feint attack upon the out-posts in front of Anglet, appeared in about half an hour afterwards moving up the slope of the hill on which the picquets were stationed. They advanced upon this point in two columns, and rushing forward with loud cries of "*En avant,*" quickly broke the line of posts between St. Etienne, and St. Bernard, while another column advancing direct upon the village of St. Etienne, cleared the place, killing the sentries, dispersing the picquets, and throwing the whole into the greatest confusion.

General Hinüber, who had not failed to warn his brigade of the expected attack, and had assembled the several regiments on the alarm place, no sooner heard the firing on the other side of the river, than he led forward the first, second and fifth line battalions of the legion, in fine order, upon the village of St. Etienne. This place was then in full possession of the enemy. The first brigade of the fifth division, which held it, had been driven back, as well as the picquets of the guards, and second light battalion of the legion, which were posted on the ground between the Bourdeaux road and the Adour. Of the picquets in St. Etienne about twenty men under ensign Oliver of the thirty-eighth, had alone recovered from the shock,

1814.

April.

Narratives &c.

and these, gallantly joining the second line battalion of the legion, advanced with it to the attack. Hinüber directed the fifth line to march straight upon the church-yard of St. Etienne; the first battalion to press forward on its right, and the second to attack by the high road from Peyhorade to Bayonne. Four companies of the latter under major Chüden, supported by three companies of the first light battalion under captains von Goeben, Gilsa, and lieutenant Hartwig, favored by the nature of the ground, came first in contact with the enemy, and charging furiously with the bayonet, soon obtained possession of the village. The guards, and three companies of the second light battalion of the legion under captains Holtzermann, Wackerhagen, and Frederick Wynecken, charged with equal success upon the right, and before four o'clock, not only was St. Etienne again in complete possession of the allies, but the whole of the ground from whence they had been driven, between the Bourdeaux road and the Adour.

The French made many attempts to renew the attack on the British line, sending out swarms of tirailleurs, and masses of men to renew the fight; but these were invariably driven back; a field piece was now brought to bear upon the retreating columns, and by six o'clock the firing had altogether ceased.

The British sustained a considerable loss in this unfortunate and unnecessary engagement, and several disasters happened among the principal officers in command. General Hay was killed, sir John Hope and his staff were severely wounded and made prisoners, general Stopford was also wounded, and the whole loss in killed, wounded, and missing was estimated at eight hundred. Among these the German legion were severe sufferers: captain Frederick von Drechsel, brigade-major to general Hinüber, a young officer of high acquirements and great promise, was killed; major Chüden, captain Müller, lieutenants Meyer and Köhler were also killed; colonel von Beck, captains Hulsemann, Frederick Wynecken,* Notting, Wackerhagen, lieutenants Behne, Fleisch, and Wolrabe were wounded, the greater number severely, and about one hundred and eighty non-commissioned officers and soldiers were killed, wounded, and missing: lieutenant-colonel Hartmann, commanding the artillery, was also wounded.

On the 27th, an official communication at length reached general Thouvenot, containing a copy of the convention, and marshal Soult's adhesion to the Bourbon government; the white flag floated above the citadel on the following day, and three hundred

---

*Frederick Wynecken,—as brave a soldier as ever commanded a company, —was very severely wounded by one of the last shots; he had volunteered his services in the charge on the right; and so great was the estimation in which he was held by the men of the light brigade of the legion, that, on his being carried past the camp in a litter, a few days after the fight, both battalions voluntarily turned out before their tents, and gave him three cheers: an honor which although it might not, perhaps, be considered extraordinary among English soldiers, was very remarkable in a German corps.—Notes of captain Christoph Heise, MSS.

rounds from the French artillery, welcomed the
restoration of their legitimate sovereign†.

† The mortified feelings of the French officers at the termination of the war, led them to frequent acts of unprovoked insult towards the officers of the allied army; duels were of constant occurrence, and among the rest an affair in which lieutenant von Düring of the fifth line battalion of the legion was concerned, excited considerable notice. In this case the French officer had invited several ladies "to see him shoot a British officer;" but they only assembled to see the vain braggart fall; for the Frenchman's pistol missed fire, and Düring's ball killed his opponent on the spot. This duel had the good effect of stopping all further insult on the part of the officers of the garrison of Bayonne, who, it is but justice to the French army generally to add, reckoned amongst them many men who had been lately promoted from among the non-commissioned officers and the ranks.

CHAPTER XVI.

OPERATIONS OF THE ANGLO-SICILIAN ARMY.

1814.

March.

While the successes of Wellington's gallant soldiers in the south of France were thus drawing the war to a close, the operations against the French in the Italian states were carried on with vigour, as well by king Murat,—now co-operating with the Austrians against Beauharnois,—as by the anglo-Sicilian army under lord William Bentinck. On the 9th of March a force of eight thousand men landed from Palermo at Leghorn, where lord William, taking the command, issued a proclamation, in which he called upon the Italians to unite with him in effecting the deliverance of their country. This was met by considerable reinforcements from the Italian states, and a force of more than fifteen thousand men was soon assembled at Leghorn. Among the troops employed in this service were the third, sixth and eighth line battalions of the German legion under major-generals von Barsse and von Hohnstedt; captain Bindseil of the German artillery had the charge of a rocket battery; some gunners of the third German battery

Annual
Register
1814.

Narrative
of major
Schaedler
MSS.

Journal of
3d foot
battery.
MSS.

also accompanied the expedition, and the following
officers of the legion served on the staff of the army :

Captain Münter, seventh line battalion, aide-de-
camp to lieutenant-general Macfarlane; captain
Delius, seventh line battalion, aide-de-camp to major-
general von Hohnstedt; captain von Hohnstedt, third
line battalion, brigade-major to major-general von
Barsse; captain Chüden, aide-de-camp to major-
general von Barsse; lieutenant Appuhn, third line
battalion, brigade-major to major-general von Hohnstedt; lieutenant Schaedler, sixth line battalion,
deputy-assistant-quarter-master-general.

Leaving major-general von Barsse as commandant
in Leghorn, lord William Bentinck proceeded
towards Spezia, and on the 20th of March, his
advanced guard under lieutenant-colonel Travers,
reached Sarzana on the river Magra. The skirmishers
of the eighth line battalion of the legion under captain
Charles Poten, led the advance, and found, on
arriving at the river, that the enemy had taken over
all the boats to the other side. Poten called out for
volunteers to swim across and bring over a boat, and
immediately three spirited fellows of the company,
Ehmann, Deppelt, and Fürstenberg, presented
themselves, and plunging into the rapid stream,
although exposed to the enemy's fire, gained the other
side and brought back the desired means of conveyance. The skirmishers then crossed, and driving
back the enemy, captured several guns, and a
considerable quantity of ammunition.

1814.

March.

On the 24th, fort Santa Croce situated at the mouth of the river Magra was stormed and carried by Poten's skirmishers in gallant style, and on the 27th, the advanced guard under colonel Travers occupied Spezia. The neighbouring fort of Santa Maria, however, held out until the 30th, when breaching batteries having been erected against it, and an effective fire poured upon the enemy's artillery-men by the German skirmishers*, it capitulated, and the allies were enabled to advance. Lord William Bentinck, having been informed that there were only two thousand troops in Genoa, determined upon making a rapid advance upon that city, and endeavouring to gain possession of it; but on arriving at Sestri he learned that the garrison had been reinforced, and now consisted of between five and six thousand men; he proceeded, however, on his march, but, owing to the bad state of the roads, was not able to concentrate his army until the 14th.

Lord William Bentinck's despatch

The country is extremely mountainous and difficult, and the troops met with considerable obstruction from

---

* Serjeant Schultz was conspicuous for his intelligence and gallantry during these operations. In the attack upon fort Santa Croce he was one of the first to volunteer his services, and in the succeeding investment of Santa Maria, he and a few other fearless men of the company, voluntarily brought away several casks of powder which were discovered in a house between the place and the allied lines, (exposing the besiegers to considerable danger,) and with great expertness, applied the powder to supply the troops with cartridges, of which they were much in want. He afterwards volunteered to pick off the enemy's gunners, and, assisted by seven other good marksmen of the company, succeeded so completely that the artillery-men abandoned their guns, and sought the protection of their infantry—Guelphic Archives. MSS.

the enemy; on the 8th of April, however, the allies dislodged them from the strong country near Sestri; on the 12th, general Montressor's division drove the French from Monte Faccia and Nervi, and on the following day, established itself in the advanced position of Sturla. On this occasion the eighth line battalion of the legion under lieutenant-colonel von Schroeder, bore a conspicuous part, and suffered a loss of twenty-seven men in killed, wounded, and taken.

The French now took up a very strong position in front of Genoa, resting their left upon the forts Richlieu and Teckla; their centre occupying the village of St. Martino, and their right extending to the sea, through a most difficult country, thickly covered with country houses, the only communications to which were by narrow lanes, bounded by high walls. On the 16th, dispositions were made by the British commander for a general attack, which he purposed to carry into execution on the following morning. The eighth line battalion of the legion formed with the thirty-first English regiment, the left advance, commanded by major-general Montressor; the right was directed by lieutenant-colonel Travers; the third and sixth battalions of the legion, forming the brigade of major-general von Hohnstedt, were directed to move round by the mountains on the north of the fortress, for the purpose of cutting off the enemy's retreat; the second line of attack was commanded by major-general Macfarlane, and the sixty-second regiment formed the reserve. With the exception of

1814.

March.

Journal of 8th line battalion. MSS.

Lord William Bentinck's despatch

Notes of lieut.-col. Münter. MSS.

1814.

April.
another English regiment, (the twenty-first,) a detachment of the twentieth dragoons, three batteries of English artillery, a rocket battery, and a detachment of the staff corps and engineers, the rest of the troops were Italian, Calabrian and Greek levies.

The attack opened at day-break on the 17th along the whole line; the third Italians under lieutenant-colonel Ceravignac, carried with great spirit, a height in front of fort Teckla,—drove off the enemy, and took three mountain guns; part of the same regiment then moved up the hill towards fort Richelieu, while colonel Travers with the Calabrians, Greeks, and Poten's skirmishers*, descended from Monte Faccia, and got possession of the highest part of the hill above the fort. Some of the advance pushed forward to the foot of the wall, which so alarmed the garrison, that, fearing to be taken by escalade, they surrendered. Fort Teckla was now hastily evacuated, and the greater part of the garrison made prisoners, the consequence of which was, that the enemy's left, being exposed, immediately fell back.

Lord William Bentinck's despatch.

The movements against the French right were not less successful. The thirty-first regiment and the eighth line battalion of the legion led the attack, under the immediate orders of general Montressor, and became sharply engaged at the church-yard of St. Francisco de Albaro, where the eighth battalion lost some men, and lieutenant Brinckmann, the

Notes of lieut.-col. Münter. MSS.

---

* Narrative of captain Charles Poten. MSS.

adjutant, was wounded. This post, which formed the key of the enemy's right, was, for some time, firmly held, but the twenty-first regiment, having been sent forward from the second line by general Macfarlane, it was soon after evacuated. The houses and gardens from thence to the sea also afforded the enemy considerable means of resistance, and a detachment under lieutenant Schaedler mainly contributed to turn this flank*; however little serious stand was offered after the fall of the church-yard, and the enemy's left being turned, they at last retired precipitately into the town†.

During these operations the gun boats from the English ships of war, which had accompanied the expedition, opened upon the enemy's sea batteries, which were soon deserted, and the whole of their sea line without the walls was taken possession of by the English sailors and marines‡: a battery which had been planted on the cliff of the Albaro, and which had hitherto escaped observation, was luckily discovered by colonel A'court and captain Münter, and was immediately secured by two English companies.

By ten o'clock the allies were in full possession of the whole ground before Genoa, and at noon they took up a position within six hundred yards of the town, at a point from whence the defences could be easily destroyed. Preparations were immediately

1814.

April.

Notes of lieut.-col. Münter. MSS.

Lord William Bentinck's despatch.

---

* Appendix No. XVIII.　　† Lord W. Bentinck's despatch.
‡ Sir Josias Rowley's despatch.

made for erecting the necessary batteries; Sir Edward Pellew's squadron entered the harbour and anchored in front of Nervi, and it was expected that the assault would be given on the following day.

Lord
William
Bentinck's
despatch.
But in the evening a deputation of the inhabitants waited upon lord William Bentinck, with a request that he would agree to a suspension of arms until the expected intelligence of peace having been concluded, should arrive.   Lord William replied that these were arguments to use with the French commandant, but not with him; the next morning several communica-

Notes of
lieut.-col.
Münter.
MSS.
tions were conveyed by captain Münter between the governor (count de Fresias,) and the British general, and at length a convention was agreed on, according to which, Genoa was to be given up to the English and Sicilian troops.

A considerable quantity of naval and military stores, as well as six ships of war fell into the hands of the allies on this occasion; the French troops marched out with the honors of war on the 21st, taking with them six pieces of cannon, and a safe passage to their own country was secured to them.

The late events at Paris became now known in Italy; all hostilities ceased, and the allied troops broke up in different directions: the eighth

Journals of
battalions
MSS.
line battalion of the legion was removed to Corsica, and in the following June both this and the third battalion proceeded to England under the command of major-general von Barsse; the sixth and seventh line battalions, as well as the third foot battery still

remained in the Mediterranean, being stationed in
Genoa, Sicily, and the island of Ponza; captain
Kronenfeldt of the sixth battalion who, during the
two preceding years, had been acting as assistant
adjutant-general to major-general Mackenzie's division in Catalonia, was, after the surrender of Genoa,
left in charge of the adjutant-general's department in
that place; Genoa remained in the hands of the
British until the month of December, when it was
made over to the king of Sardinia, and the allied
troops were directed to act as auxiliary to that
sovereign.

CHAPTER XVII.

CAMPAIGN OF WATERLOO.

In accordance with the arrangement which had been made by the allied sovereigns at the treaty of Paris, Napoleon embarked for his reduced sovereignty of the island of Elba, on the 28th of April; a treaty of peace was ratified between France and the allied powers on the 30th of the following month, and on the 20th of June, peace was proclaimed in London.

The claims of the several powers were now to be discussed, and for that purpose a congress assembled at Vienna in the month of October.

Thither the victorious British chief, now raised to the dignity of Duke, repaired as Minister Plenipotentiary from Great Britain. Meantime the several armies broke up to return to their respective countries, and a happy termination to the sanguinary and protracted struggle seemed at length to have arrived.

The greater part of the British infantry embarked at Bourdeaux in the month of July, but the cavalry marched to the northern parts, from whence they could be conveyed to England without crossing the bay of Biscay.

1814.

April.

The cavalry and artillery train of the King's German Legion, however, were sent to Flanders, where also strong garrisons of English troops were left. The infantry of the legion had been increased by the arrival from Catalonia of the fourth line battalion, and the whole embarked for England about the middle of July.

Journals of
legion
MSS.

The restoration of Louis XVIII. to the throne of his ancestors, was not viewed with such feelings throughout France as gave much prospect of permanent tranquillity. The military class, which had advanced to a high degree of reputation under the victorious guidance of the fallen Emperor, became restless and discontented under the tame dynasty of the pious Bourbon, and panted for the excitement and glory of war. Other classes saw in the proceedings of the legislature a design to restore the old monarchical principles of government; the factious aggravated these feelings, and thus a mass of secret dissension and discontent accumulated and became diffused throughout the kingdom.

In England all was joyful anticipation of the blessings of peace; and the brave soldiers who had so much contributed to produce the desired result, were received with that warmth and admiration which their noble bearing deserved.

The Prince Regent, in order to mark in as especial

manner His Royal Highness's sense of the "valour, perseverance and devotion of His Majesty's forces during the long and arduous contest in which they had been engaged," issued a proclamation on the 2d of January extending the order of the Bath. By this arrangement the order was formed into three classes consisting of knights grand crosses, knights commanders, and knights companions, the two first ranks bearing the title of knighthood.

The distinction of knight commander was conferred upon the following officers of the King's German
Legion:—

> Lieutenent-general count von Wallmoden Gimborn.
>
> Lieutenant-general count von Linsingen.
>
> Major-general sir Charles von Alten.
>
> Major-general sir Sigismund von Löw
>
> Major-general sir Henry von Hinüber.
>
> Major-general sir William von Dörnberg.
>
> Major-general sir Colin Halkett.
>
> Colonel sir Frederick von Arentschildt.
>
> Lieutenant-colonel sir Julius Hartmann.

Six months had nearly elapsed since the congress assembled at Vienna, had commenced its proceedings, yet the various interests were found so difficult to arrange, that no important result had been announced; but suddenly an event occurred which united the opinions and concentrated the energies of all the plenipotentiaries.

The sovereign of Elba, notwithstanding the supervision of English and French cruizers, had contrived to maintain a communication with France, and now availing himself of the discontented state of that country, and the protracted discussions at Vienna,—but chiefly relying on the personal attachment of the military,—he determined upon making an effort to recover his lost empire; and embarking at Porto Ferrajo on the 26th of February, with about a thousand men, he landed at Cannes on the 1st of March.

No opposition was offered to his progress; on the 7th, reaching Grenoble, he was joined by Labedoyére with two battalions, and obtained possession of a train of artillery; on the 9th he entered Lyons amid cries of *Vive l' Empereur;* Macon, Chalons, Dijon and almost all Burgundy now acknowledged him as Emperor, and halting at Lyons, he issued decrees for the arrangement of his new administration.

Scott's life of Napoleon.

Ney had been sent forward by the king, with the troops of the neighbouring garrisons to oppose Napoleon's progress, and confidently declared that he would bring him back a prisoner; but the marshal, as well as his soldiers went over to their former chief; the remaining army of the Bourbons soon followed their example, and on the 20th,—the king having precipitately retreated to Lille in the preceding night,—Buonaparte made his triumphant entry into the French capital!

The news of this event reached the congress of Vienna in the middle of their deliberations, and tended immediately to concentrate their attention upon a subject of such paramount importance to the whole of Europe.

The representatives of the allied sovereigns issued a manifesto on the 13th of March, declaring that by breaking the convention which established him in the island of Elba, Buonaparte had " destroyed the only legal title on which his existence depended,— had deprived himself of the protection of the law, and manifested to the universe that there could be neither peace or truce with him."

By a subsequent document signed on the 25th of March, the allied sovereigns declared themselves resolved to maintain entire the treaty of Paris, and bound themselves each to keep constantly in the field a force of one hundred and fifty thousand men, "and not to lay down their arms but by common consent, nor until Buonaparte shall have been rendered absolutely unable to create disturbance, and to renew his attempts for possessing himself of the supreme power in France."

Batty's campaign of 1815.

The exertions of the different states fully corresponded with the spirit of their declaration. Troops from the most distant parts of the Austrian dominions began their march towards the Rhine on the 2d of April. The Russians scarcely arrived on their frontier, traversed back the whole of Germany; the Prussians assembled to the number of one

hundred and twenty-three thousand men and one
hundred and thirty-four pieces of cannon*; Bavaria,
Baden, and the minor states of Germany made
similar preparations, and reinforcements from
England were rapidly added to the British force in
Belgium.

These preparations were carried on with such
activity, that towards the end of May, about five
hundred thousand men had assembled on the French
frontier.

According to the original agreement entered into
between the British government and the King's
German Legion†, their period of service had expired,
and the whole might have returned to their homes
six months after the treaty of Paris; however very
few availed themselves of this position, and a new
engagement for six months was voluntarily offered
by the legion, and accepted by the British government, in the month of March.

This brought nearly the whole of the German
legion to Flanders; for the third and eighth line
battalions had arrived there from the Mediterranean
in the preceding October; those which had landed
at Portsmouth from France in July, were soon after
re-shipped for Ostend, and before the opening of the
campaign of 1815, the following regiments and

---

* Von Zech. Feldzug von Waterloo.

† See Letter of Service addressed to His Royal Highness the Duke of
Cambridge, Vol. 1. Appendix No. IV.

batteries of this corps were assembled in the
Netherlands :—

ENGINEERS.

Captain Appuhn.
Captain Wedekind.
Captain Meinecke.
Captain Schweitzer.
Lieutenant Unger.

ARTILLERY.

LIEUT.-COL. SIR JULIUS HARTMANN, COMMANDING.

First Horse battery,........ brevet-major Augustus Sympher.
Second horse battery, ... brevet-major Kuhlmann.
Fourth foot battery. .... captain Cleeves.
First and second companies.. lieutenant-colonel Bruckmann.

CAVALRY.

First dragoons,........ lieutenant-colonel von Bülow.
Second dragoons,...... lieutenant-colonel de Jonquières.
First hussars, ... lieutenant-colonel von Wissel.
Second hussars, ... lieutenant-colonel von Linsingen.
Third hussars,........ lieutenant-colonel Meyer

INFANTRY.

First light battalion,...... lieutenant-colonel von dem Bussche.
Second light battalion,.... major Baring.
First line battalion, ... major von Robertson.
Second line battalion,.... major Müller.
Third line battalion...... lieutenant-colonel von Wissel.
Fourth line battalion, ... major Reh.
Fifth line battalion, ... lieutenant-colonel von Linsingen.
Eighth line battalion, ... lieutenant-colonel von Schroeder.

These troops were brigaded as follows:—

The batteries of major Kuhlmann, major Sympher, and captain Cleeves were attached to the first, second Appendix No. XX. and third divisions respectively; the remaining companies of legion artillery*, were employed to supply the deficiencies in the other batteries, as also to furnish some officers and non-commissioned officers to two new raised batteries of Hanoverian artillery. The latter were attached to the fourth and fifth divisions under the command of captains von Rettberg and Braun of the legion artillery, superintended by major Louis Heise of the same corps, and both these and the legion batteries were placed under the chief command of sir Julius Hartmann.

The first and second dragoons of the legion were brigaded with the twenty-third English dragoons under major-general sir William von Dörnberg.

The first hussars were brigaded with the tenth and eighteenth English hussars under major-general sir Hussey Vivian; the second hussars with the seventh and fifteenth under major-general sir Colquhoun Grant, and the third hussars were brigaded with the thirteenth dragoons under colonel sir Frederick von Arentschild. The two light battalions of the legion were brigaded with the fifth

---

* The first and second companies of legion artillery, had been sent from England without horses or *matériel*, and were stationed in the fortresses under the command of lieutenant-colonel Bruckmann. From these companies, lieutenants Schulzen, Hugo, Heise, Haardt, and Lewis Heise were transferred to the Hanoverian artillery. Notes of captain Christoph Heise. MSS.

and eighth line battalions under colonel von Ompteda, and placed in the third division commanded by sir Charles Alten, and the remaining line battalions formed the first German brigade under colonel du Plat, in the second division commanded by sir Henry Clinton.

Batty's
campaign
of 1815.

The whole of the British, German and Belgian force, which was called the army of the Netherlands, and placed under the chief command of the duke of Wellington, amounted to seventy-five thousand men, of which about twelve thousand seven hundred were cavalry, and the artillery numbered about one hundred and sixteen guns*; of these troops little more than thirty three thousand were English, and those principally young second battalions, many of the most efficient regiments having been sent to America;

Appendix.
No. XX.

the German legion numbered seven thousand men with eighteen guns, and the remainder consisted of the troops of Brunswick, Nassau and Belgium, and the new raised Hanoverian levies.

The latter consisted of a subsidiary corps of fourteen thousand men, including two regiments of cavalry and twelve guns, and a reserve corps of nine thousand men with one regiment of hussars; the subsidiary corps, which was principally composed of regular regiments, had been stationed in the Netherlands since the termination of hostilities in the

---

* Batty gives the force of the English—German legion—and Hanoverian artillery present at the battle of Waterloo at one hundred and eight guns; to these the two batteries of the duke of Brunswick's corps have been added.

preceding year, but the reserve corps, which was in the pay of Hanover, consisted chiefly of militia (landwehr) and had been rapidly organized in Hanover by general von der Decken, immediately previous to the opening of the campaign; several officers and non-commissioned officers of the legion were transferred for temporary duty to the new raised Hanoverian regiments, and the third and fourth Hanoverian brigades were commanded by colonel Hugh Halkett of the seventh, and colonel Best of the eighth line battalion of the legion.

With the exception of the reserve, which remained under the orders of general von der Decken, and was not intended to be immediately employed in the field,—the whole of the Hanoverian troops were placed under the command of sir Charles von Alten.*

The entire army of the Netherlands was divided into two corps and a reserve; the first, under the prince of Orange, occupied Enghien, Braine le comte,

---

* In consequence of the general inexperience of the officers and non-commissioned officers of the new levies, a proposition was made to the Hanoverian government by sir Charles Alten, suggesting that the new raised troops should be allowed to volunteer into the infantry regiments of the legion, according to the practise of the British government with regard to the militia. This proposition was declined, and it therefore, became necessary to make another arrangement, according to which the legion battalions, then consisting each of ten companies, were formed into six companies, and the supernumerary officers and non-commissioned officers transferred for temporary duty to the Hanoverian landwehr,—chiefly to the battalions of the subsidiary corps: the captains of the legion thus removed, served as field officers; the subalterns took rank according to the dates of their commissions.—Notes of captain Christoph Heise. MSS

Nivelles and Soignies; the second, under lord Hill,
stood in Ath, Lens, Oudenarde, Grammont and the
neighbourhood; the reserve was placed at Ghent,
Brussels, and the adjacent places.

The chief command of the whole allied cavalry
was given to lieutenant-general the earl of Uxbridge:
the immediate superintendence of the Hanoverian
cavalry was entrusted to major-general Victor von
Alten.

Buonaparte left Paris on the 12th of June, and
seeing the importance of attacking the British and
Prussian troops before the Russians and Austrians
could come to their assistance, marched rapidly
upon Flanders, and by the 14th, concentrated
upwards of one hundred and twenty-seven thousand
men, and three hundred and fifty pieces of cannon,
in three large divisions close to the frontier*.

But although Napoleon, by wonderful exertions,
had been able to bring up this large army to the
Flemish frontier, his numbers were unequal to cope
with the united forces of Wellington and Blucher,
which exceeded the French by more than ninety
thousand men and two hundred pieces of cannon†;
he therefore, determined upon endeavouring to
separate the two opposing armies, which would
enable him to attack one with his principal force,
while the other could be kept in check by a detached
corps.

With this view the several army-corps were

* Batty.   † Von Zech: Feldzug von Waterloo.

put in motion for the Sambre at three o'clock on the morning of the 15th, their march being directed upon Marchiennes, Charleroi, and Chatelet. The extent of frontier which the advanced corps of Prussians under general Ziethen had to cover, rendered it impossible for him to offer any effective resistance; he made gallant efforts however, to delay the progress of the enemy, and thus give time to marshal Blucher to assemble his army, but was eventually obliged to retreat upon Fleurus, where he took up a position for the night. Meantime Ney had been directed to move with the first, and three divisions of the second army-corps, and the cavalry of Kellermaun and Lefebvre* straight upon the Brussels high road, and establish himself at Quatre-bras, where that road is crossed by the one leading from Nivelles to Namur.

A brigade of the army of the Netherlands under the prince of Saxe Weimar was stationed at Frasnes in front of Quatre-bras, and between five and six o'clock in the evening it was attacked and forced back by the enemy's leading column; but Ney hearing a heavy cannonade on his right flank, where Ziethen was opposing the progress of the French upon Blucher's position, discontinued his advance, and placed his troops for the night in Frasnes, Marchiennes and Gosselies.†

* Von Zech.

† Von Zech, who gives this detached corps at forty-two thousand two hundred and twenty men and eighteen guns.

1815.

June.

Muffling's
Geschichte
des Feld-
zugs.

The duke of Wellington received notice of the advance of the French in Brussels in the evening of the 15th; and immediately issued orders for all the allied troops to hold themselves in readiness to march*, but, expecting an attack in the direction of Mons, the duke did not give his final orders until near midnight, when the reserve was directed to pass the forest of Soignies on the Charleroi road.

Meantime the prince of Orange had collected his corps at Nivelles, and early on the morning of the 16th, reinforced the troops at Quatre-bras by part of the second division of the Netherlands under general Perponcher.†   The duke of Wellington was himself on the spot by eleven o'clock; he found the enemy weak in the neighbourhood of Frasnes, but received intelligence from prince Blucher stating that considerable masses were moving against him, and that he had taken up a position near Sombref, where he expected to be attacked.

The duke wishing to give every aid to his ally, ordered up the whole army to Nivelles and Quatre-bras, but as they could not arrive before four o'clock, he rode off to consult with marshal Blucher, whom he found at the windmill of Bry, about five miles distant, just as the French had commenced an attack upon the Prussian troops, which appeared to be their main object.

The duke proposed driving in the troops before

---

* Wellington's despatch, June 19, 1815.   † Batty.

Quatre-bras, and marching upon Gosselics, but the
allied divisions being so far distant this could
scarcely be effected in the course of the day, and
meantime Blucher ran the risk of being pressed by
the whole French army. It was therefore, decided
that the army of the Netherlands should advance to
the support of the Prussians on the Quatre-bras
road.

But meanwhile the French troops at Frasnes had
been considerably reinforced, and on the duke's
return to Quatre-bras, about three o'clock, they
appeared in considerable masses, which threatened to
penetrate between both armies.

The second division of the Netherlands, as has
been stated, furnished the first reinforcement to the
troops at Quatre-bras, which arriving early in the
morning, regained part of the ground that had been
lost, and secured the communication between the
British and Prussian positions*; the fifth English
division followed under sir Thomas Picton†, together
with the greater part of the duke of Brunswick's
corps‡, which reached the scene of action about three
o'clock.

1815.

June.

*Muffling's
Geschichte
des Feld-
zugs.*

* Wellington's despatch.

† The fifth division was composed of the eighth and ninth British brigades
under sir James Kempt and sir Denis Pack, and the fifth Hanoverian
brigade under colonel Vincke, but owing to some mistake, the fourth Hanoverian brigade under colonel Best held the place of the latter in the fifth
division both at Quatre-bras and Waterloo.—Notes of captain Christoph
Heise. MSS.

‡ Geschichte des Braunschweigschen Armée-corps.

BATTLE OF QUATRE BRAS.

Notizen
vom König:
Hannov:
General—
Commando
MSS.
Quatre-bras consists of a farm-building, standing at the intersection of the roads leading from Brussels to Charleroi and from Nivelles to Namur; a few hundred yards to the right of the Charleroi road, lies the wood of Bossu, which stretching for about three quarters of a mile in the same direction, then trends to the right towards the village of Pierrepont; on the opposite side of the Charleroi road stands the farm of Gemioncourt, which was occupied by the enemy ; following the Namur road for about a mile the little village of Piermont lies about eight hundred paces on the right, and a wood extends from thence in a direction nearly parallel to the one on the opposite side. This village formed a point of support for the allied left wing, while the wood of Bossu protected their right, but the two woods, running nearly parallel with the Charleroi road, also offered considerable protection to the advance of an enemy.

Batty's
campaign
of 1815.
The fifth English division was formed to the left, and on the great Namur road, as well as in the corn fields extending to the wood of Bossu, and in the Geschichte
des Braun-
schweig:
Armée-
corps. ditch bordering the great road ; a light battalion of Brunswickers was sent towards Piermont, to cover the left flank ; two picked rifle companies of the same corps were posted in the wood of Bossu, and on the right of these some cavalry detachments were placed in observation: the remainder of the Brunswick

troops took post in second line in rear of the British division.

The whole of the allied troops thus assembled, amounted to about eighteen thousand nine hundred men, but of these about four thousand five hundred only were British infantry; the cavalry little exceeded two thousand, and only two batteries of artillery had yet been able to come up*.

The enemy stood upon the heights behind Gemioncourt on both sides of the great road, with a force which, at the lowest computation, amounted to sixteen thousand veteran infantry, three thousand cavalry, and forty-four guns†; the remainder of Ney's corps was left behind at Frasnes for the purpose either of aiding the main attack upon the Prussians or reinforcing that against Quatre-bras, as might be required‡.

Scarce were the dispositions which have been mentioned, made of the allied reinforcements, when the Belgian cavalry having failed in a charge, were driven back in some disorder upon the troops in rear,

---

* Belgian and Nassau infantry,.........5,200.—Batty.
Fifth English divison, ...6,900.—Ibid.
Brunswickers................•••••••...4,722.--Geschichte &c.
—————
Total infantry,...........16,822
Belgian cavalry........ ....1,200.—Batty.
Brunswick cavalry .... 922.—Geschichte &c.
—————
Total cavalry...............2,122.
With captain von Rettberg's Hanoverian and one English battery of artillery

† Mem: Histor: de Napoleon.   ‡ Von Zech.

and the French advanced with two columns of infantry, and nearly all their cavalry, supported by a heavy fire of artillery*. The British infantry, after a destructive fire in line, formed square to resist the cavalry, but some lancers, coming unperceived upon the forty-second Highlanders cut off two companies†,

Notizen vom Hannov: General Commando. MSS.

and then falling upon part of the Hanoverian landwehr battalion Verden, which had been deployed for attack, cut down or captured the greater number. Encouraged by this success, the French horsemen were about to cross the Namur road, when the landwehr battalions Lüneburg and Osterode, which lay concealed in the ditch, opened upon them such a fire that they instantly wheeled about; Rettberg's and the English battery assailed their flank, and the discomfited horsemen retiring with precipitation, the allied centre remained unbroken.

Geschichte des Braunschweig: Armée-corps.

Three battalions and two rifle companies of the duke of Brunswick's corps, were now sent forward on the Charleroi road, and a line of skirmishers thrown out from thence to the wood of Bossu, communicating with the light troops there; and in rear of these a regiment of Brunswick hussars, and a squadron of lancers were placed. The enemy immediately brought up a battery of artillery in front of these troops, who being altogether unprovided

---

* Pringle, in Scott's Life of Napoleon, Vol. IX.

† Scott.

with guns*, suffered considerably,—particularly the
hussar regiment which stood in line. The gallant
duke of Brunswick, wishing to give an example of
courage and steadiness to his young soldiers, remained
upon this spot quietly smoking his pipe and giving
his orders for fully an hour, until at length seeing the
continued destruction caused by the enemy's fire, he
begged that an English battery might be sent to his
assistance. Four guns were accordingly moved
forward and posted on the right of the Brunswick
infantry; but the French artillery redoubled their
fire, and two of the guns were soon dismounted.

The French, having failed on the left, now
prepared to attack the right of the allied position, and
two formidable columns, each from two to three
thousand men, supported by cavalry and artillery,
were seen advancing in succession along the edge of
the wood of Bossu. The head of the leading column
soon drove in the light troops in its front; the duke
of Brunswick led his lancers bravely against the
advancing mass, but a destructive fire of musquetry
forced back the horsemen, and the duke seeing the
overpowering onset with which he was threatened,
directed the whole of his troops to fall back upon
Quatre-bras. The French followed rapidly,—their
artillery showering balls among the retreating troops,

1815.

June.

Geschichte
des Braun-
schweig:
Armée-
corps.

---

* The Brunswick artillery (two batteries of eight guns each) were quartered
at Assche nine or ten miles on this side of Brussels, and could not, therefore
receive the order of march in time to admit of their coming up with the rest
of the corps.—Geschichte des Braunschweig: Armée-corps.

while their cuirassiers advanced in formidable numbers to the charge. This threw the Brunswickers into some confusion; the duke, seeking to restore order, became exposed to the enemy's fire, and while in the act of rallying his men, the gallant Prince was struck from his horse, and fell mortally wounded*.

* Frederick William, Duke of Brunswick-Lüneburg, Oels and Bernstadt stands conspicuous in the history of Napoleon's occupation of Germany, for a display of patriotism, firmness, and military constancy which has seldom been equalled. At the commencement of the French war with Austria in April 1809, he raised a corps of volunteers in Bohemia, and made an incursion into Saxony, but Jerome Buonaparte, the then king of Westphalia, came against him with a strong force, and he was obliged to fall back. On the armistice being concluded at Znaim on the 12th of July, the Austrians retired across the frontier; but the duke of Brunswick, declining the alliance of the emperor Francis, advanced with his little corps of eight hundred cavalry and seven hundred infantry, towards Leipsic. After a slight skirmish with the weak garrison there, he proceeded to Halle, where he arrived on the 27th, and on the 30th reached Halberstadt, which place was entered the same morning by a battalion of Westphalian infantry under colonel Wellingrode. These troops made a bold resistance, but eventually gave way; their colonel was taken prisoner, and now the duke pressed on for Brunswick. Here the corps arrived on the 31st, and bivouacked outside the town,—their chief lying in his cloak upon some straw on the ramparts. Little time, however was afforded him for repose; for his enemies were closing round him on all sides:—The Westphalian general Reubel was with four thousand men at Ohof, in the neighbourhood; general Gratien had put a division in march against him from Erfurth, and the Danish general Ewaldt had crossed the Elbe at Gluckstadt to prevent his passage of that river. The duke engaged Reubel at the village of Oelper near Brunswick on the 1st of August, when a memorable action took place, in which the Westphalian corps of nearly four thousand men, was defeated by the duke's little band of scarcely fifteen hundred ! This opened the only road by which the Brunswickers could escape, and their chief, having given the enemy reason to suppose that he intended marching upon Celle, turned short towards Hanover, where he arrived on the 2d, and the same day went on to Nienburg. Here he crossed the Weser, breaking the bridge after him, and pressed down the left bank of the river to Hoya, which he reached on the 4th. Meantime part of his corps made a false demonstration upon Bremen, into which place the *black hussars* entered on the 5th and seized the gates, but left it on the following

Such was the state of the action, when two brigades of the third division, under sir Charles Alten numbering about four thousand six hundred men*, opportunely arrived upon the field. These troops consisting of the fifth English brigade under sir Colin Halkett, and the first Hanoverian brigade under count Kielmansegge, had come up after a forced march of nine leagues from their cantonments

1815.

June.

Notizen von Han-nov: General Com-mando. MSS. Narrative of count Kielman-segge. MSS.

morning. The duke continued his march with the main body through Oldenburg, and appeared as if he sought to embark on the coast of East Friesland; but contrary to this expectation, he suddenly crossed the Hunte, a small stream running into the Weser,—seized all the merchant ships and empty river craft that he could find,—impressed the necessary number of seamen, and, with the exception of the horses, embarked his corps on the night of the 6th !

In the morning he put to sea under an English flag,—landed on the 8th at Heligoland, and on the 11th sailed from thence for England, where the whole arrived in safety.

The sea alone had saved the gallant little corps; for Reubel reached Bremen the very day on which the duke left the river, and the enemy's advanced guard was engaged with the hussars that were left to cover the embarkation.

His serene Highness was received in England with great sympathy; his corps was taken into the English service, and until the peace of 1813 restored to him his hereditary dominions, a pension of £6000 sterling was granted to him by the British government.

In 1815, the Duke of Brunswick brought into the field eight battalions of infantry, one regiment of hussars, a squadron of lancers, and two batteries of artillery,—making together a corps of seven thousand men, with sixteen pieces of cannon.—[See Real Encyclopædie; Geschichte des Braunschweigschen Armée-corps.]

* This reinforcement is erroneously given in colonel Batty's Appendix as six thousand two hundred and eighty-three, the second brigade of the King's German Legion being included; but this brigade, as will be seen, did not arrive on the field until after the action : captain Pringle has also been led into the same error, conceiving that the whole of the third division were present.

1815.

June.

Notizen,
&c. MSS.
round Soignies; they were followed by captain Cleeve's battery of German artillery, and the whole immediately entered into action. Kielmansegge's brigade was sent forward in prolongation of the left,—then only defended by an English battalion, and a detachment of Brunswickers,—while the British brigade reinforced the right, at the farm and wood of Bossu.

The Hanoverians had to pass under the fire of thirty pieces of cannon, in order to reach the point where their assistance was required, and the French infantry, already arrived upon the high road, met the head of their column with a destructive musquetry fire; but Kielmansegge, forcing on, threw out the field-battalion Lüneburg in skirmishing order, and closing with the enemy's advance, launched into a fierce contest with the opposing masses. The French made an obstinate resistance, and tenaciously held the corner of a wood close to the village of Piermont; but the Lüneburgers being reinforced by the field-battalion Grubenhagen, this point was cleared, and the enemy were finally driven as well from all the fields adjoining the road, as from the village of Piermont itself.

Batty's
campaign
of 1815.
But the main attack of the enemy was upon the allied right, and here they had gained considerable advantages:—Advancing in heavy columns, and with a preponderating force of artillery, they endeavoured to gain possession of the wood of Bossu and the out-buildings in front of Quatre-bras; a most

destructive fire fell upon Halkett's brigade,—the French artillery swept his ranks,—their horsemen riding fiercely against the weakened infantry forced them to seek safety in the wood; many gallant soldiers were struck down, and the enemy's light troops had almost succeeded in establishing themselves on the high road to Nivelles.

At this critical moment the English division of guards, nearly four thousand strong, arrived on the field of action. Major Kuhlman's horse battery of German artillery was attached to this division, and its zealous commander, pressing forward with great activity from his distant quarters between Ath and Enghien, preceded the rest of the division, and brought his guns to bear in front of Quatre-bras, just as the French cuirassiers, charging down the road, were carrying all before them. Two guns under lieutenant Speckmann were posted on the little rising ground close to the intersection of the road, and the Lüneburg landwehr battalion lined the ditch; these reserved their fire until the cavalry had arrived within a few paces distance, and then sending a shower of shot and grape among the horsemen, strewed the ground with killed and wounded, and drove the remainder back in confusion*.

Notizen &c MSS.

Notes of captain Christoph Heise MSS.

* Gunner Meyer and Bombardier Nolte of the legion artillery were distinguished for the coolness and bravery with which they worked the guns to which they were attached. Meyer, who was placed with a howitzer on the Charleroi road; beat off several attacks of the French cavalry, and Nolte, although surrounded by the horsemen, manfully held his ground,—saving himself under the gun carriage until the enemy were driven off.— Guelphic Archives. MSS.

It was about half past six o'clock when the guards

arrived, and tired as they were, two battalions in-

stantly formed line, and, entering the wood of Bossu, drove the enemy before them in the most gallant style. A well formed line of infantry met them on the other side, but, pressing onward, although their line had been broken by the intricacy of the wood, they caused these also to give way, and actually drove them up the opposite rising ground! But now the French cavalry seeing that the guards were un-supported, and that their formation had been broken,—suddenly formed on the heights, and dashed down upon the gallant battalions. To attempt forming square would have been in vain, so retiring to the wood, they ranged themselves along its skirts, from whence they sent forth so destructive a fire among the horsemen, that these retreated in disorder, leaving many of their numbers killed and wounded on the field. Again the French troopers charged, and again they were driven back. The artillery and two remaining battalions of the Brunswick corps now reached the scene of action[*], and on a fresh charge of the French, the latter skilfully covered the retreat of the guards into the wood, by forming a flêche towards the enemy.

The crisis of the battle had passed, and the allied troops remained masters of the field. Night was fast approaching, and Ney seeing no prospect of

---

[*] Geschichte des Braunschweig: Armée-corps.

restoring the fight, drew back his discomfited troops to Frasnes. The reserve which had been left there under count d'Erlon was taken off by Napoleon at four o'clock to reinforce his attack against the Prussians at St. Amand, and when, after repeated orders from Ney, it returned by Villiers to Quatre-bras, the battle had been already decided*.

The remainder of the allied troops came up to Quatre-bras in the evening and during the night; amongst the rest colonel Ompteda's brigade of the German legion, which had been detached from the third division, when on its march from Soignies, and halted in observation on the Mons road, near the village of Arguennes.

Wyneck-en's narrative. MSS.

The important object of securing the means of communication between the Prussian and Anglo-Belgian army, had thus been accomplished, but not without a considerable sacrifice on the part of the allies; the superiority of the French in cavalry and artillery gave them great advantages throughout the day, and although the allies remained masters of the field, their loss nearly equalled that of the enemy† : the loss of the Hanoverians amounted to seventeen officers and three hundred and eighty-eight non-commissioned officers and men, including killed, wounded, and missing, and lieutenants von Goeben

Notizen &c. MSS.

---

* Von Zech.

† The movements of the 17th and the battle of the 18th, rendered it difficult to obtain an exact account of the loss at Quatre-bras, but it is supposed to have been between four and five thousand men.—Muffling.

and Hartmann of the German artillery, were severely wounded.

The allied divisions had been seventeen hours
under arms, partly in march, partly in action, and
during the whole time had received scarcely any
other food but dry biscuit†; and they now sank
exhausted on the ground, glad of the relief
which even a lowering night and dreary bivouac
offered.

Sir Charles Alten and sir Colin Halkett of the
German legion are enumerated in the duke of
Wellington's account of this action among those who
had "highly distinguished themselves," and the
battalion of Hanoverians (Lüneburg landwehr) is
classed with those regiments deserving of being
particularly mentioned‡; the efficient service rendered

Notes of
captain
Christoph
Heise.
MSS.
by the latter was mainly attributable to captain von
Heimburg, brigade-major to colonel Best's brigade,
who by cautioning the young soldiers to reserve their
fire, and giving them the word of command at the
critical moment, enabled them to pour forth a volley,
which carried destruction among the enemy's horsemen.

The nature of the attack upon the duke of
Wellington's position at Quatre-bras prevented the
possibility of his rendering the promised assistance
to prince Blucher; but the Prussians gallantly

† Geschichte des Braunschweig : Armée-corps.

‡ Despatch, June 19, 1815,

maintained their ground against great disparity of numbers, from three o'clock in the afternoon until dusk, when, unable longer to withstand the fresh masses of troops which were continued to be brought against them, they commenced their retreat. Blucher, however, with wonderful activity and firmness, formed them again at a short distance from the field of battle, and retiring in the night, without being pursued, he ably concentrated the whole Prussian army at Wavres on the left bank of the Dyle.

An officer who had been despatched in the night to Quatre-bras, with intelligence of these events, was shot on the road, and it was not until seven o'clock on the morning of the 17th that the duke of Wellington received notice of the Prussian retreat*.

It was now evident that if the allied troops remained in their present position, they would be exposed to the attack of the entire French army, and that a retrogade movement on their part was also required, in order to renew their communications with the Prussians ; the duke of Wellington, therefore, directed the whole to retire through Genappe to a position which he had selected in front of the forest of Soignies and village of Waterloo.

The information received from prince Blucher at nine o'clock shewed how little the efficiency of his army had been effected by their retreat; he only

---

* Muffling.

expressed a wish for "sufficient time to furnish provisions and ammunition to his men".*

The Duke, upon this, proposed to him to send two divisions of the Prussian army to the assistance of the allies in the position of Waterloo, where, in that case, he would accept a battle on the 18th; the gallant veteran replied that "he would not come with two corps, but with his whole army, either to assist the Duke, if attacked, or to unite with him in attacking the enemy on the 19th†.

The troops at Quatre-bras were called to arms at daylight by the enemy's skirmishers, who, attacking the out posts at Piermont, kept up for some time the expectation of a general engagement. Kielmansegge's Hanoverian brigade, and some of the Brunswick light troops were here sharply engaged, and a picquet of the field-battalion Bremen suffered considerably‡; however no forward movement was attempted by the enemy, and before eleven o'clock the allies, leaving some cavalry and light troops to mask the movement, commenced their retreat.

The army marched in three columns: the first, under lord Hill, by the Nivelle road to Braine la leud; the second, consisting of the corps under the prince of Orange and the reserve, by Genappe; and the third, composed of general Colville's division, the Dutch Indian brigade, the first Belgian division, and

---

* Muffling.   † Muffling.

‡ Notizen, &c. MSS.

the Hanoverian cavalry brigade,—was detached to Hal, being intended to cover Brussels, should the enemy seek to reach it by a flank march in that direction*.

The main column,—being the first corps and the reserve,—took the straight high road leading to Brussels by Genappe; the retreat of the infantry was covered by the third division under sir Charles Alten, to which were added two light battalions of Brunswickers†, and the rear-guard of the whole army was formed of part of major-general Grant's and lord Edward Somerset's brigades of cavalry.

Alten's division took a by-road leading through Sarta Mavelines and Bezy into the great road near Genappe, and the admirable manner in which it was conducted, prevented the enemy, who followed slowly, from gaining any advantage over it‡; the cavalry rearguard, however, was pressed by the French advance: the seventh hussars attempted to drive back the enemy's lancers as they debouched, along the hollow road from Genappe, but without success, and the French horsemen were advancing to attack their opponents, when the English horse-guards charged, and completely overthrew them §.

* Muffling.

† Gesch: des Braunsch: Armée-corps.

‡ "The third division retreated from Sarta Mavelines upon Bezy, and thence into the great road near Genappe, and the excellent order in which it was conducted, in the broad face of day, prevented the enemy from deriving any advantage from it."—Batty's campaign of 1815, page 70.

§ Batty.

Time was thus obtained for the infantry to take up their ground, and, about eight o'clock the whole army had reached its position on the table land in front of Mont St. Jean*.

Batty's
campaign
of 1815.

The French did not arrive upon the opposite heights of Belle Alliance until nearly seven o'clock when they brought up some batteries, and opened a fire upon the allied rearguard; this was quickly silenced by the English artillery, and hostilities ceased for the night.

† The first light battalion of the legion having been halted, with the rest of the rear-guard, for a short time, at Genappe, colonel Bussche was occupied in placing picquets; but the march was, soon after, directed to be resumed, and serjeant Lindenau was charged to convey the order to colonel Bussche, with directions as to the road he was to take. The colonel, however, joined his battalion by another route, and Lindenau found himself, suddenly, surrounded by the enemy's cavalry skirmishers. His presence of mind did not forsake him, and he endeavoured to escape by taking advantage of the ground; but soon the French horsemen, pressing rapidly forward, were close at his heels, and he saw no other mode of saving himself, but by facing about and firing; a lucky shot brought one of his pursuers from his horse, and the other now hesitating, Lindenau took advantage of the favorable moment to decamp over a neighbouring hedge.

Here he re-loaded, and crept on for some time through the cornfields unobserved,—the French cavalry swarming around. But his trials were not yet ended; for suddenly he fell in with two chasseurs of the Imperial Guard, who had just made prisoner of an English officer of dragoons. Lindenau instantly shot the horse of one of the Frenchmen from under him, and clapping the sword upon his rifle, captured, with the assistance of the officer, both the rider and his comrade. The officer now advised him to abandon the prisoner,—mount the remaining horse, and make the best of his way to his regiment; but Lindenau would not listen to so tame a proceeding, and stabbing the horse, he quietly re-loaded his rifle, and threatened to shoot the first chasseur who attempted to escape. He then drove the two Frenchmen before him to the allied position, which, although five or six miles distant, and only to be approached through the enemy's light troops,—he reached that evening in safety, and delivered his prisoners to the battalion: the chasseurs were afterwards examined by the adjutant, and fully corroborated the statement of the gallant rifleman.—Guelphic Archives. MSS.

1815.

June.

An oppressive heat had rendered the march of the allied troops fatiguing during the early part of the day, and in the afternoon, cold and violent rain deluged the ground and rendered their progress still more difficult. The rain continued, with little intermission, throughout the night; but few fires could, consequently, be lighted; the ground was trampled into mud;—many of the regiments were labouring under the privation of having had little or no food since the 15th[*], and before morning the cold and comfortless condition of the bivouac was excessive.

BATTLE OF WATERLOO.

The dawn of the 18th of June opened with a more favorable appearance of the weather, and the sufferings of the preceding night were soon lost sight of in the active preparations which the approaching contest required: fires were lighted;—musquets put in order;—provisions, to a certain extent, cooked and distributed[†], and soon all were in readiness to meet the attack which, it was understood, Napoleon intended to make on the allied position.

The ground selected by the duke of Wellington for the scene of this eventful contest, is a gentle ridge lying in front of the little village of Mont St. Jean, where the high roads unite which lead from

Notizen vom Hannov: General Commando. MSS.

[*] Journal of first line battalion. MSS.

[†] "Every possible provision was made for men and horses, which, however, was very insufficient."—Gesch: des Braunsch: Armée-corps.

Charleroi and Nivelles to Brussels,—that from Charleroi running directly through the middle of the ridge. On similar and nearly parallel heights, at about cannon shot distance, stood the army of Napoleon. A hollow, varying in depth, divides the two ridges of ground, that in front of the French position being, in general, less steep than the other; but everywhere the field was practicable for cavalry and artillery.

The right wing of the allied army stood towards the Nivelles road where the ridge terminates, but occupied also the hamlet of Braine la leud, still farther on the right; the left wing rested upon the hamlets of Papelotte and la Haye.

On the right of the ridge ran a hollow, crossing the one in front nearly at right angles; this was fully commanded by the troops stationed here, who thus secured the right wing from being turned; but this formation of the ground rendered it necessary that the right wing should be thrown back.

In front, where the centre joined the refused right wing, stood the farm of Hougoumont, having a walled garden on its left, and a small wood and orchard on the side nearest the enemy's position: the upper story of the buildings, as well as the garden wall was loop-holed.

In the hollow in front of the centre, immediately upon the Charleroi road, stood the farm of la Haye Sainte, to which, on the French side, was attached an orchard, and on this side a small garden, both

fenced by stout hedges; fences of the same description 1815.
ran straight from the high road at this point to the June.
slope of the heights at Papelotte, upon which the Notizen,
left wing rested, serving as well for breastworks to &c. MSS.
this part of the line, as protection to the advanced
skirmishers; along the principal hedge ran a cross
road leading to Smohaim, a considerable part of
which led through a hollow way or ravine; where
the hedges commenced on the Charleroi road, a
strong barricade was formed of felled trees.

The right wing being thus thrown back, and the
left protected in a great measure by the hedges and
hollow road, the part of the position most open to
attack was that which lay between the two farms of
Hougoumont and la Haye Sainte; the terminus of
the left wing, also, offered facilities to an assailant;
for Papelotte lies low, and is not, as the hollow on
the right, commanded by the neighbouring ground.

The whole of the ridge upon which the allied
troops were posted, being of narrow dimensions, and
sloping gradually towards front and rear, gave their
commander the advantage of being able to place his
second line in a position sheltered from cannon fire.

The enemy's right wing rested upon the heights
opposite Papelotte, and their left upon the Nivelles
road; the Charleroi road, as in the allied position,
intersected their centre.

The army of the Netherlands was formed in two Batty's
lines, with the cavalry in the rear, and the several campaign of 1815.
divisions were posted in the following order:—

The centre composed of the first division under major-general Cooke, and the third division under sir Charles Alten, together with the troops of Brunswick and Nassau,—the whole under the immediate command of the Prince of Orange, held the heights between Hougoumont and la Haye Sainte, as well as these farms, which marked their flanks; a battalion of the English guards; a company of Nassauers; a company of Hanoverian field-riflemen and a detachment of a hundred men from count Kielmansegge's brigade*,—occupied Hougoumont; and la Haye Sainte was entrusted to the second light battalion of the German legion, under the command of major Baring.

The right wing was composed of the second division under lieutenant-general Clinton, and part of the fourth division under lieutenant-general Colville,—the whole being under the orders of lord Hill; the left wing was formed of sir Thomas Picton's and the sixth division, and the Belgian troops were posted on the extreme flanks.

The cavalry were principally stationed in rear of the left wing, and left of the centre; general Grant's hussar brigade† was posted in rear of the right division; lord Edward Somerset's heavy brigade immediately behind the left of sir Charles Alten's

---

* Notizen, &c. MSS.

† The second hussars of the legion, which formed part of this brigade, were not brought up to Waterloo, but left in occupation of a line of posts on the French frontier, extending from Courtray, through Menin, Ypres, Loo, and Fürnes, to the North sea: this line they had held since the end of March.—Journal of second hussars. MSS.

division, having in its rear the light brigade of sir William Dörnberg, and in rear of these was placed a new raised regiment of Hanoverian hussars.

Sir William Ponsonby's heavy brigade was posted on the left of the great road leading to Genappe and Charleroi; general Vandeleur's light brigade in rear of the left of sir Thomas Picton's division, and on the extreme left of the whole line was the hussar brigade of major-general Vivian.

The artillery were stationed in front of the centre and left, and in rear of the right wing; captain Cleeves' battery of German artillery stood with two English batteries in front of sir Charles Alten's division; major Kuhlmann's was posted with an English battery, about four hundred paces to the left of Hougoumont; captain von Rettberg's stood on the extreme left in front of colonel Best's Hanoverian brigade; major Sympher's was posted behind the left wing of the second division, and captain Braun's was in reserve with the brigade of general Lambert.

The whole of the troops thus assembled on the position of Waterloo, amounted to fifty-five thousand and eighty-eight men*, and one hundred and sixteen pieces of cannon; the remainder of the army numbering about fifteen thousand four hundred, were stationed in a position covering the approach to Brussels through Hal, and stood under the command of prince Frederick of the Netherlands.

* Batty.

But of the allied troops thus assembled at Waterloo, the British and King's German Legion alone could be considered as trained or experienced soldiers, and these did not amount to more than about thirty-two thousand*, opposed to which now stood the veteran army of Napoleon numbering seventy-five thousand fighting men†, with two hundred and forty pieces of cannon‡. A corps of thirty-two thousand men under marshal Grouchy had been despatched by the Emperor at twelve o'clock on the 17th, in pursuit of the Prussians, but these did not arrive at Gembloux until the evening, and meantime Blucher, as has been shewn, ably concentrated his army at Wavres.

Batty's campaign of 1815.

Thus were the contending armies circumstanced on the eventful morning of the 18th of June; the weather became more favorable as the day advanced, and about ten o'clock the French were distinctly seen moving down to their respective positions in front of the allied line.

About half-past eleven o'clock, the expected attack was commenced§: a strong line of French infantry bore down obliquely upon the wood of Hougoumont, throwing out skirmishers as they advanced, which soon covered the whole of their

---

* Pringle, in Scott's life of Napoleon, Vol. IX. page 373.

† Ibid. Batty reduces the French force at Waterloo to sixty-nine thousand five hundred, but captain Pringle shews that taking Buonaparte's own account as given in the Memoires Historiques, Liv. IX, it must have exceeded seventy-four thousand.

‡ Batty.   § Notizen &c. MSS.

left wing, and the light troops that were posted on
the skirts of the wood, and along the front of the enclosure, became engaged with the enemy's tirailleurs.

The firing soon increased to an incessant roll of
musquetry. The French columns approached
nearer the wood to support their light troops, and
now captain Cleeves' battery of German artillery
from the right front of sir Charles Alten's division,
opened the allied cannonade*. The English and
German batteries on the heights in front of the first
division quickly followed, and the French guns in
vain endeavoured to silence the fire. Persevering
with steady aim the artillery-men kept up a furious
cannonade against the approaching infantry, and
one column was completely dispersed by the shells
from the allied howitzers†.

The French light troops, however, succeeded in Batty's campaign of 1815.
penetrating into the wood, driving before them the
greater part of the Nassau troops; and the light companies of the first and second brigade of guards had
to sustain the furious onset of the enemy's columns.

Availing themselves of the natural defences of the
place, the guards made an effective resistance to the
efforts of the enemy at this point, and the French,
changing the direction of their attack, now attempted
to get in rear of the buildings; but the light troops
of the Coldstream and third guards, met this assault
with firmness, and, after a severe contest, drove
them off, regaining a part of the wood.

* Notizen &c. MSS.   † Batty.

During this contest at Hougoumont, a movement was also made by the enemy against Papelotte*, but it was not earnestly continued, and it was evident that Napoleon's attention was not directed to this vulnerable part of the line.

A galling fire from the French artillery however, blazed along the centre, and gradually extended itself to the left†. This was most successfully returned by the allied guns. Favored by the nature of the ground, and directed with a degree of precision that reflected the highest credit upon the artillery officers, the English and German batteries were everywhere more effective than those of the French‡; however the allied troops standing on the slope of the hill, were also severe sufferers, from the cannon fire, and the duke of Wellington, therefore, between one and two o'clock, moved back the centre about two hundred yards to the reverse slope of the hill, leaving the artillery in advance§.

Pringle's
Remarks.

It is probable that Napoleon considered this movement as the commencement of a retreat, and therefore determined upon attacking the left centre, in order to get possession of the village of Mont St. Jean, which commanded the approach to Brussels; for four columns of infantry, thirty pieces of artillery and a large body of cuirassiers advanced on, and by the side of the Genappe road. The French cavalry

---

* Notizen &c. MSS.   † Pringle.

‡ Batty.   § Pringle.

led the attack, and had advanced considerably up the slope of the allied position near la Haye Sainte, when the duke of Wellington ordered the life-guards to charge, and the cuirassiers were driven back into their own position. Here, between the steep banks of the high road, ensued a fierce contest which was continued for some minutes, but the enemy bringing down some light artillery from the heights, the British cavalry were obliged to retire.

Meantime the French infantry had pushed forward on the allied left of the Genappe road, beyond la Haye Sainte, and a brigade of Belgian infantry giving way, these columns crowned the position. Sir Thomas Picton now moved up general Pack's brigade from the second line, while part of general Ponsonby's heavy cavalry brigade wheeling round the infantry, took the column in flank, and a total route ensued. Many of the enemy were killed, and several pieces of artillery, as well as two eagles and two thousand prisoners were taken; but the British horsemen pursuing their successes too far, were in their turn assailed by the French cavalry, and were forced to retire with considerable loss, abandoning the captured guns. The gallant sir Thomas Picton and general Ponsonby were killed, in this part of the engagement.

While this conflict was carried on by two divisions of the French army in the valley between the high road and Papelotte, another division attacked the farm of La Haye Sainte.

1815.

June.

Pringle's Remarks.

Batty.

1815.

June.

See Plan,
No. 5.

Appendix
No. XX.

This important post, situated about mid-way
between the contending armies, and on which rested
the left of the centre of the allied line, was, it will
be remembered, entrusted to the second light battalion
of the King's German Legion, under the command of
major Baring. The farm lies close to the right side
of the road leading from Brussels to Genappe, and
consisted of a dwelling-house, barn, stable, orchard,
and garden; one side of the buildings abutted on the
road; the orchard bounded by a hedge was on that
side looking towards the enemy's position, and the
garden, fenced on the road-side by a low wall, and
on the other sides by a hedge, lay immediately in
rear of the whole.

From the court and buildings two doors and three
large gates led to the exterior; two of these entrances
were on the road, one opened into the garden, and
the others, being the barn and farm-yard gates, were
on the west side or allied right of the buildings: of
the latter however, the barn gate had unfortunately
been destroyed previous to the arrival of the
German battalion.

This consisted of six companies, amounting,
inclusive of serjeants, to three hundred and seventy-
six men. Of these, major Baring posted three
companies in the orchard, two in the buildings, and
one in the rear garden.

The means of defence which this post presented
were very limited, and even these could not be
rendered available; for the pioneers of the battalion

had been removed to Hougoumont, and the troops
in la Haye Sainte were left without as much as a
hatchet.

The men, however, made every possible exertion
to put the place in a state of defence; some loop-holes
were made in the wall, and a scaffolding placed
behind, in order to enable them to fire over it; but
the broken gate of the barn presented an insurmountable difficulty, and it was found impracticable to
place any effective obstruction at this opening.

Thus was the German battalion circumstanced
when the attack commenced against the allied left
wing; the French division which had been directed
against the farm of la Haye Sainte, moved forward in
column, from whence a dense cloud of skirmishers
issued, and crowded on the orchard in front.

One of the first shots from the enemy's tirailleurs
broke the bridle of major Baring's horse, close to his
hand, and another killed major Bösewiel, who stood
near him; the columns quickly followed their
advanced troops, one marching direct against the
buildings, while the other forced in mass upon the
orchard. Baring had directed his men to lie down
and reserve their fire until the near approach of the
enemy, upon whom they now opened; but the
French regardless of this opposition, forced on
in such overpowering numbers, that it was utterly
impossible for the small detachment to maintain the
orchard, and they fell back into the barn.

The companies of captain Christian Wynecken

Y

1815.

June.

Wynec-
ken's
Narrative.
MSS.

and captain von Goeben, of the first light battalion, under the command of major Hans von dem Bussche, as well as a company of Hanoverian riflemen under major von Sporken,—the whole of whom had been placed in skirmishing order to the right of the farm, poured a severe fire upon the assailants, as they advanced; suddenly however, some squadrons of cavalry appeared on their right flank, and the detached troops hastily attempted to collect together.

But at this moment the light battalion Lüneburg, under colonel von Klencke, which had been detached from the left flank of count Kielmansegge's brigade, came up in close column to support the skirmishers, and interposing between the scattered files, completely prevented their connexion. The cuirassiers charged, and these troops as well as major Baring's battalion were thrown into the greatest confusion; for the latter encouraged by the approaching reinforcement, had attempted to re-establish themselves in the orchard, and now the whole becoming mingled together and dispersed, endeavoured to gain the main position of the army. But the French had already got possession of the garden, driving the legion company into the buildings, and the Germans suffered a severe loss in officers and men. Besides captain Holtzermann who fell at the opening of the cannonade, captains von Goeben, Schaumann and ensign Robertson of the legion light brigade were killed, and six other officers were wounded.

Of Baring's battalion the greater part reached the

1815.

June.

main position; the rest secured themselves in the farmyard and buildings, where under the firm guidance of lieutenants Groeme, Carey, and Frank, they gallantly maintained their ground against every effort of the enemy.

The troops in position immediately in rear of la Haye Sainte were also, at this time, attacked by a strong column of the enemy's infantry, which advanced straight upon the seventy-ninth regiment. The highlanders cheered, and rushed on their opponents with the bayonet, while the first light battalion of the legion, which had been posted in the hollow way behind the farm, and was now ordered forward by the duke of Wellington in person,— crossing the high road, took the column in its left flank, and the eighth and fifth line battalions, bringing forward their right, also advanced to the charge. The French had already turned, and their brave opponents were driving them down the heights, when a body of cuirassiers, after an unsuccessful attack upon the left square of Kielmansegg's brigade, came upon the right-flank of the legion battalions; the first light and fifth line protected by the British cavalry, were enabled to form square, but the eighth battalion, being in the act of charging when the cuirassiers appeared upon the height, was completely surprised, and the greater part either cut down or dispersed: colonel von Schroeder who commanded the battalion was mortally wounded; captains Voigt, Westernhagen, lieutenant Marenholtz and thirty

Notes of captain Christoph Heise. MSS.

Notizen, &c. MSS.

1815.

June.

Journal of
8th line
battalion.
MSS.

Notizen,
&c. MSS.

non-commissioned officers and men were killed ; captains Sander and Rougemont, lieutenant Sattler, adjutant Brinckmann, and sixty men were wounded, the officers severely, and ensign Moreau, who carried the King's colour, being also wounded, as well as the serjeant who afterwards held it, the colour fell into the enemy's hands.* Notwithstanding this disaster, the battalion was ably rallied by major von Petersdorf, and re-formed behind the hollow road ; but it had been rendered incapable of undertaking any further active movement. In the charge of the first light battalion, lieutenant Christoph Heise was severely wounded.

Meantime part of the same body of cuirassiers had attacked the rest of the third division, and rode fiercely against Kielmansegg's Hanoverian brigade, which was formed in two squares on the right of the legion battalions. The new levies shewed great steadiness : implicitly following the orders which they had received to reserve their fire until the enemy had arrived within twenty or thirty paces, they then poured forth a volley, which sent the horsemen back in disorder. But the cuirassiers soon returned, and not meeting the fire at the point they expected, swarmed around the squares ; then was the destructive shower repeated, and they rode off as before, followed by the allied cavalry.

---

* Ensign Moreau received three severe wounds ; the colour, however, was found a few days after the battle, and brought back to the battalion by a Hanoverian cavalry soldier.—Notizen, &c. MSS.

'The great mass of the French cavalry had now been launched against this part of the allied position, and twelve thousand horsemen[*] are said to have swarmed in their front. These boldly mounted the crest of the position, and passing the intervals of the squares, penetrated to the second line; but the British household brigade under lord Edward Somerset, heedless of the defensive armour of their opponents, rushed boldly against the intruders, and, as they retreated from the fire of the squares[†], drove them up the opposite heights back into their own line. Colonel Ponsonby, also with the twelfth light dragoons made a most brilliant charge upon part of the division of Durutte, which he broke and dispersed, causing the enemy a severe loss; and some Belgian cavalry following, added to the slaughter : the twelfth were afterwards obliged to retire before the French lancers, leaving the gallant Ponsonby desperately wounded on the field; but the enemy's main object of attack had been completely defeated, and although the allies were severe sufferers, the loss of the enemy was much greater.

The second light battalion of the legion now re-occupied the farm of la Haye Sainte ; the first light battalion the hollow road, and with the exception of the continued cannonade, a momentary pause ensued in this part of the line [‡]

1815.

June.

Batty's campaign of 1815.

* Rogniat, as quoted by Pringle p. 368.

† Wynecken. MSS.

‡ Ibid.

1815.
June.
Appendix
No. XXI.

Major Baring having lost in the first attack upon la Haye Sainte, many officers and men in killed and wounded, applied for a re-inforcement, upon which two companies of the first light battalion under captains von Gilsa and Henry Marschalck were sent to his assistance. To these and a part of his own battalion he gave the defence of the garden, and placed the remainder of his force in the buildings, under the charge of the three officers who had already so gallantly defended them.

Batty's
campaign
of 1815.

Meantime the French had renewed their efforts against Hougoumont, and they succeeded in setting fire to the dwelling house and adjoining straw stacks; a hard struggle ensued; the enemy's columns endeavoured to surround the building, but the guards silenced their fire, and charging, drove them through the wood with great loss; many brave soldiers were destroyed by the fire, and some of the French infantry daringly burst the gate and penetrated into the court yard; but these venturous assailants were all slain; the gates were again secured, and the enemy never gained possession of either the garden or dwelling house.

Notizen,
&c. MSS.

The contest again raged along the centre;—the third and fifth divisions were repeatedly attacked, and the brigades of count Kielmansegge, sir Colin Halkett and colonel Ompteda, had to sustain many a furious onset of the enemy's cavalry. But the steadiness of the British and German battalions was not to be shaken; relying on their invincible formation,

they reserved their fire until the near approach of
the cavalry, and then opened a volley upon the
leading horsemen, which carried destruction into
their ranks; the allied cavalry, taking advantage of
the disorder thus created, then charged the retreating
horsemen, while the artillery-men, issuing from the
squares, in which they had sought shelter on the
advance of the cavalry, completed the discomfiture of
the intruding squadrons.

But the French horsemen constantly re-formed, and
led forward with the most chivalrous bravery by their
gallant officers, continued to dash against the squares,
or seek vainly for some opening which would give
them a chance of success. On one occasion, becoming
bolder, and having observed how much the infantry
reserved their fire, they sent out skirmishers, who, to
provoke a volley, rode close to the squares and
killed or wounded many with their carbines; this
was borne for a short time, but at length picked
marksmen were placed outside the squares, who soon
drove off the cavalry skirmishers*.

The combat continued at la Haye Sainte, and the

---

* A body of cuirassiers made repeated attacks upon the square formed by
the fifth line battalion of the legion; after each unsuccessful charge, they
retired into a hollow where they were protected from the fire of the square,
while the commanding officer, with great coolness remained in observation on
a little rising ground, moving his horse about *en vedette*, and watching for a
favorable opportunity to renew the attack. Colonel Ompteda, who was in
the square, called upon several of the men to rid him of the Frenchman's
observation, but all the shots failed, and for the fifth time, the charge was
repeated. At length a rifleman of the first light battalion, named John Milius,
who had been severely wounded and brought into the square, hearing what
was required, begged that he might be carried to the front, and here the
devoted soldier, although with a broken leg, and faint from the loss of blood—
levelling his trusty rifle, brought the officer lifeless from his horse in the first
shot!—Guelphic Archives. MSS.

first light battalion fired with great effect upon the troops which advanced against it from the road, but their loss was considerable, and several officers were wounded*.

In the attacks made by the allied cavalry at this time of the day, about four o'clock, the first dragoons and third hussars of the legion were conspicuously engaged : the second dragoons had been detached to Braine la leud for the purpose of observing some of the enemy's cavalry who had shewn themselves in that direction, and sir William Dörnberg's brigade was therefore reduced to the two remaining regiments, namely: the first dragoons of the legion, and the twenty-third English dragoons; these made some brilliant charges, both in column of squadrons and in line, and although outnumbered and obstinately resisted by the French cavalry, succeeded on each occasion in eventually causing them to fall back; but their loss was severe: captain Peters, lieutenants Levetzow and Kuhlmann were killed, colonel von Bülow, majors von Reitzenstein, and Sichart, captains von Bothmer and Hattorf, lieutenants von Hammerstein, Nanne, Trittau, Mackenzie, Bosse, Fricke (adjutant) were wounded, the greater number severely, and sir William Dörnberg commanding the brigade, was also wounded.

The third hussars of the legion exhibited their wonted intrepidity : this regiment, it will be remembered, formed with the thirteenth English dragoons the brigade of sir Frederick Arentschild, but it so

* See Appendix XX.

happened, that the two regiments never came together during the whole of the day, and the third with only seven troops present, stood alone in rear of the centre. Colonel Meyer, who commanded the regiment, was mortally wounded by a cannon shot in the early part of the day, and the command devolved upon captain von Kerssenbruck; this officer with only three troops of the hussars, made so vigorous a charge upon two squadrons of the cuirassiers that they were completely overthrown; the remaining troops were, at the same time, led forward by Arentschild against two regiments of the enemy's cavalry, but the contest was too unequal to admit of the hussar's success, and although they drove back that part of the enemy's line that was immediately opposed to them, they were soon outflanked and suffered a severe loss. The brave captain Jansen was here killed, adjutant Brüggemann and cornet Deichmann also fell; lieutenants Oelkers, True and von Dassel were so severely wounded that they were obliged to leave the field; captains von Goeben, Schuchen, cornets Floyer and Hans von Hodenberg were also wounded, and so great a number of men and horses had fallen, that on re-forming, the whole seven troops could not muster more than about sixty file !

The invincible squares, however, resisted every effort of the enemy's horsemen, and Baring's resolute soldiers still held the buildings of la Haye Sainte. Napoleon therefore, seeing that any attempt against the centre would be ineffectual without the possession

1815.

June.

Notizen, &c. MSS. Journal of 3d. hussars MSS. Narrative of major Heise. MSS.

Batty.

of this farm, directed a second formidable attack to
be now made against it.

It was about five o'clock*.   The attack was made
by a preponderating force of not less than three divisions of the French army†, which advancing in close
Appendix
No. XXI. column, surrounded the place. Baring's soldiers
met the onset with firmness, levelling their trusty
rifles with certain aim against the dense masses of
the enemy ; every bullet took effect, and often more
than *one* assailant fell before the single ball of a
German rifleman.

The French, however, advanced with unshaken
firmness.   Regardless of the fire, they threw themselves against the walls of the buildings, and
endeavoured to wrest the arms from the hands of the
Germans through the loop holes, or rushing upon
the open gateway, braved the bayonets of the
defenders.   This being a weak point, the assailants
See Plan,
No. 5. seemed confident of being able to force in, but the
little garrison knew its value, and not an opening
was given.   Man after man was bayoneted by
Baring's unyielding soldiers at this gateway, until the
slain actually formed a rampart for the assailants;—
but still no entrance was given, and the furious
contest continued to rage.

On examining into the state of his ammunition,
major Baring found that the continual firing had
reduced it one-half, and he immediately sent an officer
to the brigadier with a request for a fresh supply.

* Wynecken. MSS.   † Batty.

But no rifle ammunition was to be had; the 1815. cart which should have brought it, was upset in the June. general confusion that existed on the Brussels road, Notes of captain Christoph Heise MSS. and no other means of supply were at hand. This calamity was unknown to major Baring, and some time having elapsed without the expected arrival, he despatched another officer to the rear, with the same request.

The skirmishers of the fifth line battalion under Appendix XXI. captain von Wurmb were now sent to his assistance; Wurmb was killed at the head of his men. Serviceable as this detachment was, it could not compensate for the want of ammunition, and after maintaining an uninterrupted contest for half an hour longer, a third messenger was sent off for a supply; this proved as fruitless as the two former requisitions, however two hundred Nassau troops were added to the numbers of the little garrison, and the desperate struggle raged on.

The principal contest was carried on at the open entrance to the barn; against this every effort that the most determined courage, and the most untiring exertion could make, was directed by the enemy; but in vain: every Frenchman who attempted to cross the threshhold fell a sacrifice to his temerity.

At length the assailants finding themselves completely baffled at the gateway, gave up the hope of being able to effect an entrance into the buildings by direct assault, and resorted to the expedient of setting the barn on fire. A thick smoke soon issued

1815.

June.

Appendix
XXI.

from the thatch, and spread alarm among the defenders, for although there was no want of water in the court, all means of conveying it had been broken up, and the greatest consternation prevailed.

Luckily a happy expedient suggested itself to major Baring, who, observing the large cooking kettles that were carried by the Nassau troops, tore one of them from the back of a soldier, and filled it with water; several officers did the same; the men followed this example, and, facing almost certain destruction, boldly carried the water to the flaming barn. Soon all the kettles of the Nassauers were employed in this work, and the fire was eventually extinguished; but many a brave man had fallen, and many more, covered with wounds, continued to expose themselves with a degree of devotion beyond all praise. Among the most conspicuous was Frederick Lindau, a private of the second light battalion, who although bleeding profusely from two wounds in the head, stood firmly at the small door of the barn, and from thence defended the main entrance. Baring, seeing that the cloth about his head was not sufficient to stop the effusion of blood, repeatedly called upon him to go back; but Lindau regardless of his wounds, as of a large bag of gold which he had taken from the enemy, and carried about his person, refused to stir from the spot, "saying: "He would be a scoundrel that deserted you, so long as his head is on his shoulders"! This gallant fellow was afterwards taken prisoner and lost his treasure*.

More than an hour was occupied in this second assault of the farm, and now the French, tired from their fruitless efforts, again fell back. The relief thus given to the Germans may be well imagined, but the anxiety of their commander was little diminished ; every new attack served more and more to impress upon him the importance of the post, and more clearly to place before his eyes the deep responsibility of the command with which he had been entrusted. Placed with a small body of men in an isolated position, on the retaining of which the lives of his soldiers,—his own honour,—perhaps the safety of the whole army depended ; and where he would, in all probability be called upon to make a decision involving all these considerations—major Baring, could not but feel a painful anxiety for the result, which none of the means at his disposal were adequate to remove.

On counting the remaining cartridges he found that the men had not, on an average, more than from three to four each ! The gallant fellows made light

---

* Dahrendorf and Lindhorst of the same battalion, also distinguished themselves in the defence of la Haye Sainte : The former, although suffering from three bayonet wounds, was one of the first to assist in quenching the fire, and remained in the building to the last, when, in endeavouring to reach the position, a case shot shattered his leg, and he was left senseless on the field ; Lindhorst defended a breach which the enemy had made in the wall of the court yard with such determination, that when the ammunition failed, he maintained himself for a considerable time, alternately, by means of his rifle-sword, a large stick, and a brick which he had torn out of the wall !—Guelphic Archives. MSS.

of their wounds, and bodily fatigue ; they spared no exertion to repair the fractured walls and defences of the place, but they could not be insensible to the helpless condition in which they were placed by the want of ammunition, and made the most reasonable remonstrances to their commanding officer on the subject. These were not wanting to cause urgent representations of his critical situation to be sent in by major Baring, and he finally reported that without another supply of ammunition, he would be utterly unable to sustain another attack. But all was in vain ; no ammunition arrived, and the enemy's columns were again seen advancing on the farm !

"At this moment," says the gallant officer, " I would have blessed the ball that came to deprive me of life ;"—but more than life was at stake." The conduct of the second light battalion of the legion on this memorable day,—their complete abandonment of all consideration for their personal safety,—the enthusiasm with which they rallied round their brave leader,—the devotion with which they voluntarily sacrificed themselves to the cause of Europe, and their country,—may have been equalled, but has certainly never been excelled. On Baring exhorting his men to courage, and economy of their ammunition, one unanimous reply broke from them :—"No man will desert you; we will fight and die with you"!—But this history would assume the garb of romance were the various traits of heroism to be recorded here, which distinguished the soldiers of the

King's German Legion on the memorable field of
Waterloo.

The French columns again closed upon the devoted farm, and irritated at the protracted opposition
which was made, renewed the attack with redoubled
fury. Finding the same resistance at the open gate
way, they again attempted to fire the barn, but this
was defeated by the same means which had succeeded before; now, however, every shot fired by
the brave defenders, rendered their situation more
critical, and Baring, for the last time, sent an officer
to the rear, saying "that he must, and would give up
the place, if no ammunition was sent him": the same
cause which first prevented a supply, rendered this
message also ineffectual.

The fire of the defenders now gradually diminished;
they called loudly on their commander for ammunition,
adding "we will readily stand by you, but we must
have the means of defending ourselves."—Baring's
feelings may be imagined!—The officers now represented to him the utter impossibility of retaining the
place under the existing circumstances, and the
French, at the same time, mounting the roof and walls,
and pressing through the open gateway, which could
no longer be defended,—he reluctantly gave the
order to retire from the yard into the rear garden.

Wishing, however, to counteract the bad impression which this movement was likely to make upon
the men, he left the dwelling house occupied, and
under the charge of the same officers, who had

proved themselves so worthy of the trust. The passage to the interior of this house was very narrow and many of the men, while crowding in, were overtaken by the enemy, who vented their rage upon them in the lowest abuse, and the most brutal treatment. Here it was that ensign Frank, who had already been wounded, was furiously attacked by two French soldiers; the first he ran through with his sabre, but, at the same moment his left arm was broken by a ball from the second; in this condition he sought safety in one of the inner rooms of the house, and managed to conceal himself behind a bed. Two men of the battalion also endeavoured to secure themselves in the same room, but the French followed, refusing quarter, and shot them both before his face; Frank, however, had the good fortune to remain concealed until the farm was retaken by the allies.

The dwelling house being now in the hands of the enemy, Baring saw that it would be impossible to retain the garden, and therefore directed the men to retire, as well as they could, to the main position; the detachments that had joined him as reinforcements, returned to their respective corps, and with the remnant of his brave followers, he joined the first light battalion in the hollow road behind the farm.

Here the combat again raged, and many men and officers were struck down: of the first light battalion, captain Henry von Marschalck, who throughout the day had exhibited a degree of coolness and

bravery that could not be exceeded, was killed; 1815.
lieutenant Albert also fell; captain von Gilsa had his June.
right arm shattered; lieutenants Wolrabe, Leonhardt, Appendix XX.
Behne, Miniussir; captain Christian Wynecken, lieutenants Koester, Gibson, Genzkow, and Adolph Heise
were wounded, the three first severely ; of the second
light battalion lieutenants Frederick Kessler, Luidam,
Riefkugel, Timmann (adjutant), Knop and Meyer,
were wounded, the greater number severely, and the Appendix XXI.
gallant lieutenant Grœme, as he swung his cap in the
air to cheer on the men, had his right hand shattered.
In the retreat from the buildings captain Holtzermann
and lieutenant Tobin had been taken prisoners, the
latter as well as lieutenant Carey being wounded ;
major Hans von dem Bussche, of the first light battalion, was also severely wounded in the right arm,
and was afterwards obliged to suffer amputation ;
major Baring had many narrow escapes : four balls
entered the cloak which was strapped in front of the
saddle of the dragoon horse which he accidentally
happened to meet with when his own was shot; another
ball knocked off his hat, and just at the moment
when he had alighted to pick it up, a sixth ball
entered his saddle!

The main impediment to the enemy's advance upon Batty's campaign of 1815.
the allied centre having been removed by the evacu-
ation of la Haye Sainte, a large body of cuirassiers
moved down into the valley between that farm and
Hougoumont, where, almost entirely sheltered from
the fire of the opposing batteries, they could readily

take advantage of any disorder that might occur in the allied line; some horse-artillery were also brought up to the rise of the ground behind la Haye Sainte, and now Napoleon made furious efforts to establish himself in the centre of the British position. His cavalry made repeated charges, while column after column of infantry pressed forward to feed the attack. On the right centre the guards were assailed by the cuirassiers of Kellermann, who, under cover of a tremendous cannonade, repeatedly penetrated between the squares, but were as often driven back; the Brunswickers also, who had been moved down to Hougoumont, received the horsemen with admirable steadiness, and on all points Napoleon's powerful efforts were baffled, and the ground was covered with his slain.

Journal of 5th line battalion. MSS. Wyncken's Narrative. MSS.

But not without immense losses to the brave troops which made this effective resistance, and the fight fell heavily upon the German legion and Hanoverian battalions of the third division: The fifth line battalion of the legion stood in square, behind the hollow road which has been before mentioned, and a column of French infantry having debouched from la Haye Sainte upon this point, sir Charles Alten sent colonel Ompteda directions to deploy, if possible, the fifth battalion, and attack the column. Ompteda represented that such a movement could not be made without a useless sacrifice of men, more particularly as a body of the enemy's cavalry lay in wait on the other side of the ravine. At this moment the prince of Orange rode up and ordered colonel Ompteda to

1815.

June.

deploy; on the same representations being made to his royal highness, he impatiently repeated the order, upon which Ompteda instantly mounted his horse, gave the fatal word of command, and led forward the battalion. His gallant men jumped cheerfully over the ravine in their front, and fell upon the French column with a loud hurrah!;—the column gave way, and fled,—but just at the same moment, the enemy's horsemen rushing from their ambuscade, came thundering down upon the flank and rear of the German battalion! The consequence may be imagined;—the battalion was literally ridden over, and the slaughter was tremendous. The brave colonel Ompteda, an officer as distinguished for personal courage, as for all the higher qualities of a soldier and a man, was killed; the adjutant Schuck also fell; captain Sander, lieutenants von Berger, von Bothmer, Klingsöhr, von Witte, Meyer, Walther, Winckler were all wounded, and about one hundred and thirty serjeants and soldiers were struck down: in short, lieutenant-colonel von Linsingen and about eighteen men were all of the battalion that remained together after this fatal charge.

Encouraged by this success the French cuirassiers advanced upon the centre of the position; but the German riflemen from the hollow road, saluted them with a volley which checked their progress, and they wheeled about. Sir Frederick Arentschild now led forward the third hussars of the legion, and dashed after the cuirassiers, but these quickly made

Journal of 3d. hussars. MSS.

front, and a furious combat ensued between the contending regiments.

This was continued for nearly a quarter of an hour, with little advantage on either side, when some squadrons of the enemy's lancers appearing in rear of the hussars, they were obliged to withdraw, having their numbers reduced to forty files,* and with the loss of their leader, the brave captain von Kerssenbruch.†

The two squares formed by count Kielmansegg's brigade were terribly mutilated by this attempt of the enemy to break the centre, and an opening was almost effected in this part of the allied line; for one flank of the right square, formed by the field-battalions Bremen and Verden, was swept away,—the square being reduced to the form of a triangle, and the left square, consisting of the field-battalions Grubenhagen and Duke of York, fell back nearly broken. The commanding officers, also, of both these squares, had been struck down;—the ammunition had begun to fail;—sir Charles Alten,

---

* Notizen, &c. MSS.

† An interesting incident occurred on this occasion : a corporal of the third hussars had been surrounded, and carried away by the enemy's cavalry, but having had the adroitness to make his escape, was returning to his regiment, when he met a cuirassier who was similarly circumstanced with regard to the hussars. The corporal, although bleeding from a wound, instantly attacked the cuirassier, who was not less bold in meeting his opponent, and a single combat took place in sight of both regiments, neither of which attempted to interfere. The hussar was suffering much from loss of blood, but his activity gave him the advantage over his opponent; he gained the cuirassier's left side,—gave him a cut in the face, and with a second blow, brought him to the ground. He then rode quietly to his regiment, which received him with well merited cheers.—Narrative of General Baring. MSS.

sir Colin Halkett, and the prince of Orange had been all wounded, and of the brigadiers of the third division, count Kielmansegge alone was left to rally and re-organize the shattered remnants of the division. This, the gallant officer executed with great bravery and firmness, and the troops being, as far as it was possible, provided with ammunition, he resolutely led them back to their place in the position.

The light batalions of the legion had also been forced back; a third horse had been killed under major Baring, and falling upon him, nearly deprived him of the use of his leg; he managed, however, to creep to a farm-house, where he was assisted on another horse, and although almost distracted with the pain of his wound, sought the remnant of his brave battalion. But they had been obliged to leave the field from the want of ammunition !.

Appendix XXI.

The right wing of the fifth division was now thrown back, and the landwehr battalions Giffhorn and Hameln from colonel von Vincke's Hanoverian brigade, were brought up from the left, and placed on the high road in rear of the centre.

The allied army at this eventful period of the day, was reduced to about thirty-four thousand men*,

---

* "Our loss had been severe, perhaps not less than ten thousand killed and wounded. Our ranks were further thinned by the numbers of men who carried off the wounded, part of whom never returned to the field. The number of Belgian and Hanoverian troops, many of whom were young levies, that crowded to the rear, was very considerable, besides the number of our own dismounted dragoons, together with a proportion of our infantry, some of whom, as will always be found in the best armies, were glad to escape from the field. These thronged the road leading to Brussels in a manner that none

but although thus thinned in numbers, and somewhat forced back from their position, they still maintained a firm countenance; the right wing had as yet been but little engaged; the duke of Wellington shewed no anxiety as to the result;* and no doubt could be entertained that the arrival of the Prussians would speedily turn the scale of victory in favour of the British chief.

The Prussians had been expected at one o'clock†, but delayed by a fire which broke out at Wavres, and the difficulties of the road in the defiles of St. Lambert, it was past five o'clock before the fire of Bulow's corp was observed from the allied posi-tion‡, and about half-past six when the first Prussian corps came into communication with the allied extreme left near Ohain.§

Meantime intelligence reached Blucher that his third army-corps under general Thielmann had been attacked at Wavre by a considerable force of the

but an eye-witness could have believed, so that, perhaps, the actual force under the duke of Wellington at this time, (half-past six), did not amount to more than thirty-four thousand men."—Pringle's Remarks, pages 371—2.

Muffling makes a still further reduction: "It may be calculated," says he "that up to this time (half-past six o'clock,) the army of the duke of Wellington had already lost more than eighteen thousand men in killed and wounded; that, as is the case in all battles, particularly where young troops are engaged,—as many more were occupied with the transport of the wounded, and finally, that several thousand young, or badly commanded troops, had left the field; hence it follows that the duke of Wellington at this period of the day, had but some thirty thousand disposable men."—Geschichte des Feldzug's, p. 34.

* Pringle.   † Batty.

‡ Pringle.   § Pringle.

enemy, who were already disputing the possession of the town ; but the marshal did not allow himself to be distracted by this intelligence, and seeing that in his front only was the day to be decided, he continued his march*, and directed the third corps to remain on the Dyle, and maintain themselves as well as they could†.

Napoleon sent his sixth corps, and two regiments of cavalry against the Prussian advance, and now seeing the powerful diversion which had been commenced by Blucher, and the desperate situation of his army, he resolved on making a last effort against the British centre with the infantry of the imperial guard.

These troops had hitherto been held in reserve, and almost out of the reach of fire, and they were now moved down to the bottom of the declivity of Belle Alliance, and formed under Napoleon's own eye into two columns of attack‡. As a means of encouragement Buonaparte imposed upon them the fiction that the Prussians whom they saw on the right were the troops of Grouchy, and, standing on one side of the road as the dauntless soldiers passed in review before him, he is reported to have said, pointing to the direction of their march, "That is the road to Brussels,"

It was about seven o'clock when the French guards were thus brought into action§. They consisted of six

* Armée Bericht der Preussischen Armée vom neider Rhein.

† Muffling.　　　　‡ Scott.　　　　§ Wellington's Despatch.

battalions of the grenadiers of the old guard, which advanced in contiguous columns of companies led by the distinguished Ney, while eight battalions of the chasseurs of the guard formed another attack on their left. Supported by a heavy cannonade, these intrepid soldiers ascended to the British position ; Ney's horse was killed under him as he advanced, but the gallant veteran marched on foot at the head of the columns, leading the attack in a manner worthy of the reputation of so distinguished a soldier. General Maitland's brigade of British guards was wheeled up in four deep to meet this attack. These troops waited the
near approach of the enemy with firmness, and then commenced a fire upon the heads of the columns which never ceased for a moment. Notwithstanding the loss and severe check which they suffered from this fire, the French still advanced, and, arriving within about fifty yards of the British line, attempted to deploy. But the fire of the guards closed around them ;—they staggered,—gave way ;—the attempt to deploy was in vain, and a confusion arose in their ranks which was not to be allayed.

Napoleon watched intently the progress of his chosen soldiers, and on seeing the attacking columns stagger, and become confused, his face became pale as that of a corpse ; he muttered to himself "they are mingled together," and then saying to his attendants "all is lost for the present," he rode away from the field.

The English guards now charged and broke the

disordered columns in their front; but the chasseur
battalions from the enemy's left, threatened the right
flank of general Maitland's brigade, and he, therefore,
changed front, and prepared to meet the attack.
Meantime the allied right wing, which had been
brought forward by the duke of Wellington during
the contest in the centre, came to the assistance of
the guards. The British brigade of the second division,
under general Adam, attacked the chasseurs on ther
left flank, while Maitland charged them in front, and
thus placed between two fires, the French guard soon
fell into disorder, which was quickly communicated
to the troops in their rear. Meantime the Prussians
after meeting with some check at Frischemont* had
begun to operate with considerable effect; Bulow's
artillery was heard in rear of the enemy's right; the
French sixth corps, as well as the young guard had
become warmly engaged with the Prussian advance,
and now Wellington seeing that the long wished-for-
moment had arrived for the allies to become the
assailants,—gave orders for the whole army to
advance.

The cavalry brigades of sir Hussey Vivian and sir
Ormsby Vandeleur, which had previously been
moved to the rear of the right centre, formed along
the crest of the position, and charged down upon the
retiring masses; general Adam's brigade closely followed by that of general Maitland, pressed after the

* Muffling.

1815.

June.

Batty's
campaign
of 1815.

1815.
——
June.

discomfited guard; colonel du Plat's brigade of the German legion, and colonel Halkett's Hanoverian brigade drove before them the troops in their front; and soon the whole allied army from its different positions, pressed forward on the great road leading to Genappe.

Batty's campaign of 1815.

Four battalions of the old guard still bravely held their ground, and formed squares near Belle Alliance to check the pursuit, but they also were eventually carried away in the overwhelming confusion which prevailed; the village of Planchenoit, in the enemy's rear, which had been long obstinately defended, was now carried by storm by the Prussian troops, and the retreat became a flight*; the panic spread through every part of the enemy's ranks;—the entire army became a mass of confusion†;—whole columns threw down their arms and fled, and the cannon, ammunition, with the entire matériel of this once brilliant army fell into the hands of the victorious allies.

Wellington's unequalled soldiers were joined on the heights of Planchenoit by the advance of Bulow's corps, and prince Blucher, meeting the duke at Belle Alliance, undertook to follow the enemy " with his last horse and man"‡ throughout the night.

Narrative of captain Hesse. MSS.

The German legion and part of the Hanoverian brigade of the second division, as well as major Sympher's horse-battery of German artillery were conspicuously engaged during the advance of the

---

* Armée Bericht, &c.   † Bulletin, Monitéur, June 21.

‡ Armée Bericht, &c.

1815.

June.

Narrative
of captain
Hesse.
MSS.

right wing. These brigades had stood in column
without being employed, during the early part of the
day, but when, about four o'clock, the enemy's cavalry, passing through the intervals of the squares,
penetrated to the second line, their front was changed,
and they were moved in the direction of Hougoumont. The second line battalion being at the head
of the column, was enabled to give timely protection
to the artillerymen of a battery which had been attacked by the French cuirassiers, while the skirmishers
of the brigade, who stood on the right flank, poured
upon the horsemen a volley, which instantly drove
them back. A new line of French cavalry afterwards
appeared in front, driving the allied squadrons before
them, but Sympher, quickly unlimbering his guns,
fired with such effect through the intervals of the
column, that the horsemen fled.

Notes of
captain
Christoph
Heise.
MSS.

At this time also, about seven o'clock, the first and
third line battalions, formed in one square, beat off a
powerful charge of the enemy's cavalry, as did the
fourth battalion, which formed another square.

Narrative
of captain
Hesse
MSS.

The second line battalion presssed on towards
Hougoumont, from the garden of which a hot fire
was poured upon them, but rushing forward they
threw themselves into the ditch by which the place
was surrounded, and then, aided by the skirmishers
of the brigade, charged into the garden, and
progressively drove the enemy before them in the
direction of Belle Alliance; the remaining battalions
advanced in a line of four deep on the left of the farm,

and a large battery of the enemy's artillery was deserted by the gunners as they approached.

The first brigade of the legion suffered a severe loss in these movements: colonel du Plat, who commanded the brigade was killed; his brigade major, captain Wiegmann, of the second light battalion, also fell; captain von Saffe, Charles von Holle, and ensign Lücken, of the first line, as well as captains Tilee, of the second, Diedel of the third, and ensign Cronhelm of the fourth battalion were killed; major George Chüden, brevet major Leue, and captain George Heise of the fourth, as well as lieutenants Jeinsen and Leschen of the third line were mortally wounded; major von Robertson, captain von Schlutter, lieutenants Müller, von Einem, Henry Wilding and adjutant Schnatt of the first; captain Purgold, lieutenants von der Decken and Fischer of the second; major Boden of the third, and lieutenants de la Farque and Hartwig of the fourth line battalion were severely wounded; several other officers of the brigade were slightly wounded, and the casualties among the non-commissioned officers and men of these battalions alone, amounted to nearly five hundred.

The battalion Salzgitter of Halkett's brigade, made a gallant charge with the bayonet in the wood of Hougoumont on the right of the legion battalion, while the battalion Osnabrück, leaving the farm on its right, advanced under the immediate guidance of colonel Halkett, and attacked and broke a square of the enemy's imperial guard. This square formed part of the brigade of general Cambronne, who was captured by colonel Halkett with a degree of chivalrous daring that has seldom been exhibited in modern warfare. :—

Colonel Halkett's brigade consisted of new raised troops, the greater part of whom were then, for the first time, in presence of an enemy, and they became exposed to a destructive fire from the brigade of general Cambronne, which formed the extreme left of the French final attack. Halkett pushed forward his skirmishers to meet the enemy's advance; Cambronne's horse was shot under him, and Halkett, seeing the French general in front, cheering on his men, thought that a good opportunity was thus afforded him for inspiring his young soldiers with confidence, and dashing forward alone, towards the French general, he threatened to cut him down. But Cambronne dropped his sword, and surrendered himself to the gallant colonel, who proceeded with his prize to the British lines. Halkett's horse now received a ball, and fell, and on disengaging himself from the animal, he found, to his dismay, that the French general was coolly walking back to his own troops !—By great exertion, however, he brought the horse again upon his legs;—overtook his prisoner, and thrusting his hand into the general's aiguilette, dragged him off at a canter to the allied lines*.

* And yet, it was, this very brigade of the French guard, with general Cambronne at its head that figured in the poetic fiction about "*La garde meurtmais ne se rende pas:*" The above anecdote is given on the authority of an eye witness.

The second dragoons of the German legion made a brilliant charge upon the enemy's cavalry during the allied advance : This regiment it will be remembered, had been detached from sir William Dörnberg's brigade, in the early part of the day, for the purpose of watching a body of the enemy's cavalry which shewed itself in the neighbourhood of Braine la leud; but these withdrawing about half-past six, the regiment returned to the field, and soon after received orders to charge a large body of the enemy's cuirassiers and chasseurs, which stood in a most favourable position behind a ditch.

The French received the charge with a carbine fire from their rear ranks, and then went about, followed by the Germans. The superior numbers of the enemy, however, enabled them to wheel round upon the flanks and rear of their pursuers, who were thus thrown into disorder, and lieutenant-colonel de Jonquiéres and Meydell were both wounded. At this

Appendix
XXII.

critical moment major Friederichs, on whom the command of the regiment devolved, rallied round him a few of the dispersed men, and made front to the enemy; the rest of the scattered horsemen soon placed themselves on his flanks, and led by the gallant officer, again advanced upon their opponents whom they put to flight, capturing a gun and making many prisoners : they also retook those of the regiment who had been made prisoners in the first charge.

For his distinguished conduct on this occasion major Friederichs received the special thanks of the

duke of Wellington, as well as of sir William 1815.
Dörnberg, who commanded the brigade. June.

Captain von Bülow, and cornet Drangmeister Journal of 2d dragoons MSS.
were killed in these attacks, and captain von Harling,
lieutenant Ritter, and cornet Lorentz were severely
wounded.

The loss of the German artillery, although effectively engaged throughout the day, was not considerable: lieutenant von Schultzen was killed, and
captain Braun, lieutenant Erythropel, major Sympher
and lieutenant Lewis Heise were wounded, the two
first severely.

The reader will, perhaps, be interested in learning Appendix XXI.
how the day closed with the gallant major Baring, whom
we left in search of the remnant of his brave battalion : after riding about for some time in an almost
distracted state of mind, smarting from the pain of
his wound, and vainly seeking some trace of his men,
he was accidentally informed that they had been
obliged to leave the field, from the want of ammunition;
soon afterwards the cry of "Victory"; met his ear;
—the allied line advanced ;—Baring, having now no
men to command, joined the first hussars of the
legion, and, with them, followed the enemy in the
final pursuit by the cavalry brigade of sir Hussey
Vivian.

The halt having taken place, he again sought his
battalion, and anxiously enquired after the missing
officers and men. The invariable reply was " killed";
—" wounded;" out of three hundred and seventy

veteran soldiers with which he had commenced the battle, a mere handful remained effective. Depressed by feelings of bitter regret for the loss of his brave companions, and 'exhausted from the pain of his wound, he lay down to rest upon some straw which the men had collected for his use : on waking the next morning he found himself lying between a dead man and a dead horse !*

Armée
Bericht &c.

After the last unsuccessful attempt made by the reserve of the imperial guard, at the village of Planchenoit a wild scene of confusion ensued among the panic-stricken fugitives. Hurrying from Blucher's impatient soldiers, they became completely disorganized ; the high road, strewed with innumerable guns, waggons, arms, and fragments of every description, presented the appearance of an immense shipwreck ; those who attempted to rest in the hope of a less rapid pursuit, were driven from bivouac to bivouac ; —in some villages they attempted to make a stand, but on the first sound of the Prussian drums and bugles, they fled, or threw themselves into the houses, where they were cut down or taken prisoners. The moon shone clear and bright, as the excited Prussians, full of the remembrance of French oppression, followed their luckless victims, and the wild chace continued,—fierce, merciless, and unceasing.

* This distinguished officer has since been raised to the dignity of baron in his own country, and now commands the garrison of Hanover with the rank of major-general. The gallant Krauchenberg, also, who holds so conspicuous a place in the first volume of this history, has been similarly ennobled and promoted.

In Genappe, the fugitives attempted to check the pursuit by barricading the place with guns, ammunition waggons and overturned carriages, and a sharp musquetry fire was poured upon the Prussian advance at the entrance; but a few cannon shots and a hurrah! immediately cleared the place. Here, among other equipages, was found the carriage of Napoleon, which he had just left, to throw himself on horseback, and in which, in his hurry, he had left his sword and hat. Thus was the pursuit continued until daylight.

1815.

June.

Armée
Bericht&c.

The losses of the contending armies in this great battle were enormous. Out of seventy-five thousand French soldiers, scarce forty thousand effected their escape*, and six hundred officers, and fifteen thousand men were killed and wounded in the army of Wellington†. The brunt of the action fell chiefly upon the British and King's German Legion‡: of the legion alone one hundred and twenty-nine officers, and one thousand three hundred and forty-three non-commissioned officers and men were killed and wounded, and the loss of the Hanoverian battalions,—

---

* Armée Bericht, &c.　　　　† Scott.

‡ "The brunt of the action was chiefly sustained by the troops of the British, and King's German Legion, as their loss will shew. In stating this, it must be allowed that much support was afforded by the other contingents, but they were chiefly raw levies, newly raised, who could not be depended on in a situation of importance: some behaved ill, as is publicly known."— Pringle, in Scott's life of Napoleon, Vol. IX. page 377.

particularly of count Kielmansegge's brigade,—was considerable*.

Scott's life of Napoleon.

Napoleon, hearing that Grouchy's corps had been destroyed, and that marshal taken prisoner, made no attempt to rally his beaten troops, but leaving directions for the relics of the army to be brought together under Soult at Avesnes, he continued his flight through Charleroi and Philippeville to Paris, to which capital, on the night of the 20th he brought the news of his own discomfiture.

Pringle's Remarks.

Grouchy, however, after an obstinate conflict with Thielmann at Wavre on the 18th, had retreated with great ability before the second corps of the Prussian army, which had been detached to intercept his march, and the Prussians suffered severely in their attempts to press upon his rear-guard at Namur; he rallied many of the fugitives, and finally brought his army to Paris without loss,

Scott's life of Napoleon.

Napoleon's star of good fortune had now set, to rise no more, and his political existence was hurried rapidly to a close: a committee of the chamber of deputies declared that his abdication was absolutely necessary;—he made a vain attempt to resign in favour of his son;—a provisional government was formed, and arrangements were made for conveying him to America. These however were frustrated by the vigilance of the English cruizers, and he

* Count Kielmansegge's brigade, consisting of the field-battalions Bremen, Verden, Lüneburg, Grubenhagen, and duke of York, lost twenty-three officers and four hundred and ninety-eight men in killed and wounded.— Narrative of count Kielmansegge. MSS.

surrendered himself to captain Maitland of his majesty's ship Bellerophon, from whence he was transferred to the Northumberland, and, under the care of admiral sir George Cockburn, finally removed to the island of Elba.

The armies of Soult and Grouchy were driven under the walls of Paris by the British and Prussian troops, who storming some of the French fortresses, and blockading others, marched straight upon the capital. Some resistance was made at Issy, but on the 3d of July an armistice was concluded, according to which, Paris was surrendered to the allies, and the French army drawn behind the Loire.

On the 7th of July the allied armies took military possession of Paris, and the following day Louis XVIII re-entered his capital.

The victory of Waterloo at once terminated the war, and gave peace and freedom to Europe, and now the time drew near when the King's German Legion, agreeable to the conditions under which they had been enrolled in the British ranks, were, to bid adieu to their brothers in arms, and seek repose and recompense in the bosom of their fatherland. Few parted from their brave companions without regret; twelve long years of friendly intercourse,—of mutual toil and suffering— had served to cement those feelings of respect and esteem, which the participation in the dangers and successes of actual warfare, never fails to generate in the hearts of the brave ;—together they had fought ;— together they had conquered ;—led by the same chief whose brilliant victories have placed him on the highest pinnacle of military fame, they strove together for the cause of freedom, and of right;—together they shared the perils and the glories of a long and sanguinary war, and finally, together tore from its ambitious height the proud eagle that floated over oppressed mankind !

Appendix XXIII. G.

By a proclamation of the prince regent of England, acting in the name of his majesty, and dated the 24th of December 1815, the King's German Legion was ordered to be disbanded on the 24th day of the month in which each regiment should arrive in the kingdom of Hanover.

In pursuance of the orders which had been issued respecting the disbandment, that part of the legion attached to the Anglo-Belgian army, broke up from the neighbourhood of Paris towards the end of the year, and were marched to the several places in the kingdom of Hanover, which had been fixed on for carrying the orders into effect; the infantry moved in two successive divisions, entering their native land at Osnabrück, and were disbanded in the villages on the left bank of the Weser; the artillery and first hussars were disbanded in Hanover; the first dragoons at Celle; the second at Embden in East Friesland; the second hussars at Quackenbrück, and the third at Nordheim.

The whole of these regiments were disbanded from the British service on the 24th of February, 1816.

The sixth and seventh line battalions and third

foot battery which, it will be remembered, had been
left in Italy when the rest of the legion were removed
to Flanders, embarked from Genoa in the beginning
of February, and the infantry, arriving in the Ems
about the end of April, were disbanded at Norden
on the 24th of May.

The veteran battalion was disbanded at Osnabrück
on the 24th of February, and the greater part of the
men were placed upon the list of the Chelsea out-
pensioners.

In accordance with the letter of service under
which the legion was raised*, all the officers were
placed upon half-pay from the day of their reduction,
and the non-commissioned officers and privates were
allowed a gratuity of six kreutzers per league in aid of
their travelling expenses to their respective homes; Appendix
XXIII. G.
in addition to these allowances, each officer actually
present at the disbandment, was allowed two month's
full-pay from that date.

Although the engineer corps of the legion, from
having been broken into detachments, and employed
upon various distant services during the war, has not
been brought before the reader in any connected or
conspicuous point of view, yet it would be unjust to
the zeal and ability of its officers, to pass unnoticed
the responsible commands and important under-
takings with which many of them were entrusted:
captain Berensbach held the appointment of chief
engineer in the Ionian isles during the year 1813.

* See Vol. I. Appendix IV.

1816.

February

Notes of
services of
engineer
officers.
MSS.

and the construction of several public works, both civil and military, was commenced under his superintendence; being obliged in March 1814 to return to England, in consequence of ill health, his duties fell upon lieutenant Luttermann, under whose directions a considerable extent of road was completed in the island of Zante, and the construction of an aqueduct, a mole, and other important works, carried forward in the same island.

Captain Prott, after having been engaged in the construction of Martello towers on the coast of Sussex, was appointed, in the year 1807, second officer of engineers in the island of Jersey, where a citadel to protect the harbour of St. Hellier, was constructed under his superintendence. Both this officer and captain Berensbach also served at the siege of Copenhagen, and in the north of Germany under lord Cathcart.

Captain Meinecke shared in the sufferings of sir John Moore's army in 1808,—assisted at the siege of Flushing in the following year, and in the lines of Lisbon; he served in the trenches during the two first sieges of Badajos,—was afterwards appointed to an important engineer command on the Tagus, and, on the advance of the allied armies to Paris, after the battle of Waterloo, served under prince Augustus of Prussia, in his operations against the French fortresses.

Captain Appuhn served with the British army on the eastern coast of Spain; was in July 1814

appointed chief engineer in the Ionian isles, and the
following year, held the same situation at Antwerp
and its dependencies.

Captain Schweitzer was attached to the corps
under general Lyon in the north of Germany, in the
year 1813,—was afterwards commissioned to examine
and report upon the fortresses on the Scheldt, and
was subsequently entrusted with placing Mons in a
state of defence.

Lieutenant Unger, after serving with distinction
in the German artillery, with part of which corps he
was present at the battles of Talavera, Busaco, and
Albuera, became an engineer officer under captain
Meinecke in the lines of Lisbon; he assisted at the
first siege of Badajos, and afterwards directed the
works which had been commenced to aid the
navigation of the upper Douro. In April 1815 he
was employed under captain Meinecke at the fortifi-
cations of Ath, and subsequently became adjutant to
the siege equipment of the second Prussian army-
corps, which under prince Augustus of Prussia,
carried the several French fortresses on the advance
of the allied armies to Paris.

The members of the Hanoverian representative body, Appendix
XXIII. C.
called together by the prince regent in December,
1814, had expressed, in terms teeming with the
most elevated sentiments, " the feelings of high
respect, and deep felt acknowledgment" with which
their country was impressed towards the gallant
soldiers of the King's German Legion,—an address

most ably answered by sir Henry von Hinüber*;—
a second manifestation of their feelings was issued
by the same body on the 5th of February, 1816,
when they requested the duke of Cambridge to assure
the legion that "the assembled representatives of
the kingdom of Hanover, will never forget the great
deserts which this distinguished corps has won;—
by which the Hanoverian name has been rendered
glorious, and they will mark the moment of their
return to the common fatherland, as the happiest and
most joyful epoch in the annals of their history!".

But it remained for the legion's noble chief,—the
kind and estimable duke of Cambridge,—to soothe
the last moments of separation of his gallant corps,
by that consoling retrospect of their services, and those
earnest assurances of his personal esteem, which will
be found to accompany, in eloquent terms, the
following high testimonial from the commander-in-
chief of the British army :—

GENERAL ORDERS.

HEAD QUARTERS, HANOVER,
February 1, 1816.

" Field-marshal, his royal highness the duke of Cambridge,
is much gratified in communicating to the King's German Legion,
previous to their disbandment, the following letter, which he has
received from his royal highness the commander-in-chief."

HORSE GUARDS, Dec. 21, 1815.

Sir,

" His Majesty's government has notified to me that the King's
German Legion is forthwith to be transferred from the service of

* See Appendix XXIII. F.

Great Britain to that of Hanover, and I cannot allow this highly distinguished corps to pass from under my command, without expressing to you, as its colonel in chief, the very strong feeling of approbation and regard with which my mind is impressed by its uniform good conduct."

"In the various services in which the British army has been engaged during the course of the late eventful war, the King's German Legion has borne its ample part."

"It has participated in those achievements which have conferred the highest lustre on the British arms, and is justly entitled to share in the renown, with which they have been rewarded."

"When opposed to the enemy in the field, the bravery of the officers and soldiers of the King's German Legion has been eminently conspicuous, nor have their discipline, regularity, and good conduct, in whatever station they have occupied, whether in Great Britain or its dependencies, less given them a claim to my warmest acknowledgement and to the gratitude of the country."

"I request that your royal highness will communicate these my sentiments to every officer and soldier belonging to the King's German Legion, and assure them, that whatever may be their future destination, they will individually and collectively, ever retain my very sincere regard and earnest wishes for their honor and happiness."

I am Sir,

Your royal highness's

most affectionate brother,

FREDERICK.

To Field-marshal his royal highness   Commander-in-Chief.
the duke of Cambridge, K. G.,
&c. &c. &c.

"However unequal the duke of Cambridge feels himself to enhance the highly honorable testimony thus afforded by the commander-in-chief to the services and merits of the King's German Legion, his royal highness finds it impossible to separate from them, without adding the assurance of his lasting esteem."

"In taking a retrospective view of the variety of service in which it has been the good fortune of the legion to be engaged, during the eventful period of their employment as a British corps, the duke of Cambridge recollects with feelings of exultation, the frequent occasions, upon which their bravery and discipline have called forth the applause and commendation of the general officers, under whose command they have been placed ; still less would it become their colonel to forget their having so frequently been distinguished by the thanks of their sovereign and of the parliament of Great Britain."

"His royal highness cannot avoid, however, adverting, in particular, to the trying and ever memorable campaigns, in which the legion bore their share, while forming part of the British army in the Peninsula. In the fields of Talavera, Salamanca, and Vittoria, rendered immortal by the combined exertions of British and German valour, they have laid the imperishable foundation of a renown, which their country and the world will long contemplate with grateful admiration."

" To the completion of the brilliant detail of these services, the battle of Waterloo was alone capable of adding an increased splendour. There, encouraged by the presence of the illustrious chieftain, under whom they had so often before been led to victory, the King's German Legion nobly supported the reputation they had acquired, and powerfully aided the cause of Europe and their sovereign."

" Although the duke of Cambridge cannot view without sincere regret, the dissolution of a corps, to the formation and command of which, he will ever look back with peculiar pleasure, yet this feeling is very considerably diminished, when, as their colonel, he sees them returning victoriously to their native country, rewarded by the encomiums of their sovereign, and decorated with the honorable distinctions bestowed for their courage and good conduct."

" His royal highness would, however, deem this order very deficient, without its containing, in his own name, and in the name of the officers and men of the King's German Legion, an expression of the gratitude and respect, which the treatment they have experienced from the British government, cannot but have inspired. Participating, as they have done, in all the advantages, as well as the glory of British soldiers, the duke of Cambridge is convinced that they will long reflect, with pride and satisfaction, on their service in the cause of a nation, whose conduct towards them has been equally conspicuous for its justice and liberality."

"Recompenced by the blessings of peace,—to the restoration of which they have so greatly contributed;—cheered by the consciousness of having faithfully and nobly served their sovereign and their country,—their colonel congratulates the legion on the glorious and successful termination of their exertions; and in taking a final leave of them, the duke of Cambridge would be wanting to the feelings by which he is animated, if he did not assure both the officers and men, of the interest he will never fail to take in their welfare and prosperity."

By command of

Field marshal his royal highness

THE DUKE OF CAMBRIDGE.

J. H. REYNETT, Lieut.-Colonel,

Military Secretary.

We have thus traced the career of the distinguished legion from that period when foreign invasion first drove them from their native land, to the time when the glorious termination of a successful war restored them to their country and their homes. In the hour of danger;—in the day of death;—on the troubled ocean;—in the tented field;—sunk by privation, or stimulated by success, we behold them firm, fearless, temperate, brave;—faithful to their king; devoted to their country;—spurning the proffered bribe of dishonourable servitude;—sacrificing their dearest interests to the cause of freedom and of right.—We have seen them in the soft repose of social intercourse;—in the depressing moments of adverse fortune;—we have marked them protecting the retreat, and leading

the battle;—rescuing their comrades with chivalrous
bravery;—sharing their last morsel with the noblest
of animals.—We have watched them amid the chilling
snows of Galicia,—among the pestilential swamps of
Holland,—in northern tempests,—under a southern
sun;—but whether among the mountains of Spain,
the marshes of Holland, or under an Italian sky;
whether in social repose, or in warlike exertion;—
whether in the fury of the tempest, or the whirlwind
of the battle—at all times, and in all places—it is
still the same gallant, gentle, patient, faithful,
honorable German soldier!

It would be gratifying to add that the close of the
career of the King's German Legion was marked by
a disposal of the corps commensurate with the
services which the brave men had rendered to their
country; but a far different fate awaited them.

*   *   *   *   *

It was the intention of His Majesty George III,
and the prince regent of England, that the king's
German legion should constitute the basis of the
army to be formed for the service of Hanover, at the
termination of the war. Nothing could be more
natural than this design. The legion sprung directly
from the electoral army which had been dissolved at
Lauenburg in 1803, and whose most valuable relics,
with the true feelings of loyal and patriotic soldiers,
gave themselves up to the service of their sovereign,

and by a long and continuous course of faithful and gallant bearing, won for themselves a high place in the annals of a protracted and sanguinary war. The hope of liberating their country, and again returning to it in peace, was the motive by which the greater number of these brave men were actuated, and no stronger proof of this devotion could be given than was evinced by those, who, after the French occupation of Hanover, left their country, risking the loss of their property,—nay even of their lives—to serve under the British standard.

In the year 1815 the legion stood forth,—a corps which by its high degree of military discipline, and its long-tried and distinguished services, had gained the lasting acknowledgments of the English nation, and of the memorable commander under whose eyes it had fought. On the other hand we see, in the years 1813 and 1814, a country which for more than ten years had been systematically robbed and plundered by the enemy,—make a first exertion to form an army. The incorporation of the most discordant elements was inevitable, and a glance at the facts shews clearly how difficult it must be to mould such mixed and self-contending parts into a united body. Although the patriotism of a few, and the existing hatred of the French might justify good expectations, yet the time was too short, and the renewal of the war too recent to look for any certain result. Even the excellent—nay distinguished conduct, which several of the Hanoverian battalions

exhibited at the battle of Waterloo, furnished no
complete security for a long continued war. Besides
the greater part of these troops were not brought into
action. The legion, on this day, confirmed and increased the reputation which their former services
had won.

If, notwithstanding all these circumstances, the
disposal of the King's German Legion by the
Hanoverian government was not regulated by such
favorable conditions, either for the individuals who
were transferred to the Hanoverian service, or for
that service itself, as the nature of the case, and the
repeated expressions of royal and official authorities
gave reason to expect,—the cause must be considered
to rest upon a combination of individual facts, which
have occurred too near the present time, to enable us
confidently to pronounce judgment upon them, and
the discussion here would, perhaps, only excite
painful recollections. A reason often put forward
was the circumstance of the new raised officers
having been furnished with permanent royal commissions, the value of which, it was said, was not to be
diminished by the amalgamation of the legion with
the Hanoverian army. Thus officers of long and
distinguished service, found themselves given the
painful alternative of either retiring, in their best
days, upon their English half-pay, or submitting to be
placed under individuals, who, from the most varied
civil occupations, had just entered upon a military
life, or were in the enemy's ranks when the legion

were acting with distinction in the service of His
Majesty.

*　*　*　*　*　*

Thus terminated the career of a corps, which had commenced its course under the most unfavourable auspices,—which, by the moral power of its officers and men, led by one of the first commanders of the age, had reached a high degree of military importance and reputation,—but finally sunk under those influences which peace, and extraneous circumstances so often exercise on the most prominent features of war.

While we contemplate with feelings of regret the fate of those distinguished soldiers, of whose memorable services this history offers a feeble record, the motto of the present volume involuntarily presents itself to the mind :—

> " Wir, wir, haben von seinem Glanz und Schimmer
> Nichts, als die Müh' und als die Schmertzen,
> Und wofür wir uns halten in unserm Hertzen."

NATIONAL MONUMENT
TO MAJOR GENERAL
J.R.MACKENZIE
AND BRIGADIER GENERAL
E. LANGWERTH
WHO FELL AT
TALAVERA
JULY 28. M.DCCC.IX.

C.MANNING Sculptor

Victory laments the loss of her heroes, while the sons of
Britain recount their valiant achievements. — Against
the tomb are two wreaths, intimating the fall of two
warriors. — One of the boys bears the broken French
Imperial Eagle, which he is displaying to the other.
The helmet on the one boy, and the wreath of oak
on the other, imply the Military Service, connected
with its honors and rewards, in the sons of Britain.

This Monument occupies the upper ledge of the north transept in St Pauls Cathedral, London.

London J. & W. Boone 1837

Plate 1.

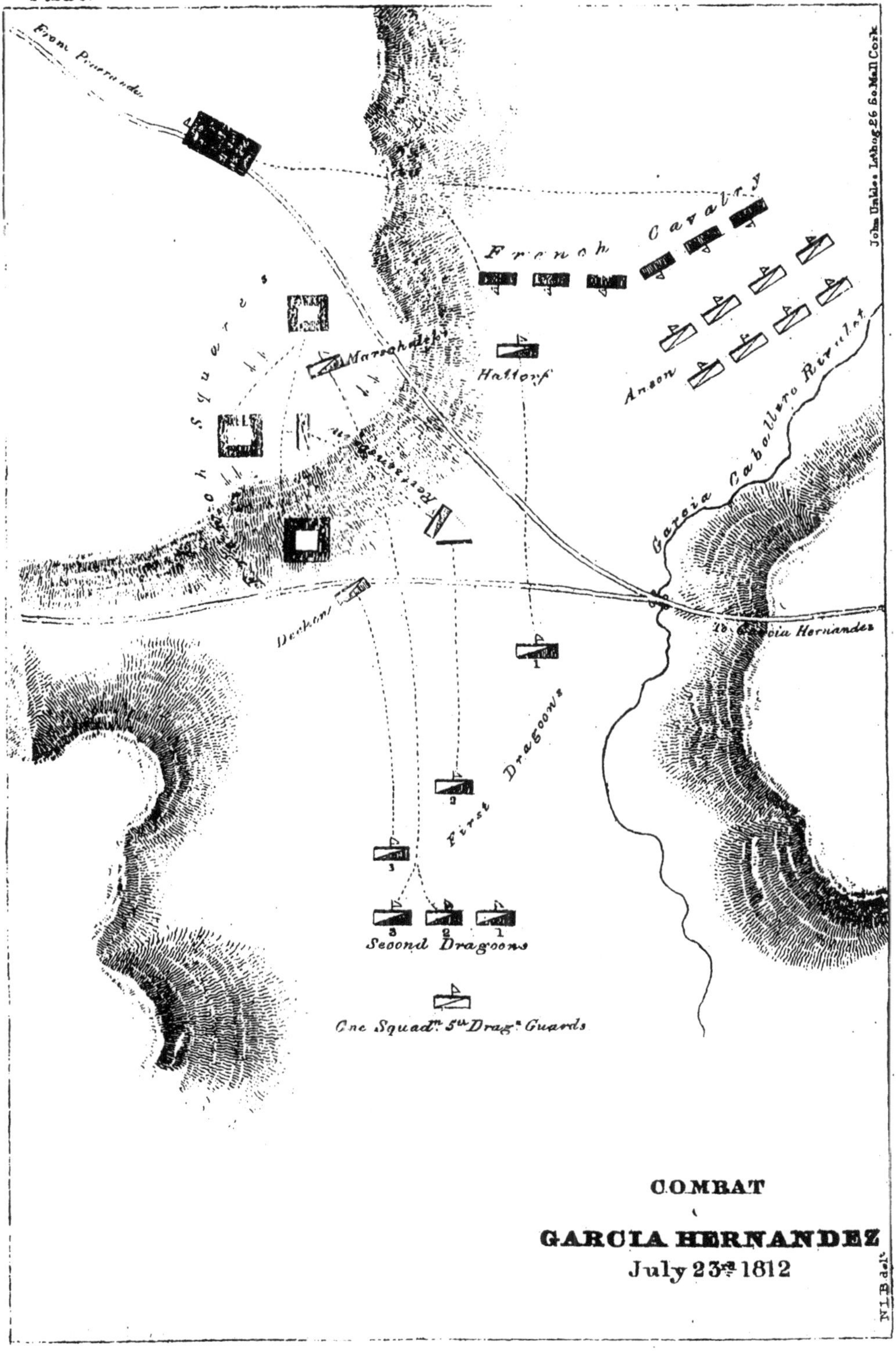

From Piarende

From Piarende

French Cavalry

Anson

Garcia Caballero Rivulet

Marshdeh

Hallort

To Garcia Hernandez

Deshon

First Dragoons

Second Dragoons
3   2   1

One Squad⟨n⟩. 5⟨th⟩ Drag⟨n⟩. Guards

COMBAT

GARCIA HERNANDEZ
July 23⟨d⟩ 1812

John Unilies Lethog. 26 Go Mall Cork

N.L.B del⟨t⟩

Plate II

From Ernani

From Tophic Lithr 2 G Gd Nov Cov.

Spaniards

Block House

Dispersed Troops

Canal

H. House

Block House

Canal

Vittoria Gate

Light Battalions

High Wall

Convent

Line Battalions

To Pamplona

Convent

Block House

From Vittoria

ATTACK
ON
TOLOSA
June 25ᵗʰ 1813

M.L.B fec.ᵗ

Plate III

BATTLE OF THE GOHRDE
16th Sepr 1813
Oldendorff
High Road from Lüneburg to Dannenberg
French Squares
Lutzow and Reiche
3d Hussars
Eichdorff
French in retreat
Nieperfitz
Lüben
Dübenkolde
Göhrde Castle
To Dannenberg
Allied Artillery
Forest

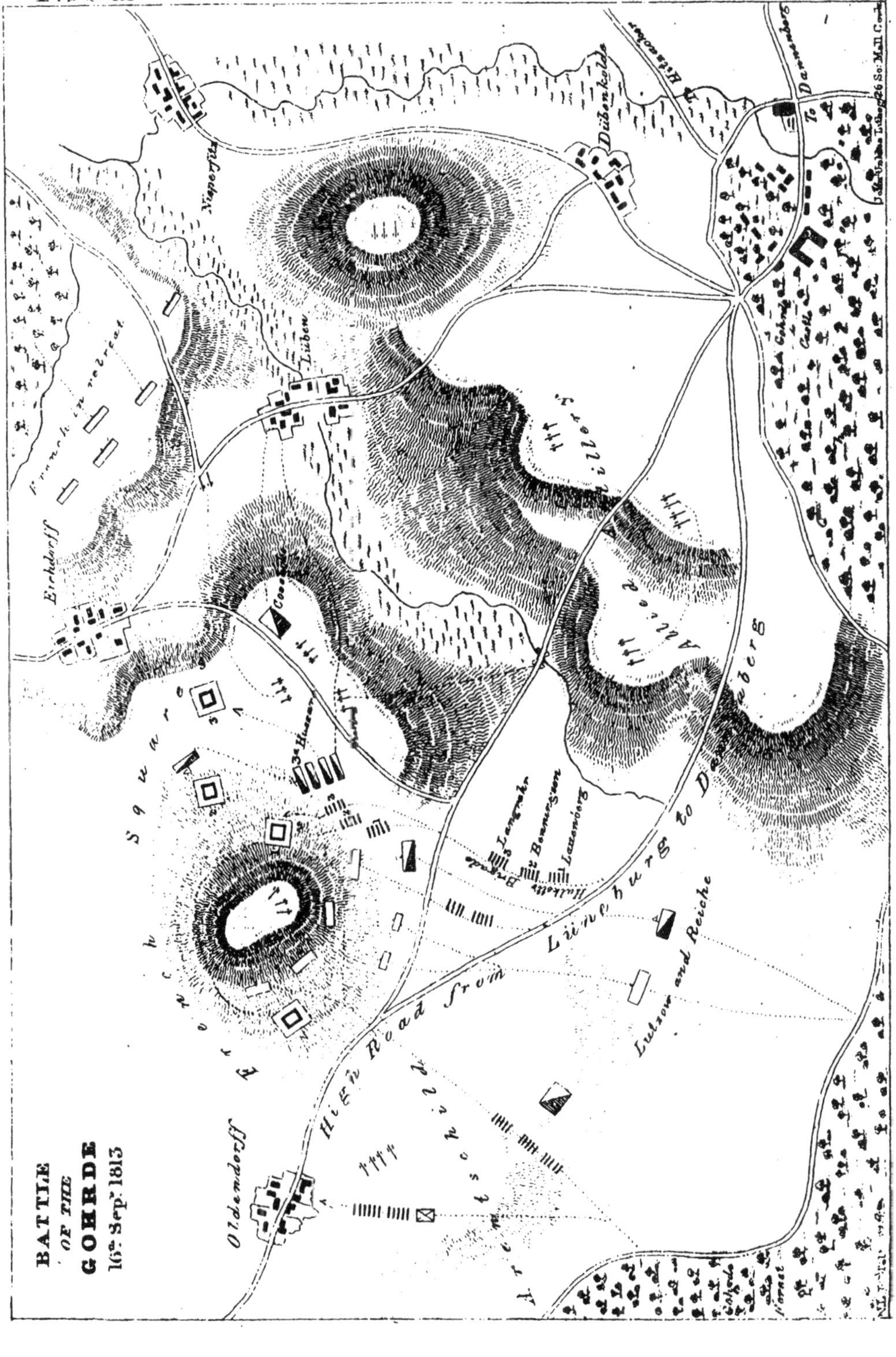

Plate V

Farm of
LA HAYE SAINTE
Defended by the 2.ᵈ Light Battalion
of the KING'S GERMAN LEGION
June 18.ᵗʰ 1815.

Belle Alliance

Barricade

Pond

Yard

Gateway

Principal Entrance *Small door* Back Entrance

Piggery

Wicket

Yard

Dwelling

House

Garden

High Road from Waterloo to

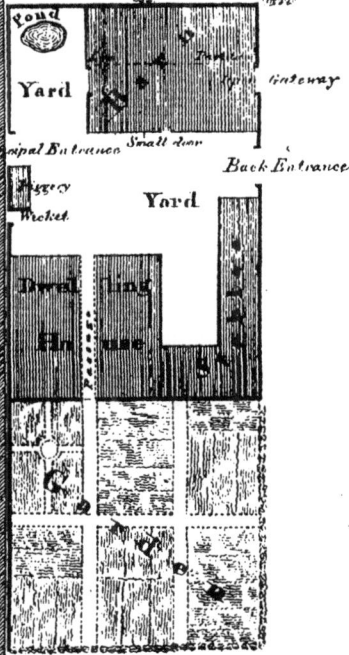

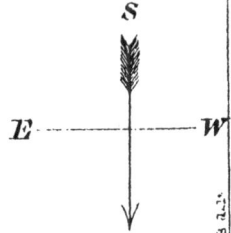

Ravine
held
by 95.ᵗʰ Reg.ᵗ

S

E ———— W

N

APPENDIX.

APPENDIX.

No. I.

EL BODON.

Extract from General Orders, dated Adjutant-general's Office,
RICHOSA, *2d October*, 1811.

* • • • • • • •

3.—The commander of the forces is desirous of drawing the attention of the army to the conduct of the second battalion 5th, and 77th regiments, and the 21st Portuguese regiment, and major Arentschildt's Portuguese artillery under the command of the honorable major-general Colville, and of the 11th light dragoons, and 1st hussars under major-general Alten, in the affair with the enemy on the 26th ultimo. These troops were attacked by between thirty and forty squadrons of cavalry with six pieces of cannon, supported by a division consisting of fourteen battalions of infantry, with cannon.

* * * * * * * * * *

5.—While these actions were performed, major-general Alten's brigade, of which there were only 3 * squadrons on the ground were engaged on the left, with numbers infinitely superior to themselves. These squadrons charged repeatedly, supporting each other, and took above twenty prisoners; and notwithstanding the immense superiority of the enemy, *the post would have been maintained,* if the commander of the forces had not ordered the troops to withdraw from it, seeing that the action would become

---

* This is probably a misprint in the published document for 5, which was the number of squadrons on the ground ; namely, 3 of hussars, and 2 of the 11th light dragoons.

still more unequal, as the enemy's infantry were likely to be engaged in it, before the reinforcement ordered to the support of the
post could arrive.

6.—The troops then retired with the same determined spirit,
and in the same good order with which they maintained their post
—the second battalion fifth regiment and seventy-seventh in one
square, and the twenty-first Portuguese regiment in another, supported by major-general Alten's cavalry and the Portuguese
artillery.

*   *   *   *   *   *   *   *   *   *   *

7.—The commander of the forces has been particular in stating
the details of this action in the general orders, as in his opinion, it
affords a memorable example of what can be effected by steadiness, discipline and confidence.   It is impossible that any troops
can, at any time, be exposed to the attack of numbers relatively
greater than those which attacked the troops under major-general
Colville and major-general Alten on the 25th of September ; and
the commander of the forces recommends the conduct of these
troops to the particular attention of the officers and soldiers of the
army, as an example to be followed in all such circumstances.

No. II.

DOCUMENTS RELATING TO THE HEAVY CAVALY BRIGADE OF THE KING'S GERMAN LEGION

A

Cornet von Hugo to captain von Bothmer.

TRANSLATION.

CLONMEL, 17th July, 1811.

MY DEAR BOTHMER,

You have so often, as well verbally as by letter, had the
kindness to offer me your friendly assistance, that it will not be
necessary for me to apologise for now availing myself of your offer
by requesting your advice and,—should you not be opposed to my

project,—your assistance respecting a matter in which I feel much interested. You have, no doubt, as well as myself, flattered yourself with the hope, that before many weeks we should leave this country, and embark for foreign service; but, alas! this hope seems to have completely vanished, for it appears the Irish gentlemen are far too anxious to keep us for attending executions, *(zum aufhängen)* and escorting the mail. I am sure that you, as well as every other right minded man, who has not entered the English service for the mere purpose of being provided with easy quarters, look with indignation upon this placing of our brigade behind every other regiment of the legion, and I, therefore, venture to lay before you a plan which may, perhaps, lead us to the desired object, and upon which I now request your opinion.

Namely: that an address be presented to the prince regent, setting forth our loyal sentiments, and begging that his royal highness's attention may be directed to us, with reference to foreign service.

Although I see clearly that this must be drawn up with the greatest consideration and care, yet I am of opinion that if these conditions be fulfilled, it cannot but serve us, and gain us respect; at least it can do us no injury in the estimation of the prince regent.

As it will naturally be very difficult to unite the opinions of the whole of our corps upon this point, I think the best plan would be, —provided you are not averse to the proposition,—to send round a circular, something in the shape of the annexed, in both regiments, which, however, I submit to your mature judgment; with this, in my opinion, your regiment, being the senior, should commence.

You will, no doubt, find many immediately to assent to the plan, and when a few have signed, be good enough to send me a copy of the circular, with the names, and I can certainly promise you, that in a few days, the names of two-thirds of the officers of this regiment will appear underneath: the rest will then soon follow.

Taken this matter into consideration, my dear Bothmer, and let me have your opinion as soon as possible.

A great part of my comrades here enter with heart and soul into this project, and unite with me in begging your assistance ; although they only know you by repute, yet is this sufficient to secure their confidence in you, in such a business.

They only wait the example of a regiment which is held in the high consideration that yours doubtless is by the whole legion,— to follow immediately themselves.

I shall look forward to the arrival of your answer with the greatest impatience.

Should you reject my plan, as being too immaturely considered, you will, I trust, allow my good intentions to stand as some excuse for this long letter.

Your friend and cousin,

LUDOLPHUS VON HUGO.

B.

PLAN.

The undersigned officers are firmly convinced that it has always been the anxious wish of their brother officers to prove their loyalty and devotion to his majesty, our most gracious king, in an active manner in battle against the common enemy, and, at the same time, to acquire for themselves, a part of the fame, which all the other regiments of the King's German Legion on foreign service have gained, and are daily gaining.

The late happy events in Spain and Portugal, and the not improbable prospect of a war in the north of Europe have rendered each more alive to these feelings. We can, without being suspected of self-love, presume that the government, after five year's experience, is convinced that we have performed every service with which we have been entrusted, with zeal and punctuality, and cannot, therefore but believe that the expression of the above wish will not be attributed to discontent with our present service, but from a zealous desire to prove ourselves still more worthy of the protection which has already, in so distinguished a manner, been afforded us by his most gracious majesty, and to give our best assistance to the success of the common cause; therefore that it will only be considered as the loyal expression of our feelings.

Presupposing that the whole of our brother officers unite with us in this opinion, we take the liberty of humbly submitting the following:—

I.—A deputation, consisting of a field officer, captain, lieutenant and cornet, to be named for the purpose of preparing an humble memorial to his royal highness the duke of Cambridge, setting forth our devotion to his majesty, and our anxious wish to testify the same, in an active manner, on foreign service, against the common enemy.

II.—To request the assistance of colonel von der Decken in preparing this memorial, and recommending it to the consideration of his royal highness the duke of Cambridge; and to beg that all our brother officers who are interested in the measure, will sign their names, and, as soon as possible, forward the document to those officers of our regiment who may be nearest at hand.

C.

Captain von Bothmer to Cornet von Hugo.

BALLINASLOE, *July 26th*, 1811.

MY DEAR HUGO.

Your letter of the 17th of July reached me a few days since, and I read its contents with the greatest pleasure.

In order that nothing should be left undone towards the accomplishment of our wish to be sent on active service, general Bock has had the kindness to draw up a petition for us, which, after it has gone round for signature in our regiment, will be immediately forwarded to yours for the same purpose. Bock will then, as brigadier, send, with our common petition, a letter from himself strongly supporting our request. I believe the quickest mode will be to send it by the post to the staff of your regiment.

Your sincere friend and cousin,

BERNHARD VON BOTHMER.

D.

REPLY.

CLONMEL, July 28, 1811.

MY DEAR BOTHMER.

I cannot describe to you with what anxiety I looked for, and with what pleasure I read the letter which I received from you yesterday. I may be justly proud of the friendship of a man like yourself, and in my own name, as well as in the name of all my friends in this regiment, I return you my heart-felt thanks for your prompt execution of our common object. Our colonel, as well as all the officers with whom I have spoken on the subject, think that the best and most expeditious mode is, to send your memorial after it has been signed, to us, which can be done in the quickest manner, by relays, through Roscrea, where, you know, a detachment of ours is stationed. We will send it round immediately on receipt, and after a few days, you will receive it back with the signature of all our officers. Our colonel will then request general Bock to prepare the memorial in the name of the brigade, and send it forward.

Send it to us therefore as soon as you possibly can.

Again I must apologise for the trouble which I have given you, and for which you will ever retain the gratitude of,

Your faithful friend and cousin,

LUDOLPHUS VON HUGO.

E.

Major-general von Bock to His Royal Highness the duke of Cambridge.

BALLINASLOE, ·*August* 9, 1811.

SIR,

Allow me most dutifully to request your royal highness, in laying before you the enclosed memorial of the officers of the first and second heavy dragoons of the King's German Legion, addressed to his royal highness the commander in chief, in which they petition that those regiments may be employed on active service,—that you will be pleased to approve of the memorial, and condescend to recommend it to the gracious consideration of his royal highness the duke of York.

The petitioners have every due sense of your royal highness's gracious encouragement to their anxious desire, which I took the liberty to represent not long since, in a private manner, which desire the men certainly have, in common with their officers, that these regiments might not be kept at home, when almost all the other troops of the legion are on service at present.

The officers, therefore, indulge themselves in hoping, that your royal highness will not be displeased at the present dutiful application to convey, through your medium, their humble petition to his royal highness the commander in chief.

I have, &c. &c.

G. VON BOCK,
Major-general.

To H. R. H. the duke of Cambridge, K.B.
colonel in chief, &c. &c.

F.

H. R. H. the duke of Cambridge, to major-general von Bock.

LEGION OFFICE, LONDON,
August 22, 1811.

SIR,

I have received your letter of the 9th instant, enclosing a memorial from the officers of the first and second regiment of heavy dragoons of the King's German Legion, addressed to his royal highness the commander in chief, requesting to be employed on active service. The manner in which the officers have expressed their wish, has met with my entire approbation, and I beg you will assure them of my thanks, and how much I am pleased with the expression of their laudable zeal for his majesty's service.

I immediately recommended their memorial to the favorable consideration of his royal highness the commander in chief, and I send you herewith enclosed, the copy of my letter, with his royal highness's answer to it.

> I am, Sir,
> Your's very sincerely,
> ADOLPHUS FREDERICK,
> *General and colonel in chief.*

To major-general von Bock,
&c. &c. &c.

G.

H. R. H. the duke of Cambridge to H. R. H. the commander-in-chief.

> LEGION OFFICE, LONDON,
> 16th *August*, 1811.

SIR,

I have the honor of transmitting to your royal highness, a letter from major-general von Bock, commanding the first and second heavy dragoons of the King's German Legion, now in Ireland, with a memorial from all the officers of those regiments, addressed to your royal highness, petitioning that the brigade might be employed on active service.

The manner in which the corps of officers volunteer their services will, I trust, meet with your royal highness's approbation, and I beg leave to add that, if the state of things in Ireland will admit of their being removed from that country, it would be a great advantage to the brigade to be employed on active service.

I have, &c. &c.

ADOLPHUS FREDERICK.

General and colonel-in-chief.

To Field-marshal H. R. H. the
duke of York, commander-
in-chief, &c. &c.

H.

H. R. H. the commander-in-chief to H. R. H. the duke of Cambridge.

HORSE GUARDS,
London, August 19, 1811.

SIR,

I lose no time in acknowledging the receipt of your royal highness's letter of the 26th inst., with its enclosures, and in assuring you that I am fully sensible of the zeal manifested by the first and second heavy dragoons of the King's German Legion in their expression of their desire to be employed on active service, conveyed through their commanding officer; and I have to desire that your royal highness will be pleased to convey my thanks to major-general von Bock, and those regiments of the brigade under his command, with an intimation of my readiness to give such favorable consideration to the object of their most laudable wishes, as the existing military arrangements will admit.

I am, &c. &c.

FREDERICK,

Commander-in-chief.

To H. R. H. the duke of Cambridge, K.B.
Colonel-in-chief, K. G. Legion, &c. &c.

I.

GENERAL ORDERS, SOUTH EASTERN DISTRICT.

Assistant Adjutant-Gen's. Office,
Kilkenny, Dec. 11, 1811.

The second heavy dragoons of the King's German Legion being under orders to embark for foreign service, lieutenant-general Wynyard takes this occasion of expressing his warm approbation of the exemplary good conduct of this regiment, which has been stationed for upwards of two years in the south-eastern district.

It is a circumstance highly creditable to this excellent corps, that during the whole of this period, dispersed, as it has been, in small parties through the most disturbed part of the country; frequently exposed to insult and attacks in the performance of its duty on the one hand, and to the temptation to inebriety and irregularity on the other,—*not a single instance* of neglect of duty, or of disorderly conduct has ever occurred, to the lieutenant general's knowledge, on the part of any individual belonging to it.

Lieutenant-general Wynyard desire that colonel von der Decken, and all the officers and men of the second heavy dragoons of the King's German Legion, will accept of his best wishes for their future welfare and success: such a regiment cannot fail of proving a most valuable acquisition to the army of the Peninsula, of which it is ordered to form a part.

By order of LT. GEN. WYNYARD.

JOHN HARVEY, major and A. A. general.

No. III.

RESERVE ORDERS.

Camp Before Badajos,
April 1, 1812.

" It having been reported to the commanding officer by the commanding engineer that the batteries, with the exception of that commanded by lieutenant von Goeben, did not fire at the breach last night, according to orders given, he is determined to report every officer to Lord Wellington who shall neglect this duty."

ADJUTANT GENERAL'S OFFICE,
Celerico, *March* 31, 1811.

G. O.

Lieutenant-colonel Offeney of the seventh line battalion, King's German Legion, is appointed to act as assistant in the department of the quarter-master-general.

ADJUTANT GENERAL'S OFFICE,
Villa Formosa, *May* 9, 1811.

G. O.

3.—Captain Heise of the second light battalion, King's German Legion, is appointed to act as brigade-major to the brigade of infantry under the command of major-general Alten.

ADJUTANT GENERAL'S OFFICE,
Fuente de Guinaldo, *August* 23, 1811.

G. O.

Captain Baron Decken, of the first hussars, King's German Legion, is appointed aide-de-camp to lieutenant-general sir Stapleton Cotton.

ADJUTANT GENERAL'S OFFICE,
Fuente Guinaldo, *May* 2, 1812.

G. O.

Major-general Charles baron Alten is appointed to command the light division.

No. IV.

ALMARAZ.

A.

Colonel Framingham to major Hartmann.

FUENTE GUINALDO,
May 27, 1812.

MY DEAR SIR,

"It is with the deepest concern I inform you of the death of lieutenant Thiele of the king's German artillery, who, anxious to

fulfil the great object with which he was entrusted, unfortunately
perished in the explosion attending the blowing up of the tower of
Ragusa.

It must be unnecessary for me to point out to you the merits of
this young man. The service has lost an officer who possessed
every requisite and qualification to render himself an ornament to
his profession and useful to his country, and his friends and
acquaintances will have to lament one so much esteemed and
beloved.

It is a grateful though melancholy consolation to know how
highly he has been thought, and spoken of by lieutenant-general
sir Rowland Hill, major-general Howard and lieutenant-colonel
Dickson, under whose immediate command he was serving, and
I herewith transmit you a copy of his letter to me, and of major
general Howard's orders, that you may make such extracts to
send his relatives as will tend to alleviate their grief and distress."

B.

Colonel Dickson to major Hartmann.

TRUXILLO, *May* 23, 1812.

" You will have heard of the successful expedition against
Almaraz, but it is with great grief and concern I have to inform
you of the death of lieutenant Thiele by a most unfortunate accident, after the affair was over.

He had been encharged with the operation of destroying the
ordnance in fort Ragusa, and blowing up the tower and magazines
of the same. The first part he performed with success, but, in
executing the latter, from some unfortunate circumstance, the
tower blew up while he was still in it, and not the smallest vestige
of him could be afterwards found.

Poor fellow ! In the preceding service he had acquitted himself in the most gallant and satisfactory manner, and it was not
more than an hour previous to his death that sir Rowland Hill
personally thanked him for his exertions during the day.

With a detachment of artillery men, he accompanied one of the columns to the assault of fort Napoleon, and I cannot sufficiently applaud the rapidity with which he assisted in turning the guns of that fort against fort Ragusa.

*   *   *   *   *   *   *   *

C.

Colonel Dickson to colonel Framingham.

*   *   *   *   *   *   *   *

" Thiele was charged to destroy the ordnance, and blow up the tower and magazines in Ragusa. He had effectually disabled all the guns and proceeded to blow up the tower.

From eight to ten hundred weight of powder was lodged in the lower part, and after examining his dispositions, I left him to carry them into execution. He said he would light his port-fire himself to prevent the possibility of accident. While we were expecting the explosion, he came across and told me that having tried the French port-fire, he found it so bad that he feared it would not answer. I furnished him with an English one and he then returned * * * He went into the tower, staid some time, came out again, left the fort with his men, soon returned, went into the tower again, and scarcely entered the door when the explosion took place, and he was blown to atoms. I find that instead of going into the tower with slow match, he took a lighted port-fire up with him, the sparks of which must have communicated with the powder in some manner."

*   *   *   *   *   *   *   *

No. V.

BATTLE OF SALAMANCA.

Official Report of lieutenant-colonel von Arentschildt of the first hussars, King's German Legion.

NEAR CALVARASSA,
July 23, 1812.

Sir,

The movements of major-general Victor Alten's brigade (under my command since he was wounded,) during the attack of the

enemy's left wing yesterday afternoon, not having been made
under your eyes, I beg leave to state the particulars thereof:—I
was ordered to support the attack of the third division, and to
cover their right flank, which I did by marching completely on
their flank. During the attack of the first hill, the enemy's
cavalry (six to seven squadrons) approached our front and seemed
determined to attack us. I immediately ordered them to be
charged, which was done with great success. They were thrown
back, but another body took them up, and they began to rally,
during which time another squadron of the enemy made a feeble
attack upon the right wing of our infantry, but on receiving their
fire, they retired; and this was the moment when the brigade
under my command, charged the whole body again, threw them
into confusion, and pursued them to a great distance, taking
many prisoners. About this time our heavy cavalry fell upon the
French infantry from the other side, and I ordered the hussars to
keep on the extremity of the left wing of the enemy's infantry, and
cut off whatever they could, *following myself with the fourteenth
in close order*. The hussars were then a great way in front,
doing great execution among the enemy's infantry, and, according to the nature of the service and ground, (this being in the
wood,) very much dispersed—when about two squadrons of the
French third hussars came up to attack them. But major
Gruben, Krauchenberg and other officers rallied, by great exertion,
a body strong enough to oppose the enemy, though they were
all mixed; some hussars, some fourteenth, and even some
Portuguese. They then fell upon the enemy and drove them
back, on which occasion some French officers were cut down; and
from that moment the French cavalry never shewed their faces
again on that side. The pursuit of the infantry was then renewed
together with some advanced parties of general le Marchant's
brigade, until they came close to the large hill under the French
batteries where you have seen them; four guns have been sent
back to the rear by the hussars. I annex a receipt for two; the
men who brought back the other two forgot to ask for receipts.
Two colours have been taken likewise. I cannot make out, at this

moment, what became of one; another I have sent to lord Wellington. The number of prisoners is not to be ascertained, for they were driven back in crowds.

The result speaks for the exertions and bravery of the officers and men, and I only have to mention that colonel Harvey, commanding the fourteenth light dragoons, and major Gruben, commanding the first hussars, not only led their respective regiments in the most handsome manner, to the several attacks, but made the greatest, and I am happy to say, successful exertions to rally the men after the charges. The hussars had five officers wounded, as you will see by the return; I hope none of them badly.

I am not able to send a return of the fourteenth, but they have lost no officer.

I have the honor to be,
F. VON ARENTSCHILDT,
Lieutenant-colonel.

To lieutenant-general sir Stapleton Cotton,
  commanding the cavalry.

No. VI.

Killed, wounded, and missing of the King's German Legion in action with the enemy at Salamanca. July 22, 1812.

Corps.	Officers. Killed.	Officers. Wounded.	Serjeants. Wounded.	Rank & File Killed.	Rank & File Wounded.	Rank & File Missing.	Horses. Killed.	Horses. Wounded.
1st hussars.........	,,	6	1	6	19	,,	11	18
1st light battalion..	,,	2	,,	,,	7	,,	,,	,,
2d do	1	1	,,	,,	9	,,	,,	,,
1st line battalion ..	,,	,,	1	1	7	3	,,	,,
2d ditto......	,,	2	4	,,	36	4	,,	,,
5th ditto......	,,	2	1	1	16	,,	,,	,,
Artillery.	,,	,,	,,	2	4	,,	5	2
TOTAL, ...	1	13	7	10	98	7	16	20

Name of officer killed.

Lieutenant Fincke 2d line battalion.

Names of officers wounded.

RANK AND NAME.	REGIMENT.	REMARKS.
Major-general Victor von Alten.	1st hussars.	.... severely
Captain Müller	ditto,	. .. slightly.
———— Frederic von der Decken	ditto,	.... ditto.
Lieutenant Teuto, ...	ditto,	.... severely.
———-- Cordemann, ...	ditto,	.... slightly
Cornet Behrens	ditto,	... ditto.
Captain Hülsemann..........	1st light battalion,	.... severely.
Lieutenant Hartwig, ...	ditto,	.... ditto,
Captain Haasmann	2d ditto,	.... slightly.
———— Scharnhorst,..........	2d line battalion,	.... severely.
Lieutenant Ripke............	ditto,	.... mortally.
Captain Langrehr, ...	5th ditto,	.... ditto.
Lieutenant von Brandis, ...	ditto,	.... slightly.

No. VII.

Killed, wounded and missing of the heavy cavalry brigade of the King's German Legion, in action with the enemy near Garcia Hernandez in Spain, July 23d, 1812.

Corps.	Officers.		Sergeants.			Rank & File.			Horses.		
	Killed.	Wounded.	Killed.	Wounded.	Missing.	Killed.	Wounded.	Missing.	Killed.	Wounded.	Missing.
1st dragoons,......	3	1	1	3	1	27	24	4	40	23	1
2d dragoons, ...	1	1	1	1	,,	19	28	1	27	23	3
TOTAL, ...	4	2	2	4	1	46	52	5	67	46	4

Names of officers killed.

RANK AND NAME.	REGIMENT.	REMARKS.
Captain Gustavus von der Decken	1st dragoons.	.... "
Lieutenant Voss,.......	ditto,	.... "
————Hcugel,...............	ditto,	.... "
Captain von Uslar,...............	2d dragoons,	.... "

Names of officers wounded.

Lieutenant Fumetty, ...	2d dragoons	.... slightly.
Cornet Tappe,.................	1st ditto,	.... severely.

No. VIII.

Killed, wounded, and missing of the King's German Legion, in the siege of the castle of Burgos, from the 19th September to 18th of October, 1812.

Corps.	Officers.			Serjeants.		Rank and File.		
	Killed.	Wounded.	Missing.	Killed.	Wounded.	Killed.	Wounded.	Missing.
1st line battalion,	2	3	"	3	4	54	97	"
2d ditto, ...	3	5	"	1	3	30	89	1
5th ditto, ...	"	5	1	3	1	25	38	"
TOTAL......	5	13	1	7	8	109	224	1

Names of officers killed.

RANK AND NAME.	REGIMENT.	REMARKS.
Major Adolphus von Wurmb, ..	2d line battalion,	.... "
Captain Scharnhorst, ...	ditto,	.... "
——— von Saffe, ...	1st line battalion,	.... "
Lieutenant Hansing, ...	2d ditto,	.... "
——————von Bothmer, ...	1st ditto,	.... "

Wounded.

Captain Breymann, ...	2d line battalion,		.... slightly.
—— Langrehr, ...		ditto,	.... severely.
—— Lodders, ...	5th	ditto,	.. . ditto,
—— La Roche, ...	1st	ditto,	. .. dangerously
—— Bachmeister, ...	5th	ditto,	.... mortally.
Lieutenant Rossing, ...	1st	ditto,	.. . severely.
———Meyer, ...	1st	ditto,	.... ditto,
———Schauroth, ...	5th	ditto,	.... slightly.
———Wynecken, ...	2d	ditto,	.... severely.
———Goeben, ...	5th	ditto,	.... ditto,
———Hesse, ...	2d	ditto,	.... ditto,
———Quade, ...		ditto,	.... ditto,
———Schlaeger, ...	5th	ditto,	.... slightly.

Missing.

Lieutenant Winckler .... 5th line battalion,

No. IX.

DESTRUCTION OF THE RETIRO AT MADRID.

A.

HEAD QUARTERS, MADRID,
August 31, 1812.

Memorandum of orders received from lord Wellington for major Hartmann.

Major Hartmann to remain and receive directions to make such arrangements of the ordnance and stores of all descriptions, in the Retiro, as will provide either for their preservation, or the facility of destroying the whole on short notice, and will assist in burning the building.

The carriages outside must be placed close to each other in the closest possible order, within the interior line.

The guns must be placed on the ground in such a manner, relatively to each other, as that the fire of one will destroy the other.

The ammunition must be laid ready by each class, in order that they may be loaded, and their destruction take place without loss of time.

The shells must be laid in the yard in the interior of the building, and all the previous arrangements made for loading each of them with half a charge, and firing a train to each with long fuze.

The shot to be piled in different lower parts of the building, in order that they may be buried under the ruins, whenever it shall be burnt.

The musquets must be placed in store, in a place convenient and easy to be got at, so as that they may be broken without loss of time.

A place must be fixed upon, and means previously arranged for destroying the powder without explosion, or incurring the risk of injuring the town.

Combustibles must be fixed in different parts of the building, so as to make it certain that when the order shall be given, the whole, with all its contents, shall be destroyed by fire.

This memorandum to be considered as secret, and to be communicated only to the commanding officer of the troops here, and the commandant of the fort.

The boats and wheels to be moved up to the Retiro, and put with the other carriages.

Major Hartmann will apply for working parties, and the use of the men and horses of the brigade remaining here, to carry these orders into execution.

Any demands made by Don Carlos d' Espagna for removal of any parts, particularly shells, to be complied with.

(*Signed,*)

WILLIAM ROBE,
Lieutenant-colonel
Commanding Royal Artillery.

To major Hartmann,
    Commanding King's German Artillery.

Added by order of lord Wellington, upon seeing him after visiting the fort:—

Should the principal building not be found susceptible of ready destruction, the angles and other parts to be blown up by small charges of powder, only sufficient to ruin the building, without causing great explosion, or injuring the town.

W. ROBE,
Lieutenant-colonel.

B.

Lord Fitzroy Somerset to lieutenant-colonel Hartmann.

CABEÇON, *October* 27, 1812.

SIR,

As soon as you receive this letter, you will be pleased to destroy the Retiro, and the stores at Madrid, according to the orders which have been given to you on the subject.

You will also be so kind as to deliver the enclosed letters to Mr. Guillen and Don Carlos d' Espana.

If the latter should have quitted Madrid, you will open the letter addressed to him, and explain its contents to the civil and military authorities in that city.

I have the honor to be,

Sir,

Your most obedient servant,

FITZROY SOMERSET.

To lieutenant-colonel Hartmann,
King's German Artillery.

C.

Lieutenant-colonel Hartmann to lord Fitzroy Somerset.

MADRID, *October* 29, 1812.

MY LORD,

I have the honor to acknowledge the receipt of your lordship's letter dated Cabeçon, October 27, of the contents of which I have informed lieutenant-general sir Rowland Hill; and I have begun upon the execution of the order which it conveyed.

The letter to Don Carlos d' Espana I have delivered to him myself; Don Carlos charged himself with that for senor Guillen.

I have the honor to be,

My Lord,

Your lordship's most obedient

humble servant

G. J. HARTMANN.

Lieutenant-colonel K. G. Artillery.

To lieutenant-colonel lord Fitzroy Somerset,
Military Secretary, &c. &c.

No. X.

SECOND HUSSARS.

GENERAL ORDERS.

ADJUTANT GENERAL'S OFFICE,
Castroneritz, June 12, 1813.

I.—The commander of the forces omitted to return his thanks to the second hussars for their services in this country, when he was lately under the necessity of ordering that their horses should be drafted from them.

II.—There is no corps in the army, of whose services and merits the commander of the forces entertains a higher opinion than of the second hussars, and he assures them that the measures which have deprived the commander of the forces of their assistance in this country, were adopted with regret, as far as they were concerned, and were occasioned solely by views for the general benefit of the army.

(Signed)

AYLMER,

Deputy Adjutant-general.

B.

Lisbon, June 5, 1813.

DEAR SIR,

I was very sorry to find upon my return to this country, that the second hussars were ordered to England. In taking leave of the excellent regiment, under your command, I have to regret very much the loss of a corps which has always conducted itself so much to my satisfaction, and which has distinguished itself upon all occasions. I beg you will be pleased to communicate my sentiments to the officers, non-commissioned officers and privates of the second hussars, and to assure them that they have my best wishes for their welfare and prosperity.

I have the honor, &c.

(Signed.)

STAPLETON COTTON,

Lieutenant-general,

Commanding the Cavalry.

To major von Wissel, commanding
second hussars, K. G. Legion.

No. XI.

BRIGADING OF THE ANGLO-PORTUGUESE ARMY.

1814 and 1815.

CAVALRY.

Lieutenant-general sir Stapleton Cotton.

Major-general von Bock.	{ 1st dragoons, King's German Legion. { 2d do. do.
Major-general Victor von Alten.	{ 1st hussars, King's German Legion, { 18th hussars.
Major-general Fane,	{ 3d dragoon guards. { 1st dragoons.
Major-general Vandeleur,	{ 12th light dragoons. { 16th do.

Colonel Grant,	{ 13th light dragoons. 14th do.
Major-general O'Loghlin,	{ 1st life guards. 2d do. Royal horse guards.
Major-general hon. Wm. Ponsonby	{ 5th dragoon guards. 3d dragoons. 4th do.
Major-gen. lord Edward Somerset,	{ 7th hussars. 10th do. 15th do.
Major general d'Urban, .	{ 1st Portuguese. 6th do. 11th do. 12th do.
Colonel Campbell,	{ 4th Portuguese. 10th do.

HORSE ARTILLERY.

Lieutenant-colonel Frazer.

One battery light six-pounders,	. . . .	major Bull.
One ditto,	. . . .	major Gardiner.
One ditto,	. . . .	captain Beans.

INFANTRY.

FIRST DIVISION.

Lieutenant-general, sir Thomas Graham.

(After the 7th October, 1813 — lieutenant-general sir John Hope.)

Major-general Howard,	{ 1st guards, 1st battalion. 1st do. 3d do. 1 company 60th, 5th battalion.
Major-general hon. Edw. Stopford,	{ 2d guards, 1st battalion. 3d do. 1st do. 1 company 60th, 5th battalion.
Colonel Halkett, afterwards Major-general von Hinüber.	{ 1st light battalion King's G. Legion. do. 2d do. do. 1st line do. do. 2d do. do. 5th do. do.

One nine-pounder battery, royal artillery . . . . . . captain Dansey.

SECOND DIVISION.

Lieutenant-general, sir Rowland Hill.

Lieutenant-general, the honorable William Stewart.

Major-general Walker,
{ 50th regiment, 1st battalion.
71st do. do.
92d do. do.
1 company 60th, 5th battalion.

Major-general Byng,
{ 3d regiment, 1st battalion.
57th do. do.
31st 4 companies, } 1 battalion.
66th 4 do. }
1 company 60th, 5th battalion.

Major-general Pringle,
{ 28th regiment, 1st battalion.
34th do. 2d do.
39th do. 1st do.
1 company 60th, 5th battalion.

Colonel Ashworth,
{ 6th regiment Portuguese line, 2 batt.
18th do. do.
6th Caçadores, 1 battalion.

One nine-pounder battery, royal artillery.... captain Maxwell.

THIRD DIVISION.

Lieutenant-general Thomas Picton.

Major-general hon. Chas. Colville,
{ 5th regiment, 1st battalion.
83d do. 2d do.
87th do. 2d do.
94th one battalion.
3 companies 60th, 5th battalion.

Major-general Brisbane,
{ 45th regiment, 1st battalion.
74th one battalion.
88th 1st battalion.

Major-general Power,
{ 9th regt. Portuguese line, 2 battalions
21st do. do.
12th caçadores, one battalions.

One nine pounder battery, royal artillery....... captain Douglas.

FOURTH DIVISION.

Lieutenant-general, the honorable sir Lowry Cole,

Major-general William Anson,
{ 27th regiment, 3d battalion.
40th do. 1st do.
48th do. 1st do.
2d 4 companies. } one battalion.
53d 4 do. }
1 company 60th, 5th battalion.

Major-general Ross,
{ 7th regiment, 1st battalion.
20th do. one battalion.
23d do. 1st battalion.
1 company Brunswick oels riflemen.

Colonel Stubbs
{ 11th regiment Portuguese line, 2 batt.
23d do. do.
7th caçadores.

One nine-pounder battery, King's German Artillery...major Sympher.

FIFTH DIVISION.

Lieutenant-general sir James Leith.

Major-general Hay,
{ 1st regiment, 3d battalion.
9th do. 1st do.
38th do. 1st do.
47th do. 2d do.
1 company Brunswick oels light infan.

Major-general Robinson,
{ 4th regiment, 1st battalion.
59th do. 2d do.
84th do. 2d do.
1 company Brunswick oels light infan.

Major-general Spry,
{ 3d regiment Portuguese line, 2 batt.
15th do. do.
8th caçadores.

One heavy six-pounder battery, royal artillery.... captain Lawson.

SIXTH DIVISION.

Lieutenant-general Henry Clinton.

Major-general Pack,
{ 42d regiment, 1st battalion.
79th do. do.
91st do. do.
1 company 60th regiment 5th battalion

Major-general Lambert.
{ 11th regiment, 1st battalion.
32d do. do.
36th do. do.
61st do. do.

{ 8th regt. Portuguese line, 2 battalions.
12th do. do.
9th caçadores, one battalion.

One nine-pounder battery, royal artillery.... captain Brandreth.

SEVENTH DIVISION.

Lieutenant-general, the earl of Dalhousie.

Major-general Barnes,
- 6th regiment, 1st battalion.
- 24th do. 4 companies ⎱ one
- 58th do. do. ⎰ battalion.
- 9 companies Brunswick oels light infan.

Major-general Inglis,
- 51st regiment, one battalion
- 68th do. do.
- 82d do. 1st battalion.
- Chasseurs Brittaniquer, one battalion.

Brigadier-general le Cor,
- 7th regt. Portuguese line, 2 battalions.
- 19th do. do.
- 2d caçadores, one battalion.

One nine-pounder battery, royal artillery....captain Carnes.

LIGHT DIVISION.

Major-general Charles von Alten.

Major-general Kempt,
- 43d regiment, 1st battalion.
- 95th do. 2d do.
- 17th Portuguese line.

Major-general Skerret,
- 52d regiment, 1st battalion.
- 95th do. do.
- 1st Portuguese caçadores.
- 3d do. do.

One battery of horse artillery, royal artillery..lieutenant-colonel Ross.

PORTUGUESE DIVISION.

Major-general, the Conde de Amarante.

Brigadier-general de Costa,
- 2d regiment Portuguese line, two battalions.
- 14th do. do.

Brigadier-general Campbell,
- 4th do. do.
- 10th do. do.
- 10th caçadores, one battalion.

One nine-pounder battery, Portuguese Artillery....captain Michell.

One six-pounder do. do. major Cuntra.

UNATTACKED.

Major-general lord Aylmer,	⎧ 37th regiment, one battalion. ⎪ 62d do. 2d do. ⎨ 76th do. one do. ⎪ 77th do. do. do. ⎩ 85th do. do. do.
Major-general Bradford,	⎧ 13th Portuguese line, two battalions. ⎨ 24th do. do. ⎩ 5th caçadores, one battalion.
Brigadier-general Wilson,	⎧ 1st Portuguese line, two battalions ⎨ 16th do. do. ⎩ 4th caçadores do.

RESERVE OF ARTILLERY.

Lieutenant-col. Hartmann—King's German Artillery.

One nine-pounder battery, horse artillery, royal artillery—major W. Smith.

One eighteen-pounder battery, royal artillery—captain Morrisson.

One nine-pounder battery, royal artillery—captain Mitchell.

One nine-pounder battery, Portuguese artillery—major Arenga.

AMMUNITION.

1st division gun ammunition	. . . .	captain Hutchinson.
2d	do.	. . . .	captain Cleeves, K. G. A.
3d	do.	. . . .	captain Bentham.
4th	do.	. . . .	captain Thompson.
1st division small arm ammunition	. . . . .	lieutenant Preussner, K. G. A.
2d	do.	. . . .	captain Faddy.

COMMANDING OFFICERS OF ARTILLERY.

Lieutenant-colonel Fisher, to the end of May, 1813.

Colonel Alexander Dickson, to the end of the war, 1814.

No. XII.

*Copies of the documents relating to the formation and Esta-
blishment of the foreign veteran battalion of the King's
German Legion.*

HORSE GUARDS,
January 26, 1813.

SIR,

I am directed by the commander-in-chief to acquaint your royal
highness, that the prince regent has been pleased, in the name
and on the behalf of his majesty, to approve of a veteran battalion
being formed to receive the worn-out men of the King's German
Legion. The battalion in the first instance, to consist of the
numbers stated (in page 433), and upon its exceeding four hundred, to be established at six companies of one hundred rank and
file each, and another field-officer, and, upon a further augmen-
tation of effectives, it be established at ten companies of one
thousand rank and file, with the usual number of officers and non-
commissioned officers. I am therefore commanded to request
your royal highness will form the men mentioned in the enclosed
statement, into a battalion ; and his royal highness also desires,
that you will be pleased to recommend such officers of the King's
German Legion, who, from their services, are unfit for active
duty, but whom you may consider capable of doing garrison duty,
at the same time communicating to such officers, who may be
removed to the veteran battalion, that they are not to look for any
further progressive promotion.

I have the honor to be, with the most profound respect,

Sir,

Your royal highness's

most obedient humble Servant,

(Signed,)

H. TORRENS.

General his royal highness the duke
of Cambridge, K.G. &c. &c. &c.
London.

Statement of men of the different corps of the Legion in the Peninsula, unfit for active service.

1st regiment of hussars, ...	„	serjeants ..	1	corporal, ..	15	privates.
3d do. do.	„	do. ..	„	do.	.. 5	do.
2d do. dragoons	3	do. ..	2	do.	.. 4	do.
1st light battalion	5	do. ..	2	do.	.. 86	do.
2d do.	6	do. ..	2	do.	.. 47	do.
1st line battalion, .. ,	3	do. ..	2	do.	.. 53	do.
2d do.	11	do. ..	1	do.	.. 71	do.
5th do.	4	do. ...	1	do.	.. 50	do.
Detachments of the light infantry and infantry of the line at Bexhill, ..	7	do. ..	4	do.	.. 33	do.
TOTAL, ...	39	serjeants	15	corporals	364	privates

HORSE GUARDS,
February 8, 1813.

SIR,

I have the honor to transmit herewith a copy of the memorandum concerning the veteran battalion to be formed for the reception of the worn-out men of the King's German Legion, enclosed in your royal highness's letter of the 29th ultimo, with the commander-in-chief's remarks and decisions thereon.

I have, &c. &c.

(*Signed*)

H. TORRENS.

General his royal highness, the duke
of Cambridge, K.G. &c &c

London.

MEMORANDUM

Concerning the veteran battalion to be formed to receive the worn-out men of the King's German Legion.

I.—It is proposed to draft the officers, non-commissioned officers and privates of the independent garrison company attached to the King's German Legion now serving in Portugal, into that battalion, on account of that company being likewise composed of worn-out men.

Agreed to

2.—Orders have been sent to the regiments of cavalry and battalions of infantry of the King' German Legion serving in the Peninsula and in Sicily, to send in returns of officers who are qualified for garrison duty, but as it will require a considerable time before these returns can arrive, and meanwhile the officers of that description in this country, will be appointed to that battalion, it is proposed to establish the rule, *that all the officers appointed to that veteran battalion are to take their rank according to the dates of their commission in the King's German Legion,* and not according to the dates of their appointment to the said battalion.

Under these circumstances the commander in chief approves of the officers transfered to the veteran battalion, taking rank according to the dates of their commissions in the King's German Legion.

3,—It appears that *Bexhill* will be a proper place for the formation of the veteran battalion.

Approved.

4.—No date for the establishment of the veteran battalion, being fixed, it is proposed to establish it from the *25th February* next.

Agreed to.

5—Whether off-reckonings will be granted for that battalion.

No off-reckonings to be granted; to be clothed in the same manner as the veteran battalions in the British service.

HORSE GUARDS,
February 11, 1813.

SIR,

I have had the honor of laying before the commander-in-chief your letter of the 10th instant, and in reply have it in command to signify to you, that the prince regent has been pleased to approve of the same description of clothing, being provided for the veteran battalion of the King's German Legion, which is about to be formed, as is worn by the veteran battalions of the British army, and you will be pleased to communicate the same to his royal highness the duke of Cambridge.

I have, &c.

(*Signed*,)

HARREY CALVERT,
Adjutant-general.

Major-general F. Decken,
&c. &c. &c.
London.

ESTABLISHMENT.

Number of companies of 100 rank and file each.	Colonel.	Majors.	Captains.	Lieutenants.	Ensigns.	Paymaster.	Adjutant.	Quarter-master.	Surgeon.	Assistant-surgeon.	Serjeant-major.	Quarter-master-serjeant.	Paymaster-serjeant.	Armourer-serjeant.	Serjeants.	Corporals.	Drum-major.	Drummers.	Privates.	TOTAL.
4	1	1	4	4	4	1	1	1	1	1	1	1	1	1	20	20	1	7	380	451

WAR OFFICE, FOREIGN DEPARTMENT,
December 22, 1812.

SIR,

I have the honor to acquaint your royal highness, that his royal highness the prince regent has been pleased in the name and on the behalf of his majesty, to order, that the depôt company of the King's German Legion, under your command, shall be discontinued on the establishment from the 25th instant inclusive.

I have further to acquaint your royal highness, that the officers of the said company will be borne as supernumeraries on the general establishment of the legion, and paid according to their respective ranks, until vacancies occur, to which they are to succeed.

I have, &c.

(*Signed,*)

PALMERSTON.

General his royal highness the duke of
 Cambridge, K. G. colonel-in-chief
 of the King's German Legion, &c.
 London.

HORSE GUARDS,
February 15, 1813.

SIR,

With reference to the correspondence which has taken place relative to the depot company of the King's German Legion, I am directed to transmit to you, for the information of the duke of Cambridge, the copy of a letter from Mr. Merry, and to acquaint you, that if the circumstances are as represented by the secretary at war, the commander-in-chief is not possessed of grounds upon which he could urge the re-establishment of the depot company.

I have, &c.

(*Signed,*)

H. TORRENS.
Military Secretary.

To major-general F. Decken,
 &c. &c. &c.
 London.

WAR-OFFICE, FOREIGN DEPARTMENT,
January 28, 1813.

SIR,

I have the honor to acknowledge the receipt of your letter of the 12th instant, enclosing copy of one from his royal highness the duke of Cambridge, relative to the depôt company of the King's German Legion, and I am directed by the secretary at war, to state for the information of the commander-in-chief, that it would appear from documents at this office, that the greatest part (if not

all) of the recruits who were enlisted for the legion in the course
of last year from the prisoners of war in this country, were at once
forwarded to Bexhill or Ipswich, without being intermediately
sent to the depôt company, nor is it understood that any difficulty has thereby been occasioned in respect of the settlement for
bounty. The depôt at Bexhill, to which a paymaster has been
especially attached, was formed before the additional companies
of the infantry battalions were ordered to be raised, and it is presumed that after these companies shall be sent to join their regiments, it will still be necessary to keep up some establishment
upon the same footing. It should seem however, that such an
establishment cannot be accommodated with barracks in the Isle
of Wight, and on the other hand the secretary at war apprehends,
that it can scarcely be requisite to continue the depôt company,
merely for the purpose of receiving such recruits as may occa-
sionally be sent to that island. In regard to the men who are
forwarded thither from the foreign depôt, the transfer may very
probably be more the consequence of the depôt company being
actually stationed in the isle of Wight, than of any inconvenience
incident to their proceeding at once to Bexhill or Ipswich; those
who may arrive in the island from other quarters, will it is imagined, be but few in number, and might immediately be sent to
Lymington, whither, lord Palmerston is still of opinion it would
be advisable that all foreign recruits should be forwarded for final
approval.

Upon the whole, therefore, the secretary at war cannot but
consider it as desirable that the depôt company should be reduced,
the expense thereof not being, in his view of the subject, coun-
terbalanced by any exclusive advantage attending its establishment.

I have, &c.

(*Signed,*)

W. MERRY.

To colonel Torrens,
&c. &c.

Horse Guards,
                            March 16, 1813.

Sir,

I have to acknowledge the receipt of your royal highness's letter of 22d ultimo, and to acquaint you in reply, that under the principle of no promotion being given in the invalids, such serjeants and corporals of the different regiments and battalions of the King's German Legion, who are reported to be unfit for active service, but fit for garrison duty, can only be placed as supernumeraries in the veteran battalion on privates' pay, with the view of succeeding to vacancies as they occur. It strikes me that these non-commissioned officers and corporals might be usefully employed, for the present, at the depôts of their respective corps.

I remain, Sir,

Your royal highness's most affectionate brother,
(*Signed,*)
FREDERICK.
Commander-in-chief.

General his royal highness the duke
of Cambridge, K.G. &c. &c.
London.

Horse Guards,
                            January 20, 1814.

Sir,

I am directed by the commander-in-chief to acquaint you, that in consequence of the effective rank and file of the veteran battalion of the King's German Legion exceeding its present establishment of four hundred, that battalion will be augmented from the 25th ultimo, to six companies of one hundred rank and file each, and which has been accordingly notified to the war office.

I have, &c.
(*Signed,*)
H. TORRENS.
Military Secretary

To lieutenant-general baron
Linsingen, &c. &c.
London.

By the secretary of war's letter of the 2d of February, 1814, to lieutenant-colonel Belleville, commanding the veteran battalion, the battalion is to be increased from four hundred to six hundred rank and file, from 25th December, 1813, and to consist of:—

ESTABLISHMENT.

6 Companies of 100 rank & file each.	1 Colonel.	1 Lieut.-colonel.	1 Majors.	6 Captains.	6 Lieutenants.	6 Ensigns.	1 Paymaster.	1 Adjutant.	1 Quarter-master.	1 Surgeon.	1 Assistant-Surg.	1 Serjeant-major.	1 Quar.-mas.-serjt.	1 Paymaster-serjt.	1 Armourer-serjt.	1 School-mas.-serjt.	30 Serjeants.	30 Corporals.	1 Drum-major.	11 Drummers.	570 Privates.	673 TOTAL, ...

HORSE GUARDS,
August 5, 1815

SIR,

I am directed by the commander-in-chief (in the absence of major-general sir Henry Torrens,) to acquaint you that, as it appears by a return received this day at the adjutant-general's office, the effective rank and file of the first foreign veteran battalion greatly exceeds its present establishment of six hundred, that battalion will be augmented from the 25th of June last to ten companies of 100 rank and file each, and which has been accordingly notified to the war-office.

ESTABLISHMENT.

10 Companies of 100 rank & file each,	1 Colonel.	1 Lieut.-colonel.	2 Majors.	10 Captains.	10 Lieutenants.	10 Ensigns.	1 Paymaster.	1 Adjutant.	1 Quartermaster.	1 Surgeon.	2 Assistant-surg.	1 Serjeant-major.	1 Quar.-mast.serjt.	1 Paymaster-serjt.	1 Armourer-serjt.	1 School-mas.-serjt.	50 Serjeants.	50 Corporals.	1 Drum-major.	19 Drummers.	950 Privates.	1115 TOTAL, ...

I have, &c.

W. MALING.

(*Signed*,)

To lieutenant-colonel W. Linsingen,
   Deputy-adjutant-general, K.G.L.
   Legion-Office,   *Chelsea.*

DEPOT COMPANY OF THE KING'S GERMAN LEGION

The formation of this company was approved of by his royal highness the commander-in-chief, on the 24*th November*, 1803, and ordered to consist of : —

1 Captain,
2 Lieutenants,
2 Ensigns,
6 Serjeants,
5 Corporals,
2 Drummers,

TOTAL,.... 18 Men

It was first under the command of captain Peter de Salve, and afterwards under captain Colin Pringle.

From the 25*th December*, 1812 inclusive, the company was discontinued on the establishment of the army, (per lord viscount Palmerston's letter of the 22*d December*, 1812,) and from the 25*th February*, 1813, the officers and men were transferred to the veteran battalion and battalions of the line.

Its station was the vicinity of Portsmouth, Lymington, Isle of Wight, &c. but it accompanied the expenditure to Hanover in 1805-6, also the expedition to the Baltic in 1807.

INDEPENDENT GARRISON COMPANY OF THE KING'S GERMAN LEGION.

This company was placed on the establishment of the army, 25*th March*, 1805, and ordered to consist of one hundred rank and file, with the usual proportion of officers, non-commissioned officers, and drummers.

On the above date it was formed at Lymington by colonel Howard, and the establishment was : —

1 Captain,
2 Lieutenants,
1 Ensign,
5 Serjeants,
5 Corporals,
2 Drummers,
95 Privates,

TOTAL,.. ..111 Men.

But on the 25th *December*, 1806, this establishment was re-duced and fixed from that date, at 1 captain, 2 lieutenants, 1 ensign, 4 serjeants, 3 corporals, 2 drummers, 47 privates,—*Total*,—60 men.

The commandant of this company was, first, captain Frederick Plate, and next captain Frederick Bothe.

On the 25th *February*, 1813, the officers (with the exception of lieutenant Charles Christoph Hünicken) and men were trans-ferred to the veteran battalion, and the company was discontinued on the establishment of the army, from 25th *March*, 1813, inclusive, per war-office letter, 29th *April*, 1813.

This company was in the expeditions to Hanover in 1805-6, and to the Baltic in 1807—to Sweden in 1808—proceeded from thence to Portugal, and returned from that country on being transferred to the veteran battalion.

Both depôt and garrison company wore the uniform of the infantry of the line of the King's German Legion.

Return of the number of serjeants, corporals, drummers and privates transferred from the different corps of the King's German Legion, to the foreign veteran battalion, from 25th Feb. 1813, to the reduction of the battalion, 24th Feb. 1816.

Transfers Received	Serjeants	Corporals	Drummers	Privates	TOTAL	Dead	Deserted	CASUALTIES. DISCHARGED. Before Reduction With Pension	Without Pension	At the Reduction With Pension or recommended for the same.	Without Pension
From the Infantry.	80	52	10	832	974	55	30	56	147	316	370
From the Cavalry.	26	6	0	134	166	15	7	2	35	36	71
TOTAL,	106	58	10	966	1140	70	37	58	182	252*	441

Two privates attached to major-generals Cooke, and sir Colin Halkett, were killed in the battle of Waterloo.

* Of these a great number was rejected by the Chelsea board.

Hanover, December 22, 1830.

LEWIN BENNE.

No. XIII.

NIVELLE.

Killed, wounded, and missing of the King's German Legion, in action with the enemy at the passage of the Nivelle, November 10, 1813.

Corps.	Killed.			Wounded.				Missing.			Total.	Remarks.
	Officers.	Drummers.	Rank & file.	Officers.	Serjeants.	Drummers.	Rank & file.	Serjeants.	Rank & file.			
1st light battalion,	,,	,,	2	1	2	1	22	,,	,,	28		
2d do......	,,	,,	15	2	4	,,	60	,,	,,	81		
1st line do.	1	1	7	,,	,,	,,	11	,,	,,	20		
2d do......	,,	,,	3	1	2	,,	20	1	2	30		
5th do......	,,	,,	,,	1	,,	,,	12	,,	2	15		
Total,......	1	1	27	5	8	1	125	1	4	174		

Officer killed.
1st line battalion...........Lieutenant George Boyd.

Officers wounded.

REGIMENT.	NAME.	REMARKS.
1st light battalion.	captain William Heimbrüch,	severely, left arm amputated.
2d do.	lieutenant Lewis Behne,	severely.
	adjutant Bernhard Riefkugel,	slightly.
2d line battalion	lieutenant Chas. v. d. Decken,	ditto.
5th do.	lieutenant Charles de Witte,	severely.

No. XIV.

BAYONNE.

A

Return of killed, wounded, and missing, of the infantry brigade of the King's German Legion, in action with the enemy before Bayonne, from the 27th of February to the 1st of March, 1814.

		Killed.			Wounded.							Missing.		Total.
Dates.	Corps.	Lieutenants.	Serjeants.	Rank & file.	Majors.	Captains.	Lieutenants.	Staff.	Serjeants.	Drummers.	Rank & file.	Serjeants.	Rank & file.	Total.
	1st light battalion,	,,	,,	7	,,	1	2	1	2	,,	18	,,	,,	31
	2d do.	,,	,,	5	,,	2	3	,,	6	1	44	1	5	67
Feb. 27,	1st line battalion,	,,	2	7	,,	3	4	,,	7	1	59	,,	,,	83
	2d do.	1	,,	3	1	,,	1	,,	2	2	24	,,	,,	34
	5th do.	,,	,,	2	,,	2	5	,,	5	,,	89	,,	,,	113
	TOTAL	1	2	34	1	8	15	1	22	4	234	1	5	328
	1st light battalion,	1	,,	1	,,	,,	,,	,,	,,	,,	10	,,	,,	12
	2d do.	,,	1	1	,,	,,	,,	,,	2	,,	3	,,	1	8
Feb. 28,	1st line battalion,	,,	,,	2	,,	,,	,,	,,	,,	,,	9	,,	,,	11
	2d do.	,,	,,	1	,,	,,	,,	,,	,,	,,	8	,,	,,	9
	5th do.	,,	,,	,,	,,	,,	,,	,,	1	1	1	,,	,,	3
	TOTAL, ...	1	1	5	,,	,,	,,	,,	3	1	31	,,	1	43
	1st light battalion	,,	,,	,,	,,	,,	,,	,,	,,	,,	2	,,	,,	2
	2d do.	,,	,,	1	,,	,,	1	,,	1	,,	5	,,	,,	8
Mar. 1.	1st line battalion,	,,	,,	,,	,,	,,	,,	,,	,,	,,	1	,,	,,	1
	2d do.	,,	,,	,,	,,	,,	,,	,,	1	,,	2	,,	,,	3
	5th do.	,,	,,	,,	,,	,,	,,	,,	1	,,	,,	,,	,,	1
	TOTAL, ...	,,	,,	1	,,	,,	1	.,	3	,,	10	,,	,,	15
	GENERAL TOTAL, ...	2	3	40	1	8	16	1	28	5	275	1	6	386

REMARKS.

Five rank and file of the fifth line battalion taken prisoners, and returned among the wounded.

Names of officers killed.

DATE.	RANK AND NAME.	REGIMENT.
Feb. 27, ...	lieutenant Charles Meyer, ...	2d line battalion.
—— 28, ...	lieutenant George Elderhorst, ...	1st light do.

Names of officers wounded.

DATE.	RANK AND NAME.	REGIMENT.	REMARKS.
Feb. 27,	Captain Rautenberg. ..	1st light battalion,	severely.
	Lieutenant Heimbruch,	ditto,	do, since dead
	—— Wolrabe,	ditto,	slightly.

	Adjutant Fahle,	ditto,	severely.
	Captain F. Wynecken,.. 2d light battalion	slightly
	Lieutenant Holtzermann,	ditto,	do.
	———— Witzendorf	ditto,	severely, taken prisoner, since dead.
	———— Tobin,	ditto,	severely.
	———— Marwedel,	ditto,	do.
	Captain von Petersdorf... 1st line battalion,	slightly.
	———— von Borstel	ditto,	severely.
	———— von Rettberg.	ditto,	do.
Feb. 27,..	Lieutenant Rössing,	ditto,	dangerously.
	———— Wilding,	ditto,	severely.
	———— Drysdale,	ditto,	do.
	———— Wiechmann,	ditto,	slightly.
	Major Chüden, .. 2d line battalion,	severely:
	Lieutenant von der Decken, ditto,	slightly.
	Captain Rautenberg, .. 5th ditto,	severely.
	———— von Linsingen	ditto,	do.
	Lieutenant Augustus Meyer, ditto,	do.
	———— Rothardt,	ditto,	do.
	———— Scharnhorst,	ditto,	slightly.
	———— Korscham,	ditto,	do.
	———— Klingsöhr	ditto,	do.
Mar. 1, ...	———— Atkins,	2d light battalion,	slightly.

(*Signed*)

FREDERICK DRECHSEL.
Major of brigade.

B.

CORRESPONDENCE RELATIVE TO THE CONDUCT OF THE KING'S GERMAN LEGION, BEFORE BAYONNE, ON THE 27TH FEB. 1814.

H. R. H. the duke of Cambridge to major-general von Hinüber

HANOVER,
April 4, 1814.

SIR,

I have to acknowledge the receipt of your letter containing the account of the gallant conduct of the battalions under your command before Bayonne, and I request that you will express to all the officers and men, my public approbation of their conduct, and the satisfaction which I feel in being at the head of such a corps.

I cannot conclude without returning to you my thanks for the distinguished manner in which you have acted in the command of this corps, and sincerely hope that your wound may not impair your health.

(Signed,)

ADOLPHUS FREDERICK,

To major-general von Hinüber,
&c. &c. &c.

C.

General Hinüber to the duke of Cambridge.

CHATEAU LA VIELLE,
May 15th, 1814.

SIR,

I had the honor of receiving your royal highness's most gracious letter of the 4th ultimo, and humbly request to be permitted in the name of the battalions of his majesty's German Legion here, and for myself, to express the sentiments of sincerest gratitude, for the highly flattering and honorable notice which your royal highness has had the condescension to take of my conduct on the 27th of February last.

If it were possible to raise our zeal for his majesty's service, the honor conferred upon us would have been the most powerful incentive to new exertions, and will certainly always be the greatest encouragement we could receive for exerting our utmost endeavours to deserve the honor which your royal highness's gracious letter has conveyed to us.

The only circumstance which gives us pain on this occasoin is, that from the silence of lord Wellington with regard to the legion, your royal highness must necessarily suspect, either that I have much over-rated their gallantry on the day abovementioned, or that at least, something or other must have occurred which was not perfectly correct, and which had produced his lordship's neglect of us.

In order to remove any such impression from the mind of your royal highness, I wrote an official letter on the subject to the adjutant-general, and beg leave to subjoin a copy of that letter, together with the original of the reply which I received.

This is certainly as cold a letter as ever issued from an office, and I partly attribute it to the latter part of my own, which I knew contained a fact that would be unwelcome, but which under the neglect we experienced, I could not deny the satisfaction to my battalions to mention.

At all events the candid testimony of his lordship to the conduct of the legion on all occasions, proves that nothing of a censurable nature has taken place, which is all that I am desirous your royal highness should be convinced of.

I have the honor to be
with profound respect,
Your royal highness's
most devoted humble servant,
HINUBER.
Major-general,

To Field-marshal his royal highness,
the duke of Cambridge, &c. &c.

D.

General Hinüber to the Adjutant-general.

St. Etienne, *April* 25, 1814.

SIR,

The attention which his excellency the commander of the forces has always been pleased to pay to the conduct of the troops, and the notice which he has had the condescension to take of it, whenever it has met with his approval, in his public despatches, led the battalions of the King's German Legion fondly to hope that their conduct and exertions on the 27th of February last, in taking and maintaining the fortified position of St Etienne, close to the enemy's intrenched camp, and under the guns of the citadel of Bayonne might have obtained for them that most honorable distinction. They were the more sanguine in their hopes on this occasion, as my report on the above operation was transmitted by major-general Howard with his approval to lieutenant-general sir John Hope, who expressed himself pleased with the manner in which the service had been performed, and would submit it to the eye of his excellency the commander of the forces.

Yet we have seen his lordship's despatch on the subject of the various occurrences on the day before mentioned, but without even naming the corps by whom the position of St. Etienne had been taken, although the battalions of the King's German Legion executed that service, and not without struggling hard for it, as the return of killed and wounded sufficiently proves*.

The silence of his lordship in this instance cannot be attributed to casual omission, but must be founded on some particular reason, and the only one which we can at all guess at,—however painful to our feelings—is that from some circumstance unknown to us, we have incurred his lordship's displeasure, and that labouring under such, we must necessarily be precluded from the honors which a public notice of our services, would otherwise have bestowed upon us.

In consequence of this conviction, I beg leave Sir to address myself to you, and to request that you would be pleased to endeavour to discover from his lordship the subject of his displeasure, and to acquaint me with the cause which may have drawn upon the battalions under my command, the unhappy predicament in which they find themselves placed; to the end that, by redoubled exertion in the execution of their duty, they may succeed to restore themselves to the favorable opinion with which his excellency the commander of the forces was formerly pleased to honor them, and to return to which, they flatter themselves they may have acquired a small claim, having, on the morning of the 14th instant, retaken the village of St. Etienne, after it had been left to the enemy by

* See Return XIV. A.

detachments of the fifth division under whose charge it had been placed.

I have the honor to be,

Sir,

Your most obedient humble servant,

HINUBER,

Major-general.

To major-general the honorable
sir Edward Packenham, K. B.
Adjutant-general, &c. &c.

E.

The Adjutant-general to general Hinüber.

TOULOUSE, *May* 6, 1814.

DEAR SIR,

I mentioned to my lord Wellington the sentiments expressed in your letter of the 25th ultimo, and am desired to observe that his excellency has ever had pleasure in being satisfied with the conduct of the legion, during the service of the corps composing it under his orders. I am in no way authorized to enter into further explanation on the subject to which your communication relates, but I should recommend you to subdue any anxiety that may have arisen on account of his excellency's good opinion of the legion, which he has always taken occasion to express, when called upon to speak of the corps.

I have the honor to be

Dear Sir,

Your very obedient servant,

EDWARD PACKENHAM

Adjutant-general.

To major-general Hinüber.
&c. &c.

No. XV.

FIRST HUSSARS.

Near Toulouse,
April 11, 1814.

CAVALRY ORDERS.

Lieutenant-general sir Stapleton Cotton cannot too much applaud the gallant conduct of the first hussars in forcing the bridge of Montaudran yesterday, which was strongly barricaded and occupied by a superior force.

The lieutenant-general has to return his best thanks to major Gruben, captain Schaumann, and the rest of the officers, non-commissioned officers and hussars who were engaged upon this occasion.

Captain Poten will accept the lieutenant-general's best thanks for the gallantry he displayed yesterday, as also for the support which he gave to the eighteenth hussars, near the bridge of Croiz d'Orade on the 8th instant.

(Signed.)

J. ELLEY.
Colonel,
Assistant-adjut.-general.

No. XVI.

FIRST HUSSARS.

MOURVILLES, *April* 14, 1814.

BRIGADE ORDER.

Colonel von Arentschildt feels highly gratified in publishing the following letter which he received this morning from the general commanding the cavalry, and he feels very proud of having so long had the honor to command a regiment on which so much praise is bestowed, and he begs major Gruben, the officers, non-commissioned officers and men, will accept the assurance of the high sense that he entertains of the merits of the corps.

CARAMAN, *April* 14, 1814.

My Dear Colonel,

I have to acknowledge the receipt of your letter of the 13th instant, with major Gruben's and captain Poten's reports.]

The first hussars of the King's German Legion since I have had the pleasure of knowing that regiment, and have had the honor of commanding the cavalry, has always conducted itself much to my satisfaction.

I have upon many occasions witnessed the gallantry of the corps, and have to acknowledge the great service it has rendered to this army during the last five years, by the intelligence and activity for which it has been conspicuous in performing the outpost duties; and notwithstanding the short periods of rest from very harassing field duties, which the regiment has experienced, it has always been in an efficient state, and has been the admiration of the army.

Our labours are now over, and I must take this opportunity of returning my warmest acknowledgments to you, major Gruben, and all the officers, non-commissioned officers and privates, for the very great assistance which I have at all times derived from the intelligence, zeal, and gallantry of the first hussars.

Wishing that every happiness and success may attend you and the corps,

> I remain,
> My dear colonel
> &c. &c. &c.
> STAPLETON COTTON.
> *Lieutenant-general*
> Commanding the cavalry.

No. XVII.

SORTIE FROM BAYONNE.

Return of killed, wounded and missing of the infantry brigade of the King's German Legion, at a sortie made by the enemy from the citadel of Bayonne, on the 14th of April, 1814.

Corps.	Majors.	Captains.	Lieutenants.	Serjeants.	Rank and file.	TOTAL.	Lieut.-colonels.	Captains.	Lieutenants.	Serjeants.	Drummers.	Rank and file.	TOTAL.	Captains.	Serjeants.	Drummers.	Rank and file.	TOTAL.
			Killed.						Wounded							Missing.		
1st light battalion,	,,	,,	,,	1	6	7	,,	2	1	,,	1	16	20	,,	,,	,,	1	1
2d do.	,,	,,	,,	1	19	20	,,	1	1	5	,,	36	43	1	1	2	25	29
1st line do.	,,	,,	,,	,,	4	4	,,	,,	,,	,,	,,	5	5	,,	,,	,,	,,	,,
2d do.	1	1	,,	,,	12	14	1	,,	1	,,	,,	21	23	,,	,,	,,	5	5
5th do.	,,	,,	2	,,	7	9	,,	2	,,	,,	1	10	13	,,	,,	,,	,,	,,
GENERAL TOTAL,	1	1	2	2	48	51	1	5	3	5	2	88	101	1	1	2	31	35

☞ The missing are all prisoners of war.

Names of officers killed.

RANK AND NAME.	REGIMENT.	REMARKS.
Brigade-major F. von Drechsel,	Staff,	{ not included in the above.
Major Paul Chüden, ...	2d line battalion,	
Captain Henry Müller, ...	ditto,	
Lieutenant John Meyer, ...	5th ditto,	
Lieutenant Charles Köhler, ..	ditto,	

Names of officers wounded.

Lieutenant-colonel von Beck,..	2d line battalion,	slightly.
Captain Frederick Hulsemann,	1st light battalion,	severely.
———— Frederick Wynecken,	2d ditto,	dangerously.
———— Julius Bacmeister, ..	5th line battalion,	slightly.
———— George Nötting, ...	5th ditto,	ditto.
———— Christian Wynecken..	1st light ditto,	ditto.
Lieutenant Lewis Behne	2d light battalion,	severely.
————Hermann Wolrabe,	1st light ditto,	ditto.
————Ernest Fleisch, ...	2d line ditto,	slightly.

Name of officer Missing.

Captain George Wackerhagen,	2d light battalion	severely.

(*Signed,*)

H. WIEGMANN,
Major of brigade.

No. XVIII.

GENOA.

(Copy.)

A.

LONDON, *Oct.* 1, 1818.

I hereby certify that from the time I assumed the command in the Mediterranean to the latter end of 1814, captain Schaedtler served as assistant deputy quarter-master general. In the various active services upon which he was engaged, his conduct always deserved my entire approbation.

His conduct in the Riviere de Gênes particularly excited my attention, and it was in a great measure owing to a detachment which he conducted, that the right of the enemy on the 17th of April was turned.

I recommend him strongly to the gracious favor of his sovereign.

(*Signed.*)

W. BENTINCK,
Lieutenant-general.

B.

(Copy.)

ISLE OF WIGHT,
September 13, 1818.

DEAR SIR,

In reply to your letter of the 24th ultimo, it is but justice on my part to state, that during the time you acted under my orders as a deputy assistant quarter-master general with the Mediterranean army, I had every reason to be satisfied with the attention paid by you to the duties of the department, and zeal for the service in general ; your having attended me during the short campaign in Italy, afforded me the opportunity of witnessing your conduct in the field, particularly on the 13th of April, 1814, near Sturla, and on the 17th following, when you volunteered to lead the companies directed to turn the right of the enemy strongly posted near St. Francisco d'Albaro.

I have further to state for your satisfaction, that whilst you were attached to the division of the army under the orders of major general Montresor at Messina, and generally employed by that officer in communications with the enemy in Calabria, your conduct was such as to induce the major-general to signify to me his entire approbation of it, and to regret the necessity of your removal to head quarters.

I have the honor to remain,

Dear Sir,

Your's faithfully,

Signed and Sealed,

R. ROBERTS.

Lieut.-colonel.

Captain Schaedtler, Hanoverian staff,

    &c. &c. &c.

The above copies were taken from the originals by the undersigned.

CHRISTOPH HEISE,

Captain R. H. Rifle Guards.

Hanover, October 23, 1836.

No. XIX.

LIST OF INDIVIDUALS OF THE KING'S GERMAN LEGION UPON WHOM THE ORDER OF THE BATH HAS BEEN CONFERRED.

G.C.B. Knight grand cross.——K.C.B. Knight commander.——
C.B. Knight companion.

The individuals marked (*) belong to the first nomination in January, 1815

Staff,	His royal highness the colonel in chief, Adolphus Frederick duke of Cambridge.	G.C.B.*
Artillery,	Major (Br. Lt.-col.) sir Julius Hartmann,	K.C.B.*
,,	Capt. (Br. major.) Kuhlmann,	C.B.
,,	—— (Br. Lt.-col.) A. Sympher,	C.B.
,,	—— (Br. major.) sir Victor von Arentschildt,	C.B.

1st *Dragoons*,	Col. com. (Br. Lt.-gen.) count Wallmoden,	K.C.B.*
,,	————— (major-gen.) sir William Dörnberg,	K.C.B.*
,,	Lieutenant-colonel von Bülow,	C.B.
,,	Major, (Br. Lt.-col) von Reitzenstein,	C.B.
2d *Dragoons*.	Lieutenant-colonel de Jonquières,	C.B.
,,	Major (Br. Lt.-col.) Friedrichs,	C.B.
1st *Hussars*	Col. com. (Lt.-gen.) count von Linsingen,	K.C.B.*
,,	Lieutenant-colonel A. von Wissell,	C.B.
,,	Major (Br. Lt.-col.) von Gruben,	C.B.
3d *Hussars*,	Col. com. sir Frederick von Arentschildt,	K.C.B.*
,,	Major (Br. Lt.-col.) baron Krauchenberg,	C.B.
1st *light battalion*,	Col. com. (major-gen.) count von Alten,	G.C.B.*
,,	Lieutenant-colonel von Hartwig,	C.B.
,,	Major (Br. Lt.-col.) H. von dem Bussche,	C.B.
2d *light battalion*,	Col. com. (major-gen.) sir Colin Halkett,	K.C.B.*
,,	Major (Br. Lt.-col.) baron Baring,	C.B.
,,	Captain (Br. Lt.-col.) Augustus Heise,	C.B.
1st *line battalion*,	Lieutenant-colonel Bodecker,	C.B.
,,	Major (Br. Lt.-col.) v. Robertson,	C.B.
2d *line battalion*,	Lieutenant-colonel von Beck,	C.B.
,,	——————— Aly,	C.B.
,,	Major (Br. Lt.-col.) Müller,	C.B.
3d *line battalion*,	Col. com. (major-gen.) sir Harry v. Hinüber,	K.C.B.*
,,	Lieutenant-colonel von Wissell,	C.B.
,,	Major (Br. Lt.-col.) Luttermann,	C.B.
4th *line battalion*,	Col. com. (major-gen.) sir Sigismund v. Löw,	K.C.B.*
,,	Major (Br. Lt.-col.) Reh.	C.B.
5th *line battalion*,	Lieutenant-colonel L. von dem Bussche,	C.B.
,,	Lieutenant-colonel W. von Linsingen,	C.B.
7th *line battalion*,	Lieutenant-colonel Hugh Halkett,	C.B.
8th *line battalion*,	Major (Br. Lt.-col) von Petersdorf,	C.B.
,,	Major Breymann,	C.B.

Captain de Bosset, formerly of the 2d line battalion, K. G. L. latterly Lieutenant-colonel, half-pay, 50th, is likewise a C.B.

RETURN of the Corps, Effective Strength and Commanders of the King's German Legion, who served in the Battle of Waterlo[o]

DISTRIBUTION OF THE CORPS On the 16th, 17th and 18th of June, 1815.	CORPS.	OFFICERS WHO COMMANDED THE DIFFERENT CORPS.	Commissioned Staff	Serjeants	
	PERMANENT STAFF. [Brigade Majors.]				
	Staff,...........................	Brevet lieut.-col. [major] sir George J. Hartmann, K.C B.	,,	3	,,
Attached to the 2d division of infantry,........... Ditto, ... 1st do. do. .... Ditto, ... 3d & 4th do. do.	Artillery,.... 1st troop of horse artillery, ... 2d do. .... 1st company of foot artillery, ... 4th, 5th & 6th do (detachments)	Brevet major .. [captain] Augustus Sympher, ... Ditto, .. [captain] Henry Jacob Kuhlmann, .. 2d captain, ... Frederick Erythropel, .. Captains, ... { Andrew Cleeves, ... Charles von Rettberg,......	21	3	14
1st light dragoons, 3d brigade under the command of 2d do. of major-general 23d do. ..British cavalry, sir Wm. von Dörnberg, K.C.B.	1st light dragoons,...........................	Lieutenant-colonel John von Bülow, ...	27	6	50
	2d ditto, ...	Ditto, ... Charles de Jonquières, ...	26	6	31
	1st hussars,........................	Ditto, ... Augustus von Wissell, ...	26	7	45
2d hussars .... 7th do. 5th do... under command of 15th do....British major-general sir Colquhoun Grant, K.C.B.	2d do. Major-general Victor von Alten,........ superintending the duties of the Hanoverian cavalry Captain,...... Anthony von Streauwitz, ... Ditto,...... August Krauchenberg, ... aide-de-camps, Lieutenant,.. Hermann, S.G.F.A. v Estorff Two serjeants and six privates employed as orderlies by different generals, The regiment itself was on duty at Ypres.		4	,,	2
1st hussars, ... 10th do. 6th do.. under command of 18th do....British major-general sir Hussey Vivian, K.C.B.	3d do. .. 7 troops ; the other 3 troops being detached towards Condé under the command of major George Krauchenberg, Lieut.-col. Fred. Lewis Meyer, severely wounded succeeded by Capt. Agatz von Kersenbruch, killed ; the command devolved upon captain Quintus von Goeben,	32	6	48
3d hussars, ... 7th do. under command of colonel sir 13th light drag. Br F. von Arentschildt, K.C.B.	1st light battalion, ... Lieut.-colonel Lewis von dem Bussche, succeeded to the command of the 2d brigade and Brevet lieut.-colonel Fred. Wm. von Hartwig to the command of the battalion, ...	39	6	44
1st line battalion, 1st brigade under command of col. Charles 2d do.	2d do. ..... Major George Baring, ...	33	12	39
2d do....... of infantry du Plat; after being severely	1st line battalion, ... Major William von Robertson, after being severely wounded, succeeded by Captain Frederick von Goeben, ...	34	6	42
3d do....... King's Ger wounded, the command devolved upon 4th do....... man legion lieut.-col. Fred. von Wissell, of the 3d. line battalion.	2d do. ... Major George Müller, ...	34	5	46
	3d do. ... Major Frederick von Lutterman to the command of the battalion,...................	34	5	40
	4th do. .. Major Frederick Reh, ...	40	5	43
1st light battalion under command of colonel C. v. Ompeda; after being killed in a charge at the head of his 2d do. own, the 5th line, battalion, 5th line battalion, 2d do. Lieut.-colonel Lewis von dem 8th do. Bussche, of the 1st light battalion, succeeded him in the command of the brigade, ..	5th do. .. Lieutenant-colonel William von Linsingen, ...	30	5	43
	6th do. .. { detachment ; the battalion being { on service in the Mediterranean. } was attached to different battalions, ...	5	,,	,,
	7th do. .. .. ditto, ... ditto, ...	9	2	2
	8th do. ..{ Lieut.-col. John Christian von Schröeder, of the 2d line battalion, and on being severely { wounded, the command devolved upon major C. von Petersdorff of the 8th do.....	35	5	47
	Of foreign veteran battalion two privates were attached to major-generals G. Cooke and sir C. Halkett, both killed	,,	,,	,,
		TOTAL..............	430	82	536

Field Marshal his Grace the Duke of Wellington, together with the casualties during the actions on the 16th, 17th and 18th June 1815.

Troop Horses & Mules	Colonel	Brevet-colonel	Lieutenant-colonels	Major	Brevet-majors	Captains of troops	Captains of companies	Captain and Brigade major	Lieutenants	Lieutenants and adjutants	Cornets	Ensigns	TOTAL	Serjeant-major	Serjeants of artillery	Serjeants of cavalry	Serjeants of infantry	Corporals of artillery	Corporals of cavalry and infantry	Bombardiers	Trumpeters	Drummers	Gunners	Dragoons	Hussars	Riflemen	Musqueteers	Smiths, Drivers of artillery	TOTAL	GRAND TOTAL	Troop horses and mules	Colonels	Lieutenant-colonels	Majors	Captains and second captains	Lieutenants	Cornets and ensigns	Brigade major	Adjutants	Serjeants	Trumpeters, Buglemen and drummers	Rank and file	TOTAL	Troop horses and mules	Serjeants	Drummers	Rank and file	TOTAL	Troop horses and mules
																															1									2				2						
620	,,	,,	,,	,,	,,	,,	,,	1	,,	,,	1	,,	1	,,	1	,,	,,	1	,,	4	,,	,,	10	,,	,,	,,	1	5	19	20	51	,,	,,	,,	3	3	,,	,,	,,	1	,,	50	57	,,	,,	,,	4	4	,,
521	,,	,,	,,	1	,,	2	,,	,,	3	,,	3	,,	,,	4	,,	1	,,	22	,,	,,	,,	,,	30	33	53	1	1	1	3	2	,,	1	7	1	82	102	95	,,	,,	6	6	,,
458	,,	,,	,,	1	,,	,,	1	,,	2	,,	,,	1	,,	,,	1	,,	18	,,	,,	,,	,,	20	22	30	,,	2	,,	2	1	1	,,	6	,,	45	57	36	,,	1	1	22
547	,,	,,	,,	,,	,,	,,	,,	,,	,,	,,	,,	,,	,,	,,	3	,,	,,	,,	,,	3	3	9	,,	,,	,,	1	,,	,,	5	6	13	1	,,	2	3	3
8	,,	,,	,,	,,	,,	,,	,,	,,	,,	,,	,,	,,	,,	,,	,,	,,	,,	,,	,,	,,	,,	,,	,,	,,	,,	,,	,,
704	,,	1	,,	,,	2	,,	,,	1	1	,,	5	,,	,,	2	,,	2	,,	1	,,	,,	26	,,	,,	,,	,,	31	36	63	,,	,,	2	2	3	,,	9	1	103	120	24	,,	,,	15
,,	,,	,,	,,	3	,,	1	,,	,,	4	,,	,,	3	5	,,	,,	41	,,	,,	,,	,,	49	53	,,	1	,,	1	2	7	4	,,	6	3	73	97	,,	,,	13	13
,,	,,	,,	1	,,	2	,,	,,	1	4	,,	,,	7	4	,,	,,	35	,,	,,	46	50	,,	1	,,	1	7	2	,,	1	8	1	111	132	,,	2	,,	27	29
,,	,,	,,	2	,,	,,	1	3	1	,,	2	3	,,	1	,,	,,	27	,,	34	37	,,	1	1	3	1	,,	1	6	,,	63	75	,,	1	16	17
,,	,,	1	,,	,,	1	,,	,,	,,	2	,,	1	3	,,	,,	13	,,	17	19	,,	,,	1	4	,,	4	,,	75	82	1	,,	6	7
,,	,,	,,	1	,,	2	,,	,,	3	,,	1	4	,,	,,	32	,,	37	40	,,	1	,,	2	,,	2	1	90	96	,,	31	31
,,	1	,,	1	1	,,	1	,,	1	5	,,	2	2	,,	19	,,	23	28	,,	1	3	1	3	,,	74	83	1	13	14
,,	1	,,	,,	1	,,	1	,,	3	,,	1	3	,,	37	,,	41	44	,,	1	2	,,	6	1	40	50	,,	74	74
,,	,,	,,	,,	,,	1	,,	1	1	,,	1	,,	1	,,	,,	,,	4	5	,,
,,	,,	,,	2	1	,,	3	,,	2	1	,,	24	,,	28	31	,,	1	1	1	,,	1	4	,,	76	84	,,	1	2	13	16
,,	,,	,,	,,	,,	,,	,,	2	,,	2	2	,,
2858	1	1	2	1	2	17	1	9	2	3	39	1	1	6	19	1	31	1	5	311	1	5	382	421	206	3	3	4	18	40	15	2	5	62	8	891	1051	168	5	4	206	215	40

(brackets above totals: 4 13 / 7 2 over 17; 3 2 10 40 29 76 156 over 311; 90 and 961 under brackets)

I. KILLED.

Staff	Brigade-major, captain Charles von Bobers (attached to the 7th brigade of cavalry) killed in the battle, 18th of June 1815.
Artillery,	1st lieutenant Charles Detlef von Schultzen, (was attached to the 1st battery of Hanoverian artillery) killed in the battle, 18th June 1815.

1st dragoons, ... { Captain Frederick Peters................
Lieutenant F. C. Lewis von Levetzow,..
2d do........ { Ditto, Otto Kuhlmann, ... } killed in the battle, 18th June.
Captain Frederick von Bülow, ...
Cornet Henry Drangmeister, ...

3d hussars ...... { Lieutenant-colonel Fred. Lewis Meyer, died at Brussels, 6th July 1815, of the wounds he received in the battle of Waterloo, 18th of June 1815.
Captain Agats von Kerssenbruch, ...
—— George Janssen, ...
Lieutenant & adjutant Henry Brüggemann,
Cornet William Deichmann, ... } killed in the battle, 18th June, 1815.

1st light battalion, { Captain Philip Holtzermann, ...
—— Henry von Marschalck ...... }
Augustus Alexander von Goeben,
Lieutenant Anton Albert, ...

2d do........ { Captain (Brevet-major) Adol. Böswiel, ..
—— Fred. Melchior Wm. Schauman, }
—— Henry Wiegmann, (acting as major of brigade to the 1st brigade of infantry K. G. Legion) killed in the battle, 18th June, 1815.

1st line battalion, { Ensign Fred. von Robertson, —— } killed in the battle, 18th June,
Captain Charles von Holle, — } 1815.
—— Augustus von Saffe, (his hat and horse found on the field of battle, but he himself could not immediately be traced) killed in the battle, 18th June, 1815.
Ensign Hartwich von Lücken,—— killed in the battle 18th June 1815.

2d do........ { Lieut.-colonel John Christian von Schröder, died at Brussels, 22d June 1815, of the wounds received in the battle of Waterloo, 18th of June 1815.
Captain George Tileo, —— } killed in the battle, 18th June 1815.

3d do........ { —— Frederick Didel, —— } killed in the battle, 18th June 1815.
Lieutenant Frederick von Jeinsen, } died at Brussels, 28th June 1815, of their
—— Frederick Leschen,— } wounds received in the battle of Waterloo, 18th of June 1815.

4th do........ { Lieut.-col. (brevet-col.) G. C. August du Plat { commanded the 1st brigade of infantry K.G. Legion) died at Brussels 21st June 1815, of the wounds he received in the battle of Waterloo, June 18, 1815.
Major G. Cyriacus Chüden died at Brussels 19th June 1815 of their wounds received in the battle of Waterloo, June18,1815
Captain (brevet-Major) G. Lewis Leue do. 23d do.
—— George Heise .. do. 27th do. }
Ensign Edward Theodore von Cronhelm, killed in the battle 18th June 1815.

5th do. ...... { Colonel Christian von Ompteda (commanded the 2d brigade of infantry K. G. Legion,) killed in the battle 18th June 1815.
Captain Ernest Christian Chas. von Wurmb,
Lieutenant and Adjut. John Lewis Schuck,

8th do. ...... { Captain Augustus William von Voigt } killed in the battle 18th Jun. 1815
—— Thilo von Westernhagen
Lieutenant William von Marenholtz,

II. WOU[NDED]

Staff, ...	Brigade, major, captain Gottfried von Einem, severely (was attached to the 2d brigade of infantry.)	
	Ditto, do. Moritz von Cloudt, ...	slightly. do 3d cavalry.

Artillery, ... { Captain (brevet major) Augustus Sympher, ... slightly.
2d captain William Braun, severely { was attached to the 1st battery of Hanoverian artillery, wounded in the beginning of the action.
—— Frederick Erythropel, ... severely.
1st lieutenant William von Goeben, ... severely.
—— Henry Hartmann, ... severely.
2d—————Lewis Heise .... slightly.

1st dragoons, ... { Major-general sir Wm. von Dörnberg, K.C.B. ..... severely.
Lieutenant-colonel John von Bülow .... severely.
Major Augustus von Reizenstein, ... severely.
Captain Philip von Sichart, ... severely.
—— George von Hattorf, ... severely.
Bernard von Bothmer, ... right leg amputated.
Lieutenant Wm. Mackenzie, ... slightly.
—— and adjutant William Fricke, ... severely.
—— Otto von Hammerstein, ... severely.
—— Henry Bosse, ... severely.
Cornet Staats Henry Nanne, ... very severely.
—— Edward Trittau, ... severely.

2d do. ...... { Lieutenant-colonel Charles de Jonquières, ... slightly.
—— Charles von Maydell, ... very slightly.
Captain C. Theodore Leopold George von Harling, ... very severely.
—— Lewis Lüderitz, ... slightly.
Lieutenant Hermann Henry Conrad Rittor, ... severely.
Cornet Ferdinand Lorentz .... severely.

1st hussars, ... Lieutenant George Baring, ... slightly.

3d do. ...... { Captain Quintus von Goeben, ... slightly.
—— Wm. von Schneben, ... slightly.
Lieutenant Hermann True, ... very severely.
—— Christian Oehlkers, ... very severely.
Cornet Frederick Hoyer .... slightly.
—— Conrad von Dassel, ... severely.
Hans von Hodenberg, ... severely.

1st light battalion, { Major-general Charles count Alten, K.C.B. .... very severely.
Major Hans von dem Bussche, ... right arm amputated.
Captain Frederick von Gilsa, ... very severely.
—— Christian Wyneken, ... slightly.
Lieutenant Augustus Wahrendorff, ... slightly.
—— Christoph Heise, ... severely.
—— Hermann Wollrabe, ... severely.
—— Ernest F. A. Koester, ... slightly.
—— Harry Leonhart, ... severely.

1st light battalion,	Lieutenant Nicholas de Miniussir,	....	slightly.
	—— Edgar Gibson,	....	slightly.
	Ensign Gustavus Best,	....	severely.
	—— Adolphus Augustus von Gentzkow,	....	slightly.
	—— Charles Behne,	....	slightly.
	—— Adolphus Heise,	....	slightly.
2d do.	Major-general sir Colin Halkett, K.C.B.	....	severely.
	Captain Ernest Augustus Holtzermann,	....	slightly, and taken prisoner,—rejoined
	Lieutenant George Meyer,	....	slightly.
	—— F. G. T. Kessler,	....	slightly.
	—— Ole Lindam,	....	severely.
	—— Bernhard Rieckugel	....	slightly.
	—— Marius T. H. Tobin,	. .....	slightly, taken prisoner,—rejoined.
	—— George Drummond Graeme,	....	slightly.
	—— and adjutant Wm. Timmann	....	severely.
	—— Thomas Carey,	....	slightly.
	Ensign George Frank,	....	severely.
	—— Augustus Knop,	....	slightly.
1st line battalion,	Major William von Robertson,	....	severely
	Captain Gerlach von Schlütter,	....	very severely.
	Lieutenant and adjutant Frederick Schmuth,	....	severely.
	Lieutenant Augustus Müller,	....	very severely.
	—— Diederich von Einem	....	severely.
	—— Henry Wilding, jun.	....	severely.
	Ensign Chas. Aug. von der Hellen,	... ...	slightly.
2d do.	Captain Frederick Purgold,	....	severely.
	Lieutenant Claus von der Decken,	....	severely.
	—— Charles Fischer,	....	severely.
	—— Francis la Roche,	....	slightly.
	—— Aug. Ferdinand Ziel,	....	slightly.
3d do.	Major Anthony Boden,	... .	severely.
	Lieutenant Augustus Kuckuck,	....	slightly.
	—— Harry Edward Kuckuck,	....;...	slightly.
4th do.	Captain William Heydenreich,	....	slightly.
	Lieutenant Caspar von Both,	....	slightly.
	—— and adjutant Adolphus von Hartwig,	......	leg amputated.
	—— Wm. Lewis de la Farque,	....	leg amputated.
	—— Adolphus von Langwerth	....	slightly.
	Ensign Arnold Appuhn,	....	slightly.
5th do.	Captain Frederick Sander,	... .	very severely.
	Lieutenant Charles Berger,	....	slightly.
	—— George Klingsöhr,	....	slightly.
7th do.	—— George Klingsöhr,	....	slightly.
8th do.	Captain Charles Emanuel Wilhelm Rougemont,	....	slightly
	Lieutenant and adjutant Frederick Brinckmann,	....	severely.
	—— Christian Sattler,	....	slightly.
	Ensign William von Moreau,	....	very severely

MEMORANDUM.

Lieutenant-general Charles count Alten, K.C.B. (major-general and colonel commandant 1st light battalion K. G. Legion,) commanded the 3d division of the British-Hanoverian army.

Major-general sir Colin Halkett, K.C.B. ...... (colonel commandant 2d light battalion, K. G. Legion,) commanded the 5th British brigade of infantry.

Colonel Hugh Halkett, ... (lieutenant-colonel 7th line battalion K.G. Legion) commanded the 3d Hanoverian brigade of infantry.

Colonel Charles Best, ..., ... (lieutenant-colonel 8th line battalion K.G. Legion) commanded the 4th Hanoverian brigade of infantry.

Major-general Victor von Alten, ... (colonel commandant 2d hussars K. G. Legion) superintended the duties of the Hanoverian cavalry, under the orders of lieutenant-general the earl of Uxbridge, G. C. B. who commanded the whole of the British and Hanoverian cavalry.

In consequence of the diminutive state of the battalions of the King's German Legion, they were, per general orders, dated Brussells, 25th of April 1815, formed into six companies each battalion: and the rank and file and drummers of each battalion distributed among these companies; but the officers and serjeants who became supernumerary by this arrangement, were disposable for service with other corps, and ninety officers and one hundred and four serjeants were ordered to do duty with the Hanoverian corps and attached to the battalions in the third, fourth, fifth and sixth Hanoverian brigades, per general orders dated Brussells, 9th May 1815.

The names of all the killed (including those who died of their wounds) returned in column* are engraved on the monument erected in the Waterloo-place at Hanover, in commemoration of the battle of Waterloo, with the exception of the two men of the foreign veteran battalion, who, by accident were omitted.

The names of the two privates killed of the sixth and seventh line battalions, and who were attached to the second and fourth line battalions, are included with those battalions on the Waterloo monument.

(Signed) LEWIS BENNE.

Hanover, February 1831.

No. XXI.

RELATION OF THE PART TAKEN BY THE SECOND LIGHT BAT-
TALION OF THE KING'S GERMAN LEGION IN THE BATTLE
OF WATERLOO, BY MAJOR-GENERAL BARON VON BARING.
(From the Hanoverian Military Journal. Part II. 1831.)

TRANSLATION.

*   *   *   '*   *   *   *   *   *   *

The farm of la Haye Sainte lies, as is well known, close by the
side of the high road which leads from Brussels to Genappe, in
the centre of the two positions, and about midway between them.

The dwelling-house, barn, and stables were surrounded by a
rectangular wall, forming a court in the interior.   Towards the
enemy's side was an orchard, surrounded by a hedge, and in rear
was a kitchen-garden, bounded by a small wall towards the road,
but on the other sides by a hedge.   Two doors and three large
gates led from the court to the exterior ; but of these, that of
the barn had been unfortunately broken and burned by the troops.

The battalion consisted of six companies, which did not number
four hundred men ; I posted three companies in the orchard, two
in the buildings, and one in the garden.

Important as the possession of this farm apparently was, the
means of defending it were very insufficient, and besides, I was
ordered, immediately on arriving there, to send off the pioneers of
the battalion to Hougoumont, so that I had not even a hatchet ;
for unfortunately the mule that carried the entrenching tools, was
lost the day before.

As day broke on the 18th of June, we sought out every possible
means of putting the place in a state of defence, but the burned
gate of the barn presented the greatest difficulties.   With this
employment, and cooking some veal which we found in the place,
the morning was past until after eleven o'clock, when the attack
commenced against the left wing.

Every man now repaired to his post, and I betook myself to the orchard, where the first attack was to be expected : the farm lies in a hollow, so that a small elevation of the ground immediately in front of the orchard, concealed the approach of the enemy.

Shortly after noon, some skirmishers commenced the attack. I made the men lie down, and forbad all firing until the enemy were quite near. The first shot broke the bridle of my horse close to my hand, and the second killed major Bösewiel, who was standing near me. The enemy did not stop long skirmishing, but immediately advanced over the height, with two close columns, one of which attacked the buildings, and the other threw itself in mass into the orchard, shewing the greatest contempt for our fire. It was not possible for our small disjointed numbers fully to withstand this furious attack of such a superior force, and we retired upon the barn, in a more united position, in order to continue the defence: my horse's leg was broken, and I was obliged to take that of the adjutant.

Colonel von Klencke now came to our assistance with the Lüneburg battalion. We immediately recommenced the attack, and had already made the enemy give way, when I perceived a strong line of cuirassiers form in front of the orchard ; at the same time captain Meyer came to me and reported that the enemy had surrounded the rear garden, and it was not possible to hold it longer. I gave him orders to fall back into the buildings, and assist in their defence. Convinced of the great danger which threatened us from the cuirassiers, in consequence of the weak hedge, so easy to break through, I called out to my men, who were mixed with the newly arrived Hanoverians,—to assemble round me, as I intended retiring into the barn. The number of the battalion which had come to our assistance, exceeded, by many degrees, that of my men, and as, at the same time, the enemy's infantry gained the garden,—the skirmishers having been driven out by a column attack,—the former, seeing the cuirassiers in the open field, imagined that their only chance of safety lay in gaining the main position of the army. My voice, unknown to them, and also not sufficiently penetrating, was, notwithstanding all my exertions, unequal to halt and collect my men together; already overtaken by the cavalry, we fell in with the enemy's infantry, who had surrounded the garden, and to whose fire the men were exposed in retiring to the main position. In this effort a part succeeded. Notwithstanding this misfortune, the farm-house itself was still defended by lieutenants George Groeme and Carey, and ensign Frank. The English dragoon guards now came up,—beat back the cuirassiers,—fell upon the infantry, who had already suffered much, and nearly cut them to pieces.

In this first attack I lost a considerable number of men, besides three officers killed, and six wounded; on my requisition for support, captains von Gilsa and Marschalck were sent to me, with their companies of the 1st light battalion; to these, and a part of my own battalion, I gave the defence of the garden, leaving the buildings to the three officers who had already so bravely defended them: the orchard I did not again occupy.

About half an hour's respite was now given us by the enemy, and we employed the time in preparing ourselves against a new attack; this followed in the same force as before; namely, from two sides by two close columns, which, with the greatest rapidi-ty, nearly surrounded us, and, despising danger, fought with a degree of courage which I had never before witnessed in French-men. Favored by their advancing in masses, every bullet of ours hit, and seldom were the effects limited to one assailant; this did not, however, prevent them from throwing themselves against the walls, and endeavouring to wrest the arms from the hands of my men, through the loop-holes; many lives were sacrificed to the defence of the doors and gates; the most obstinate contest was carried on where the gate was wanting, and where the enemy seemed determined to enter. On this spot seventeen Frenchmen already lay dead, and their bodies served as a protection to those who pressed after them to the same spot.

Meantime four lines of French cavalry had formed on the right front of the farm: the first cuirassiers, second lancers, third dra-goons, and fourth hussars, and it was clear to me that their intention was to attack the squares of our division in position, in order by destroying them to break the whole line. This was a critical moment, for what would be our fate if they succeeded! As they marched upon the position by the farm, I brought all the fire possible to bear upon them ; many men and horses were over-thrown, but they were not discouraged. Without in the least troubling themselves about our fire, they advanced with the greatest intrepidity, and attacked the infantry. All this I could see, and confess freely that now and then I felt some apprehension. The manner in which this cavalry was received and beaten back by our squares, is too well known to require mention here.

The contest in the farm had continued with undiminished violence, but nothing could shake the courage of our men, who, following the example of their officers, laughing, defied danger. Nothing could inspire more courage or confidence than such conduct. These are the moments when we learn how to feel what one soldier is to another ;—what the word "comrade" really means ;—feelings which must penetrate the coarsest mind, but which he only can fully understand, who has been witness to such moments!

When the cavalry retired, the infantry gave up also their fruit-less attack, and fell back, accompanied by our shouts, and derision. Our loss, on this occasion, was not so great as at first ; however, my horse was again shot under me, and as my servant, believing me dead, had gone away with my other horse, 1 procured one of those that were running about.

Our first care was to make good the injury which had been sustained ; my greatest anxiety was respecting the ammunition, which, I found, in consequence of the continued fire, had been reduced more than one half. I immediately sent an officer back with this account, and requested ammunition, which was pro-mised. About an hour had thus passed when I discovered the enemy's columns again advancing on the farm ; I sent another officer back to the position with this intelligence, and repeated the request for ammunition.

Our small position was soon again attacked with the same fury, and defended with the same courage as before. Captain von Wurmb was sent to my assistance with the skirmishers of the fifth line battalion, and I placed them in the court ; but welcome as this reinforcement was, it could not compensate for the want of ammunition, which every moment increased, so that after half an hour more of uninterrupted fighting, I sent off an officer with the same request.

This was as fruitless as the other two applications; however, two hundred Nassau troops were sent me. The principal contest was now carried on at the open entrance to the barn ; at length the enemy, not being able to succeed by open force, resorted to the expedient of setting the place on fire, and soon a thick smoke was seen rising from the barn! Our alarm was now extreme, for although there was water in the court, all means of drawing it, and carrying it were wanting,—every vessel having been broken up. Luckily the Nassau troops carried large field cooking kettles ; I tore a kettle from the back of one of the men ; several officers followed my example, and filling the kettles with water, they carried them, facing almost certain death, to the fire. The men did the same, and soon not one of the Nassauers was left with his kettle, and the fire was thus luckily extinguished;—but alas ! with the blood of many a brave man ! Many of the men, although covered with wounds, could not be brought to retire. " So long as our officers fight, and we can stand," was their constant reply, " we will not stir from the spot."

It would be injustice to a skirmisher named Frederick Lindau, if I did not mention him : Bleeding from two wounds in the head and carrying in his pocket a considerable bag of gold which he had taken from an enemy's officer, he stood at the small back barn door, and from thence defended the main entrance in his front. I told him to go back, as the cloth about his head was not sufficient to stop the strong flow of blood ; he, however, as regardless of his wounds as of his gold, answered : " He would be a scoundrel that deserted you, so long as his head is on his shoulders." This brave fellow was afterwards taken, and lost his treasure.

This attack may have lasted about an hour and a half, when the French, tired from their fruitless efforts, again fell back. Our joy may be well imagined. With every new attack I became more convinced of the importance of holding the post. With every attack also, the weight of the responsibility that devolved upon me increased. This responsibility is never greater than when an officer is thus left to himself, and suddenly obliged to make a decision upon which, perhaps, his own as well as the life and honor of those under him,—nay even more important results,— may depend. In battles, as is well known, trifles, apparently of little importance, have often incalculable influence.

What must have been my feelings, therefore, when, on counting the cartridges, I found that, on an average, there was not more than from three to four each! The men made nothing of the diminished physical strength which their excessive exertions had caused, and immediately filled up the holes that had been made in the walls by the enemy's guns, but they could not remain insensible to the position in which they were placed by the want of ammunition, and made the most reasonable remonstrances to me on the subject. These were not wanting to make me renew the most urgent representations, and finally to report specifically that I was not capable of sustaining another attack in the present condition. *All was in vain!* * With what uneasiness did I now see two enemy's columns again in march against us! At this moment I would have blesssed the ball that came to deprive me of life.—But more than life was at stake, and the extraordinary danger required extraordinary exertion and firmness. On my exhortations to courage and economy of the ammunition, I received one unanimous reply:—"No man will desert you,—we will fight and die with you!"—No pen, not even that of one who has experienced such moments, can describe the feeling which this

---

* It must be observed that the battalion were armed with rifles, and, therefore, could not make use of the ordinary infantry ammunition. This circumstance explains what occurred; but at the same time, shews how dangerous it may prove to have fire arms of different calibres.—Note of the Editor of the Hanoverian Military Journal.

excited in me ; nothing can be compared with it !—Never had I felt myself so elevated ;—but never also placed in so painful a position, where honor contended with a feeling for the safety of the men who had given me such an unbounded proof of their confidence.

The enemy gave me no time for thought; they were already close by our weak walls, and now, irritated by the opposition which they had experienced, attacked with renewed fury. The contest commenced at the barn, which they again succeeded in setting on fire. It was extinguished, luckily, in the same manner as before. Every shot that was now fired, increased my uneasiness and anxiety. I sent again to the rear with the positive statement that I must and would leave the place if no ammunition was sent me. This was also without effect.

Our fire gradually diminished, and in the same proportion did our perplexity increase ; already I heard many voices calling out for ammunition, adding :—" We will readily stand by you, but we must have the means of defending ourselves!" Even the officers, who, during the whole day, had shewn the greatest courage, represented to me the impossibility of retaining the post under such circumstances. The enemy, who too soon observed our wants, now boldly broke in one of the doors ; however, as only a few could come in at a time, these were instantly bayonetted, and the rear hesitated to follow. They now mounted the roof and walls, from which my unfortunate men were certain marks ; at the same time they pressed in through the open barn, which could no longer be defended. Inexpressibly painful as the decision was to me of giving up the place, my feeling of duty as a man overcame that of honor, and I gave the order to retire through the house into the garden. How much these words cost me, and by what feelings they were accompanied, he only can judge who has been placed in a similar situation !

Fearing the bad impression which retiring from the house into the garden would make upon the men, and wishing to see whether it was possible still to hold any part of the place, I left to the before-mentioned three officers the honor of being the last. The passage through the house being very narrow, many of the men were overtaken by the enemy, who vented their fury upon them in the lowest abuse, and the most brutal treatment. Among the sufferers here was ensign Frank, who had already been wounded: the first man that attacked him, he ran through with his sabre, but at the same moment, his arm was brokenby a ball from another; nevertheless he reached a bed room, and succeeded in concealing himself behind a bed. Two of the men also took refuge in the same place, but the French followed close at their heels, crying *Pas de pardon a ces B—— verds !*, and shot them before his face: Frank had himself the good luck to remain undiscovered until the place again fell into our hands.

As I was now fully convinced, and the officers agreed with me, that the garden was not to be maintained when the enemy were in possession of the dwelling house, I made the men retire singly to the main position. The French, pleased, perhaps, with their success, did not molest us in retreat. The men who had been sent to me from other regiments, I allowed to return, and with the weak remnant of my own battalion I attached myself to two companies of the first light battalion, which, under lieutenant-colonel Lewis von dem Bussche, occupied the hollow road behind the farm. Although we could not fire a shot, we helped to increase the numbers. Here the combat recommenced with increased fury, the enemy pressing forth from the farm, and I had the pain to see captain Henry von Marschalck fall—a friend whose distinguished coolness and bravery on this day I can never forget; captain von Gilsa also had his right arm shattered; lieutenant Albert was shot, and lieutenant Groeme, as he swung his cap in the air to cheer on the men, had his right hand shattered; neither would go into the hollow road, notwithstanding all my persuasions, but remained above upon the edge. On the retreat from the buildings captain Holtzerman and lieutenant Tobin were taken, and lieutenant Carey was wounded, so that the number of my officers was very much reduced. I rode a dragoon horse, in front of whose saddle were large pistol holsters and a cloak, and the firing was so sharp that four balls entered here, and another the saddle, just as

I had alighted to replace my hat which had been knocked off by a sixth ball.

The fifth line battalion which stood on our right, were now ordered to attack the enemy with the bayonet   *   *   *   *

The cuirassiers thought this a good opportunity to break through the line, not, perhaps, being aware of the presence of our men in the hollow road ; however when they had arrived within about twenty paces, they received such a fire that they wheeled about in the greatest disorder, well marked by our men ; at this moment the third hussars advanced.

*   •   *   *   *   *   •   *

Fresh columns of the enemy again advanced, and nothing seemed likely to terminate the slaughter but the entire destruction of one army or the other. My horse, the third which I had had in the course of the day, received a ball in his head; he sprung up, and in coming down again, fell on my right leg, and pressed me so hard into the deep loamy ground, that, despite of all exertion, I could not extricate myself. The men in the road considered me dead, and it was not till after some little time that one of them came out to set me free. Although my leg was not broken, I lost the use of it for the moment ; I begged most urgently for a horse, offering gold upon gold, but men who called themselves my friends, forgot the word, and thought only of their own interest ! I crept to the nearest house behind the front. An Englishman was charitable enough to catch a stray horse,—place a saddle upon him, and help me up ; I then rode again forward, when I learned that general Alten had been severely wounded. I saw that the part of the position, which our division had held, was only weakly and irregularly occupied. Scarce sensible, from the pain which I suffered, I rode straight to the hollow road, where I had left the rest of the men ; but they also, had been obliged to retire to the village in consequence of the total want of ammunition, hoping there to find some cartridges. A French dragoon finally drove me from the spot, and riding back, in the most bitter grief, I met an officer, who gave me the above information of the battalion. I directed him to bring my men forward, if there were only two of them together, as I had hopes of getting some ammunition. Immediately after this, there arose throughout the whole line, the cry of "victory"! victory"!, and with equal enthusiasm "forward"! "forward!"—What an unexpected change! As I had no longer any men to command, I joined the first hussars, and with them followed the enemy until dark, when I returned to the field of battle.

The division, which had suffered dreadfully, remained, during the night, on the field. Out of nearly four hundred men, with which I commenced the battle, only forty-two remained effective. Whoever I asked after, the answer was "killed",—"wounded"! I freely confess that tears came involuntarily into my eyes at this sad intelligence, and the many bitter feelings that seized upon me. I was awakened from these gloomy thoughts by my friend major Shaw, assistant-quarter-master-general to our division. I felt myself exhausted to the greatest degree, and my leg was very painful. I lay down to sleep, with my friend, upon some straw which the men had collected together for us : on waking we found ourselves between a dead man, and a dead horse!—But I will pass over in silence the scene which the field of battle, with all its misery and grief, now presented.

We buried our dead friends and comrades ; amongst the rest colonel von Ompteda, the commander of the brigade, and many brave men. After some food was cooked, and the men had, in some measure, refreshed themselves, we broke up from the field to follow the enemy.

B.

Return of officers of the second light battalion, two companies of the first light battalion, and the skirmishers of the fifth line battalion of the King's German Legion, who were present at the defence of the farm of la Haye Sainte, June 18, 1815.

SECOND LIGHT BATTALION.

MAJORS.

George Baring,	....
A. Bösewiel,	.... killed.

CAPTAINS.

E. Holtzermann,	.... taken prisoner.
W. Schaumann,	.... killed.

LIEUTENANTS.

F. Kessler,	.... wounded.
C. Meyer,	....
O. Lindam,	.... wounded.
B. Riefkugel,	.... wounded.
A. Tobin,	.... taken prisoner.
T. Carey,	.... wounded.
E. Biedermann,	....
D. Groeme,	.... wounded.
S. Earl,	....

ENSIGNS.

F. Von Robertson,	.... killed.
G. Frank,	.... wounded.
W. Smith,	....
L. Baring,	....
Lieutenant and adjutant W. Timmann,	.... wounded.
Surgeon G. Heise,	....

FIRST LIGHT BATTALION.

CAPTAINS.

Von Gilsa	.... wounded.
Von Marschalck,	.... killed.

LIEUTENANT.

Kuntze,	....

ENSIGN.

Baumgarten,	....

SKIRMISHERS OF FIFTH LINE BATTALION

Captain von Wurmb,　　　　　　　........ killed.

LIEUTENANTS.

Witte,　　　　　　　　　　........ wounded.
Schläger,　　　　　　　　　........

ENSIGN.

Walther,　　　　　　　　　....... .. wounded.

No. XXII.
SECOND DRAGOONS AT WATERLOO.

A.

Certificate of lieutenant-general sir William von Dörnberg,
K.C.B.

(Copy.)

I do hereby certify that lieutenant colonel Friederichs, of the late second light dragoons King's German Legion, behaved most gallantly in the memorable battle of Waterloo, and that he rallied and led the regiment against the enemy, when it had been put into disorder by a charge of French cuirassiers,—in a most conspicuous manner.

Dated Celle, the 16th June, 1820.

　　　　　　　　　　　　　v. Dörnberg,
　　　　　　　　　　　　　　Lieutenant-general.

(L.S.)

B.

Lieutenant-colonel de Jonquières to Lieutenant-colonel
Friederichs.

Emden, *March* 11, 1816.

Sir,

Having lost the rough copy, I am sorry that I am not able, as you desire, to provide you with a copy of my letter, in which, some time after the battle of Waterloo, I wrote to colonel the earl of Portarlington, the particular circumstances concerning you in that battle ; but it is with the greatest pleasure I can assure you that I reported in that letter to the earl :—

" That after the regiment had made the first charge upon the French cavalry, and was obliged to fall back, you immediately renewed the attack with that part of the regiment which you had re-assembled, not far from the place where the regiment first met the enemy".

And I am confident that by this conduct, you prevented the men who were wounded and dismounted in the first charge, from ill treatment by the enemy.

I have the honor to be,
Sir,
Your obedient humble servant,
C. de JONQUIERES,
Lieutenant-colonel.

To lieut.-colonel Friedrichs, &c. &c.

No. XXII.

ARMY OF THE NETHERLANDS.

COMMANDED BY FIELD-MARSHAL HIS GRACE THE DUKE OF WELLINGTON. JUNE 1815.

CAVALRY.

1st brigade-major-general lord Edward Somerset.	1st life guards. 2d do. royal horse guards. 1st dragoon guards.
2d brigade-major-general sir William Ponsonby.	1st dragoons. 2d do. 6th do.
3d brigade-major-general sir William von Dörnberg.	1st dragoons, K. G. L. 2d do. 23d dragoons.

4th brigade-major-general sir Ormsby Vandeleur, { 11th light dragoons, 12th do. 16th do.

5th brigade-major-general sir Colquhoun Grant. { 2d hussars, K. G. L. 7th hussars, 15th do.

6th brigade-major-general sir Hussey Vivian. { 1st hussars, K. G. L. 10th hussars. 18th do.

7th brigade-colonel sir Frederick von Arentschildt { 3d hussars, K. G. L. 13th light dragoons.

1st Hanoverian brigade { Bremen and Verden hussars. Lüneburg hussars.

INFANTRY.

FIRST CORPS COMMANDED BY GENERAL HIS ROYAL HIGHNESS THE PRINCE OF ORANGE.

1st division major-general Cooke {

1 battery, K. G. horse artillery—major Kuhlmann.
1 do. royal foot do. —captain Sandham.

1st brigade major-general Maitland. { 1st foot guards, 2d battalion. 1st do. 3d do.

2d brigade major-general Byng, { Coldstream guards, 2d battalion. 3d guards, 2d battalion.

3d divsion lieut.-general sir Charles von Alten. {

1 battery royal horse artillery—major Lloyd.
1 ditto, K. G. foot do. —captain Cleeves.

5th brigade, major-general sir C. Halkett. { 30th foot, 2d battalion. 33d do. 69th do. 2d battalion. 73d do. ditto,

K. G. L. 2d brigade colonel von Ompteda. { 1st light battalion, K. G. L. 2d do. do. 5th line battalion do. 8th do. do.

Hanoverian 1st brigade major-general count Kielmansegge { field batt. duke of York ——— Bremen ——— Verden. ——— Grubenhagen. ——— Lüneburg.

Belgians.
{
1 battery horse artillery.
1 do. foot do.
7 regiments cavalry.
2d and 3d divisions infantry.
Nassau brigade.
}

SECOND CORPS—LIEUTENANT-GENERAL LORD HILL.

2d division
Lieutenant-general
sir Henry Clinton
{

1 battery, K. G. horse artillery—major Sympher.

1 do royal foot do. —captain Napier.

3d brigade
major-general
Adam,
{
52d foot, 1st battalion.
71st do. do.
95th do. 2d battalion.
95th do. 3d do.
}

K. G. L.
1st brigade,
colonel
du Plat.
{
1st line battalion, K. G. L.
2d do. do.
3d do. do.
4th do. do.
}

Hanoverian
3d brigade.
col. Halkett.
{
landwehr batt. —Bremervörde
——————————Saltzgitter.
——— ———Osnabrück
——— ———Quackenbrück.
}
}

4th division.
lieutenant-general
sir Chas. Colville.
{

1 battery royal foot artillery—major Bromes

1 do Hanoverian do. —captain von Rettberg.

4th brigade
col. Mitchell,
{
14th foot, 3d battalion.
23d do.
51st do.
}

6th brigade
major-gen.
Johnstone.
{
35th foot, 2d battalion
54th do.
59th do. 2d battalion.
91st do. 1st do.
}

Hanoverian
6th brigade
major-general
Lyon.
{
field batt. ——Calenberg.
——— ——— Lauenburg.
landwehr batt. Hoya.
——————— Nienburg
——————— Bentheim.
}
}

Belgians
Prince Frederick
of Orange.
{
1 battery horse artillery
1 do. foot do.
1st infantry division.
Indian brigade
}

RESERVE.

1 battery royal foot artillery—major Rogers,

1 do.   Hanoverian do.   —captain Braun.

5th division
lieutenant-general
sir Thomas Picton

8th brigade
major-general
sir
James Kempt.
- 28th foot.
- 32d do.
- 79th do. 1st battalion.
- 95th do.   do.

9th brigade
major-general
sir
Denis Pack.
- 1st foot 3d battalion,
- 42d do. 1st   do.
- 44th do. 2d   do.
- 92d do.   do.

Hanoverian
5th brigade
colonel
von Vincke.
- landwehr batt. —Hameln.
- ————————Hildesheim.
- ————————Peina.
- ————————Giffhorn.

6th division.

1 battery royal foot artillery—major Unett.

10th brigade
major-general
Lambert
- 4th foot 1st battalion.
- 27th do.   do.
- 40th do.   do.
- 81st do. 2d   do.

Hanoverian
4th brigade
colonel Best
- Landwehr batt. —Lüneburg.
- ————————- Verden.
- ————————-Osterode.
- ——————————Münden.

7th brigade
major-general
M'Kenzie.
- 25th foot, 2d battalion.
- 37th do.   do.

8th brigade,
- 13th veteran battalion.
- 1st foreign   do.

RESERVE ARTILLERY.

Three batteries royal foot artillery.

One battery eighteen pounders   do.

BRUNSWICK CORPS COMMANDED BY HIS SERENE HIGHNESS THE DUKE OF BRUNSWICK.

Artillery,
major Mahn.
{ 1 battery horse artillery.
{ 1 do.   foot   do.

Cavalry,
{ 1 regiment of hussars.
{ 1 squadron of lancers.

Advanced guard
major von Rauschenplatt.
{ 2 companies riflemen.
{ 2   do.   light infantry

Light brigade,
lieut.-col. von
Buttlar,
{ 1st light battalion.
{ 2d   do.
{ 3d   do.

Line brigade,
lieut.-colonel
von Specht.
{ 1st line battalion.
{ 2d   do.
{ 3d   do.

HANOVERIAN RESERVE CORPS—LIEUTENANT-GENERAL VON DER DECKEN.

CAVALRY.

Cumberland hussars—lieutenant-colonel von Hacke.

INFANTRY.

1st brigade, lieut.-col. von
Benningsen, afterwards
lieut.-col. von Wissel.
{ field battalion—Hoya.
{ landwehr, do.—Mölln.
{ ————————Bremerlehe.

2d brigade, lieut.-colonel
von Beaulieu.
{ landwehr battalion—Nordheim.
{ ————————Alfeldt.
{ ————————Springe.

3d brigade, lieut.-colonel
von Bülow,
{ landwehr battalion —Otterndorf.
{ ————————Zelle.
{ ————————Ratzeburg.

4th brigade, lieut-colonel
von Bodecker,
{ landwehr battalion—Hanover.
{ ————————Uelzen.
{ ————————Neustadt.
{ ————————Deipholtz.

No. XXIII.

DOCUMENTS RELATING TO THE ORGANIZATION, SERVICES, AND
FINAL REDUCTION OF THE KING'S GERMAN LEGION.

A.

Proclamation of Lieutenant-general Don,

TRANSLATION.

I George Don, lieutenant-general in the service of his majesty
the king of the united kingdom of Great Britain and Ireland, &c.,
commanding a corps of British troops on the continent, consider
it my first duty hereby to explain, and publicly to make known to
the inhabitants of the electorate of Hanover, that the operations
of the corps which I have the honor to command, have for their
chief object the evacuation of his majesty's German province by
the enemies of his majesty, and the defence of the same.

The universally acknowledged discipline of the troops under
my command, is the best security to me of their good conduct
towards the subjects of their sovereign; should, however, contrary
to my expectations, any well founded complaint upon this subject
be brought before me, the same shall be investigated, with the
greatest impartialily, and immediately redressed.

His majesty, my most gracious master, is fully confident that
his majesty's much loved German subjects will receive his troops
in friendship; and in the name, and under the express orders of
his majesty, I invite all those whose circumstances admit of their
entering into military service, and *particularly those who formerly served in the royal electoral army*—to assemble, without
delay, under the British standard, where all the advantages will
be secured to them, which are enjoyed by the King's German
Legion. With united strength we will then put a stop to the unjust
demands of the enemy, and can with so much the more confidence anticipate success, as we take up arms for a just cause—
for our king,—and for our country !

Given at Stade, the 20th of Nov., 1805.

(*Signed.*)

GEORGE DON,
Lieutenant-general.

B.

Regulations under which the Hanoverian officers were gazetted to the King's German Legion.

TRANSLATION.

From the time of the formation of the King's German Legion in the year 1803 until the return of the corps from the north of Germany in 1806, the seniority of the officers was, by the order of his majesty, directed to be entirely regulated by the position which they had held in the late electoral army. In pursuance of this order, many officers who joined the legion several years after its formation, were placed above those who had entered the corps at an earlier period; among others, all those who first entered the service on the return of the legion from the north of Germany in the winter of 1805-6; as for instance: the first commission of lieutenant-colonel von Hartwig of the first light battalion is dated the 13th of October 1803, although he did not enter the legion until the 21st of January 1806, and then as captain, while major Hans von dem Busshe had been gazetted as captain in the same battalion since the 17th of November 1803, consequently had served some years longer than him in the same rank.

The order according to which this regulation was prescribed is dated horse-guards, 9th of February, 1804, and states as follows :—

" I have further to inform your royal highness, that his majesty has been pleased to authorize your royal highness to place the officers according to their succession, but, at the same time, so to regulate the date of each commission, that it may express the rank which the individual *formerly* held in the Hanoverian service, in order that the officers of the King's German Legion may take rank in their present corps according to their Hanoverian seniority."

This order remained in force until the 14th July 1806, when, it being presumed that all the Hanoverian officers had joined, who were capable of complying with the invitation to enter the service in the legion,—the commissions were from that time dated from the day of appointment.

(*Signed*)

CHRISTOPH HEISE.

Captain, R. H. Rifle-Guards.

C.

Address from the Hanoverian Chamber of Deputies to his royal highness the duke of Cambridge.

TRANSLATION.

MAY IT PLEASE YOUR ROYAL HIGHNESS !

The history of our time is rich in great events and glorious deeds, which posterity alone will be able adequately to appreciate and value according to their merits. But the examples of heroic firmness in the greatest dangers,—the most cheerful sacrifices of the dearest possessions of life for the good of the country and mankind—are too recent and too apparent not to move us, as contemporaries, to offer our thanks and reverence to those, who have elevated themselves to this high degree of virtue, full of the noblest pride, and loudly to express these our sentiments.

These, most gracious prince, were the feelings which your royal highness excited in the breasts of all, on the day of the solemn opening of the first meeting of the representatives of this kingdom, when you made honorable mention of the achievemeuts by which our country's sons have won undying fame, in the contest for freedom, for right, and the benefit of mankind, now gloriously terminated. United with the brave and conquering Britons, these noble warriors, whom we are proud to call brothers,—led by the first commander of the age, have inflicted one defeat after another upon an haughty enemy, who had presumed to consider himself invincible, and broken the chains which, by a preponderating force and daring artifice, he had succeeded in drawing around the half of Europe.

But it is not the merit of bravery alone which the fatherland values in its courageous defenders; great sacrifices have been brought upon a great part of the army, as also on the country, by their separation during ten years and more from their paternal hearth, and all that is most dear to the civilized and feeling man, in order to support the contest for freedom,—gathering their laurels in distant climes, exposed to numerous dangers and fatigues.

Instigated by a like praiseworthy zeal, a not inconsiderable number of noble youths unconnected with the military profession have, out of feeling for the good cause, torn themselves from the circle of their peaceful occupations, and, on the first call that was made upon the people to save their country, joined the bands of the veteran soldiers and bravely fought by their side.

They have all, with perseverance and firmness, contended for the holy cause of freedom, and have obtained a peace, which has again united us under our beloved monarch, and his exalted representative our much honored prince regent, under whose protection, and mild paternal government, we confidently look forward to a happy and prosperous future.

It is the unanimous wish of the deputies of the kingdom here assembled, that the sentiments of high respect, and deep-felt acknowledgment with which their grateful country is impressed, for the distinguished services of the brave Hanoverian soldiers, should be made known to the officers, non-commissioned officers and men, as well of the King's German Legion as of the other army-corps who have come forward for the deliverance of the country.

May it please your royal highness graciously to approve of this wish expressed through the representatives of the Hanoverian people and the respectful request that the contents of this unanimous resolution may be communicated from the general government to the troops, in the manner that may be deemed most fitting by your royal highness.

Signed in the name of the united deputies of the kingdom, in parliament assembled.

G. VON DEM SCHULEMBURG WOLFSBURG.

J. H. MEYER,

Secretary-general

HAVOVER, *Dec.* 27, 1814.

D.

Lieutenant-general Frederick von der Decken to major-general sir Henry von Hinüber.

TRANSLATION.

HANOVER, *Dec.* 30, 1814.

The deputies of the kingdom of Hanover here assembled, have presented an address to his royal highness the duke of Cambridge a copy of which is annexed, in which they express their high respect and acknowledgement for the distinguished services of the Hanoverian soldiers.

His royal highness begs that you will send a copy of the enclosed, to the infantry battalions of the King's German Legion which are in the Netherlands, and direct the commanding officers of the same to assure the officers, non-commissioned officers and soldiers, in the name of the duke of Cambridge, that it has afforded his royal highness great pleasure to see publicly acknowledged, in so honorable a manner by the deputies of the country to which the most part of them belong,—the great merits of the King's German Legion.

(*Signed,*)

FR. V. D. DECKEN,

Lieutenant-general.

E.

Division Orders.

A. A. GENERAL'S-OFFICE,
TOURNAY, *Jan.* 12, 1815,

TRANSLATION

It affords major-general sir Henry von Hinüber the greatest pleasure to have received the commission to communicate the thanks which the assembled deputies of the kingdom of Hanover, by means of an address to his royal highness the duke of Cambridge, have expressed for the brave and glorious conduct of the legion, and requested that the same may be made known to the different corps.

To have attained the unanimous approbation of our country, and to see this expressed in so flattering a manner by the deputies of the entire land, is the greatest reward for the dangers and fatigues of the past war, that we could hope to obtain.

The major-general, therefore, requests that the brigadiers will give general publicity to the annexed address of the Hanoverian deputies, and he has no doubt that all will be impressed with the deepest gratitude for the distinguished manner in which the kingdom of Hanover has acknowledged our services.

The value of the address is still further highly increased by the flattering communication with which his royal highness has caused it to be accompanied. His royal highness is pleased not only to look upon the services of the legion as "great" but expresses a peculiar pleasure at the country having publicly acknowledged them in so honourable a manner.

(*By order*)

FR. BREYMANN,
Major and A. A. general.

F.

Major-general sir Henry von Hinüber to his royal highness
the duke of Cambridge.

TRANSLATION.

MAY IT PLEASE YOUR ROYAL HIGHNESS!

Your royal highness has been graciously pleased to have communicated to the infantry of the King's German Legion, now
stationed in the Netherlands, the unanimous resolution of the deputies of the kingdom of Hanover, passed at their general meeting
on the 27th of December last. Your royal highness's orders have
been followed.

To express in a manner commensurate with their dignity and
our feelings, the united sentiments of the corps upon the honorable approbation of the representatives of the land, would be as
difficult, as sacred a duty, did we not hope to see in the same royal
chief through whom a rare reward has been bestowed upon us,
the gracious medium of our obligations. Your royal highness
knows us : may it please your royal highness to speak for us, and
we shall feel assured that the exalted assembly to which the expressions are directed, will acknowledge our ardent desire to prove
ourselves thankful, in a manner worthy of them, for the honorable
distinction with which we have been noticed.

May it please your royal highness to bear witness for us,
that far from founding claims upon the exertions and sacrifices,
which, existing under the first commander of the age, and under
British colours,—would be easy, and which can alone find an adequate compensation in the remembrance,—we rest our merits upon
this :—that during a separation of more than eleven years, our
country has never been absent from our sight. The many
benefits in which we have participated in Britain's happy isle, or
in the midst of her victorious armies, in the most distant quarters
of Europe, have been always accompanied by the bitter recollec-

tion of the fate of our unhappy land ;—our most heartfelt joy has been derived from that patriotic spirit, which, outliving all oppression, finally broke, by the powerful force of united Germany, the long and heavy chain, of the first links of which,—although far distant from our own frontiers,—it was our happy lot, to aid the destruction.

May these sentiments answer for the feeling with which we view the beneficial regulations of the glorious regent of the Guelphic states, by which far extended future good has been prepared by calling together the parliament, in which the voice of the people can raise itself with freedom, but with order. May we not err in seeing a happy presage of the future in a solemn expression of the noble president of this assembly :—that directly from the throne, which governs the kingdom, where the features of the old German constitution are respected and revered, the "holy fire" will spread over the whole German nation ! May a time approach when this nation, then only happy, great, and safe in self-dependence, can develop each restrained ability and power ;—when, in the closest political union with the great German houses, she will be governed by such regents as those, under whose dominion, in a former age, the British kingdom raised itself to the most glorious and happy of the earth !

With the deepest respect,

Your royal highness's, &c. &c.

HINUBER,

Major-general.

G.

Proclamation directing the disbandment of the King's German Legion

GEORGE P. R.

By his Royal Highness the Prince Regent of the United Kingdom of Great Britain and Ireland.

Whereas we have been pleased in the name, and on the behalf of his majesty, to order our German legion, commanded by our most dearly beloved son and councillor, field marshal his royal highness Adolphus Frederick duke of Cambridge, K. G.—to be disbanded and discontinued on the establishment of the army, our will and pleasure therefore is, that you do proceed to disband the cavalry and infantry regiments of the said legion accordingly, on the 24th day of the month in which each regiment shall arrive at Hanover, and that in the execution of this service the following rules be strictly observed.

I.—You are to cause an exact muster to be taken by the respective paymasters of the several troops or companies of the said regiments, up to the day of disbandment inclusive.

II.—Each officer actually present at the disbandment of his regiment, will be allowed two month's full pay from the date of such disbandment. The non-commissioned officers and private soldiers will be allowed the gratuity specified in the 11th article of the letter of service for raising the said legion, in aid of their travelling expenses to their respective homes; viz: two pence English money, or two kreutzers of the empire per league, the same to be calculated from the place of disbandment.

A return of the men who are disabled by wounds or infirmities contracted in our service is to be sent to our secretary at war, with a view to their being placed on the out-pension of our royal hospital at Chelsea.

III.—The accounts of the men are to be made up and completely settled to the day of the disbandment of each regiment.

IV.—It is our pleasure that each non-commissioned officer, trumpeter, drummer, and private man hereby to be disbanded, be permitted to carry away with him his knapsack and his regimental clothing; but if, from any circumstance, the clothing for the respective periods terminating on the 24th December, 1815, has not been, and cannot be delivered to the men before the day of disbandment; then, and in such case only, the men are to receive compensation in lieu thereof, for the periods of their several claims, at the rates prescribed for the regulations for clothing, the amount of which is of course to be paid by the agent on the part of the colonel, and is not to be charged by the paymasters in their public accounts.

V.—The officers will be placed upon half-pay from the date of the termination of their full pay.

VI.—The great coats in wear will be allowed to be taken away by the non-commissioned officers and men who may be discharged, if the same shall have been actually worn for the space of two years, but if not, they are to be delivered into store, and an inventory thereof is to be sent to our secretary at war.

VII.—The arms and appointments of the soldiers of both cavalry and infantry, who shall be present at the disbandment, and the troop horses of the cavalry, with their full military equipment are to be delivered over to the Hanoverian government.

VIII.—The sums required for the payment of the officers and men are to be drawn from the deputy paymaster-general.

IX.—And to the end that the said non-commissioned officers, trumpeters, drummers, and private men may be sensible of the care we have taken of them upon their discharge, you are to cause these our directions to be read at the head of each troop or company.

Given at our court at Carlton-house this 24th day of December 1815, in the fifty-sixth year of his majesty's reign.

By command of his royal highness the prince regent, in the name and on the behalf of his majesty.

(Signed,)

PALMERSTON.

(A true Copy)

J. H. REYNETT,
Lieutenant-colonel, Military Secretary.

H.

Second Address of the Hanoverian deputies.

TRANSLATION

HANOVER, *February* 7, 1816.

I hasten to communicate to the King's German Legion a proof of the universal esteem with which their distinguished conduct has inspired their fellow citizens.

The assembled representatives of the kingdom have presented me with the following flattering expression of their thanks, and requested me to communicate it to the whole corps of the legion.

ADOLPHUS FREDERICK.

MAY IT PLEASE YOUR ROYAL HIGHNESS!

The assembled deputies of the kingdom of Hanover would neglect their most holy and most pleasing duty, if at the moment when the victorious English (German) Hanoverian Legion returned to their fatherland, and made their festive entrance into the capital—they did not express to them feelings of admiration and acknowledgment.

If the legion have contributed by their acknowledged glorious deeds, and enduring bravery, to the great end that has been accomplished,—earned the admiration of the present age, and of posterity, the satisfaction of his royal highness the prince regent, our master, and the thanks of the great English nation,—they are indebted for a great part of these distinguished rewards to your royal highness their chief, by whose untiring zeal and powerful protection, this distinguished corps was alone enabled to acquire that high degree of fame in the ever-memorable campaigns in the Spanish peninsula, and add, if possible, to this reputation in the battle of Waterloo.

Deeply impressed with feelings of reverence and gratitude towards your royal highness, the chief of the royal English-Hanoverian-Legion, the assembled deputies of the kingdom of Hanover venture respectfully to repeat their sentiments, and humbly to request that your royal highness will be pleased to express the feelings of the assembled deputies, to all the officers, non-commissioned officers and soldiers of the royal English (German)—Hanoverian legion, on their joyful return to their fatherland, and their festive entrance into the capital; and to add the assurances that the assembled representatives of the kingdom of Hanover will never forget the great deserts which this distinguished corps has won; by which the Hanoverian name has been rendered glorious, and that they will mark the moment of their return to the common fatherland, as the happiest and most joyful epoch in the annals of our history.

We remain with the deepest respect,

Your royal highness's

most obedient humble servants,

the deputies chosen by the kingdom for the general assembly,

J. H. MEYER,

Court counsellor & Secretary-general.

L. VON BAR,

President.

Hanover, Feb. 5, 1816.

I.

Principles upon which the seniority of the officers of the King's German Legion in the Hanoverian service, has been determined.

TRANSLATION.

I.—All those officers of the legion who enter the Hanoverian service with the rank which they held in the legion, shall retain the date of their English commissions. The position in which they formerly stood with regard to those Hanoverian officers, who may have served before in the legion, does not effect this condition.

II.—Those officers who enter the Hanoverian service with promotion, will receive commissions dated posterior to those of the Hanoverian officers of similar rank who are already placed. With regard to Hanoverian officers promoted at the same time, the place of both will be determined by the dates of their respective commissions or brevets in the English and Hanoverian service.

G 7

III.—It having been determined by article I, that those officers of the legion, who enter the Hanoverian service, shall retain the date of their English commissions or brevet, the case will, in some instances, arise where young brevet officers of the legion, as well as those who have already received commissions in the Hanoverian army, will come to be placed above their seniors in the legion.

This evil could not be remedied without counteracting the principles which have been above laid down; in order, however, to restore their seniority to the officers thus prejudiced it has been determined:—

IV.—That those who are advanced out of their turn, either by brevet, or an earlier Hanoverian commission, shall not be promoted in future until those over whom they have been thus advanced, shall have been placed in the same rank.

V.—When, however, two legion officers enter the service with *promotion*, one of whom, either by brevet, or from official mistake, or from causes which no longer exist,—has already been placed above the others in the legion, he who has had the seniority in the *next lower grade*, in the legion, shall retain the same seniority in the Hanoverian service.

VI—In Nos. I. and III. it has been stated that the brevet officers shall be enrolled according to the dates of their brevet. This principle is not, however, applicable, when an officer has received two successive brevets, and has been thereby considerably advanced above his seniors. In this case the date and rank of the first brevet will alone be considered.

However, the possibility is not hereby precluded of his entering the Hanoverian service with the rank of his *second* brevet, as it might occur that those who are his seniors, may in like manner, reach by promotion, the same rank.

K.

Comparative return of the strength of the King's German Legion and Hanoverian army previous to, and after the new organization of the latter in February 1816.

Previous to new organization.   After new organization.

ARTILLERY.

	Batteries.		*Batteries.*
K. G. Legion horse batteries......	2	K. G. Legion and Hanoverians	
Ditto, foot do.........	6	amalgamated.	
Hanoverian do,...........	2	————————horse batteries,	2
		————————foot do. ..	8
Total batteries, ...	10	Total batteries,......	10

CAVALRY.

	Troops.		*Troops.*
K. G. Legion, 4 regiments of		K. G. Legion, 5 regiments of	
5 squadrons, (10 troops) each,	40	4 troops each, ...	20
Dittto, 1 regiment of 6 squadrons	12	Hanoverians 3 do. of do, ...	12
Total legion, ...	52		
Hanoverians,.. 3 regiments of 4			
squadrons (8 troops) each,... .	24		

INFANTRY.

	Companies.		*Companies.*
K. G. Legion, 11 battalions of 10		K. G. Legion, 4 battalions	
companies each, ...	110	of guards, 6 companies	
		each, *.................	24
Hanoverians, 8 field battalions of		3 battalions landwehr of 4	
4 companies each, ...	32	companies each, ...	12
		Total legion companies, ...36	

* In 1817, the battalions of guards were reduced to four companies each.

31 landwehr   do. of   do. 124   Hanoverians, 6 field battalions
                          ———   of 4 companies each, ... 24
Total Hanoverian companies,   156   27 landwehr, do. of do.,... 108

                                Total Hanoverian companies, 132

Summary of the above.

Artillery and Engineers,———no reduction.

CAVALRY.

	Troops.		Troops.
Legion before reduction, ...	52	Hanoverians before reduction,..	24
———— after do.	20	———————— after do. ..	12
Legion loss, ...	32	Hanoverian loss......	12

INFANTRY.

	Companies		Companies
Legion before reduction	110	Hanoverians before reduction,	156
———— after do.	36	———————— after do. ·	132
Legion loss, ...	74	Hanoverian loss,....	24

The present strength of the Hanoverian army (1837) is ten batteries of artillery; four regiments of cavalry of 6 squadrons each; 16 battalions of infantry of five companies each, besides some engineers and land dragoons.

No. XXIV.

A.

KING'S GERMAN LEGION PENSION FUND.

The establishment of a fund for the relief of the invalided soldiers, as well as the widows and orphans of the King's German Legion, was originally proposed to the corps by major Cordemann of the hussar guards; and, under the sanction of his royal highness the duke of Cambridge, circular letters were issued on the 29th of March 1819, inviting the officers of the late legion to contribute four days half pay per annum, for this benevolent purpose. To this call, the officers with few exceptions immediately responded: His Majesty the king of Hanover ; their royal highnesses the dukes of Cambridge and Cumberland, and the Hanoverian government, became liberal contributors, and a committee of five officers was appointed to manage the distribution. By the following abstract, bringing the accounts of the Society down to 1836, it appears that six hundred and fifty-seven individuals received relief ;—that the present income amounts to about 4,300 dollars per annum, and that the sum distributed from the first formation of the fund in March 1819, to December 1836, amounted to upwards of 73,000 dollars, or about £10,500.

The establishment and steady support of this fund, is in the highest degree creditable to the officers of the King's German Legion, shewing a benevolent consideration for their more humble companions in arms, many of whom, although sharers in their dangers and fatigues, would have been left to the misery of a premature old age, dragged on in penury and wretchedness, had not this timely aid been afforded them. To these officers the value of a brave soldier was well known, and they have considered this expression of their acknowledgment, a sacred duty which devolved upon them, when the termination of the war threw so many of their humble associates upon the world, without health, employment, or means of support.

B.

Abstract of the receipts and expenditure of the King's German Legion Pension Fund.

	Dollars.	Grosch.
Invalids and widows of the 1st class, per month	1	,,
Ditto, and do. of the 2d do.	,,	18

EXPENDITURE.

	Men.	Widows and orphans.	Dollars.
1 Paid in the district of Hanover, ...	111	55	1018
2————————Celle by lt.-col. Wyneken,	50	16	399
3————————Hildesheim by capt. Schnath	16	5	123
4————————Hameln by capt. Kirch,....	25	13	225
5————————Nienburg by capt. Best,.....	28	8	213
6————————Verden by lieut. Croon,.....	11	2	78
7————————Osnabrück by cap. Dorndorf	12	1	81
8————————Münden by cap. Falkmann,	16	5	123
9————————Göttingen by lient. Schuster	45	6	312
10————————Nordheim, lt.-col. v Schnehen	18	6	141
11————————Einbeck by capt. Braun....	17	4	123
12————————Hertzberg by lieut. Seffers...	14	4	102
13————————Uelzen by cap. v. Weyhe,..	20	2	129
14————————Lüchow by capt. Töbing, ..	14	2	96
15————————Harburg, lt.-col. Schaumann	2	2	36
16————————Lüneburg by cap. Kuckuck	10	0	57
17————————Grethem, lt.-col v Hodenberg	11	7	108
18————————Emden by capt. Poten,.....	10	8	111
19————————Stade by capt. Bostelmann,	13	4	102
20————————Meinersen by capt. Fischer,	12	2	87
21————————Hoya by Dr. Heise, ...	28	10	225
22————————Diepholtz, lieut. Diestelhorst	10	2	72
Total,........	493	164	3961

657

Miscellaneous expenses.

	Dollars.	gr.	d.
Clerk of the committee from 1st Jan. to 31st Dec. 1836,	74	,,	,,
Postage, books, and transport of money,..............	41	21	7
Brought down as above,...........	3961	,,	,,
Total expenses,....... Dollars,	4076	21	7

RECEIPTS.

			Dollars.	grosch.	d.
His majesty the king (William IV.)		....	684	13	,,
Royal treasury,		....	616	24	,,
Royal princes,		....	369	30	,,
General staff,	.. 10 officers,	....	74	20	,,
Artillery,	.. 29	....	178	12	,,
Engineers,	.. 6	....	40	,,	,,
1st dragoons,	.. 20	....	174	20	,,
2d do.	.. 15	....	101	14	,,
1st hussars,	.. 17	....	132	30	,,
2d do.	.. 15	....	94	12	,,
3d do.	.. 25	....	170	4	,,
1st light battalion,	.. 23	....	161	34	,,
2d do.	.. 16	....	114	20	,,
1st line battalion,	.. 20	....	147	24	,,
2d do.	.. 17	....	101	10	,,
3d do.	.. 20	....	115	4	,,
4th do.	.. 17	....	129	18	,,
5th do.	.. 26	....	175	31	,,
6th do.	.. 18	....	114	30	,,
7th do.	.. 22	....	129	16	,,
8th do.	.. 14	....	79	20	,,
Veteran battalion,	.. 10	....	68	24	,,

352 officers.

Extraordinary contributions,	....	40	,,	,,
Balance in hand, December 1835,	....	358	17	5
Total receipts, ... Dollars, ...	4373	31	5
Expenses as detailed,	.. ..	4076	21	7
Balance remaining 1st January 837,	Dollars,	297	9	6

COMMITTEE.

C. W. KRONENFELDT.   **C. ELDERHORST.**   **S. MIELMANN.**
Colonel grenadier guards.   Lieut.-col. 2d dragoons.   Captain, artillery.

R. RIEFKUGEL.   **W. RUHSE.**
Captain, rifle-guards.   Captain and regimental quarter-
                                master, rifle-guards.

N.B.—Individuals entitled to receive relief must have served in the legion until its disbandment in 1816, and not be in receipt of any pension from the British government.

GUELPHIC ARCHIVES.

Extracts from the Guelphic Archives not detailed in the text.

The Guelphic medal, accompanied by a monthly pension of two dollars, was given to those non-commissioned officers and soldiers of the King's German Legion, who had distinguished themselves by extraordinary services during the war, which services are set forth in attested memorials in the following manner.

☞ *The number and date affixed to each memorial denote its position in the archives.*

TRANSLATION.

Serjeant-major FERDINAND NIENBURG of the artillery, serving at the battle of Talavera, July 28th 1809, with the battery of captain von Rettberg, under the immediate command of Lieutenant Braun, distinguished himself by persevering bravery, inasmuch as, although severely wounded in the head, and requested to go back, in order that his wounds might be bound up, he continued to perform his laborious duty at the battery, until the end of the battle, when he was brought away quite exhausted.

81.—1819. Attested by lieut.-col. v. Rettberg lieut.-col. Braun, and captain Speckmann.

Also at the battle of Quatre-bras on the 16th June 1815, Nienburg distinguished himself by great bravery throughout the day ; he recovered two English guns which had been dismounted, going forward of his own accord with the team, and bringing them out of the enemy's fire.

Serjeant HUNTE of the artillery. On the repeated attacks of the enemy's cavalry at the battle of Waterloo, Hunte was always the last to leave the battery to which he belonged, and, continuing the fire of the guns to the last possible moment, he did considerable injury to the enemy : on one of these occasions he rescued the limber of the gun which he commanded. On the whole, his conduct, upon every occasion in which he was engaged before the enemy, and which comprised fifteen principal engagements, was always so distinguished, that he was reckoned amongst the best non-commissioned officers of the regiment.

24.—1819. Attested by captain Pfannkuche, and lieutenant Ludowig.

159—1818   Serjeant GEORGE KAHRMANN, 1st hussars.   In the battle of Salamanca

Attested by sir F. von Arents-childt, and baron Krauchen-berg.
the 1st hussars were ordered to attack the left wing of the enemy's cavalry. In order to reach this point, it was necessary to pass a defile, at the end of which the enemy awaited them in superior force, and pressed upon the hussars with such impetuosity, that their retreat would have been endangered, had not Kahrmann and a few men who followed him, thrown themselves into the midst of the French column, and thus opened a free passage for the regiment.   On the 12th of June 1813, being in command of a picquet, consisting of six hussars, he fell upon the French rear guard and captured a gun.

148—1818   Serjeant-major HENRY MATTHIAS, 1st hussars.   On the 18th of March

Attested by major M. von Müller and capt. Teuto.
1811, the third squadron of the regiment formed the advanced guard at Ponte Murcella, and Matthias, with a hussar named Bollewien of the fourth troop, went forward as volunteers on two different occasions : the first time they brought back a French captain of engineers, with his covering party, consisting of a corporal and four men, and the next time, an infantry detachment of two serjeants and ten men, which they had cut off, and taken prisoners.   At the battle of Thoulouse, 10th of April 1814, Matthias with eleven hussars, charged 40 of the enemy's cavalry, overthrew them, and captured six men and horses.

Attested by lieut.-col. count v. d. Decken.
Serjeant FREDERICK WESTERMANN, 1st hussars.   On the 16th of Sept. 1810, the 1st hussars formed the rear guard of the allied army, then retreating into the lines of Lisbon.   The enemy's army defiled through Celorico upon Fornos, pressing upon the hussars a strong corps of cavalry, and at Villa Cortes, a serious combat took place.   The horse of lieutenant George von der Decken was shot ; he was surrounded by the enemy, and must inevitably have fallen into their hands, had not Westermann, jumping from his own horse, given it to lieutenant Decken, and thus saved him : the serjeant was himself lucky enough to meet with a stray horse, which enabled him to escape, and he continued to take an active part in the combat.

On the morning of the 27th of September 1811, during a thick fog, general sir Stapleton Cotton made a reconnoisance towards Ciudad Rodrigo, and went forward in front of the chain of outposts, accompanied only by his staff, and a picquet of twelve men.   The party were soon surrounded by a strong column of the enemy's cavalry, and the general, depending on the swiftness of his horse, sought to reach the position of El Bodon by cross roads.   In leaping a ditch, he was thrown, and would inevitably have fallen into the enemy's hands, had not his escort, led forward with the greatest bravery by his aide-de-camp, captain von der Decken,—thrown themselves against the superior force of the enemy, and stopped their progress.

Westermann was much distinguished on this occasion; he was cut from his horse, taken prisoner, and carried to Rodrigo, where he remained, until the successful storm of that fortress by the allies in the following January, restored him to the regiment.

Hussar HENRY MERTENS, 1st hussars. At Albuquerqe in the month of June 1811, lieutenant George v. d. Decken with a patrole of five men, surprised a column of French cavalry, which had halted in a plain, having left a foraging party behind. The latter was attacked by lieutenant Decken. In consequence of a ditch which interposed, hussars Mertens and Schroeder were the only men, who were able to follow the lieutenant, and they, keeping together, attacked the enemy's leading horsemen, and captured two men out of eight.
147—1818 Attested by lieut.-col. count v. d. Decken.

Serjeant KOHLENBERG, 1st hussars. On the 21st of January 1813, serjeant Kohlenberg and six men were sent on patrole towards Vittoria; on the road they fell in with a detachment of the enemy's infantry, which they attacked, and brought in twenty-six men prisoners.
145—1818 majors Müller and Cordemann.

Serjeant WEISSMANN, 1st hussars. In the month of February 1811, Weissmann with some more hussars, was on patrole with a detachment under the command of captain Cocks of the sixteenth English light dragoons, between Ascaldas, and Alcobaça. The patrole was attacked by a superior force of the enemy's cavalry, and overthrown. Captain Cock's horse stumbled, and he was surrounded by the enemy, and taken; however Weissmann and a few hussars dashing forward against the French horsemen, rescued him.
144—1818 Attested by lieut.-col. count v. d. Decken.

Corporal HENRY THIELE, 1st hussars,—was on a foraging party under lieutenant v. d. Wisch in the neighbourhood of Santarem, 28th of February 1811, and learned that in a village half a league from thence, was an enemy's cavalry detachment of twelve men. Lieutenant Wisch, with four hussars, one of whom was Thiele, surprised the enemy. Thiele particularly distinguished himself; he captured alone, two of the enemy's vedettes who were posted in front of the place —then rushed with the rest into the village, where two men and four mules were taken.
142—1818 Attested by major v. d. Wisch, and capt. Teuto.

At Quinta de Toro on the 9th of October 1810, during the retreat into the lines, the rear-guard of the 1st hussars was severely pressed ; the horse of lieutenant Wisch fell, wounded, and the lieutenant himself was only saved from capture, by the sacrifice made by corporal Thiele, who gave up to him his own horse, and escaped with great difficulty on foot.

141—1818
Major v. d.
Wisch.

Corporal GEORGE OELMANN, 1st hussars,—was sent on patrole with eleven hussars under the command of lieutenant Wisch, on the 13th of March 1811, to Coimbra, and, on the road, attacked a detachment of the enemy's cavalry consisting of twenty men. Oelmann particularly distinguished himself; he disarmed the enemy's officer, and the whole detachment were brought in prisoners.

140—1818
Major
Cordemann.

Corporal BREITHAUPT, 1st hussars, was sent on patrole with hussar Rohde, on the 20th of June 1813, in the neighbourhood of Vittoria ;—they fell in with a patrole of the enemy's infantry, which they attacked, and captured sixteen men.

130—1818
184—1819
Lieut.-col.
Krauchenberg.

Serjeant HISCHE, 1st hussars.   On the 19th of March 1811, during Massena's retreat from the lines of Lisbon, captain Aly's squadron attacked the French rear-guard at Ponte Murcella, with great success, and made a number of prisoners.   Hische finding that a body of infantry were posted in a wood, attacked them with only forty hussars, and after an obstinate contest, succeeded in making thirty prisoners.   On the 3d of April 1811, when on patrole under lieutenant Strenuwitz, he again distinguished himself, and it was mainly owing to his intrepidity that eighteen men of the enemy's infantry, who made an obstinate resistance, were captured.

121—1818
Captain
Teuto.

Corporal SUBTHUT, 1st hussars.   In a charge of the regiment at Canizal on the 18th of July 1812, where the hussars were engaged with a far superior force of the enemy's cavalry, Subthut was cut off, and surrounded by ten French dragoons.   He received two severe wounds, and his horse three ; but nevertheless, he cut two of his opponents from their horses, and made his escape to the regiment.

117—1818
Major
Cordemann.

Serjeant LICHTE, 1st hussars,—was on a detachment under lieutenant Cordemann in October 1812, for the purpose of observing the army of marshal Soult, which advanced from Andalusia towards Madrid.

This army marched in three columns, in the neighbourhood of the Tagus ; lieutenant Cordemann placed himself in rear of the right column, and gave

Lichte orders to march cautiously with three hussars, between this and the centre column, until he was able to discover at what point the latter should pass the Tagus.

As it was broad day, this duty was not a little difficult. Lichte detached two hussars to his right flank, and retained the other by himself, but the former were soon discovered and driven off by the enemy's flank patroles.

After he had marched for some distance with the enemy's column, and attained his object, he was also discovered, and was surrounded by five chasseurs; but although wounded in the right hand, he cut his way through, and brought back the required information. Lord Wellington was so pleased with the serjeant's conduct, that he proposed making him an officer; Lichte, however, declined the promotion, upon which his lordship presented him with a gratuity of fifty piastres.

Hussar SCHROEDER, 1st hussars. On the 10th of December 1814 397—1821 Schroeder formed one of a detachment of twenty-four men, composed of equal Baron numbers of the first hussars and eighteenth English hussars, which were at-Krauchen-berg. tached to the light division, under the command of lieutenant Blumenhagen. After the action of the 9th of December, this detachment was placed in rear of the infantry picquets, and stationed in a village, where they were quartered in two houses. Schroeder was with the half under the command of the serjeant of the 18th, who, with his men, made themselves comfortable, and, believing the enemy far distant, went to sleep.

Schroeder, accustomed from long outpost duty to wake towards morning, went, about this time, out of the house, upon the road. Day had just broke, when he heard two shots in the direction of the line of outposts, and nearly at the same moment, French infantry charged into the village, having surprised and captured the allied infantry picquet in front.

Schroeder instantly re-entered the house,—woke up his comrades—jumped on his horse, which he had timely made ready, and dashed out on the road against the enemy, calling out and making signals with his sword, as if an entire squadron was in his rear.

The scattered French hesitated, and notwithstanding their fire, Schroeder succeeded in keeping them at bay, until the English serjeant and his detachment were out of the house. These then hurried to lieutenant Blumenhagen, and, notwithstanding the surprise, escaped without losing a man. To the bravery, vigilance, and presence of mind of Schroeder, whose clothes were pierced with many balls,—this was alone to be ascribed.

Schroeder was at another time, Nov. 15 1812, on detachment under lieut. Teuto, who led the rear-guard near Salamanca, and was sent to the assistance of a village, which lay on the left. Here he met hussar Stobe, who had been sent from another picquet for the same purpose. On searching the village they found six of the enemy's infantry, who were also aware of the presence of the hussars, and retired behind a ditch outside the place. Schroeder called upon his comrade to join him in attacking them,—gallopped forward, —received their fire,—jumped over the ditch, and obliged them to throw down their arms, and surrender. As the two hussars were proceeding with their prisoners to the regiment, they found that it had fallen back, and that the enemy were between them. They were, therefore obliged to follow the army,—then retreating on Ciudad Rodrigo,—by cross roads, and, concealing themselves in woods during the day, and marching by night, they finally succeeded in bringing their prisoners to the army.

396—1821 Major Cordemann.

Hussar BLANKE, 1st hussars. In the year 1813, Blanke was one of a patrole consisting of four hussars and four English dragoons under captain Cordemann, who learned from a Spanish peasant, that a village in his front was occupied by two companies of the enemy's infantry. Arrived before the village, they saw four men posted in a garden, which was surrounded by a wall. Blanke, and one of the English dragoons volunteered to attack these men, but the Englishman's horse would not jump the wall, and Blanke entered the garden alone. The French soldiers fired, but without effect, and Blanke riding at them in full gallop, shot one with the pistol,—cut another down, and obliged the rest to lay down their arms, and surrender. The alarm was now sounded in the village, and the enemy retired hastily in square, leaving the patrole in possession of thirty horses and mules.

395—1821 Major Cordemann.

Serjeant SCHRADER, 1st hussars, was orderly to general Craufurd at Barba de Puerco, in the month of April 1809, when suddenly in the night, the enemy, having surprised the outposts, pressed into the place. Schrader dashed boldly against them, and checked the progress of several horsemen in the narrow streets, until assistance reached him. His bravery and presence of mind were much praised by general Craufurd.

In the month of June 1813, on the advance of the army to Vittoria, lieutenant Strenuwitz, having learned that a picquet of thirty of the enemy's cavalry occupied a neighbouring village, begged permission to call for volunteers for the purpose of cutting them off. This was assented to, and Schrader with twenty-five hussars offered their services. The lieutenant gave Schrader the command of half the body, which was to press into the village from different directions. The enemy were probably aware of this design, for they were found formed up in the middle of the place. Schrader gallopped in with his men, and favoured by the darkness, fell upon them, and cut the officer from his horse. Lieutenant Strenuwitz soon came to his assistance, and the whole of the French picquet were either cut down or taken prisoners. Two of the enemy's horsemen endeavoured to save themselves by flight, but Schrader pursued them alone, and came up with them, at some distance from the village. Here one made front, and wounded him in the bridle arm, but, at the same time received from the serjeant a cut in the shoulder which caused him to surrender. Schrader now gave his prisoner in charge of a hussar who, following him, had just come up, and set off in chace of the other whom the light of the moon soon shewed, making the best of his way in front. Schrader dashed on, and had nearly reached his object, when his horse tumbled into a ditch, and fell upon him. The chasseur now wheeled about and called upon Schrader to surrender. Meantime the horse of the latter sprung up, and got out at the other side of the ditch. Schrader ran after it, and the animal being accustomed to him, easily allowed itself to be caught. The ditch was an insurmountable barrier to the Frenchman, who contented himself with firing his pistol at his pursuer; but Schrader, being now mounted, cleared the ditch, and obliged the chasseur to surrender.

On the evening of the battle of Waterloo, the squadron in which Schrader served, was on picquet, and he, with another hussar, patrolling during the night, saw four cavalry soldiers riding at a short distance. They appeared not to observe the hussars, and Schrader directed his comrade to attack them with shouts from one side, while he assailed them on the other. But the enemy were not to be surprised, and they boldly met the attack. They proved to be

Major Cordemann, and lieut.-col. F. von der Decken.

cuirassiers, whose armour and superior force prevented the hussars from gaining any advantage over them ; Schrader, therefore, resorted to a stratagem : he took his comrade away at a gallop, and thus induced the French to follow, but after a time, seeing his pursuers dispersed, he suddenly turned his horse round on the nearest, and dealing him a sabre cut in the face, brought him to the ground. Meantime the hussar was engaged with two others, and the serjeant now hurried to his help. A fourth cuirassier came up at this moment. Schrader cut one of them on the neck, upon which he fell forward on his horse ; the others throwing away their swords begged for quarter ; and finally, the serjeant and his comrade brought 'back the four cuirassiers prisoners, to the squadron.

303—1830
Lieut.-col.
Krauchen-
berg.

Hussar FREDERICK BOCK, 1st hussars. In the month of July 1810, a patrole of the first hussars was sent out in the neighbourhood of Pinhel, to obtain intelligence of the enemy. Some peasants, who met the patrole, stated that the place was strongly occupied by the French. In order to learn their strength with as little loss as possible, the commander of the patrole called for two volunteers to alarm the enemy. Bock offered to do the required duty alone, and riding rapidly forward, he drove before him the French vedette, who seeing him coming on at full speed, fired,—made a signal, and fled into the place.

Bock followed close at his heels, and both arrived almost at the same moment, in an open place, where a picquet of cavalry stood dismounted, and the neighbouring houses were occupied with infantry. Bock halted ;—fired both pistols at the two first men who attempted to mount,—turned his horse round, receiving a salvo from the infantry, and galloped off, closely followed by the enemy, whose strength he had thus discovered. He reached his detachment without further injury than his clothes sustained from several balls by which they had been pierced.

309—1820
Major
Schau-
mann.

Serjeant FREDERICK LEIMERS, 1st hussars. Near Ponte Murcella, on the 19th of March 1811, Leimers, and hussar Fricke of the fifth troop, were directed to seek for a patrole of two men which had been a long time out, without any tidings having been received from it. Having found the men, they learned from them that some twenty of the enemy had halted to bake bread in a neighbouring village. Leimers persuaded the three hussars to join him in attempting a *coup* upon the Frenchmen, and having arrived at the village, he placed one of the men upon a height, with orders to give notice to the rest, by firing, if any of the enemy should enter the village by the other side. With the other two men, who followed him, at the distance of a horse's length, he rode cautiously into the village. In a farm yard in the middle of the place, he found a quantity of burning straw, and saw a Frenchman looking out of the window of the farm-house. Leimers dismounted,—gave his horse to one of the hussars, and ran up the steps of the house with his carbine in his hand. On entering the room, he found sixteen French infantry soldiers seated at table, each of whom had his arms near him. Although now seeing that he had been somewhat too bold, he collected himself with great presence of mind, and called out, that "if they did not surrender on the spot, and instantly give up their arms, and go down into the yard, they should be all put to the sword."

Luckily for Leimers a corporal of the French horse artillery, who understood German, was among the party, and he translated to them the requisition, upon which the whole, on condition of not being given up to the Portuguese peasants, surrendered, and went unarmed into the court. Besides the sixteen men, Leimers captured the horse of the artilleryman.

After the battle of Orthes, in March 1814, a corps of the allied army under marshal Beresford advanced towards Bourdeaux. Arrived on the left bank of the Garonne, the town of Langen was occupied by a brigade of infantry under general Inglis, and a squadron of the first hussars. A company of infantry was sent in small boats to the right bank, in order to occupy the little town of St. Macaire, and to this company Leimers and six hussars were attached, and directed to patrole for four leagues on the right bank. According to orders he set off with his patrole from St. Macaire, two hours before daybreak, but on his return found that not only was St. Macaire in possession of the enemy, but the whole right bank of the Gironde; for just before daybreak, the French had surprised the place, and taken the English prisoners. Leimers now drew back his patrole, and kept them concealed for two days and nights in the midst of the enemy. At length, on the third day, he succeeded in taking them to the left bank in fishing boats, from the neighbourhood of Bourdeaux, and joined the company without the loss of a single man or horse.

Col. Aly,
lieut.-col.
F. von der
Decken.

H 8

310—1820   Hussar NEBEL, 1st hussars.   Nebel was on picquet with a corporal and
col. Aly.
six men of the eighteenth English hussars, near Hasparren, in France, in
the month of January 1814; double vedettes were posted, and as Nebel was
relieved from this duty, the corporal directed him, and the other hussar, to
ride into a wood on the left, and see if there was any appearance of the enemy
in that direction.

Arrived in front of the wood, they branched off on opposite sides, but
managed to keep each other in sight.   French hussars had concealed themselves behind the underwood, and suddenly an officer and twelve men dashed
out towards Nebel.   He was about to wheel round, but saw that his road was
stopped, he, therefore, rode forwards, but soon was unable to proceed from
the nature of the ground.   The French surrounded him; Nebel levelled his
carbine at the officer, who called out to him in German: "Fellow, surrender,
and you will not be hurt, but if you are not quiet, you will be cut to pieces."
Nebel refused to surrender,—cut about him fiercely,—brought one of his
opponents to the ground, and seeing a lucky opening, rushed through, and
made for the picquet, having received two sword cuts.   The officer and a
hussar pursued him, and being better mounted, followed close at his heels.

Nebel soon perceived that these two had separated themselves from the
rest, and suddenly turning his horse round, he dealt the hussar a blow on the
head.   The officer now took to flight, and, although the approach of the rest
prevented Nebel from bringing away the wounded man a prisoner, he succeeded
in regaining the picquet.

327—1820   Hussar BLIEDONG, 1st hussars.   On the march of the allied army to
col. Aly.
Vittoria, June 18, 1813, captain Aly's squadron formed the advanced guard,
in front of the light division near St. Milan.   Skirmishers were sent out under
serjeant Kahrmann, and after they had passed a defile, perceived the third
French hussars in their front.   Three hussars of this regiment rode towards
the right flank of the German skirmishers, and the serjeant called out: "Who
will go and attack the fellows?", upon which, Bliedong immediately rushed
forward.

One of the French horsemen met him boldly, the two others remaining a
few paces behind.   Bliedong had the luck to give the first a cut in the face
before the others came up, and dealing one of these a blow in the right arm,

the third fled towards his regiment. Bliedong followed, but the enemy were too near to admit of his catching him; the two others he brought back prisoners.

On the evening of the 22d of June 1813, Bliedong formed one of a picquet which was sent out under serjeant Oelzen. As the night was very dark, and no one was acquainted with the country, the serjeant called for volunteers to patrole. Bliedong and hussar Heinrichs offered their services, and arrived, in about half an hour, at a river of considerable width. They rode down the bank, listening, and soon saw something move on the opposite side. Bliedong called out :—"Who goes there?" which was answered by musquet fire. The hussars fell back a few paces, and again listened. They distinguished several voices, and notwithstanding the darkness, made out that the enemy were not in great force. Bliedong, therefore, determined on riding up the river,—swimming across, and attacking the enemy in flank, while his comrade alarmed them on the other side. This was done. He rushed upon them with a loud shout,—the other hussar hallooed on the opposite bank;—the enemy's fire was without effect;—Bliedong cut down one of the party, and the rest, five in number, throwing away their arms, surrendered, and were brought in prisoners to the picquet.

Serjeant-major Louis Engel. In July, 1810, at the bridge of Gallegos, which the squadron under captain Krauchenberg defended with so much success against a superior force of the enemy, Engel particularly distinguished himself, cutting a French officer from his horse, and taking another prisoner. _198—1820 baron Krauchenberg._

Corporal Knigge, 1st hussars,—was in 1811, with three men of the regiment, on a patrole which followed the French rear-guard. At Tamames, they fell in with a body of the enemy, which they attacked, and killed three; and the rest taking refuge in the houses, Knigge dismounted, and forced eighteen men and three English deserters to surrender, the whole of whom were brought to head quarters. _361—1821 col. Aly._

Serjeant Christian Schauss, 1st hussars—was on patrole with ten men, the 19th of June 1815, and observed that the enemy's troops were in a wood at some distance. He led his men against them, and although the enemy, protected by rough ground, made an obstinate resistance, he succeeded in taking prisoners a captain, trumpeter, and eighteen infantry soldiers, together with two horses, the whole of whom were delivered to the regiment. _153—1820 col. Aly. lieut.-col. count v. d. Decken._

298—1820
captain
Blumen-
hagen.

Hussar HENRY BECKER, 1st hussars. On the 13th of April 1814, the day after the battle of Thoulouse, a detachment of twenty-four men under lieutenant Blumenhagen, followed a body of French *gen's d' armerie* with such perseverance, that they finally captured twenty-nine out of forty men, of which the division consisted. Hussars Becker, and Anton Bartels were always the foremost on this occasion, and thus took the greater number of the prisoners.

296—1820
lieut.-col,
count v. d.
Decken.

Corporal FREDERICK WINDEL, 1st hussars. At Langen, in the month of April 1814, five days before the battle of Thoulouse, eighteen men of the first hussars were attached to the seventh division, in order to act as a patrole, and advancing about a league and a half, they halted in front of a village, which was occupied by the enemy. At day-break corporal Windel and hussar Stille were sent forward to learn further information, having effected which, they were returning towards the village, when six of the enemy's dragoons fell upon them. After an obstinate contest, Windel and his comrade succeeded in defeating this superior force, and having wounded several, made them all prisoners. But just at the moment when the prisoners had laid down their arms, and were about to return with the patrole, the enemy's light infantry, hurrying from the village, fell upon them, and Stille was shot. The prisoners now took courage, seized their side arms, and attacked Windel, who received a wound in the shoulder, but was fortunate enough to cut his way through the assailants, and rejoin his party.

286—1820
major v. d.
Wisch.

Coporal CHRISTOPH RANGENIER, 1st hussars. In a combat which the first hussars had with the French cavalry at Francosa, in the month of August 1810, lieutenant Teuto's horse was severely wounded, and the lieutenant would certainly have fallen into the enemy's hands, had not Rangenier given him his own horse, and thus saved his officer from being taken prisoner.

281—1820
major-gen.
v. Gruben,
captain v.
Ilten.

Hussar LUDOLPHUS KRAUEL, 1st hussars. At the battle of Fuentes Onoro, May 5th 1811, the squadron of captain von Gruben was many times charged by a superior force of the enemy. The captain having been severely wounded, and obliged to leave the field, the command of the squadron devolved upon lieutenant von Ilten, who again led the men forward to new attacks. Krauel was particularly distinguished by his bravery on this occasion, and being one of the oldest, and most experienced soldiers in the regiment, his example had the effect of inspiring the young soldiers with courage and confidence.

At Baziage in the south of France, on the 12th of April 1814, when captain Poten's squadron was engaged with a brigade of French cavalry, and took from this superior force thirty men and horses, Krauel distinguished himself in a remarkable manner, above all his comrades, and, according to the evidence of his captain, greatly contributed by his example of bravery, to encourage and stimulate the rest of the squadron.

Lieut.-col. E. Poten.

Serjeant BERGMANN, 1st hussars. At Leiria, on the 5th of October 1810, the regiment made several charges, and Bergmann took a French officer prisoner, but received at the same time, a severe wound in the head. However, notwithstanding the loss of blood, and the exhaustion which followed this wound, he rescued two of his comrades, who were surrounded by several French dragoons — cutting one from his horse, and making the rest prisoners.

257—1819 baron Krauchenberg.

Hussar GRAUE, 1st hussars. At Castello Branco, on the 5th of April 1812, captain Aly's squadron was on picquet, and Graue was sent out with hussar Ehlers, to notify to corporal Oelmann who had been sent on patrole, that he was to come in, as the enemy were pressing on in force. These two men were cut off, on the way, by twelve of the enemy's chasseurs a cheval, and they had no alternative but to surrender, or attack them. They boldly resolved upon the latter,—fell upon the foremost,—wounded several, and brought off one man and horse prisoner: Graue received a severe cut on the hand.

155—1819 col. Aly.

In the month of June 1813, a short time after the battle of Vittoria, Graue, and serjeant Kahrmann were on a patrole, which was hard pressed and pursued by the enemy, and obliged to cross a wide ditch, into which one of the men fell. Five of the enemy's chasseurs immediately surrounded him, and he would inevitably have been lost, had not Graue alone, re-crossed the ditch,—cut one of the chasseurs from his horse,—mortally wounded another, and put the rest to flight.

Corporal ALMSTEDT, 1st hussars. At the bridge of Gallegos, 4th of June 1810, when the rear-guard under captain Krauchenberg, opposed the superior numbers of the enemy with such persevering bravery, corporal Almstedt particularly distinguished himself. He was always one of the foremost in

139—1819 baron Krauchenberg, major Cordemann.

repelling the attacks, and saved the life of serjeant Bergmann, who, surrounded and wounded, was rescued by his cutting down several of those who were
taking the serjeant away a prisoner, and putting the rest to flight. In general,
upon all occasions when volunteers were required, Almstedt was the first to
offer himself.

127—1819
sir F. von
Arents-
childt,
baron
Krauchen-
berg und
major
Corde-
mann.

Hussar CHARLES GÖHRDER, 1st hussars. In the year 1813, Göhrder was
on picquet with a corporal and three English dragoons. They were attacked
by four French dragoons; the Englishmen galloped off, and Göhrder alone
faced the enemy. He allowed them to come up singly towards him,—wounded
two—took two prisoners, and brought these to the regiment, where he received
public thanks for his conduct.

126—1819
sir F. von
Arents-
childt.

Corporal HEUER, 1st hussars. In the year 1810, Heuer was on picquet
with serjeant Schumacher. The inhabitants of a neighbouring village begged
assistance against French infantry, who had marched in there, to levy supplies.
As the number of the enemy was given at eighty men, and the serjeant had
only six under his command, he at first declined complying with the request,
but, on the pressing entreaties of Heuer, finally consented, and the picquet
advanced in double files upon the village. Heuer and his coverer chose for
themselves the most difficult part of the attack, being that upon the two vedettes on the high road ; however when Heuer dashed towards one of these
his comrade rode off, and he was left quite alone.

The Frenchman shot, but missed, and was taken; without losing a moment
Heuer attacked the other, who met with the same fate. He now heard infantry in his rear ;—made a signal for his comrades to advance, and as soon
as they appeared upon the height, the French fled through the village leaving
behind them a large quantity of provisions which they had collected.

In the year 1813, Heuer was one of a flank patrole of eight men who captured
two French infantry soldiers, who were plundering in a village in front of
their line. From these they learned that twelve more were about half a
league in advance; six hussars immediately set off after them, and fell in
with nine men, who were carrying away a quantity of plundered articles on
mules. After a short resistance these were all taken. The remaining three
(non-commissioned officers) had already crossed a hill in front of the valley
where the French army stood; Heuer went after them *alone*,—cut off their

retreat, and notwithstanding their resistance, made all three prisoners.

Four days afterwards Heuer was again on patrole, under the command of an English officer; he took a French infantry soldier prisoner, and learned from him that five more were in the neighbourhood. Giving the prisoner up to the rest of the patrole, he sent three men to the right,—rode himself to the left, and soon fell in with the five men, whom he attacked before they had time to fire, and made prisoners. From these again he learned that twelve men more of the same division, were about a quarter of a mile distant; he delivered his prisoners to the commander of the patrole, and requested a few men to support him; without waiting for these, he straightway rode forward, and came in sight of the twelve men, from whom, however, he kept so far distant that they could not see him. As they were all armed with musquets, he considered that it would be an act of fool-hardiness, to make a direct attack, so suddenly shewing himself, he shouted out, and made a signal with his sword as if calling to his comrades in the rear. The French immediately took fright, and Heuer, availing himself of the moment, dashed upon them, upon which they laid down their arms and surrendered. With the help of four men, who came, soon after, to his assistance, he was enabled to bring back the prisoners.

In the month of July 1813, after the battle of the Pyrenees, Heuer was attached to assistant quarter-master-general Campbell, and was one day with him in a village near St. Estevan, where twelve of the enemy's infantry, who had been betrayed by the inhabitants, were taken prisoners by them. On this occasion, Heuer was wounded. A few days after he captured eight men from the head of an advanced guard of the enemy, and brought written testimonials of both these facts to the regiment, from general Campbell. *Sir F. von Arents-childt, and baron Krauchen-berg.*

Corporal BAECKEFELD, 1st hussars—was during four years continuously, orderly to the duke of Wellington, and distinguished himself, as well by his exemplary conduct in general, as by his bravery. *125—1819 sir F. von Arents-childt, and major-gen. von Linsin-gen.*

He furnished a proof of the latter at El Bodon: The duke of Wellington had given orders that major-general Victor von Alten's brigade should attack the enemy as soon as they had arrived at a certain point, and rode, with his staff, some distance to the rear, from whence he could have a clear view of the action. As soon as Baeckefeld saw that his regiment were about to attack, he begged permission from the duke to join his comrades, which was granted, and hurrying to his squadron he fought in every charge that it made during the day.

At the battle of Vittoria, on the 21st June 1813, while acting as orderly to the duke of Wellington, who was always at the head of his army, he captured two French dragoons, who came too near the duke's staff.

In the battle of Thoulouse, 12th of April 1814, Baeckefeld rushed out from among the duke of Wellington's staff, and liberated an English officer, who was attacked by two French cavalry soldiers;—cutting one of them from his horse, and making the other prisoner, although wounded himself.

114—1819
baron
Krauchen-
berg, and
count G.
von der
Decken.

Corporal SCHRELL, 1st hussars. At Celerico in the month of September 1810, captain George von der Decken had his horse shot under him, and was immediately surrounded by the enemy, which being observed by corporal Schrell, he voluntarily dashed forward from the ranks, and with the most distinguished bravery, rescued captain Decken from the enemy's hands.

61.—1819
sir F. von
Arents-
childt, and
major
Schau-
mann.

Hussar GOTHARD, 1st hussars. On the 1st of October 1810, during the retreat of the allied army into the lines of Lisbon, the first hussars formed the rear-guard, and were hotly pressed by the enemy's cavalry behind Coimbra. In one of the charges Gothard was taken prisoner, and carried to the rear. While his escort were occupied in dividing the booty which they found upon him, he seized the opportunity to turn his horse round, and attempt his escape. Four reserve parties and a line of skirmishers were to be passed ; he was without arms, and quite defenceless ; numbers of the enemy pursued him, while others endeavoured to stop his progress, and he received thirty-four sword cuts,—yet, none of them proved serious, and leaning over his horse's neck he managed to effect his escape. On the whole, hussar Gothard had gained such a reputation in the regiment for his extraordinary bravery, that his commanding officer, colonel Arentschildt, many times offered to promote him, which, however, with great humility, he always declined.

36—1819.
major
Corde-
mann.

Corporal MEYER, 1st hussars,—was sent on patrole with three hussars to Alcobaça, in the month of February 1811,—fell in with the enemy upon the way, and captured eight chasseurs.

baron
Krauchen-
berg.

In July 1813, in the Pyrenees, captain Krauchenberg called for a volunteer to carry a despatch to the duke of Wellington,—a very difficult and dangerous duty at that moment. Meyer offered his services, and executed the task with the greatest boldness and circumspection.

Corporal BERTRAM, 1st hussars. On the advance of the allied army to Salamanca, in June 1812, the first hussars formed the advanced guard, and were engaged in a skirmish with the enemy, who formed an extended line of skirmishers, and made great exertions to out-flank the right wing of the hussars. On this occasion corporal Bertram's bravery and firmness were remarkable: he instantly rallied the nearest men,—rushed against the advancing enemy, and not only prevented their design, but captured, with the far inferior number under his command, fourteen chasseurs. *199—1819 capt. Leonhardt.*

Hussar REUSCH, 1st hussars. On the 4th of April 1814, Reusch formed one of a patrole, which was detached from the squadron in the neighbourhood of Laverdac. They had a wood to pass, which was occupied by a French volunteer-corps, and Reusch was sent forward, with another hussar, to reconnoitre. He had ridden about a quarter of a league, when suddenly a loud shout met his ear; he rode towards the sound,—found the baggage of the squadron surrounded by a strong force of the enemy, with whom the weak escort were vainly contending. Reusch instantly hurried to their assistance,—cut one of the assailants from his horse, and made two prisoners; and the charge having been sounded in the enemy's rear at the same moment, they took to flight. It afterwards appeared that serjeant Severin and trumpeter Lange had accidentally arrived near the spot, and had hit upon this happy expedient, by means of which fifty of the enemy were put to flight. The whole baggage guard consisted of only four effective men: Reusch was wounded by a sword cut in the right arm. *182—1819 lieut.-col. F. v. d. Decken.*

Serjeant CHRISTOPH MEYER, 1st hussars. At the battle of Fuentes Onoro, May 1811, general sir Lowry Cole was much in need of information respecting the movements of the enemy, and Meyer was, therefore, sent out by captain Moritz von Müller, with six men, in order if possible to make some prisoners. He fell in with an officer and twenty French cavalry—charged them, and captured seven men and horses, which he delivered to the general. *260—1819 sir F. von Arentschildt and baron Krauchenberg.*

Hussar FREDERICK KUNZE, 1st hussars. On the 3d April 1811, during the retreat of the French army from the lines of Lisbon, Kunze was sent with two hussars to patrole in the neighbourhood of Sabugal, and he succeeded in *143—1810 major Schaumann.*

capturing a detachment of fifteen men of the enemy's infantry, having previously been exposed to their fire.

132—1819 major Buertling.   Serjeant AUGUSTUS FISCHER, 1st hussars. In the combat near Almeida, July 1810, when the English light division and the first hussars were driven by the enemy over the Coa, serjeant Fischer rescued lieutenant-colonel Smith of the English rifle-corps, who was severely wounded, and would certainly have fallen into the enemy's hands, had not Fischer, at the risk of his own personal safety, given him his horse, and submitted to make his own way on foot. General Craufurd, who was witness to this occurrence, sent a handsome remuneration to the serjeant on the following day.

Col. Aly.   On the 19th March, 1811, Fischer alone captured, at Ponte Murcella, a corporal and nine French infantry.

131—1819 capt. Teuto   Corporal THIELBÖRGER, 1st hussars,—being on picquet under lieutenant von Bobers, April 11th 1814, was sent with a few men to patrole. They found the enemy in a village. The corporal in order to make his force appear greater, caused his men to approach the village in different directions, upon which the enemy left it. Thielbörger immediately collected his men,—dashed through the place,—attacked the French, and made ten men prisoners.

130—1819 count G. von der Decken.   Corporal DEEKE, 1st hussars. On the 1st of October 1810, the squadron to which Deeke belonged, was on picquet near Coimbra, and was attacked many times by the French, at a defile, which the squadron had to pass, and in order to clear which, the hussars were obliged frequently to charge superior numbers of the enemy's cavalry. Deeke distinguished himself on this occasion by great bravery and presence of mind. In one charge he and three other hussars, were entirely cut off. He did not therefore give himself up for lost, but, together with two of his comrades, boldly cut his way through : one of the hussars was killed, and Deeke and the two others were both wounded.

113—1820 sir F. von Arents- childt, and major-gen. v. Gruben.   Corporal GERLACH, 1st hussars, On the 9th of October 1810, during the retreat of the allied army into the lines of Lisbon, Gerlach was wounded, and taken prisoner. Having been brought, with fourteen others, into a convent, he formed a plan to effect their escape. He formed a rope of rags, and let himself down from the fourth story to the ground; the rest followed, and after experiencing much fatigue and danger for a period of eight days, they succeeded in regaining the regiment. Altogether Gerlach was known in the first hussars, as a particularly brave and confidential soldier, who distinguished himself in almost every engagement by some bold action : On the retreat of the enemy from the lines, he captured an officer and two men ; another time, under lieutenant Strenuwitz, he brought in several of the enemy's flankers, as also on many other occasions.

Hussar Frederick Meyer, 1st hussars. At the battle of Salamanca, June 22d 1812, Meyer many times distinguished himself by his bravery. He dragged a French officer of infantry out of the ranks with his own hands, and captured a gun, having been the first to cut the traces of the horses, and thus prevented it from being carried away. 136—1820
major-gen.
v. Gruben.

Corporal Frederick Lange, 1st hussars. On the 13th of March 1811, during the pursuit of the French army under Massena, captain von dem Wisch was sent with eighteen men on patrole to Coimbra. Lange and two hussars were in advance. They perceived at some distance, between Condeixa and Coimbra, several fires, and Lange, having reported the circumstance to his officer, received directions to approach the spot with caution, and ascertain the cause. As they approached, the enemy's vedette fired, but Lange, pursued him to the French picquet, making a shouting and noise with his men, as if a whole squadron followed. Captain Wisch had in the mean time formed up the rest of his men on hearing the shot, and following rapidly, attacked the enemy's picquet, overthrew them, and made the whole prisoners. 154—1820
major v. d.
Wisch.

Corporal Schröder, 1st hussars. In the month of June 1811, near the Mondego, five leagues from Badajos, captain George von der Decken with four hussars, fell in with an enemy's foraging party of ten dragoons, who formed behind a ditch, as soon as they perceived the hussars. Schröder was the first to cross this broad ditch, and attack the enemy, who, after a few more had crossed, took to flight, and Schröder captured two men and horses. 135—1819
count G.
von der
Decken.

At the battle of Salamanca, June 22d 1812, the line of skirmishers of the first hussars was hard pressed by the enemy's skirmishers, and Schröder, rushing into the middle of the latter, cut the commanding officer on the head, and brought him off a prisoner, upon which the enemy's skirmishers gave way, and immediately drew back. Baron
Krauchen-
berg, lieut-
col. F. v.d.
Decken.

10.—1819.
captain
Meyer.

Corporal FREDERICK STUCKE, 2d hussars. In the year 1814, Stucke was one of a picquet under cornet Meyer, in front of Antwerp, and being on patrole, perceived four waggons laden with provisions, which, were proceeding towards the fortress, under an escort of the enemy's infantry. Stucke followed them with two men,—overtook them close by Antwerp,—drove off the far superior force of the enemy, and brought in the waggons, which proved to be laden with wheat.

13.—1819.
col. Aly, &
major von
Stoltzen-
berg.

Serjeant RÜMPEL, 2d hussars—was, in January 1814, with five men, on patrole in the neighbourhood of Antwerp, and fell in with an enemy's detachment of seven men, which he attacked, and the greater part were cut down and taken.

14.—1819.
major-gen-
Victor von
Alten.

Corporal DETTMER, 2d hussars—was on a patrole under lieutenant Meister in June 1811, which attacked and overthrew an enemy's detachment of twice the strength. Dettmer particularly distinguished himself on this occasion, and captured two of the enemy's dragoons.

16.—1819.
col. Aly, &
lieut.-col.
v. Düring.

Serjeant-major AUGUSTUS KLARE, 2d hussars. In the month of February 1814, just before the attack upon the village of Merxen near Antwerp, the commanding general, lord Lynedock, wished to gain information respecting the position of the enemy, whose right wing was covered by a height occupied by a detachment of infantry. Serjeant Klare, with great bravery and presence of mind, undertook to gain the height. He drove off the infantry,—took sufficient time to look all round, and brought the required information to the general.

18.—1819.
lieut.-col.
Cleve, and
capt.Meyer

Serjeant SPREINE, 2d hussars. A detachment of the 2d hussars under cornet Meyer, formed the advanced guard of a reconnoisance which was made on the 14th of March 1814, towards the village of Merxen, and by which the enemy were driven in. After the desired object had been accomplished, and the reconnoitering party were on their return, the enemy followed slowly on the high road, but sent a strong detachment to the flank, in order to cut off cornet Meyer's advance. Cornet Meyer divided his men into two parts,—left one half on the high road, and dashed forward with the rest, consisting of nine hussars, by a cross road against the enemy. In consequence of the high hedges, the strength of the latter could not be ascertained ; but according to all appearance it was far superior to that of the hussars. The enemy were nevertheless attacked, and completely overthrown and dispersed. Spreine particularly distinguished himself on this occasion,— cutting several of the enemy from their horses, and making many prisoners : these could not, however, be brought away, as reinforcements came to their assistance. The strength of the French detachment, which was thus attacked by nine of the 2d hussars, consisted of thirty-six men, being lancers of the imperial guard.

Hussar HENRY STENZIG, 3d hussars. On the attack of the French squares at the battle of the Göhrde, September 16th 1813, Stenzig and his horse, which had received five wounds, fell in the midst of the enemy ; he succeeded, however, in cutting his way through the square, on foot. 22.—1818.
lieut.-col.
Bremer.

Hussar WILLIAM FRANCIS, 3d hussars. In December 1813, Francis was on a night patrole with a non-commissioned officer and six men near Eckernförde in Holstein. Going forward alone, he fell in with three of the enemy's patrole, whom he made prisoners, and learned from them that a detachment of one hundred and fifty men, would follow in the course of an hour ; upon hearing which he placed himself as vedette. 29.—1818.
capt. Meyer
and lieut.
Götte.

The detachment arrived,—was challenged by him, and upon the answer "Danes!" he fired and rode back. Having reached the patrole, he gave the word of command with a loud voice—"Threes right wheel! gallop! march!" and directed his comrades to extend their files and fire quickly, in order to deceive the Danes as to their strength ; this was done, and the enemy's detachment were induced to retreat.

Corporal FREDERICK LIBERTY, 3d hussars. At the first charge made by the regiment on the French cuirassiers at the battle of Waterloo, June 18th 1815, Liberty's horse was wounded in the head, and the head stall and reins of the bridle were cut in two, so that he was, for the moment, unable to manage his horse, which ran straight into the French line with him. He was followed by three cuirassiers, from whom he freed himself one after another, but, at last, fell among the French infantry, and was taken prisoner by two lancers. These placed him with a crowd of other prisoners, and in the hurry, left his horse with him. He took advantage of the circumstance to put his bridle together as well as he could,—jumped on his horse, and galloped back to the allied position. Immediately after this he took part in another charge, which 32.—1821.
captain
Friederichs was made by his squadron, and liberated hussar Meyer, who was surrounded by four French chasseurs,—bringing one from his horse by a shot, and putting the rest to flight with his sword.

17.—1821.
capt. von Hodenberg

Hussar FREDERICK GRAMMÜSCH, 3d hussars. At the fourth charge of the regiment on the French cavalry, 18th June 1815, lieutenant von Hodenberg was surrounded, and in the greatest danger of being taken prisoner, when Grammüsch, who observed his situation, cut the lieutenant free, receiving nine wounds in the act.

294—1820
serjeants Nervo and Rüsse-meyer.

Hussar JOHN SCHWANN, 3d hussars. At the charge made by captain von Hugo, with such distinguished bravery, upon two French squares at the battle of the Göhrde, September 16th 1813, hussar Schwann was *the first* who entered the square with him. He received, thereby, many severe wounds, which rendered him an invalid for life.

194—1816
lieut.-col. v. Bremer.

Corporal CHRISTIAN SCHAPER, 3d hussars. Captain Hugo was severely wounded in the attack upon the squares at the Göhrde, and lay on the ground. Several of the enemy, rushing out of the square, held their bayonets to his breast. Schaper was lying under his horse, a few paces distant; he worked his way out.—fired at the different assailants with his carbine,—drove them back into the square, and succeeded, notwithstanding the heavy fire, in bringing captain Hugo away in safety.

73.—1819.
col. Küper

Serjeant ANDREW WEDEMEYER, 3d hussars. At the attack of the third hussars on the French squares at the battle of the Göhrde, hussar Heymann's horse was shot, just as the square was broken, and he took advantage of the position in which he was thus placed, to seize general Milozinsky, who commanded the square, and with the help of serjeant Wedemeyer, who cut down those who attacked him with the bayonet,—he succeeded in holding the general fast, and bringing him off a prisoner.

108—1819
capt. H. v. Hodenberg

Hussar HENRY BERGMANN, 3d hussars. In the battle of Waterloo, a French cavalry regiment stood opposite the third hussars. Bergmann dashed out from the ranks of his own accord,—attacked the commanding officer of the regiment,—cut him from his horse in front of his men, and returned to his place in the ranks.

30.—1819.
Count Wallmo-den.

Hussar SCHELLER, 3d hussars. At the combat between Sehestedt and Cluvensik, December 10th 1813, the Danish cavalry, rushing out of the village of Schestedt, overthrew the allied infantry, posted on the road. At the head of this body of infantry was general Wallmoden, and, having in vain endeavoured to keep them together, he and his small staff soon became involved in the fight. The bravery of some of his orderly dragoons, among whom Scheller particularly distinguished himself, alone enabled him to escape unhurt, for these throwing themselves against the enemy's leading horsemen, drove them back, and thus enabled the general to reach the nearest infantry support in the direction of Osterade.

Corporal GEORGE DUNTEMANN, 3d hussars. In the battle of the Göhrde, September 16th 1813, Duntemann, who had exhibited great gallantry in the attack on the squares—succeeded with the assistance of hussars Wrede, Holle and Driege,—the two first of whom were killed—in capturing a gun, which was defended by the enemy with the greatest obstinacy.

103—1819 lieut.-col. v. Bremer. captain Oehlkers.

Hussar OTTO BASEDAU, 3d hussars. On sir John Moore's retreat, December 1808, Basedau was one of the allied rear-guard, which was severely pressed by the French cavalry. In one of the charges, hussar Greberg of the second troop, was wounded, and carried off by the enemy. Basedau, seeing him surrounded by twelve of the enemy's hussars, rushed forward, although the rest of the regiment had, meantime, fallen back,—and rescued his comrade from their hands.

26.—1819. lieut.-col. v. Goeben.

Serjeant HOFMEISTER, 1st dragoons. In one of the charges which this regiment made at the battle of Waterloo, the commanding officer, lieutenant-colonel von Bülow, was wounded, and just at the same moment, the regiment was forced back by the superior numbers of the enemy, Hofmeister, who was in rear, and severely pressed by the French, seeing his commanding officer lying bleeding on the ground, braved the destruction, with which the least delay threatened him,—pulled up his horse,—dragged the colonel out of the fight; then placed him on his own horse, and made him ride away. Hofmeister continued on foot until he met with a stray horse, upon which he rejoined his regiment, and fought during the rest of the battle.

174—1819 colonel von Reitzenstein.

Serjeant ERDFELDER, 2d dragoons. On the 20th of July 1812, the third squadron of the second dragoons covered the retreat of the allied army from the Duero upon Salamanca; several Portuguese infantry soldiers were taken by the enemy, and Erdfelder begged for four men, in order that he might liberate them, which he effected with the greatest bravery.

203—1819 captain A. Poten.

9.—1819.   Trumpeter Louis Zietz, 2d dragoons. In one of the charges made by this
colonel
Friederichs regiment at the battle of Waterloo, Zietz noticed one of the enemy's field-
officers retiring with their discomfited cavalry; he pursued him, attacked,
and made him prisoner, and delivered him to colonel Friederichs. The
officer proved to be an aide-de-camp of Napoleon's; his gold watch and well
filled purse remained untouched in his possession, bearing honorable testimony
to the disinterestedness of the trumpeter.

346—1820 Corporal Diedrich Schlemm, 1st light battalion. On the 28th February
colour serjt 1814, the company of captain Henry von Marschalck was on picquet before
Nolte.
Bayonne, and the enemy were busied in erecting a battery near the spot,
which was likely to prove very injurious to the besiegers. Volunteers were,
therefore, called out to drive off the workmen; Schlemm undertook the duty
alone, and creeping forward, brought down the workmen shot after shot, unti[1]
at length, the enemy gave up their design.

In the following night captain Marschalck called for volunteers to seize a
small house which was occupied by the enemy. Schlemm offered himself as
leader of the party, and took the place with distinguished bravery, This
house served afterwards for a night post.

Lieut.-col.   At the battle of Waterloo, when the 1st light battalion drove back a heavy
C. Wyne-
ken, and   column of the enemy's infantry, with the bayonet, Schlemm distinguished
captain C.   himself as one of the foremost in the attack. He afterwards went, with nine
Heise.
men to the extreme point of the garden of la Haye Sainte, from whence, by
his well directed fire, he did great service, nor did he cease until a shot
which he received in the lungs, obliged him to leave the field.

97.—1819.   Corporal Henry Müller, 1st light battalion. During the battle of
general v.   Waterloo the company in which Müller served, was detached for a short
d. Bussche,
lieut.-col.   time, to la Haye Sainte. The enemy advanced in close column to the
Wyneken,   attack. Müller obtained permission from lieutenant Albert, who commanded
and lieut.
Macdonald   the company, to go to the extreme end of the garden, and endeavour to shoot
the French commanding officer, who rode in front of the column. He took
with him the skirmishers Sasse and Schülermann, who loaded the rifles for
him, and he succeeded not only in bringing the officer from his horse in the
first shot, but in further doing considerable injury to the enemy. When
the French were afterwards driven from the position, and made another attempt

in close column upon the place, they were led by an officer on foot, who, waving his sword, encouraged them to advance. This officer was also shot by Müller, and the column instantly gave way, and fell into disorder. Altogether Müller was one of the best shots in the battalion and distinguished himself on many occasions by his bravery, and effective fire in the field.

Serjeant FREDERICK LÜLLEMANE, 1st light battalion. On the 28th February 1814, the company in which Lüllemann served was on picquet in front of Bayonne under the command of captain von Both. The French had taken possession of, and strongly occupied a house, which the battalion had taken the day before ; and, at dusk Lüllemann begged permission to attempt its re-capture with a few volunteers. Captain Both allowed him to take 14 men, with which he made so determined an attack, that the enemy, although far superior in number, were drive out of the place. 110—1820 lieut.-col. Wyneken,

Serjeant CONRAD SCHULTZE, 1st light battalion. On the attack of the enemy's position on the Bidassoa, October 7th 1813, Schultze particularly distinguished himself. He rushed in front of a strong French column, in the moment of attack, shot the commanding officer from his horse, and by his subsequent effective fire, threw the column into disorder, and obliged them to retreat. 126—1820 general v. d. Bussche, lieut.-col. Wyneken, and capt. Buhse.

On the 9th of December 1813, his bravery was equally conspicuous : Accompanied by a few men, he stormed and gained possession of a house, which was strongly occupied by the enemy.

Corporal WILLIAM WIESE, 2d light battalion. At the battle of Waterloo an *abattis* was constructed near a Haye Sainte, to impede the progress of the enemy's cavalry. This was defended, with great bravery, by a few men under corporal Wiese, until, overpowered by numbers, he was obliged to fall back into the farm-yard. He was wounded, but continued under fire, and contributed much to the defence of the place. When the barn was set on fire, he and Dahrendorf, rushing into the midst of the enemy's balls, brought water many times in their caps to quench the flames. 169—1820 lieut Frank

Corporal HENRY HOFMEISTER, 2d light battalion. At the false attack which was made by the light brigade of the legion on the enemy's right wing, November 10th 1813, a company of the second light battalion, which was engaged skirmishing under lieutenant Behne, was driven back by a superior 160—1820 major Behne.

force of the enemy, and hotly pursued; at this moment, lieutenant Behne was severely wounded by a cannon shot, and would inevitably have fallen into the enemy's hands, had not Hofmeister, with distinguished bravery, rallying the men, led them boldly against the enemy, and rescued his officer.

178—1819 captain Riefkugel. Serjeant DIEDRICH MEYER, 2d light battalion. At the sortie from Bayonne, April 14th 1814, Meyer commanded the sixth company of the battalion, and distinguished himself by the fearlessness and perseverance with which he defended the post that had been entrusted to him, from all the attacks of the enemy.

Captain Graeme. At the defence of the farm of la Haye Sainte, June 18th 1815, Meyer was one of the last who, under lieutenant Graeme, defended the rear building, and when the lieutenant had ventured too far, and the enemy had rushed upon him with the bayonet, and were about to take him prisoner,—Meyer hurried to the spot, and liberated him. He received, however, in the act, a blow on his head from the butt end of a musquet, which struck him to the ground, and he was taken prisoner.

150—1810 captain Riefkugel. GOTTLIEB KIESTLING, 2d light battalion. At the storming of St. Sebastian, February 27th 1814, a detachment under lieutenant von Witzendorf which had been sent towards the Adour, drove the enemy close under the citadel of Bayonne. A house occupied by his men under lieutenant von Marwedel, was soon after attacked by great numbers, who, favored by the ground, succeeded in blockading our men in it. The greater number of these, however, among whom was Kiesling, succeeded in fighting their way through. Lieut. Marwedel was, on this occasion, severely wounded on the head, and two Frenchmen were about to take him prisoner, when Kiesling, hurrying to the spot, shot one of the assailants,—knocked the others down with his rifle, and brought away his officer,—receiving himself, at the same time, a shot through the right leg.

81.—1818. lieut.-col. v. Rettberg HENRY FREYHÖFER, 1st line battalion, (Band.) At the storming of the churchyard of St. Etienne by the skirmishers of the line brigade of the legion under captain von Rettberg, Freyhöfer, being one of the foremost, sprung upon two of the enemy, who were about to level their musquets against captain von Rettberg and brigade-major von Drechsel, and, although himself wounded and unarmed, made them both prisoners.

CHRISTIAN HALLEGO, 2d line battalion. At the siege of Burgos, October 9l.—1818. 1812, Hallego was employed in the trenches, under the command of a captain *capt. Hesse* of the 24th English infantry. The detachment had to defend an outwork which had been taken, and were exposed to the fire of the place, at forty yards distance. Hallego rushed forward voluntarily on the parapet, and with the greatest contempt of danger, placed several heavy beams upon it,—bored loop holes underneath, and by these means saved the lives of many of his comrades. On his return from the trenches, he was specially recommended to the commander of the battalion, by the English captain.

At the storming of the castle of Burgos, 18th October 1812, Hallego volunteered for the forlorn hope, and was one of the foremost among those who forced on to the third line.

On the 18th June 1815, when the garden of Hougoumont, strongly occu- *Major von* pied by the enemy, was re-taken by the allies, Hallego particularly distin- *Wencks-* *tern.* guished himself, being the first who rushed in, seized two Frenchmen and made them prisoners, and with powerful blows of the butt end of his musquet, cleared the way before him.

Corporal CHRISTIAN BRINKMANN, 3d line battalion. At the defence of *163—1820* the garden and wood of Hougoumont, June 18th 1815, the enemy's line of *captain* *Dehnel &* tirailleurs was close to the outer hedge, led by an officer of the staff. Brink- *captain von* mann, jumped suddenly over the hedge,—seized the officer's horse by the *Soden.* bridle, and took him prisoner in the sight of his own men.

HANOVERIAN HONOR AND HONESTY.

When, in the beginning of the year 1806, lord Cathcart found himself obliged to re-embark the army which had been landed in the ports of the Weser in the preceding December, many cases of desertion, caused by various influences, occurred, as is well known, among the troops of the King's German Legion that were attached to the expedition. (See Vol I. p. 89.)

Among others the fourth and fifth troops of the first hussars, suffered particularly. From these, in pursuance of a previous understanding, some 20 men deserted in one day, taking with them their horses and appointments, after selling which, they returned to their homes.

Among the deserters was a young hussar named Schumann, a native of Mahlen in the district of Hoya, who one morning at day-break appeared before his father's house, in order to seek shelter behind the plough, from the danger to which he would be subjected by serving in foreign climes against "cannibals", and other imaginary evils, with which ill disposed persons had filled his mind. The father, however, firmly devoted to his king and country, could not reconcile himself to his son's conduct, and having heard his story, and made enquiry whether it was possible for him to return to his regiment, he handed him a letter to his captain (the late colonel Aly,) enclosing the price of the horse that had been sold—" in order that neither he nor his son should be so disgraced as to have stolen from the king,"—and sent the deserter back to his regiment.

The son, now repentant, obeyed the orders of his father, but before he could reach the regiment, it had already been embarked. The gallant fellow, however, did not hesitate to continue his honest course, and notwithstanding the danger that threatened all those who attempted to enter the English service, he followed the regiment, and arrived safe in England.

But the regiment had been removed to Ireland before his arrival, and to this country also the persevering youth repaired; he reported himself to his captain in Gort, and faithfully delivered the money.

This remarkable proof of honesty in both father and son, could not fail to attract the attention of the superior officers, in consequence of which the money was returned to the hussar.

Schumann endeavoured by his good conduct to atone for his youthful error, and now lives at Mahlen, a pensioned corporal, after having, until lately, continued his service in the hussar-guards, and afterwards in the first dragoons.

COMPLETE LIST

OF ALL THE OFFICERS WHO WERE ACTUALLY SERVING

IN

THE KING'S GERMAN LEGION,

AT THE DISBANDMENT OF THE CORPS IN 1816;

Together with

A SPECIFICATION OF THEIR SERVICES, WOUNDS, HONORARY DISTINCTIONS, & ULTIMATE CONDITION.

COMPILED BY

CHRISTOPH HEISE, H.G.O.3.—H.W.C.

&c. &c.

Captain, Royal Hanoverian Rifle Guards.

MEMORANDUM.

The names, and dates of commissions were furnished by captain Lewis Benne, of the Hanoverian Staff, whose valuable aid in preparing various elaborate Lists and Returns for this work, has been noticed in the preface to the 1st Volume.

TABLE

Shewing the services abroad of the different Corps of the King's German Legion.

ARTILLERY.

1st Foot Battery,   Expedition to Hanover, 1805-6.
                      Expedition to the Baltic, 1807.
                      Expedition to the Baltic, 1808.
                      Peninsula (stationed at Lisbon & Neighbourhood, 1808-9-10-11-12-13-14.)
                      Battle of Waterloo and campaign of 1815.

2d Foot Battery,   Expedition to Hanover, 1805-6.
                      Expedition to the Baltic, 1807.
                      Campaign in the Peninsula, 1808-9-10-11-12-13.
                      Campaigns in the south of France, 1813-14.
                      Station in the Netherlands, 1814.
                      Battle of Waterloo and Campaign of 1815.

3d Foot Battery,   Expedition to Hanover, 1805-6.
                      Station in the Mediterranean (Sicily) 1808-9-10-11-12-13-14-15-16.
                      (including expedition to the Gulf of Naples, 1809, and expedition to the continent of Italy, 1814 and 1815.)

4th Foot Battery,   Expedition to the Baltic, 1807.
                      Expedition to the Baltic, 1808.
                      Campaign in the Peninsula, 1808-9-10-11-12-13.
                      Campaigns in the south of France, 1813-14.
                      Station in the Netherlands, 1814.
                      Battle of Waterloo and Campaign of 1815.

1st Horse Battery,   Expedition to Hanover, 1805-6.
                      Expedition to the Baltic, 1807.
                      Campaigns in north of Germany, 1813-14.
                      Station in the Netherlands, 1814.
                      Battle of Waterloo and Campaign of 1815.

2d Horse Battery,   Expedition to Hanover, 1805-6.
Campaign in the north of Germany, 1813-14.
Station in the Netherlands, 1814.
Battle of Waterloo and Campaign of 1815.

Engineers,   (Compare text and nominal list of officers.)

CAVALRY.

1st Dragoons,   Expedition to Hanover, 1805-6.
Campaigns in the Peninsula, 1812-13.
Campaign in the south of France, 1813-14.
Station in the Netherlands, 1814.
Battle of Waterloo and Campaign of 1815.

2d Dragoons,   Campaigns in the Peninsula, 1812-13.
Campaigns in the south of France, 1813-14.
Station in the Netherlands, 1814.
Battle of Waterloo and Campaign of 1815.

1st Hussars,   Expedition to Hanover, 1805-6.
Expedition to the Baltic, 1807.
Campaigns in the Peninsula, 1809-10-11-12-
   13.
Campaigns in the south of France, 1813-14.
Station in the Netherlands, 1814.
Battle of Waterloo and Campaign of 1815.

2d Hussars,   Expedition to the Baltic, 1807.
Expedition to the Scheldt, 1809.
Campaigns in the Peninsula, 1810-11-12-13.
Station in the Netherlands, 1814.
Campaign of 1815.

3d Hussars,   Expedition to the Baltic, 1807.
Campaigns in the Peninsula, 1808-9, (form-
   ing part of sir John Moore's army—the
   regiment came home from Corunna, leav-
   ing detachments in the Peninsula), left
   Peninsula end of May, 1813.
Campaign in the north of Germany, 1813-14.
Station in the Netherlands, 1814.
Battle of Waterloo and Campaign of 1815.

INFANTRY.

1st Light Batt.
Expedition to Hanover, 1805-6.
Expedition to the Baltic, 1807.
Expedition to the Baltic, 1808.
Campaigns in the Peninsula, 1808-9, (forming part of sir John Moore's army—the battalion came home from Vigo, leaving detachments in the Peninsula.)
Expedition to the Scheldt, 1809.
Campaigns in the Peninsula, 1811-12-13.
Campaigns in the south of France, 1813-14.
Station in the Netherlands, 1814.
Battle of Waterloo and Campaign of 1815, (detachments of the battalion were employed in the campaign in the north of Germany, 1813-14.)

2d Light Batt.
Expedition to Hanover, 1805-6
Expedition to the Baltic, (5 companies) 1807
Expedition to the Baltic, 1808.
Campaigns in the Peninsula, 1808-9 (forming part of sir John Moore's army—the battalion came home from Vigo, leaving detachments in the Peninsula.)
Expedition to the Scheldt, 1809.
Campaigns in the Peninsula, 1811-12-13.
Campaigns in the south of France, 1813-14.
Station in the Netherlands, 1814.
Battle of Waterloo and Campaign of 1815, (detachments of the battalion were employed in the campaign in the north of Germany, 1813-14.)

1st Line Batt.
Expedition to Hanover, 1805-6.
Station in the Mediterranean, (Gibraltar) 1806-7.
Expedition to the Baltic, 1807.
Expedition to the Baltic, 1808.

Campaigns in the Peninsula, 1808-9-10-11-12-13.

Campaigns in the south of France, 1813-14.

Station in the Netherlands, 1814.

Battle of Waterloo and campaign of 1815, (detachments of the battalion were employed in the campaign in the north of Germany, 1813-14.)

2d Line Batt. Expedition to Hanover, 1805-6.

Station in the Mediterranean, [Gibraltar] Expedition to the Balic, 1807.

Campaigns in the Peninsulo, 1808-9-10-11-12-13.

Campaigns in the south of France, 1813-14.

Station in the Netherlands, 1814.

Battle of Waterloo and Campaign of 1815, (detachments of the battalion were employed in the campaign in the north of Germany, 1813-14.)

3d Line Batt. Expedition to Hanover, 1805-6.

Expedition to the Baltic, 1807.

Station in the Mediterranean, (Sicily) 1808-9-10-11-12-13-13-14, (including expedition to the Gulf of Naples, 1809,) grenadier and light company, operations in Catalonia, 1812-13.

Expedition to the continent of Italy, 1814.

Station in the Netherlands, 1814.

Battle of Waterloo and campaign, of 1815.

4th Line Batt. Expedition to Hanover, 1805-6.

Expedition to the Baltic, 1807.

Station in the Mediterranean (Sicily)1808-9-10-11-12, (including

Expedition to the Gulf of Naples, 1809).

Campaigns in the Peninsula, 1812-13-14, the battalion forming part of the allied army in Catalonia.)

South of France, 1814.

Station in the Netherlands, 1814.

Battle of Waterloo and Campaign of 1815.

5th line Batt.

Expedition to the Baltic, 1805-6.

Expedition to Hanover, 1807.

Expedition to the Baltic 1808.

Campaigns in the Peninsula, 1808-9-10-11-12-13.

Campaigns in the south of France, 1813-14.

Station in the Netherlands, 1814.

Battle of Waterloo and Campaign of 1815,

(detachments of the battalion were employed in the Campaigns in the north of Germany, 1813-14.)

6th Line Batt.

Expedition to the Baltic, 1807.

Station in the Mediterranean (Sicily) 1808-9-10-11-12-13-14-15-16. (including expedition to the Gulf of Naples (1809) and the continent of Italy, 1814-15.)

Campaigns in the Peninsula, 1812-13, (the battalion forming part of the allied army in Cataonia,)

7th Line Batt.

Expedition to the Baltic, 1807.

Expedition to the Baltic, 1808.

Campaigns in the Peninsula, 1808-9-10-11.

Station in the Mediterranean (Malta and Sicily) 1812, 13, 14, 15, 16; light company, operations in Catalonia, 1812-13.

8th line Batt.

Expedition to the Baltic, 1807.

Station in the Mediterranean, (Sicily) 1808-9-10-11-12-13-14, including expedition to the continent of Italy and to Corsica, 1814)

Station in the Netherlands, 1814; grenadier and light company—operations in Catalonia, in 1812-13.

Battle of Waterloo and Campaign of 1815.

Foreign Veteran Battalion.

Station in the Netherlands, 1814-15.

DESIGNATION OF SERVICES.

Expedition to Hanover in 1805 . . . . .H. 1805

Expedition to the Baltic in 1807 and 1808 . . . . . .B. 1807-8.

Mediterranean: Stations & Expeditions, (including Gibraltar, Sicily, Malta, Corsica, and
continent of Italy,) 1806-7-8-9-10-11-12-13
14-15-16. . . . . } M. 1806-7-&c.

Peninsular Campaigns, (including operations in
Catalonia, which are marked *) 1808-9-10
11-12-13. . . . . } P. 1808-9-&c.

Expedition to the Scheldt, 1809. . . . . .S. 1809.

Campaign in the south of France, 1813-14 . . . .S.F. 1813-14.

Campaign in the north of Germany, 1813-14.
(The officers not actually present with general
Wallmoden's corps are marked †) . . . . } N. G. 1813-14.

Netherlands, 1814-15. . . . . .N. 1814-15.

Battle of Waterloo and campaign of 1815. . . . . . .W.C. 1815.

Campaign 1815. . . . . ,C. 1815.

MEMORANDUM,

The names of such Individuals only are marked H. 1805, who
actually served in the legion at the period of its embarkation in
November 1805, and who formed the first basis of the corps.

Designation of Honorary Distinctions.

1. Grand-cross, 2. Commander, 3. Companion or Knight, 4. Knight of 2d
Class, 5. Knight of 3d Class.

BRITISH.

B. B. O. 1. 2. 3.	Order of the Bath,
B. K. G.	Order of the Garter,
G. M. B. I. O.	Ionian Order, (Grand Master.)
B. G. C. 1. 2.	Gold Cross (with clasps,) for Battles.
B. G. M. 1. 2. 3.	Gold Medal (with clasps,) for Battles.
B. W. M.	Waterloo Medal.

HANOVERIAN.

H. G. O. 1. 2. 3.	Guelphic Order.
H. W. M.	Waterloo Medal.
H. W. C.	King William's Cross.

AUSTRIAN.

A. M. T. 1. 2. 3.	Order of Maria Theresa.
A. L. O. 1. 2. 3.	Order of Leopold.
A. I. C. 1. 2· 3.	Order of the Iron Crown.
A. S. St. 1.	Order of St. Stephen.

BADEN.

Bn. F. O. 1. 2.	Order of Fidelity.
Bn. Z. L. O. 1. 2. 3.	Order of the Lion of Zähringen.

BRUNSWICK

Br. G. C.	Gold Cross for distinguished services.
Br. H. L. O. 1. 2. 3.	Order of Henry the Lion.

BAVARIAN.

Ba. H. O.	Order of St. Hubert.
Ba. M. I. 1. 2. 3.	Order of Maximilian Joseph.

DANISH.

D. D. O. 1. 2. 3. 4	Order of Danebrogh.

FRENCH

F. St. L. 1. 2. 3.	Order of St. Louis.
F. L. H. 1. 2. 3. 4. 5.	Order of the Legion of Honor.

HANSEATIC.

H. M.	Medal for Campaign of 1813-14.

HESSIAN.

He. G. L. 1. 2. 3.	Order of the Gold Lion.
He. M. M.	Order of Military Merit.
He. I. H.	Order of the Iron Helmet.
He. M.	Medal for Campaigns.
He. D. L. 1. 2. 3.	Order of Ludewig of Hesse Darmstadt.

MECKLENBURG.

M. M.	Medal of Merit.

NETHERLANDS.

N. L. O. 1. 2. 3.	Order of the Lion of the Netherlands.
N. W. O. 1. 2. 3.	Military Order of William.
Be. O. L. 1. 2. 3.	Order of Leopold:

POLISH.

Po. St. O. 1. 2. 3. 4.	Order of Stanilaus.
Po. W. E. 1. 2. 3.	Order of the White Eagle.

PORTUGUESE.

P. T. S. 1. 2.	Order of the Tower and Sword.
P. C.	Cross for distinguished services.

PRUSSIAN.

Pr. B. E.	Order of the Black Eagle.
Pr. R. E. 1. 2. 3. 4.	Order of the Red Eagle.
Pr. I. C.	Order of the Iron Cross, *(second class)*
Pr. I. O.	Order of St. John of Jerusalem.
Pr. M. O. M.	Order of Military Merit.
Pr. M.	Medal for Campaigns.
Pr. C.	Cross for distinguished services.

RUSSIAN.

R. A. O.	Order of St. Andrew.
R. A. N. O.	Order of Alexander Newsky.
R. St. A. O.* 1, 2, 3, 4.	Order of St. Anne. (the order marked by asterics has an additional decoration in diamonds)
R. St. G. O. 1, 2, 3, 4, 5.	Order of St. George,
R. St. W. O. 1, 2, 3, 4,	Order of St. Wladimir.
R. M.	Medal for Campaigns.
R. P. M.	Medal for Capture of Paris.
R. T. M.	Medal for Turkish Campaign.
R. G. M. M.	Gold medal of merit.
R. Sw. of H.	Sword of honor for gallantry in the field

SARDINIAN.

S. M. L. 1, 2, 3,	Order of St Maurice and St. Lazare.

SWEDISH.

Sw. N. St. 1, 2, 3,	Order of the North Star.
Sw. Sw. O. 1. 2, 3,	Order of the Sword.
Sw. Sw. M.	Medal of the order of the Sword.
Sw.	Medal for distinguished services.

SICILIAN.

Si. C. G. O.	Order of Constantine and St. George.
Si. F. O. 1, 2, 3,	Order of St. Ferdinand.
Si. I. O.	Order of St. January.

SPANISH.

Sp. C.	Cross for distinguished services.

WURTEMBERG.

W. M. M. 1, 2, 3,	Order of military merit.
W. M.	Medal for distinguished services.
W. O. C. 1, 2, 3.	Order of the Crown.
W. S. C.	Cross for services.
W. D. (1815),	Distinction for Campaign, 1815.

MARKS AND ABBREVIATIONS.

The mark (*) preceding the number attached to each officer in the list, denotes those who contribute to the Pension Fund, according to the return of December 1836. The first date represents the date of the first commission in the legion; the second date the date of gazettment, or commencement of pay, and the third, the date of brevet rank in the British army.

¶ Served without permanent rank until the battle of Salamanca, July 1812.

N. C. O. Entered the service as cadet, or served as non-commissioned officer.

H. S. Hanoverian Service.

h. p. Hanoverian pension.

r. l. Hanoverian retired list.

ret. retired.

res. resigned.

br. brevet.

† died.

in Han. in the kingdom of Hanover.

COMPLETE LIST,

&c.

STAFF

COLONEL IN CHIEF.

*1, *His Royal Highness Adolphus Frederick Duke of Cambridge*, 17th Nov. 18‍73.. Field Marshal 26th Nov. 1813. [N. G.† 1813-14,] H. G. O. 1.—B. B. O. 1.—B. K. G.— G. M. B. I. O.—Pr. B E. 1.—Pr. R. E. 1.—He G. L. 1. R. A. O.—Br. H.L.O. 1.—Po. W. E. 1.—N.L. O. 1.—R. A. N. O. 1.—R. St. A. O. 1.—H. W. C.— late viceroy of Hanover.

BRIGADE MAJORS.

*2, *Ernest von Kronenfeldt*, 26th Jan.—4th Feb. 1806..capt. 20th Feb. 1813, [B. 1807, M. 1808-9-10-11-12-13-14- 15, P.* 1812-13.] Si. F. O. 2,—H. W. C. lieut.-col. H. S. 1st line battalion.

*3, *Gottfried von Einem*, 25th—28th Jan. 1806..captain 28th April 1814, [M. 1806-7, B. 1807-8, P. 1808-9-10-11- 12-13, S. F. 1813-14 N.1814, W. & C. 1815,] severely wounded 18th June 1815, at Waterloo. H. G. O. 3.— B. W. M.—H. W. C. lieut-col. H. S. 1st line battalion.

*4, *Frederick von Heimburg*, 16th June 1804..captain 26th July, 1815. [H. 1805, B. 1807, M. 1808-9-10-11-12- 13, S. F. 1814, N. 1814, W. & C. 1815.] H. G. O. 3. B. W. M.—H. W. C. major by br. h. p. town major at Hanover.

5, *Hermann Segeband Gotthelf Friedrich August von Estorff*, 14th—21st March, 1807...capt. 28th July 1815. [B. 1807. S. 1809. P. 1811. N. G. 1813-14. N. 1814. W. & C. 1815.] severely wounded, 29th Dec. 1811, at La Nava, B. W. M. † et Osnabrück, 28th April, 1827, a captain H. S. 2d regt. of hussars.

K 10

*6, *John Frederick Lewis Benne*, N. C. O. 6th—17th March 1812..captain 8th August, 1815. [H. 1805, B. 1807.] H. G. O. 3, captain h. p. at Hanover.

7, *William von Rantzau*, 28th Jan. 1806...captain 15th Aug. 1815, [B. 1807. M. 1808-9-10-11-12. P.* 1812-13-14, S. F. 1814. N. 1814. W. & C. 1815.] H. G. O. 3.-B. W. M. † at Hildesheim, in Han. 27th Dec. 1822, a captain H. S. 3d infantry regiment.

*8, *George Baring*, N. C. O., 23d Nov.—6th Dec. 1808, captain 20th Nov. 1815. [H. 1805, B. 1809-10-11-12-13, S. F. 1813-14, N. 1814, W. & C. 1815,] slightly wounded 18th June, 1815 at Waterloo, H. G. O. 3, B. W. M.—H. W. C. captain H. S. 2d regt of dragoons.

CHAPLAINS OF BRIGADES.

*9, *Henry Frederick Rambke*, 17th March 1804. [H. 1805, M. 1806-7. B. 1807,] Pastor at Grossen-munzel, in Han.

10, *George Henry Gündell*, 17th March 1804, [P. 1812-13.- S. F. 1813-14, N. 1814, C. 1815,] H. G. O. 3, † field-chaplain and superintendent at Wunstorf, in Han. 17th April, 1835.

11, *Frederick Daniel Buchholz*, 20th June 1806, [B. 1807, M. 1808-9-10-11-12-13-14-15-16,] at Hanover.

12, *Frederick Albrecht Pohse*, 20th July, 1806. [B. 1807, M. 1808-9-10-11-12-13-14, N. 1814, C. 1815.] † at Eitzendorf near Hoya, in Han. 1st Jan. 1823, Pastor at Eitzendorf.

13, *Henry Andrew Meyer*, 25th Dec. 1807. [B. 1808, P. 1808-9-10-11-12-13, S. F. 1813-14, N. 1814, C. 1815.] † at Auleben in Schwarzburg-Rudolstadt, 5th Nov. 1820.

ENGINEERS.

FIRST CAPTAINS.

14, *Augustus Berensbach*, ¶ 20th—21st April, 1804...major 4th June, 1814. [H. 1805, B. 1807, M. 1808-9-10-11-12-13-14-15.] † at Eimbeck, in Han. 23d Sept 1819.

*15, *Victor Prott*, ¶ 20th—21st April, 1804...captain, 23d March, 1805. [H. 1805, B. 1807.](1808-9-10-11-12-13, at Jersey on the Staff of general Don) N. G.† 1813-14.] H. G. O. 2.—H. W. C. colonel H. S. and quartermaster-general.

*16, *Charles Ernest Appuhn*, 21st March, 1804...captain 25th Nov. 1808. [H. 1805, B. 1807-8, M. 1810-11-12-14 P.* 1812-13-14, N. 1814-15,] at Hanover.

17, *Charles Wedekind*, 21st April 1804, captain 12th Oct. 1809. [H. 1805, B. 1807-8, P. 1808-9:10-11-12-13, N. 1814-15.] br. lieut.-col. h. p. at Harburgh.

SECOND CAPTAINS.

*18, *George Frederick Meinecke*, 16th June, 1804..captain 24th Nov. 1810. [H. 1805, B. 1807-8, P. 1808-10-11-12-13-14, C. 1815, with the Prussian 2d army-corps.] H. G. O. 3.—H. W. C. lieut.-col. Han. engineers.

*19, *Augustus Schweitzer*, 6th—9th February, 1805...capt. 15th July, 1812, [H. 1805, B. 1807, N. G.† 1814, N. 1814-15] H. W. C. br. lieut.-col. Han. Engineers.

20, *William Müller*, 24th April—20th May, 1809...captain 13th Dec. 1812. (S. 1809, employed to survey the coast between the river Elbe and Boulogne sur mer, N. G. 1813-14.) br. major h. p. at Stade, in Han.

21, *Frederick von Gaugreben*, 14th—29th Nov. 1809...capt. 5th March, 1814, (1811, stationed in Jersey; 1813-14-15, stationed in Canada) † at Cassel, electorate of Hessia, 6th Jan. 1822.

FIRST LIEUTENANTS.

*22, *William Unger*, N. C. O., 25th March—4th April, 1807. (M. 1806-7, B. 1807-8, P. 1808-9-10-11, (1812-13-14, employed on the lines in front of Lisbon, and on the upper Douro, C. 1815, with the Prussian 2d army-corps.) H. G. O. 3.—H. W. C. captain Han. engineers.

*23, *John Luttermann*, 21st Jan. 1806. (B. 1807, M. 1808-9-10-11-12-13-14-15-16, P.* 1812-13) H. G. O. 3—H. W. C. captain Han. engineers.

ARTILLERY.

HORSE:—"*Waterloo, Göhrde.*"   FOOT:—"*Peninsula, Waterloo.*

COLONEL COMMANDANT.

*24, *Frederick count von der Decken,* colonel of the King's
German regiment, 28th July 1803..deputy adjutant-gen.
King's German legion 17th Nov. 1803..colonel of horse
artillery King's German legion, 1st January 1804,
lieut.-gen. 4th June, 1814. (H. 1805. B. 1807,—on a
diplomatic mission to the Peninsula in 1808, N. G.†
1813-14, N. 1815.) H. G. O. 1.—He. G. L. 1. general
h. p. at Hanover.

LIEUTENANT-COLONEL

25, *Augustus Röttiger,* ¶ 8th Nov. 1803,—17th Nov. 1804...
colonel 4th June, 1814. (H. 1805, B. 1807. N. G.†
1813-14.) H. G. O. 2.—H. W. C. lieut.-gen. H. S.
Director of the Ordnance department.

MAJORS.

*26, *George Julius Hartmann,* ¶ 9th Nov. 1803.—24th Jan.
1804...lieut.-col. 17th Aug. 1812. (H. 1805, B. 1808,
P. 1808-9-10-11-12-13, S. F. 1813-14, N. 1814,
W. & C. 1815.) slightly wounded 28th July 1809, at
Talavera; slightly wounded, 14th of April 1814, before
Bayonne. B. G. C. 1. 2. Talavera, Albuera, Salamanca,
Vittoria, St. Sebastian, Nive. B. B. O. 2.—H. G. O. 2.—
B. W. M.—H. W. C.—lieut.-gen. Han. artillery.

27, *F. Henry Brückmann,* ¶ 3d—17th Nov. 1803...lieut.-col.
4th June 1814. (H. 1805, B. 1807, N. G. 1813-14,
N. 1814, C. 1815.) H. G. O. 2.—R. St. W. O. 4. †
at Stade, in Han. 27th October 1834, a major-gen. h. p.

FIRST CAPTAINS.

28, *Henry Jacob Kuhlmann,* ¶ 16th June, 1804..major 4th
June 1814. (H. 1805, N. G. 1813-14, N. 1814, W. & C.
1815) B. B. O. 3.—H. G. O. 3.—B. W. M. † at Stade, in
Han. 19th March, 1830, (a br. lieut.-col, Han. artillery.

29, *Augustus Sympher*, ¶ 17th Nov. 1804..lieut.-col. 18th June, 1815. (H. 1805, B 1807, N G 1813-14, N 1814, W & C 1815,) slightly wounded, 18th June 1815, at Waterloo. B. B. O. 3.—H. G. O. 3.—B. W. M. † at Hanover 11th Dec. 1830, a br. lieut.-col Han. artillery.

30, *Victor von Arentschildt*, ¶ 13th—24th Jan. 1804..major 25th Nov. 1813. [H. 1805, B. 1807-8, P. 1808-9-10-11-12-13. (in the Portuguese service since 1809,) S. F. 1813-14.] B. G. M. 1, 2. Busaco, Fuentes de Onoro, Toulouse.—B. B. O. 3.—P. T. S. 2.—P. C.—H. G. O. 2. major-gen. by br. h. p. at Münden, in Han.

31, *Bernhard Busmann*, ¶ 2d July 1805—captain 2d July1805, H. 1805, M. 1808-9-10-11-12-13-14-15.) † at Hanover, 15th Feb. 1828, a br. lieut.-col. Han. artillery.

32, *Charles von Witzleben*, ¶ 20th—21st March, 1804—captain 23d Dec. 1805. [H. 1805, B. 1807, S. 1809, N. G. † 1813-14.] H. G. O. 3.—H. W. C. colonel H. S. 1st line battalion, and assistant-adjutant-general to the Hanoverian infantry.

33, *Charles von Rettberg*, ¶ 2d—5th May, 1804..captain, 12th April 1806 (H. 1805, B. 1807, P. 1808-9-10-11-12-13-14, W. & C. 1815.) B. G. M. 1, 2. Talavera, Busaco, Badajoz, H. G. O. 3.—B. W. M.—H. W. C. colonel Han. artillery.

34. *Andrew Cleeves*, 14th—17th Nov. 1803—major, 18th June 1815. (H. 1805, B. 1807-8, P. 1808-9-10-11-12-13. S. F. 1813-14, N. 1814, W. & C. 1815,) severely wounded, 31st October 1812, at the Retiro, B. G. M. Albuera, H. G. O. 3,—B. W. M. † at Selby, county of York, in England, 8th June, 1830, a br. lieut.-col. Han. artillery.

*35, *Lewis Daniel*, 21st March, 1804—captain, 26th Nov. 1808. (H. 1805, B. 1807, P. 1809-10-11-12-13, S. F. 1813-14, N. 1814-15.) B. G. M. 1. Orthes, Toulouse, H. G. O. 3. br. lieut.-col. h. p. at Harburg.

SECOND CAPTAINS.

* 36 *George Wiering*, 20th—21st April 1804..captain, 23d
Nov. 1809, (H. 1805, B. 1807, N. G. 1813-14, N.
1814, W. & C. 1815. II G O 3.—B. W. M.—H. W. C.
lieut.-colonel Han. artillery.

37, *Charles Meyer*, ¶ 23d March 1805. (H. 1805, B. 1807-8,
P. 1808-9, M. 1810-11-12-13-14, N. 1815.) † at Gal-
horn, Amt Rotenburg. 27th April, 1833, a major by br.
h. p.

38, *William Braun*, 5th May, 1804. (H. 1805, B. 1807-8, P.
1808-9-1(-11-12, (in the Portuguese service from 1810
to 1812) N. G.† 1813-14, W & C 1815,) severely wounded 18th June, 1815 at Waterloo. B. G. M. Albuera, P.C.
Sp. C.—H. G. O. 3.—B. W. M.—H. W. C. br. lieut.-
col. Han. artillery.

39, *Augustus Bindseil*, 7th July, 1804. (H. 1805, B. 1807,
M. 1808-9-10-11-12-13-14 15.) † at Hanover 7th Nov.
1817. a captain Han. artillery.

*40, *Lewis Jasper*, 7th—9th Feb. 1805. (H. 1805, B. 1807,
N. G. 1813-14, N. 1814-15.) H. W. C. major Han.
artillery.

*41, *William von Schade*, 8th—9th Feb. 1805. (H. 1805, N.G.
1813-14.) slightly wounded 6th Oct. 1813, at Büchen
on the Stecknitz, H. G. O. 3.—H. W. C. br. major Han.
artillery.

42, *Ernest Lüchow*, N. C. O. 9th Feb. 1805. (H. 1805, P.
1809-10-11-12-13-14, † at Hanover, 12th March 1822,
a captain Han. artillery.

43, *Frederick Erythropel*, 23d March, 1805. (H. 1805, B.
1807, N. G. 1813-14, N. 1814. W. & C. 1815.) severely
wounded 18th June, 1815, at Waterloo, B. W. M. major
by br. h. p. at Basbeck, Amt Bremervörde, in Han.

FIRST LIEUTENANTS.

44, *Victor Preussner*, N. C. O. 20th August, 1805. (H. 1805, P. 1812-13, S. F. 1813-14, N. 1814-15.) captain by br. r. l. at Langenhagen near Hanover.

* 45, *Ferdinand von Brandis*, 24th Dec. 1805. (H. 1805, B. 1807-8, P. 1808-9-10-11-12-13-14, N. 1815.) H. W. C. captain Han. artillery.

*46, *Henry Mielmann*, N. C. O. 7th,—10th May, 1806. (H. 1805, B. 1807-8. P. 1808-9-10-11-12-13. S. F. 1813-14, N. 1814, W. & C. 1815,) slightly wounded, 22d July, 1812, at Salamanca; severely wounded, 17th July, 1813, before St. Sebastian, H. G. O. 3.—B. W. M.—H. W. C. captain Han. artillery.

47, *Theodore Speckmann*, N. C. O. 8th,—10th May, 1806. (H 1805, N. G. 1813-14, N. 1814, W. & C. 1815.) B. W. M. Sw. M † at Stade, 17th Sept. 1834, a captain h. p.

*48, *Lewis Stöckmann*, N. C. O. 9th,—10th May 1806, . . lieut. 19th Sept. 1810. (H. 1805, B. 1807, P. 1808-9-10, N. G. 1813-14, N. 1814, W. & C. 1815.) † at Wunstorf, in Han. 1st Feb. 1822, a captain Han. artillery.

49, *Carl Anthony Hugo*, N. C. O. 5th—18th June 1807. (B. 1807, M. 1812-13-14, W. & C. 1815.) B. W. M. † at Stade, 28th Jan. 1826, a captain Han. artillery.

50, *Henry Stöckmann*, N. C. O. 8th—18th June 1807.(H. 1805, M. 1808-9-10-11-12-13-14-15,) captain h. p. at Stade.

*51, *William Rummel*, N. C. O. 28th Sept.—9th Oct. 1807. (B. 1807-8, P. 1808-9-10-11-12-13, S. F. 1813-14, N. 1815.) H. W. C. captain Han. artillery.

*52, *William von Goeben*, 8th Nov.—5th Dec. 1808.—P. 1809-10-11-12-13, S. F. 1813-14, N. 1814, W. & C. 1815.) severely wounded 7th May 1812, at assault of Badajos, severely wounded 16th June 1815 at Quatre-bras, H. G. O. 3,—B. W. M. major by br. r. l. at Celle.

53, *William von Scharnhorst*, 24th Nov.—30th Dec. 1809. (Pr. 1811-12-13, N. 1814, W. & C. 1815.) slightly wounded, 20th June 1812, before the forts of Salamanca, Pr. R. E. 3—Pr. I. C.—Pr. C.—R. St. G. O. 4—R. St W. O. 4—Sw. Sw. O. 3,—N. W. O. 3,—B. W. M. colonel Prussian artillery.

54, *Frederick Drechsler*, N. C. O. 19th Sep.—8th Oct. 1810. (H 1805, M 1808-9-10 11-12-13-14-15.) captain by br. r. l.

*55, *Augustus Pfannkuche*, N. C. O. 14th,—29th Oct. 1811 (P 1812-13, S F 1813-14, N 1814-15, W & C 1815,) H. W. C. captain Han. artillery.

*56, *Henry Hartmann*, N. C. O. 17th Apr.—5th May, 1811. (P 1811-12-13, S F 1813-14, N. 1814, W & C 1815) severely wounded, 16th June 1815, at Quatre-bras, H. G. O. 3,—B. W. M.—H. W. C. captain Han. artillery.

57, *George Meyer*, N. C. O. 15th Aug.—11th Sep. 1811. (H 1805 N. G. 1813-14, N. 1814, W & C 1815.) B. W. M. † in Hanover, 12th July 1831, a captain h. p.

*58, *Henry Bostelmann*, N. C. O. 31st Jan.—29th Feb. 1812 (H 1805, B 1807-8, P 1808-9-10-11-12. N G† 1813-14.) H. W. C. captain Han. artillery.

59, *Henry Heise*, 30th Jan. 21st July, 1812. (N G† 1813-14. W & C 1815.) B. W. M. † at Hanover, 9th Oct. 1832, a captain Han. artillery.

SECOND LIEUTENANTS.

60, *Frederick Lücke*, N. C. O. 11th—26th Dec. 1812. (H 1805, N G 1813-14,) † at Osnabrück, 11th Feb. 1819.

*61, *Frederick Seinecke*, N. C. O. 12th—26th Dec. 1812. (H. 1805, B 1807,) captain r. l. at Stade.

*62, *Henry Köhler*, 13th, 26th Dec. 1812. (H 1805, N. G. 1813-14,) captain h. p. at Elze, in Han.

*63, *Lewis Haardt*, N. C. O. 14th,—26th Dec. 1812. (N. G† 1813-14. W. & C. 1815.) B. W. M. captain by br. h. p. at Osnabrück.

*64, *Lewis Heise*, 15th—26th Dec. 1812.(N G† 1813-14, W &
C 1815.) slightly wounded, 18th June 1815, at Waterloo.
B W M, captain h. p. at Hanover.

*65, *Lewis Scharnhorst*, N C O. 15th—29th Nov. 1813.(H 1805,
N G† 1813-14.) H W C...captain Han. artillery.

*66, *Lewis von Wissell*, 30th Nov.—16th Dec. 1813 (N 1814, W
& C 1815) H. G. O. 3—B. W. M.—H. W. C. captain
Han. artillery on the staff.

67, *Charles Hermann Ludowieg*, 16th Feb.—3d March, 1814.
(W & C 1815) B. W. M. captain by br. h. p. at Stade.

68, *Edward Hartmann*, 23d March—13th April 1814 (C. 1815)
† at Hanover, 5th March 1818.

*69, *Augustus Capelle*, 19th—28th May 1814,...captain Han.
artillery.

*70, *John Frederick Schlichthorst*, 20th—28th May, 1814, H. G.
O. 3. captain Han. artillery.

71, *Edward Michaelis*, 20th Oct.—18th Nov. 1814 † at Ostro-
lencka in Poland, May 1831, a lieutenant h. p.

72, *Charles du Plat*, 25th Nov. 15th Dec. 1814,...major by br.
r. l.

*73, *Franz Röttiger*, 26th Nov. 15th—Dec. 1814, (C. 1815,)
captain Han. artillery.

*74, *Adolphus Rechtern*, 24th July,—3d Aug. 1815..captain
Han. artillery.

*75, *Lewis Hagemann*, 25th July,—3d Aug. 1815..captain
Han. artillery.

CAPTAIN COMMISSARY.

76, *Frederick Rehwinkel*, ¶ 4th—5th May 1804,..captain 28th
Sept. 1807 (H. 1805, B 1807, N G† 1813-14, N. 1815)
major by br. r. l. † at Hanover, 29th Dec. 1836.

ADJUTANT.

*77 *Ernest Thielen*, N. C. O. 10th May, 1806,..1st lieutenant
16th April 1811, (H. 1805, M 1808-9-10 11-12, N G†
1813-14.) H. G. O. 3.—H. W. C. captain Han. artillery
and brigade-major.

L 11

PAYMASTER.

78, *John Blundstone*, 9th April 1805, H. 1805, B. 1807, N G†
1813-14, N 1814, C 1815.

QUARTERMASTER.

79, *Henry Hoyns*, N. C. O. 5th—13th Feb. 1807. (H. 1805, B.
1807, N G† 1813-14,) † at Hanover 10th March, 1821,
a captain and quartermaster, Han. artillery.

SURGEON.

80, *Henry Kels*, ¶ 18th Dec. 1805, (B 1807, P. 1810-11-12-
13, N 1814-15,) at Liebenau, in Han.

ASSISTANT SURGEONS.

a, Horse artillery.

81, *Christian Friederich Gottlieb Edward Schmersahl, M. D.*
30th Dec. 1805. (B 1807, N G† 1813-14,) † at Hanover,
12th Oct. 1829, a surgeon Han. artillery.

82, *George Crone*, 10th—20th Feb. 1810. (N. G. 1813-14, N.
1814, W. & C. 1815.) B. W. M. Surgeon by br. h. p. at
Wunstorf, in Han.

b. Foot artillery.

83, *Christ. Adolph Rentzhausen*, 15th—27th April 1813. (N.
1814, W. & C. 1815.) B. W. M. † at Hameln, in Han.
15th December 1826.

84, *John Christopher William Beyer*, 16th Jan.—16th May
1814. (N. 1814, W. & C. 1815.) B. W. M. † at Berge-
dorff, in Han. 31st May 1819.

VETERINARY SURGEON.

*85, *John Frederick Hilmer*, 22d Aug. 1805—25th Nov. 1806.
B. 1807, N. G. 1813-14, N. 1814-15.) H. W. C. br.
lieutenant and veterinary surgeon, H. S. 3d dragoons.

FIRST DRAGOONS.

" Peninsula, Waterloo, Garcia Hernandez."

COLONEL COMMANDANT.

*86, *William von Dörnberg,* ¶ col. commdt. of the Brunswick hussars 25th Sept. 1809,.. K. G. legion as colonel commandant, 24th June 1815,.. major-general 1st Jan. 1812. (N. G. 1813-14, N. 1814, W. & C. 1815.) severely wounded 18th June 1815, at Waterloo, H. G. O. 1,—B. B. O. 2,—R. A. N. O,—R. St. A. O. 1,—R. St. G. O. 3,—He. G. L. 1,— Pr. M. O. M,—N. W. O. 3,—He. I. H,—B. W. M,— R. M, R. P. M,—R. T. M,—H. M.—He. M. lieutenant-general r. l. ambassador at St. Petersburg.

LIEUTENANT-COLONEL.

*87, *John von Bülow,* 3d Sept. 1803, King's German regiment, 17th Nov. 1803, King's German legion, (H. 1805, S. 1809, P. 1812-13, S. F. 1813-14, N. 1814, W. & C. 1815.) severely wounded 18th June 1815 at Waterloo, B. G. M. 1. 2, Salamanca, Vittoria, Toulouse B. B. O. 3,—B. W. M,—H. G. O. 3, colonel by br. r. l. at Wolfenbüttel dutchy of Brunswick.

MAJORS.

88, *Augustus von Reizenstein,* ¶ 3d Jan. 1804,.. lieut.-colonel, 18th June 1815, (H. 1805, P. 1812-13, S. F. 1814, N. 1814, W. & C. 1815.) severely wounded, 18th June 1815 at Waterloo, B. B. O. 3,—H. G. O. 2,—B. W. M,† at Celle in Han. 6th Nov. 1830, a br. colonel H. S. Garde du corps, and aide-de-camp to his majesty the King.

*89, *Philip von Sichart,* ¶ 18th—21st Jan. 1806. (S. F. 1813-14, N. 1814, W. & C. 1815.) severely wounded, 18th June 1815 at Waterloo, B. G. M. Toulouse, H. G. O. 3. B. W. M. colonel by br. h. p..commandant at Osnabrück, † 23d of August 1836.

CAPTAINS.

*90, *Hans von Hattorf,* ¶ 8th—14th Feb. 1804. (H 1805, P. 1812-13, S F 1813-14, N 1814, W & C 1815.) Pr. I. O. H. G. O. 2. B. W. M. H. W. C. colonel on the staff, H. S.

*91, *Frederick von Uslar* ¶ 9th—14th Feb 1804..captain 3d Jan 1809 (H 1805, P 1812-13, S F 1813-14, N 1814. W & C 1815,) slightly wounded, 11th Aug 1812, at Majalahonda. B. G. M. Vittoria. H. G. O. 3. B. W. M. H. W. C. colonel H. S. 2d regiment of dragoons.

*92, *Bernhard von Bothmer,* 30th Jan.—14th Feb. 1804. (H 1805 P. 1812-13, S. F. 1813-14, N. 1814, W & C 1815) severely wounded,—leg amputated,—18th June, 1815, at Waterloo. H. G. O. 3. B. W. M. br. lieut.-col h. p. at Hanover.

*93, *George Henry von Hattorf,* 3d—14th Feb. 1804. (H 1805, P 1812-13, S F 1813-14, N 1814, W. & C. 1815) severely wounded, 11th Aug. 1812, at Majalahonda; severely wounded, 18th June 1815, at Waterloo. H. G. O. 3. B. W. M. H. W. C. br. lieut.-colonel, H. S. 3d regiment of dragoons.

94, *George von Ramdohr,* ¶ 15th—22d Dec. 1804. (H. 1805, N. 1814, W. & C. 1815.) B. W. M. at Kirchwehren, Amt. Blumenau, in Han.

*95, *Charles Elderhorst,* N. C. O. 17th Nov. 1804. (H. 1805, P. 1812-13, S. F. 1813, N. 1814. W. & C. 1815.) H.G.O.3, B. W. M, H. W. C. br. lieut.-colonel H. S. 2d dragoons.

*96, *Hartwig von Witzendorf,* 19th—23d April 1805. (H. 1805, P. 1812-13, S. F. 1813-14, N. 1814-15.) severely wounded, 11th Aug. 1812, at Majalahonda, H. G. O. 3,—H. W. C. br. lieut.-colonel H. S. Garde du corps, and adjutant to the division of cavalry.

*97, *Moritz von Cloudt,* 15th Feb. 1806,..captain 17th Sept. 1813. (P. 1812-13, S. F. 1813-14, N. 1814, W. & C. 1815.) slightly wounded, 18th June 1815 at Waterloo, Pr. I. O.—B. W. M.—H. W. C. br. major H. S. Garde du corps.

'98, *Benedix von der Decken*, N. C. O. 12th Oct. 1805...captain
18th September 1813. (II. 1805, P. 1812-13, S. F. 1813-
14, N. 1814, W. & C. 1815), slightly wounded 23d Oct.
1812, at Venta del Poço, B. W. M. major by br. r. l. at
Laak in Han.

99, *Henry Lefftreu*, 25th Nov.—9th Dec. 1809. (P. 1812-13,
S. F. 1813-14, N. 1814, W. & C. 1815.) B. W. M. †
at Clausdorff in Prussia, in 1827.

LIEUTENANTS.

*100, *August Fischer*, 26th—28th Sept. 1810. (P. 1812-13,
S. F. 1813-14, N. 1814, W. & C. 1815.) B. W. M.
captain h. p. at Ahnsen, amt Meinersen, in Han.

101, *Frederick Natermann*, N. C O. 25th May—3d June 1811.
(P. 1812-13, S. F. 1813-14, N. 1814, C. 1815.) captain
by br. r. l. at Holle, amt Wohldenberg in Han.

102, *Charles Lindes*, N. C. O. 11th—12th March 1812. (II.
1805, B. 1807, S. F. 1814, N. 1814, W. & C. 1815.)
B. W. M. † at Brunswick 12th Sept. 1819.

103, *William Makenzie*, 10th—21st April 1812. (S. F. 1813-
14, N. 1814, W. & C. 1815.) slightly wounded, 18th
June, 1815 at Waterloo. B. W. M. † at Wienhusen near
Celle, 9th June 1824, a captain H. S. cuirassier guards.

104, *Henry Bosse*, N. C. O. 27th May,—6th June 1812. [H.
1805, P. 1812, N. 1814, W. & C. 1815.] severely wounded 18th June, 1815, at Waterloo, B. W. M. † at Gielde,
amt Staden, in Han. 18th Sept. 1818, a captain by br.
h. p.

*105, *Otto von Hammerstein*, 27th Aug.—11th Sept. 1813.
(N. 1814, W. & C. 1815.) severely wounded, 18th June,
1815, at Waterloo, B. W. M.—H. W. C...captain H. S.
garde du corps.

*106, *Conrad Poten*, 28th Aug.,—11th Sept. 1813. (N. 1814,
W. & C. 1815.) B. W. M.—H. W. C. captain H. S.
garde du corps.

*107, *Staats Henry Nunne,* 22d Sept.—5th Oct. 1813. [N. G. 1813, N. 1814, W. & C. 1815.] very severely wounded 18th June 1815 at Waterloo, B. W. M. captain by br. r. l. at Bederkesa, in Han.

*108, *Lewis Kirchner,* 27th Oct.—9th Nov. 1813. [N. 1814, W. & C. 1815.] B. W. M. captain by br. h. p. at Bergen in Han.

109, *William Jones,* 25th Nov.—7th Dec. 1813...br. lieut.-colonel r. l. A. D. C. to his royal highness the duke of Cambridge.

CORNETS,

*110, *Frederick Breymann,* N. C. O. 15th—29th March 1814, (N. G. † 1814, N. 1814, W. & C. 1815.) B. W. M. at Bockenem, in Han.

*111, *Charles von der Decken,* 18th—30th April 1814...capt. H. S. garde du corps.

*112, *Lewis von Müller,* 22d April—3d May 1814. [N. 1814, W. & C. 1815.] B. W. M. captain H. S. garde du corps.

*113, *Hanasch Leschen,* 27th May—5th July 1814. (N. 1814, W. & C. 1815.) B. W. M. at Celle.

*114. *George von Uslar,* 13th—27th May 1815. [C. 1815.] captain H. S. 3d dragoons.

115, *Edward Trittau,* 14th—27th May 1815. [N. 1814, W. & C. 1815.] severely wounded 18th June 1815, at Waterloo, B. W. M.—H. M...lieut. by br. r. l. at Hildesheim, in Han.

*116, *Ernest Lewis Gropp,* 6th—22d July 1815,..lieut. H. S. garde du corps.

*117, *Henry Anthony Frederick Cleve,* 7th—22d July 1815. (C. 1815.) H. W. M. captain by br. h. p. at Dieckhorst, amt Meinersen in Han.

118, *Richard Halpin,* 8th—22d July 1815. [C. 1815.]

*119, *Hans Christian von Bülow,* 25th Oct.—4th Nov. 1815... lieutenant H. S. r. l. at Tessin, Grand dutchy of Mecklenburg.

PAYMASTER.

120, *William Halpin*, 6th January 1807. P. 1812-13, S. F. 1813-14, N. 1814, C. 1815.

ADJUTANT.

*121, *William Fricke*, N. C. O. 26th May—6th June, 1812,.. lieutenant 6th Oct. 1813. [II. 1805, P. 1812-13, S. F. 1813-14, N. 1814, W. & C. 1815.] severely wounded, 18th June 1815, at Waterloo, B. W. M. captain h. p. at Celle.

QUARTERMASTER.

122, *Henry Kranz*, N. C. O. 14th July, 29th Aug. 1809. (II. 1805, P. 1812-13, S. F. 1813-14. N 1813, W. & C. 1815.) B. W. M. † at Celle in Ian. 6th Nov. 1830, a captain and quartermaster Han. garde du corps.

ASSISTANT SURGEON.

123, *N. Daniel Meyer*, 31st March,—10th April, 1810. (N. 1814, W. & C. 1815.) B. W. M. at Hamburg.

124. *John Penry Christoph Friderici, M. D.* 2d—17th Mar. 1812. (P. 1812-13, S. F. 1813-14, N. 1814, W. & C. 1815.) B. W. M. † at Merseburg, in Prussia, 6th June, 1826.

VETERINARY SURGEON.

*125, *Ludolph Heuer*, N. C. O. 25th May, 1805. (II. 1805, P. 1812-13, S. F. 1813-14, N. 1814, W. & C. 1815.) B. W. M..lieutenant by br. h. p. at Celle.

SECOND DRAGOONS.

" Peninsula, Waterloo, Garcia Hermandez."

COLONEL COMMANDANT.

126, *John Augustus von Veltheim*, ¶ 17th April, 1804,—21st Jan. 1806,..major-general, 25th July, 1810. Pr. I. O. † at Hildesheim, in Han. 15th Feb. 1829, a lieut-general by br. h. p.

LIEUTENANT COLONEL.

127, *Charles Frederick de Jonquières*, ¶ 20th April 1804—21st
Jan. 1806, (P. 1812, N. 1814, W. & C. 1815.) slightly
wounded, 18th June, 1815, at Waterloo, B. B. O. 3.—
B. G. M. Salamanca—H. G. O. 3.—B. W. M. † at Plate
near Lüchow, in Han. 12th Oct. 1831, a major-gen. r. l.

MAJORS.

128, *Augustus Friedrichs*, ¶ 19th Oct. 1803,—23d Nov. 1805.
..lieut.-colonel, 18th June, 1815. (H. 1805, B. 1807,
S. 1809, P. 1810-11-12-13, S. F. 1813-14, N. 1814.—
W. & C. 1815.) B. B. O. 3.—B. G. M. Toulouse, H.
G. O. 3.—B. W. M...colonel by br. r. l. at Hameln, in
Han.

129, *Ernest Lewis Wilmerding*, ¶ 25th Dec. 1805,—21st
Jan. 1806. (P. 1812-13, S. F. 1813-14, N. 1814, W.
& C. 1815.) B. W. M. † at Stöckheim, Amt Rotenkirchen
in Han. 15th April, 1819.

CAPTAINS.

* 130, *Charles Baron von Marschalck*, 29th Jan.—14th Feb.
1804..captain, 24th Nov. 1809. (H. 1805, P. 1812-13,
S. F. 1813, N. G. † 1813-14, N. 1814, W. & C. 1815,)
severely wounded, 22d June, 1806, at Tullamore, H. G.
O. 3,—B. W. M...colonel by br. h. p. at Geesthof, in
Han.

131, *Conrad George Wilhelm Auhagen*, ¶ 29th Dec. 1805,
21st Jan. 1806. N. 1814, W. & C. 1815.) B. W. M. †
at Lemie, Amt Wenningsen, in Han. 21st Jan. 1828, a
major by br. r. l.

132, *Lewis Thiele*, ¶ 30th Dec. 1805,—28th Jan. 1806. (P.
1812, S. F. 1813-14, N. 1814, W. & C. 1815.) B. W. M.
† at Göttingen, 3d July, 1834.

133, *Lewis Wilhelm Lüderitz* ¶ 16th—21st Jan. 1806. (N. 1814,
W. & C. 1815.) slightly wounded, 18th June, 1815, at
Waterloo, B. W. M. † at Bovenden, near Göttingen,
18th November, 1832.

134, *William Quentin*, 3d—21st Jan. 1806. (N. 1814, W. & C. 1815.) B. W. M. † at Limmer near Han. 20th May, 1824.

*135, *William Seeger*, 15th—21st Jan. 1806. (P. 1812-13, S. F. 1813-14, N. 1814. W. & C. 1815.) H. G. O. 3.— B. W. M. br. lieut.-col. h. p. at Leer, in Han.

136, *Christian Theodore Leopold George von Harling*, 17th Jan.—8th Feb. 1806, P. 1813, S. F. 1813-14, N. 1814, W. & C. 1815.) very severely wounded, 18th June, 1815, at Waterloo, B. W. M. † at Hanover, 7th Nov. 1823.

*137, *George Braun*, N. C. O. 15th—17th May, 1806. (H. 1805, P. 1812-13, S. F. 1813-14, N. 1814, W. & C. 1815.) B. W. M...major by br. h. p. at Esens, in Han.

*138, *August Poten*, N. C. O. 16th—17th May, 1806. (H. 1805, P. 1812-13, S. F. 1813-14, N. 1814, W. & C. 1815,) slightly wounded, 11th Aug. 1812, at Majalahonda. H. G. O. 3, — H. W. C.—B. W. M...captain Han. garde du corps.

139, *Ernest Heinrich August Bergmann*, 17th May, 1806. (P. 1813, S. F. 1813-14, N. 1814, W. & C. 1815.) B. W. M. † at Isernhagen, near Hanover, 5th April, 1827.

LIEUTENANTS.

*140, *Ludolph von Hugo*, 10th—17th May, 1806. (P. 1812-13, S. F. 1813-14, N. 1814, W. & C. 1815.) slightly wounded, 23d Oct. 1812, at Venta del Poço, B. W. M...captain h. p. at Harburg.

*141, *Joannes Justinus von Fümetty*, N. C. O. 27th Feb.—4th March, 1809. (B. 1807, P. 1812-13, S. F. 1813-14, N. 1814, W. & C. 1815.) slightly wounded, 23d July. 1812. at Garcia-Hernandez, H. G. O. 3.—H. W. C.—B.W.M. ..captain Han. garde du corps.

*142, *Augustus Kuhls*, N. C. O. 4th—18th April, 1809. (H. 1805, P. 1812-13, S. F. 1813-14, N. 1814, C. 1815.) severely wounded, 11th Aug. 1812, at Majalahonda. H. G. O. 3.—H. W. C.. captain 2d Han. dragoons.

*143, *Charles Schaeffer*, 23d April—7th May 1811. (P. 1812, N. 1814, W. & C. 1815.) severely wounded 23d October 1812, at Venta del Poço. Br. G. C.—B. W. M...captain by br. r. l. at Campen, dutchy of Brunswick.

M 12

144, *Hermann Heinrich Conrad Ritter*, 24th—31st March
1812. (P. 1813, S. F. 1813-14, N. 1814, W. & C. 1815.)
severely wounded, 18th June 1815, atWaterloo. B. W. M.
at Hamburg.

*145, *Ernest Meier*, N. C. O. 9th—19th May 1812. (P. 1813,
S. F. 1813-14, N. 1814, W. & C. 1815.) Br. G. C.
B. W. M...captain by br. r. l. at Brunswick.

146, *John Uesseler*, 21st—28th July, 1812. (P. 1813, S. F.
1813-14, N. 1814, W. & C. 1815.) † at Carraccas di
Leon, in America, a colonel in the Columbian service.

147, *Charles Montague Pocock*, 8th—29th August 1812.
(S. F. 1813-14, N. 1814, W. & C. 1815.) B. W. M.

*148, *Ferdinand Küster*, 5th—26th Sep. 1812. (N. G. 1813-
14, N. 1814, W. & C. 1815.) B. W. M...captain h. p.
at Herzberg in Han.

149, *Frederick Rumann*, 21st May—1st June 1813. (N. 1814-
15) † at Nordheim, in Han. 10th May 1834, a lieut. h. p.

CORNETS.

*150, *Otto von Bülow*, 8th—23d Oct. 1813. (N. 1814, W. &
C. 1815.) B.W. M—H. W. C...cap. Han. garde du corps.

151, *Frederick von Wissell*, 6th—29th March, 1814, † at Hameln, in Han. 18th March, 1826, a lieutenant Han. hussar-
guards.

152, *Ferdinand August Lorentz*, 11th July—6th August, 1814.
N. 1814, W. & C. 1815.) severely wounded, 18th June
1815, at Waterloo. B. W. M. † at Detmold, 2d Oct. 1831,
a capt. by br. r. l.

*153, *Edmund Kulhs*, 10th—29th April, 1815..captain 3d
Han. dragoons.

154, *Friedrich Ernest von Hedemann*, 25th May—3d June,
1815...captain Han. garde du corps, and A. D. C. to
his majesty the King of Hanover.

155, *Henry Frederick Gropp*, 3d—22d July, 1815, lieutenant
Han. garde du corps.

*156, *Ernest von Voss*, 4th—22d July, 1815. (C. 1815.) H.
W. C...lieut. Han. garde du corps.

157, *Ferdinand von Berger*, 24th Oct.—4th Nov. 1815, .lieut.
Han. garde du corps.

*158, *Ferdinand von Stoltzenberg*, 21st Nov.—9th Dec. 1815..
lieut. 2d Han. dragoons,..captain with local rank out of
kingdom of Hanover.

*159, *Christian Carl Rudolph Julius Schaumann*, N. C. O.
23d Nov.—9th Dec. 1815. (C. 1815.)..lieut. Han. garde
du corps.

PAYMASTER.

160, *Warren Hastings White*, 21st—30th Sept. 1815. N.
1815.

ADJUTANT.

161, *John George Augustus Niess*, N. C. O. 26th Nov.—7th
Dec. 1813. (P. 1812-13, S. F. 1813-14, N. 1814, W. &
C. 1815) B. W. M. † at Hanover, 4th June, 1825, a
lieutenant 1st Han. cuirassiers.

QUARTERMASTER.

162, *Henry Gropp*, N. C. O. 15th July,—29th Aug, 1809. (P.
1812-13, S. F. 1813-14, N. 1814, W. & C. 1815.) B.
W. M. † at Aurich in East-Friesland, 22d Sept. 1831, a
captain and quartermaster, 1st Han. cuirassiers.

SURGEON.

*163, *Daniel Frederick Detmer*, 27th Dec. 1805, (P. 1812-13,
S. F. 1813-14, N. 1814, W. & C. 1815) B. W. M.—H.
W. C. surgeon, Han. garde du corps.

ASSISTANT SURGEONS.

164, *John Diederich Lange*, 6th—20th Oct. 1812. (P. 1813,
S. F. 1813-14, N. 1814, W. & C. 1815.) B. W. M. † at
Papenburg, in Han. 27th Jan. 1826, an assistant-surgeon,
1st Han. cuirassiers.

165, *Charles Thalacker*, 26th Oct.—9th Nov. 1813. [P. 1813,
S. F. 1813-14, N. 1814, W. & C. 1815.] B. W. M. †
at Rudolstadt, 3d April 1821.

VETERINARY SURGEON.

166, *Henry Hogreve*, N. C. O. 12th July—12th August 1806.
[P. 1812-13, S. F. 1813-14, N. 1814, W. & C. 1815.]
B. W. M. veterinary surgeon 15th hussars, British service.

FIRST HUSSARS.

"Peninsula, Waterloo, El Bodon."

COLONEL COMMANDANT.

167, *Charles Christian count Linsingen,* ¶ 18th Aug. 1804..
lieut.-gen. 4th June 1811. (H. 1805, B. 1807.) H. G.
O. 1.—B. B. O. 2.—Pr. R. E. 1. † at Herrenhausen
near Hanover, 5th Sept. 1830, a general H. S., inspector
of Han. cavalry and colonel commandant hussar-guards.

LIEUTENANT-COLONEL.

*168, *Augustus von Wissell,* ¶ 15th Oct. 1803—21st Jan.
1806. (P. 1811-12-13, N. 1814, W. & C. 1815.) B. B.
O. 3.—H. G. O. 2.—B. W. M. major-gen. h. p. at Verden.

MAJORS.

169, *Philip Moritz von Gruben,* ¶ 8th Nov. 1803—22d Dec.
1804...lieut.-col. 18th June 1815. [H. 1805, B. 1807,
P. 1809-10-11-12-13, S. F. 1813-14, N. 1814, W. & C.
1815.] slightly wounded 5th May 1811, at Fuentes de
Onoro. B. G. M. 1. 2. Salamanca, Orthes, Toulouse.
B. B. O. 3.—H. G. O. 2.—B. W. M. † at Diepholz in
Han. 13th Oct. 1828, a major-gen. H. S. & colonel comm.
2d regiment of hussars.

170, *Moritz von Müller,* ¶ 14th Feb. 1804. (H. 1805, B. 1807.
P. 1809-10-11-12-13, S. F. 1813-14, N. 1814, W. & C.
1815,) slightly wounded 18th June 1812 at Canizal;
slightly wounded 22d July 1812 at Salamanca—B. W. M.
† at Hameln, 18th February 1835.

CAPTAINS.

171, *William count Linsingen,* 13th Oct. 1804...lieut.-colonel
29th June 1815, local rank of colonel on the continent
28th Feb. 1822. [H. 1805, B. 1807, S. 1809.] † at
Hildesheim, 4th Jan. 1837.

*172, *George count von der Decken,* 11th—14th Feb 1804.
(H. 1805, B. 1807, P. 1809-10-11-12-13, S. F. 1813-
14, N. 1814, W. & C. 1815.) severely wounded, 10th
Dec. 1813 at Bidart; severely wounded 27th Feb. 1814 at
Orthes, H. G. O. 3.—B. W. M.—H. W. C. br. lieut.-
colonel 1st Han. dragoons.

*173, *Ernest Poten*, 18th—21st March, 1804. (II. 1805, B. 1807, P. 1809-10-11, S. F. 1813-14, N. 1814, W. & C. 1815) severely wounded 28th July, 1809, at Talavera; severely wounded, [arm amputated] 25th September, 1811, at El-Bodon—B. G. M. Toulouse H. G. O. 3.— B.W. M.—H. W. C...lieut.-col. by br. r. l...commandant at Göttingen.

*174, *Frederick von der Decken*, 13th—17th Nov. 1804. (II. 1805, B. 1807, P. 1809-10-11-12-13, S. F. 1813-14, N. 1814, W. & C. 1815.) slightly wounded, 22d July, 1812, at Salamanca—H. G. O. 3.—B. W. M.—H. W. C...br. lieut.-colonel 1st Han. dragoons.

*175, *Lewis Krauchenberg*, 22d—24th Jan. 1804. (II. 1805, B. 1807, P. 1809-10-11, N. G. 1813-14, N. 1814, W. & C 1815.) severely wounded, 5th May, 1811, at Fuentes de Onoro. R. St. W. O. 4,—H. G. O. 3.—B. W. M.—H. W. C...br. lieut.-colonel 3d Han. dragoons.

176, *Ernest Cordemann*, N. C. O. 9th Feb. 1805. (H. 1805, B. 1807, P. 1809-10-11-12-13, S.F. 1813-14, N. 1814, W. & C. 1815) slightly wounded 22d July 1812 at Salamanca, H. G. O. 3.—B. W. M. † at Langenhagen in Han. 27th Sept. 1833, a lieut.-col. by br. h. p.

*177, *Gustavus Schaumann*, N. C. O. 1st March 1806. (H. 1805, B. 1807, P. 1809-10-11-12-13-, S. F. 1813-14, N. 1814. W. & C. 1815.) slightly wounded, 1st October, 1810, at the Passage cf the Mondego, H. G. O. 3.—B.W. M.—H. W. C. br. major 3d Han. dragoons.

*178, *Frederick Baertling*, N. C. O. 10th—17th May 1806. [II. 1805, B. 1807, P. 1809-10-11-12-13, S. F. 1813-14, N. 1814, W. & C. 1815.] H. G. O. 3.—B. W. M.. major by br. h. p. at Celle.

*179, *Hieronimus von der Wisch*, 8th Feb. 1806..captain 6th April 1814. (B. 1807, P. 1809-10-11-12-13, S. F. 1813-14, N. 1814, W. & C. 1815.) slightly wounded 18th July 1812, at Canizal, H. G. O. 3.—B. W. M.. major by br. h. p. at Verden in Han.

180, *Bernhard Teuto*, N. C. O. 18th—26th Jan. 1808. (II. 1805, B. 1807, P. 1809-10-11-12-13, S. F. 1813-14,

N. 1814, W. & C. 1815.) slightly wounded 28th July 1809, at Talavera; severely wounded, 22d July, 1812, at Salamanca. H. G. O. 3.—B. W. M. † at Bredenbeck near Han. 10th March, 1820...a captain Han. hussar guards.

*181, *Conrad Poten*, N. C. O. 16th—24th March, 1810. (P. 1809-10-11-12-13, S. F. 1813-14, N. 1814, W. & C. 1815.) slightly wounded, 10th April, 1814, at Toulouse, H. G. O. 3.—B. W. M.—H. W. C...captain 1st Han. dragoons.

182, *Adolphus George Hermann von Ilten*, 17th—29th Aug. 1809. (P. 1809-10-11-12-13, S. F. 1813-14, N. 1814, W. & C. 1815.) slightly wounded, 30th July, 1813, near Pampelona, H. G. O. 3.—B. W. M. † at Harburg, 3d of Nov. 1829...a captain Han. garde du corps.

183, *Leopold Schulze*, N. C. O. 17th—22d Sept. 1810. (B. 1807, P. 1809-10-11-12-13, S. F. 1813-14, N. 1814, W. & C. 1815.) B. W. M. at Lüneburg.

*184, *Frederick Holtzermann*, 8th—16th July, 1811. (P. 1812, N. 1814-15.) severely wounded, 16th June, 1812, near Salamanca...captain by br. h. p. at Osnabrück.

*185, *Henry Behrens*, N. C. O. 25th July,—6th Aug. 1811. (H. 1805, B. 1807, P. 1812-13, S. F. 1813-14, N. 1814, W. & C. 1815.) slightly wounded, 16th June, 1812, near Salamanca; slightly wounded, 22d July, 1812, at Salamanca, B.W.M..capt by br. r. l. atBurgwedel in Han.

186, *Adolphus Frederick James William count Wallmoden-Gimborn*, 7th—17th Sept. 1811. (P. 1812-13, S. F. 1813-14, N. 1814, W. & C. 1815.) B. W. M. † at Prague in Bohemia, 3d. Dec. 1825...a capt. Han. hussar guards, and A.D.C. to his royal highness the duke of Cambridge.

187, *Frederick William Trittau*, 9th—17th Sept. 1811. (P. 1812-13, S. F. 1813-14, N. 1814, W. & C. 1815.) B. W. M † at Port-au-prince, St. Domingo, 27th Feb. 1822, a captain by br. r. l.

188, *Frederick Gottfried Ludewig Blumenhagen*, N. C. O. 16th—25th March 1809. (H. 1805, P. 1809-10-11-12-13, S. F. 1813-14, N. 1814, W. & C. 1815.) severely wounded, 28th July, 1809, at Talavera, H. G. O. 3.—B. W. M. † at Hameln, in Han. 1st Jan. 1826...a capt.h.p.

189, *George Leonhardt*, N C. O. 31st Jan.—11th Feb. 1812. (B. 1807, P. 1809-10-11-12-13, S. F. 1813-14, N. 1814, W. & C. 1815.) severely wounded, 16th Sept. 1810, at Cortiçao ; severely wounded 8th May, 1812, at Castello Branco. II. G. O. 3—3. W. M. † at Hanover 4th May, 1833,. . a captain h. p.

190, *Lewis Versturme*, 9th—22d Dec. 1812. (N. 1814, W. & C. 1815.) B. W. M. . . captain by br. r. l. and captain h. p. British service.

CORNETS.

191, *Otto Heise*, 23d July—31 Aug. 1813. (S. F. 1814, N. 1814, W. & C. 1815.) B. W. M. captain r. l. in the Brazils.

192, *George Leopold Conze*, 11th Nov.—7th Dec. 1813. (N. 1814, W. & C. 1815,) B. W. M. † at Hanover, 11th May, 1832. . a captain, h. p.

*193, *Ludewig Friederich George Augustus count Kielmansegge*, 4th,—22d Jan. 1814. (W. & C. 1815.) II. G. O. 3. B. W.M.—H. W. C. . . captain Han. garde du corps.

*194, *Francis von Oldershausen*, 27th Jan.—1st March 1814. (W. & C. 1815) B. W. M. . capt. 1st Han. dragoons.

*195, *William Theodore Gebser*, 14th Feb.—5th March 1814. (N. 1814, W. & C. 1815.) B. W. M. . . capt. 1st Han. dragoons.

196, *Frederick Jacob Rahlwes*, 26th April,—10th May 1814. (N. 1814, W. & C. 1815.) B. W. M. . at Bremen.

*197, *William von Hassell*, 13th Sept.—1st Oct. 1814. (N. 1814, W. & C. 1815) B. W. M.—H. W. C. . . captain 1st Han. dragoons.

198, *Christian Weitemeyer*, N. C. O. 25th Jan—11th Feb. 1815. (H. 1805, B. 1807.) veterinary surgeon, r. l. at Volkmarshausen, Amt Münden, in Han.

199, *George Lewis count Oeynhausen senior*, 5th—22d July, 1815. . captain h. p. at Hameln.

200, *Lewis count Oeynhausen jun.* 22d Nov.—9th Dec. 1815. . lieut. Han. garde du corps.

PAYMASTER.

201, *James William Longmann*, 27th—28th Sept. 1810. (P. 1811-12-13, S. F. 1813-14, N. 1814, W. & C. 1815.) B. W. M. † in England 14th August 1831.

ADJUTANT.

202, *Siegesmund Freudenthal,* N. C. O. 12th Dec. 1810—16th Feb. 1811..lieut. 27th March 1813. (H. 1805, B. 1807, P. 1809-10-11-12-13, S. F. 1813-14, N. 1814, W. & C. 1815.) B. W. M. captain by br. r. l. at Kirchboitzen, amt Rethem on the Aller, in Han.

QUARTERMASTER.

203, *Henry Cohrs,* N. C. O. 20th—31st Dec. 1811. (H. 1805, B. 1807, P. 1809-10-11-12-13, S. F. 1813-14, N. 1814, W. & C. 1815.) B. W. M. at Burgwedel in Han.

SURGEON.

204, *Frederick Fiorillo,* M. D. 12th—29th Dec. 1807. (P. 1809-10-11-12-13, S. F. 1813-14, N. 1814, W. & C. 1815.) B. W. M. † at Hanover 31st March 1817, surgeon Han. hussar guards.

ASSISTANT SURGEON.

*205, *Frederick Deppe,* 6th Dec. 1805, (B. 1807-8, P. 1808-9-10-11-12-13, S. F. 1813-14, N. 1814, W. & C. 1815.) B. W. M. surgeon by br. h. p. at Gestorf, amt Calenberg, in Han.

206, *Henry Gehse,* M. D. 3d—17th March, 1812, (P. 1813, S. F. 1813-14, N. 1814, W. & C. 1815.) B. W. M. Surgeon by br. r. l. at Grossen Aschersleben, near Halberstadt, Prussia.

VETERINARY SURGEON.

207, *Thomas Power,* 20th July—6th Aug. 1811..(P. 1812-13, S. F. 1813-14, N. 1814, W. & C. 1815.)—B. W. M.

SECOND HUSSARS.

" Peninsula, Barossa."

COLONEL COMMANDANT.

208, *Victor von Alten,* ¶ 15th Nov. 1803—21st April 1804.. major-general 25th July 1810, (H. 1805, B. 1807, S. 1809, P. 1811-12-13, N. 1814, W. & C. 1815.) severely wounded, 22d July 1812, at Salamanca, B. G. M. 1. Salamanca, Vittoria, H. G. O. 2.—B. W. M. † at Osnabrück, 23d Aug. 1820, a lieut.-general H. S. and colonel commanding 2d regiment of hussars.

LIEUTENANT COLONEL.

209, *Augustus Henry von Linsingen*, ¶ 5th Oct. 1803—5th
Jan. 1805..lieut.-col. 4th June 1813, (H. 1805, B. 1807-
8, P. 1808-9, N. 1814, C. 1815.) † at Verden, 12th
Dec. 1817..col. H. S. commanding Cumberland hussars.

MAJORS.

*210, *Werner von dem Bussche*, ¶ 9th Nov. 1803—21st March
1804. (H. 1805, B. 1807, S. 1809, P. 1810-11-12-13,
N. 1814, C. 1815.) H. G. O. 2.—H. W. C. major-gen.
H. S. and commandant at Osnabrück.

211, *William Aly*, ¶ 15th—16th June 1804. (H. 1805, B.
1807, P. 1809-10-11-12-13, S. F. 1813-14, N. 1814,
C. 1815.) slightly wounded, 9th Oct. 1810, at Quinta de
Torre; severely wounded, 18th July, 1812, at Canizal.
H. G. O. 2. † at Osnabrück, 26th March 1833..colonel
Han. 6th dragoons, (lancers.)

CAPTAINS.

212, *George von Donop*, ¶ 1st—5th May 1804, (H. 1805, B.
1807, S. 1809.) at Wübbel, principality of Lippe-Detmold.

213, *John Janssen*, ¶ 22d October 1805..captain 2d August
1810. (H. 1805, B. 1807, S. 1809, P. 1810, N. 1814,
C. 1815.) † at Bergedorf near Hamburg 21st May 1823.

*214, *Urban Cleve*, ¶ 20th—21st Jan. 1806. B. 1807, S. 1809
P. 1810-11-12-13, N. 1814, C. 1815.) H. G. O. 3.—H.
W. C.—Br. H. L. O. 3. br. lieut-col. Han. garde du corps.

215, *John Diederich von Düring*, 17th—21st March 1804. (H.
1805, B. 1807, S. 1809, P. 1810-11-12-13, N. 1814,
C. 1815.) H. G. O. 3 † at Osnabrück, 7th May 1832..
br. lieut.-col. Han. 2d hussars.

216, *George Meister*, 30th April—5th May 1804. (H. 1805, B.
1807, S. 1809, P. 1811, C. 1815.) slightly wounded, June
13, 1811 at Los Santos, † at Evensen in Han. 2d Dec. 1820.

*217, *William von Issendorff*, 11th—17th Nov. 1804. (H. 1805,
B. 1807, S. 1809, P. 1811-12-13, N. 1814, C. 1815.)
slightly wounded, 29th Dec. 1811, at la Nava, H. G. O. 3
H. W. C. br. lieut.-col. Han. 2d dragoons.

*218, *Theodore von Stoltzenberg*, 5th April 1806. (B. 1807,
S. 1809. P. 1811-12-13, N. 1814, C. 1815.) major by br.
h. p. at Lutmersen, amt Neustadt am Rübenberge, in Han.

219, *Anthony von Streeruwitz*, 15th—22d Sept. 1810. . captain
11th Nov.1813. (P. 1810-11-12-13.) at Silberstadt, Miesz,
in Bohemia.

220, *Lewis Koch*, N. C. O. 14th—17th May 1806. (H. 1805,
B. 1807, S. 1809, P. 1810-11-12-13, N. 1814, C.1815.)
II. G. O. 3. † at Walsrode in Han. 18th July 1833. .
captain Han. 3d hussars.

221, *Augustus Krauchenberg*, N. C. O. 22d August—2d Sept.
1806. (B. 1807, S. 1809, P. 1810-11-12-13, N. 1814,
W. & C. 1815.) B. W. M. † at Celle in Han. 14th April
1818, . . captain Han. 2d hussars.

LIEUTENANTS.

*222, *Daniel Borchers*, N. C. O. 11th July—29th Aug. 1809.
(H. 1805, B. 1807, S. 1809, P. 1811-12-13, N. 1814,
C. 1815.) slightly wounded, 23d June 1811, at Quinta de
Gremezia, H. G. O. 3.—H. W. C. capt. 2d Han. dragoons.

223, *Christoph Fahrenkohl*, N. C. O. 14th—23d Oct. 1810.
(H. 1805, B. 1807, S. 1809, P. 1811, N. 1814, C. 1815.)
† at Brunswick, May 29th 1836.

*224, *Frederick Grahn*, N.C.O. 16th—26th Feb. 1811.(S. 1809,
P. 1810-11-12-13, N. 1814-15.) capt. h. p. at Göttingen.

225, *Charles Wiebold*, N. C. O. 10th—21st May 1811. (P.
1811-12-13, N. 1814, C. 1815.) captain by br. r. l. at
Baden, grand dutchy of Baden.

226, *Frederick Roeders*, N. C. O. 28th July—6th Aug. 1811.
(P. 1812-13, N. 1814, C. 1815.) † at Nienburg, in Han.
19th April, 1822.

227. *Michael Löning*, N. C. O. 30th July,—6th Aug.1811. (P.
1811-12-13, N. 1814, C.1815.) at Manheim, grand dutchy
of Baden.

228, *Moritz von Thümmel*, 8th—17th Sept. 1811. (P. 1811-12-
13, N. 1814, C. 1815.) slightly wounded, 16th March 1812,
at Merida. II. G. O. 3. . captain by br. r. l. at Amsterdam.

229, *George Siegfried Christian Trefurt*, 28th Sept.—8th Oct.
1811. P. 1811-12-13, N. 1814, C. 1815.) † at Hoya, in
Han. 11th April, 1830.

230, *Lewis von Witte*, N. C. O. 12th—19th March, 1811. (B.
1807, P, 1808-9-10-11-12-13, N. 1814, C. 1815.)
slightly wounded, 13th Jan. 1812, before Cuidad Rodrego,
F. L. H. 5. † at Nienburg, 21st June, 1823. . captain by
br. h. p.

231, *Charles Holmström*, Feb. 28,—March 10, 1812, N. 1814, C. 1815.

CORNETS.

*232, *James Hay*, 12th—24th Nov. 1812. N. 1814, C. 1815. II. G. O. 3, II. W. C. capt. Han. garde du corps, A. D. C. to his royal highness the duke of Cambridge.

233, *Hermann Meyer*, 16th—29th Dec. 1812. (N. 1814, C. 1815.) II. G. O. 3...captain h. p. at Suhlingen in Han.

234, *Maurice Prendergast*, 22d Feb.—9th March, 1813. (N. 1814, C. 1815.

235, *Henry Fricke*, N. C. O. 3d—16th March, 1813. (II. 1805, B. 1807, S. 1809, C. 1815.) † at Markoldendorf near Eimbeck, in Han. 23d April 1820.

*236, *Ernest Soest*, Nov. 27—Dec. 7, 1813. (N. 1814, C.1815.) major by br. r. l. and district commissary at Melle, in Han.

*237, *Hermann Westfeld*, 23d March—9th April, 1814. (N. G.† 1814, N. 1814, C. 1815.) II. W. C...captain Han. 2d dragoons.

*238. *Victor von Alten*, 27th April—10th May 1814. [N. 1814, C. 1815.] captain Han. 2d dragoons. A. D. C. to his majesty the king of Hanover.

239, *Ernest von Bothmer*, 20th Oct.—15th Nov. 1814, at Lüneburg.

*240, *O. Theodore von Marschalck*, 28th July—5th August 1815..lieut. h. p. at Klint, Gericht Hechthausen in Han.

PAYMASTER.

241, *William Mitchell*, 13th—29th Aug. 1812. (P. 1812-13, N. 1814, C. 1815.

ADJUTANT.

*242, *Henry Götz*, N. C. O. 29th March—16th April 1811.. lieut.March 28 1812. (II. 1805, B. 1807, S. 1809, P. 1811-12-13, N. 1814, C. 1815,) capt. h. p. at Weetzen, in Han.

QUARTERMASTER.

243, *George Henry Müller*, N. C. O. 16th July—6th August, 1814. (II. 1805, B. 1807, S. 1809, P. 1810-11-12-13, N. 1814, C. 1815,) † at Osnabrück, 22d Dec. 1820.

ASSISTANT SURGEONS.

*244, *William Holscher*, *M. D.* 19th April 1806. (B. 1807, S. 1809, P. 1810-11-12-13, N. 1814, C. 1815,)—II. W. C. surgeon Han. 11th line battalion.

245, *Joseph Ader*, M.D. May 25—June10, 1809. (P. 1809-10-11-12-13, N. 1814, C. 1815.) † at Hanover, 30th Dec. 1819, assistant-surgeon, Han. rifle-guards.

VETERINARY SURGEON.

*246, *Frederick Eicke*, 2d—13th Jan. 1807, (B. 1807, S. 1809, N. 1814, C. 1815,) at Vahrenwald near Hanover.

THIRD HUSSARS.
"Peninsula, Waterloo, Göhrde,"
COLONEL COMMANDANT.

247, *Frederick Levin August von Arentsschildt*, ¶ 12th Nov. 1803—25th Sept. 1804..col. 4th June 1813. (H. 1805, B. 1807, P. 1809-10-11-12-13, S. F. 1813-14, N. 1814, W. & C. 1815.) B. G. C. 1. Talavera, Fuentes de Onoro, Salamanca, Vittoria, Toulouse. B. B. O. 2.—H. G. O. 2.—P. T. S. 2.—R. St. A. O. 2.—N. W. O. 3.—B. W. M. † at Nordheim, in Han. 10th Dec. 1820..major-general H. S. and col. commanding 3d hussars.

LIEUTENANT-COLONEL.

248, *Charles von Maydell*, ¶ 1st Oct. 1803—24th Aug. 1804.. lieut.-col. 26th April 1813. (H. 1805, P. 1812-13, S. F. 1813-14, N. 1814, W. & C. 1815.) very slightly wounded, 23d Oct. 1812, at Venta del Poço, very slightly wounded, 18th June 1815, at Waterloo, B. W. M...at Bourdeaux, in France.

MAJORS.

*249, *George baron Krauchenberg*, ¶ 28th Jan. 1804..lieut.-col. 18th June 1815. (H. 1805, B. 1807, P. 1809-10-11-12-13, S. F. 1813-14, N. G. 1814, N. 1814, W. & C. 1815.) severely wounded, 1st Oct 1810, at the passage of the Mondego; slightly wounded 5th May 1811 at Fuentes de Onoro; slightly wounded, 18th July 1812, at Canizal. B. B. O. 3.—H. G. O. 2.—B. W. M.—H. W. C. major-general H. S. commanding 1st brigade of cavalry.

*250, *Ernest von Linsingen*, ¶ 17th Nov. 1804..major 4th June 1814. (H. 1805, B. 1807, P. 1809-10-11-12-13, N. G.† 1813-14.) slightly wounded, 9th Oct. 1810, at Alcoentre, H. G. O. 2.—H. W. C. major-general H. S. and adjutant-general to the Hanoverian cavalry.

CAPTAINS.

*251, *Frederick baron Poten*, ¶ 16th—24th Jan. 1804. (H.
1805, B. 1807, N. G. † 1813-14.) H. G. O. 3.—Pr. R.
E. 3.—He. D. L. 2.—Pr. I. O.—H. W. C..lieut.-col.
Han. 1st dragoons, and A. D. C. to his majesty the king
of Hanover.

*252, *Charles Bremer*, ¶ 20th—24th Dec. 1805. (B. 1807-8
P. 1808-9, N. G. 1813-14, N. 1814-15.) H. G. O. 3.—
H. W. C.. lieut.-col. Han. 3d dragoons.

*253, *Quintus von Goeben*, ¶ 24th Dec. 1805. (B. 1807-8, P.
1808-9, N. G. 1813-14, N. 1814, W. & C. 1815.)
slightly wounded, 18th June 1815, at Waterloo, H. G. O. 3,
—H. W. C.- B. W. M. br lieut.-col. Han garde du corps.

*254, *Christian Heise*, 22d—24th December 1805. (B. 1807-
8, P. 1808-9, N. G. 1813-14, N. 1814, W. & C. 1815.)
slightly wounded, 16th September 1813, at the Göhrde,
B. W. M. major by br. r. l. at Hanover.

*255, *William von Schneken*, 10th—17th Nov. 1804. (H.
1805, P. 1812-13, N. 1814. W. & C. 1815.) slightly
wounded, 18th June 1815, at Waterloo, H. G. O. 3.—B.
W. M.—H. W. C. br. lieut.-col Han. garde du corps.

*256, *Ivan Gottlieb Friederich von Hodenberg*, 24th Dec.1805,
(B. 1807, N. G. 1813-14.) lieut.-col. by br. r. l. at
Linden near Hanover.

257, *Augustus von Harling*, N. C. O. 6th Feb.—5th April
1806, (B. 1807-8, P. 1808-9, N.G. 1813-14, N. 1814,
W. & C. 1815.) B. W. M. major by br. r. l. at Lohnde,
amt Burgwedel, in Han.

*258, *George Meyer*, N. C. O. 7th—8th Feb. 1806. (B. 1807-
8, P. 1808-9, N G. 1813-14, N. 1814, W. & C. 1815.)
H. G. O. 3.—B. W. M.—H. W. C. br. major Han. 3d
dragoons.

*259, *William von der Hellen*, N. C. O. 6th—14th Oct. 1806.
(B. 1807-8, P. 1808-9, N. G. 1813-14, N. 1814, W. &
C. 1815.) B. W. M. at Wellen near Beverstedt, in Han.

260, *Gustavus Meyer*, N. C. O. 8th—20th June 1807. (B.
1807-8, P. 1808-9, N. G. 1813-14, N. 1814.) major by
br. h. p. at Moringen in Han.

261, *Francis Power*, N. C. O. 30th April—7th May 1808
(B. 1807, P. 1808-9, N. G. 1813-14, N. 1814, W. & C
1815.) B. W. M..major unatt. British service.

262, *Heinrich Eberhard Friedrichs*, N. C. O. 26th Nov.—2d
Dec. 1809, (N. G. 1813-14, N. 1814, W. & C. 1815.)
B. W. M. † at Hildesheim in Han. 25th April 1820..
captain Han. cuirassier guards.

LIEUTENANTS.

*263, *Frederick Nanne*, N. C. O. 31st May—2d June 1810,
(N. G. 1813-14, N. 1814, W. & C. 1815.) B. W. M.—
H. W. C. captain Han. 1st dragoons.

*264, *Henry von Humboldt*, 9th—16th Oct.1810,(N. G. 1813-
14,N.1814,W.& C. 1815.)slightly wounded at the Görde.
R.St.A.O.4.—B.W.M. capt. by br. r. l. at Aschaffenburg.

*265, *Augustus Reinecke*, 25th—30th Oct. 1810, (N. G. 1813-
14, N. 1814, W. & C. 1815.) B. W. M.—H. W. C.
captain Han. 2d dragoons.

266, *Hermann True*, N. C. O. 16th—25th Feb. 1812. (B.
1807-8, P. 1808-9, N. G. 1813-14, N. 1814, W. & C.
1815.) very severely wounded, 18th June 1815, at Waterloo, B. W. M. † at Wannebergen near Verden, in Han.
31st July 1821.

*267, *Christian Oehlkers*, N. C. O. 12th Nov.—1st Dec. 1812.
(B. 1807-8, P. 1808-9, N. G. 1813-14, N. 1814, W.&
C.1815.) slightly wounded, 16th Sept.1813, at the Göhrde;
very severely wounded, 18th June 1815, at Waterloo, H.
G. O. 3.—B. W. M.—R. St. A. O. 4. captain h. p. at
Moringen in Han.

268, *Lewis Krause*, N. C. O. 13th Nov.—1st Dec. 1812, (P.
1808-9, N. G. 1813-14, N. 1814, W. & C. 1815.) B.
W. M. captain h. p. at Nordheim in Han.

269, *Frederick Zimmermann*, 26th Dec. 1812—12th Jan, 1813.
(N. G. 1813-14, N. 1814, W. & C. 1815.) B. W. M. at
Strasburg.

270, *Eberhard Gerstlacher*, 4th—16th March 1813. (N. G.
1813-14, N. 1814, W. &. C. 1815.) B. W. M. captain
by br. r. l. at Carlsruhe.

*271, *Anthony Frederick Hoyer*, 22d—30th March 1813.
(N.G. 1813-14, N.1814,W. & C. 1815.) slightly wounded,
18th June 1815, at Waterloo. B. W. M.—H. W. C..
captain Han. 3d dragoons.

272, *Frederick du Fresnoy*, 15th—27th April 1813. (N. G.
1813-14, N. 1814, W. & C. 1815.) B. W. M.

*273, *Philip Volborth*, N. C. O. 6th—21st August 1813. (B. 1807-8, P. 1808-9, N. G. 1813-14, N. 1814-15.) at Niedersachswerfen, Harzstein, in Han.

CORNETS.

*274, *Alexander von Hammerstein*, 9th—23d Oct. 1813. (N. G. 1813-14, N. 1814, W. & C. 1815.) B. W. M.—H. W. C. capt. Han. 3d dragoons, and adjt. 2d cavalry brigade

*275, *Rudolphus Friedrichs*, 10th—23d Oct. 1813. (N. G. 1813-14, N. 1814, W. & C. 1815.) B. W. M.—H. W. C. captain Han. 3d dragoons.

*276, *Conrad von Dassel*, 22d Oct.—9th Nov. 1813. (N. G. 1813-14, N. 1814, W. & C. 1815.) severely wounded, 18th June 1815, at Waterloo, H. G. O. 3.—B. W. M.—H. W. C. lieut. Han. 3d dragoons.

*277, *Charles von der Hellen*, 28th Nov. 7th Dec. 1813. .lieut. r. l. † at Wellen near Beverstedt in Han.2d Ap. 1837.lieut.h.p.

278, *Augustus von Hodenberg*, 30th Nov.—7th Dec. 1813, (N. G. 1813-14, W. & C. 1815.) B. W. M. † at Wiedenhausen amt Ahlden, in Han. captain by br. r. l.

*279, *Hons von Hodenberg*, 1st—7th Dec. 1813, (N. G. 1813-14, W. & C. 1815.) severely wounded, 18th June 1815, at Waterloo, B. W. M. captain by br. h. p. at Wathlingen, in Han.

280, *Ernest von der Decken*, 27th Dec. 1813—8th Jan. 1814, (N. 1814, W. & C. 1815.) B. W. M.—He. D. L. 2.—Pr. I. O. stallmaster at Hanover.

*281, *Julius Meyer*, 5th—.7th May 1814. .lieut. and quartermaster Han. 3d dragoons.

*282, *Charles D. Urban O. F. Cleve*, 9th—22d July 1815, (C. 1815.) H. W. M. captain by br. r. l. at Diekhorst in Han.

*283, *Charles Frederich Deichmann*, 23d Oct.—4th Nov. 1815 . .lieut. Han. 3d dragoons.

284, *Jacob Frederick Charles von Karsseboom*, N. C. O., 30th Oct.—21st Nov. 1815. [W. & C. 1815.] B. W. M. † at Baden, near Rastadt 28th March 1829. .lieut. Han. hussarguards.

PAYMASTER.

285, *John William Wieler*, 20th Aug.—15th Oct. 1811, (N. G. 1813-14, N. 1814, W. & C. 1815.) B. W. ... major by br. r. l. at Augustenburg in Holstein.

ADJUTANT.

286, *Henry Brandis*, N. C. O. 31st July—5th Aug. 1815.. cornet 31st July 1815, (H. 1805, B. 1807, P. 1809-10-11-12-13, S. F. 1813-14, N. 1814, W. & C. 1815.) B. W. M. † at Nordheim in Han. 31st Oct. 1825..lieut. and adjutant Han. 3d hussars.

QUARTERMASTER.

287, *William Hoppe*, N. C. O. 4th—13th Jan. 1810. (B, 1807) 8, P. 1808-9, N. G. 1813-14, N. 1814, W. & C. 1815. B. W. M. † at Dörverden, near Verden, in Han. 24th Jan. 1834.

SURGEONS.

288, *George Ripking*, 25th Nov. 1805. (B. 1807-8. P. 1808-9, N. G. 1813-14, N. 1814, W. & C. 1815.) H. G. O. 3.— B. W. M. † at Celle, 21st October 1824,..surgeon h. p.

ASSISTANT SURGEONS.

289, *Gerhard Lewis Wahl*, 25th Nov.—16th Dec. 1805. (B. 1807-8, P. 1808-9, N. G. 1813-14.) † at Bovenden, near Göttingen, 6th Dec. 1827, asst.-surgeon r. l.

290, *Lewis Bauermeister*, 7th Sept. 1813. (N. G. 1813-14, N. 1814, W. & C. 1815.) B. W. M. at Hamburg.

VETERINARY SURGEON.

291, *Frederick Eidmann*, N. C. O. 12th July 1806. (B. 1807-8, P. 1808-9, N.G. 1813-14, N. 1814, C. 1815, at Bremen.

FIRST LIGHT BATTALION.

"Peninsula, Waterloo, Venta del Poço."

COLONEL COMMANDANT.

*292, *Charles count Alten*, ¶ 16th—17th Nov. 1803..major-general 25th July 1810. (H. 1805, B. 1807-8, P. 1808-9-10-11-12-13, S. 1809, S. F. 1813-14, N. 1814, W. & C. 1815.) very severely wounded, 18th June 1815, at Waterloo, B. G. C. 1. 2. 3. Albuera, Salamanca, Vittoria, Nivelle, Nive, Orthes, Toulouse. B. B. O. 1,—R. A. N. O.—R. St. A. O. 1.—Pr. R. E. 1.—F. L. H. 2.—P. T. S. 2.—N. W. O. 3.—B. W. M.—H. G. O. 1.—A. S. St. 1. H. W. C. general H. S. Inspector-general of the Hanoverian forces, and minister at war.

LIEUTENANT COLONEL.

293, *Frederick William von Hartwig*, ¶ 13th Oct. 1803—21st January 1806, lieut. colonel 21st June 1813. (B. 1807-8, S. 1809, P. 1811-12-13, S. F. 1813-14, N. 1814, W. & C. 1815,) slightly wounded, 16th May 1811, at Albuera. B. G. M. 1. Albuera, Nive. B. B. O. 3.—H. G. O. 3.—B. W. M. † at Hameln, 16th Nov. 1822.

MAJORS.

* 294, *Hans von dem Bussche*, ¶ 20th Oct.—17 Nov. 1803, lieut. colonel 18th June 1815, (H. 1805, B. 1807-8, P. 1808-9-10-11-12-13, S. F. 1813-14, N. 1814, W. & C. 1815,) severely wounded (arm amputated), 18th June 1815, at Waterloo. B. G. M. Busaco.—B. B. O. 3.—H. G. O. 2—B. W. M.—H. W. C. major general and adjutant general H. S.

* 295, *Henry Dammers*, ¶ 14th—15th Sept. 1804, major 4th Jan. 1814, (H. 1805, B. 1807, M. 1808-9-10-11-12-13-14, N. 1814-15,) H. W. C. Lr. colonel h. p. and commandant at Nienburg.

CAPTAINS.

* 296, *Henry Frederick Hülsemann*, ¶ 12th—17th Nov. 1803, major 18th June 1815, (H. 1805, B. 1807-8, P. 1808-9-11-12-13, S. 1809, S. F. 1813-14, N. 1814, W. & C. 1815) severely wounded, 22nd July 1812, at Salamanca ; slightly wounded 7th Oct. 1813 on the Bidassoa ; severely wounded 14th April 1814, before Bayonne. H. G. O. 3.—B. W. M. H. W. C. lieut. colonel h. p. commandant at Lingen, in Han.

* 297, *George Lewis Rudorf*, ¶ 16th—17th Nov. 1803, major 18th June 1815, (H. 1805, B. 1807- 8, P. 1808-9-11-12-13 S. 1809, S. F. 1813-14, N. 1814, W. & C. 1815,) slightly wounded, 16th May 1811, at Albuera. H. G. O. 3—B. W. M. lieut. colonel Han. 2d light battalion, † 25th Dec. 1836 at Eimbeck, in Han.

* 298, *Frederick von Gilsa*, ¶ 19th—22d Dec. 1804. (H. 1805, B. 1807-8, P. 1808-9-11-12-13, S. 1809, S. F. 1813,-14,

N. 1814, W. & C. 1815) very severely wounded, 18th June 1815, at Waterloo. H. G. O. 3—B. W. M. –H. W. C. br. lieut-colonel h. p... commandant at Eimbeck.

*299, *Christian Wyneken*, 20th Dec. 1803. (H. 1805, B. 1807-8, P. 1808-9-11-12-13. S. 1809, S. F. 1813-14, N. 1814, W. & C. 1815) slightly wounded, 25th June 1813, at Toloza ; slightly wounded 14th April 1814, before Bayonne ; slightly wounded. 18th June 1815, at Waterloo.—H. G. O. 3 B. W. M.—H. W. C.—lieut. colonel Han. land dragoons.

*300, *Gustavus von Marschalck*. 5th Jan. 1805 (H. 1805, B. 1807-8, P. 1808-9-11-12-13, S. 1809, S. F. 1813, N. G.† 1814, N. 1814, W. & C. 1815.) H. G. O. 3—B. W. M.— H. W. C. lieut. colonel Han. 7th line battalion.

301, *Frederick Ludewig von Both*, 26th—28th Jan. 1806. (B. 1807-8, P. 1808-9-10-11-12-13, S F. 1813-14, N. 1814, W. & C. 1815.) H. G. O. 3.—B. W. M. † at Hanover, 9th June 1806, captain Han. rifle guards,

302, *George Ferdinand Schaedtler*, N. C. O. 20th—28th Nov. 1807. (B. 1807-8, P. 1808-9-11-12-13, S. 1809, S. F. 1814, N. 1814, W. & C. 1815.) B. W. M. † at Niewport, in Flanders, 27th Sept. 1826.

* 303, *Augustus Wahrendorf*, 17th—25th July 1809. (S. 1809, P. 1811-12-13, S. F. 1813-14, N. 1814, W. & C 1815.) severely wounded, 24th June 1813, at Villafranca ; severely wounded, 7th Oct. 1813, on the Bidassoa ; slightly wounded, 18th June 1815, at Waterloo, H. G. O. 3.—B. W. M.— H. W. C. captain Han. 4th line Battalion.

304, *Frederick von Hartwig*, N. C. O. 28th Sept.—17th Oct. 1809, (S. 1809, P. 1811-12-13, S. F. 1813-14, N. 1814, W.&C. 1815)severely wounded, 16th May 1811, at Albuera ; severely wounded, 22d July 1812, at Salamanca. B. W. M. captain h. p. at Egestorff, Amt Wennigsen, in Han.

* 305, *Christoph Heise*, 5th—14th April 1810, (P. 1811-12-13, S. F. 1813-14, N. 1814, W. & C. 1815) slightly wounded, 25th June 1813, at Toloza ; severely wounded, 18th June 1815, at Waterloo. H. G O. 3.—B W. M.—H. W. C. captain Han. rifle guards.

LIEUTENANTS.

*306, *George Breymann*, N. C. O. 19th Jan.—16th Feb. 1811,
(P. 1811-12-13, S. F. 1813-14, N. 1814, W. & C. 1815,)
B. W. M... captain by br. h. p. at Osterode in Han.

* 307, *William von Heugel*, 30th Oct.—5th Nov. 1811, (P. 1813,
N. G.† 1814, N. 1814, W. & C. 1815,) severely wounded
(arm amputated) 25th June 1813, at Tolozn. H. G. O. 3—
B. W. M. major by br. r. l. at Kentschkau near Breslau in
Silesia.

* 308, *John Baumgarten*, N. C. O. 29th Feb —10th March 1812
(H. 1805, B. 1807-8. P. 1808-9-11-12-13. S. 1809, S. F.
1813-14, N. 1814, W. & C. 1815,) B. W. M. captain by
br. r. l. at Lübeck.

309 *Charles Kessler*, N. C. O. 30th March—7th April 1812, (S.
F. 1813-14, N. 1814, W. & C. 1815,) B. W. M. captain
h. p. H. S.

* 30, *Ernest Frederick Adolphus Koester*, 9th—19th May 1812,
(N. G. 1813-14, N. 1814, W. & C. 1815,) slightly wounded
18th June 1815, at Waterloo. B. W. M.—H. W. C. captain
Han. 6th line battalion.

311, *Nicholas de Miniussir*, 12th—26th May 1812, (P. 1812-13,
S. F. 1813-14, W. & C. 1815,) slightly wounded, 18th June
1815, at Waterloo, (did duty with the Spanish Army) B. W.
M. colonel in the spanish service.

* 312, *Harry Leonhart*, 13th—26th May 1812, (N. G. 1813-14,
N. 1814, W. & C. 1815,) severely wounded, 18th June 1815,
at Waterloo. B. W. M.—H. W. C. captain Han. 2nd light
battalion.. adjutant to the 1st division of infantry.

313, *Edgar Gibson*, 5th—15th Dec. 1812. (S. F. 1813-14, N. 1814
W. & C. 1815,) slightly wounded, 7th Oct. 1813, on the
Bidassoa ; slightly wounded, 18th June 1815, at Waterloo.
B. W. M. captain 52d light Infantry, British service.

314, *Stephen Macdonald*, 22d—29th Dec. 1812, (N. G. 1813-14,
N. 1814, W. & C. 1815,) slightly wounded, 10th Dec. 1813,
at Sehestedt. B. W. M. captain by br. r. l. at Dover,
England

* 315, *John Frederick Kuntze*. 20th—29th June 1813,(N. G. 1813 N. 1814, W. & C. 1815,) B. W. M. at Ratzeburg, kingdom of Denmark.

316, *John Henderson*, 3d—10th Feb. 1813, (S. F. 1813-14, N. 1814-15,) captain by br. r. l.

ENSIGNS.

317, *William Rubenz*, 7th—21st Aug. 1813, (N. G.† 1814, N. 1814, W. & C. 1815) B. W. M. at Darmstadt.

* 318, *Gustavus Best*. 25th Nov.—7th Dec. 1813, (N. G.† 1813-14 N. 1814, W. & C. 1815,) severely wounded, 16th June 1815, at Quatre-Bras. B. W. M. captain by br. h. p. at Hanover.

* 319, *Lewis von Reden*, 26th Nov.—7th Dec. 1813, (N. 1814, W. & C. 1815,) B. W. M, lieutenant r. l. at Winsen on the Aller, in Han.

* 320, *Adolphus Augustus von Gentzkow*, 27th Nov.—7th Dec. 1813, (N. 1814, W. & C. 1815,) slightly wounded, 18th June, 1815, at Waterloo. B. W. M.—H. W, C. captain Han. rifle guards.

321, *Frederick Heise*, 29th Jan.—1st March 1814, (N. 1814, W. & C. 1815,) B. W. M. died at Langenhagen near Hanover, 12th March 1822.

322, *Charles Behne*, 6th—17th May 1814, (N. 1814, W. & C. 1815,) slightly wounded, 18th June 1815, at Waterloo. B. W. M. lieutenant by br. r. l. Dr. of laws, and advocate, at Diepholtz in Han.

*323, *Otto von Marschalck*, 16th—31st May 1814,(N. 1814, W. & C. 1815,) B. W. M. lieutenant r. l. at Hechthausen, in Han.

*324, *Adolphus Heise*, 28th May—5th July 1814, (N. 1814, W. & C. 1815,) slightly wounded, 18th June 1815, at Waterloo. B. W. M. Dr. of laws, and advocate, at Hoya, in Han.

ⁿ25, *A. Lewis von Hartwig*, 12th—29th April 1815, lieutenant Han. 10th line battalion.

* 326, *Charles Martin Adolphus Heckscher*, 20th Aug.—9th Sept. 1815, at Hamburg.

PAYMASTER.

327, *Adolphus Nagle*, 28th April 1804, (H. 1805, B. 1807-8, P. 1808-9-11-12-13, S. 1809, S. F. 1813-14, N. 1814, W. & C. 1815,) B. W. M. † at Hanover, 2rd Feb. 1819, paymaster of Chelsea pensioners on the Continent.

ADJUTANT.

* 328, *William Buhse*, N. C. O. 29th May—3rd June 1815, ensign 29th May 1815, (B. 1807-8, P. 1808-9-11-12-13, S. 1809, S. F. 1813-14, N. 1814, W. & C. 1815,) severely wounded, 7th Oct. 1813, on the Bidassoa. H. G. O. 3.— B. W. M.—H. W. C. captain and quartermaster Han. rifle guards.

QUARTERMASTER.

329, *John Christoph Rudolph Hüpeden*, N. C. O. 19th—23rd June 1810, (B. 1808, P. 1811-12-13, S. F. 1813-14, N. 1814, W. & C. 1815,) B. W. M. † at Hanover 5th May 1817, lieutenant and quartermaster Han. rifle guards.

SURGEON.

330, *John Grupe*. ¶ 25th Dec. 1805, (B. 1807-8, P. 1808-9-11-12-13, S. 1809, S. F. 1813-14, N. 1814, W. & C. 1815,) B. W. M. † at Hanover 21st Oct. 1833.

ASSISTANT SURGEONS.

331, *Daniel Fehlandt M. D.* 9th Dec. 1805, (B. 1807-8, P. 1808-9-10-11-12-13, S. F. 1813-14, N. 1814, W. & C. 1815,) B. W. M. † at Hanover, 6th March 1829, surgeon Han. hussar guards.

332, *George Henry Düvel,* 12th— 29th Dec. 1807, (B. 1807-8, P. 1808-9-11-12-13, S. 1809, S. F. 1813-14, N. 1814, W. & C. 1815,) B. W. M. † at Uslar in Han. 1st Oct. 1822, assistant surgeon r. l.

SECOND LIGHT BATTALION.

" *Peninsula, Waterloo, Venta del Pogo.*"

COLONEL COMMANDANT.

* 333, *Colin Halkett*, 17th Nov. 1803, major-gen. 4th June 1814. (H. 1805, B. 1808, P. 1808-9-11-12-13, S 1809, S. F. 1813, N. 1814, W & C. 1815,) severely wounded, 18th

June 1815, at Waterloo. B. G. C. Albuera, Salamanca,
Vittoria, Nive. B. B. O. 2.—H. G. O. 1.—P. T. S. 2.—
Ba. M. I. 2.—B. W. M.—N. W. O. 3.—B. W. M. lieut.
general British service—lieutenant general by br. r. l.

LIEUTENANT COLONEL.

334, *David Augustus Louis Martin*, ¶ 17th Jan.—25th May 1805,
(H. 1805, B. 1807-8, P. 1808-9. S. 1809, N. G. 1813-14,
N. 1814-15,) H. G. O. 2.—R. St. W. O. 4.—H. M. † in
Hanover 4th April 1829, major general and adjutant
general H. S.

MAJORS.

*335, *George Baron Baring*, ¶ 10th—17th November 1803, lieut.
colonel 18th January 1815, (H. 1805, B. 1807-8, P. 1808-
9-11-12-13, S. 1809, S. F. 1813-14, N. 1814, W. & C.
1815,) slightly wounded, 16th May 1811, at Albuera. H. G.
O. 2.—B. B. O. 3.—N. W. O. 3.—B. W. M.—H. W. C.
major general H. S. commanding 1st brigade of infantry,
and commandant at Hanover.

* 336, *Ernest von Düring*, ¶ 14th—17th November 1803, major,
30th Sept. 1813 (H. 1805, B. 1807-8, P. 1808-9, S. 1809,
N. G.† 1813-14, N. 1814-15,) slightly wounded, 25th Aug.
1807, before Copenhagen. H. G. O. 3.—Pr. M. O. M.—
H. W. C. major general H. S. commanding 2nd brigade of
infantry.

CAPTAINS.

337, *Augustus Heise*, 3d Sept. 1803, King's German Regiment—
17th Nov. 1803, King's German Legion,.. lient. colonel 4th
Dec. 1815, (H. 1805, B. 1807-8, P. 1808-9-11-12-13, S.
1809, S. F. 1813-14, N. 1814, W. & C. 1815,) severely
wounded, 9th Dec. 1813, at Cambo on the Nive. B. G. M.
1. 2. Pyrenees, Nivelle, Nive.—B. B. O. 3.—H. G. O. 3.—
B. W. M. † at Tübingen in Würtemberg, 1st Aug. 1819,
lieut. colonel H. S. on the Staff.

338, *George Haasmann*, 11th—17th Nov. 1803, (H. 1805, B.
1807-8, P. 1808-9-10-11-12-13, S. F. 1813-14, N. 1814,
W. & C. 1815,) slightly wounded, 22nd July 1812, at
Salamanca, B. W. M.

* 339, *William Stolle*, ¶ 21st—23rd April 1805. (H. 1805, B. 1807-8, P. 1808-9-10-11-12-13, S. F. 1813-14, N. 1814, W. & C. 1815,) severely wounded, 27th Sept. 1810, at Busaco. B. W. M.—H. W. C. br. lieut. colonel h. p. commandant at Emden.

* 340, *Ernest Augustus Holtzermann*, 21st—24th January 1804, (H. 1805, B. 1807-8, P. 1808-9-11-12-13, S. 1809, S. F. 1813-14, N. 1814, W & C. 1815,) slightly wounded, 18th June 1815, at Waterloo. H. G. O 3.—B. W. M.—H. W. C. lieut. colonel Han. 2nd line battalion.

341, *Alexander Home*, N. C. O. 3rd—4th Feb. 1806. (H. 1805, B. 1807-8, P. 1808-9-11-12, S. 1809, N. G.† 1814, N. 1814, W. &. C. 1815,) B. W. M. † at Hanover, 12th Oct. 1821, captain Han. rifle guards.

342, *Frederick Theodore Kessler*, N. C. O. 7th—13th May 1809, (B. 1807, S. 1809, P. 1811-12-13, S. F. 1813-14, N. 1814 W. & C. 1815,) slightly wounded, 24th June 1813, at Villa-franca ; slightly wounded, 18th June 1815, at Waterloo.— H. G. O. 3.—B. W. M. † at Hanover, 28th January 1833, major by br. h. p.

343, *George Meyer*, 18th—25th July 1809, (S. 1809, P. 1811-12-13, S. F. 1813, N. G.† 1814, N. 1814, W. & C. 1815,) severely wounded, 9th Dec. 1813, before Bayonne ; slightly wounded, 18th June 1815, at Waterloo. B. W. M. † at Otterndorf, in Han, 16th March 1832, captain h. p.

* 344, *Charles Meyer*, 19th—25th July 1809, (S. 1809, P. 1811-12-13, N. G.† 1814, N. 1814, W. & C. 1815,) B. W. M. —H. W. C. captain Han. 2nd line battalion.

* 345, *Lewis Behne*, 5th—13th Jan. 1810, (P. 1811-12-13, S. F. 1813-14, N. 1814, C. 1815,) severely wounded, 10th Nov. 1813, at Urugne ; severely wounded, 14th April 1814, before Bayonne. H. G. O. 3. major by br. r. l. at Fallersleben, in Han.

346, *George Richter*, 25th Dec. 1815—16th Feb. 1816. . as captain 1st Ceylon regiment, 22nd July 1813. (C. 1815.) B. W. M. † at Darmstadt, 23rd May 1833, major by br. r. l.

LIEUTENANTS.

347, *Ole Lindam*, N. C. O. 15th—19th May 1810, (P. 1811-12-13, S. F. 1813-14, N. 1814, W. & C. 1815,) severely wounded, 18th June 1815, at Waterloo. H. G. O. 3.—B. W. M. major by br. r. l. in Devonshire, England.

* 348, *Bernhard Riefkugel*, N. C. O. 25th Nov.—30th Dec. 1809 (B. 1807, P. 1808-9-10-11-12-13, S. F. 1813-14, N. 1814 W. & C. 1815,) slightly wounded, 10th November 1813, at Urugue ; severely wounded, 18th June 1815, at Waterloo. H. G. O. 3.—B. W. M.—H. W. C. captain Han. rifle guards.

349, *Marius T. H. Jobin*, N. C. O. 25th—28th Sept. 1810, (P. 1811-12-13, S. F. 1813-14, N. 1814, W. &. C. 1815,) slightly wounded, 27th Feb. 1814, before Bayonne ; slightly wounded, 18th June 1815, at Waterloo. B. W. M. † at Surinam in 1825.

350, *J. Charles Baron Mervede*, 8th—21st May 1811, (P. 1813, S. F. 1813-14, N. 1814, W. & C. 1815,) severely wounded 27th Feb. 1814, before Bayonne ; slightly wounded 7th Oct. 1813, on the Bidassoa. B. W. M...in the Dutch service.

351, *Thomas Carey*, 1st—9th July 1811, (P. 1811-12-13, S. F. 1813-14, N. 1814, W. & C. 1815,) slightly wounded, 18th June 1815, at Waterloo. H. G. O. 3—B. W. M. captain by br. r. l.

252, *Emanuel Biedermann*, 5th—26th November 1811, (N. G. 1813-14, W & C. 1815.) B. W. M. † at Steinhütte near Winterthür in Switzerland, Oct. 17th 1836.

353, *John Frederick von Meuron*, 15th—28th April 1812, (S. F. 1813-14, N. 1814, W. & C. 1815,) B. W. M... in Switzerland.

* 354, *George Drummond Graeme*, 14th—26th May 1812, (P. 1813, S. F. 1813-14, N. 1814, W. & C. 1815,) slightly wounded, 18th June 1815, at Waterloo. H. G. O. 3—B. W. M.—H. W. C. captain Han. grenadier guards.

355, *John Leopold von Ingersleben*, 2d.—11th Sept. 1818. . lieutenant 5th battalion 60th British foot, 31st Oct. 1810, (P. 1813, S. F. 1813-14, N. 1814, W. & C. 1815.) B. W. M. † at Meve, West-Prussia 21st Nov. 1834, captain by br. r. l.

356, *Salomon Earl*, 10th.—20th April 1813, (N. 1814, W. &. C. 1815.) B. W. M.

357, *Alexander Macbean*, 25th April—4th May 1813, (S. F. 1813-14, N. 1814-15,) slightly wounded, 9th Dec. 1813, before Bayonne.

* 358, *Thomas William Döring*, 17th—27th July 1813, (S. F. 1813-14, N. 1814, W. & C. 1815.) B. W. M... captain by br. r l. at Münden, in Han.

ENSIGNS.

359, *Lewis Bolomey*, 26th Sept.—5th. Oct. 1813, (N. 1814, W. & C. 1815.) B. W. M.

360, *Augustus Friedrichs*, 29th Nov.—7th. Dec. 1813, (N. 1814. W. & C. 1815.) B. W. M. † in Hanover, 10th Jan. 1820.

* 361, *George Frank*, 5th—22d Jan. 1814, (N. 1814, W. &. C. 1815,) severely wounded, 18th June 1815, at Waterloo. H. G. O. 3.—B. W. M... captain by. br. h. p. at Liebenburg, in Han.

362, *August Knop*, 14th—29th Jan. 1814, (N. 1814, W. & C. 1815,) B. W. M. slightly wounded, 18th June, 1815, at Waterloo. lieutenant r. l. at Celle.

363, *William Smith*, 8th Feb.—1st March, 1814. (N. 1814, W. & C. 1815.) B. W. M.

364, *Charles von Goedke*, N. C. O 17th—29th March, 1814. (N. G. 1813-14, N. 1814-15,) at Heppenheim, Grand duchy of Hesse Darmstadt.

* 365, *Lewis Baring*, 11th—30th April, 1814. (N. 1814, W. & C. 1815.) B. W. M. lieutenant Han. rifle guards.

366, *Charles Mejer*, 12th July—6th Aug. 1814. (N. 1814, W. & C. 1815,) B. W. M. † at Schöningen, amt Uslar, in Han. 11th June, 1829.

* 367, *George le Bachelle*, 13th—29th April 1815, (C. 1815,) at Holzminden, dutchy of Brunswick.

p 14

* 368, *Augustus Behne*, 26th June—22nd July, 1815, (C. 1815.)
H. G. O. 3. lieutenant by br. r. l. at Neustadt am Ruben-
berge, in Han.

PAYMASTER.

369, *John Knight*, 20th—29th Jan. 1814, (S. F. 1814, N. 1814,
W. &. C. 1815,) B. W. M.

ADJUTANT.

370, *William D. Timmann*, N. C. O. 25th Sept.—5th Oct. 1813,
lieutenant 13th April 1815. (H. 1805, B. 1807-8, P. 1808-
9-11-12-13, S. 1809, S. F. 1813-14, N. 1814, W. &. C.
1815,) severely wounded, 18th June, 1815, at Waterloo.
B. W. M. † at Hamburg in 1818.

QUARTERMASTER.

371, *James Palmer*, 10th—18th Nov. 1809, (P. 1811-12-13, S. F.
1813-14, N. 1814, W. &. C. 1815,) B. W. M. † at
Brompton in England, 12th November, 1831,

SURGEON.

372, *Ernest Nieter*, 3rd May 1804, (H. 1805, S. 1809, P. 1811,
N. 1814, C. 1815,) † at Celle 3d March, 1825.

ASSISTANT SURGEONS.

373, *Henry Frederick August Müller*, 9th Dec, 1805, (B. 1807-8,
S. 1809, P. 1808-9-11,N. 1814, W. & C. 1815,) B. W. M.
† at Lüneburg, 5th June, 1819.

374, *Joseph Tholon*, 6th—21st Oct. 1815, C. 1815.

FIRST LINE BATTALION.
" Peninsula.   Waterloo."
COLONEL COMMANDANT.

* *His Royal Highness the Commander in Chief*, (vide No. 1.)

LIEUTENANT COLONEL.

375, *Rudolphus Bodecker*, ¶ 18th Sept.'1803—21st March, 1804,
(H. 1805, M. 1806-7, B. 1807-8, P. 1808-9-10-11-12-13,
S. F. 1813-14, N. 1814, C. 1815,) slightly wounded, 28th
July, 1809, at Talavera, B. G. C. Talavera, Salamanca,
Vittoria, Nive. B. B. O. 3.—H. G. O. 2. † at Emden, 17th
January, 1831, major general H. S. and col. commanding
10th regiment of infantry.

MAJORS.

* 376, *William von Robertson*, ¶ 25th Oct. 1803—21st March, 1804 lieut. colonel, 18th June, 1815, (H. 1805, M. 1806-7, B. 1807-8, P. 1808-9-10-11-12-13, S. F. 1813-14, N. 1814, W. & C. 1815,) severely wounded, 18th June, 1815, at Waterloo. B. B. O. 3.—H. G. O. 2.—B. W. M. at Hamburg.

* 377, *Charles von Kronenfeldt*, ¶ 17th—20th Dec. 1803, (H. 1805 B. 1807, M. 1808-9-10-11-12-14-15, P.* 1812-13-14,) H. G. O. 3.—H. W. C. colonel Han. grenadier guards.

CAPTAINS.

* 378, *Lewis von Borstel*, ¶ 17th—21st March 1804, (H. 1805, M. 1806-7, B. 1807-8, P. 1808-9-10-11-12-13, S. F. 1813-14,) severely wounded, 27th Feb. 1814, before Bayonne. H. G; O. 3... major by br. r. l. at Buxtehude, in Han.

379, *George von Düring*, ¶ 18th—21st March, 1804.. major 21st June 1813. (H 1805, M. 1806-7, B. 1807-8, P. 1808-9-10-11-12-13, S. F. 1813-14,) H. G. O. 3. colonel by br. r. l. at Horneburg, in Han.

* 380, *Andreas von Schlütter*, 2d—14th Feb. 1804, (H. 1805, M, 1806-7, B. 1807-8, P. 1808-9-10-11-12, N. G.† 1814, N. 1814, W. & C. 1815,) slightly wounded, 28th July, 1809, at Talavera. H. G. O. 3.—B. W. M... lieut. colonel h. p. at Stade, in Han.

* 381, *Frederick von Goeben*, ¶ 9th—21st Jan. 1806, (N. 1806-7, B. 1807-8, P. 1808-9, N. 1814, W. &. C. 1815,) severely wounded, 28th July, 1809, at Talavera. B. W. M... major by br. r. l. at Otterndorf, in Han.

382, *George von Goeben*, ¶ 17th—21st Jan. 1806, (M. 1806-7, B. 1807-8, P. 1808-9-10-11, N. G.† 1814, N. 1814, W. & C. 1815,) B. W. M... major by br. r. l. at Bremen,

383, *Gerlach von Schlütter*, 8th—14th Feb. 1804, (H. 1805, M. 1806-7, B. 1807-8, P. 1808-9-10-11-12-13, S. F. 1813-14, N. 1814, W. & C. 1815,) very severely wounded, 18th June 1815, at Waterloo. B. W. M. † at Stade, 29th June 1818. major by br. r. l.

* 384, *Leopold von Rettberg*, 14th—15th Sept. 1804, (H. 1805, M. 1806-7, B. 1807-8, P. 1808-9-10-11-12-13, S. F. 1813-14, N. 1814, W. & C. 1815,) severely wounded, 27th Feb. 1814, before Bayonne. H. G. O 3.—B. W. M.—H. W. C... lieut. colonel Han. rifle guards.

* 385 *Ernest von Hodenberg*, 22d—23d April 1805, (H. 1805, M. 1806-7, B. 1807-8, P. 1808-9-10-13, S. F. 1813-14, N. 1814, C. 1815,) severely wounded, 28th July 1809, at Talavera. H. G. O. 3.—H. W. C... lieut. colonel by br. h. p. commandant at Verden.

* 386, *Diederich Lewis von Holle*, 26th—28th Jan. 1806, (M. 1806-7, B. 1807-8, P. 1808-9-10-11-12-13, S. F. 1813-14, N. 1814, W. & C. 1815,) H. G. O. 3.—B. W. M. at Hanover.

* 887, *Ferdinand Christian von Rössing*, 28th Jan. 1806, (M. 1806-7, B. 1807-8, P. 1808-9-10-11-12-13, S. F. 1813-14, N. 1814, W. & C. 1815,) severely wounded, 22d Sept. 1812, before Burgos ; slightly wounded, 31st Aug. 1813, before St. Sebastian. H. G. O. 3.—B. W. M... lieut. colonel by br. r. l. at Rössing near Calenberg, in Han.

LIEUTENANTS

* 388, *Christian Henry von Düring*, 30th May—9th June, 1807, (B. 1808, P. 1808-9-10-11-12-13, S. F. 1813-14, N. 1814, W. & C. 1815,) slightly wounded, 27th Sept. 1810 at Busaco. H. G. O. 3.—B. W. M.—H. W. C... captain Han. 6th line battalion.

*389, *Ludolph Kumme*, N. C. O. 14th—31st Oct. 1807, (M. 1806-7 P. 1808-9-10-11-12-13, S. F. 1813-14, N. 1814, W. & C. 1815.) B. W. M. at Eschede, in Han.

390, *Thomas Allen*, 1st—11th Feb. 1809, (P. 1809-10-11-12-13,) S. F. 1813-14, N. 1814, W. & C. 1815,) slightly wounded, 28th July, 1809, at Talavera. B. W. M. † at Springfield in England, Nov. 1833.

* 391, *Ernest Wilding*, 1st July, 1806.. lieutenant 22d May, 1811, (B. 1807, M. 1808-9-10, P. 1811-12-13, S. F. 1813-14, N. 1814, C. 1815,) severely wounded, 27th Feb. 1814, before Bayonne. H. G. O. 3... major by br. h. p. in Sicily.

* 392, *Charles Lewis Best,* 18th—26th Jan. 1808, (N. G. 1813-14, N. 1814. W. & C. 1815.) B. W. M... captain h. p. at Nienburg in Han.

* 393, *William Schroeder,* 26th Aug.—2d Sept. 1809, (P. 1809-10-11-12-13, S. F. 1813-14, N. 1814-15.) H. W. C.. captain Han. 12th line battalion.

394, *Diederich von Einem,* 7th—19th Sept. 1809, (P. 1810-11-12-13, S. F. 1813-14, N. 1814, W. & C. 1815.) severely wounded, 18th June, 1815, at Waterloo,) B. W. M. at Hanstedt near Zeven in Han.

* 395, *George baron Wichmann,* 20th—28th Sept. 1810, (P. 1811-12-13, S. F. 1813-14, N. 1814, W. & C. 1815,) slightly wounded, 27th Feb. 1314, before Bayonne. H. G. O. 3.—B. W. M.—Be. O. L. 3... lieut. colonel h. p. at Brussels.

* 396, *Charles von Weyhe,* N. C. O. 18th—31st Dec. 1811, (B. 1807, P. 1808-9-13, S. F. 1813-14, W. & C. 1815,) B. W. M.—H. W. C... captain Han. 1st. line battalion.

397, *Conrad William Meyer,* N. C. O. 5th—19th May, 1812, (P. 1812-13, S. F. 1813-14, N. 1814, C. 1815,) † at Bremerlehe, in Han. 26th Sept. 1826.

398, *Benjamin Fellows,* 2d—14th Nov. 1812, (S.F. 1813-14,N. 1814 W. & C. 1815,) B. W. M. † in England, 16th April 1824.

* 399, *William Wolff,* N. C. O. 24th Nov,—8th Dec. 1812, (P. 1811-12-13, S, F, 1813-14, W. & C. 1815,) B. W. M,—H. W. C... captain and quartermaster Han. grenadier guards.

* 400, *Adolphus von Arentsschildt,* 7th—29th Aug. 1812, (N, G. 1813-14, N. 1814, W. & C. 1815,) B, W. M.—H. W. C. captain Han. 5th line battalion.

401, *William Drysdale,* 8th—23d Jan. 1813, (S. F. 1813-14, N, 1814, W. & C. 1815,) slightly wounded, 27th Feb. 1814, before Bayonne, B. W, M. † in London, 13th April 1823,

* 402, *August Müller,* N. C. O. 23d—30th March, 1813, (H. 1805, B. 1807, P. 1809-10-11, N. G.† 1814, N. 1814. W. & C. 1815,) severely wounded, 28th July, 1809, at Talavera ; very severely wounded, 18th June, 1815, at Waterloo. H. G. O. 3.—B. W. M... captain by br. r. l. at Osterholz, in Han.

* 403, *William Best*, 24th April—4th May, 1813, (N. G. 1813, N. 1814, W. & C. 1815,) B. W, M.—H. W. C... captain Han. grenadier guards.

404, *Henry Wilding*, 15th—29th May, 1813, (N. 1814, W, & C. 1815,) severely wounded, 18th June, 1815, at Waterloo. B. W. M. † at Idstein near Frankfort 16th May 1820, lieutenant Han. 3d battalion of guards,

405, *Alexander Carmichel*, 12th—22d Dec. 1812, (S. F. 1813-14, N. 1814, W. & C. 1815.) B. W. M,.. captain 97th British foot.

ENSIGNS,

406, *Francis Leslie*, 31st May—8th June, 1813, (S. F. 1813-14, N. 1814, W. &. C. 1815.) B. W, M. † in England, 27th July, 1831.

407, *Augustus baron le Fort*, 9th—25th Sept. 1813, (N. 1814, W. & C. 1815.) B. W. M. at Wendhof, Grand dutchy of Mecklenburg.

*408, *August von Brandis*, 6th—22d Jan. 1814, (N. 1814, W. & C. 1815.) B. W. M... lieutenant Han. land dragoons.

* 409, *Arnold Wilhelm Heise*, 7th—22d, Jan. 1814, (N. 1814, W. & C. 1815.) B. W. M... captain by br. h. p. at Hameln.

410, *Augustus Frederick Kersting*, 19th Feb.—5th March, 1814, (N. 1814, W. & C. 1815.) B. W. M. in the Brazils.

411, *George ChristophLodemann*, 18th—29th March, 1814, (N. 1814 W. & C. 1815,) B. W. M. † in Hanover, 21st May, 1825, lieutenant and adjutant Han. grenadier guards.

* 412, *Adolphus von Beaulieu*, 21st March—9th April, 1814, (N. 1814, C. 1815,) at Göttingen.

413, *August von Reiche*, 12th—30th April, 1814, (N. 1814, W. & C. 1815,) B. W. M. at Celle.

* 414, *Charles August von der Hellen*, 7th.—17th May, 1814, (N. 1814, W. & C. 1815,) slightly wounded, 18th June, 1815, at Waterloo. B, W. M. at Latzen near Hanover.

415, *Ferdinand von Weddig*, 7th—22d. July, 1815, † in the Brazils, PAYMASTER.

416, *Thomas Teighe*, 8th Sept. 1804, (H. 1805, M. 1806-7, B. 1807-8, P. 1808-9-10-11-12-13, S. F. 1813-14, N. 1814, W. & C. 1815.) B. W. M.

ADJUTANT.

* 417, *Frederick Schnath,* N. C. O, 10th—23d. Sept. 1809. . lieut. 18th March, 1812, (H. 1805, M. 1806-7, B. 1807-8, P. 1808-9-10-11-12-13, S. F. 1813-14, N. 1814, W. & C. 1815,) severely wounded, 18th June, 1815, at Waterloo. B. W. M.. . captain by br. r. l. at Hildesheim.

SURGEON.

418, *Gottlieb Jacob Hieronimus Wetzig,* M. D. 19th April, 1806, B. 1807, M. 1808-9-10-11, P. 1813, S. F. 1813-14, N. 1814, W. & C 1815.) B. W. M. † at Hildesheim, 6th Feb. 1830. . surgeon Han. 3d infantry regiment.

ASSISTANT SURGEONS.

*419, *Frederick Harzig,* M. D. 7th Dec. 1805, (H. 1805, M 1806-7 B. 1807-8, P. 1808-9-10-11-12-13, S. F. 1813-14,) surgeon h. p. in Han.

420, *Philip Langeheineken,* M. D. 31st Jan.—31st Dec, 1811, (P. 1812-13, S. F. 1813-14, N. 1814, W. & C. 1815,) B. W. M. at Rethem on the Aller, in Han.

SECOND LINE BATTALION.

" *Peninsula, Waterloo.*"

COLONEL COMMANDANT.

421, *Adolphus von Barsse,* ¶ 15th Nov. 1803—14th Feb. 1804,. . major general, 25th July, 1810, (H, 1805, M. 1806-7..13-14, B. 1807-8,) † in Hanover, 19th May, 1834,. . lieut. general by br. h. p.

LIEUTENANT COLONEL.

422, *Charles August Aly,* ¶ 19th Oct. 1803—21st Jan. 1806, (H. 1805, B. 1807-8, P. 1808-9-10-11-12, N. 1814, C. 1815,) B. G. M. Fuentes de Onoro. B. B. O. 3.—H. G. O. 3. † at Osterode in Han. 18th March, 1832.

MAJORS.

*423, *George Müller,* ¶ 2d Nov. 1803—5t hMay, 1804. . lieutenant colonel, 18th June 1815, H. 1805, M. 1806-7, B. 1807-8, P. 1808-9-10-11, N. G. 1813-14, N. 1814, W. & C. 1815,) severely wounded, 5th May, 1811, at Fuentes de Onoro, B. G. M.—Talavera—B. B. O. 3.—H. G. O. 2—B. W. M.— H. W. C.. major general by br. h. p.. commandant at Celle.

424, *Gebhardus Timaeus*, ¶ 1st Nov. 1803—23d April, 1805. . major
20th Oct. 1812. (H. 1805, B. 1807, † at Lüneburg, 27th
Jan. 1830.

CAPTAINS.

*425, *William von der Decken*, ¶ 4th—14th Feb. 1804. . major 18th
June, 1815, (H. 1805, M. 1806-7, P, 1808- 9-10-11-12-13,
B. 1807-8, S. F. 1813-14, N. 1814, W. & C. 1815,) severely
wounded, 5th May, 1811 at Fuentes de Onoro, H. G. O. 2.
B. W. M . colonel h, p. in Han.

* 426, *Augustus Hartmann*, ¶ 10th—14th Feb. 1804, (H. 1805, M.
1806-7, B. 1807-8, P. 1808-9-10-11-12, N. G,† 1814, N.
1814, W. & C. 1815,) B, W. M . lieut. colonel h. p. at
Hildesheim.

427. *Frederick Purgold*, ¶ 15th—21st March 1804, (H. 1805, M.
1806-7, P. 1808-9-10-11-12-13, S. F. 1813-14, N. 1814,
W. & C. 1815,) severely wounded, 18th June, 1815, at
Waterloo, B. W. M . lieut. colonel h. p. † at Lüneburg,
March 3d. 1836.

428, *Charles Beurmann*, ¶ 12th Jan.—1st March, 1806, (P. 1808-9-
10-11-12-13, S. F. 1813-14, N. 1814, W. & C. 1815,)
severely wounded, 28th July, 1809, at Talavera ; severely
wounded, 25th June, 1813, at Toloza, B. W. M. † at
Waltzen near Hoya, in Han. 26th Aug. 1817.

429, *Ernest Claus Henry Wyneken*, 12th—14th Feb. 1804, (H.
1805, M. 1806-7, B. 1807-8, P. 1808-9-10-11-12-13, N.
G.† 1814, N. 1814, W. & C. 1815,) severely wounded, 8th
Oct. 1812, before Burgos, H. G. O. 3.—B. W. M. † in
Hanover, 18th Oct. 1818, captain Han. grenadier guards.

* 430, *Frederick von Wenckstern*, 19th—21st April, 1804, (H. 1805
M. 1806-7, B. 1807-8, P. 1808-9-10-11-12-13, S. F. 1813-
14, N. 1814, W. & C. 1815,) slightly wounded 28th July,
1809, at Talavera, H. G. O. 3.—B. W. M.. . major by br. r.
l. at New Strelitz in Mecklenburg. . lieut. col. Mecklenburg
service.

431, *Frederick Elderhorst*, ¶ 14th—28th Nov. 1807, (B. 1808, P.
1808-9-10-11-12-13, S. F. 1813-14, N. 1814-15,) † in
Hanover, 19th June, 1837,. . major by br. r. l.

432, *George Ludewig Julius Heinrich Wolkenhaar*, N. C. O. 22d Dec. 1804. (H. 1805, B. 1807-8, P. 1808-9-10-11-12-13, S. F. 1813-14, N. 1814, W. & C. 1815.) B. W. M. † at Kirchhorst near Hanover 27th July 1818.

433, *Ferdinand Adolphus von Holle*, 19th—20th August 1805. (H. 1805, M. 1806-7, B. 1807-8, P. 1808-9-10-11-12-13, S. F. 1813-14, N. 1814-15.) severely wounded, 28th July 1809, at Talavera; severely wounded 25th June 1813 at Toloza. H. G. O. 3. major by br. r. l. at Hanover.

434, *Claus von der Decken*, 24th—28th Jan. 1806. (M. 1806-7, B. 1807-8, P. 1808-9-10-11-12-13, S. F. 1813-14, N. 1814, W. & C. 1815.) slightly wounded 10th Nov. 1813, at Urugne; slightly wounded, 27th Feb. 1814 before Bayonne; severely wounded, 18th June 1815 at Waterloo, B. W. M. † at Oerichsheil near Stade, 15th Sept. 1834.

LIEUTENANTS.

435, *William Kulemann*, N. C. O. 25th March—4th April 1807. (M. 1806-7, B. 1807-8, P. 1808-9-10-11-12-13, S. F. 1813-14, N. 1814, W. & C. 1815.) B. W. M. captain by br. r. l. at Bevern, near Holzminden, dutchy of Brunswick.

*436, *Godfried Tiensch*, N. C. O. 27th Nov.—5th Dec. 1807. [H. 1805, M. 1806-7, B. 1807-8, P. 1808-9-10-11-12-13, S. F. 1813-14, N. 1814, W. & C. 1815.] slightly wounded, 28th July 1809, at Talavera, B. W. M. captain by br. r. l. at Hoya in Han.

437, *Ernest August Jonas Fleisch*, 28th Nov.—5th Dec. 1807. (H. 1805, M. 1806-7, B. 1807-8, P. 1808-9-10-11-12-13, S. F. 1813-14, N. 1814, W. & C. 1815.) slightly wounded, 14th April 1814, before Bayonne. B. W. M. † at Buxtehude in Han. 21st December 1817.

438, *Augustus Schmidt*, N. C. O. 28th Jan.—2d Feb. 1808. M. 1806-7, B. 1807-8, P. 1808-9-10-11-12-13-14, N. 1815.) slightly wounded, 28th July 1809, at Talavera.

439, *Charles Billeb*, N. C. O. 26th August—3d Sept. 1808. (H. 1805, M. 1806-7, B. 1807-8, P. 1808-9-10-11-12-13-14, N. 1814, W. & C. 1815.) severely wounded, 28th July 1809, at Talavera, B. W. M. captain by br. r. l. at Göttingen.

Q 16

440, *George Meyer*, N. C. O. 5th—19th Sept. 1809, (H. 1806, M. 1806-7, B. 1807-8, P. 1808-9-10-11-12-13, S. F. 1813-14, N. 1814, W. & C. 1815.) B. W. M at Hohne amt Bedenbostel in Han.

441, *August Kathmann*, N. C. O. 12th—22d Oct. 1811, (P. 1813, S. F. 1813-14, N. 1814, W. & C. 1815.) B. W. M. † at Soltau in Han. 10th June 1827.

442, *George Frederick Paschal*, 17th—31st March 1812. (S. F. 1813-14, N. 1814, W. & C. 1815,) B. W. M. captain h. p. unattached, British service.

443, *Adolphus Kessler*, N. C. O. 31st March—7th April 1812. (S. F. 1813-14, N. 1814, W. & C. 1815.) B. W. M. † at Hanover 4th May 1825, lieut. Han. grenadier guards.

444, *William Dawson*, 6th—19th May 1812. (P. 1813, S. F. 1813-14, N. 1814, W. & C. 1815.) B. W. M.

445, *Alexander Patterson*, 25th July—4th Aug. 1812. (S. F. 1813-14, N. 1814-15.)

446, *James Hamilton*, 26th July—4th Aug. 1812. (P. 1813, S. F. 1813-14, N. 1814, W. & C. 1815.) B. W. M.

447, *Patrick Gairdner*, 27th July—4th August 1812, (S. F. 1813-14, N. 1814, W. & C. 1815.) B. W. M.

448, *Carl Fischer*, N. C. O. 10th—22d Dec. 1812. (P. 1808-9-10-11-12-13, S. F. 1813-14, N. 1814, W. & C. 1815.) severely wounded, 18th June 1815, at Waterloo, B. W. M. † at Hamburg 23d March 1818.

449, *Francis La Roche*, 23d—29th Dec. 1812, (S. F. 1813-14, N. 1814, W. & C. 1815.) slightly wounded, 18th June 1815, at Waterloo. B. W. M. in Switzerland.

450 *George Fabricius*, N. C. O. 12th—23d Nov. 1813. N. G.† 1814, N. 1814-15.

451, *George Lowson*, 15th—23d Nov. 1813.(N. 1814, W. & C. 1815.) B. W. M. † in London, May 28 1836.

452, *Augustus Ferdinand Ziel*, 14th—29th January 1814. (N. 1814, W. & C. 1815.) slightly wounded, 18th June 1815 at Waterloo,...at Göttingen.

*453, *Lewis Henry von Sichart*, 15th Feb.—5th March 1814, [N. 1814, W. & C. 1815.] B. W. M. captain Han. 4th line battalion,..on the staff.

ENSIGNS.

*454, *Charles Lewis von Sichart*, 16th Feb.—5th March 1814, [N.1814, W.&C. 1815.] B.W.M. lieut. h.p. at Hildesheim.

455, *Adolphus Lynch*, 1st—12th April 1814. [N. 1814, W. & C. 1815.] B. W. M. ensign 63d British infantry.

*456, *Frederick Diestelhorst*, N. C. O. 14th—30th April 1814, [H. 1805, B. 1807-8, P. 1808-9-11-12-13, S. 1809, S. F. 1813-14, N. 1814, W. & C. 1815.] severely wounded, 7th Oct. 1813, on the Bidassoa; severely wounded, 14th April 1814, before Bayonne, B. W. M..lieut. by br. r. l. at Wagenfeld, amt Diepholz, in Han.

*457, *Gustavus Hartmann*, 8th—17th May 1814, [N. 1814, W. & C. 1815.] B.W.M. lieut. by br. r.l. at Rethem, amt Han.

*458, *Henry Bergmann*, 17th—31st May 1814, [N. 1814, W. & C. 1815.] B. W. M. ensign r. l. at Hanover.

*459, *Henry Garvens*, 24th—31st May 1814, [N. 1814, W. & C. 1815.] B. W. M. lieut. h. p. at Steyerberg in Han.

*460, *Thilo von Uslar*, 29th May—5th July 1814, [N. 1814, W. & C. 1815.) B. W. M. lieut. Han. 1st line battalion.

461, *August Lüning*, 17th June—9th July 1814. [N. 1814, W. & C. 1815.] B. W. M. at Neuhaus on the Oste in Han.

462, *Ferdinand von Lasperg*, 28th May—3d June 1815.. ensign r. l. at Dissen, amt Iburg, in Han.

*463, *David Brauns*, 13th—29th Aug. 1815, [C. 1815.] at Brunswick.

PAYMASTER.

464, *Thomas Small*, 8th—17th Sept. 1814, [N. 1814, W. & C. 1815.] B. W. M. † at Brompton, 28th April 1837.

ADJUTANT.

*465, *Adolphus Hesse*, N. C. O. 30th Nov.—5th Dec. 1807.. lieut. 17th March 1812. (B. 1807-8, P. 1808-9-10-11-12-13, S. F. 1813-14, N. 1814, W. & C. 1815.) severely wounded, 18th Oct. 1812, at Burgos; severely wounded, 7th Oct. 1813, on the Bidassoa. H. G. O. 3.—B. W. M.— H. W. C. captain Han. rifle-guards.

QUARTERMASTER.

466, *John Schilvester*, 21st March 1801, (H. 1805, M. 1806-7,
B. 1808, P. 1808-9-10-11-12-13, S. F. 1813-14, N.
1814, W. & C. 1815.) B. W. M. † at Homburg on the
Ohm, 14th February 1830.

SURGEON.

*467, *Charles Thompson*, M. D. ¶ 3d Sept. 1805, (H. 1805,
M. 1806-7, B. 1807-8, P. 1808-9-10-11-12-13, S. F.
1813-14, N. 1814, W. & C. 1815.) H. G. O. 3—B. W.
M—H. W. C..staff surgeon Han. rifle guards.

ASSISTANT SURGEON.

*468, *Henry Rathje*, M. D. 7th December 1805, (M. 1806-7,
B. 1807-8, P. 1808-9-10-11-12-13, S. F. 1813-14, N.
1814, W. & C. 1815.) B. W. M..surgeon h. p. at Celle.

THIRD LINE BATTALION.

" Waterloo."

COLONEL COMMANDANT.

469, *Henry von Hinüber*, ¶ 9th—17th Nov. 1803..major-
general 4th June, 1811, (H. 1805, B. 1807, M..1808-9-
10-11-12-13, S. F. 1813-14, N. 1814-15.) B. G. M. Nive.
B. B. O. 2.—H. G. O. 1. † at Frankfort, 2d Dec. 1833,
lieut.-general H. S. comm. 2d. division of infantry.

LIEUTENANT-COLONEL.

470, *Frederick von Wissell*, ¶ 24th May. 1806,..lieut.-colonel
4th June 1813, (B. 1807, M. 1808-9-10-11-12, P. 1813,
S. F. 1813-14, N. 1814, W. & C. 1815.) B. B. O. 3,—
H. G. O. 2.—B. W. M. † at Wiesbaden, grand dutchy of
Nassau, 16th Dec. 1820..br. colonel H. S. comm. 2d
battalion of guards.

MAJORS.

471, *Gottlieb Frederick von Luttermann*, ¶ 19th Oct. 1803—
21st Jan. 1806..lieut.-col. 18th June 1815, (B. 1807-8,
M. 1808-9-10-11-12-13-14, N. 1814, W. & C. 1815.)
B. B. O. 3.—H. G. O. 3.—B. W. M. † at Gelliehausen,
near Göttingen, 15th Sept. 1831.

172, *Anthony Everhard Charles Boden*, ¶ 7th Nov. 1803—
21st Jan. 1806. (B. 1807, M. 1808-9-10-11-12-13-14, N.
1814, W. & C. 1815.) severely wounded, 18th June, 1815,
at Waterloo. B. W. M. † at Göttingen, 19th Feb. 1831.

CAPTAINS.

*173, *George von Hohnhorst*, ¶ 13th—16th June, 1804. (H.
1805, B. 1807, M. 1808-9-10-11-12-13-14, N. 1814,
W. & C. 1815.) B. W. M.—H. W. C...lieut.-col. h. p.
commandant at Lüneburg.

*174, *Lewis von Dreves*, ¶ 12th—24th May, 1806..major,18th
June, 1815. [B. 1807, M. 1808-9-10-11-12-13-14, P*
1812-13, N. 1814, W. & C. 1815.] B. W. M..lieut.-col.
h. p. at Celle.

175, *Augustus Ferdinand David Curren*, ¶ 30th Dec. 1805—
21st January 1806, [B. 1807-8, P. 1808, M. 1809-10-11-
12-13-14, N. 1814, W. & C. 1815.] B. W. M. † at
Emden, 6th March 1830...lieut.-colonel Han. 10th
infantry regt.

176, *Eberhard Magnus Ludewig Lueder*, ¶ 15th—16th June,
1804, [H. 1805, B. 1807, M. 1808-9-10-11-12-13-14,
P.* 1812-13, N. 1814, W. & C. 1815.] B. W. M. † at
Hameln, 19th March, 1816..br. major Han. landwehr
battalion Peine.

477, *Charles Leschen*, ¶ 15th Sept. 1804, [H. 1805, B. 1807,
M. 1808-9-10-11-12-13-14, N. 1814, W. & C. 1815.]
B. W. M. † at Walsrode, in Han. 19th Feb. 1820.

478, *William Carl Heinrich von Schleicher*, ¶ 16th—22d Dec.
1804, [H. 1805, B. 1807, M. 1808-9-10-11-12-13-14,
N. 1814, W. & C. 1815.] B. W. M. † at Drebber, amt
Diepholz, in Han. 11th April, 1826.

*479, *Albertus Cordemann*, 13th—16th June 1804, [H. 1805,
B. 1807, M. 1808-9-10-11-12-13-14, N. 1814, W. & C.
1815.] B. W. M..major by br. r. l. at Han.

*480, *Frederick Erdmann*, 21st March, 1804, [H. 1805, B.
1807, M. 1808-9-10-11-12-13-14-15, P.* 1812-13.]..
major by br. r. l. at Nienburg.

*481, *Hans von Uslar*, 2d—5th May, 1804, [II. 1805. B. 1807,
M. 1808-9-10-11-12-13-14, P.* 1812-13, N. 1814, W.
& C. 1815.] H. G. O. 3.—B. W. M.—H. W. C...capt.
Han. 2d. line battalion.

*482, *George Appuhn*, 14th—16th June 1804, [II. 1805, B.
1807, M. 1808-9-10-11-12-13-14, N. 1814, W. & C.
1815.] H. G. O. 3.—B. W. M.—H. W. C. captain
Han. 1st line battalion.

LIEUTENANTS.

*483, *Lewis Pauli*, 15th—16th June 1804, [II. 1805, B. 1807,
M. 1808-9-10-11-12-13-14-15, P.* 1812-13.] H.G.O.3.
S. M. L. 3. lieut.-col. by br. r. 1..consul general at Genoa

*484, *George William Ferdinand von Weyhe*, 23d April 1805,
[B. 1807, M. 1808-9-10-11-12-13-14, N. 1814-15.]..
captain by br. r. 1. at Eimke, near Ebstorf, in Han.

*485, *William Appuhn*, N. C. O. 8th—23d September 1806,
B. 1807, M. 1808-9-10-11-12-13-14, P.* 1812-13, N.
1814-15.]..severely wounded, 12th April 1813, near Biar,
in Spain—H. G. O. 3. † at Hanover, 4th July 1837...
captain Han. rifle guards.

*486, *Charles Brauns*, N. C. O. 4th—19th Sept. 1807, [B. 1807,
M. 1808-9-10-11-12-13-14, N. 1814, W. & C. 1815.]
B. W. M.—H. W. C..captain Han. 2d light battalion.

487, *Christian von Soden*, N. C. O. 30th Oct.—7th Nov. 1807,
(B. 1807, M. 1808-9-10-11-12-13-14, P.* 1812-13, N.
1814, W. & C. 1815.) B. W. M..capt. by br. r. 1. at
Blomberg, Lippe-Detmold.

488, *Lorenz Heise*, N. C. O. 19th—23d July 1808, (II. 1805,
B. 1807, M. 1808-9-10-11-12-13-14, N. 1814, C. 1815.)
at Wustrow, in Han.

489, *Weypart von Laffert*, 1st—2nd June 1810, (M. 1810-11-
12-13-14, N. 1814, W. & C. 1815.) B. W. M. † at
Hildesheim, 7th October 1820, lieut. Han. rifle guards.

*490, *Augustus Kuckuck*, N. C. O. 14th—22d Sept. 1810,
(N. G. 1813-14, N. 1814, W. & C. 1815.) slightly
wounded. 18th June 1815, at Waterloo.—H. W. C..capt.
Han. 3d line battalion.

491, *Julius Brinkmann*, 19th Dec. 1810—20th Feb. 1811, (M. 1811-12-13-14, N. 1814, W. & C. 1815.) B. W. M. at Diepholz, in Han.

*492, *Henry Dehnel*, 28th April—5th May 1812, (N. G. 1813-14, N. 1814, W. & C. 1815.) B. W. M.—II. G. O. 3.—Br. G. C.—II. W. C., captain Han. artillery.

*493, *Louis le Bachellè*, 3d—14th July 1812. (M. 1813-14, N. 1814, W. & C. 1815.) B. W. M., captain by br. r. l. at Döhren, amt Hanover.

494, *Harry Edward Kuckuck*, 10th—20th Oct. 1812, N. G. 1813, N. 1814, W. & C. 1815.) slightly wounded, 18th June 1815, at Waterloo.—B. W. M., captain by br. r. l. at Göttingen.

495, *Thomas Cutting*, 9th—23d January 1813, M. 1813-14, N. 1814, C. 1815.

ENSIGNS.

*496, *Frederick von Storren*, 18th Feb—9th March 1813, (N. 1814, W. & C. 1815.) B. W. M.—II. W. C., lieutenant Han. rifle guards.

*497, *Frederick von Schlütter*, 6th—18th May 1813, (N. G. 1813, N. 1814, W. & C. 1815.) B. W. M.—II. W. C., lieut. Han. rifle guards.

498, *William von Brandis*, 25th July—3d August 1813, (N. G. 1813, N. 1814-15. † at Imbsen, near Dransfeld, in Han. 29th March 1830.

499, *Charles Augustus von der Sode*, 30th Nov.—7th Dec. 1813, (N. 1814, W. & C. 1815.) B. W. M. † at Hanover, 1st March 1835, lieutenant 2d light battalion.

500, *August William Kuckuck*, 8th—22d January 1814, (N. 1814, W. & C. 1815.) B. W. M., at Vienna.

*501, *Richard Hüpeden*, 9th—22d January 1814, (N. 1814, W. & C. 1815.) B. W. M., lieut. Han. artillery.

502, *Ernest Wilhelm Carl Rodewald*, 17th Feb.—5th March 1814, (N. 1814, W. & C. 1815.) B. W. M. † at Brake, near Detmold, 5th August 1830.

503, *Adolphus Lewis Breymann*, 20th—29th March 1814,
    (N. 1814, W. & C. 1815.) B. W. M..lieutenant r. l. at
    Lüchow, in Han.

504, *Frederick von Rönne*, 21st—29th March 1814. (N. 1814,
    W. & C. 1815.) B. W. M...Prussian consul-general and
    chargé d'affaires in the U. S. of America.

505, *Ernest John Beurmann*, 13th Sept.—1st Oct. 1814. (N.
    1814, W. & C. 1815.) B. W. M.

PAYMASTER.

506, *William Anderson*, 13th—18th May, 1813. (M. 1813-14,
    N. 1814, C. 1815,)..major by br. r. l. in Scotland.

ADJUTANT.

*507, *Frederick Bernhard Schneider*, 14th—18th Nov. 1809,
    lieutenant, 18th March, 1812. (M. 1810-11-12-13-14,
    N. 1814, W. & C. 1815.) B. W. M...captain, r. l. at
    Verden.

QUARTERMASTER.

*508, *Frederick Levien*, N. C. O. 20th—23d July, 1808, (H.
    1805, B. 1807, M. 1808-9-10-11-12-13.14, N. 1814, W.
    & C. 1815.) B. W. M. † 5th Feb. 1837..captain by br.
    r. l. at Osterode, in Han.

SURGEON.

*509, *Lewis Stunz, M.D.* ¶ 14th Aug. 1805, (H. 1805, B.
    1807, M. 1808-9-10-11-12-13-14, N. 1814, W. & C.
    1815.) B. W. M. at Hanover.

ASSISTANT SURGEONS.

510, *Charles Schuntermann*, 25th Oct. 1805, (H. 1805, B.
    1807, M. 1808-9-10-11-12-13-14, P.* 1812-13, N.
    1814, W. & C. 1815.) B. W. M. † at Manheim, grand
    dutchy of Baden, 1837.

511, *Francis Degenhart*, 7th—12th Oct. 1813. (M. 1813.14,
    N. 1814, W. & C. 1815.) B. W. M. at Vienna.

FOURTH LINE BATTALION.
"Peninsula , Waterloo."

COLONEL COMMANDANT.

*512, *Siegesmund von Löw,* ¶ 20th Dec. 1804—21st January
1806..major-general 25th July 1810. [B. 1807-8, P.
1808-9-10-11-12.] B. G. M. 1. Talavera, Salamanca,
B. B. O. 2.—H. G. O. 2..lieut.-general by br. h. p. at
Löwenruhe near Offenbach on the Rhine.

LIEUTENANT COLONEL.

*513, *George Soest,* ¶ 19th Oct. 1803—21st Jan. 1806. (B.
1807, M. 1808-9-10-11-12-13-14-15.) colonel by br. h. p.
at Hasede near Hildesheim

MAJORS.

514, *Ferdinand von Marschalck,* ¶ 3d—17th Nov. 1803. (H.
1805, M. 1806-7, B. 1807-8, P, 1808-9-10-11, N. 1814,
C. 1815.) severely wounded, 28th July 1809, at Talavera,
† at Klinthoff, dutchy of Bremen, 20th May 1819.

515, *Henry William August Delius,* ¶ 29th Dec. 1805—21st
Jan. 1806. (B. 1807, M. 1808-9-10-11-12-13-14, N.
1814-15.) † at Eimbeck in Han. 23d Jan. 1825,..lieut.-
colonel h. p.

CAPTAINS.

516, *William Heydenreich,* ¶ 9th May 1806. [B. 1807, M.
1808-9-10-11-12, P.* 1812-13-14, S. F. 1814, N. 1814,
W. & C. 1815.] B. W. M. slightly wounded, 18th June
1815, at Waterloo..major h. p. in Hanover.

517, *George Ludewig,* ¶ 20th— 25th Sept. 1804, [H. 1805, B.
1807, M. 1808-9-10-11-12, P.* 1812-13-14, S. F. 1814,
N. 1814, W. & C. 1815.] B. W. M. lieut.-colonel h.p. at
Emden.

*518, *Augustus Rumann,* ¶ 2d—3d Jan. 1804. (H. 1805, B.
1807, M. 1808-9-10-11-12, P.* 1812-13-14, S. F. 1814,
N. 1814, W. & C. 1815.) H. G. O. 3.—B. W. M. † in
Hanover, 16th July 1837..lieut.-colonel h. p.

519, *Augustus Frederick von Brandis,* ¶ 15th—17th Nov.
1804, [H. 1805, B. 1807, M. 1808-9-10-11-12, P • 1812-
13-14, S. F. 1814. N. 1814, W. & C. 1815.] B. W. M.
† at Altona in Holstein, 28th Jan. 1820.

*520, *Conrad Schlichthorst*, ¶ 8th—21st Jan. 1806, [H. 1805,
    B. 1807, M. 1808-9-10-11-12, P. *1812-13-14, N. 1814,
    W. & C. 1815.] B. W. M. at Hittfeld near Harburg.

521, *Frederick Otto*, 23d—25th Sept. 1804. [H. 1805, B. 1807,
    M. 1808-9-10-11-12, P.* 1812-13-14, S. F. 1814, N.
    1814, W. & C. 1815.] B. W. M..captain h. p. at Osterode
    in Han.

*522, *Frederick Kessler*, 12th—17th Nov. 1804, [H. 1805, B.
    1807, M. 1808-9-10-11-12, P.* 1812-13-14, S. F. 1814,
    N. 1814, W. & C. 1815.] B. W. M..major by br. h. p.
    at Emden.

*523, *Christian Bacmeister*, 5th—10th Dec. 1805. [H. 1805,
    B. 1807, M. 1808-9-10-11-12, P. *1812-13-14.] severely
    wounded, 13th Sept. 1813, at the pass of Ordal. II. G. O. 3.
    at Misburg near Hanover.

524, *Justus Tormin*, ¶ 12th—21st Jan. 1806..captain 9th June
    1815. (B. 1807, M. 1808-9-10-11-12-13-14, N. 1814,
    W. & C. 1815.) B. W. M..capt. h. p. at Achim in Han.

525, *William Pape*, 5th—10th Dec. 1805. [B. 1807, M. 1808-
    9-10-11-12, P. *1812-13-14, S. F. 1814, N. 1814, W.
    & C. 1815.] B. W. M..captain h. p. at Adelhorn, amt
    Diepholz, in Han.

LIEUTENANTS.

*526, *Caspar von Both*, 27th—28th Jan. 1806. [B. 1807, M.
    1808-9-10-11-12, P.* 1812-13-14, N. 1814, W. & C.
    1815.] slightly wounded, 18th June 1815, at Waterloo.
    B. W. M..major by br. h. p. at Kalkhorst, grand dutchy
    of Mecklenburg.

527, *Augustus Freudenthal*, N. C. O. 6th—14th Oct. 1806.
    [H. 1805, B. 1807, M. 1808-9-10-11-12, P.* 1812-13-
    14, S. F. 1814, N. 1814, W. & C. 1815.) B. W. M. † in
    South America, date and place unknown.

528, *Frederick William Krietsch*, N. C. O. 10th Aug.—1st Sept.
    1807. [B. 1807, M. 1808-9-10-11-12, P.* 1812-13-14,
    S. F. 1814, N. 1814, W. & C. 1815.] B. W. M. † at
    Nette amt Wohldenberg in Han. 28th May 1830,..
    lieutenant r. l.

529, *Christian Lichtenberger*, N. C. O. 9th—20th Oct. 1807. (M. 1808-9-10-11-12, P.* 1812-13-14, S. F. 1814, N. 1814, W. & C. 1815.) B. W. M, † at Wiesbaden, grand dutchy of Nassau, 5th Oct. 1821.

530, *Adolphus von Hartwig*, N. C. O. 2d—12th Nov. 1808. (M. 1808-9-10-11-12, P.* 1812-13-14, S. F. 1814, N. 1814, W. & C. 1815.) severely wounded, (leg amputated) 18th June 1815, at Waterloo. B. W. M. † at Duderstadt in Han. 7th Dec. 1836...captain by br. r. l.

531, *Charles von Lasperg*, 30th March—8th April 1809. (M. 1809-10-11-12, P.* 1812-13-14, S. F. 1814, N. 1814, W. & C. 1815.) B. W. M. † at Neustadt am Rübenberge, in Han. 3d June 1828,..captain Han. rifle-guards.

532, *Frederick von Jeinsen*, N. C. O. 10th—23d Dec. 1809. (B. 1807, M. 1808-9-10-11-12, P.* 1812-13-14, S. F. 1814, N. 1814, W. & C. 1815.) B. W. M. † at Eldagsen amt Calenberg, in Han. 29th Nov. 1831.

533, *Theodore Adolphus Rumann*, 2d June 1810. (M. 1810-11-12, P.* 1812-13-14, S. F. 1814, N. 1814, W. & C. 1815.) B. W. M. † in Hanover, 1st June 1819.

*534, *Adolphus Ludewig*, N. C. O. 1st—12th Nov. 1811. [M. 1812, P.* 1812-13-14, S. F. 1814, N. 1814, W. & C. 1815.] B. W. M. at Evensen amt Bergen in Han.

*535, *Henry von Witte*, N. C. O. 1st—7th Jan. 1812. [B. 1807, M. 1808-9-10-11-12, P.* 1812-13-14, S. F. 1814, N. 1814, W. & C. 1815.] B. W. M.—H. W. C..captain Han. rifle-guards.

536, *George Frederick Siebold*, N. C. O. 11th-24th March 1812, [H. 1805, B. 1807, M. 1808-9-10-11-12, P.* 1812-13-14, S. F. 1814, N. 1814, W. & C. 1815.] B. W. M. † at Celle, 25th Dec. 1824.

537, *William Lewis de la Farguc*, N. C. O. 30th June—7th July 1812. [N. G. 1813-14, N. 1814, W. & C. 1815.] severely wounded, (leg amputated,) 18th June 1815, at Waterloo, B. W. M. † at Doesberg, Netherlands, Jan. 1833.

*538, *Ernestus Brinckmann*, 4th—14th July 1812. [N. 1814, W. & C. 1815.] B. W. M.—H. W. C..captain Han. 7th line battalion.

*539, *Charles Frederick William von Lasperg*, 5th—14th July
 1812. (S. F. 1814, N. 1814, W. & C. 1815.) B. W. M.
 major by br. r. l. at Bernburg, principality of Anhalt-
 Bernburg.

540, *William Shea*, 6th—15th Dec. 1812. [P.* 1813-14, S. F.
 1814, N. 1814, W. & C. 1815.] B. W. M. † in England
 4th April 1833.

541, *Frederick Heitmüller*, N. C. O. 14th—23d Feb. 1813. (H.
 1805, B. 1807, M. 1808-9-10-11-12, P.* 1812-13-14,
 S. F. 1814, N. 1814-15.) † at Holdenstedt, near Ueltzen
 in Han. 22d June 1830, captain by br. r. l.

ENSIGNS.

542, *William Lüning*, 7th—18th May 1813. (N. 1814, W. & C.
 1815.) B. W. M. at Neuhaus on the Oste, in Han.

*543, *Frederick Augustus Schulze*, 15th—22d June 1813 (S.F.
 1814, N. 1814-15.) at Wolfskuhle near Bremen.

*544, *Frederick von Brandis*, 26th July—3d Aug. 1813. (N. G.
 1813, N. 1814, W. & C. 1815.) B. W. M..lieut, Han.
 1st light battalion.

*545, *James Mannsbach*, 21st Sept.—5th Oct. 1813. (H. 1805,
 B. 1807. M. 1808-9-10-11-12, P.* 1812-13-14, S. F.
 1814, N. 1814, W. & C. 1815·) B. W. M...at Verviers,
 Netherlands.

546, *William Schaefer*, 8th—21st Dec. 1813. (N. 1814, W. &
 C. 1815.) B. W. M. † in Bessarabia, 5th Sept. 1829.

*547, *Ferdinand von Uslar*, 30th May—5th July 1814. (N.
 1814, W. & C. 1815.) B. W. M..lieutenant.Han. grenadier guards.

548, *Arnold Appuhn*, 6th June—5th July 1814. (N. 1814, W.
 & C. 1815.) slightly wounded, 18th June 1815, at Waterloo, B. W. M. at Harburg.

549, *Frederick Freudenthal*, 14th—29th April 1815. (N. 1814,
 W. & C. 1815.) B. W. M. at Lamspringe, in Han.

550, *Lewis von Soden*, 25th May—3d June 1815. (N. 1814,
 W. & C. 1815.) B. W. M. at Ohrdruf, near Gotha.

551, *George von Brandis*, 21st June—22d July 1815..lieut.
 Han. 4th line battalion.

PAYMASTER.

552, *Thomas Jones*, 8th Dec. 1804. (H. 1805, B. 1807, M. 1808-9-10-11-12, P.* 1812-13-14, S. F. 1814, N. 1814, W. & C. 1815.) B. W. M.

ADJUTANT.

*553, *Adolphus von Langwerth*, 31st Oct.—12th Nov. 1811... lieut. 19th March 1812. (N. G. 1813-14, N. 1814, W. & C. 1815.) slightly wounded 18th June 1815 at Waterloo, B. W. M..major h. p. at Eltville on the Rhine.

QUARTERMASTER.

554, *Augustus Becker*, 25th Sept. 1804, (H. 1805, B. 1807, M. 1808-9-10-11-12, P.* 1812-13-14, S. F. 1814, N. 1814, W. & C. 1815.) B. W. M..at Neustadt am Rübenberg, in Han.

SURGEON.

555, *George Günther, M. D.* 21st April 1804, (H. 1805, B. 1807, M. 1808-9-10-11-12, P.* 1812-13-14, S. F. 1814, N. 1814, W. & C. 1815.) B. W M. † at Nienburg, 10th January 1830.

ASSISTANT SURGEONS.

556, *John Daniel Matthaei.* 12th Dec. 1805, (H. 1805, B. 1807, M. 1808-9-10-11-12, P.* 1812-13-14, S. F. 1814, N. 1814, W. & C. 1815.) B. W. M. † at Lüneburg, 15th March 1836.

557, *John Henry Wicke, M. D.* 28th Feb.—10th March 1812, (B. 1807, M. 1808-9-10-11-12, P.* 1812-13-14, S. F. 1814, N. 1814, W. & C. 1815.) B. W. M..assistant surgeon, h. p. at Wustrow, in Han.

FIFTH LINE BATTALION.

" Peninsula, Waterloo."

COLONEL COMMANDANT.

*558, *Lewis von dem Bussche*, ¶ 14th Feb. 1804..lieut.-col. 29th March 1809, (H. 1805, B. 1807-8, P. 1808-9-10-11-12-13, S. F. 1813-14, N. 1814, W. & C. 1815.) B. G. M. 1..Vittoria, Nive—B. B. O. 3—N. W. O. 3—H. G. O. 1—B. W. M.—H. W. C..lieut.-general, H. S. comm. 1st division of infantry

LIEUTENANT-COLONEL.

*559, *William von Linsingen*, ¶ 6th Oct. 1803—25th May 1805,
lieut.-colonel 4th June 1813—H. 1805, B. 1807. M. 1808-
9-10-11-12-13-14, P.* 1812-13, N, 1814, W. & C. 1815.)
B. B. O. 3—H. G. O. 2—B. W. M..lieut.-general h. p.
at Hildesheim.

MAJORS.

*560, *Augustus Kuckuck*, ¶ 15th Sept. 1804..major, 4th June
1814. (H. 1805, B. 1807, M. 1808-9-10-11-12-13-14,
N. 1814, W. & C. 1815.) Pr. R. E. 4—B. W. M.—H.
W. C..colonel by br. h. p. and commdt. at Hildesheim.

561, *Philip Mejer*, ¶ 22d—25th Sept. 1805..major, 4th June
1814. (H. 1805, B. 1807, M. 1808-9-10-11-12, P.* 1812-
13-14, S. F. 1814, N. 1814, W. & C. 1815.) B. W. M.
at Lauenburg, kingdom of Denmark.

CAPTAINS.

*562, *Frederick Sander*, ¶ 6th—21st Jan. 1806. (B. 1807-8,
P. 1808-9-10-11, N. G.† 1814, N.1814, W. & C. 1815)
—very severely wounded, 18th June 1815, at Waterloo.
B. W. M..major by br. r. l. at Harburg.

563, *William Meyer*, ¶ 20th—21st Jan. 1806. (B. 1807-8, P.
1808-9-10-11, N. G.† 1814, N. 1814-15, W. & C. 1815.)
B. W. M..at Westheim, near Paderborn, in Prussia.

564, *Frederick Heinemann*, ¶ 21st—28th Jan. 1806. (B. 1807-8,
P. 1808-9-10-11-12-13, S. F. 1813 14, N. 1814-15.)
H. G. O. 3. † at Lüneburg, in Han. 13th Dec. 1833..
major by br. r. l.

*565, *George Nötting*, 24th—25th May 1805. (H. 1805, B.
1807-8, P. 1808-13, S. F. 1813-14, N. 1814, W. & C.
1815.) slightly wounded, 14th April 1814, before Bayonne.
B. W. M. † at Bremen, 11th Feb. 1837..major by br. r. l.

566, *Charles von Linsingen*, 7th—10th Dec. 1805. (H. 1805,
B. 1807-8, P. 1808-9-10-11-12-13, S. F. 1813-14.)—
severely wounded, 28th July 1809, at Talavera; severely
wounded, 27th Feb. 1814, before Bayonne..major by br.
r. l. at Ritterhude, in Han.

*567 *Ernest von During*, 26th—28th Jan. 1806. (H. 1805, B. 1807-8, P. 1808 9, S. F. 1814, N. 1814, W. & C. 1815.) severely wounded, 28th July 1809, at Talavera, where he was taken prisoner; leg amputated in consequence of a wound in 1831. B. W. M...major by br. h. p. at Hildesheim.

*568, *Charles von Bothmer*, 27th—28th Jan. 1806. (B. 1807-8, P. 1808 9-10-11-12-13, S. F. 1813-14, N. 1814, W. & C. 1815.) B. W. M. † at Celle, 27th Feb. 1837.

569, *John Henry von Dachenhausen*, 20th—21st March 1804. captain, 8th Dec. 18'3. (H. 1805, B. 1807, M. 1808-9-10-11-12-13, C. 1815. at Hanau, electorate of Hessia.

*570, *Eberhard von Brandis*, N. C. O. 29th Sept.—10th Oct. 1807. (B. 1807-8, P. 1808-9-10-11-12-13, S. F. 1813-14, N. 1814, W. & C. 1815.)..slightly wounded, 28th July 1809, at Talavera; slightly wounded, 22d July 1812, at Salamanca. H. G. O 3.—B. W. M.—H. W. C..capt. Han. 12th line battalion.

*571, *Charles Berger*, N. C. O. 26th July—2d August 1808. (H. 1805, B. 1807-8, P. 1808-9-10-11-12-13, S. F. 1813-14, N. 1814, W. & C. 1815.) slightly wounded, 18th June 1815, at Waterloo. B. W. M..at Harburg.

LIEUTENANTS.

572, *George Buhse*, N. C. O. 6th—19th Sept. 1809. H. 1805, B. 1807-8, P. 1808-9-10-11-12-13, S. F. 1813-14, N. 1814, W. & C. 1815. B. W. M...captain by br. r. l. at Hainholz near Hanover.

*573, *George von Schauroth*, 19th—28th Oct. 1809. (P. 1810-11-12-13, S. F. 1813-14, N. 1814, W. & C. 1815.) slightly wounded, 4th Oct. 1812, before Burgos; slightly wounded, 27th Feb. 1814, before Bayonne. B. W. M... major by br. r. l. at Rudolstadt.

*574, *Charles von Witte*, N. C. O. 9th—23d Dec. 1809. (B. 1807-8, S. 1809, P. 1808-9-10-11-12-13, S. F. 1813-14, N. 1814, W. & C. 1815.) severely wounded, 10th Nov. 1813, at Urugne—H. G. O. 3—B. W. M..captain h. p. at Hanover.

575, *Augustus Winckler*, N. C. O. 1st—4th August 1810 (P.
1811-12, S. F. 1814, N. 1814, W. & C. 1815.) B. W. M.
captain by br. h. p. at Holzminden, dutchy of Brunswick.

*576, *Charles Schlaeger*, N. C. O. 22d—28th Sept. 1810. (H.
1805, B. 1807-8, P. 1808-9-10-11-12-13, N. 1814, W.
& C. 1815.) slightly wounded, 18th October 1812, at
Burgos. H. G. O. 3—B. W. M.—H. W. C...captain
Han. grenadier guards.

*577, *George Klingsöhr*, 6th—14th Jan. 1812. (S. F. 1813-14,
N. 1814, W. & C. 1815.) severely wounded, 27th Feb.
1814, before Bayonne; slightly wounded, 18th June 1815,
at Waterloo. B. W. M.—H. W. C...capt. Han. grenadier
guards.

578, *Theodor Gallenberg*, N. C. O. 4th—17th Jan. 1809..
lieut. 26th Sept. 1811. H. 1805, B. 1807.

579, *Lewis von Geissmann*, 6th—29th August 1812. (P. 1812-
13, S. F. 1813-14, N. 1814, W. & C. 1815.) B. W. M.

*580, *Lewis Jaenicke*, 15th August—1st Sept. 1812. (N. G.
1813-14, N. 1814-15.) at Stendal in Prussia.

581, *Edmund Wheatley*, 23d October—3d Nov. 1812. (S. F.
1813-14, N. 1814, W. & C. 1815.) B. W. M.

582, *Henry Vassmer*, N. C. O. 17th—29th Dec. 1812. (P.
1811-12-13, S. F. 1813-14, N. 1814, W. & C. 1815.)
B. W. M. † at Steyerberg, in Han. 1st June 1831.

*583, *George Wischmann*, N. C. O. 26th Jan.—13th Feb. 1813.
(H. 1805, B. 1807, P. 1808-9, N. G. 1813-14, N. 1814,
W. & C. 1815.) B. W. M...at Rotenburg, in Han.

*584, *Bernhard Croon*, N. C. O. 10th—23d Feb. 1813. (H.
1805, B. 1807-8, P. 1808-9-10-11-12-13, S. F. 1813-14,
N. 1814, W. & C. 1815.) B. W. M...at Verden.

585, *Charles Ferdinand Christian Albrecht Weiss*, N. C. O.
11th—23d Feb. 1813. (P. 1811-12-13, S. F. 1813-14,
N. 1814, W. & C. 1815.) B. W. M. † at the Bruchhof,
near Stadthagen, principality of Bückeburg, 30th May 1818

ENSIGNS.

*586, *Ferdinand Scharnhorst*, 27th March—6th April 1813.
(N. 1814, W. & C. 1815.) B. W. M...lieut. h. p. at
Eimke, amt Bodenteich, in Han.

587, *Julius von Reinbold*, 11th—23d Oct. 1813. (N. G. 1813-N. 1814, W. & C. 1815.) B. W. M...in South America, retired colonel in the Columbian service.

*588, *Charles Christian Winckler*, 10th—22d Jan. 1814. (N. 1814, W. & C. 1815.) B. W. M...at Bleckede, in Han.

*589, *William Lewis Klingsöhr*, 22d—29th March 1814. (N. 1814, W. & C. 1815.) B. W. M..lieut. and adjt. Han. grenadier guards.

590, *Ernest Baring*, 25th—31st May 1814. (N. 1814, W. & C. 1815.) B. W. M...at Duderstadt, in Han.

*591, *Adolphus Scharnhorst*, 7th—5th July 1814. (W. & C. 1815.) B. W. M..lieut. Han. 4th line battalion.

*592 *George Charles August von Loesecke*, 15th—29th April. 1815. (N. 1815.) lieut. Han. rifle-guards.

593, *Arnold Meier*, 16th—29th Ap. 1815. (C. 1815.) at Brunswick.

594, *Rudolphus Carstens*, 15th—27th May 1815. (W, & C. 1815.) B. W. M. at Stellingen near Hamburg.

595, *John Christian Goebel*, N. C. O. 15th—29th Aug. 1815. (H. 1805, B. 1807-8, P. 1808-9-10-11-12-13, S. F. 1813-14, N. 1814, W. & C. 1815.) B. W. M. † at Münden in Han. 16th June 1827..captain and quartermaster, 1st regiment of infantry.

PAYMASTER.

596, *Henry Knight*, 2d July 1805. (H. 1805, B. 1807-8, P. 1808-9-10-11-12-13, S. F. 1813-14, N. 1814. W. & C. 1815.) B. W. M..paymaster 9th lt. drag. British service.

ADJUTANT.

*597, *William Walther*, N. C. O. 22d Nov.—7th Dec. 1813.. ensign 22d Nov. 1813. (P. 1811-12-13, S. F. 1813-14, N. 1814, W. & C. 1815.) H. G. O. 3—B. W. M..capt. and quartermaster h. p. at Stade, in Han.

QUARTERMASTER.

598, *John Frederick Lewis Armbrecht*, N. C. O. 12th—27th Oct. 1807. (H. 1805, B. 1807, P. 1811-12-13, S. F. 1813-14, N. 1814-15.) † at Echte near Nordheim, in Han. 15th March 1830.

ASSISTANT SURGEONS.

599, *Gerf. Herm. Gerson, M. D.* 9th Aug.—6th Sept. 1811.
(P. 1811-12-13, S. F. 1813-14, N. 1814, W. & C.
1815.) B. W. M. at Hamburg.

600, *John Henry Erdmann Meyer,* 8th—21st Oct. 1815. (C.
1815.) † at Wolfenbüttel, dutchy of Brunswick 25th
Dec. 1822.

SIXTH LINE BATTALION.
"Peninsula."
COLONEL COMMANDANT.

601, *Augustus von Houstedt,* ¶ 15th Dec. 1804—21st Jan.
1806..major-general, 25th July 1810. (B. 1807, M.
1808-9-10-11-12-13-14-15-16, P.* 1812-13.) H. G. O. 2.
† in London 31st Oct. 1821..major-general h. p.

LIEUTENANT-COLONEL.

*602, *J. William von Ulmenstein,* ¶ 12th Jan. 1805. (H. 1805.
M. 1806-7, B. 1807, M. 1808-9-10-11-12-13-14-15-16,
P.* 1812-13.) major-gen. by br. r. l. at Celle.

MAJORS.

*603, *Melchoir von der Decken,* ¶ 9th Nov. 1803—21st Jan.
1806..major 4th June 1814. (B. 1807, M. 1808-9-10-
11-12-13-14-15-16, P.* 1812-13.) H. G. O. 3—H. W.
C...major-general by br. h. p. commandant at Hameln.

604, *Colin Pringle,* ¶ 17th Nov. 1803..major 4th June 1814.
(H. 1805, B. 1807, M. 1814-15 16.)..at Edinburgh, br.
lieut.-col. British service.

CAPTAINS.

605, *George William Frederick Wolckenhaar,* ¶ 30th Dec.
1805.—21st Jan. 1806. (B. 1807, M. 1808-9-10-11-12-
13-14-15-16, P.* 1812-13.) † at Burgwedel near
Hanover, 2d Dec. 1827, major by br. r. l.

606, *Ferdinand Rougemont,* ¶ 1st—21st Jan. 1806. (B. 1807,
M. 1808-9-10-11-12-13-14-15.) † at Condé in France,
12th April 1818, major Han. light infantry battalion Hoya.

*607, *Charles von Brandis,* ¶ 2d—21st Jan. 1806. (B. 1807,
M. 1808-9-10-11-12-13-14-15-16, P.* 1812-13.) major
h. p. at Burgdorf in Han.

608, *Johann Christian Ketler*, ¶ 6th—28th Jan. 1806. (B.
1807, M. 1808-9-10-11-12-14-15-16, P.* 1812-13.)
† at Verden, 21st Feb. 1821.

*609, *Christian Anthony*, ¶ 19th—21st Jan. 1806. [B. 1807,
M. 1808-9-10-11-12-13-14-15-16, P.* 1812-13.] major
by br. r. l. at Mellendorf, in Han.

*610, *Ernest von Magius*, 5th—21st Jan. 1806. [B. 1807, M.
1808-9-10-11-12-13-14-15-16, P.* 1812-13.] major by
br. h. p. in Hanover.

611, *Johann Christian Strüver*, 6th—21st Jan. 1806. (B. 1807,
M. 1808-9-10-11-12-13-14-15-16, P.* 1812-13.) † at
Lüneburg, 29th June 1820.

*612, *Eberhard Kuntze*, 10th—21st Jan. 1806. [B. 1807, M.
1808-9-10-11-12-13-14, P.* 1812-13.)..major h. p. at
Harburg.

613, *George von Düring*, 13th—21st Jan. 1806. (B. 1807. M.
1808-9-10-11-12-13-14-15-16, P.* 1812 13.)..captain
h. p. at Frankfort, o. m.

*614, *Barthold von Honstedt*, 19th—28th Jan. 1806. (B. 1807,
M. 1808-9-10-11-12-13-14-15-16, P.* 1812-13.) H. G.
O. 3—H. W. C..capt. Han. 8th line battalion.

LIEUTENANTS.

615, *Joseph Kersting*, 21st Jan. 1806. (B. 1807, M. 1808-9-
10-11-12-13-14-15-16, P.* 1812-13.)..capt. by br. r. l.
at Hildesheim.

*616, *John Anton Schaedtler*, 12th—17th May 1806. (B. 1807,
M. 1808-9-10-11-12-13-14, N. 1814, C. 1815.) F. St.
L. 3..major by br. h. p. at Burgdorf, in Han.

*617, *Ernest von Heimburg*, 13th—17th May 1806. (B. 1807,
M. 1808-9-10-11-12-13-14-15, P.* 1812-13.) at Dresden.

*618, *Otto Schaumann*, 3d June 1806. (B. 1807, M. 1808-9-
10-11-12-13-14-15-16, P.* 1812-13.)..capt. h. p. in Han.

*619, *Arnold Völger*, N. C. O. 12th—25th Nov. 1806. (B.
1807, M. 1808-9-10-11-12-13-14-15-16, P.* 1812 13.)
H. W. C...capt. Han. 9th line battalion.

620, *Christian Fedden*, N. C. O. 11th August—1st Sept. 1807.
(B. 1807, M. 1808-9-10-11-12-13-14-15-16, P.* 1812-13)
capt. by br. h. p. at Dorum, in Han.

*621, *Frederick Hurtzig*, 31st March—8th April 1809. (B. 1807, M. 1808-9-10-11-12-13-14-15-16, P.* 1812-13.) II. G. O. 3..captain by br. h. p. at Verden.

622, *William Benthien*, N. C. O. 28th May—10th June 1809. (B. 1807, M. 1808-9-10-11-12-13-14-15-16, P.* 1812-13) capt. by br. r. l. † at Vahrenwaldt near Han. 2d Dec. 1835.

*623, *Henry Kirch*, N. C. O. 21st—28th Sept. 1810. (B. 1807, M. 1808-9-10-11-12-13-14-15-16, P.* 1812-13.)..capt. by br. r. l. at Hameln.

*624, *Ernest Mensing*, N. C. O. 25th Jan.—16th Feb. 1811. (B. 1807, M. 1808-9-10-11-12-13-14-15-16, P.* 1812-13) at Reifenhausen, amt Friedland, in Han.

625, *Ludewig Klauer*, N. C. O. 15th—23d April 1811. (B. 1807, M. 1808-9-10-11-12-13-14-15-16, P.* 1812-13.) † in Hanover, 21st August 1818..lieut. Han. landwehr battalion Emden.

626, *Ferdinand Leopold Schaefer*, 10th—19th May 1812. (N. G. 1813-14, N. 1815.) † at Wolfenbüttel, dutchy of Brunswick, 7th July 1821.

627, *Francis Baron Acton*, 17th—26th May 1812. M. 1812-13-14-15, P.* 1812-13.

*628, *Christian Ludewig von Ompteda*, 22d—30th June 1812. (N. 1814, W. & C. 1815.) B. W. M.—H. W. C...capt. Han. rifle guards.

629, *Charles Frederick Apfel*, N. C. O. 7th—14th July 1812. (M. 1811-12-13-14-15-16.) † at Blankenburg on the Harz, 11th April 1823.

ENSIGNS.

630, *Christian Seelhorst*, N. C. O. 16th Oct.—3d Nov. 1812. (Never joined the battalion, but did duty with the Italian levy.)..at Dankelshausen, near Münden, in Han.

631, *Augustus Fleischmann*, 29th April—11th May 1813. (N. 1814, W. & C. 1815.) B. W. M.

*632, *Adolphus William Stieglitz*, 22d March—9th April 1814. (N. 1814, W. & C. 1815.) B. W. M...capt. by br. r. l. in Hanover.

633, *Alexander Autran*, 2d—12th April 1814. M. 1814-15-16

*634, *Lewis Albrecht von Ompteda*, 15th—30th April, 1814.
(N. 1814, W. & C. 1815.) B. W. M...brevet captain,
Han. grenadier guards, on the staff, and A.D.C. to H.M.
the King of Hanover.

635, *Adolphus von Uslar*, 31st May—5th July, 1814. (N.
1814, W. & C. 1815.) B. W. M. † in Hanover, 6th
Dec. 1827...lieut. Han. rifle guards.

636, *William Gustav Friedrich von Linsingen*, 1st June—5th
July, 1814, at Celle in Han.

637, *Hermann Frederick Schwencke*, 8th June—5th July,
1814, (N. 1815.) lieut. by br. r. l. in Hanover.

638, *Edward von Brandis*, 9th—24th June, 1815..lieut. r. l. at
Burgdorf, in Han.

PAYMASTER.

639, *Henry James Amey*, 1st March, 1806, B. 1807, M.
1808-9-10-11-12-13-14-15-16, P.* 1812-13.

ADJUTANT.

640, *Mathias Debs*, N. C. O. 18th—26th January, 1808—lieut.
25th Feb. 1812. (M. 1808-9-10-11-12-13-14-15. P*
1812-13.) capt. by br. r. l. at Naples.

QUARTERMASTER.

*641, *John Charles Krüger*, N. C. O. 6th—14th July, 1812,
B. 1807, M. 1808-9-10-11-12-13-14-15-16, P.* 1812-13,
in Hanover.

SURGEON.

642, *Henry Neumann, M. D.* 1st Dec. 1805, (B. 1807, M.
1808-9-10-11-12-13-14-15-16, P.* 1812-13, † at Leeste
near Bremen, 19th Jan. 1831.

ASSISTANT SURGEON.

643, *Ernest August Ruhstradt*, 30th Dec. 1805, (B. 1807,
M. 1808-9-10-11-12-13-14-15-16, P* 1812-13,) † at
Verden, 24th Oct. 1819..br. surg. Han. landwehr batt.
Verden.

644. *S. T. Einthoven*, 29th Feb.—10th March, 1812, (M.
1812-13-14-15-16, P* 1812-13,)..at Gröningen, Netherlands.

SEVENTH LINE BATTALION.
" Peninsula."
COLONEL COMMANDANT.

645, *Frederick Charles von Drechsel*, ¶ 21st Jan. 1806..
lieut.·gen. 4th June, 1811, (B. 1807,) H. G. O. 1, †
in Hanover, 12th Jan. 1827...general by br. h. p. and
commandant of Hanover.

LIEUTENANT-COLONEL.

*646, *Hugh Halkett*, 21st Oct.—17th Nov. 1803..lieut.-col.
1st Jan. 1812. (H. 1805, B. 1807-8, P. 1808·9-11-12,
S. 1809, N. G. 1813-14, N. 1814, W. & C. 1815.) B. G·
M. 1..Albuera, Salamanca. B.B.O. 3—R. St. A.O. 2.
Sw. Sw. O. 3—B. W. M.—H. W. C...lieut.-general
H. S. comm. 2d division of infantry.

MAJORS.

*647, *William Chüden*, ¶ 4th Nov. 1803—5th May 1804· (H.
1805, B. 1807, M. 1808·9-10-11-12-13·14-15 16.)—
lieutenant-colonel h. p. in Hanover.

648, *August Levin von Harling*, ¶ 20th July 1804...major,
4th June 1814. (H. 1805, B. 1807, M. 1808-9-10-11-
12-13-14-15-16, P.* 1812-13.) † in Hanover, 10th Oct.
1829..lieut.-colonel h. p.

CAPTAINS.

649, *Frederick Christian Ruperti*, ¶ 27th Dec. 1805—21st
Jan. 1806. [B. 1807-8, P. 1808-9-10-11, M. 1812-13-
14-15-16.] † at Papenburg, in Han. 27th May 1829..
lieut.-colonel by br. r. l.

650, *Alexander William Isenbart*, ¶ 3d—21st Jan. 1806. [B.
1807-8, P. 1808-9-10-11, M. 1812-13-14-15-16.] † at
Eimbeck in Han. 30th Aug. 1831..major by br. r. l.

*651, *William Völger*, ¶ 10th—21st Jan. 1806. [B. 1807-8,
P. 1808-9·10-11, M. 1812-13-14-15-16.] slightly wounded, 28th July 1809, at Talavera..major h. p. at Aurich,
in Han.

652, *Frederick von Sichart*, ¶ 14th—21st January 1806. [B.
1807-8, P. 1808-9-10-11, M. 1812-13-14-15·16.] † at
Stade in Han. 27th Dec. 1827...major Han. 6th regiment
infantry.

*653, *Arnold Bacmeister*, ¶ 26th—28th Jan. 1806. [B. 1807, M. 1812-13-14-15-16.]..lieut.-colonel by br. h. p. at Lüneburg.

654, *Frederick Ludwig Ernst August von Sebisch*, 14th—21st Jan. 1806. [B. 1807-8, P. 1808-9-10-11, M. 1812-13-14 15 16.] † at Wandsbeck, near Hamburg, 22d Dec. 1821..captain h. p.

*655, *Frederick Münter*, 4th—14th Feb. 1804..capt. 21st Sept. 1810. [H. 1805, B. 1807, M. 1808-9-10-11-12-13-14-15-16.] Si. F. O. 2—H. W. C..lieut.-colonel Han. 12th line battalion.

*656, *Ferdinand von Hugo*, 21st Jan. 1806. [B. 1807-8, P. 1808-9-10-11, P.* 1812-13, M. 1812-13-14, N. 1815.] H. W. C..captain Han. 8th line battalion.

*657, *Gottlieb von Hartwig*, 23d—24th June 1806. [B. 1807-8, P. 1808-9-10-11, M. 1812-13-14-15-16.] H. W. C.. captain Han. 10th line battalion.

LIEUTENANTS.

658, *Charles von Windheim*, N. C. O. 12th—25th Nov. 1806. [B. 1807-8, P. 1808-9-10-11, N.G. 1813-14, N. 1814-15] H. G. O. 3..lieut.-colonel by br. h. p. at Osnabrück.

*659, *Leopold von Mutio*, 8th—16th May 1807. [B. 1807-8, B. 1809-10-11, M. 1812-13-14-15-16.]..captain h. p. at Hanover.

660, *George Luttermann*, N. C. O. 17th—26th Jan. 1808. [B. 1807-8, P. 1808-9-10-11, M. 1812-13-14-15-16.] † at Oldersum, in Eastfriesland, 1st April 1818..captain Han. landwehr battalion, Emden.

661, *John Bohn*, N. C. O. 5th—13th Feb. 1808. [B. 1808, P. 1808-9-10-11, M. 1812-13-14, N. 1815.] † in the Morea in 1822—date unknown.

662, *Frederick William Conring*, N. C. O. 6th—13th Feb. 1808. [B. 1807-8, P. 1808-9-10-11, M. 1812-13-14-15-16.]— † at Hanover 8th Sept. 1824..captain Han. landwehr battalion, Emden.

663, *Augustus von Offen*, N. C. O. 20th Dec.—3d Jan. 1809. [P. 1809-10-11, M. 1812-13-14-15-16.] severely wounded, 28th July 1809, at Talavera. H. W. C...captain Han. 7th line battalion.

*664, *Frederick von Diebitsch*, 28th October—7th Nov. 1809. [P. 1810-11, M. 1812-13-14, N. G.† 1814.] H. W. C.. captain Han. 4th line battalion.

665, *George William Ernst la Bachellé*, N. C. O. 17th—27th Jan. 1810. (S. 1809, P. 1810-11, N. G. 1813-14, N. 1814, W. & C.1815.) severely wounded, 5th May 1810, at Fuentes de Onoro; severely wounded, 13th May 1813, at Zollenspiker. H. G. O. 3.—B. W. M.—II. M. † at Wilhelminenholz, near Aurich, 28th July 1825, captain Han. 1st regiment infantry.

*666, *Charles Poten*, 10th—17th July 1810. [P. 1810-11, N. G. 1813-14, N. 1814, W. & C. 1815.] B. W. M..capt. h. p. at Eimbeck.

667, *William Corlien*, N. C. O. 13th—19th March 1811. [B. 1807-8, P. 1808-9-10-11, M. 1812-13-14-15-16.] † at Osnabrück, 31st Jan. 1819, lieut. Han. landwehr battalion Aurich.

*668, *Theodor von Sebisch*, 27th March—2d April 1811. [P. 1810-11, P.* 1812-13, M. 1812-13-14-15-16.] II. W. C. captain Han. 11th line battalion.

*669, *Frederick Ebell*, N. C. O. 7th—18th June 1811. (B. 1807, P. 1809-10-11, M. 1812-13-14-15-16.) captain h. p. at Hameln.

670, *Anthony Rüden*, N. C. O. 18th..23d Sept. 1811. (H. 1805, B. 1807-8, P. 1808-9-10-11.) † at Verden, Dec. 19, 1835...captain by br. r. l.

671, *Charles Helmrich*, 27th Jan.—4th Feb. 1812. (N. G. 1813-14, N. 1814, W. & C. 1815.) slightly wounded, 18th June 1815, at Waterloo. B. W. M. † at Hofglaubzahl near Hungen in the Wetterau, 15th Feb. 1834, capt. by br. r. l.

672, *William Leopold*, 26th June—7th July 1812. [P. 1812, M. 1813-14, N. 1814, C. 1815.] † at Eystrup, amt Hoya, in Han. 11th July 1834.

673, *Charles Blöttniz*, 27th June—7th July 1812. [P. 1812, M. 1813-14-15-16.] at Gr. Glogau in Silesia.

674, *Christian Eichhorn*, N. C. O. 14th—21st July 1812. (B. 1807-8, P. 1808-9-10-11, P.* 1812-13, M. 1812-13-14-15-16.) at Düsseldorf in Prussia.

675, *John Hunt*, 11th—22d Dec. 1812. M. 1813-14-15-16.

*676, *August Steffens*, N. C. O. 15th—23d Feb. 1813. (B. 1807-8, P. 1808-9, P. 1808-9-11-12-13, S. 1809, M. 1813-14-15-16.) at Kirchteimke, amt Ottersberg, in Han.

677, *William von Lösecke*, 8th—18th May 1813. [N. G. 1813, N. 1814, W. & C. 1815.] B. W. M. † at Hitzacker. in Han. 28th Aug. 1832.

ENSIGNS.

678, *Erich Backhaus*, 18th—27th July 1813, (N. 1814, W. & C. 1815,) B. W. M. . lieutenant h. p. at Barnstorf amt Diepholz, in Han.

* 679, *Gottlieb von Suckow*, 23d March—9th April, 1814, (N. 1814, W. & C. 1815,) Sw. Sw. M.—M. M.—B. W. M. . captain h. p. at Bellinghausen, near Leer, in Han.

680, *Adolphus F. W. Grahn*, 6th—19th April, 1814, (N. 1815,) † at Lilienthal, near Bremen, Aug. 4th. 1835, lieutenant h. p.

* 681, *Ernest Frederick Charles Neuschäfer*, 19th—30th April, 1814 (N. 1814, W. & C. 1815,) B. W. M.—H. W. C... lieut. and quartermaster Han. 12th line battalion.

* 682, *Frederick Backhaus*, 29th April—10th May, 1814, (W. & C. 1815,) B. W. M... lieutenant Han. 10th line battalion.

* 683, *Augustus von Hodenberg*, 2d June—5th July, 1814, (N. 1815) lieutenant Han. 2d dragoons.

684, *Charles Martin*, 19th June—5th July, 1814, (N. 1814, W. & C. 1815,) B. W. M. † at Heidelberg, grand dutchy of Baden, 2d Dec. 1822.

685, *Henry Charles Soest*, 7th—29th April, 1815. H. W. M. † at Osterode in Han. 3d Feb. 1817.

686, *Gustavus von Behr*, 27th May—3d June, 1815, (N. 1815,) † at Hertzberg, August 15th 1836, captain by br. r. l.

687, *Charles Ernest Bernhard Christoph von Langwerth*, 26th Oct.— 4th Nov. 1815, † in Hanover, 17th Sept. 1829. . captain 46th British foot.

PAYMASTER.

688, *Henry Cowper*, 1st March 1806. B. 1807-8. P. 1808-9-10-11, M. 1812,-13-14-15-16.

ADJUTANT.

* 689, *John Stutzer*, N. C. O. 16th—26th Jan. 1808. . lieutenant 29th Oct. 1809, (B. 1807-8, P.1808-9-10-11, M. 1812-13-14-15-16,). . captain h. p. at Emden.

QUARTERMASTER.

* 690, *Gustavus Hagenberg*, N. C. O. 9th July—12th Aug. 1806, (H. 1805, B. 1807-8, P. 1808-9-10-11, M. 1812-13-14-15-16,). . captain r. l. in Hanover.

SURGEON.

691, *John Frederick Hering*, 1st Dec. 1804, (H. 1805, B. 1807, P. 1809-10-11, M. 1812-13-14-15-16,) † at Göttingen, 10th November, 1832.

ASSISTANT SURGEONS.

692, *Casper Henry Brüggemann*, 30th Dec. 1805, (B. 1807-8, P. 1808-9, N. G. 1813-14, N. 1814, W. & C. 1815.) B. W. M. † at Nordheim, in Han. 3d March, 1816.

693, *Henry Schuchardt, M. D.* 16th Jan.—31st May, 1814, (N. 1814, W. & C. 1815,) B. W. M. at Cassel electorate of Hessia.

EIGHTH LINE BATTALION.

" *Waterloo.*"

COLONEL COMMANDANT.

694, *Peter Joseph du Plat*, ¶ 18th Sept. 1804—24th Sept. 1806.. major general, 25th July 1810, (B. 1807, M. 1808-9-10-11-12-13-14-15-16,) S. I. O. † at Celle 19th March, 1824, lieut. general by br. h. p.

LIEUTENANT COLONEL.

695, *Charles Best*, ¶ 1st Oct. 1803—15th Sept. 1804.. lieut. colonel 1st Jan. 1812, (H. 1805, B. 1807-8, P. 1808-9, S. 1809, N. G.† 1814, N. 1814, W. &. C. 1815,) H. G. O. 2.—B. W. M † at Verden, 5th Dec. 1836, major general h. p.

MAJORS.

696, *Charles von Petersdorff*, ¶ 9th Nov. 1803—21st March 1804, lieut. colonel, 18th June, 1815, (H. 1805, M. 1806-7, B. 1807-8, P. 1808-9-10-11-12-13, S. F. 1813-14, N. 1814, W. & C. 1815,) slightly wounded, 28th July, 1809, at Talavera. B. B. O. 3—H. G. O. 2—B. W. M. † at Witzenhausen, electorate of Hessia, 13th March, 1834.

697, *Frederick Leopold Breymann*, ¶ 11th—17th Nov. 1803.. major 4th June, 1814, (H. 1805, M. 1806-7, B. 1807-8, P. 1808-9-10-11-12-13, S. F. 1813-14, N. 1814, W. & C. 1815,) slightly wounded, 28th July, 1809, at Talavera; slightly wounded, 22d Sept. 1812, before Burgos, B. B. O. 3—H. G. O. 3—B. W. M. † at Tesperhude near Lauenburg, Denmark, 24th Jan, 1821.

698, *Julius Brinckmann*, ¶ 7th—24th May, 1806, (B. 1807, M. 1808-9-10-11-12-13-14, P.· 1812-13, N. 1814, W. & C. 1815,) B. W. M. † at Nienburg, 2d Sept. 1825, br. lieut. colonel Han. 9th infantry regiment.

699, *Siegmund Brauns*, ¶ 14th—15th Sept. 1804, B. 1807, M. 1808-9-10-11-12-13-14, P.·1812-13, N. 1814, W. & C. 1815,) H. G. O. 3—B. W. M. † at Otterndorf, in Han. 7th Oct. 1817, major Han. landwehr, battalion, Otterndorf.

700, *John Henry Oehme*, ¶ 19th—23d March, 1805. (B. 1807, M. 1808-9-10-11-12-13-14, N. 1814, W. & C. 1815,) B. W. M. † at Wilsdorf near Harburg, 11th May, 1820, major by br. r. l.

* 701, *Frederick Marburg*, 23d March—24th May, 1806, (B. 1807, M. 1808-9-10-11-12-13-14, N. 1814, W. & C. 1815,) B. W. M. at Walsrode, in Han.

702, *Charles Emanuel Wm. Rougemont*, 28th Feb.—1st March, 1806 (B. 1807, M. 1808-9-10-11-12-13-14, N. 1814, W. & C. 1815,) slightly wounded, 18th June, 1815, at Waterloo, B. W. M. † at Nienburg, 12th Dec. 1821, major h. p.

* 703, *George Delius*, 29th Sept.—1st Oct. 1805. (H. 1805, B. 1807, M. 1808-9-10-11-12-13-14, N. 1814, W. & C. 1815) B. W. M. major by br. h. p. at Münden in Han.

* 704, *George Hotzen*, 30th Sept.—1st Oct. 1805, (H. 1805, B. 1807, M. 1808-9-10-11-12-13-14, N. 1814, W. & C. 1815) H. G. O. 3—B. W. M.—H. W. C. captain Han. grenadier guards.

* 705, *Frederick Lüderitz*, 2d—3d June, 1806, (B. 1807, M. 1808-9-10-11-12-13-14, N. 1814, W. & C. 1815,) B. W. M.—H. W. C. captain Han. 4th line battalion.

* 706, *Charles Poten*, 15th Sept. 1804, (H. 1805, B. 1807, M. 1808-9-10-11-12-13-14, P.· 1812-13, N. 1814, W. & C. 1815,) B W. M.—H. W. C. captain Han. 10th line battalion.

* 707, *Lewis von Hodenberg*, 16th—21st Jan. 1806. B. 1807, M. 1808-9-10-11-12-13-14, N. 1814, W. & C. 1815,) B. W. M. captain h. p. at Herrenhausen, near Hanover.

LIEUTENANTS.

* 708, *Charles Ferdinand von Weyhe*, 26th June—1st July 1806, (B. 1807, M. 1808-9-10-11-12-13-14, N. 1814, W. & C. 1815,) B. W. M.—H. W. C.. captain Han. 12th line battalion.

709, *William Wilkens*, 29th Jan.—1st July, 1806, (B. 1807, M. 1808-9-10-11-12-13-14, N. 1814, W. & C. 1815,) B. W. M.. captain by br. r. l. † 13th June, 1837, at Germerode, near Waldcappeln, electorate of Hessia.

710, *David Frederick le Bachelle*, N. C. O. 6th—19th Aug. 1806, (B. 1807, M. 1808-9-10-11-12-13-14, N. 1815,) at Klötze, Prussia,

711, *Johann Christian Sattler*, N. C. O. 5th—10th Feb. 1810, (B. 1807, M. 1808-9-10-11-12-13-14, P.* 1812-13, N. 1814, W. &*C. 1815,) slightly wounded, 18th June, 1815, at Waterloo. B. W. M. † at Winsen, near Celle, 16th June, 1817.

712, *Frederick Wm. Ziermann*, N. C. O. 30th April—5th May, 1810, (B. 1807, M. 1808-9-10-11-12-13-14, N. 1814, W. & C. 1815,) B. W. M.. captain by br. h. p. at Stade.

713, *Christian Adolph Ernest Werner Grahn*, N. C. O. 18th—27th Jan. 1810, (S. 1809, M. 1811-12-13-14, N. 1814, W. & C. 1815,) B. W. M. † in Hanover 7th Sept. 1831, captain by br. r. l.

714, *Otto Brüel*, 26th—30th Oct. 1810. (B. 1807, M. 1808-9-10-11-12-13-14, N. 1814, W. & C. 1815,) B. W. M. † at Celle, 12th March, 1817, lieutenant Han. 3d battalion of guards.

715, *Franz Schmidts*, N. C. O. 17th—26th Feb. 1811, (B. 1807, M. 1808-9-10-11-12-13-14, P.* 1812-13, N. 1814, W. & C. 1815,) B. W. M. † [supposed in Sicily,] 16th May, 1831.

* 716, *Christopher Bernhard Bertram*, N. C. O. 22d. May—1st June 1811, (H. 1805, B. 1807, M. 1808-9-10-11-12-13-14, N. 1814, W. & C. 1815,) B. W. M.. captain by br. r. l. at Burgwedel, in Han.

717, *Valentine Büchler*, 20th June—2d July, 1811, (M. 1812-13-14 N. 1814-15,) † at Badenweiler, grand dutchy of Baden 8th May, 1829, captain by br. r. l.

718, *J. Henry Schlichting*, N. C. O. 20th Aug.—6th Sept. 1811,
H. 1805, B. 1807, M. 1808-9-10-11-12-13-14, N. 1814,
W. & C. 1815,) B. W. M. † at Harburg, 15th Sept. 1829,
captain by br. r. l.

719, *Frederick Müller*, N. C O. 3d—10th March, 1812, M. 1812-
13-14, N. 1814, W. & C. 1815,) B. W. M.

720, *Franz Schultz*, 11th—19th May, 1812, (N. G. 1813-14, N.
1814, C. 1815,) † at Döhren, near Hanover, 22d Sept. 1818.

721, *Augutt Helmich*, N. C. O. 11th—14th July, 1812, (B. 1807,
M. 1808-9-10-11-12-13-14, N. 1814, W. & C. 1815,) B.
W. M. at Bielefeld, in Prussia.

ENSIGNS.

* 722, *Frederick Dorndorf*, N. C. O. 12th—14th July, 1812, (B.
1807, M. 1808-9-10-11-12-13-14, P. ˙ 1812-13, N. 1814,
W. & C. 1815, B. W. M—H. W. C . captain and quartermaster Han. 2d dragoons.

* 723, *Gotlieb Kunoth*, N. C O. 13th—14th July, 1812, (B. 1807
M. 1808-9-10-11-12-13-14, P. ˙ 1812-13, N. 1814, W. & C.
1815,) B. W. M . lieuteuant h. p. at Bremen.

724, *William de Moreau*, 11th—20th Oct. 1812, (M. 1812-13-14,
N. 1814, W. & C. 1815,) very severely wounded, 18th June
1815, at Waterloo. H. G. O. 3—B. W. M . captain r. l. at
Brussels.

725, *Edward Stanley*, N. C. O. 12th—20th Oct. 1812, (M. 1812.
13-14, N. 1814, W. & C. 1815,) B. W. M.

* 726, *August Spiel*, 23d—29th March, 1814, (N. 1814, W. & C.
1815,) B. W. M . ensign r. l. at Celle.

727, *Frederick Henry Müller*, 13th—30th April, 1814, (N. 1814,
W. & C. 1815,) B. W. M. at Wasdahl, amt Bremervörde,
in Han.

* 728, *Henry Seffers*, N. C. O. 3d June—5th July 1814, (H.
1805, B. 1807-8, P. 1808-9-11, N. 1814, W. & C. 1815,)
B. W. M . lieutenant by br. r. l. at Herzberg, in Han.

729, *John Ernest David Bornemann*, N. C. O. 10th Sept.—1st
Oct. 1814, (B. 1807, M. 1808-9-10-11-12-13-14, N. 1814-
15,) † at Frankfort o. m. 15th April 1824.

730, *George Lunde*, N. C. O. 12th Sept.—1st Oct. 1814, (B. 1807, M. 1808-9-10-11-12-13-14, N. 1814, W. & C. 1815) B. W. M.. lieutenant by br. r. l. at Stolzenau. in Han.

731, *Frederick Sander*, 25th Nov.—6th Dec. 1814, (N. 1814, W. & C. 1815,) B. W. M. † at Kula, near Stade, in Han. 19th Feb. 1820.

PAYMASTER.

732, *James Harrison*, 12th July 1806, (B. 1807, M. 1808-9-10-11-12-13-14, N. 1814, W. & C. 1815,) B. W. M.

ADJUTANT.

* 733, *Frederick Brinckmann* 30th June—1st July, 1806,.. lieut. 10th April 1811, (B. 1807, M. 1808-9-10-11-12-13-14, N. 1814, W. & C. 1815,) slightly wounded, 17th April, 1814, at Genoa ; severely wounded, 18th June 1815, at Waterloo, B. W. M.—H. W. C... captain Han. grenadier guards.

QUARTERMASTER.

734, *Christian Tübing*, N. C. O. 14th—19th Dec. 1807, (H. 1805, B. 1807. M. 1808-9-10-11-12-13-14, N. 1814, W. &. C. 1815,) B. W. M.. captain by br. r. l. at Lüchow, in Han.

SURGEON.

735, *John August Frederick Ziermann*, ¶ 17th July, 1806, (B. 1807, M. 1808-9-10-11-12-13-14, N. 1814, W. & C. 1815) B. W. M. † at Celle, 13th January 1831.

ASSISTANT SURGEONS.

736, *Ernest Sander*, 4th—5th July 1806, (B. 1807, M. 1808-9-10-11-12-13-14, N. 1814, W. & C. 1815,) B. W. M. at Döhren near Hanover.

737, *John Christian Lewis Ziermann, M. D.* 5th July 1806, (B. 1807 M. 1808-9-10-11-12-13-14, N. 1814, W. & C. 1815,) B. W. M. † at Celle, 8th April 1825, assistant surgeon r. l.

FOREIGN VETERAN BATTALION.

COLONEL COMMANDANT.

738, *Claus Benedictus von der Decken*, ¶ 18th May 1804—22d Oct. 1805,. colonel 4th June 1813. † at Osnabrück, 9th Feb. 1823

LIEUTENANT COLONEL.

739, *Charles de Belleville*, ¶ 16th Sept. 1803—5th May 1804.
lieut. colonel 7th Dec. 1809, (H. 1805, B. 1807-8, P. 1808-
9-10-11, N. 1814-15,) B. G. M. Talavera. slightly wounded,
28th July 1809, at Talavera. † at Hameln 30th April,
1826.

MAJOR.

740, *Charles August Thalmann*, ¶ 9th Oct. 1803—2d July 1805,.
major 18th Jan. 1808, (H. 1805, B. 1807-8, P. 1808-9-10-
11, M. 1812, N. 1814-15,) B. G. M. Talavera. † at Hameln
30th April 1826.

CAPTAINS.

* 741, *Frederick Bothe*, ¶ 2d—21st Jan. 1806. . captain 4th April
1809, B. 1807-8, P. 1808-9-10-11-12, N. 1814-15, in Hanover.

742, *Charles Ebell*, ¶ 27th—28th Jan. 1806. . captain 23d March
1812, (B. 1807-8, P. 1808-9, N. G.† 1814, N. 1814-15,)
at Echte, Gericht Oldershausen, in Han.

743, *Frederick Dolge*, ¶ 19th—21st Jan, 1806,. . captain 19th Jan.
1806, (B. 1807. M. 1808-9-10-11-12, P.* 1812-13, N. 1814-
15,) † at Bremen, 2d January, 1832.

744, *Augustus Maimburg*, ¶ 20th Dec. 1803. . captain 5th April
1810, H. 1805, B. 1807-8, P. 1808-9-11-12-13, S. F. 1813,
N. 1814-15, † at Paris, January 5th 1836.

745, *George Schrader*, ¶ 22d—28th Jan. 1806. . captain 12th May,
1812, (B. 1807, M. 1808-9-10-11-12, N. 1814-15,) † at
Verden, 28th June 1828.

* 746, *Frederick Wyneken*, 19th—20th Dec. 1803. . captain 8th
July 1811, (H. 1805, B. 1808, P. 1808-9-11-12-13, S. 1809
S. F. 1813-14, N. 1815,) severely wounded, 22d June 1812,
at Morisco; slightly wounded, 9th Dec. 1813, before Bayonne; very severely wounded, 14th April, 1814, before Bayonne. H. G. O. 3. . lieut. colonel by br. h. p. at Celle.

* 747, *George Rautenberg*, ¶ 12th—21st Jan. 1806. . captain 17th
March, 1812, (B. 1807-8, P. 1808-9-11-12-13, S. 1809, S.
F. 1813-14, N. 1814-15,) severely wounded, 7th Oct. 1813,
on the Bidassoa; severely wounded 27th Feb. 1814, before
Bayonne. H. G. O. 3. . major by br r. l. in Hanover.

748, *Frederick George Wilhelm Hotzen*, ¶ 5th—21st Jan. 1806. .
captain 4th March 1813, (B. 1807, M. 1808-9-10-11-12.
P.· 1812-13-14, S. F. 1814, N. 1814, W. & C. 1815,) B.
W, M. † at Hemmendorf, near Hanover, 14th April, 1830.

* 749, *Christian von Goeben*, 8th—10th Dec. 1805. . captain 27th
Feb. 1815, (B. 1807-8, P. 1808-9-10-11-12, N. G.† 1814,
N. 1814-15,) severely wounded, 8th Oct. 1812, before
Burgos. . at Oppershausen near Celle,

*750, *Augustus von der Wense*, ¶ 15th—24th May 1806. . captain 26th
Oct. 1810, B. 1807, M. 1808-9-10-11-12-13-14, N. 1814-
15,) † 24th June 1836, at Oppershausen. near Celle.

LIEUTENANTS

751, *Frederick Schnering*, ¶ 20th 22d—Oct. 1805. . lieutenant 20th
Oct. 1805, (H. 1805, B. 1807, N. 1814-15,) † at Osterholz
in Han. 14th July 1829, captain by br. r. l.

752, *Theophilus Thalmann*, 25th May 1805. . lieutenant 22d July,
1806, (H. 1805, B. 1807, M. 1808-9-10-11-12, N. 1814-15-
† at Hameln, 24th Sept. 1832.

* 753, *John Tatter*, 1st—12th Nov. 1808. . lieutenant 19th Aug.
1809, (B. 1808, P. 1808-9-10, N. 1814-15,) in Hanover.

754, *Lewis von Weyhe*, ¶ 8th—23d Dec. 1809. . lieutenant 8th Dec.
1809, (P. 1810-11-12, N. G.† 1814, N. 1814-15,) † at
Dissen, near Osnabrück, 13th April 1834.

755, *Frederick Quade*, N. C. O. 4th—19th Sept. 1809. . lieutenant
17th March 1812, (H. 1805, M. 1806-7, B. 1807-8, P.
1808-9-10-11-12, N. 1814-15,) severely wounded, 18th
Oct. 1812, before Burgos. † at Walsrode, in Han. 16th
May 1826, captain by br. r. l.

756, *George von Witte*, N. C. O. 19th—26th Jan. 1808. . lieutenant
20th Aug. 1811, (B, 1807, M. 1808-9-10-11-12, N. 1814-
15,) at Döhren, near Hanover.

757, *Augustus Meyer*, N. C. O. 1st—8th Aug. 1809. . lieutenant
1st Dec. 1810, (P. 1808-9-10-11-12-13, S. F. 1813-14, N.
1814, W. & C. 1815,) severely wounded, 27th Feb. 1814,
before Bayonne. B. W. M. † at Tournay in the Netherlands,
28th Sept. 1826.

758, *William Atkins*, 9th—17th March 1810. . lieutenant 2d July
1811, (P. 1811-12-13, S. F. 1813-14, N. 1814-15,) slightly
wounded, 7th Oct. 1813, on the Bidassoa; slightly wounded,
28th Feb. 1814, before Bayonne. . . captain 75th British foot.

* 759, *William Fahle*, N. C. O. 22d Feb.—3d March 1810. .
lieutenant 14th March 1812, (H. 1805, B. 1807-8, P. 1808-
9-11-12-13, S. 1809, S. F. 1813-14, N. 1814-15,) slightly
wounded, 16th May 1811, at Albuera; severely wounded,
27th Feb. 1814, before Bayonne. . captain by br. h. p. at
Lüneburg.

760, *Frederick von Fincke*, N. C. O. 30th Nov. 1810—16th Feb.
1811. . lieutenant 20th March 1812, (P. 1811-12-13, N.
1814, W. & C. 1815,) severely wounded, 25th June 1813,
at Toloza. B. W. M. . . captain by br. r. l. at Potsdam, in
Prussia.

ENSIGNS.

761, *George Rumann*, N. C. O. 25th June—7th July 1812. . ensign
25th June 1812. (H. 1805, B. 1807-8, P. 1808-9-11-12,
S. 1809, N. G. 1813-14, N. 1814-15,) slightly wounded,
16th May 1811, at Albuera. . captain by br. r. l. at Bösing-
hausen near Göttingen.

762, *Charles Dedecke*, N. C. O. 5th—16th March 1813, (B. 1807-
8, P. 1808-9, S. 1809, N. G. 1813-14, N. 1814-15,) † at
Over, near Harburg, 10th December 1833.

763, *Joseph Kopetzky*, N. C. O. 13th—28th Aug. 1813. H, 1805,
M. 1806-7, B. 1807-8, P, 1808-9-10-11-12, N. 1814-15.

764, *William Riddle*, N. C. O. 30th Jan.—1st March 1814. (H.
1805, B. 1807-8, P. 1808-9-10-11-12-13, S. F. 1813-14,
N. 1814-15,) severely wounded, 10th Nov. 1813, at Urugne.
. . at Delft in Holland.

765, *Henry Brockmeyer*, N. C. O. 31st Jan.—1st March 1814,
(H. 1805, B. 1807, P 1809-10-11, N. 1814-15,) at Gnad-
enberg, near Hamburg.

* 766, *William Müller*, N. C. O. 17th—29th Aug. 1815, (H. 1805, B. 1807-8, P. 1808-9, N. 1814-15,) at Osnabrück.

767, *John Wegener*, N. C. O. 18th—29th Aug. 1815, (H. 1805, M. 1806-7, B. 1807-8, P. 1808-9-10-11-12-13, S. F. 1813-14, N. 1814, W. & C. 1815,) B. W. M... at Hamburg.

768, *Gottfried Henry Oppermann*, N. C. O. 19th—29th Aug. 1815, (H. 1805, B. 1807-8, P. 1808-9-10-11-12-13. S. F. 1813-14, N. 1814-15,) † at Hameln, 20th March 1818.

769, *Frsderick Schultze*, N. C. O. 20th—29th August 1815, (B. 1807-8, P. 1808, 9-10-11, M. 1812-13-14-15, N. 1815,) at Brunswick.

PAYMASTER.

770, *Thomas Finlayson*, 28th April 1804, (H. 1805, M. 1806-7, B. 1807-8, P. 1808-9-10-11, N. 1814-15,) † at Boulogne in 1830.

ADJUTANT.

* 771, *Henry Schaefer*, N. C. O. 12th July—29th Aug. 1809.. lieutenant 15th Feb. 1813, H, 1805, B. 1807-8, P. 1808-9-10. N. 1814-15,) at Abbensen, amt Meinersen, in Han.

QUARTERMASTER.

772, *John Henry James Behnsen*, N. C. O. 24th—30th October 1810. (H. 1805. B. 1807, N. 1814-15,) † at Hainholz near Hanover, 14th Dec. 1822.

SURGEON.

773, *George Kessler*, ¶ 25th Dec. 1805, (M. 1806-7, B. 1807, P. 1809-10-11-12, N, 1814-15,) † in Hanover, 25th June 1837.

ASSISTANT SURGEONS.

* 774, *T. C. F. Fischer*, 17th Feb.—1st March 1814, (N. 1814-15) at Ochsenwerder, near Hamburg.

775, *George Charles Meyer*, 15th—28th Dec. 1813, (N. 1814, W. & C. 1815,) B. W. M, † at Remoulins, south of France, 5th November 1823.

List of Casualties,

IN THE CORPS OF OFFICERS

OF THE

KING'S GERMAN LEGION,

From its Formation in 1803, to its Dissolution in 1816.

STAFF.

KILLED IN BATTLE.

776, *brigade major Frederick von Drechsel*, 2d—14th Feb. 1807.
captain 18th July 1810, (B. 1807, P. 1810-11-12-13, S. F.
1813-14.) killed in a sortie, made by the French garrison
of Bayonne, on the morning of the 14th April 1814.

777, *brigade major Charles von Bobers*, 10th—20th Sept. 1808..
captain 13th Sept. 1814, (P. 1809-10-11-12-13, S. F. 1813-
14, N. 1814, W. & C. 1815,) B. W. M. killed in the battle
of Waterloo, 18th June 1815.

LOST AT SEA, OR DROWNED BY SHIPWRECK.

778, *chaplain Martin Christoph Färber*, 21st Oct. 1804, H. 1805,
B. 1807.) Lost by the wreck of the "Eagle Packet," in the
Queen's channel, on the return of the expedition from
Copenhagen, in November 1807, (with his wife and children.)

DIED BY ILLNESS.

779, *brigade major Peter de Salve*, ¶ 3rd Sept. 1803.. as lieutenant
in the king's German regiment, 3d Sept. 1803, and in the
K. G. Legion, 17th Nov. 1803.. captain of depot company
K. G. Legion, 24th Dec. 1804, (H. 1805, B. 1807-8, P. 1808-
9-10,) † at Lisbon 6th May 1810.

780, *brigade major Ferdinand von Ompteda*, ¶ 19th—21st March
1804.. captain 24th April 1808. (H. 1805, B. 1807-8, P.
1808-9,) † at Egham in Surrey, 31st Oct. 1809.

781 *brigade major Augustus von Ompteda,* ¶ 20th Dec. 1803, (H. 1805, B. 1807-8, S. 1809, P. 1808-9-11,) † at Elvas in Portugal, 21st April 1811.

ENGINEERS.

782, *captain Julius Hussebroick,* ¶ 18th—21st April 1804, (H. 1805, B. 1807.. on a diplomatic mission to the Peninsula in 1808, attached to general von der Decken.) † in London 19th Jan. 1814.

RESIGNED AND RETIRED.

783, *captain George Frederick Schaeffer,* ¶ 10th Dec. 1804.. resigned 4th Dec. 1806.. killed in action near Dannenberg, 14 Aug. 1813, captain Han. engineers.

784, *2d captain Frederick Kunze,* ¶ 21st Jan. 1806. R. St. W. O. 4.—H. G. O. 3.—H. W. M... resigned 19th June 1806.. lieut. colonel h. p. at Schloss Ricklingen, in Han.

ARTILLERY.

KILLED IN BATTLE.

785, *captain Frederick Sympher,* ¶ 14th Feb. 1804.. major 17th Aug. 1812, (H. 1805, P. 1810-11-12-13, S. F. 1813-14,) B. G. C. 1. 2. Salamanca—Vittoria—St. Sebastian—Pyrenees.—Nivelle—Orthes.. killed in the battle of Orthes, 27th February 1814.

786, *lieutenant Charles Edmund Blumenbach,* 21st Jan. 1806, (B. 1807-8, P. 1808-9-10-11-12-13, S. F. 1813-14,) slightly wounded, 16th May 1811, at Albuera.. killed in the battle of Toulouse, 10th April 1814.

787, *lieutenant Charles Detlef von Schulzen,* N. C. O. 22d April—1st May 1807, (B. 1807-8, P. 1808-9-10-11-12-13, S. F. 1813-14, N. 1814, W. & C. 1815,) B. W. M... killed in the battle of Waterloo, 18th June 1815.

788, *2d lieutenant Henry Thiele*, N. C. O. 21st April—1st May 1807, (B. 1807-8, P. 1808-9-10-11-12,) severely wounded, 16th May 1811, at Albuera; slightly wounded, 1st April 1812, before Badajos; killed by the explosion of a Tower, in Fort Ragusa, near Puente d'Almaraz in Spain, 19th May 1812.

DIED FROM ILLNESS.

789, *captain Anthony Tieling*. ¶ 22d Dec. 1804, (H. 1805, B. 1807 P. 1808-9.) † at Langenhagen near Hanover, when on leave of absence from Portugal for the recovery of his health, 10th Oct. 1809.

790, *2d captain Charles Flügge*, 19th—21st April 1804, (H. 1805,) † at Fareham near Porchester, Hants, 20th May 1807.

791, *lieutenant Charles Ueberfeld*, ¶ 9th July 1805, (H. 1805, M. 1808-9-10-11.) † at Taormina in Sicily, 12th Jan. 1811.

792, *lieutenant Augustus Friderici*, 15th—16th June 1804, (H. 1805, B. 1807.) † at Lögten in Danish Zealand, 14th Oct. 1807.

PLACED ON HALF-PAY

793, *captain George Gesenius* ¶ 20th—23d March 1805, (H. 1805, B. 1807-8, P. 1808-9-10-11-12-13, S. F. 1814.) placed on half-pay, 1st May 1815. † in Hanover, 14th Feb. 1830, major by br. r. l.

RESIGNED AND RETIRED

794, *lieut. colonel Frederick von Linsingen*, ¶ 6th Oct. 1803—21st March 1804. (H. 1805, B. 1807.) retired 5th Dec. 1808. † at Oldenburg.

795, *major Daniel Ludowig*, ¶ 9th July 1805, (H. 1805.) retired 12th April 1806. . major h. p. in Hanover.

796, *captain Henry Lewis Heise*, ¶ 16th—17th Nov. 1804, (H. 1805, B. 1807-8, P. 1808-9-10) B. G. M.—Talavera. H. G. O. 3.—H. W. M. resigned 19th Sept. 1810. † in Hanover, 1st Dec. 1818. . br. lieut. colonel Han. artillery.

797, *captain John Frederick Ruperti*, ¶ 8th Nov. 1803—24th Dec.
1805, (H. 1805.) retired 17th May 1806. † at Bremen,
15th Jan. 1831, major commanding Hanseatic infantry of
Bremen.

798, *2d lieutenant John Charles August Galle*, N. C. O. 1st—17th
Sept. 1810, (B. 1807-8, P. 1808-9-10.) resigned 29th
October 1810.

799, *captain commissary Lewis Kersting*, ¶ 18th—21st April 1804,
(H. 1805,) retired 9th Oct 1807.. in the Brazils.

800, *assistant surgeon Julius Welhausen*, 24th Sept. 1805, (H.
1805,) retired 9th April 1806. † in Hanover, 19th April
1809.

CAVALRY.

KILLED IN BATTLE.

801, *3d hussars, captain Agatz von Kerssenbruch*, ¶ 5th Jan. 1805.
(H. 1805, B. 1807-8, P. 1808-9, N. G. 1813-14, N. 1814,
W. & C. 1815.) B. W. M.. killed in the battle of Waterloo,
18th June 1815.

802, *3d hussars, captain George Janssen.* ¶ 23d—24th Dec. 1805,
(B. 1807-8, P. 1808-9, N. G. 1813-14, N. 1814, W. & C.
1815,) slightly wounded, 29th Aug. 1807, at Kiöge. B. W.
M... killed in the battle of Waterloo, 18th June 1815.

803, *1st dragoons, captain Frederick Peters*, 16th—21st March
1804, (N. 1814, W. & C. 1815,) slightly wounded, 22d
Aug. 1806, at Tullamore. B. W. M.. killed in the battle
of Waterloo, 18th June 1815.

804, *2d dragoons, captain Frederick von Uslar*, 2d—21st Jan.
1806, (P. 1812,) killed in the combat of Garcia Hernandez,
23d July 1812.

805, 2d *dragoons, Captain Frederick von Bülow*, 21st Jan. 1806,
(P. 1812-13, S, F. 1813-14, N. 1814, W. & C. 1815.)
B. W. M. killed in the battle of Waterloo, 18th June 1815.

806, 2d *hussars, lieutenant Charles von Gruben*, 21st—22d Oct.
1805, (H. 1805, B. 1807, S. 1809, P. 1811-12,) killed in
a skirmish with the enemy in front of Ribeira in Spain, 1st
August 1812.

807, 1st *dragoons, lieutenant Augustus von Voss*, 5th May 1804,
(H. 1805, P. 1812,) killed in the combat of Garcia Hernandez, 23d July 1812.

808, 3rd *hussars, lieutenant Henry Brüggemann*, N. C. O. 30th
Nov.—5th Dec. 1807. lieutenant 16th Feb. 1812, (B. 1807-
8, P. 1808-9, N. G. 1813-14, N. 1814, W. & C. 1815,)
slightly wounded, 16th Sept. 1813, at the Göhrde. B. W.
M... killed in the battle of Waterloo, 18th June 1815.

809, 1st *dragoons, lieutenant Charles von Heugel*, N. C. O. 19th—
24th Feb. 1810, (P. 1812,) killed in the combat of Garcia
Hernandez, 23d July 1812.

810, 1st *dragoons, lieutenant Frederick Charles Lewis von Levetzow*,
22d Sept.—8th Oct. 1811, (P. 1812-13, S. F. 1813-14, N.
1814, W. & C. 1815,) B. W. M... killed in the battle of
Waterloo, 18th June 1815.

811, 2d *dragoons, lieutenant Robert Droege*, 11th—19th Feb. 1811
(P. 1812,) killed in an affair with the enemy's cavalry, near
Venta del Poço in Spain, 23d October 1812.

812, 1st *dragoons, lieutenant Otto Kuhlmann*, 11th—21st April
1812, (S. F. 1813-14. N. 1814, W. & C. 1815.) B. W. M.
killed in the battle of Waterloo, 18th June 1815.

813, 2d *dragoons*, *cornet Frederick William Kohlstedt*, N. C. O. 12th—19th May 1810, (P. 1812,) killed at the combat of Majalahonda in Spain, 11th Aug. 1812.

814, 2d *dragoons*, *cornet Henry Drangmeister*, N. C. O. 2d—13th Oct. 1812, (P. 1812-13, S. F. 1813-14, N. 1814, W. & C. 1815,) B. W. M. killed in the battle of Waterloo, 18th June 1815.

815, 3d *hussars*, *cornet William Deichmann*, 18th Feb.—5th March 1814, (N. G. 1813-14, N. 1814, W. & C. 1815,) B. W. M. killed in the battle of Waterloo, 18th June 1815

DIED OF WOUNDS.

816, 3d *hussars*, *lieut. colonel Frederick Lewis Meyer*, ¶ 10th Oct. 1803,—24th Dec. 1805, (B. 1807-8, P. 1808-9-11-12-13, N. 1814, W. & C. 1815,) slightly wounded, 5th May 1811, at Fuentes de Onoro. B. W. M... † at Brussels, 6th July 1815, of the wounds he received in the battle of Waterloo, 18th June 1815.

817, 1st *dragoons*, *major John Christian Diedrich Fischer*, ¶ 2d, Oct. 1803—21st Jan. 1806, (P. 1812,) † in French captivity at Burgos, 27th Oct. 1812, of the wounds he received in a combat with the enemy's cavalry near Venta del Poço, 23d October 1812.

818, 1st *dragoons*, *captain Gustavus von der Decken*, ¶ 7th—17th Nov. 1803, (H. 1805, P. 1812,) † at Salamanca 16th Sept. 1812, of the wounds he received in the combat of Garcia Hernandez, 23d July 1812.

819, 2d *hussars*, *captain Frederick von Voss*, ¶ 9th—17th Nov. 1803, (H. 1805, B. 1807, S. 1809, P. 1810-11,) † 5th March 1811, of the wounds he received that day in the battle of Barossa.

820, 3d hussars—*captain Ernest von Biela*, ¶ 6th--10th Dec.
1805. (B. 1807-8, P. 1808-9, N. G. 1813.) † 11th Nov.
1813, at Grabow in Mecklenburg, of the wounds he received in the battle of the Göhrde, 16th Sept. 1813.

821, 3d hussars—*captain Court von Hugo*, 15th—21st March
1804. (H. 1805, B. 1307-8, P. 1808-9, N. G. 1813.) †
17th Sept. 1813, of the wounds he received in the battle
of the Göhrde, 16th Sept. 1813.

822, 1st hussars—*captain George Bergmann*, 20th Dec. 1803.
(H. 1805, B. 1807, P. 1809-10-11.) † 17th Oct. 1811,
of the wounds he received in the combat of El Bodon in
Spain, 25th September 1811.

823, 3d hussars—*captain William von Both*, 20th—22d Oct.
1805. (H. 1805, B. 1807-8, P. 1808-9, N. G. 1813.)
† 3d Jan. 1814, at Grabow in Mecklenburg, of the wounds
he received in the battle of the Göhrde, 16th Sept. 1813.

824, 1st hussars—*lieutenant Ernest Rudorf*, 7th—14th Feb.
1804. (H. 1805, B. 1807.) † of the wounds he received
at Kiöge in the isle of Danish Zealand, 29th Aug. 1807.

825, 3d hussars—*lieutenant George Cremer*, N.C.O. 27th Sept.
8th Oct. 1811. (N. G. 1813.) † 18th Sept. 1813, of the
wounds he received in the battle of the Göhrde, 16th Sept.
1813.

LOST AT SEA OR DROWNED BY SHIPWRECK.

826, 1st dragoons—colonel commandant—*Eberhardt Otto
George von Bock*, ¶ 21st Ap. 1804..major-general 25th
July 1810. (H. 1805, P. 1812-13, S.F. 1813.) B.G.M.1.
Salamanca—Vittoria. Lost by the wreck of the "Bellona"
transport, No. 342, on the 21st of Jan. 1814, on his way
from Passages in Spain, to England, on the rocks of Tulbest
near the coast of Pleubian, Arrondissement de Paimpol
in France: he was found on the shore of Pleubian, where
he was buried.

827, 2d hussars, *captain Ludolphus Baring*, ¶ 21st March,
1804. [H. 1805, B. 1807.] drowned in Yarmouth roads
on the return of the expedition from Copenhagen, 2d Nov.
1807, having been on shore, and the boat upsetting when
rejoining his transport in a heavy sea.

828, 1st dragoons—*captain Charles von Hodenberg,* ¶ 17th Nov. 1803..captain 12th Oct. 1805. (H. 1805, P. 1812-13, S. F. 1813.)..lost with major-general von Bock on board the Bellona transport, No. 342, on the 21st Jan. 1814. [vide above.]

829, 2d hussars—*captain Lewis von Bock,* 20th—21st January 1806..captain 28th March 1812. (B. 1807, S. 1809, P. 1810-11-12-13, S. F. 1813)..severely wounded, 5th March 1811, at Barossa; lost with his father, major-general von Bock, on board the Bellona transport, No. 342, on the 21st Jan. 1814. [vide above.]

DIED BY ILLNESS.

830, 3d hussars—*lieut.-col. Ulrich von Töbing,* ¶ 20th—21st April 1804. (H. 1805. N. G. 1813.) † 3d Sept. 1813, at Wismar in Mecklenburg.

831, 3d hussars—*major Frederick Valentini,* ¶ 23d Feb. 1804 24th Dec. 1805. † 1st June 1807, at Guilford Barracks, Surrey.

832, 2d dragoons—*major Otto Henry Volger,* ¶ 25th Sep. 1803—10th Dec. 1805. (P. 1812.) † 19th Sep. 1812, at Santarem in Portugal.

833, 2d dragoons—*major Frederick Lueder,* ¶ 5th Oct. 1803—21st Jan. 1806. (P. 1812.) † 16th April 1812, at Estremoz in Portugal.

834, 1st dragoons—*captain Frederick von Oldershausen,* ¶ 7th Nov. 1803—9th Feb. 1805. (H. 1805.) † 22d Dec. 1808, at Tullamore in Ireland.

835, 3d hussars—*captain Gabriel Wilhelm Heise,* 7th Nov. 1803—22d Oct. 1805. (H. 1805, B. 1807-8, P. 1808-9.) † 2d Jan. 1810, at Ipswich, Suffolk.

836, 2d hussars—*captain Frederick Wiering,* ¶ 22d Dec. 1804. captain 21st Dec. 1804. (H. 1805, B. 1807, S. 1809, P. 1811.) slightly wounded, 23d June 1811, at Quinta de Gremezia. † 19th July 1811, at the hospital of Zabucca de Vide in Portugal.

837, 2d husssars—*captain George von der Wense,* ¶ 12th—21st March 1804..captain 11th Oct. 1805. (H. 1805, B. 1807, S. 1809, P. 1810-11-12-13.) † 24th Feb. 1814, at Ipswich, Suffolk.

838, 3d hussars—*captain Ulrich Hoyer,* ¶ 21st—24th Dec. 1805. (B. 1807-8, P. 1808-9, N. G. 1813-14, N. 1814, W. & C. 1815.) B. W. M. † 16th Oct. 1815, at Abbeville in France.

839, 2d hussars—*captain George Lewis Schultze,* ¶ 18th—20th Dec. 1803. (H. 1805, B. 1807, S. 1809, P. 1811-12) slightly wounded, 28th Oct. 1811, at Aroya-Molinos. † 3d Oct. 1812, at Truxillo in Spain.

840, 2d dragoons — *captain George von Weyhe,* ¶ 27th Dec. 1805—21st Jan. 1806. (P. 1812-13, S. F. 1813-14, N. 1814-15.) † 15th February 1815, at Tournay in the Netherlands.

841, 2d dragoons—*captain Otto Friesland,* ¶ 15th—21st Jan. 1806. (P. 1812.) † 24th Aug. 1812, at Madrid.

842, 2d hussars—*captain Charles Koch,* ¶ 19th—28th Jan. 1806. (B. 1807, S. 1809, P. 1810-11.) † 12th Dec. 1811, at Belem in Portugal.

843, 1st dragoons—*captain George von Issendorf,* 3d—5th May 1804. (H. 1805, P. 1812-13.) † 13th Feb. 1813, at Lisbon.

844, 1st hussars—*lieut. Charles Krauchenberg,* 17th—24th Jan. 1804. (H. 1805.) † 25th Nov. 1806, at Ballinrobe, county of Mayo, in Ireland.

845, 2d hussars—*lieut. & adjt. Gustav von Gruben,* 22d Oct. 1805..lieut. 16th July 1810. (H. 1805, B. 1807, S. 1809, P. 1811.) slightly wounded, 25th June 1811, at Quinta de Gremezia—† 14th Oct. 1811, at Castello Branco in Portugal.

846, 3d hussars—*lieutenant Joachim Henry Thumann,* N. C. O. 2d—14th May 1811. (B. 1808, P. 1808-9, N. G. 1813-14, N. 1814, W. & C. 1815.) B. W. M. † 23d Dec. 1815, at St. Leger in France.

847, 3d hussars—*cornet Charles Baring*, 23d—24th Dec. 1805. † 28th Sept. 1806 at Guilford, Surrey.

848, 2d hussars—*cornet August Thiele*, 18th—21st Jan. 1806. † 5th Sept. 1806, at Canterbury in England.

849, 1st dragoons—*cornet Joseph Cruise*, 5th—12th May 1810. † 31st March 1811 at Loughrea in Ireland.

850, 2d hussars—*cornet James Parodi*, 5th—16th June 1812. (N. 1814, C. 1815.) † 16th Dec. 1815, at St Denis, near Paris.

851, 3d hussars—*cornet Albrecht von Arentsschildt*, 29th July— 5th Aug. 1815. (C. 1815.) † 23d Nov. 1815, at Abbeville in France.

852, 1st hussars—*paymaster Mathias O'Toole*, 7th Feb. 1804. (H. 1805.) † 22d April 1807, at Gort in Ireland.

853, 2d hussars—*paymaster Richard Richardson*, 24th Dec. 1805. (B. 1807, S. 1809, P. 1811.) † 3d Oct. 1811, at Castello Branco in Portugal.

854, 1st hussars—*veterinary surgeon Frederick Precht*, 20th Oct. 1804. (H. 1805, B. 1807, P. 1809-10.) † 15th Dec. 1810, at Belem in Portugal.

855, 2d hussars— *veterinary surgeon Frederick Neynaber*, N. C. O. 28th Jan. 1806. † 29th Oct. 1806, at Canterbury in England.

PLACED ON THE REDUCED ALLOWANCE.

856, 3d hussars—*colonel commandant John George von Reden*, ¶ 18th Dec. 1804—9th Feb. 1805. (H. 1805, B. 1807-8, P. 1808.) retired on an allowance of 7s. 6d. per day, 19th May 1810, † at Pattensen, amt Calenberg, in Han. 12th Aug. 1811.

857, 3d hussars—*lieutenant-colonel John Daniel Crusius*, ¶ 18th Feb. 1804—24th Dec. 1805. (B. 1807.) retired on an allowance of 5s. per day, 25th Feb. 1809. † at Hankesbüttel, amt Isenhagen in Han. 3d Sep. 1819.

858, 1st hussars—*major George von Plessen*, ¶ 12th Oct. 1805. (H. 1805, B. 1807, P. 1809-10.) retired on an allowance of 5s. per day, 2d June 1810. † at Wilhelmsburg, near Harburg, 12th Aug. 1827.

859, 2d dragoons—*captain William Bergmann,* ¶ 8th Oct. 1803—21st Jan. 1806, retired on an allowance of 3s. per day, 19th May 1810. † at Isernhagen near Hanover, 21st June 1818.

860, 2d dragoons -*capt. Frederick Lüderitz,* ¶ 10th Oct. 1803 —21st Jan. 1806, retired on an allowance of 3s. per day, 7th July 1810, † at Celle, 19th June 1833, major by br. h.p.

861, 1st hussars—*captain Ernest count Kielmansegge,* ¶ 3d Jan. 1804. (H. 1805. B. 1807.) H. G. O. 2. retired on an allowance of 3s. per day, 16th Feb. 1811. colonel by br. h. p. at Blumenau near Hanover.

862, 1st dragoons—*lieutenant Augustus Frederick Ernest von Leyser,* ¶ 13th—21st March 1804. (H. 1805.) retired on an allowance of 2s. per day, 5th May 1810. † at Döhren near Hanover 21st June 1816.

863, 2d hussars—*cornet Charles Pollmann,* N. C. O. 30th Nov. 5th Dec. 1807. (S. 1809.) retired on an allowance of 2s. per day, 21st May 1811. † at Laak, dutchy of Brunswick, 22d March 1823.

864, 1st hussars—*paymaster William Darcy Todd,* 18th June —28th July 1807. (P. 1809-10.) H. G. O. 3. retired on an allowance of 5s. per day, 8th Aug. 1810.

PLACED ON HALF-PAY.

865, 2d hussars—*lieutenant-colonel William Charles Rodewald* ¶ 16th Dec. 1804— 8th Feb. 1806 . . colonel 4th June 1813, [B. 1807, S. 1809.] placed upon half-pay 29th June 1813. † at Herzberg, in Han. 10th April 1819.

866, 3d hussars—*major Ernest von Burgwedel,* ¶ 28th Sep. 1803—24th Dec. 1805. [B. 1807-8, P. 1808-9.] severely wounded 29th Dec. 1808 at Benavente, B. G. M.—Benavente, placed upon half-pay 14th May 1811, † at Goldberg, grand dutchy of Mecklenburg, 16th Nov. 1832.

867, 2d hussars—*major Johann Conrad Victor von Müller,* ¶ 5th Oct. 1803—21st Jan. 1806. (S. 1809.) placed upon half-pay 12th March 1811. † at Wrestorf near Lüneburg 15th March 1832.

868, 1st hussars—*major Charles Otto*, ¶ 7th Oct. 1803—21st
    Jan. 1806. (B. 1807-8, P. 1808-9-10-11.) B. G. M.
    Fuentes de Onoro, placed upon half-pay 17th March 1812.
    † in Hanover 4th March 1821.

869, 2d hussars—*major Augustus Frederick von dem Bussche*,
    ¶ 8th Oct. 1803—10th Dec. 1805. (H. 1805, B. 1807-8,
    P. 1808-9-10-11-12.) slightly wounded, 28th Oct. 1811,
    at Arroya Molinos. B. G. M. Barossa. H. G. O. 2.—H.
    W. M.—H. W. C. placed upon half-pay 9th March 1813,
    lieut.-general h. p. commandant at Stade.

870, 3d hussars—*major John Charles Küper*, ¶ 17th—22d Oct.
    1803. (H. 1805, B. 1807-8, P 1808-9, N. G. 1813-14.)
    H. G. O. 3—R. St. W. O. 4. placed upon half-pay 17th
    Sept. 1814, † at Verden 3d July, 1824, lieut.-colonel by
    br. r. l.

871, 1st dragoons—*major Otto Frederick von Gruben*, ¶
    18th Oct. 1803—9th Feb. 1805. (H. 1805, N. 1814-15),
    placed upon half-pay, 25th Oct. 1815, † at Lüneburg,
    29th July, 1831, lieutenant·colonel by br. r. l.

872, 2d dragoons—*major Frederick von Ziegesar*, ¶ 18th
    Oct. 1803—21st Jan. 1806. (P. 1812-13, S. F. 1813-14,
    N. 1814-15.) B. G. M.—Vittoria, placed upon half-pay,
    25th Oct. 1815, † at Hagen—Ohsen, near Hameln, 24th
    Feb. 1825, major h. p.

873, 1st hussars—*captain George von Müller*, ¶ 16th June, 1804
    ..major, 4th June, 1814. (H. 1805, B. 1807, P. 1809-
    10.) placed upon half-pay, 25th June, 1814...at Loccum,
    in Han.

874, 2d dragoons—*captain George Frederick Meyer*, ¶
    28th Dec. 1805—21st Jan. 1806, placed upon half pay,
    25th Feb. 1812 † at Lüneburg, 7th March, 1830.

875, 2d dragoons—*captain E. A. W. F. C. von Lenthe*, ¶
    29th April—5th May, 1804..captain, 25th Nov. 1809.
    (H. 1805, P. 1812.) placed upon half-pay, 25th Oct.
    1815, † in Hanover, 2d Aug. 1818, major by br. r. l.

876, 2d dragoons—*captain Charles Leschen*, ¶ 8th—21st Jan.
    1806, placed upon half-pay, 6th July, 1814. † at Celle,
    Sept. 17th 1836, major by br. r. l.

877, 2d hussars—*captain Charles Schanz*, ¶ 19th—22d Oct. 1805. (H. 1805, B. 1807, S. 1809), placed upon half-pay, 25th June, 1814...at Syke, in Han.

878, 1st dragoons—*lieutenant Charles Tappe*, N. C. O. 25th Nov.—10th Dec. 1811. (H. 1805, P. 1812, N. 1814-15), severely wounded, 23d July, 1812, at Garcia Hernandez; placed upon half-pay, 25th April, 1815... at Salzhausen, amt Winsen on the Luhe, in Han.

879, 1st dragoons—*lieutenant Charles Sprebach*, N. C. O. 3d—15th Dec. 1812. (H. 1805, N. 1814-15), placed upon half pay, 25th Oct. 1815, † at Predoht, amt Lüchow, in Han. 10th April, 1816.

880, 2d. dragoons—*cornet William von Kalckreuth*, 28th Aug.—15th Sept. 1812; placed upon half-pay, 25th Feb. 1815.

881, 2d dragoons — *cornet Hermann Voss*, N. C. O. 1st—13th Oct. 1812. (H. 1805, B. 1807, N. 1814-15) placed upon half-pay, 25th Sept. 1815. † at Holsten amt Hoya, in Han. 29th Oct 1826.

882, 2d dragoons—*paymaster Wm. Armstrong*, 1st May, 1806. (P. 1812-13, S. F. 1813-14, N. 1814-15), placed upon half-pay, 30th Sept. 1815

883, 2d hussars—*quartermaster James Hauschildt*, N. C. O. 17th—21st July, 1810. (B. 1807, S. 1809, P. 1811-12-13, N. 1814, C. 1815.) placed upon half-pay, 6th Aug. 1814, † at Ipswich in England, 10th May, 1819.

884, 1st hussars—*surgeon Henry Wm. Bergmann*, M. D. 16th Dec. 1805. (B. 1807, P. 1809-10 11-12.) placed upon half-pay, 27th July, 1813, † at Alten Bruchhausen, in Han. 25th Sept. 1830.

RESIGNED AND RETIRED

885, 1st dragoons—*col. comm. count Wallmoden Gimborn*, ¶ 17th—22d March 1814..lieut.-general 21st Jan. 1813. (N. G. 1813-14.) A. M. T. 3—R. St. A. O. 1—R. St. W. O. 2—R. St. G. O. 3—B. B. O. 2—Pr. R. E. 1—Pr. M. O. M.—Sw. Sw. O. 1—Si. F. O. 1—Si. C. G. O. 1—H. G. O. 1. resigned 24th June 1815..fieldmarshal lieut. Austrian service, commanding at Milan.

886, 2d dragoons—*col. comm. Otto. von Schutte,* ¶ 21st Jan 1806..major-general 16th August 1814—resigned 4th August 1810. † at Burg-Sittensen, in Han. 2d Aug. 1826.

887, 2d dragoons—*major Frederick von Heimburg,* ¶ 19th Feb. 1804—·21st Jan. 1806..resigned, 1st May 1807. major h. p. at Nord-Goltern, in Han.

888, 2d hussars—*major Henry Niemann,* ¶ 20th Feb. 1804— 28th Jan. 1806. (B. 1807.) retired 25th March 1809— † in Hanover 16th Feb. 1823.

889, 1st hussars—*major Otto von Grote,* ¶ 2d Oct. 1803—21st Jan. 1806. (B. 1807, P. 1809.) H. W. M..resigned 30th Oct. 1810, 27th Jan. 1834..col. h. p. and commandant at Nienburg.

890, 2d dragoons—*captain Justus Klare,* ¶ 24th Sep. 1803 —21st Jan. 1806, never joined ; retired 17th May 1806. † at Göttingen 2d Sep. 1816.

891, 2d hussars—*captain Jürgen Melchior von Issendorff,* ¶ 2d—22d Oct. 1805, (H. 1805.) retired 3d April 1807. † at Stade, 18th Feb. 1830, colonel h. p. and commandant at Stade.

892, 2d hussars—*captain Frederick Ernest von Stoltzenberg,* ¶ 4th—14th Oct. 1805. [H. 1805.] retired 17th May 1806. H. W. C. lieut.-colonel by br. h. p. and commandant at Harburg.

893, 1st dragoons—*captain Augustus von dem Knesebeck,* ¶ 6th Nov. 1803—14th Feb. 1804. (H. 1805.) resigned 7th Sep. 1810, colonel h. p. at Lüneburg.

894, 1st hussars—*captain Charles von Bischoffshansen,* ¶ 22d 24th Jan. 1804. (H. 1805, B. 1807, P. 1809-10.) resigned 24th March 1810, at Cassel.

895, 2d hussars—*captain Clamor von dem Bussche,* ¶ 5th— 17th Nov. 1803. (H. 1805, B. 1807, S. 1809.] resigned 21st July 1810, † 30th July 1816..major Han. 4th hussars.

896, 1st dragoons—*captain Adolphus von Hake,* ¶ 25th Sep. 1804, captain 25th Sep. 1804. (H. 1805, B. 1807,) resigned 2d Dec 1809, .at Ohr, near Hameln.

897, 3d hussars—*captain Hieronimus von der Decken*, ¶ 14th—
21st March 1804. (H. 1805, B. 1807-8, P. 1808-9.) H.
G. O. 2—H. W. M.—H. W. C..resigned 21st July 1810,
major-general H. S. comm. 2d brigade of cavalry.

898, 1st hussars—*lieut. Hermann von der Beck*, ¶ 16th—21st
March 1804. (H. 1805, B. 1807, P. 1809-10.) resigned
22d Sep. 1810..major by br. h. p. at Podendorf, amt
Moisburg, in Han.

899, 2d hussars—*lieut. George von Werlhof*, ¶ 21st—22d Oct.
1805...retired 10th May 1806. †

900, 3d hussars—*lieut. Hannach von Linsingen*, ¶ 19th—24th
Dec. 1805. (B. 1807.) resigned 7th May 1808..captain
h. p. at Schafstall, near Lüneburg.

901, 2d dragoons—*lieut. George Bornemann*, 30th December
1805—21st Jan. 1806. resigned 25th Nov. 1806.

902, 1st hussars—*lieut Bernhard Cropp*, 4th—5th May 1804.
(H. 1805, B. 1807.) resigned 9th June 1810, † at Mis-
burg, near Hanover, 7th March 1824.

903, 3d hussars—*lieut. Anton D. von Wersebe*, 1st—5th May
1804. (H. 1805, B. 1807-8, P. 1808-9.) resigned 3d Nov.
1812, † at Frensdorfsmühlen, dutchy of Bremen, 2d
March 1819.

904, 1st hussars—*lieut. Christian von Heimbruch*, 7th—9th
Feb. 1805. (H. 1805, B. 1807, P. 1809-10.) resigned
22d Sep. 1810. H. W. C...capt. Han. 7th line battalion.

905, 1st dragoons—*lieut. George von Hattorf*, 17th—22d Dec.
1804. (H. 1805.) resigned 19th March 1811..captain
r. l. Prussian service at Pöckelsheim near Paderborn, in
Prussia.

906, 1st dragoons—*lieut. Harlow Phibbs*, 30th April—7th May
1808. (P. 1812.) slightly wounded, 23d Oct. 1812, at
Venta del Poço..resigned 22d June 1813.

907, 1st dragoons—*lieut. Charles von Assig*, 5th—17th March
1812. P. 1813, S. F. 1813-14.) resigned 5th July 1814,
† in England in 1828.

908, 1st hussars—*lieut. Augustus von Scharnhorst*, 16th—22nd
Sep. 1810. retired 6th April 1814; † in 1827..captain
in the Prussian service.

909, 1st dragoons—*lieut. Ulrich von Barner*, 4th—19th May 1812. (P. 1812-13.) Pr. R. E. 3—Pr. I. C.—R. St. A. O. 2—Pr. C.—K. St. W. O. 3—Pr. I. O.—Po. St. O. 2. resigned 23d Oct. 1813...major-gen. Prussian service.

910, 1st hussars—*lieut. John Charles Rahlwes*, 10th—16th July 1811. (P. 1813.) resigned 29th Nov. 1813. † at Baltimore in 1820.

911, 1st hussars—*cornet Gottlieb von Heimbruch*, 9th July, 1805. (H. 1805. B. 1807, P. 1809-10,) severely wounded, 27th June 1809, at Talavera ; resigned 22d Sept. 1810. † at Stelligte, in Han. 6th June 1822, captain Han. 8th regt. infantry.

912, 2d dragoons—*cornet Wm. Christian Alexander Decker*, 4th—21st Jan. 1806..retired 17th May 1806.

913, 2d hussars—*cornet Ernest von Bülow*, 19th—21st Jan. 1806, did not join the regt..resigned 1st Sept. 1806.

914, 3d hussars—*cornet Charles Adolphus von Estorff*, N. C. O. 8th Feb. 1806. (B. 1807-8, P. 1808-9.) H. W. M... resigned 2d Dec. 1809..colonel h. p. at Teindorf, near Uelzen, in Han.

915, 2d hussars—*cornet Christian count Bothmer*, 5th—19th Aug. 1806...resigned 26th Feb. 1811...in Holstein.

916, 2d dragoons—*cornet John Christian Heinssen*, 28th May—2d June, 1810...resigned, 19th Feb. 1811.

917, 2d hussars—*cornet Adolphus Schröder*, 17th—23d Sept. 1811...resigned 16th June, 1812.

918, 1st hussars—*cornet Frederick Klein*, 20th—28th April, 1812. R. St. A. O. 2. Bn. F. O.—R. St. W. O. 4.— R. P. M...Pr. M. O. M.—R. Sw. of H...resigned 25th April, 1813..retired colonel, Russian service.

919, 1st dragoons — *cornet Augustus von Münchhausen*, 5th—19th May, 1812..resigned, 1st Sept. 1812.

920, 2d dragoons, *cornet Valentine von Massow*, 6th— 19th May, 1812. [P. 1812-13.] severely wounded, 23d Oct. 1812. at Venta del Poço. Pr. I. O.—Pr. I. C.—Pr. C. B. B. O. 2.—F. L. H. 5.—He. G. L. 3.—Po. St. O. 3.— R. St. W. O. 4.—R. St. A. O.* 2.—H. G. O. 2.—Pr. K. E. 4...resigned, 16th May, 1813..colonel Prussian service, A. D. C. to his majesty the king of Prussia.

921, 2d hussars—*cornet Frederick von Forer*, 7th—19th May, 1812..resigned, 25th Oct. 1813.

922, 3d hussars—*cornet Frederick James Horn*, 14th Oct.— 3d Nov. 1812..resigned, 16th March, 1813, H. W. C... major, Han. 6th line battalion.

923, 1st hussars—*cornet Frederick von Petersdorff*, 30th Jan. 13th Feb. 1813..resigned, 16th May, 1813.

924, 1st hussars—*cornet George Schreiber*, 6th—20th April, 1813...resigned, 12th Dec. 1813, promoted cornet, by purchase, 11th British light dragoons, 23d Dec. 1813.

925, 1st hussars—*cornet Joost Kops*, 24th July—3d Aug. 1813, resigned, 29th Sep. 1814.

926, 2d dragoons—*cornet Frederick Nanne*, 29th Aug.—11th Sep. 1813..resigned, 7th Dec. 1813.

927, 1st dragoons—*cornet Philip Augustus Warton*, 14th— 23d Nov. 1813..resigned 3d May 1814.

928, 1st dragoons—*paymaster Ernest von Schmiedern*, 5th May 1804. (H. 1805.) H. G. O. 3..resigned 5th Dec. 1806..major unattached, British service.

929, 1st dragoons—*assistant-surgeon William Heise, M.D.* 19th April 1806. (P. 1812.)..resigned 17th March 1812, ..in Ireland.

SUPERSEDED, BEING ABSENT WITHOUT LEAVE.

930, 3d hussars—*lieutenant-colonel Albrecht von Estorff*, ¶ 19th May 1804—24th Dec. 1805. [H. G. O. 2—H. W. M.] superseded, 20th June 1807..lieut.-general h. p. at Veerssen, near Uelzen in Han.

931, 2d dragoons—*lieutenant Charles von Siegroth*, 15th—25th Feb. 1812. [P. 1813.] superseded 15th March 1814.

932, 2d hussars—*cornet Daniel Schultze*, N. C. O. 14th Aug. —6th Sep. 1811. [P. 1811.] superseded 21st Aug. 1813.

933, 1st dragoons—*cornet Henry Struensee*, 19th Aug.—1st Sep. 1812..superseded, 5th Oct. 1813.

934, 1st dragoons—*cornet Jacob Hoenes*, N. C. O. 4th—15th Dec. 1812. [S. F. 1813-14, N. 1814-15.] superseded, 27th April 1815.

935, 1st dragoons—*cornet William Edward Rudolph*, 24th March—6th April 1813..superseded, 29th March 1814.

936, 3d hussars—*cornet Ferdinand von Heymert*, 29th Nov.—7th Dec. 1813..superseded, 17th May 1814, not having joined since appointed.

937, 1st hussars—*cornet Frederick von Quiter*, 22d July—12th Aug. 1814..superseded, 22d July 1815.

938, 2d dragoons—*assistant-surgeon Cramer, M.D.* 30th Dec. 1805..superseded, 25th Oct. 1806.

939, 2d dragoons—*veterinary-surgeon Koch*, 21st Jan. 1806.. superseded, 12th Aug. 1806. † at Harburg, 27th April 1833.

DISMISSED HIS MAJESTY'S SERVICE.

940, 3d hussars—*paymaster Harris Power*, 9th December 1806. [B. 1807.]..dismissed, 5th July 1811.

NAMES OF THE OFFICERS WHO WERE GAZETTED, BUT WHOSE APPOINTMENT DID NOT TAKE PLACE, AS THEY NEVER JOINED THE CORPS.

941, 2d hussars—*lieut.-colonel Crusen*, ¶ 20th May 1804—28th Jan. 1806..appointment cancelled, 8th Feb. 1806.

942, 2d dragoons—*cornet J. W. von Struve*, 1st—21st Jan. 1806. H. G. O. 3—H. W. M. appointment cancelled, 15th Feb. 1806. † at Behrensen, near Hameln, 17th Nov. 1834, colonel by br. h. p.

943, 1st hussars—*cornet von Reichmeister*, 3d—14th Feb. 1807. appointment cancelled 16th May 1807.

944, 1st dragoons—*cornet Charles von Reden*, 9th—18th July 1807..appointment cancelled, 12th May 1810. † in 1813, in consequence of wounds received in the battle of Leipzig..captain in the Prussian service.

945, 2d hussars—*cornet Schulze*, 2d—16th Feb. 1813...appointment cancelled, 2d March 1813.

946, 1st dragoons—*cornet Adolphus von Bock*, 20th—29th June 1813. H. W. M.—H. W. C...appointment cancelled 30th April 1814...lieut. and adjt. 2d Han. dragoons.

947, 2d dragoons—*Frederick von Veltheim*, 9th—29th April 1815...appointment cancelled, 3d June 1815...at Nordheim, in Han.

948, 3d hussars—*cornet Buch*, 10th—22d July 1815,..appointment cancelled 4th November 1815.

NAMES OF OFFICERS WHO LEFT THE LEGION, EITHER
BY PROMOTION, OR TRANSFER TO BRITISH REGIMENTS,
OR APPOINTMENTS UPON THE STAFF OF THE ARMY,

949, Staff—*brigade-major Joseph Seeliger*, 16th—17th Nov.
1803. captain 16th Nov. 1803.(H. 1805.) appointed captain of a company in the 83d regt. of infantry, 27th Aug.
1805. † in London, 18th June 1819.

950, Artillery—*assistant-surgeon Augustus Romhield*, 3d Jan.
1804. [H. 1805.) promoted surgeon in de Roll's regt. 29th
Dec. 1804...at Genoa,

951, 2d hussars—*captain Augustus Heiliger*, 3d Sep. 1803,
K's German regiment,..17th Nov. 1803, King's German
legion. [H. 1805.] transferred to 15th light dragoons
25th March 1806. † at sea off Corunna Jan 1809,
whilst serving on the staff of sir John Moore's army.

952, 1st hussars—*lieut. William von der Osten*, ¶ 10th—17th
Nov. 1803. (H. 1805.) H. G. O. 3—B. W. M. transferred to the 16th light dragoons 5th Nov. 1808..major and
lieut.-colonel à la suite H. S.

953, 1st hussars—*lieut. Lewis von Düring*, 5th May 1804. (H.
1805.) transferred to the 15th light dragoons, 23d July
1805...major.

954, 1st dragoons—*lieut. and adjutant William von Bock*,
13th—21st March 1804..lieut. 12th Oct. 1805. (H.1805.)
transferred to the 8th garrison battalion, 17th Nov. 1807.

955, 1st dragoons—*cornet John Peters*, 14th—21st March 1804.
[H. 1805.] promoted lieutenant in the Scot's Greys, 13th
April 1805...lieut.-colonel half-pay unattached at Wen-
nebostel, in Han.

956, 3d hussars—*cornet Charles Holborn*, N. C. O. 9th—20th
June 1807. (B. 1807-8, P. 1808-9.) promoted lieut. 10th
light dragoons, 11th Feb. 1812...at Hamburg.

957, 1st dragoons—*cornet Charles Auchmuty*, 20th Aug.—3d
Sep. 1808..promoted lieut. 7th regt. of foot, 19th August
1809.

958, 1st dragoons—*cornet Govert Roepel*, 21st—28th Jan. 1809, promoted lieut. 60th regiment of foot, 3d March 1812.

959, 1st dragoons—*cornet Edward Adams*, 19th—23d June 1810..transfered to 3d dragoons, 17th Nov. 1812.

960, 1st Dragoons—*cornet Frederick von Loen*, 21st Sep.—8th Oct. 1811..promoted lieut. 10th light dragoons, 5th Nov. 1811, and again transferred to the 15th light dragoons, 10th Dec. 1811.

961, 1st dragoons—*surgeon John Gottlob Meusel, M.D.* ¶ 5th May 1804. (H. 1805, M. 1807.) promoted surgeon to the forces, 25th July 1805, and physician to the forces, 20th June 1807. † in Hanover 26th March 1817.

962, 1st hussars—*surgeon Christian Brandes*, ¶ 3d Nov. 1804. (H. 1805, B. 1807, M. 1808-9-10-11-12-13-14.) promoted surgeon to the forces, 4th June 1837..at Hainholz near Hanover.

963, 3d hussars—*surgeon Charles Grosskopf, M. D.* ¶ 25th Nov. 1805..deputy inspector of hospitals to the forces on the continent of Europe only, 22d Feb. 1816. (B. 1807-8, P. 1808-9, N. 1814, C. 1815.) H. G. O. 3—H. W. C.. promoted surgeon to the forces, 13th Feb. 1813..staff surgeon H. S. at Hanover.

964, 2d dragoons—*surgeon Victor Sergel, M. D.* ¶ 30th Dec. 1805..physician to the forces on the continent of Europe only, 22d Feb. 1816. (P. 1810-11-12-13, S. F. 1813-14, N. 1814-15.) promoted surgeon to the forces, 8th Aug. 1809...at Osnabrück.

965, 2d dragoons—*surgeon John Taberger, M. D.* 3d Nov. 1804. (H. 1805, B. 1807-8. P. 1808-9-12-13, S. F. 1813-14, N. G.† 1814.) promoted surgeon to the forces, 22d Jan. 1814...at Hanover.

966, 1st dragoons—*surgeon John Frederick Grosskopf, M. D.* 21st April 1804. (H. 1805, P. 1812-13, S. F. 1813-14, N. 1814, W. & C. 1815.) B. W. M..promoted surgeon to the forces, 22d Feb. 1816. † at Celle, 21st April 1823, surgeon Han. cuirassier guards

967, 2d hussars—*surgeon Frederick William Wollring, M. D.* 3d Dec. 1805. (H. 1805, B. 1807, S. 1809, P. 1811-12-13, N. 1814, C. 1815.) promoted surgeon to the forces, 22d Feb. 1816..at Diepholz in Han.

968, 1st dragoons—*asst.-surgeon Henry Waiblinger, M. D.* 13th Nov. 1803. (H. 1805.) promoted surgeon to the duke of Brunswick-Oel.'s cavalry, 17th March 1810.

969, 2d dragoons—*asst.-surgeon Frederick Seiler, M. D.* 25th October 1806. (P. 1812-13, S. F. 1813-14.) promoted assistant-surgeon to the forces, 5th Jan. 1813, and surgeon to the forces, 26th May, 1814, † at Lüde near Pyrmont, 16th April 1836.

970, 1st dragoons—*veterinary surgeon William Clarkson,* 21st Dec. 1803. (H. 1805) transferred to the 1st or King's dragoon guards, 25th March 1805.

INFANTRY.

KILLED IN BATTLE.

971, 4th line battalion—*colonel commandant Ernst Eberhard Kuno von Langwerth,* ¶ 14th Nov.—20th Dec. 1803. brigadier-gen. 1808. (H. 1805, B. 1807-8, P. 1808-9.) B. G. M. Talavera..killed in the battle of Talavera de la Reyna, in Spain, 28th July 1809.

972, 5th line batt.—*colonel commandant Christian von Ompteda,* ¶ 13th—17th Nov. 1803..colonel 4th June 1813. (H. 1805, M. 1806-7, B. 1807-8, P. 1813, S. F. 1813-14, N. 1814, W. & C. 1815.) B. G. M. 12..Vittoria,—Nive Nivelle—B. W. M..killed in the battle of Waterloo, 18th June 1815.

973, 2d line battalion—*major Adolphus Wm. von Wurmb,* ¶ 12th Oct. 1803—14th Feb. 1804. (H. 1805, M. 1806-7, B. 1807-8, P. 1808-9-10-11-12.) severely wounded, 27th Sep. 1810, at Busaco—B. G. M. 1. 2. Talavera,—Busaco, Salamanca..killed in storming the interior line of defence of the castle of Burges in Spain, 18th Oct. 1812.

974, 2d line batt.—*major Paul Gottlieb Chüden*, ¶ 18th Oct. 1803—10th Dec. 1805. (B. 1807-8, P. 1808-9-10-11-12-13, S. F. 1813-14.) severely wounded, 27th Feb. 1814, before Bayonne..killed in a sortie made by the French garrison of Bayonne in France, on the morning of 14th April 1814.

975, 2d light batt.—*captain Adolphus Böseviel*, ¶ 5th May 1804..major 4th June 1814. (H. 1805, B. 1807-8, P. 1808-9-11, S. 1809, N. 1814, W. & C. 1815.) B. W. M. killed in the battle of Waterloo, 18th June 1815.

976, 1st line batt.—*captain Charles Christian Frederick von Avemann*, ¶ 3d—14th Feb. 1804..captain 19th July 1804. (H. 1805, B. 1807-8, P. 1808-9-10-11-12-13.) killed in the battle of the Pyrenees, near Pamplona in Spain, 28th July 1813, whilst serving as brigade major in the 4th infantry division.

977, 2d line batt.—*captain Ernest Scharnhorst*, ¶ 19th—25th Sep. 1804. (H. 1805, M. 1806-7. B. 1807-8, P. 1808-9-10-11-12.) severely wounded, 28th July 1809 at Talavera; severely wounded, 22d July 1812, at Salamanca..killed 22d Sep. 1812, in the attack of the exterior line of defence of the castle of Burgos.

978, 1st line battalion—*captain William von Saffe*, ¶ 6th—17th Nov. 1803. [H. 1805, M. 1806-7, B. 1807-8, P. 1808-9-10-11-12.] slightly wounded, 28th July 1809, at Talavera..killed, 8th Oct. 1812, in the siege of the castle of Burgos.

979, 1st line battalion—*captain Charles Dettmering*, ¶ 3d Jan. 1804. [H. 1805, M. 1806-7, B. 1807-8, P. 1808-9.] killed in action before Oporto, 11th May 1809.

980, 1st line battalion—*captain Christian von Wersebe*, ¶ 12th—14th Feb. 1804, (H. 1805, M. 1806-7, B. 1807-8, P. 1808-9.) killed in the battle of Talavera de la Reyna in Spain, 28th July 1809.

981, 5th line batt.—*capt. Ernest Christian Charles von Wurmb*, ¶ 25th May 1805. (H. 1805, B. 1807-8, P. 1808-9-10-11-12-13, S. F. 1813-14, N. 1814, W. & C. 1815.) B. W. M..killed in the battle of Waterloo, 18th June 1815.

982, 8th line battalion—*captain Augustus William von Voigt,* ¶ 13th—24th May 1806. [B. 1807, M. 1808-9-10-11-12-13-14, N. 1814, W. & C. 1815.] B. W. M..killed in the battle of Waterloo, 18th June 1815.

983, 2d light battalion—*captain Henry Wiegmann,* ¶ 7th—21st Jan. 1806..captain 24th Oct. 1811. [B. 1807-8, P. 1808-9-11-12-13, S. 1809, S. F. 1813-14, N. 1814, W. & C. 1815.] B. W. M..killed in the battle of Waterloo, 18th June 1815.

984, 2d line battalion—*captain George Tilee,* ¶ 16th June 1804. [H. 1805, B. 1807-8, P. 1808-9 10-11, N. G.† 1813-14, N. 1814, W. & C. 1815.] B. W. M..killed in the battle of Waterloo, 18th June 1815.

985, 1st line battalion—*captain Augustus von Saffe,* 5th—14th Feb. 1804..major 18th June 1815, it not being known at the time that he was killed at Waterloo. (H. 1805, M. 1806-7, B. 1807-8, P. 1808-9-10-11, N. G. 1813-14, N. 1814, W. & C. 1815.) slightly wounded, 28th July 1809, at Talavera. B. W. M..killed in the battle of Waterloo, 18th June 1815.

986, 2d line battalion—*captain Henry Müller,* 19th—24th Jan. 1804. (H. 1805, M. 1806-7, B. 1807-8, P. 1808-9-10-11, S. F. 1813-14.) killed in a sortie made by the French garrison of Bayonne, on the morning of the 14th of April 1814.

987, 1st light battalion—*captain Gottlieb Thilo Holtzermann,* 23d—24th Jan. 1804. (H. 1805, B. 1807-8, P. 1808-9, S. 1809, N. G. 1813-14, N. 1814, W. & C. 1815.) B. W. M..killed in the battle of Waterloo, 18th June 1815.

988, 2d light battalion—*captain Frederick Melchior William Schaumann,* 20th—21st April 1805. [H. 1805, B. 1807-8, P. 1808-9, S. 1809, N. G. 1813-14, N. 1814, W. & C. 1815.] B. W. M..killed in the battle of Waterloo, 18th June 1815.

989, 1st line battalion—*captain Charles von Holle*, 19th—21st March 1804. (H. 1805, M. 1806-7. B. 1807-8, P. 1808-9-10-11-12-13, S. F. 1813-14, N. 1814, W. & C. 1815.) severely wounded, 28th July 1809, at Talavera, B. W. M. killed in the battle of Waterloo, 18th June 1815.

990, 3d line batt.—*captain Frederick Diedel*, ¶ 17th—22d Dec. 1804. (H. 1805, B. 1807, M. 1808-9-10-11-12-13-14, N. 1814, W. & C. 1815.) B. W. M..killed in the battle of Waterloo, 18th June 1815.

991, 1st light batt.—*captain Henry von Marschalck*, 23d March 1805. (H. 1805, B. 1807-8, P. 1808-9-11-12-13, S. 1809, S. F. 1813-14, N. 1814, W. & C. 1815.) B. W. M. killed in the battle of Waterloo, 18th June 1815.

992, 8th line battalion—*captain Thilo von Westernhagen*, 24th May 1806. (B. 1807, M. 1808-9-10-11-12-13-14, N. 1814, W. & C. 1815.) B. W. M..killed in the battle of Waterloo, 18th June 1815.

993, 1st light batt.—*captain Augustus Alexander von Goeben*, 25th—28th Jan. 1806. (B. 1807-8, P. 1808-9-11-12-13, S. 1809, S. F. 1813-14, N. 1814, W.&C. 1815.) B. W. M..killed in the battle of Waterloo, 18th June 1815.

994, 5th line battalion—*lieut. George Evert*, ¶ 7th—10th Dec. 1805. (B. 1807-8, P. 1808-9.) killed in the battle of Talavera de la Reyna, 28th July 1809.

995, 5th line batt.—*lieut. Ernest Gottlieb von Dachenhausen*, ¶ 3d Jan.—8th Feb. 1806. (B. 1807-8, P. 1808-9.) killed in the battle of Talavera de la Reyna, 28th July 1809.

996, 5th line battalion—*lieut. George Hemmelmann*, 23d—25th May 1805. (B. 1807-8, P. 1808-9.) killed in the battle of Talavera de la Reyna, 28th July 1809.

997, 2d line battalion—*lieut. Charles Gustavus Meyer*, N. C. O. 20th Aug. 1805. (H. 1805, M. 1806-7. B. 1807-8. P. 1808-9-10-11-12-13, S. F. 1813-14.) killed in action before Bayonne, 27th Feb. 1814.

998, 8th line battalion—*lieut. William von Marenholz*, 17th June 1806. (B. 1807, M. 1808-9-10-11-12-13-14, P. 1812-13 N. 1814, W. & C. 1815.) B. W. M..killed in the battle of Waterloo, 18th June 1815.

999, 2d line battalion—*lieut. Adolphus Hansing*, 28th Jan. 1806. (M. 1806-7. B. 1807-3, P. 1808-9-10-11-12.) killed in the attack of the exterior line of defence of the castle of Burgos, 22d Sep. 1812.

1000, 1st line batt.—*lieut. George Henry von Hodenberg*, 27th 28th Jan. 1806. (M. 1806-7, B. 1807-8, P. 1808-9.) killed in the battle of Talavera de la Reyna, 28th July 1809.

1001, 2d light battalion—*lieutenant Florian Sprecher*, 23d May, 1809 (S. 1809.) killed before Flushing, isle of Walcheren, 14th August, 1809.

1002, 5th line battalion—*lieutenant John Meyer*, N. C. O. 10th July—12th Aug. 1806. (H. 1805, B. 1807-8, P. 1808-9-10 11-12-13, S. F. 1813-14.) killed in a sortie made by the French garrison of Bayonne, on the morning of the 14th April 1814.

1003, 3d line battalion—*lieutenant Frederick Hasselbach*, N.C. O. 9th—23d Sep. 1806. (H. 1805, B. 1807, M. 1809-10-11-12, P*. 1812-13.) killed in action near Castalla in Spain, 13th April 1813.

1004, 5th line batt.—*lieutenant Charles Köhler*, N. C. O. 15th —21st Feb. 1809. (H. 1805, B. 1807.8, P. 1808-9-10-11-12-13, S. F. 1813-14.) severely wounded, 28th July 1809, at Talavera; killed in a sortie made by the French garrison of Bayonne, on the morning of 14th of April 1814.

1005, 2d light battalion—*lieutenant John Whitney*, 20th—25th July 1809. (P. 1811.) killed in the battle of Albuera, 16th May 1811.

1006, 1st light battalion—*lieut. George Elderhorst*, 28th Jan. 1806. (B. 1807-8, P. 1808 9.11-12-13, S. 1809, S. F. 1813-14.) slightly wounded, 9th Dec. 1813, before Bayonne; killed in action before Bayonne, 28th of Feb. 1814.

1007, 1st light battalion—*lieutenant Frederick von Klenck*, 1st March 1806. (B. 1807-8, P. 1808-9-11-12-13, S. 1809, S. F. 1813.) killed in action, on fording the river Bidassoa, south of France, 7th Oct 1813.

1008, 1st light batt. *lieutenant Anton Albert*, N. C. O. 21st— 27th May 1809. (B. 1807-8, P. 1808-9-11-12-13, S. 1809, S. F. 1813-14, N. 1814, W. & C. 1815.) B. W. M. killed in the battle of Waterloo, 18th June 1815.

1009, 2d light battalion—*lieut. James Grant*, 7th—23d Dec. 1809. (P. 1811.) killed in action when reconnoitering before Badajoz, on the 22d April 1811.

1010, 1st line battalion—*lieut. George Boyd*, 29th May—10th June, 1809. (P. 1809-10-11-12-13, S. F. 1813. slightly wounded, 25th June 1813, at Toloza, killed 10th Nov. 1813, in action near Urugne, in France.

1011, 2d light battalion—*lieut. W. Philip Augustus von Fincke*, N. C. O. 15th—23d Oct 1810. (P. 1811-12.) killed in the battle of Salamanca, 22d July 1812.

1012, 5th line battalion—*lieut. & adj. John L. Schuck*, N. C. O. 15th Oct.—3d Nov. 1812..lieutenant, 25th April 1814. H. 1805, B. 1807-8, P. 1808-9-10-11 12-13, S. F. 1813-14, N. 1814, W. &. C. 1815.) killed in the battle of Waterloo, 18th June 1815.

1013, 2d light battalion—*ensign Frederick von Robertson*, 28th Nov.—7th Dec. 1813. (N. 1814, W. & C. 1815.) B.W.M..killed in the battle of Waterloo, 18th Jun. 1815

1014, 1st line battalion—*ensign Hartwich von Lücken*, 1st Feb. 1st March 1814. (N. 1814, W. & C. 1815.) B. W. M.. killed in the battle of Waterloo, 18th June 1815.

1015, 4th line battalion—*ensign Edward Theodore von Cronhelm*, 10th June—9th July 1814. (N. 1814, W. & C. 1815.) B. W. M..killed in the battle of Waterloo, 18th June 1815.

DIED OF WOUNDS.

1016, 2d line battalion—*lieut.-colonel John Brauns*, ¶ 6th Jan. 25th May 1805. (H. 1805, B. 1807-8, P. 1808-9.) B. G. M. Talavera—† 6th Oct. 1809, of the wounds he received in the battle of Talavera de la Reyna, 28th July 1809.

1017, 4th line battalion—*lieut.-col. George Charles Augustus du Plat,* ¶ 18th Nov. 1803—17th Nov. 1804..colonel 4th June 1813. (H. 1805, B. 1807, M. 1808-9-10-11-12, P.* 1812-13-14, S. F. 1814, N. 1814, W. & C. 1815.) B. W. M. † 21st June 1815, of the wounds he received in the battle of Waterloo, 18th June 1815.

1018, 2d line battalion—*lieut.-col. John Christian von Schröder,* ¶ 8th Oct. 1803—24th May 1806..lieut.-colonel 4th June 1813. (B. 1807, M. 1808-9-10-11-12-13-14, N. 1814, W. & C. 1815. B. W. M. † 22d June 1815, of the wounds he received in the battle of Waterloo, 18th June 1815.

1019, 4th line battalion—*major George Wm. Cyriacus Chüden,* ¶ 9th Nov. 1803—9th Feb. 1805..major 4th June 1814. (H. 1805. B. 1807, N. G.† 1813-14, N. 1814, W. & C. 1815.) B. W. M. † 19th June 1815, of the wounds he received in the battle of Waterloo, 18th June 1815.

1020, 5th line battalion—*captain Ernest von Hamelberg,* ¶ 19th Oct. 1803—10th Dec. 1805. B. 1807-8, P. 1808-9.) † 11th August 1809, of the wounds he received in the battle of Talavera de la Reyna, 28th July 1809.

1021, 5th line battalion—*capt. Fred. Ernest Philip Langrehr,* ¶ 3d Nov. 1803—25th May 1805. (H. 1805, B. 1807-8, P. 1808-9-10-11-12.) † 12th Sep. 1812, at Salamanca, of the wounds he received in the battle near that place, 22d July 1812.

1022, 1st line battalion—*capt. Henry La Roche de Starkenfels,* ¶ 5th Nov. 1803—14th Feb. 1804. (H. 1805, M. 1806-7, B. 1807-8, P. 1808-9-10-11-12.) B. G. M..Ciudad-Rodrigo. † at Arevalo in Spain, 31st Oct. 1812, of the wounds he received before the castle of Burgos, 18th October 1812.

1023, 5th line battalion—*captain John Wm. Lucas Bacmeister,* ¶ 7th Nov. 1803—25th May 1805. (H. 1805, B. 1807-8, P. 1808-9-10-11-12.) † 2d Nov. 1812, at Penaranda in Spain, of the wounds he received before the castle of Burgos, 18th Oct. 1812.

1024, 2d line battalion—*captain Charles von Heldcritt*, ¶ 21st April 1804. (H. 1805, M. 1806-7, B. 1807-8, P. 1808-9.) † 3d Aug. 1809, of the wounds he received in the battle of Talavera de la Reyna, 28th July 1809.

1025, 4th line battalion—*captain George Lewis Leue*, ¶ 15th—17th Nov. 1804..major 4th June 1814. [H. 1805, B. 1807, M. 1808-9-10-11-12, P.* 1812-13-14, S. F. 1814, N. 1814, W. & C. 1815.] B. W. M. † 23d June 1815, of the wounds he received in the battle of Waterloo, 18th June 1815.

1026, 2d light battalion—*captain Frederick William Augustus du Fay*, ¶ 15th—17th Nov. 1803. (H. 1805, B. 1807-8, P. 1808-9, S. 1809.) † 11th Feb. 1810 at Porchester Hants, of the wounds he received before Flushing, ou the isle of Walcheren, on the 7th Aug. 1809.

1027, 2d light battalion—*captain George Arnold Heise*, 13th—17th Nov. 1803. (H. 1805, B. 1807-8, P. 1808-9-11.) † 10th June 1811 at Elvas in Portugal, of the wounds he received in the battle of Albuera, 16th of May 1811.

1028, 1st light battalion—*captain Lewis Cropp*, 3d Sep. 1803—King's German regt., 17th Nov. 1803, King's German legion. (H. 1805, B. 1807-8, P. 1808-9-10-11-12-13.) † 25th June 1813, of the wounds he received on that day in action near Toloza in Spain.

1029, 4th line battalion—*captain George Heise*, ¶ 18th—22d Dec. 1804. (H. 1805, B. 1807, M. 1808 9-10-11-12, P.* 1812-13-14, S. F. 1814, N. 1814, W. & C. 1815.) B. W. M.. † 27th June 1815, of the wounds he received in the battle of Waterloo, 18th June 1815.

1030, 1st line battalion—*captain Frederick Heine*, 6th—14th Feb. 1804. (H. 1805, M. 1806-7, B. 1807-8, P. 1808-9-10-11-12-13.) † 3d Sep. 1813, of the wounds he received in the storming of San Sebastian, 31st Aug. 1813.

1031, 1st line battalion—*lieut. Lewis von Bothmer*, 20th July 1804. (H. 1805, M. 1806-7, B. 1807-8. P. 1808-9-10-11-12.) † of his wounds 5th Jan. 1813, at Burgos in Spain, he being severely wounded in the assault of the castle of Burgos, and taken prisoner by the enemy on the 18th Oct. 1812.

1032, 2d line battalion—*lieut. Augustus Rypke*, 25th—28th Jan. 1806. (H. 1805, M. 1806 7, B. 1807-8, P. 1808-9-10-11-12.) † 30th July 1812, of the wounds he received in the battle of Salamanca, 22d of July 1812.

1033, 3d line battalion—*lieut. Ernestus von Freytag*, 27th—28th Jan. 1806. [H. 1805, B. 1807, M. 1808-9-10-11-12, P.* 1812-13.] † at Alicante, 13th June 1813 of the wounds he received in action near Castalla, 13th April 1813.

1034, 1st line battalion—*lieutenant Frederick von Hodenberg*, 25th—28th January 1806. (M. 1806-7, B. 1807-8, P. 1808-9.) † 30th July 1809, of the wounds he received in the battle of Talavera de la Reyna, 28th July 1809.

1035, 5th line battalion—*lieut. Paul Müller*—28th Jan. 1806. (H. 1805, B. 1807-8, P. 1808-9-10.) † 3d Nov. 1810, at Lisbon, of the wounds he received in a skirmish near Deteiro, on the 14th Oct. 1810.

1036, 1st light battalion—*lieut. Henry von Heimbruch*, 6th Aug. 1805. (H. 1805, B. 1807-8, P. 1808-9-10-11-12-13, S. F. 1813-14.) † 2d March 1814,) of the wounds he received in action before Bayonne, 27th of Feb. 1814.

1037, 3d line battalion—*lieut. Frederick von Jeinsen*, N. C. O. 13th—27th Oct. 1807. (H. 1805, B. 1807, M. 1808-9-10-11-12-14, P.* 1812-13, N. 1814, W. & C. 1815.) B. W. M. † 28th June 1815, at Brussels, of the wounds he received in the battle of Waterloo, 18th June 1815.

1038, 2d. light batt.—*lieut. Adol. von Witzendorff*, N.C.O. 8th—2d Dec. 1809. (P. 1811-12-13, S. F. 1813-14.) † 19th March 1814, of the wounds he received in action before Bayonne on the 27th Feb. 1814.

1039, 1st light battalion—*lieut. Charles von Hedemann*, 24th November—2d Dec. 1809. (P. 1811-12-13, S. F. 1813-14.) slightly wounded 21st June 1813 at Vittoria. † 30th March 1814, of the wounds he received that day in action before Bayonne.

1040, 1st line batt.—*lieut. Conrad Victor Meyer*, N. C. O. 17th 25th Feb. 1809. (M. 1806-7, B. 1807-8, P. 1808-9-10-11-12) † 18th Oct. 1812, of the wounds he received on the evening of the 4th Oct. 1812, in the assault and capture of the exterior line of defence of the castle of Burgos.

1041, 4th line battalion—*lieut. Charles Graeffe*, 29th March—8th April, 1809. (M. 1809-10-11-12, P.* 1812-13.) † 14th Sep. 1813, of the wounds he received in action on the night of the 12th and morning of the 13th Sep. 1813, in the pass of Ordal in Spain.

1042, 3d line battalion—*lieut. Frederick Leschen*, N. C. O. 8th—29th Aug. 1812. (M. 1808-9-10-11-12-13-14, N. 1814, W. & C. 1815.) B. W. M. † 28th June, 1815, at Brussels, of the wounds he received in the battle of Waterloo, 18th June 1815.

1043, 1st light battalion—*ensign Edward Schmalhausen*, 18th Jan.—16th Feb. 1811. (P. 1811.] † 9th June 1811, at Elvas in Portugal, of the wounds he received in the battle of Albuera, 16th May 1811.

1044, 1st line battalion—*ensign Ernest baron le Fort*, 8th—25th Sep. 1813. (N. G. 1813.) † 16th Sep. 1813, of the wounds he received on that day, in the battle of the Göhrde.

LOST AT SEA OR DROWNED BY SHIPWRECK.

1045, 2d line battalion—*lieut.-colonel Joachim Christian Andreas von Lösecke*, ¶ 10th Jan.—11th May 1805. [H. 1805, M. 1806-7, B. 1807.] lost by the wreck of the "Salisbury" transport on the Kentish coast, 11th Nov. 1807, on the return of the expedition from Copenhagen.

1046, 7th line battalion—*lieut.-colonel Frederick von Goldacker*, ¶ 21st April 1804. (H. 1805, B. 1807, M. 1808-9.) supposed to have perished on board the Harmony transport, which was lost in the Mediterranean about the beginning of 1810, on her voyage from Malta to England. The lieutenant-colonel and his wife took their passage in the Harmony, but the actual fate of them and the vessel has not been ascertained.

1047, 7th line battalion—*capt. Frederick Augustus de Tessier*, ¶ 12th Oct. 1803—21st Jan. 1806. (B. 1807.) lost by the wreck of the " Eagle packet" in the Queen's channel, November 1807, on the return of the expedition from Copenhagen.

1048, 7th line battalion—*captain Burchard Lewis von der Decken*, ¶ 14th Oct. 1803—21st Jan. 1806. (B. 1807.) lost by the wreck of the " Eagle packet" in the Queen's channel, Nov. 1807, on the return of the expedition from Copenhagen.

1049, 2d light battalion—*captain Bodo Wilken*, ¶ 13th—17th Nov. 1803. (H. 1805, B. 1807-8, P. 1808-9.) lost by the wreck of the "Smallbridge" transport on her return to England from Vigo, in Feb. 1809.

1050, 2d line battalion—*captain George Ritter*, ¶ 20th—24th Jan. 1804. (H. 1805, M. 1806-7, B. 1807.) lost by the wreck of the " Salisbury" transport on the Kentish coast, 11th Nov. 1807, on the return of the expedition from Copenhagen.

1051, 7th line battalion—*captain William von Coulon*, ¶ 28th Dec. 1805—21st Jan. 1806. (B. 1807.) lost by the wreck of the " Eagle packet" in the Queen's channel, Nov. 1807, on the return of the expedition from Copenhagen.

1052, 2d line battalion—*lieut. Adolphus von Hinüber*, ¶ 5th—14th Feb. 1804. (H. 1805, M. 1806-7, B. 1807.) lost by the wreck of the " Salisbury" transport, on the Kentish coast, 11th Nov. 1807, on the return of the expedition from Copenhagen.

z 24

1053, 2d line battalion—*lieutenant Frederick Ludewig Augustus Marburg,* ¶ 13th—14th Feb. 1804. (H. 1805, M. 1806-7, B. 1807.) lost by the wreck of the "Salisbury" transport, on the Kentish coast, 11th Nov. 1807, on the return of the expedition from Copenhagen.

1054, 2d line battalion—*lieutenant and adjutant Frederick von Hodenberg,* ¶ 21st April 1804. (H. 1805, M. 1806-7, B. 1807, lost by the wreck of the "Salisbury" transport on the Kentish coast, 11th Nov. 1807, on the return of the expedition from Copenhagen.

1055, 2d light battalion—*lieutenant George von Heimbruch,* ¶ 19th—23d April 1805.) H. 1805, B. 1807, P. 1808-9.) lost by the wreck of the "Smallbridge" transport, on her return from Vigo to England Feb. 1809.

1056, 7th line battalion—*lieutenant Hermann von Schlütter,* ¶ 16th—21st Jan. 1806. (B. 1807.) lost by the wreck of the "Eagle packet" in the Queen's channel, Nov. 1807, on the return of the expedition from Copenhagen.

1057, 2d line battalion—*liutenant Francis Wedemeyer,* 13th—14th Feb. 1804. [H. 1805, M. 1806-7, B. 1807.] lost by the wreck of the "Salisbury" transport, on the Kentish coast, 11th Nov. 1807, on the return of the expedition from Copenhagen.

1058, 7th line battalion—*lieutenant Leopold Wattenberg,* 8th—21st Jan. 1806. [B. 1807.] lost by the wreck of the "Eagle packet" in the Queen's channel, Nov. 1807, on the return of the expedition from Copenhagen.

1059, 2d line battalion—*lieutenant Augustus Isenbart,* 8th—9th Feb. 1805. (H. 1805, M. 1806-7, B. 1807.) lost by the wreck of the "Salisbury" transport on the Kentish coast, 11th Nov. 1807, on the return of the expedition from Copenhagen.

1060, 2d line battalion—*ensign George Leopold John Frederick Charles Greve.* 20th—21st Jan. 1806. (M. 1806-7, B. 1807.) lost by the wreck of the "Salisbury" transport, on the Kentish coast, 11th Nov. 1807, on the return of the expedition from Copenhagen.

1061, 2d light battalion—*ensign Charles Augustus Augspurg*, 4th Feb. 1806. (B. 1807, P. 1808-9.) lost by the wreck of the "Smallbridge" transport on her return from Vigo to England, in Feb. 1809.

1062, 7th line battalion—*ensign Leopoldus le Bachellé*, 24th June 1806. (B. 1807) lost by the wreck of the "Eagle packet" in the Queen's channel, Nov. 1807, on the return of the expedition from Copenhagen.

1063, 7th line battalion—*David le Bachellé*, N. C. O. 7th Sep. —8th Nov. 1806. (B. 1807.) lost by the wreck of the "Eagle packet" in the Queen's channel, Nov. 1807, on the return of the expedition from Copenhagen.

1064, 2d line battalion—*ensign Lewis Leonhard Müller*, N. C. O. 14th—21st March 1807. (M. 1806-7, B. 1807.) lost by the wreck of the "Salisbury" transport on the Kentish coast, 11th Nov. 1807, on the return of the expedition from Copenhagen.

1065, 7th line battalion—*ensign Adolphus von Spilker*, 9th—16th May 1807. (M. 1806-7, B. 1807.) lost by the wreck of the "Eagle Packet," in the Queen's channel, Nov. 1807, on the return of the expedition from Copenhagen.

1066, 2d light battalion—*ensign William Riddle*, N. C. O. 15th—28th July 1807, [H. 1805, B. 1808, P. 1808-9.] lost by the wreck of the "Smallbridge" transport, on her return from Vigo to England, in Feb. 1809.

1067, 2d light battalion—*quartermaster James Willan*, 25th March—19th April 1808. [B. 1808, P. 1808-9.] lost by the wreck of the "Smallbridge" transport on her return from Vigo to England, in Feb. 1809

DIED FROM ILLNESS OR ACCIDENTS.

1068, 5th line battalion—*colonel commandant George Henry Klingsöhr*, ¶ 17th Dec. 1804—9th July 1805...colonel 4th June 1813. (H. 1805, B. 1807, M. 1808-9, P. 1810-11-12-13.) B. G. M. 1, 2, Fuentes de Onoro,—Salamanca, Vittoria. † in the camp near Oyarzun in Spain, 4th Aug. 1813.

1069, 5th line battalion—*lieut-colonel Charles von Reinbold*, ¶ 10th Nov. 1803—25th Sept. 1804. [H. 1805, B. 1807-8, P. 1808-9.] † at Sacavom near Lisbon, 1st March 1809.

1070, 1st light battalion—*lieut-colonel Ernest Lewis Francis Leonhart*, ¶ 8th—12th Jan. 1805. [H. 1805, B. 1807-8. P. 1808-9-11-12, S. 1809.] severely wounded, 16th May 1811, at Albuera, B. G. M. 1, Albuera—Salamanca, &c. † at Escurial in Spain, 10th Sept. 1812.

1071, 7th line battalion—*lieut.-colonel William Offeney*, ¶ 17th Nov. 1803. [H. 1805, B. 1807-8, P. 1808-9-11-12, S. 1809.] B. G. M. Fuentes de Onoro. † at Belem in Portugal, 15th Aug. 1812,

1072, 8th line battalion—*lieut-colonel George von Lasperg*, ¶ 20th April 1804—21st Jan. 1806. [B. 1807, M. 1808-9-10-11-12.] † at Melazzo in Sicily, 5th Feb. 1812.

1073, 6th line battalion—*major Ferdinand Diederich von Ompteda*, ¶ 10th Oct. 1803—21st Jan. 1806. . lieutenant-colonel 4th June 1814. [B. 1807, M. 1808-9-10-11-12-13-14, P.* 1812-13.] † at Verden, 9th May 1815.

1074, 2d light battalion—*major Henry Peter Hurtzig*, ¶ 28th Oct. 1803—21st Jan. 1806. [B. 1807, M. 1808-9-10-11-12, P. 1813, S. F. 1813-14.] B. G. M. 1, Vittoria, Nive. † at St Jean de Luz in France, 11th March 1814.

1075, 2d light battalion—*major Detlef Gerber*, ¶ 31st Oct. 1803—10th Dec. 1805. [B. 1807-8, P. 1808-9-10-11-12.] slightly wounded, 28th July 1809, at Talavera. † at Majados in Spain, 19th Sept. 1812.

1076, 8th line battalion—*major Charles William Langrehr*, ¶ 5th Nov. 1803 —14th Feb. 1804. . major 21st June 1813. (H. 1805, M. 1806-7, B. 1807-8, P. 1808-9-10-11-12-13, N. G.† 1814.) severely wounded, 11th May 1809, at Grijon ; severely wounded, 8th Oct. 1812, before Burgos ; severely wounded, 25th June 1813, at Toloza. . found drowned in the river Leine near Hanover, on the 5th of May 1814.

1077, 4th line battalion—*captain Charles von Falkenberg,* ¶ 15th Oct. 1803.—25th Sep. 1805. (H. 1805, B. 1807, M. 1808.) † at Fort San Salvadore near Messina in Sicily, 24th Oct. 1808.

1078, 5th line battalion—*captain Frederick Ferdinand von Brandis,* ¶ 16th Oct. 1803—10th Dec. 1805. (B. 1807-8, P. 1808-9.) † at Attalaya near Abrantes in Portugal, 23d June 1809.

1079, 7th line battalion—*captain Edward Adolphus Engel,* ¶ 19th Oct. 1803—21st Jan. 1806. (B. 1807-8, P. 1808-9-10-11.) † at Lisbon, 11th Feb. 1811.

1080, 2d light battalion—*captain John Mackenzie,* ¶ 23d Oct. 17th Nov. 1803. (H. 1805.) † at Lymington in England, 6th July 1809.

1081, 6th line battalion—*captain Diederich Graeffe,* ¶ 30th Oct. 1803—21st Jan. 1806. (B. 1807, M. 1808-9-10-11) † at Trapany in Sicily, 20th Dec. 1811.

1082, 3d line battalion—*captain Lewis von Weyhe,* ¶ 5th Nov. 1803—16th June 1804. (H. 1805, B. 1807.) † in the isle of Danish Zealand, 11th Oct. 1807.

1083, 2d light battalion—*captain Ernest Lewis von Robertson,* ¶ 6th Nov. 1803—5th May 1804. (H. 1805, B. 1808, P. 1808-9-11, S. 1809.) † at Belem in Portugal, 28th Nov. 1811.

1084, 4th light battalion—*captain Augustus von Quernheim,* ¶ 7th Nov. 1803—25th Sep. 1805. (H. 1805.) † at Tullamore in Ireland, 19th March 1807.

1085, 3d light battalion—*captain Frederick William Nanne,* ¶ 7th Nov. 1803—16th June 1804. (H. 1805, B. 1807, M. 1808.) † at Contessa in Sicily, 27th Sep. 1808.

1086, 1st light battalion—*captain Ferdinand von Zerssen,* ¶ 18th 20th Dec. 1803. (H. 1805.) † at Stade, 27th Nov. 1805.

1087, 2d light battalion—*captain Augustus du Plat,* ¶ 3d Jan. 1804. (H. 1805, B. 1807-8, P. 1808-9, S. 1809.) † in the isle of Walcheren, 2d Sep. 1809.

1088, 7th line battalion—*captain Augustus von Berger,* ¶ 23d 24th Jan. 1804. (H. 1805, B. 1807.) † in the isle of Danish Zealand, 9th Oct. 1807.

1089, 3d line battalion—*captain Augustus Cierow*, ¶ 13th—
15th Sep. 1804. (H. 1805, B. 1807, M. 1808-9-10.)
† at Catania in Sicily, 3d July 1810.

1090, 4th line battalion—*captain Charles von Kaufmann*, ¶
25th April—5th May 1804. (H. 1805.) † at Monkstown
near Cork, in Ireland, 29th March 1806.

1091, 4th line battalion—*captain George von Reinbold*, ¶ 26th
April—5th May, 1804. (H. 1805, B, 1807, M. 1808, †
at the citadel of Messina in Sicily, 10th Oct. 1808.

1092, garrison company—*captain Frederick Plate*, ¶ 4th—17th
Nov. 1803. (H. 1805, B. 1807-8, P. 1808 9-10-11. †
at Coimbra in Portugal, 27th May 1811.

1093, 5th line battalion—*captain Frederick von Diepenbroick*,
¶ 8th—24th May 1806. (B. 1807-8, P. 1808-9-10-11.)
† at Colwell Barracks, Isle of Wight, England, 20th Sep.
1811.

1094, 1st light battalion—*captain George von Alten*, ¶ 8th—
17th Nov. 1803. (H. 1805, B. 1807-8, P. 1808-9
slightly wounded, 22d July 1806, at Tullamore, † in
London, 21st Jan. 1810.

1095, 5th line battalion—*captain Frederick von Hugo*, ¶ 23d—
25th May 1805. (H. 1805, B. 1807-8, P. 1808-
9-10-11-12.) † at San Christoval in Spain, 6th Sep.
1812.

1096, 8th line battalion—*captain Charles Frederick Wm. von
Walthausen*, ¶ 18th—24th May 1806. (B. 1807, M.
1807-9-10-11-12-13. ... murdered by brigands in the
vicinity of St. Margaritta in Sicily, 2d April 1813.

1097, 5th line battalion—*captain William Rautenberg*, ¶
22d—25th May 1805. (H. 1805, B. 1807-8. P. 1808-
9-10-11-12-13, S. F. 1813-14.) severely wounded, 27th
Feb. 1814, before Bayonne, † at Holstropp, between
Lipstadt and Hanover, while on his route to the latter
place, 27th Nov. 1814.

1098, 4th line battalion—*captain Frederick Schmidt*, 18th—
24th Jan. 1804. (H. 1805, B. 1807, M. 1808-9-10-11-
12, P* 1812-13.) † in London, 13th Jan. 1814.

1099, 2d line battalion—*lieutenant Daniel Zorn*, ¶ 6th—
14th Feb. 1804. † at Deal in England, 4th Nov. 1805.

1100, 2d light battalion—*lieutenant Henry Jenisch*, ¶ 21st
March 1804. (H. 1805.) † on board a transport, when
the battalion was on its passage from Portsmouth to
Ireland, 18th March, 1806.

1101, 4th line battalion—*lieutenant Albertus Oldenburg*, ¶
21st—25th September, 1804. (H. 1805, B. 1807, M.
1808-9.) † at Gisso in Sicily, 8th Oct. 1809.

1102, 4th line battalion—*lieutenant Ernest Clausen*, ¶ 22d—
25th September 1804. H. 1805, B. 1807, M. 1808-9-10.)
† at Augusta in Sicily, 23d Jan. 1810.

1103, 3d line battalion—*lieut. Augustus von Bruchhausen*, ¶
23d—25th Sep. 1804. (H. 1805, B. 1807, M. 1808-9-10-
11) † at Contessa, near Messina, in Sicily, 25th Jan. 1811.

1104, garrison company—*lieutenant Henry Otto*, ¶ 20th—23d
March, 1805. (H. 1805, B. 1807-8, P. 1808-9.) † at
Belem in Portugal, 6th Dec. 1809.

1105, 5th line battalion—*lieutenant Wm. Stisser*, ¶ 24th—25th
May 1805. H. 1805, B. 1807-8, P. 1808-9.) † at Talavera
la Real in Spain, 14th Sep. 1809.

1106, 5th line battalion, *lieut. Lewis von Loesecke*, ¶ 9th—10th
Dec. 1805. (H. 1805, B. 1807-8, P. 1808.) † at Belem
in Portugal, 29th Dec. 1808.

1107, 2d light battalion—*lieut. George Boden*, ¶ 6th—21st Jan.
1806, [B. 1807-8, P. 1808-9, S. 1809.] † at Bexhill,
Sussex, in England, 14th Nov. 1809.

1108, 4th line battalion—*lieut. Christian Burchard von Schlütter*, ¶ 10th—21st Jan. 1806. [B. 1807, M. 1808-9-10.]
† at Augusta in Sicily, 26th Nov. 1810.

1109, 3d line battalion—*lieut. Charles le Bachellé*, ¶ 13th—
21st Jan. 1806. (B. 1807, M. 1808-9-10.] † at Contessa
near Messina, in Sicily, 30th Jan. 1810.

1110, 6th line battalion—*lieut. William Teuto*, 18th—21st Jan.
1806. † at Winchester in England, 19th April 1806.

1111, 5th line battalion—*lieut. Just Lodemann*, ¶ 21st—25th
May 1805. [H. 1805.] † in Hanover, 15th March 1808.

1112, 2d line battalion—*lieut. Augustus von Münch*, ¶ 1st—
14th Feb. 1804. [H. 1805, M. 1806-7.] † at Gibraltar,
9th Jan. 1807.

1113, 6th line battalion—*lieut. Charles Wiering*, ¶ 20th—21st
Jan. 1806. † at Bandon in Ireland, 13th Sep. 1806.

1114, 2d line battalion—*lieut. Augustus Sothen*, 20th—21st
April 1804. [H. 1805, M. 1806-7, B. 1807-8.] found
dead in a meadow between Portsmouth and Porchester
August 1808.

1115, 2d light battalion—*lieutenant Frederick Jansen*, 14th
Feb. 1804. (H. 1805, B. 1808, P. 1808 9.) † at Bexhill
Sussex, 12th Oct. 1810.

1116, 6th line battalion—*lieut. Ernest de Tessier*, 14th—17th
Nov. 1804. [H. 1805, B. 1807, M. 1808-9-10-11. † at
Trapany in Sicily, 27th Jan. 1811.

1117, 4th line battalion—*lieut. Augustus von Reinbold*, 16th—
17th Nov. 1804. [H. 1805, B. 1807.] † in the isle of
Danish Zealand, 22d Sept. 1807.

1118, 2d line battalion—*lieut. Frederick Wessel*, 25th Jan.
1806. (B. 1807-8, P. 1808-9-10.) severely wounded,
28th July 1809, at Talavera. † in London 15th March 1814

1119, 7th line battalion—*lieut. George Balck*, N. C O. 9th—
23d Sept. 1806. [B. 1807-8, P. 1808-9-10-11-12.] †
in London, 2d April 1815.

1120, 2d line battalion—*lieut. Charles von Wyck*, 27th—28th
Jan. 1806. [M. 1806-7, B. 1807-8, P. 1808-9-10-11-
12.] severely wounded, 28th July 1809, at Talavera. † at
Lucinde in Portugal, 17th April 1813.

1121, 7th line battalion—*lieut. Gideon Wilcken*, N. C. O. 9th—
17th Nov. 1807. [B. 1807-8, P. 1808-9. † at Talavera
la Real, in Spain, 5th Oct. 1809.

1122, 2d light battalion—*lieut. Henry Balemann*, N. C. O.
7th—13th Feb. 1808. [H. 1805, B. 1807-8, P. 1808-
9.] † at Bexhill, Sussex, 4th April 1811.

1123, 2d light battalion—*lieut. James Colburne*, 6th—13th
May 1809. (S. 1809, P. 1811-12.) † at Lymington in
England, 1st May 1813.

1124, 5th line battalion—*lieut. Frederick Moeller*, N. C. O. 4th—13th Feb, 1808 [H. 1805, B. 1807-8, P. 1808-9-10.] † at Gouveia in Portugal, 14th Aug. 1810.

1125, 3d line battalion—*lieutenant Rudolphus Borgstedt*, N. C. O, 23d Aug.—2d Sep. 1809. (H. 1805, B, 1807, M. 1808-9-10-11-12.) † at Contessa, near Messina, in Sicily, 27th Jan. 1812.

1126, 5th line battalion—*lieut. Alexander Lehmann*, N. C. O. 7th—19th Sep. 1809. (II. 1805, B. 1807-8, P. 1808-9-10-11-12. † at Salamanca, 25th Sep. 1812.

1127, 6th line battalion, *lieut. Christian Polchau*, N. C. O. 21st—31st March 1812. (II. 1805, M. 1808-9 10-11-12-13-14. † at Melazzo in Sicily, 20th Oct. 1814.

1128, 2d light battalion—*ensign Charles Dettmering*, 22d—24th Jan. 1804. † at Porchester Barracks, Hants, 4th Feb. 1804.

1129. 6th line battalion—*ensign George Rumann*, 20th Jan.—15th Feb. 1806. (B. 1807.) † in the Isle of Rügen, 26th July, 1807.

1130, 3d line battalion—*ensign Lewis Hesse*, 3d—4th Feb. 1806. (II. 1805, B. 1307, M. 1808.) † at Messina, in Sicily, 27th March 1808.

1131, 8th line battalion—*ensign Lewis von Bärtling*, 27th June—1st July, 1806. (B. 1807, M. 1808-9-10.) † at Syracusa, in Sicily, 31st Jan. 1810.

1132, 6th line battalion—*ensign George Lübbern*, N. C. O. 26th March—4th April, 1807. (B. 1807, M. 1808-9.) † at Syracusa in Sicily, 27th Feb. 1809.

1133, 2d line battalion—*ensign Lewis Lindener*, N. C. O. 29th November—5th Dec. 1807. (B. 1807-8. P. 1808-9.) drowned whilst bathing near Talavera in Spain, 14th July 1809.

1134, 7th line battalion—*ensign Charles Ziegeler*, N. C. O. 11th—23d Sep. 1809. (B. 1807-8, P. 1808-9.) supposed to have died in French captivity in Spain, and ordered to be replaced per letter from the commander-in-chief's office of 20th September 1811.

a 1

1135, veteran battalion—*ensign Frederick Küster*, N. C. O. 22d
     September—6th Oct. 1812. (H. 1805, B. 1807, P. 1809,
     N. 1814-15.) † at Antwerp, 12th May 1815.

1136, 1st line battalion—*ensign Edward Leslie*, 25th Jan.—13th
     Feb. 1813. † before he joined his battalion 21st May 1813.

1137, 8th line battalion—*ensign John Baptist Weber*, 4th June
     —5th July 1814. † at Harwich in England before he
     joined his battalion, 24th Nov. 1814.

1138, 6th line battalion—*ensign George von Ulmenstein*, 19th
     Nov.—3d Dec. 1814...drowned whilst skaiting at Ver-
     den, in Han. 10th December, 1815.

1139, veteran battalion—*ensign Conrad Leue*, N. C. O. 22d
     June—22d July, 1815. (H. 1805, B. 1807-8, P. 1808-
     9-10-11-12-13, N. 1814-15.) found drowned in a canal
     at Antwerp, 31st Dec. 1815.

1140, 3d line battalion—*quartermaster Archibald Riddel*, 16th
     June 1804. (H. 1805, B. 1807.) † at Colwell barracks,
     Isle of Wight, 10th Aug. 1810.

1141, 1st light battalion—*quartermaster Henry Hesse*, 19th—
     22d Dec. 1804. (H. 1805, B. 1807-8, P. 1808-9.) † at
     Bexhill, Sussex, 11th May 1809.

1142, 5th line battalion—*quartermaster Philippe de Lichtervel-
     den*, N. C. O. 1st July, 1806. (H. 1805, B. 1807-8, P.
     1808-9-10.) † in the lines before Lisbon, 20th Nov. 1810.

1143, 7th line battalion—*quartermaster Gottfried Pape*, 25th
     28th Jan. 1806. B. 1807-8, P. 1808-9-10. † at Trancozo,
     in Portugal, 3d May 1810.

1144, 1st line battalion—*quartermaster John Carolin*, N. C. O.
     6th—18th June 1811. (H. 1805, M. 1806-7, B. 1807-
     8, P. 1808-9-10-11-12-13, S. F. 1813-14, N. 1814, W.
     & C. 1815.) B. W. M. † near Valenciennes, being on
     his march from Paris to Hanover, 18th Dec. 1815.

1145, 6th line battalion—*surgeon Henry Frederick Meyer*, ¶
     7th Dec. 1805. (B. 1807, M. 1808-9-10-11.) † at Cast Vel
     Veterano, in Sicily, 14th June 1811.

1146, 1st light battalion—*assistant surgeon Henry Rielcke*, 3d
     Jan. 1804. † at Hilsea barracks, in 1804.

1147, 6th line battalion—*assistant surgeon Frederick Lewis Philip Müller*, 7th Dec. 1805. (B. 1807, M. 1808-9-10-11.) † at Trapany in Sicily, 21st Nov. 1811.

1148, 7th line battalion—*assistant surgeon William Sander*, 10th—20th Feb. 1810. (P. 1810.) † at Lisbon, 6th Oct. 1810.

PLACED ON THE REDUCED ALLOWANCE.

1149, 5th line battalion—*colonel-commandant Ernst George von Drieberg*, ¶ 1st April 1804—10th Dec. 1805.. brigadier general, 1808. (B. 1807-8, P. 1808-9.) retired on an allowance of 7s. 6d. per day, 9th June 1810. † at Celle, in Han. 3d Jan. 1832.

1150, 8th line battalion—*lieutenant colonel Frederick von Behr*, ¶ 4th Feb. 1805—21st Jan. 1806.. (B. 1807.).. retired on an allowance of one year's full pay, 26th Jan. 1808. † at Hildesheim, 24th Oct. 1817.

1151, 8th line battalion—*lieutenant-colonel Philip Müller*, ¶ 20th April 1804—21st Jan. 1806.'(B. 1807, M. 1808.).. retired on an allowance of 5s. per day, 25th Feb. 1809. † at Darmstadt, Jan. 1837.

1152, 2d line battalion—*major Gustavus von Behr*, ¶ 20th Jan.—25th May 1805. (H. 1805, B. 1807.)..retired on an allowance of 5s. per day, 25th Feb. 1809..

1153, 5th line battalion—*major Frederick Gerber*, ¶ 24th Jan. 25th May 1805. (H. 1805, B. 1807-8, P. 1808-9.).. retired on an allowance of 5s. per day, 16th Oct. 1810.. colonel, h. p. at Delmenhorst, grand dutchy of Oldenburg.

1154, 5th line battalion—*major William von Uslar*, ¶ 5th Feb. 1805—21st Jan. 1806. (B. 1807-8, P. 1808-9.)..retired on an allowance of 5s. per day, 16th April 1811. † at Zeitz, in Saxony, 24th Nov. 1813.

1155, 7th line battalion—*major Augustus von Berger*, ¶ 18th 21st January 1806. (B. 1807-8, P. 1808-9.) slightly wounded, 28th July 1809, at Talavera. B.G.M. Talavera—H. G. O. 2—H. W. M.—R. St. W. O. 4—H. M.—R. St. A. O. 2..retired on an allowance of 5s. per day. 28th Sep. 1810..lieutenant-general, h. p. at Nienburg in Han.

1156, 1st line battalion—*captain Bernhard Frederick Augustus von Zerssen*, ¶ 7th Nov. 1803—21st March 1804. (H. 1805, M. 1806-7, B. 1807-8, P. 1808-9-10.) severely wounded, 28th July 1809, at Talavera..retired on an allowance of 3s. per day, 11th Aug. 1810. † in Italy in 1810.

1157, 2d light battalion—*captain Albrecht von Düring*, ¶ 12th 17th Nov. 1803. (H. 1805, B. 1807-8, P. 1808-9.) slightly wounded 28th July 1809, at Talavera..retired on an allowance of 3s. per day, 7th May 1811. † in Hanover, 7th June 1820, major by br. r. l.

1158, 1st light battalion—*captain Frederick August Wilhelm von Geyso*, ¶ 27th April—5th May, 1804. (H. 1805, B. 1807-8, P. 1808-9)..retired on an allowance of 3s. per day, 14th April 1810. † at Zellerfeld, in Han. 24th July 1832.

1159, 8th line battalion—*captain Victor Schaumann*, ¶ 6th— 24th May 1806. (B. 1807, M. 1808-9-10.)..retired on an allowance of 3s. per day, 6th Sep. 1811..lieutenant colonel by br. r. l. at Harburg.

1160, 6th line battalion—*captain Arnold Julius von Horn*, ¶ 31st Dec. 1805—21st Jan. 1806. (B. 1807, M. 1808-9-10-11.) retired on an allowance of 3s. per day, 26th May 1812. † in Hanover, 17th Jan. 1824.

1161, 7th line battalion—*lieutenant Charles Tormin*, ¶ 28th Jan. 1806..retired on an allowance of one year's full pay, 24th June 1806, † at Goslar, in Han. 27th Sep. 1814, captain H. S. h. p.

1162, 7th line battalion—*lieut George Severin*, ¶ 18th—21st Jan. 1806. (B. 1807.)..retired on an allowance of 2s. per day, 30th Oct. 1810. † at Eimbeck, in Han. 9th Jan. 1824, captain by br. r. l.

1163, 8th line battalion—*lieutenant Frederick Schele*, ¶ 20th— 24th May, 1806. (B. 1807, M. 1808-9.)..retired on an allowance of 2s. per day, 11th June 1811..major by br. h. p. at Gr. Eicklingen near Celle.

1164, garrison company—*lieutenant Charles Augustus Gabriel Schlütter*, 19th—20th July 1804. (H. 1805, B. 1807-8, P. 1808-9-10)..retired on an allowance of 2s. per day, 1st June 1811. † at Hitzacker in Han. 15th July, 1832.

1165, depôt company—*lieutenant Frederick Baumeister*, 15th—17th Nov. 1803. (H. 1805, B. 1807...retired on an allowance of 2s. per day, 8th Oct. 1811..killed in action near Bremerlehe, in 1813.

1166, 2d light battalion—*ensign F. William Farmer*, 25th March—19th April, 1808. (B. 1808, P. 1808-9.)..retired on an allowance of 2s. 6d. per day, 13th Jan. 1810.

1167, 7th line battalion—*surgeon Lewis Boyer, M. D.*, 7th Dec. 1805. (B. 1807-8, P. 1808-9-10.)..retired on an allowance of one year's full pay, 23d April 1811. † in Hanover in 1816.

1168, 7th line battalion—*assistant surgeon George William Suffert*, 28th—30th Dec. 1805..retired on an allowance of 2s. per day, 20th Feb. 1810 †.

PLACED ON HALF-PAY.

1199, 3d line battalion—*lieut.-colonel Frederick William Charles von Schlütter*, ¶ 14th Jan.—25th May 1805. (H. 1805, B. 1807, M. 1808-9-10-11-12-13.) placed upon half-pay 1st Oct. 1814. † at Stade, 25th May 1822.

1170, 2d line battalion—*lieut.-colonel Adolphus von der Beck*, ¶ 2d July 1805...lieut.-colonel, 1st Jan. 1812. (H. 1805, M. 1806-7, B. 1087-8, P. 1808-9-10-11-12-13. S. F. 1813-14. N. 1814.) severely wounded, 5th May 1811, at Fuentes de Onoro ; slightly wounded, 14th April 1814, before Bayonne, B. G. M. 1, Talavera—Nive, B. B. O. 3, H. G. O. 3..placed upon half-pay, 25th May 1815..at Celle, in Han.

1171, 4th line battalion—*major Honning von Luttermann*, ¶ 8th Oct. 1803—21st Jan. 1806..lieut.-colonel 4th June 1813. [B. 1807, M. 1808-9 10-11-12, P* 1812-13-14.] placed upon half-pay 1st Oct. 1814. † at Gelliehausen near Göttingen, 22d May 1829.

1172, 3d line battalion—*major David le Bachellè,* ¶ 16th Oct. 1803—24th May 1806. (B. 1807, M. 1808-9-10-11-12-13.) placed upon half-pay, 12th April 1814. † at Hameln 23d Oct. 1818.

1173, 4th line battalion—*major Frederick Reh,* ¶ 19th Oct. 1803—21st Jan. 1806..lieut.-colonel 18th June 1815. (B. 1807-8, P. 1808-9-19-11, M. 1812, P.* 1812-13-14, S. F. 1814, N. 1814, W. & C. 1815.) B. B. O. 3—H. G. O. 3—B. W. M..placed upon half-pay, 25th Sep. 1815. † at Osterode in Han. 24th July 1829.

1174, 5th line battalion—*major John George Arnhold Gerber,* ¶ 27th Oct. 1803—24th May 1806..lieut.-colonel 21st Sept. 1813. [B. 1807, M. 1808-9-10, P. 1811-12-13, S. F. 1813-14, N. 1814-15.] B. G. M.—St. Sebastian. placed upon half-pay 25th July 1815. † at Hameln, 14th March 1816.

1175, foreign veteran battalion—*major George von Coulon,* ¶ 2d Nov. 1803—17th June 1806. (B. 1807, M, 1808-9-10-11-12-13, S. F. 1814, N. 1814-15.) placed upon half-pay, 25th Oct. 1815, † at Stade, 12th Oct. 1827.

1176, 3d line battalion—*captain Henry David Christian William von Weyhe,* ¶ 1st Nov. 1803—16th June 1804. [H. 1805, B. 1807, M. 1808-9.] placed upon half-pay, 2d Sept. 1809. † at Lüneburg, 33d March 1827, lieut.-colonel by br. r. l.

1177, 4th line battalion—*captain George von Ulmenstein,* ¶ 5th Nov. 1803—25th Sept. 1805. [H. 1805, B. 1807. M. 1808-9-10-11.] placed upon half-pay, 12th Jan. 1813. † at Mariensee near Hanover, 26th Jan. 1816.

1178, 5th line battalion—*captain Charles von Wurmb,* ¶ 5th Nov. 1803—25th May 1805. (H. 1805, B. 1807-8, P. 1808-9-10-11-12.) placed upon half-pay 27th April 1813.. found drowned in Limehouse hole near London, 3d Oct. 1813.

1179, 4th line battalion—*captain George von Pufendorf,* ¶ 16th—17th Nov. 1804. (H. 1805, B. 1807, M. 1808-9-10-11-12.] placed upon half-pay, 14th Nov. 1812. † at Göttingen, 1st April 1833, major by br. r. l.

1180, 8th line battalion—*captain Frederick Balduin Corde mann,* ¶ 29th June—1st July 1806. [B. 1807, M. 1808-9-10-11-12-13-14.] placed upon half-pay, 25th May 1814. † at Verden, 10th May 1830.

1181, 7th line battalion—*captain August Friederich Charles von Döhren,* ¶ 26th Dec. 1805—21st Jan. 1806. [B. 1807-8, P. 1808-9-10, M. 1812-13.] placed upon half-pay, 21st Dec. 1813. † at Hardegsen in Han. 2d Feb. 1829.

1182, 7th line battalion—*captain Ernest von Becker,* ¶ 29th Dec. 1805—21st Jan. 1806. (B. 1807-8, P. 1808-9-10-11, M. 1812-13.) placed upon half-pay, 13th Nov. 1813. major by br. r. l. at Lüneburg.

1183, 3d line battalion—*captain Lewis Bacmeister,* ¶ 14th June 1804. (H. 1805, B. 1807, M. 1808-9-10-11-12-13-14.)..placed upon half-pay 1st Oct. 1814..in Hanover.

1184, 5th line battalion—*captain Frederick August John Lewis Lodders,* ¶ 8th—10th Dec. 1805. B. 1807-8, P. 1808-9-10-11-12.) severely wounded, 11th May, 1809, at Grijon; severely wounded, 8th Oct. 1812, before Burgos.. placed upon half-pay 25th April, 1815. † at Neuhaus on the Oste, in Han. 4th Oct. 1825..major by br. r. l.

1185, 7th line battalion—*captain Frederick William von Loesecke,* ¶ 4th—21st Jan. 1806. (B. 1807-8, P. 1808-9-10-11, M. 1812-13.) placed upon half-pay, 25th July 1815. † at Lüneburg, 23d July 1835, major by br. r. l.

1186, 8th line battalion—*captain Frederick von Becker,* ¶ 16th—24th May 1805. (B. 1807, M. 1808-9-10-11-12-13-14, N. 1814-15.) placed upon half-pay, 25th Oct. 1815..at Lüneburg.

1187, 5th line battalion—*captain Julius Bacmeister,* ¶ 10th Dec. 1805. (B. 1807-8, P. 1808-9-10-11-12-13, S. F. 1813-14, N. 1814-15.) severely wounded, 25th June 1813, at Toloza; slightly wounded, 14th April 1814, before Bayonne, H. G. O. 3. placed upon half-pay 25th July 1815..major by br. r. l. at Hanau electorate of Hessia.

1188, 2d light battalion—*captain George Wackerhagen*, ¶ 9th—21st Jan. 1806. [B. 1807-8, P. 1808-9-10-11-12-13, S. F. 1814.] severely wounded, 14th April 1814, before Bayonne..placed upon half-pay 25th May 1815,..lieut.-colonel by br. r. l. in Hanover.

1189, 2d line battalion—*captain Philip Clemens Majus*, ¶ 11th—21st Jan. 1806. [M. 1806-7, B. 1807.] placed upon half-pay 19th June 1813. † in Hanover, 23d March 1819.

1190, 4th line battalion—*captain Frederick Ludewig*, 22d—25th Sep. 1804. (H. 1805, B. 1807, M. 1808-9-10-11-12, P.* 1812-13-14, S. F. 1814.] placed upon half-pay, 25th May 1815..in Hanover.

1191, 5th line battalion—*captain George Hagemann*, 17th—28th Jan. 1806. (B. 1807-8, P. 1808-9-10-11-12-13, N. 1815.) placed upon half-pay 25th July 1815..at Hanover.

1192, 1st light battalion—*captain William von Heimbruch*, 9th—17th Nov. 1804. (H. 1805, B. 1807-8, P. 1808-9.13, S. 1809, S. F. 1813, N. 1814-15.) severely wounded.. (arm amputated) 10th Nov. 1813, at Urugne..placed upon half-pay 25th June 1815..at Stellichte near Wallsrode, in Han.

1193, 7th line battalion—*lieut. & adjt Charles Delius*, ¶ 19th—21st Jan. 1806. (B. 1807-8,P. 1808-9.) severely wounded (arm amputated) 27th July 1809, at Talavera..placed upon half-pay, 27th Jan.1810..major by br. r. l. atStade.

1194, depôt company—*lieut. Charles Wistinghausen*, 6th—10th Dec. 1805. (B. 1807) placed upon half-pay, 16th April 1814. † in Han. 17th April 1833.

1195, garrison company—*lieutenant John Charles Christoph Hünicken*, N. C. O. 14th—21st Feb. 1809. (H. 1805, M. 1806-7, B. 1807-8, P. 1808-9-10-11-12.) very severely wounded, (both legs amputated) 13th Jan. 1812, before Ciudad Rodrigo..retired on full pay of his rank, 17th Aug. 1814. † at Goslar in Han. 4th June 1824.

1196, 6th line battalion—*lieutenant William Baring*, N. C. O. 19th—28th Nov. 1807. (B. 1807, M. 1808-9-10-11-12-13-14-15.) placed on half-pay, 24th May 1816. † at Lüneburg, 14th May 1829.

1197, 1st light battalion—*lieutenant Hermann Wollrabe*, 26th March—2d April 1811. (P. 1812-13, S. F. 1813-14, N. 1814, W. & C. 1815.) severely wounded, 24th June 1813, at Villafranca; severely wounded, 14th April 1814, before Bayonne; severely wounded, 18th June 1815, at Waterloo. B. W. M..placed upon half-pay, 25th Oct. 1815. † at Pomrau near Klötze, in Han. 14th Feb. 1820.

1198, 5th line battalion—*lieut. Adolphus John Lorenz Rothardt*, N. C. O. 8th—19th Sep. 1809. (H. 1805, B. 1807-8, P. 1808-9-10-11-12-13, S. F. 1813-14, N. 1814-15.) severely wounded, 27th Feb. 1814, before Bayonne.. placed upon half-pay 25th July 1815..captain by br. r. l. at Lüneburg.

1199, 7th line battalion—*lieutenant George Münderloh*, N.C.O. 27th—30th Oct. 1810. (S. 1809.) placed upon half-pay, 4th Sep. 1813..at Hameln.

1200, 5th line battalion—*lieutenant Joseph Korschann*, N.C.O. 19th—31st Dec. 1811. (H. 1805, B. 1807-8, P. 1808-9-13, S. F. 1813-14, N. 1814-15.) slightly wounded, 27th Feb. 1814, before Bayonne..placed upon half-pay, 25th July 1815..at Znaim in Moravia.

1201, 2d light battalion—*lieut. Frederick Schaumann*, 27th July—3d Aug. 1813. (N. 1814-15.) placed upon half-pay, 25th Oct. 1815..in Hanover.

1202, 2d light battalion—*paymaster Stewart Boone Inglis*, 28th April 1804. (H. 1805, B. 1807-8, P. 1808-9-11, S. 1809.) placed upon half-pay, 29th Jan. 1814. † at Inverness in Scotland, 4th April 1828.

1203, 1st line battalion—*quartermaster Peter Stewart*, 3d Jan. 1804. (H. 1805, M. 1806.) exchanged to the half-pay of 8th garrison battalion, with quartermaster James Boyd, 19th Aug. 1806.

1204, 2d light battalion—*surgeon George Heise, M. D.* 23d July 1805. (H. 1805, B. 1807-8, P. 1808-9-10-11-12-13, S. F. 1813-14, N. 1814, W. & C. 1815.) H. G. O. 3—B. W. M.—H. W. C. . . placed upon half-pay, 25th Oct. 1815, being supernumerary . . staff surgeon Han. grenadier guards.

1205, 2d line battalion—*asst. surgeon Henry von Bremen, M.D.* 25th May 1805. (H. 1805, M. 1806-7, B. 1807-8, P. 1808-9-10-11-12-13, S. F. 1813-14, N. 1814-15.) placed upon half-pay, 25th Dec. 1815 . . lost by shipwreck in the mouth of the Elbe, 1816.

1206, 5th line battalion—*assistant surgeon Julius Balthasar Khörs,* 6th Dec. 1805. (B. 1807-8, P. 1808-9-10-11-12-13, S. F. 1813-14. N. 1814, W. & C. 1815.) B. W. M. . . placed upon half-pay, 25th July, 1815. † at Bergen on the Dumme, in Han. 1st May, 1826.

RESIGNED AND RETIRED.

1207, 8th line battalion—*lieut.-colonel Philipp von Hugo,* ¶ 23d Dec. 1804—24th May 1806 . . resigned 1st July 1806. † at Nienburg in 1819.

1208, 6th line battalion—*lieut-colonel Francis von Alten,* ¶ 3d January 1805—21st Jan. 1806. (B. 1807, M. 1808-9-10.) resigned 16th Feb. 1811. † at Wilkenburg, near Hanover, 30th Nov. 1823 . . lieutenant-colonel h. p.

1209, 8th line battalion—*major Victor Frederick von Soden,* ¶ 19th April, 1804—24th May 1806—resigned 1st July 1806. † at Stade, 1st March 1832.

1210, 2d light battalion—*major his serene highness Henry Prince Reuss,* ¶ 23d Oct.—3d Nov. 1812 . . lieut.-colonel 30th Dec. 1813. (P. 1813, S. F. 1813.) severely wounded 24th June 1813 at Villafranca, A. M. T. 3—D. D. O. 1— H. G. O. 2—Ba. H. O.—R. St. A. O. 1 . . resigned 3d June 1815 . . major general in the Austrian service . . commanding a brigade at Prague.

1211, 1st line battalion—*captain Frederick Lewis Augustus von Wurmb,* ¶ 15th Oct. 1803—24th Dec. 1805. (M. 1806-7.) H. W. M, . . retired 3d April 1807 . . killed 18th June 1815, at Waterloo. . . colonel H. S. . . commanding field battalion Grubenhagen.

1212, 8th line battalion—*captain George von Bothmer*, ¶ 17th Oct. 1803—24th May 1806. H. W. M.. retired 24th June 1806. † at Celle 31st May 1827, major h. p.

1213, 8th line battalion—*captain Ernest von Goeben*, ¶ 30th Oct. 1803—24th May 1806. [B. 1807, M. 1808-9-10-11-12.) resigned 10th March 1812.

1214, 1st line battalion—*captain William von Minnigerode*, ¶ 5th Nov. 1803—21st Jan. 1806. [M. 1806-7, B. 1807.] resigned 30th April, 1808.

1215, 2d light battalion—*captain Ludolphus von Voss*, ¶ 24th Jan. 1804. (H. 1805, B. 1807-8, P. 1808-9, S. 1809.) resigned 28th Sep. 1810. † at Diepholz, in Han. May 1819.

1216, 2d light battalion—*captain P. Arnaud Baron Trvent*, ¶ 2d—17th Nov. 1803. [H. 1805, B. 1808, P. 1808-9-11-12, S. 1809.] resigned 1st March 1814. † in Holland, 1818.

1217, 1st light battalion—*captain Augustus von Klencke*, ¶ 30th April—5th May 1804. [H. 1805, B. 1807-8, P. 1808-9, S. 1809.] H. G. O. 2.—H. W. M.—R. St. W. O. 4.. resigned 31st Dec. 1811. † at Ober-Neuland, near Bremen, 24th Jan. 1825, colonel H. S. commanding 2d regiment infantry.

1218, 7th line battalion—*captain Frederick von Dachenhausen*, ¶ 22d—25th May, 1805. [H. 1805. B. 1807-8, P. 1808-9.] H. G. O. 3.—B. W. M.—H. W. C.—resigned 23d Sep. 1809.. lieutenant-colonel Han. 8th line battalion.

1219, 2d light battalion—*captain Rudolphus Pringle*, 16th—17th Nov. 1803. [H. 1805, B. 1808, P. 1808-9-11-12-13, S. 1809, N. 1814-15.] resigned 29th Ap. 1815.. at Heidelberg, grand dutchy of Baden.

1220, 2d light battalion—*captain Burchard Neussel*, 21st April 1804. [H. 1805, B. 1807-8, P. 1808-9-11, S. 1809.] resigned 6th June 1812. † at Stadthagen, principality of Bückeburg, 10th Aug. 1820.

1221, 2d light battalion—*captain George Denicke,* 1st Oct.
1805. [II. 1805, B. 1807-8, P. 1808-9-11-12-13, S.
F. 1813-14, N. 1814-15.] resigned 16th Sep. 1815; lost
by shipwreck on the coast of France, 17th Nov. 1817.

1222, 2d line battalion—*lieut. and adjutant William Langrehr,*
¶ 7th—14th Feb. 1804. [II. 1805, M. 1806-7.]   H. W.
M..retired 31st Aug. 1807..killed 18th June 1815, in
the battle of Waterloo, lieut.-colonel H. S. commanding
field battalion Bremen.

1223, 1st line battalion—*lieut. Benedix von der Decken,* ¶ 11th
14th Feb. 1804.—retired 20th Aug. 1805. † at Schwinge
near Stade.

1224, 4th line battalion—*lieut. Charles von Heimburg,* ¶ 16th—
17th Nov. 1804. [H. 1805, B. 1807, M. 1808-9-10-11.]
H. W. M. resigned 7th Jan. 1812..captain h. p. at Eckerde,
amt Wenningsen, in Han.

1225, 1st line battalion—*lieut. Anton von Klenke,* ¶ 20th—23d
April 1805. [H. 1805.] retired 24th May 1806.

1226, 6th line battalion—*lieut. Frederick von Weyhe,* ¶ 3d—
21st Jan. 1806..retired 3d June, 1806..major h. p. at
Neustadt am Rübenberge, in Han.

1227, 5th line battalion—*lieut. George von Roden,* ¶ 4th—21st
Jan. 1806..resigned 7th Nov. 1806..major h. p. at
Latzen, near Hanover.

1228, 1st light battalion—*lieut. Andreas Delius,* ¶ 4th—21st
January 1806. [B. 1807, S. 1809.] resigned 16th Feb.
1811. † at Hamburg, 3d March 1820.

1229, 6th line battalion—*lieut Frederick Mühlenfeld,* ¶ 7th—
21st Jan. 1806. [B. 1807, M. 1808.] resigned 25th March
1809. † at Bücken, near Hoya, in Han.

1230, 7th line battalion—*lieut. George Hemme,* ¶ 11th—21st
Jan. 1806..retired 17th May 1806. † at Eimbeck, in
Han. 1825.

1231, 1st light battalion—*lieut. George von Graevemeyer,* ¶
13th—21st Jan. 1806. [B. 1807-8, P. 1808-9, S. 1800.]
H. W. M...resigned 16th Feb. 1811. † at Stade, 16th
April 1832, major H. S. 6th regiment infantry.

1232, 6th line battalion—*lieut. Frederick Lewis von Horn*, ¶
14th—21st Jan. 1806. [B. 1807, M. 1808-9-10.]
resigned 10th March 1812. † between Heligoland and the
river Elbe in 1813.

1233, 1st line battalion—*lieut. Ernst Lewis von Gerstein*, ¶
15th—21st Jan. 1806. [M. 1806-7, B. 1807, P. 1808-9.]
resigned 19th Sep. 1809. † at Moritzberg, near Hildesheim
20th April, 1826.

1234, 1st line battalion—*lieut. von Witzendorff*, ¶ 21st—
28th Jan. 1806..resigned 17th May 1806. H. W. M.
captain h. p.

1235, 2d line battalion—*lieut. Lütjen*, ¶ 21st—28th Jan. 1806.
resigned 1st March 1806.

1236, 1st light battalion—*lieut. Detleff von Uslar*, ¶ 21st—28th
Jan. 1806. [B. 1807-8, P. 1808-9.] resigned 16th Feb.
1811..amt Scharzfels, in Han.

1237, 4th line battalion—*lieut. Frederick count von Bismark*,
24th—25th Sep. 1804. [H. 1805.] W. M. M. 2.—He.
M. M.—Ba. H. O.—F L. H. 2.—R. St. G. O. 4.—W. M.
R. St. A. O. 1.—A. L. O. 3.—Pr. I. O.—Bn. F. O.—Bn.
Z. L. O.—D. D. O. 1.—Pr. R. E. 1.—W. O. C. 1.—W.
S. C.—W. D. [1815.] resigned 27th July 1807..lieut.-
general, Würtemberg service.

1238, 4th line battalion—*lieut. Helmuth Fiedler*, 25th Sep.
1804. [H. 1805, B. 1807.] resigned 26th Jan. 1808. †
at Büzow in Mecklenburg, 30th Aug. 1832.

1239, 1st light battalion—*lieut. Emilius von Düring*, 9th—14th
Feb. 1804. [H. 1805.] retired 1st March 1806. † at
Lappo in Finland, 1808.

1240, 2d light battalion—*lieut. Ernest Mayer*, 10th—14th Feb.
1804. (H. 1805, B. 1807-8, P. 1808-9, S. 1809.) F. L.
H. 5..resigned 21st May 1811..captain h. p. at Hagen,
amt Syke in Han.

1241, 1st light battalion—*lieut. William Ludowig*, 7th July
1804. (H. 1805, B. 1807-8, P. 1808-9, S. 1809.)
H. G. O. 3—H. W. M.—H. W. C. resigned 23d April
1811..lieut.-colonel Han. 6th light battalion.

1242, 8th line battalion—*lieut. Seehausen,* ¶ 10th—24th May 1806..resigned, 1806.

1243, 8th line battalion—*lieut. Gideon de Benoit, senior,* ¶ 11th—24th May 1806. did not join for duty. H. G. O. 3— H. W. M. retired 1st July 1806..major-general h. p. at Verden.

1244, 8th line battalion—*lieut. Evert,* ¶ 14th—24th May 1806.. resigned in 1806..at amt Bissendorf in Han.

1245, 7th line battalion—*lieut. G. D. von Wrisberg,* 9th—21st Jan. 1806..retired 3d June 1806.

1246, 8th line battalion—*lieut. de Benoit, jun.,* ¶ 17th—24th May 1806..retired 1st July 1806. † at Zeven in Han., captain h. p.

1247, 8th line battalion—*lieut. Hogreve,* ¶ 19th—24th May 1806..did not join for duty..resigned 12th Aug. 1806.

1248, 7th line battalion—*lieut. Frederick von Hanstein,* 11th— 21st Jan. 1806. (H. W. M.) retired 3d April 1807. † at Cassel 20th May 1828, major by br. h. p.

1249, 7th line battalion—*lieut. Clamor Ludwig Ernst Leo von Freytag,* 12th—21st Jan. 1806. (B. 1807-8, P. 1808-9.) slightly wounded, 28th July 1809, at Talavera..resigned 2d April 1811. † at Estorf, amt Stolzenau in Han. 16th Nov. 1825, captain h. p.

1250, 7th line battalion—*lieut. Lewis Hartmann,* N. C. O. 31st May—9th June 1807. [B. 1807-8, P. 1808.] resigned 28th Jan. 1809..captain h. p. at Hainholz near Hanover.

1251, 3d line battalion—*lieut. Charles von Brocktorff,* 28th Jan. 1806. (H. 1805, B. 1807, M. 1808-9.) resigned 18th Nov. 1809.

1252, 7th line battalion—*lieut. Henry Beck,* N. C. O. 15th— 26th Jan. 1808. (H. 1805, B. 1807-8, P. 1808-9-10-11, M. 1812-13.) resigned 12th April 1814. † in Hanover, 9th Oct. 1828.

1253, 4th line battalion—*lieut. Edward Sander,* N. C. O. 4th Feb. 1806. [H. 1805, B. 1807, M. 1808-9-10-11.) resigned 24th March 1812.

1254, 2d light battalion—*lieut. Nicholas Lemmers*, 7th—20th
June 1809. (S. 1809, P. 1811-12-13, S. F. 1813-14.)
severely wounded, 22d June 1812, at Morisco; slightly
wounded, 7th Oct. 1813, on the Bidassoa..resigned 10th
May 1814. † in the West Indies, 1828.

1255, 1st light battalion—*lieut. Frederick von Hedemann*, 27th
28th Jan. 1806. (B. 1807-8, P. 1808-9-11, S. 1809.)
severely wounded, 7th Aug. 1809, before Flushing..
resigned 1st Dec. 1812..lost by shipwreck on the coast
of France, 17th Nov. 1817.

1256, 8th line battalion—*lieut. George Wilding*, 28th June—
1st July 1806. (B. 1807, M. 1808-9-10-11-12-13-14.)
A. I. C. 1—Si. I. O. 1—H. G. O. 2..resigned 12th Ap.
1814..prince of Butera and Campofiorito..Neapolitan—
ambassador at the court of Petersburg.

1257, 7th line battalion—*lieut. Frederick Jericho*, N. C. O. 4th
10th December 1808. (P. 1809-10-11, M. 1812-13-14.)
resigned 12th April 1814.

1258, 7th line battalion—*lieut. Augustus Schaumann*, N. C. O.
5th—18th April 1809. (P. 1808-9-10-11-12.) resigned
21st July 1812..deputy assistant commissary general on
half-pay..in Hanover.

1259, 1st line battalion—*lieut. Ernest von Wedell*, 18th—21st
July 1810. (P. 1811-12.) resigned 7th Dec. 1813.

1260, 1st light battalion—*lieut. Augustus von Quistorp*, 7th—
20th Aug. 1811. (P. 1811-12-13, S. F. 1813-14.)..did
duty with the Spanish army. Pr. M. O. M.—Pr. I. C.—
Pr. C.—Sp. C. 2..resigned 4th Feb. 1815..lieut.-colonel
Prussian infantry.

1261, 6th line battalion—*lieut. George Sander*, N. C. O. 17th
25th March 1809. (B. 1807, M. 1808-9-10-11-12-13.)
resigned 5th July 1814. † at Bexhill, Sussex, 31st July
1814.

1262, 2d light battalion—*lieutenant I. H. von Egmont*, N.C.O.
29th July—6th Aug. 1811...resigned 1st Sep. 1812.

1263, 5th line battalion—*lieut. Henry Llewellyn*, 7th—19th May 1812. (S. F. 1813-14, N. 1814.)..resigned 2d Feb. 1815.

1264, 5th line battalion—*lieut. Jacob Wünning*, N. C. O. 28th May—13th June 1812. (B. 1807, P. 1808-9-10-11-12-13) resigned 29th March 1814. † at Leipzig, 21st February 1821.

1265, 1st line battalion—*lieut. Charles Michaelis*, 5th—29th Aug. 1812..resigned 25th June 1813.

1266, 2d light battalion—*lieut. Henry Conradi*, N. C. O. 6th— 16th June 1812. (N. 1813.) resigned 23d Oct. 1813.

1267, 2d light battalion—*lieut. Benedetto von Kienburg*, 29th Oct.—14th Nov. 1812. (N. G. 1813.) resigned 7th Dec. 1813.

1268, 2d light battalion—*lieut. Rudolphus Hurtzig*, 9th—14th July 1812. N. 1814, W. & C. 1815.) B. W. M..resigned 20th Sep. 1815.

1269, 6th line battalion—*lieut. Edward Martin Müller*, 24th July—4th August 1812. (M. 1812-13-14-15.) resigned 24th Jan. 1816.

1270, 1st light battalion—*ensign William Offeney*, 12th—17th Nov. 1803..retired 7th July 1804.

1271, 2d line battalion—*ensign George Wehner*, 20th—22d Dec. 1804..retired 9th Feb. 1805.

1272, 6th line batt.—*ensign John Frederick Lewis Müldener*, 16th—21st January 1806. H. W. M..retired 17th May 1806. † at Nienburg, 5th June 1831..captain 9th Han. infantry.

1273, 6th line battalion—*ensign Franz William Biela*, 18th— 28th Jan. 1806..resigned 24th Nov. 1806.

1274, 3d line battalion—*ensign Julius von Moeller*, 4th Feb. 1806. (B. 1807.) retired 18th Sep. 1807.

1275, 4th line battalion—*ensign William von Reden*, 14th— 26th Nov. 1808. [M. 1810-11.] resigned 12th November 1811,,at Hildesheim.

1276, 2d light battalion—*ensign William Collier*, 18th—30th March 1813..resigned 7th July 1813.

1277, 4th line battalion—*ensign Arnold Diederich Tamm*, 14th 29th May 1813. [S. F. 1814, N. 1814-15.] resigned 29th April 1815. † at Hamburg, 13 March 1827.

1278, 1st line battalion—*ensign Charles Theodore Meyer*, 24th July—3d Aug. 1813. [N. G. 1813.] resigned 5th March 1814.

1279, 1st light battalion—*ensign Henry von Welling*, 16th— 30th April 1814. [N. 1814, W. & C. 1815.] B. W. M.. resigned 9th Sep. 1815 † near Frankfort, o. m. in 1831.

1280, 2d line battalion—*ensign Edward Cropp*, 28th April— 10th May 1814. [N. 1814-15.] resigned 29th Aug. 1815

1281, 3d line battalion—*paymaster James Anderson*, 20th Oct. 1804. [H. 1805, B. 1807, M. 1808-9-10-11-12-13.] resigned in favor of his brother, William Anderson, 18th May 1813. † at Palermo, 12th Dec. 1821.

1282, 7th line battalion—*quartermaster Gerhard Baethgen*, 21st Jan. 1806..resigned 9th June 1807.

1283, 8th line battalion—*quartermaster Carl Falkmann*, 24th May 1806...resigned 1st Sep. 1806..captain h. p. at Münden, in Han.

1284, 1st line battalion—*quartermaster Henry Lasius*, 10th— 19th March 1808. [B. 1808, P. 1808-9-10-11.] resigned 18th June 1811. † in Portugal while serving in the British commissariat department, 1814.

1285, 1st light battalion—*asst. surgeon John George Stille*, 3d Nov. 1804. [H.1805, B. 1807.] resigned 29th December 1807..since dead.

1286, 2d light battalion—*asst. surgeon Philip Menzer*, M. D. 3d Nov. 1804. [H. 1805, B. 1807-8, P. 1808-9, S. 1809.] resigned 17th March 1812. † at Hameln, 20th March 1820.

1287, 3d line battalion—*asst. surgeon Lewis Kleine*, 7th Dec. 1805. (B. 1807, M. 1808-9-10-11-12-13.) resigned 12th Oct. 1813. † in Sicily.

1288, 7th line battalion—*assistant surgeon John E. Stutzer*, *M. D.* 30th Nov.—16th Feb. 1811. (B. 1807-8, P. 1808-9-10-11, M. 1812-13-14.) † at Rethmar, amt Ilten, in Han. 17th March, 1828.

SUPERSEDED, BEING ABSENT WITHOUT LEAVE.

1289, 2d line battalion—*lieut.-colonel Charles von Bennigsen*, ¶ 11th Nov. 1803—14th Feb. 1804..superseded 11th May 1805. † at Hildesheim, 15th Oct. 1830.

1290, 1st light battalion—*captain Thomas Harward*, ¶ 15th—17th Nov. 1803..absented himself without leave, 4th April 1805.

. 1291, 1st light battalion—*captain Frederick von Anderten*, ¶ 19th—24th Jan. 1804. (H. 1805, B. 1807-8, P. 1808-9, S. 1809.) superseded 23d April 1811..major r. l. at Celle.

1292, 2d line battalion—*lieut. Just Ernst Hermann Stoffregen*, ¶ 7th—21st Jan. 1806. (M. 1806-7.) superseded 31st May 1808. † at Bergen in Han. 26th May 1831, captain by br. r. l.

1293, 7th line battalion—*lieut. Hartwich Kellner*, ¶ 17th—21st Jan. 1806. (B. 1807.) superseded 10th Dec. 1808. † at Oldenburg, April 1st. 1836, major Oldenburg service.

1294, 4th line battalion—*lieut. Schestag*, ¶ 22d—28th Jan. 1806..superseded 1st Sep. 1807..lieutenant h. p. at Hildesheim.

1295, 2d light battalion—*lieut. John Dankaerts*, ¶ 20th—24th Jan. 1804. (H. 1805, B. 1807..superseded 19th Sep. 1807. † in England, 1821.

1296, depôt company—*lieut. George Scharloock*, ¶ 28th Jan. 1806..ensign 28th Jan. 1806..lieutenant 28th January 1806..superseded 27th October 1807..at Geestendorf in Han.

1297, 2d light battalion—*ensign George von Hugo*, N. C. O. 21st April 1805. (H. 1805.) H. W. M...superseded 6th Aug. 1808. † at Eimbeck, in Han. 9th October 1832, captain h. p.

1298, 2d light battalion—*ensign Antonio de Younge Bleck* 2d—9th July 1811..did not join for duty..superseded 27th April 1813.

1299, 2d light battalion—*ensign John William Home,* 15th—26th May 1812..did not join for duty..superseded 5th Oct. 1813. †

1300, 2d light battalion—*ensign A. Roell,* 23d June—7th July 1812..did not join for duty..superseded 5th Oct. 1813.

1301, 2d light battalion—*ensign J. Tulleke,* 24th June—7th July, 1812..did not join for duty..superseded 22d Jan. 1814.

1302, 1st light battalion—*ensign Gustav von Heugel,* 1st—14th July 1812..did not join for duty..superseded 27th April 1813. † at Neustadt in Bohemia, 1813, ensign Prussian service.

1303, 1st light battalion—*ensign Gustav von Lüttwitz,* 2d—14th July 1812..did not join for duty. Pr. I. C. 2—Pr. M. superseded 27th April 1813..lieutenant r. l. Prussian service..at Krintsch near Neumark in Silesia.

1304, 6th line battalion—*ensign Gustavus von Behr,* 8th—14th July 1812..did not join for duty..superseded 12th April 1814.

1305, 2d light battalion—*ensign von Braam,* 3d—13th Oct. 1812. did not join for duty..superseded 29th Jan. 1814.

1306, 2d light battalion—*ensign William Erskine Fraser,* 22d May—1st June 1813..did not join for duty..superseded 29th March 1814.

DISMISSED HIS MAJESTY'S SERVICE AND CASHIERED.

1307, 2d line battalion—*captain Frederick William Rudorff,* ¶ 21st—24th Jan. 1804. (H. 1805, M. 1806.) dismissed 13th Nov. 1806..killed in action in the French service.

1308, 2d light battalion—*lieut. Bernard Lewis von Helmoldt,* ¶ 21st—28th January 1806. (B. 1807-8, P. 1808-9.) cashiered 20th June 1809..at Grohnde near Göttingen.

1309, 7th line battalion—*lieut. Alexander von Wenckstern*,
20th—21st January 1806. (B. 1807-8, P. 1808-9-10.)
cashiered 8th June 1810.

1310, 2d line battalion—*paymaster Joseph Lancaster*, 16th—
21st July 1812. (P. 1813, S. F. 1813-14.) dismissed
10th July 1814.

1311, 1st light battalion—*quartermaster Frederick William
Reusch*, 24th Jan. 1804..dismissed 1st July 1805.

1312, 8th line battalion—*quartermaster Frederick Lewis Pollmann*, N. C. O. 22d Aug.—2d Sep. 1806. (B. 1807.)
dismissed 5th December 1807.

NAMES OF THE OFFICERS OF THE INFANTRY WHO WERE
GAZETTED, BUT WHOSE APPOINTMENT DID NOT TAKE
PLACE, AS THEY NEVER JOINED THE CORPS.

1313, 5th line battalion—*lieut. von Mandelsloh*, 5th—21st Jan.
1806..appointment not taken place..major by br. h. p.
at Wennebostel near Mellendorf, in Han.

1314, 2d line battalion—*ensign Lüderitz*, 16th—21st January
1816..appointment not taken place.

1315, 2d light battalion—*ensign George Foremann*, 9th—20th
Oct. 1807..appointment not taken place.

1316, 2d light battalion—*ensign John Lloyd*, 19th—26th Jan.
1808..appointment not taken place.

1317, 2d light battalion—*ensign D. Robinson*, 29th Sep.—28th
Oct. 1809..appointment cancelled 23d Dec. 1809.

1318, 2d light battalion—*ensign Frederick von Jenner*, 29th
March—10th April 1810..appointment cancelled 19th
May 1810.

1319, 2d light battalion—*ensign Henry von Dyck*, 16th—26th
May 1812..appointment cancelled 6th June 1812.

1320, 8th line battalion—*ensign Erik Erdm ann*, 10th—14th
July 1812..appointment cancelled 29th March 1814.

1321, 1st light battalion—*ensign Hermann Meyer*, 30th Nov.—
8th Dec. 1812..appointment cancelled 22d Dec. 1812.

1322, 1st light battalion—*ensign Charles F. W. Ebell*, 22d—
30th March 1813..appointment cancelled 6th April 1813.

1323, 6th line battalion—*ensign Charles Völger*, 31st July—
21st Aug. 1813..appointment cancelled 7th Dec. 1813.
capt. Han. 8th line battalion, R. St. W. O. 4—H. G. O.
3—H. W. M.—H. W. C.

1324, 2d line battalion—*ensign Lewis von Berger*, 30th Aug.—
11th Sep. 1813..H. W. M.—H. M.—H. W. C..appoint-
ment cancelled 10th May 1814..captain Han. 9th line
battalion.

1325, 7th line battalion—*ensign Bodo Heinsius*, 18th Feb.—
5th March 1814. H. W. M..appointment cancelled 30th
April 1814..captain by br. r. l. at Hildesheim.

1326, 2d line battalion—*ensign John Blanckardt*, 19th—29th
March 1814..appointment cancelled 30th April 1814.

1327, 2d light battalion—*ensign Augustus Alberti*, 2d—10th
May 1814..appointment cancelled 6th Aug. 1814.

1328, 6th line battalion—*ensign Ferdinand von Wurmb*, 11th
Sep.—1st Oct. 1814..appointment cancelled 18th April
1815..at Nordheim in Han.

NAMES OF THE OFFICERS OF THE INFANTRY WHO LEFT
THE LEGION EITHER BY PROMOTION OR TRANSFER
TO BRITISH REGIMENTS, OR APPOINTMENTS
UPON THE STAFF OF THE ARMY,

1329, 2d line battalion—*captain C. P. de Bosset*, ¶ 22d Oct.—
17th Nov. 1803. (H. 1805, M. 1806-7, B. 1807-8, P.
1808.) B. B. O. 3—H. G. O. 3...promoted major in de
Roll's regiment, 24th Dec. 1808..lieut.-colonel h. p. 50th
British foot..major-general 1837.

1330, 2d light battalion—*captain James M'Glashan*, 1st—11th
Nov. 1809. (P. 1811-12, N. G. 1813-14, W. & C. 1815.)
severely wounded, 22d June 1812, at Morisco. H. G. O. 3.
B. W. M..appointed captain of a company, 1st Ceylon
regiment, by exchange with captain George Richter.
† on his passage to the East Indies, 2d Dec. 1817.

1331, 2d light battalion—*lieut. & adjutant Philip von Frank*,
¶ 13th—17th Nov. 1803..appointed cornet in the 15th
light dragoons, 1805..at Schwermstedt in Han. h. p.
15th dragoons.

1332, depôt company—*lieut. Lewis Schlötzer*, ¶ 14th—17th Nov. 1803..transferred to the regiment of Malta, 2d July 1805. † in French captivity.

1333, 2d light battalion—*lieut. Lewis Hausdorff*, 12th—17th Nov. 1803. (H. 1805, B. 1807-8, P. 1808-9.) exchanged into de Watteville's regiment, with lieut. F. Sprecher, 23d May 1809.

1334, 2d light battalion—*lieut. William Riddle*, 17th Nov. 1803. (H. 1805, B. 1808, P. 1808-9, S. 1809.) promoted captain 4th Ceylon regiment, 17th March 1810.

1335, 1st light battalion—*lieut. Frederick Baring*, 24th Jan. 1804. (H. 1805, B. 1807-8, P. 1808-9.) exchanged into de Roll's regiment, with lieut. Rud. Hüpeden, 25th July 1809..lieut. 29th British foot.

1336, 1st line battalion—*lieut. George von Düring*, 18th—22d Dec. 1804. (H. 1805, M. 1806-7, B. 1807-8, P. 1808.) transferred to de Roll's regt. 24th Dec. 1808. † at Bückeburg 16th Dec. 1828.

1337, 2d light battalion—*lieut. Peter Richard Andrew von Dyck*, 14th—28th April 1812. (P. 1813.) exchanged into the 60th regt. of foot with lieut. J. L. Ingersleben, 11th Sep. 1813.

1338, 2d light battalion—*ensign Emanius Lewis von Steiger*, 28th Jan. 1806. (H. 1805, P. 1808-9) promoted lieut. in de Roll's regt. 24th Dec. 1808.

1339, 2d light battalion—*ensign Baron Tuyt de Servoskerken*, 2d—4th Feb. 1806..promoted lieut. in de Watteville's regt. 28th July 1807.

1340, 2d light battalion—*ensign Rudolphus von Steiger*, 11th 17th May 1806..promoted lieut. in de Watteville's regt. 11th July 1807.

1341, garrison company—*ensign James Boyd*, 5th—19th Aug. 1806..promoted lieut. 7th royal veteran battalion, 23d July 1811.

1342, 2d light battalion—*ensign William Nortcot*, N. C. O. 29th July—6th Aug. 1808. (P. 1808-9.) transferred to the 81st foot, 5th April 1809.

1343, 7th line battalion—*ensign Adolphus Bronkhorst*, N. C.
O. 30th April—11th May, 1813. (H. 1805.) promoted
lieut. in the 60th foot, 25th Sep. 1813.

1344, 2d line battalion—*ensign William Nagel*, N. C. O. 20—
27th July 1813—promoted lieut. in the 60th foot, 25th
Sep. 1813.

1345, 2d light battalion—*surgeon Frederick Weber*, ¶ 3d Jan.
1804. (H. 1805, B. 1807, M. 1808-9-10-11-12-13-14-
15-16.) transferred to the regt. of Malta, 11th May 1805,
in Sicily.

1346, 1st line battalion—*surgeon Henry Heine*, ¶ 21st April
1804. (H. 1805, B. 1807, P. 1808-9-10-11-12-13.)
promoted surgeon to the forces, 25th Dec. 1805..at
Manheim.

1347, 1st light battalion—*surgeon Joseph Dynely*, ¶ 2d June
1804. (H. 1805, B. 1807.) promoted surgeon to the
forces, 25th Dec. 1805.

1348, 2d light battalion—*surgeon George Denecke*, 26th Jan.
1805. H. 1805, B. 1807-8, P. 1808-9, S. 1809, N.
1814, C. 1815.) H. G. O. 3.—B. W. M.—promoted
surgeon to the forces 8th Aug. 1809, and deputy inspector
of hospitals to the forces on the continent of Europe only,
22d Feb. 1816.

1349, 5th line battalion—*surgeon Hermann Lorentz Deppen*, ¶
1st Dec. 1804. (H. 1805, B. 1807-8, P. 1808 9-10-11-
12-13, S. F. 1813, N. 1814, W. & C. 1815.) B.W.M...
promoted surgeon to the forces by commission of the 22d
Feb. 1816. † in Hanover, 29th May 1829.

1350, 1st line battalion—*assistant surgeon William Christian
Bach*, 25th May 1805. (H. 1805, M. 1806-7.) transferred
to the Cape regt. 19th April 1808. † at Stutgardt, in
Würtemberg, Nov. 1824.

MEMORANDA

Respecting the date of commission and commencement of pay of the officers of the King's German Legion; their rank when on duty with the native British officers, and the precedence of the legion, as a corps in the British army.

As it was the king's pleasure that the officers of his majesty's former Hanoverian army, should take precedence in the King's German Legion, according to their seniority in that service, it became necessary, on the formation of the legion, when so many appointments were made at once, to antedate the commissions, in order to effect a due seniority; hence the difference arises between the date of commission and that of gazettement; the latter has always been the commencement of pay, as it was the date at which the officer actually entered the British service.

Extract. (Copy.)   *Horse Guards, Feb.* 9, 1804.

I have further to inform your royal highness, that with a view to enable the officers of the King's German Legion to take *precedence*, in their present corps, according to the rank they *held* in the *Hanoverian* service, his majesty has been graciously pleased to authorize your royal highness to *post the officers as they are appointed*, and to recommend *their* commissions *bearing* such *dates*, as will place them in *their proper situations* in *point of rank accordingly.*

         (*Signed*)   FREDERICK, Commander-in-chief.

Lieut.-general his royal highness the duke of Cambridge, K. G. &c. &c. *London.*

About the middle of the year 1806, the King's German Legion was considered as formed, and as, by that time, all such officers of the late Hanoverian army as wished to join the British standard, were appointed to the legion, there was no further necessity for ante-dating commissions, and from the 14th July 1806, the date of commissions was fixed and proposed by the duke of Cambridge, at the time when new appointments or promotions were recommended by H. R. H. to the commander-in-chief for being submitted for the king's approbation; but the date of gazettement continued invariably to mark the beginning of pay.

With regard to the taking of rank of the officers of the legion when on duty with the native British officers, the following letter shews the regulation that was established :—

(COPY)   *Weymouth, August* 13, 1805.

SIR, in reply to your royal highness's letter of the 6th instant, and that enclosed from colonel baron Bock, of the King's German Legion, I beg to acquaint you, that it is decidedly established that the officers of the King's German Legion, whether their rank be permanent or temporary, shall be considered in all respects as British officers, and that, when serving together, they shall respectively take rank in all duties according to the dates of their commissions. The circumstance of colonel Anson of the fifteenth dragoons, having taken rank of colonel baron Bock in the turn of duty as colonel of the day here, must have preceded from inadvertence.   I have, &c.

         (*Signed*)   FREDERICK,

                                     Commander-in-chief.

Lieut.-general, his royal highness the duke of Cambridge, K.G. &c. &c.

And with respect to the *precedence* of the *corps composing* the K. G. Legion, the subjoined extract contains a statement of the order directed to be observed :

(COPY)   *Horse Guards, May* 18, 1812.

SIR, I have the honor to acquaint your royal highness, in answer to your letter of the 14th instant, that the several corps composing the King's German Legion take *precedence with other foreign corps*, according to the *dates* of their *repective letters of service.*

                         I have, &c.

       (*Signed*)   W. WYNYARD, D. A. General.

In the preceding list, the *transfers* or *removals* in the corps itself have not been noticed. In order to avoid a name being mentioned twice, such of the officers as entered the legion with temporary rank, or *above* the rank of second lieutenant, cornet, or ensign, have ¶ affixed to the date of their commission. Such of this class of officers as were *still serving* in the King's German Legion, on the 18th Aug. 1812, received, on that day, permanent rank in the British army, from the date of their respective commissions; vide Memorandum in the London Gazette of 18th Aug. 1812. Such of the officers as have N. C. O. affixed to their names, served in the legion either as warrant officers, non-commissioned officers, or cadets. Such as are without these letters did not serve in the legion before they received commissions.

Hanover, March 27, 1833.   LEWIS BENNE.

B. I.

NUMERICAL RETURN

Of the casualties of the K. G. Legion in the field, since the formation of the corps up to its dissolution, extracted from the official lists, the journals of brigades and battalions, &c. &c. &c.

CORPS.	KILLED — Colonel commandant	Lieut.-colonels	Majors	Captains	Lieutenants	Cornets or ensigns	Adjutants	Serjeants	Rank and file includ. trumpeters, buglem. and drummers	Horses	Total (exclusive of horses)	WOUNDED — Ccls. commandant	Lieut.-colonels	Majors	Captains	Lieutenants	Cornets or ensigns	Adjutants	Serjeants	Rank & file includ. trumpeters, buglem, and drummers	Horses	Total (exclusive of horses)	Grand Total	REMARKS.
Regt. of artillery	,,	,,	,,	1	3	,,	,,	4	49	113	57	1	,,	2	4	11	,,	,,	5	155	75	177	234	
1st dragoons	,,	,,	,,	1	4	,,	,,	4	79	155	88	1	1	3	7	6	3	2	19	171	196	203	291	
2d do.	,,	,,	,,	2	1	2	,,	4	55	90	64	1	,,	1	3	6	2	,,	9	124	134	146	210	
1st hussars	,,	,,	,,	1	,,	,,	,,	2	44	161	47	1	2	1	14	9	7	,,	17	270	247	318	365	
2d do.	,,	,,	,,	,,	1	,,	,,	2	16	41	19	,,	,,	,,	1	5	1	,,	5	110	110	126	145	
3d do.	,,	,,	1	1	1	1	,,	2	51	172	57	1	1	1	6	6	5	,,	16	236	239	271	328	
1st light infantry batt.	1	,,	,,	3	3	,,	,,	6	108	,,	120	1	1	2	14	23	7	2	33	488	,,	571	691	exclusive of detachments in the north of Germany.
2d do.	,,	,,	,,	3	4	1	1	11	123	,,	142	,,	,,	1	10	17	3	1	44	467	,,	549	691	
1st line battalion	,,	1	,,	6	2	1	,,	9	164	,,	182	1	3	3	10	20	3	1	36	595	,,	668	850	
2d do.	,,	,,	,,	3	2	2	,,	7	144	,,	158	1	3	3	13	18	5	,,	29	667	,,	738	896	
3d do.	,,	,,	,,	1	1	,,	,,	1	41	,,	44	,,	,,	1	1	6	1	,,	5	87	,,	100	144	
4th do.	,,	1	,,	,,	1	1	,,	3	27	,,	32	,,	,,	,,	3	1	1	,,	3	101	,,	116	148	
5th do.	1	,,	,,	1	5	1	,,	5	142	,,	155	,,	1	,,	11	16	3	,,	34	452	,,	516	671	ditto,
6th do.	,,	,,	,,	,,	,,	,,	,,	,,	6	,,	6	,,	,,	,,	,,	,,	,,	,,	,,	18	,,	18	24	
7th do.	,,	,,	,,	1	,,	,,	,,	2	39	,,	42	,,	,,	,,	1	3	2	1	17	97	,,	121	163	
8th do.	,,	,,	,,	2	1	,,	,,	2	39	,,	44	,,	,,	,,	1	1	2	,,	6	135	,,	146	190	
Foreign veteran batt.	,,	,,	,,	,,	,,	,,	,,	,,	2	,,	2	,,	,,	,,	,,	,,	,,	,,	,,	,,	,,	,,	2	
TOTAL	2	,,	2	27	27	6	2	64	1129	732	1259	5	9	20	99	156	43	11	278	4173	1025	4794	6043	

6043 individuals, 1757 horses. To be added the casualties of the K. G. Legion detachments in the north of Germany 1813-14,—78.

Grand Total, 6121 individuals.—1757 horses.

(*Signed*,) C. HEISE.

B. II

SUMMARY RETURN

Of casualties in the field, of the corps of officers of the King's German Legion, from the formation of the corps up to its dissolution, arranged regimentally.

		Killed.	Died of wounds.	severely wounded.	slightly wounded.	Total.
Artillery,	..	4	0	8	9	21
1st dragoons,	..	5	2	14	7	28
2d do	..	5	0	6	7	18
1st hussars,	..	1	2	10	19	32
2d do.	..	1	1	3	7	12
3d do.	..	4	5	5	9	23
1st light battalion,	..	6	5	23	23	57
2d do.	..	8	2	19	17	46
1st line battalion,	..	9	6	16	16	47
2d do.	..	7	4	24	14	49
3d do.	..	2	3	2	3	10
4th do	..	2	5	3	4	14
5th do.	..	8	4	14	12	38
7th do.	..	1	0	3	5	9
8th do.	..	3	0	3	2	8
		66	39	153	154	412

(*Signed*)

C. HEISE.

C.

RETURN of the number of officers of the King's German Legion who *were placed* and *not placed* in the Hanoverian army, either on the actual Reduction of the corps or afterwards.

DATE OF REDUCTION. 1816.	CORPS.	Colonel-in-chief	Colonel Commandant	Lieutenant Colonels	Majors	Captains of troops & companies	Brigade majors	Second captains	Lieutenants	Second lieutenants	Cornets	Ensigns	Captain Commissary	Paymasters	Chaplains	Adjutants	Quartermasters	Surgeons	Assistant surgeons	Veterinary surgeons	Total
24th February	Permanent staff,														5						5
24th February and	Corps of engineers,																				3
24th May, ...	Regiment of artillery,																				8
	1st regiment of dragoons,																				13
	2d do																				15
	1st regiment of hussars,																				15
	2d do.																				10
	3d do.																				14
24th February, ...	1st battalion of infantry,																				15
	2d do.																				17
	1st battalion of the line,																				27
	2d do.																				23
	3d do.																				31
	4th do.																				23
	5th do.																				24
24th May	6th do.																				26
	7th do.																				23
	8th do.																				18
24th February, ...	Foreign veteran battalion,																				27
Total number of officers *not placed* in the Han. army,			8	6	13	66		1	128	1	6	59	1	17	5	4	11	9	21	4	360
Total ditto, *placed* in the Han. army,		1	7	12	20	107	7	11	103	15	44	49		17		13	5	5	14	2	415
Grand Total of officers, actually serving at the time of the reduction of the King's German Legion,		1	15	18	33	173	7	12	231	16	50	108	1	17	5	17	16	14	35	6	775

(Of these a great many have since died, resigned and retired with pensions.)

(*Signed*) LEWIS BENNE.

D.

NUMERICAL RETURN

Of non-commissioned officers, trumpeters, buglemen, drummers, and rank and file of the King's German Legion, who died since the formation of the corps, up to its dissolution.—*Extracted from the official list of deaths and casualty returns.* Hanover, Jan. 1831.

CORPS.	PERIODS. FROM.	TO	Staff serjeants and Serjeants.	Trumpeters, buglemen and drummers.	Rank and file.	TOTAL.	REMARKS.
Regiment of artillery,	Formation,	25th Dec. 1815	11	1	292	304	
1st regt. of dragoons,	do.	3d Aug. 1815	13	3	240	256	
2d do.	do.	18th June 1815	13	4	226	243	
1st regiment of hussars,	do.	do.	8	2	165	175	
2d do.	do.	14th Dec. 1815	12	3	143	158	
3d do.	do.	14th July 1815	5	2	144	151	
1st light battalion,	do.	16th Oct. 1815	23	8	427	458	
2d do.	do.	25th June 1815	33	7	695	735	
1st line battalion,	29th August, 1807,	18th June 1815	19	3	398	420	The deaths in these two battalions cannot be traced prior to Aug. 1807, they having lost the regimental books by shipwreck, on the return of the Copenhagen expedition.
2d do.	do.	do.	23	3	415	441	
3d do.	Formation,	do.	10	1	249	260	
4th do.	do.	do.	11	7	234	252	
5th do.	do.	27th Nov. 1815	23	7	489	519	
6th do.	do.	10th Jan. 1816	11	3	159	176	
7th do.	do.	9th Nov. 1815	17	6	410	433	
8th do.	do.	1st May 1816	15	5	210	230	
Independent garrison comp.	25th March, 1805,	25th Mar. 1813 Dissolution	3	,,	16	19	
Foreign veteran battalion,	25th February, 1813,	24th Feb. 1816	....			70	
TOTAL, ...			253	65	4912	5300	of all ranks

N.B.—The above return includes ALL deaths whether by sickness, killed, drowned, &c. &c. amongst the non-commissioned officers and men, as far as I can trace the numbers with certainty.—But as many have died "absent sick," "in captivity," &c. of which the regiments were never informed—taking also into account, the deaths which occurred during several months prior to the reduction of the corps, of which I possess no satisfactory information—I think, the total number may be stated at 300

And if the deaths in the corps of officers be added viz:

a Killed in battle, ... 66
b Died of wounds, ... 39
c Lost, or drowned at sea, 28
d Died by sickness or accidents 115

} 248

The Grand Total of deaths in the King's German Legion will be 5848 heads.

(*Signed*) LEWIS BENNE.

KING'S GERMAN LEGION.

E.

RECRUITING FROM AMONGST THE PRISONERS OF WAR IN ENGLAND FOR THE KING'S GERMAN LEGION.

Great difficulty having been experienced, by the state of the continent since the year 1818, in procuring eligible recruits for the King's German Legion, as well as other foreign corps in the British service, numerous projects were suggested to the British government, and many experiments tried without success, until the proposal of his royal highness the duke of Cambridge to enlist, under proper restrictions, from amongst the prisoners of war in England, all such subjects as were qualified and willing to volunteer for service either in the legion or the other foreign corps. From the circumstance of these prisoners of war being for a great part conscripts of the north of Germany or of the states forming the confederation of the Rhine, and forced into the service of the Emperor of the French—it was imagined that many would be glad to seize an opportunity of gaining their liberty and avenging, in the ranks of the duke of Wellington, the grievances they and their respective countries had experienced under the iron Sceptre of Napoleon. This plan succeeded so well that, notwithstanding the great circumspection in the selection of the men, not only was the legion completed and augmented with troops and companies, but several battalions were also raised for the 60th regiment, and the other foreign corps were furnished with recruits.

On the 26th October 1811. His royal highness the Commander in Chief communicated to the duke of Cambridge the arrangement [previously proposed by his royal highness] under which the enlisting of a proportion of eligible foreigners from amongst the prisoners of war at the different Depots' in England should be effected, and by subsequent orders up to the 2*d of March* 1812, every thing was settled so far, that on the 3*d March* 1812, the duke of Cambridge could issue his instructions to the inspecting field officers, and order the parties to proceed upon their duty.

The men were to be engaged under the same conditions as those already serving in the K. G. Legion, and to receive a bounty of four guineas each. None but natives of Germany, or who spoke—or at least understood German—including all the German countries which had been incorporated with France, likewise the possessions of the house of Austria, and those which belonged formerly to Prussia and Holland were to be accepted ; and neither French, Italians, Danes, Swedes, Russians, Spaniards or Portuguese, were to be engaged. The field officers and captains employed upon this recruiting service, received an allowance of ten shillings, and the subaltern officers, five shillings per day in addition to the usual travelling expenses. The non-commissioned officers and men received marching money on their route.

On the 21*st March* 1814, it was ordered that the last recruiting parties, stationed at Hilsea barracks and Plymouth dock, should be drawn in, the circumstances of the continent rendering it unnecessary to continue to enlist for the King's German Legion in England.

The following is a Statement of the Number of Recruits enlisted from amongst the Prisoners of War in England for the K. G. Legion.

In the South West District enlisted and finally approved by lieut-colonel David Martin of the 2d light battalion, K. G. L. between the 10th March and 23d April 1812.   546

Of this number 65 were posted to the cavalry and 481 to the infantry, and were marched from Cumberland-fort, where the party under lieut-col. Martin was stationed, direct to the depots at Ipswick and Bexhill.

In the South-west district, enlisted by captain Frederick von Marschalck of the foreign veteran battalion, [stationed at Cumberland-fort from 25th July 1813, to 24th Jan. 1814] and captain George Tilee of the 2d line battalion, K. G. L. who relieved captain von Marschalck, and was then stationed at Hilsea barracks,—from 25th Jan. to 24th of March 1814, when the party was discontinued ; from 25th July 1813, to 24th March 1814, at Forton depot, Porchester, prison ships, &c. and who were finally approved by colonel John M. Mainwaring, commandant at Hilsea barracks, and forwarded by the captains direct to the depots at Ipswich and Bexhill. 542

Out of this number captain Tilee enlisted 153, of whom he sent 61 to the cavalry and 92 to the infantry.

How captain von Marschalck posted his 389 men does not clearly appear.

At Norman-cross barracks, near Peterborough, county of Northampton, enlisted by major Augustus von Linsingen, of the 3d hussars, K. G. Legion, between the 17th March and middle of May 1812, and finally approved of by him on the spot, and sent to the depots at Ipswich and Bexhill, ... 14

In the Kent, Western and Severn districts, enlisted in the course of the year 1812, by major T. H. Brückman of the artillery, K. G. Legion, and finally approved of by him and forwarded to the depots at Ipswich and Bexhill, viz.

at Chatham 45
at Dartmoor prison, ... 6 } Total,....... 675
at Plymouth, ... 593
at Stapleton prison,.... 13

Enlisted by the party stationed at Plymouth Dock, viz. *(a)* by lieut William von Schade of the artillery, K. G. Legion, from 25th Dec. 1812, to 24th May 1813, ... 58

(b) by lieut. Theodore Gattenberg of the 5th line battalion, K.G.L. from 25th May 1813, to 24th March 1814, when the party was discontinued, ... 58

The recruits enlisted by this party were finally approved of by the gen. commanding at Plymouth, and forwarded from thence direct to the depots at Ipswich and Bexhill,

On the 3d Sept. 1813, captain Andrew von Schlütter, ensigns Nagel and Bronkhorst, serjeants Krüger, Katzmann and Weiss, and three privates from the detachments at Bexhill, were ordered to Valleyfield prison at Pennycuick near Edinburgh, to recruit from amongst the German prisoners of war at that depot, for the 7th battalion of the 60th foot, and commenced their duty on the 17th of that month. The capt. enlisted at the same time 12 for the K. G. Legion cavalry and 14 for the infantry—26 men, and forwarded them in October and November to the foreign depot at Lymington, for f.nal settlement and transfer to the legion. Captain Schlütter left Edinburgh for Bexhill in the end of Nov. 1813, his party having been appointed to the 7th battalion of the 60th foot, the ensigns to lieutenantcy's, and the serjeants to ensigncy's, ...   26

In Feb. 1812, major-general Hammond, commanding at Brighton, sent from the prisoners of war at Dartmoor, 69 volunteers to Bexhill, from whom 48 were finally approved of by lieut.-colonel Best, and posted to the legion. The remaining 21 were sent to the foreign depot at Lymington, they being not eligible for the legion.   48

In Feb. 1812, there were further sent from Brighton, by the 10th light dragoons, to Bexhill, 33 men already approved of, out of whom 29 were posted to the K. G. Legion, and the other four, being Frenchmen, forwarded to the foreign depot at Lymington, ...   29

Grand total raised from amongst the prisoners of war in England, 1978

MEMORANDUM.

The total number of recruits received by the K. G. Legion, in the year

1811, is	....		 2242	men.
Ditto,	do.	do. 1812,	 3438	,,
Ditto,	do. in 1813, up to the 24th Sep.		 521	,,

[Vide report from the K. G. Legion-Office to his royal highness the commander-in-chief of 13th Oct. 1813.]

N.B.—In this statement are included all recruits from whatever source they may have been obtained. It must, however, be observed that recruiting from amongst prisoners of war, and German deserters from the French army in Spain, was, in those years, the only mode left for increasing or filling up our ranks.

All the recruits which could be procured in England from the prisoners of war and transfers from the foreign depot, being required for the re-formation of the 7th line battalion, (which was drafted in Spain, and the officers and non-commissioned officers sent to Bexhill and for the corps serving in the Peninsula, it was impossible to post any recruits to the battalions serving in the Mediterranean. But as these battalions were likewise in want of men, the commanding officers were enjoined to embrace every opportunity of obtaining recruits, and fill up the vacancies in their own battalions. Lieut.-general Lord William Bentinck the commander of the forces in Sicily, was also requested to facilitate the recruiting of the battalions of the legion under his command, and his lordship did all in his power to promote the wishes of his royal highness the duke of Cambridge in that respect.

Great praise is however due to the exertions of the brave major-general Augustus von Honstedt, colonel commandant of the 6th line battalion of the K. G. Legion, by whose intimate friendship with Lord William Bentinck, accurate knowledge of the circumstances of the country, and personal acquaintance with the men in power—the consent of the Sicilian government was obtained to the volunteering of all the foreigners serving in the Sicilian regiments, into the K. G. Legion.

(b) In the course of the war the Sicilians had enrolled into their regiments a great number of Germans, by means of agents employed in Spain, &c. who pretended to engage men for the foreign regiments in the British serivce, but on getting them to Sicily posted them to the Sicilian corps. In the month of May 1812, the meritorious general Honstedt commenced receiving the volunteers, and obtained from the regiment " Ester" alone, between the 11th and 16th May 1812,—890 fine young men, mostly conscripts of the confederation of the Rhine and of Hanover, or the then kingdom of Westphalia. There arrived at the same time 500 prisoners of war and deserters from Port Mahon, of whom a great number were found fit for service in the legion. Some recruits were also obtained from Gibraltar, Alicante, Minorca, Taragona, Malta, &c. &c. &c.

The total number of recruits obtained from the sources just detailed, and posted to the battqlions serving in the Mediterranean, is as follows :—	Serjeants.	Drummers	Privates.	
3d line batt. between the 25th Dec. 1810, and 24th June, 1814, ...	,,	2	350	
4th do. 25th do. 24th do.	,,	2	397	
6th do. 25th Jun. 1810, 24th do.	2	2	440	
7th do. 25th Dec. 1812, 24th do.	,,	1	241	1976
8th do. 25th Jun. 1810, 24 Dec.	,,	7	492	
The 3d comp. of foot artillery, about	,,	,,	40	
Total, ...	2	14	1960	

Grand Total of recruits raised from amongst the prisoners of war in England and the volunteers of the Sicilian corps, prisoners of war, &c. &c, in the Mediterranean, ... 3954 men.

Hanover, Dec. 22, 1830.

(Signed)

LEWIS BENNE.

F.

Return of the number of officers actually serving in the King's German Legion, at the time of the reduction of the corps, and who have since died.

(June, 1837.)

CORPS.	Colonel-in-chief	Col. commandants	Lieut.-colonels	Majors	Capt. of troops & com.	Brigade-majors.	Second captains	Lieutenants	Second Lieutenants	Cornets	Ensigns	Captain Commissary	Paymasters	Chaplains	Adjutants	Quartermasters	Surgeons	Assistant Surgeons	Veterinary Surgeons	Total
Permanent staff,						2								3						5
Corps of engineers,					1													3		2
Regiment of artillery,		1	1	2	4		3	5				1				1		1		21
1st regiment of dragoons,		1	1	1	6			3		2					1					8
2d ditto,		1	1	2	3			2		1						1	1	2		17
1st regiment of hussars,		1		2	5			5		1					1	1	1			14
2d ditto,		1		1	1			4		1			1		1	1	1	1		15
3d ditto,		1	1	1	3			1		3						1	1			10
1st battalion of light infantry,			1	1	5				1		1							2		10
2d ditto,		1	1	2	1			3			2		1			1	1	1		15
1st battalion of the line,		1	1	1	6			5			3					1		1		11
2d ditto,		1	1	2	4			5										1		16
3d ditto,		1	1	2	1			1			3		1			1		1		13
4th ditto,		1	1	1	3			11			1					1	1	1		17
5th ditto,		1		2	4			2			2							1		9
6th ditto,		1		2	4			4			1						1			12
7th ditto,		1		1	4			9			5					1	1	1		22
8th ditto,		1	1	2	4			7			2						1	1		19
Foreign veteran battalion,		1	1	1	5			5			2		1			1	1	1		19
Total,	„	10	9	16	61	2	4	72	3	7	22	1	4	3	3	11	10	17	„	255

C. HEISE.

G.

RETURN of the number of officers actually serving in the King's German Legion at the time of the reduction of the corps, *and who are now not serving in the Hanoverian army.* (June 1837.)

CORPS.	Colonel-in-chief	Colonels commandt.	Lieut.-colonels	Majors	Caps of troops & com.	Brigade-majors	Second captains	Lieutenants	Second-lieutenants	Cornets	Ensigns	Captain commissary	Paymasters	Chaplains	Adjutants	Quartermasters	Surgeons	Assistant surgeons	Veterinary surgeons	TOTAL
Permanent staff,						2								2						4
Corps of engineers,			1					1									1			3
Regiment of artillery,		1			2			5	6				1		1		1	1		18
1st regiment of dragoons,			1		3			7		4			1		1	1		1	1	20
2d ditto,				1				3		3			1		1	1		1	1	12
1st regiment of hussars,		1			2			5		4			1		1	1		1	1	17
2d ditto,			1		2			5		4			1		1	1		1	1	17
3d ditto,				1	3			8		3			1		1	1		1	1	20
1st battalion of light infantry,			1		2			7			7		1		1			1		20
2d ditto,				1	2			7			7		1		1			1		20
1st battalion of the line,		1		1	9			6			6		1		1			1		26
2d ditto,			1		10			5			9		1		1			1		28
3d ditto,				1	7			7			4		1					1		21
4th ditto,				1	5			10			6		1					1		24
5th ditto,		1		1	8			10			5		1					1		27
6th ditto,			1		9			10			7							1		28
7th ditto,				1	2		1	9			2							1		16
8th ditto,				1	3		1	6			7							1		19
Foreign veteran battalion,				1	5			5			7							1		19
TOTAL,		4	6	10	74	2	2	116	6	18	67		13	2	10	5	2	17	5	359

C. HEISE.

H.

RETURN of the number of officers actually serving in the King's German Legion, at the time of the reduction of the corps, *and who are now serving in the Hanoverian army.* (June 1837.)

CORPS.	Colonel in chief	Cols. commandant	Lieut.-colonels	Majors	Capt. of troops & com	Brigade majors	Second captains	Lieutenants	Second lieutenants	Cornets	Ensigns	Captain commissary	Paymasters	Chaplains	Adjutants	Quartermasters	Surgeons	Assistant surgeons	Veterinary surgeons	TOTAL
Permanent staff	1	,,	,,	,,	,,	3	,,	,,	,,	,,	,,	,,	,,	,,	,,	,,	,,	,,	,,	4
Corps of engineers	,,	,,	1	,,	1	,,	,,	2	,,	,,	,,	,,	,,	,,	1	,,	,,	,,	,,	5
Regiment of artillery	,,	,,	1	1	6	,,	,,	6	7	,,	,,	,,	,,	,,	,,	,,	1	,,	1	23
1st regiment of dragoons	,,	,,	,,	,,	4	,,	2	1	,,	4	,,	,,	,,	,,	1	,,	,,	,,	,,	12
2d ditto	,,	,,	,,	,,	,,	,,	4	,,	,,	8	,,	,,	,,	,,	,,	,,	,,	,,	,,	12
1st regiment of hussars	,,	,,	,,	2	2	,,	,,	1	,,	5	,,	,,	,,	,,	,,	,,	,,	,,	,,	10
2d ditto	,,	,,	,,	1	2	,,	,,	1	,,	3	,,	,,	,,	,,	,,	,,	,,	,,	,,	7
3d ditto	,,	1	,,	2	5	,,	,,	1	,,	5	,,	,,	,,	,,	1	,,	,,	,,	,,	15
1st battalion of light infantry	,,	,,	,,	1	4	,,	,,	3	,,	,,	2	,,	,,	,,	1	,,	,,	,,	,,	11
2d ditto	,,	,,	,,	,,	2	,,	,,	3	,,	,,	2	,,	,,	,,	,,	,,	,,	,,	,,	7
1st battalion of the line	,,	,,	,,	,,	2	,,	,,	5	,,	,,	1	,,	,,	,,	,,	,,	1	,,	,,	9
2d ditto	,,	,,	,,	,,	1	,,	,,	1	,,	,,	1	,,	,,	,,	,,	,,	,,	1	,,	4
3d ditto	,,	,,	1	,,	1	,,	,,	5	,,	,,	2	,,	,,	,,	,,	,,	,,	,,	,,	9
4th ditto	,,	,,	,,	,,	1	,,	,,	3	,,	,,	1	,,	,,	,,	,,	,,	,,	,,	,,	5
5th ditto	,,	,,	,,	,,	2	,,	,,	4	,,	,,	1	,,	,,	,,	,,	,,	,,	,,	,,	7
6th ditto	,,	,,	,,	,,	1	,,	,,	2	,,	,,	1	,,	,,	,,	,,	,,	,,	,,	,,	4
7th ditto	,,	,,	,,	,,	3	,,	,,	5	,,	,,	3	,,	,,	,,	,,	,,	,,	,,	,,	11
8th ditto	,,	,,	,,	,,	1	,,	,,	,,	,,	,,	5	,,	,,	,,	,,	,,	,,	,,	,,	6
Foreign veteran battalion	,,	,,	,,	,,	,,	,,	,,	,,	,,	,,	,,	,,	,,	,,	,,	,,	,,	,,	,,	,,
TOTAL	1	1	3	7	38	3	6	43	7	25	19	,,	,,	,,	4	,,	2	1	1	161

C. HEISE.

KING'S GERMAN LEGION.

I

SUMMARY RETURN OF ALL THE OFFICERS WHO HAVE HELD COMMISSIONS IN THE KING'S GERMAN LEGION.

A. *Before disbandment of the corps.* (575.)

Killed in battle, or died of wounds,	105
Lost at sea, or drowned by shipwreck,	28
Died from illness or accidents,	115
Placed on half-pay or reduced allowance, on account of wounds,* or other infirmities, contracted on service,	88
Resigned and retired without receiving any allowance,	136
Superseded, being absent without leave,	28
Gazetted without joining their corps,	24
Transferred to British regiments or the staff of the army,	44
Dismissed the service,	7

B. *After disbandment of the corps,* (775.)

Died since disbandment,	255
Actually serving in the Hanoverian army,	161
Actually not serving in the Hanoverian army†,	359
	1350

* Of these about two-thirds (218) reside in the kingdom of Hanover, and the rest, including several (39) individuals, whose present residence or existence could not be ascertained, reside out of the kingdom.

† Of these 60 individuals are ascertained to have died.

The grand total number of officers of the King's German Legion, actually drawing half-pay, does not exceed 500, several individuals having sold out.

C. HEISE.

THE END.

www.ingramcontent.com/pod-product-compliance
Lightning Source LLC
Chambersburg PA
CBHW070931150426
42814CB00025B/186